DATE DUE

Prostitution and Pornography

Prostitution and Pornography

Philosophical Debate About the Sex Industry

EDITED BY

Jessica Spector

STANFORD UNIVERSITY PRESS

STANFORD, CALIFORNIA 2006

Stanford University Press
Stanford, California

© 2006 by the Board of Trustees of the
Leland Stanford Junior University.
All rights reserved.

Printed in the United States of America
on acid-free, archival-quality paper

Library of Congress Cataloging-in-Publication Data

Prostitution and pornography : philosophical debate about the sex
industry / edited by Jessica Spector.
    p. cm.
Includes bibliographical references and index.
ISBN-13: 978-0-8047-4937-4 (cloth : alk. paper)
ISBN-13: 978-0-8047-4938-1 (pbk. : alk. paper)
    1. Prostitution.   2. Pornography.   3. Feminist theory.
4. Feminist ethics.   I. Spector, Jessica.
HQ115.P74 2006
306.77–dc22   2006006597

Typeset by TechBooks, New Delhi, in 10/12 Sabon.

To Michael,
for the conversation
that began this project.

Contents

Contributors

NORMA JEAN ALMODOVAR, retired prostitute and former employee of the Los Angeles Police Department, is the founder and president of ISWFACE (International Sex Worker Foundation for Art, Culture and Education) www.iswface.org. She is the author of *Cop to Call Girl* as well as numerous articles, and an international advocate for sex worker rights.

SCOTT ANDERSON is Assistant Professor of Philosophy at the University of British Columbia. He works in moral, social and political philosophy, and in particular on the nature of coercion. He also works on issues around gender and feminism, including prostitution, sexual harassment, and rape. Within moral philosophy, he is interested in neo-Aristotelian thinkers, consequentialism, action theory, and the concept of privacy.

MARGARET A. (MEG) BALDWIN is an Associate Professor of Law at Florida State University College of Law. Her scholarship and advocacy activities have long centered on advancing justice for prostituted women and girls. Professor Baldwin has represented prostituted women in civil rights and clemency cases, authored the first statute in the United States creating compensation claims for girls and women coerced in prostitution, and has written extensively on legal strategies benefiting prostituted women and girls.

VEDNITA CARTER is Executive Director of BREAKING FREE, a non-profit organization founded in 1996, that assists prostituted women and girls, and other battered women involved in the criminal justice system. BREAKING FREE provides advocacy services and educational support as an alternative to the revolving door of social services and the criminal justice system, addressing core issues of racism and sexism that keep women trapped in prostitution and violent lifestyles.

JOSHUA COHEN is Goldberg Professor of the Humanities, and professor of philosophy and political science at MIT. Cohen has written extensively on issues of democratic theory, freedom of expression, human rights, and the implications of ideas of deliberative democracy for social and political arrangements. Since 1991, he has been editor of *Boston Review*, and has edited more than 20 books in the *Review*'s New Democracy Forum series.

RONALD DWORKIN has a joint appointment at University College, London and at NYU where he is a professor both in the Law School and the Philosophy Department. Professor Dworkin is the author of many articles in philosophical and legal journals as well as articles on legal and political topics in the New York Review of Books. He has written *Taking Rights Seriously* (1977), *A Matter of Principle* (1985), *Law's Empire* (1986), *Philosophical Issues in Senile Dementia* (1987), *A Bill of Rights for Britain* (1990), *Life's Dominion* (1993), *Freedom's Law* (1996), and *Sovereign Virtue* (2000).

EVELINA GIOBBE has been Executive Director of the Commercial Sexual Exploitation Resource Institute (CSERI). CSERI was established in 1996 to answer the need for a coordinated community response to the expanding sex industry in Minnesota. Its mission is to abate commercial sexual exploitation through research, education and community organizing; to advocate for the rights of prostituted women, youth and transgender persons; and to increase opportunities for individuals to leave the sex industry.

LAURA KIPNIS is a cultural critic and theorist whose books include *Against Love: A Polemic* (Pantheon), *Bound and Gagged: Pornography and the Politics of Fantasy in America* (Duke), and *Ecstasy Unlimited: On Sex, Capital, Gender & Aesthetics* (Minnesota). She has received fellowships from the Guggenheim Foundation, the Rockefeller Foundation, and the National Endowment for the Arts, and is a professor of media and cultural studies at Northwestern University.

CATHARINE A. MACKINNON, ELIZABETH A. LONG Professor of Law at the University of Michigan, is a teacher, lawyer, writer, and activist on sex equality under constitutional and international law. Her ten books include *Sex Equality* (2001), *Toward a Feminist Theory of the State* (1989), *Only Words* (1993), and *Sexual Harassment of Working Women* (1979). She pioneered the legal claim for sexual harassment and recognition of the harms of pornography. In representing Bosnian women survivors of Serbian genocidal sexual atrocities, she established rape as an act of genocide. She co-directs The Lawyers Alliance for Women (LAW) Project of

Equality Now, an international NGO promoting sex equality. She is one of the most widely cited legal scholars in the English language.

JULIAN MARLOWE is a former escort who has also worked with Chisel Media and Pornducer.com in the Internet porn industry. Although no longer active in the sex industry, he is part of the ongoing debate and continues to challenge the inaccurate portrayal of all male participants as abusers and misogynists. His essay on male prostitution, "It's Different For Boys", appeared in the anthology *Whores and Other Feminists* (Routledge).

MARTHA NUSSBAUM is Ernst Freund Distinguished Service Professor of Law and Ethics at The University of Chicago, appointed in Philosophy, Law, and Divinity. Her most recent books are *Hiding From Humanity: Disgust, Shame, and the Law* and *Frontiers of Justice: Disability, Nationality, Species Membership*.

CAROLE PATEMAN is Professor of Political Science at UCLA, a member of the Center for Social Theory and Comparative History and a Faculty Affiliate of the Center for the Study of Women. She is a Fellow of the American Academy of Arts and Sciences and was President of the International Political Science Association. Her publications include *Participation and Democratic Theory*, *The Sexual Contract*, and, recently, articles on the idea of a basic income.

TRACY QUAN is author of the novels *Diary of a Manhattan Call Girl* and *Diary of a Married Call Girl* (Three Rivers Press). Her essays and reviews have appeared in *The Globe and Mail*, *Los Angeles Times Book Review*, *Der Tagesspiegel*, *South China Morning Post*, *The Philadelphia Inquirer*, *Lingua Franca* and other publications. More information about her work can be found at her website: www.tracyquan.net Email: *tq@tracyquan.net*

THERESA REED (AKA DARKLADY) is a full-time freelance writer who resides in Portland Oregon and has covered the flesh industry and alt sexuality beat from both the inside and the outside since the early 1990s. She is or has been an adult magazine editor, porn and sex toy reviewer, pansexual party organizer, columnist, reporter, public speaker, sex educator, professional dominant, and liaison to the adult industry for the Woodhull Freedom foundation. Learn more at www.darklady.com.

DEBRA SATZ is Associate Professor of Philosophy and, by courtesy, of Political Science at Stanford University. She is also Director of the interdisciplinary program in Ethics in Society. She teaches courses in ethics, social and political philosophy, and philosophy of the social sciences. Within these fields, her research has focused on the ethical limits of markets, theories of rational choice, democratic theory, feminist philosophy, and issues of international justice. Her articles have appeared in Ethics, Philosophy and Public Affairs, the Journal of Philosophy and the World Bank Economic Review.

SIBYL A. SCHWARZENBACH is Associate Professor of Philosophy at the City University of New York (Baruch College and the Graduate Center). She is editor of and contributor to Women and the United States Constitution; History, Interpretation and Practice (Columbia University Press, 2004) and is currently finishing a book entitled *On Civic Friendship* about the requirements of social and political cohesion. She is also the author of numerous articles in political philosophy, ethics and feminist theory.

LAURIE SHRAGE is Professor of Philosophy at California State Polytechnic University, Pomona. She is the author of Abortion and Social Responsibility: Depolarizing the Debate (Oxford 2003), Moral Dilemmas of Feminism: Prostitution, Adultery, and Abortion (Routledge 1994), and numerous articles on sex work, feminist theory, reproductive rights, and ethnic identity. She co-edited *Hypatia: A Journal of Feminist Philosophy* (1998–2003), and Race, Class, Gender, and Sexuality (Blackwell 1998). Her current projects include "How Queer is Sex Work" and "Philosophy and the Jewish Questions."

JESSICA SPECTOR has published on Locke and Hume, and lectured extensively on various aspects of the sex industry. After a career as an academic philosopher, she has moved on to become a professional writer. In 2002 she founded The Academy, which works with attorneys and business professionals on the principles of clear writing and effective argument.

CHRISTINE STARK is a poet, writer, speaker, visual artist and activist of American Indian and European ancestry. Her work has been published in numerous periodicals and anthologies. She co-edited *Not For Sale: Feminists Resisting Prostitution and Pornography*. She has spoken nationally and internationally and organized numerous community events on rape, racism, homelessness and poverty. She received an MFA in Writing and teaches at a community college.

Acknowledgments

The inspiration for this volume was a series of philosophy courses I taught while a professor at Trinity College, and work I did relating to street prostitution in Hartford, Connecticut. I am grateful to a number of people, from a variety of professions and with an array of viewpoints on the sex industry, for their generosity as I began working on some of the issues covered in this book. Judge Raymond Norko, social worker Karen Brown, Hartford Community Court Administrator Chris Pleasanton, and Hartford Police Sergeant Franco Sanzo showed me that there are people within the criminal justice system really trying to make things better for the women who too-often are marginalized by it, using creative sentencing and social services to try to alleviate the problems inherent in a system that works by punishing those most victimized. Susan Breault, of the Paul and Lisa Program and writer and activist Carol Leigh were also very generous with their time. Although their views regarding the legalization of prostitution are diametrically opposed, both Ms. Breault and Ms. Leigh are committed to bettering the lives of women in prostitution and both deserve thanks for their efforts in that arena, as well as for the time they spent talking and working with me on the issues discussed in this volume.

My students at Trinity, too, deserve thanks. In an era where much fun is made of college courses that deal with sex and pop-culture, my students rose to the expectations of them to treat these subjects with seriousness and sensitivity. It may seem incredible to say so, but I had not one student in my years of teaching about this subject who did not maturely and thoughtfully engage with the subject matter. And I had many students who surpassed the maturity of many of my professional peers in being able to talk about sex without becoming overwhelmed by the titillation factor. I am grateful in particular for the work and conversation of Jon Amory, John Canali, Caleb (Thayer) Fox, Josh Freemire, Jeff Green, Mark Gutzmer, Pamela Judkowitz, Michele Kelly, Jessica Kennett, Marli Reifman, and Elizabeth Santos-McClure.

Finally, I wish to thank my family. My husband was understanding and patient about many late nights put in at the office, on the streets of Hartford, and in other places one might not expect one's spouse to be while she is severely pregnant. My children, who were each onboard for stints along the way, may not be able to read this book for many years, but someday they may be interested to know some of the places and venues they visited prenatally. My hope and confidence is that they will all grow into adults who care about justice, freedom, and the well-being of those who can't fight for themselves.

Introduction

Sex, Money, and Philosophy

JESSICA SPECTOR

From mainstream corporate pornography to illegal street prostitution, there are billions of dollars being made each year from the sale of sex and sex-related products and activities. Who is making that money and who is benefiting from, or being harmed by, the various sex-related businesses is one of the topics of this book. But however one counts, it is clear that commerce in sex is not diminishing and that more people are involved in various aspects of the industry every day. The sex industry— a loose term for a variety of commerce in sex—is an enormous economic force in the United States and worldwide. According to one report, the American pornography industry grosses more per year than the American music and mainstream movie industries combined.[1] According to another report, Americans spend more money per year on strip clubs than on theater, opera, ballet, jazz, and classical music concerts combined.[2] General Motors (through its subsidiaries) supposedly sells more pornographic videos than Larry Flynt.[3] Estimates of the amount of money spent per day on prostitution in the United States range upward of $40 million. All these claims, although controversial in their detail, reveal a trend toward the mainstreaming of pornography and other departments of the sex industry in the United States, despite prostitution's

1. Frank Rich, "Naked Capitalists: There's No Business Like Porn Business," *New York Times,* May 20, 2001.
2. Martin Amis, "Sex in America," *Talk,* February 2001; and "A Rough Trade" *Guardian Unlimited,* March 17, 2001.
3. Timothy Egan, "Erotica Inc.: A Special Report; Technology Sent Wall Street into Market for Pornography," *New York Times,* October 23, 2000.

remaining illegal everywhere in the country except certain counties in Nevada.[4]

As the industry itself grows, so does writing and thought about it from academic and activist circles (which are sometimes the same, sometimes not). This book is about the attempt of academic and activist feminists to deal with the sex industry and the hard questions it raises for liberal feminism.[5] When one picks up a book entitled *Prostitution and Pornography: Philosophical Debate About the Sex Industry*, one probably expects a debate about whether prostitution and pornography should be legal or not. To an extent, this book delivers in that area. But this is more than a collection of arguments pro and con; it is an exploration of some of the deeper issues behind the pro and con arguments. The articles collected here focus on questions about what prostitution and pornography are, what they do, and how arguments about them involve our conceptions of the self, freedom, social responsibility, and action.

Certainly, at the center of all this are some disagreements about sex: its function, its meaning, and its proper place in one's life. But also at the center of the arguments here are disagreements about money: how it affects freedom, what it should be used for, and how its distribution should be controlled. This book is as much about the confluence of sex and money in general as it is about prostitution and pornography in particular. These issues regarding sex, money, and the self are important both to those who are talking about the details of everyday life and those who want to think about the concepts that frame those details. Indeed, the ethical questions raised by sexual commerce in general are at the heart of philosophy, while also being the most practical of questions: about who we are, what we do, why we do it, and whether or not we should.

The book begins with the so-called radical critique of feminist liberal defenses of the sex industry and its products. The second section focuses

4. A popular misconception is that prostitution is legal in Las Vegas. In fact, it is illegal in all Nevada counties over a certain population; and streetwalking is illegal everywhere in the State. Currently, brothels are the only legal form of prostitution in Nevada, and they are legal only in ten out of Nevada's seventeen counties. For an account of working conditions inside Nevada's legal brothels, see Alexa Albert, 2001, *Brothel: Mustang Ranch and Its Women* (New York: Random House).

5. Readers should note here the use of the expression "feminist liberalism" rather than the reverse "liberal feminism." This is because this collection of articles is organized around questions about the adequacy of liberalism to address the putative harms and benefits of the sex industry and its products. It is not organized around questions about the goals and limits of feminism, although these questions, of course, do come up in many of the articles.

on feminist liberal responses to the critique of prostitution, while the third section focuses on feminist liberal responses to the critique of pornography. Section Four gathers together several articles that attempt in different ways to address some of the conflicts between feminist liberals and their critics, without giving up an interest in either feminist concerns with women's condition or a liberal commitment to equality and individual choice generally.

For newcomers to these issues, it may seem that this collection of articles places them in the middle of a debate rather than at the beginning. In a sense it does. There are no articles in this volume by social conservatives, or by those on the religious right, or from those consumers of sex industry products or work who have no interest in general questions about the status of women. These may be the source of much interesting discussion elsewhere, but here the focus is on what people who are generally interested in sexual freedom, generally interested in remedying social injustice, and particularly interested in sexual freedom and social justice for women, have to say about prostitution, pornography, and what the two have to do with each other.

In this context, the reader should note the division here between feminist liberal discussions of prostitution and feminist liberal discussions of pornography in Sections Two and Three, respectively. This division is not an editor's conceit; the two aspects of the sex industry really are treated very differently in academic circles. And that brings us to another main theme of this collection: the differing treatment of prostitution and pornography in much feminist liberal academic writing and in U.S. legal/political culture. A quick comparison of legal practices and societal attitudes toward prostitution and pornography reveal a dichotomy of thought: prostitution is illegal and socially condemned in much of the United States, while pornography is generally legal and increasingly considered more socially acceptable, although both involve commerce in sex. (Even the typical explanation that this dichotomy is due to the sexual Puritanism of U.S. society fails to explain the dichotomy itself, since the same dichotomy is preserved in reverse in some societies that are thought to be more sexually liberal than the United States, such as some democracies of Western Europe.) The different attitudes toward prostitution and pornography persevere despite the fact that those with experience inside the sex industry do not tend to view various departments of the sex industry as so clearly distinct. Workers, activists, students, and scholars can all benefit from thinking about why this might be the case and what it has to do with the way the sex industry functions and why further thought about it is important.

Some of the articles included here are by people who have had direct experience in the sex industry and could be called activists—whether for or against the sex industry. Most are by academics, some of whom are also activists. All of the articles share a common interest in the ways in which feminist liberalism does or does not adequately deal with the sex industry. The idea is not to have industry veterans or survivors "teach" academics something practical so they can produce better-informed theory, or for academics to explain to industry veterans or survivors what the significance of their experiences really are. Rather, the point is to bring together an assortment of writings about the sex industry by people who are generally interested in questions about the status of women, the role of law in affecting that status, and the place of sex in our lives, in order to make some sense of the very different ways prostitution, pornography, and other parts of the sex industry are treated in U.S. culture, and to think about how the principles of feminism and liberalism conflict with and compliment one another.

That having been said, the reader should note some of the differences between the academic and nonacademic articles in this collection. Each section of the book opens with writings by people with experience inside the sex industry. This organizational structure is intended to highlight rather than gloss over the differences in emphasis between some of the academic and nonacademic pieces. The nonacademic articles tend to diverge from the academic articles in the privilege they give to anecdote and first-person experience. In some cases, this difference in style itself constitutes a kind of argument about the alienation that many activists and workers feel from academic discussions within liberal feminist circles, which often treat first-person accounts as useful simply for providing "color" to theoretical debates and for spurring classroom discussions. Since one of the themes of this collection is the question of liberalism's adequacy for addressing criticisms of the sex industry, it is important to think about whether academic divisions of the conceptual terrain of the sex industry in fact line up with the experiences of those who have lived in that terrain.

A final introductory note, before an overview of the materials collected here: it is not the goal of this collection as a whole to advance any particular agenda or set of arguments. Rather, the hope is that readers will take away from this book a deeper understanding of the complexity of questions about the sex industry and an interest in pursuing further some of the topics raised here. Of course, each of the authors included here has a view about the goods and ills of the sex industry and its products, and of course, each of the authors here would hope to make the case that her or his argument should convince the reader of some fundamentally important point about prostitution or pornography. After all, as the subtitle of this book states, this is a philosophical debate. But all of the authors here would probably describe themselves as feminists in some sense, if they were given to labeling themselves. All are interested in the welfare of women and the way it is affected by the sex industry. And minimally, all the authors here would probably describe themselves as interested in very general liberal ideals. The real disagreement is over the questions of whether and how feminist principles can be reconciled with classical liberal ideals of individual freedom and choice. Despite their widely different views on these matters, all of the authors have agreed to include their work here because they think that it is important for both a general audience and a scholarly one to pay more attention to the issues raised by prostitution and pornography, and their effects on the lives of real people.

The first section of the book is a collection of critiques of the sex industry by people concerned about the damage it does to women. The authors discuss various harms caused or perpetuated by the sex industry, all being critical of the industry in general, and all connecting different aspects of the sex industry, from stripping, to pornography, to prostitution. According to this group of authors—in an analysis often labeled "radical feminist" for its emphasis on the social fact of the gendered nature of the sex industry and the harms it causes—evidence of rampant coercion and subjugation in the sex industry supports their view that the industry is not a legitimate one. Thus, this group of authors does not use the term "sex work," which has become popular among a certain subset of Western writers on the subject, but instead refers to prostitution, in its various forms, using terms like "exploitation," "slave," and "survivor."

This section opens with Vednita Carter and Evelina Giobbe's article, "Duet: Confronting the Liberal Lies about Prostitution," which is a response to the argument that "sex work" is work just like other work. Carter and Giobbe argue that prostitution and pornography are founded upon coercion and that liberals confuse the exploitation inherent in the sex industry with free choice. An undercurrent in their argument is that there is an element of racism in the defenses of prostitution offered by "sexual liberals," and they charge academics as guilty of perpetuating the exploitation of women used in the industry by appropriating real experiences for academic debates about abstract politics.

The next article, "Stripping as a System of Prostitution," a new piece for this collection by Christine Stark, links prostitution and pornography to more socially accepted departments of the sex industry, like stripping. Stark describes how supposedly disparate forms of sexual commerce function together as a system, subjugating women and enslaving them in a cycle of sexual abuse. She challenges the notion that more socially accepted activities like stripping are any more legitimate than prostitution, arguing that the two are inseparable and that more accepted activities like stripping are in fact gateways to lure women into prostitution and pornography and keep them there.

After these descriptions of the way the sex industry systematically abuses women, Carole Pateman offers an analysis of what makes this abuse different from legitimate work. In "What's Wrong with Prostitution," from her book *The Sexual Contract*, Pateman responds to the liberal defense of prostitution offered by philosopher Lars Ericsson in his article entitled "What's Wrong with Prostitution?". Pateman answers that question by arguing that selling sex differs fundamentally from selling other labor. Her argument is that the prostitution contract must be viewed in the context of an overarching societal "sexual contract" wherein men trade sexual access to women. So for Pateman, the entire exchange is an instantiation of gender hierarchy that makes women into commodities bought and sold by men.

In a newly revised version of her article "Split at the Root: Prostitution and Feminist Discourses of Law Reform," Margaret Baldwin also attacks the theoretical bent of much of the liberal defense of the sex industry, charging that abstract academic arguments about the sex industry perpetuate an "us/them, good-woman/whore" dichotomy. Baldwin's argument is that the liberal focus on consent misleads us into thinking that prostitution is something women meaningfully choose, and so turns prostitution in particular into a problem about "other women" rather than a problem with gender and power relations.

Catharine MacKinnon, in "Equality and Speech" from her book *Only Words*, argues that pornography is not a form of protected speech but a practice of sex inequality. She claims that as such, pornography of the sort commonly sold by the pornography industry should be treated in the same way as other forms of activity that are abusive, discriminatory, or degrading. This is an innovative way of critiquing pornography because it centers the discussion on questions of equal rights rather than simply on speech. MacKinnon's argument is that pornography results from and causes injuries to equality rights, which should be promoted under the 14th Amendment to the U.S. Constitution. One common misconception about this argument is that it is a call for a ban on pornography. In fact, it is not. It is instead an argument that there should be civil remedies under the law for victims of pornography, namely, the women used in it or abused with it.

Underlying MacKinnon's argument about the injurious consequences of pornography is an approach that differs markedly from liberal treatments of the sex industry. MacKinnon's discussion of a lack of consent to the harms of pornography is not meant theoretically, but empirically. The observation is that women in pornography mainly do not in fact consent to the injuries done to them and with them. This critique of the lack of meaningful consent goes to the heart of the liberal view that "sex work" can be empowering by enabling the disadvantaged to gain control of their own labor power.

The second section of this collection focuses on feminist liberal discussions of prostitution. The articles in this section each make the case that prohibitions on prostitution are wrong, harmful, or both. The main problem with prostitution in the United States, according to many feminist liberals, is that poor women often do not have many choices and their labor conditions are generally bad. Selling sexual services is not fundamentally different from other bodily labor in this regard, and indeed, can even offer disadvantaged women more autonomy and personal control over their working conditions than many other jobs. What disadvantaged women need then, is not further restriction on economic opportunities, but fair, safe, labor conditions, and freedom from stigmatization if they choose to engage in sexual commerce. Some liberals thus think that the answer to the problem of prostitution lies in government regulation and normalization, while some more libertarian feminists think that government intervention in the sexual lives of women is itself part of the problem and should be abandoned altogether. The articles here run the gamut of these positions, but all share the view that criminalization and other forms of prohibition do more to hurt than help those who are supposed to be of primary concern: disadvantaged women with few choices.

Norma Jean Almodovar's "Porn Stars, Radical Feminists, Cops, and Outlaw Whores: The Battle Between Feminist Theory and Reality, Free Speech, and Free Spirits," is a new piece, written for this collection, which asks the reader to consider the rationality of the different treatment that prostitution and pornography receive under the law. Almodovar, a former LAPD employee and prostitute, is a libertarian activist who attacks the legitimacy of *any* governmental role in legislating sexual commerce: either through regulation as labor or through prohibition. Her argument here focuses specifically on the way pornography is considered legitimate work, while prostitution is criminalized. The same free choice can be involved in both types of sexual commerce, according to Almodovar, and laws against prostitution essentially amount to persecution of prostitutes, whose plight is often ignored by the pornography industry. Almodovar argues that the legal treatment of prostitution is neither justified theoretically nor practically, when one considers the abuse prostitutes often receive at the hands of the legal system.

In " 'Whether From Reason or Prejudice': Taking Money for Bodily Services," Martha Nussbaum argues that the main trouble with sex work is the bad working conditions that tend to characterize the lives of many sex workers—as well as the lives and work of the poor generally. This, combined with repressive attitudes about sex in general, is what makes prostitution as it is typically practiced so troubling, rather than the sale of sexual services in and of itself. Nussbaum urges us to consider sex work in comparison to other forms of bodily labor in order to investigate whether or not there really is something essential to it that sets it apart from other bodily labor. The implication here is that there is nothing about sexual activity that makes it fundamentally different from other sorts of human activity, and that the real problems with sex work are the economic necessity and low pay that also characterize some other forms of bodily labor. A centerpiece of Nussbaum's argument is a comparison among several jobs that involve varying degrees of intimacy and bodily risk, including prostitution. One of the features of this comparison is a focus on the stigmatization of prostitution that sets it apart from other jobs. According to Nussbaum, this stigmatization is itself damaging and in need of redress.

Sibyl Schwarzenbach emphasizes this thought about the damaging effects of stigmatization even more in an article that pre-dates the others in this section. In "Contractarians and Feminists Debate Prostitution," Schwarzenbach argues that the marketing of sexual services can, in fact, be an empowering force. She uses the notion of *stewardship*, which she views as central to both Locke's and Hegel's philosophical theories, and which underlies much of modern philosophical thought on property, to make the case that selling sexual labor power is much like selling certain other forms of labor power—provided, always, that strict limits are maintained. The focus here is a bit different than Nussbaum's focus on human capabilities. Especially interesting is Schwarzenbach's comparison between the work of a prostitute and that of a professional dancer, both of which involve the sale of something that may be seen as central to one's conception of self, and both of which involve bodily performance for the pleasure of others (which can be at some physical cost to the performer).

Laurie Shrage's article, "Prostitution and the Case for Decriminalization," argues in support of decriminalization, making the case that prostitution should be understood as an economic activity, which can vary according to context. In some contrast to her own earlier published piece on prostitution (as discussed in the Schwarzenbach article in this collection), Shrage does not find much value in the radical feminist critique of the sex industry, which she sees as insufficiently attentive to the way various contexts shape prostitution differently. Here Shrage develops a position intermediate between condemning prostitution as a sign of social decay and glamorizing it as libratory transgression. She argues that prohibition worsens the stigma that is one of the central problems for sex workers, and suggests that although the sex industry may be problematic, criminalization only exacerbates its damaging effects on the individuals involved. By removing legal sanctions against prostitution, Shrage thinks we might thus facilitate other moral ideals.

Section Three of this collection focuses on feminist liberal treatments of pornography and arguments for easing restrictions on it. Strikingly, the traditional academic liberal emphasis on the individual shifts when it comes to discussions of pornography. While the critic's concern remains both the person who is exchanging sex for money and the condition of women generally, the liberal focus shifts from the individual worker to the social value of expressive liberty. In my own article in Section Four of this collection, I will argue that this involves a shift from an Enlightenment model of personhood and agency—with its emphasis on individuality and rationality—to a view of the self as more socially embedded and fluid. But one need not accept that argument to notice the disparate treatment of prostitution and pornography in many academic feminist liberal discussions. This distinction is not found in many nonacademic discussions, however, and this fact alone is worth some further consideration. What the articles in this third section all have in common is their emphasis on the negative consequences of restrictions on expression, and a worry about repressing too quickly or too broadly, differing expressions of sexuality—even (sometimes especially) where such expressions are troubling or disturbing.

The first article in Section Three has been written exclusively for this collection by sex writer Theresa Reed (aka "Darklady"). In "Private Acts vs. Public Art: Where Prostitution Ends and Pornography Begins," Reed describes her experience working within the pornography industry and discusses some of the real and perceived differences between pornography and prostitution. Although concerned about the rights of individuals to engage in whatever consensual forms of sex work they choose, Reed emphasizes the important difference between the public nature involved in the creation and distribution of a tangible third-party pornography product and the private nature of the personal and individualized prostitution exchange. She expands this into the realm of artistic expression, arguing that both pornography and prostitution are capable of involving artistic expression. This is in contrast with many liberal treatments of each, which limit the pornography debate to discussion of expression rights, and the prostitution debate to discussion of labor concerns.

In "Freedom, Equality, Pornography," Jonathan Cohen responds to MacKinnon's call for legal restrictions on pornography by trying to make some space for societal interests in protecting pornography. Cohen argues that the harm pornography does can be combated in a way that preserves sexual expression. His appeal to other legal means of controlling abuse in the sex industry provides liberalism's strongest response to charges that it ignores the harmful fallout from the industry. Ultimately, Cohen is pessimistic about what strict regulation can accomplish, and he argues that the best way to deal with troubling expression is to expose it rather than try to suppress it.

Ronald Dworkin's article, "Women and Pornography," was originally written as a review of MacKinnon's book *Only Words*. In it, Dworkin criticizes MacKinnon's equality argument (laid out in Chapter Four of this book) as too broad, and dangerous in its implications. According to Dworkin, MacKinnon's argument presupposes the principle that equality requires that some tastes and preferences not be expressed at all. Such a principle is dangerous, according to Dworkin, because it could justify government prohibition of any expression that offends a disadvantaged group. Not only is Dworkin unwilling to trade liberty for this sort of equality, but he also argues that such a trade-off is not required by a commitment to First Amendment values. According to Dworkin, one of the purposes of the First Amendment is to protect the very ideal of equality that MacKinnon thinks gets short shrift in liberal defenses of pornographers' free expression rights.

In "Disgust and Desire: *Hustler* Magazine," Laura Kipnis moves the debate about pornography away from concerns about sexual abuse and gender oppression by arguing that pornography is sometimes not only about sex, but also about class. According to Kipnis, one way of understanding the revulsion to certain forms of "low" sexuality is as a mechanism for upholding bourgeois class distinctions. Using Larry Flynt and *Hustler* magazine as a case study, Kipnis explores the intersections of class antagonistic humor and graphic sexuality, arguing that *Hustler* challenges both bourgeois and feminist bodily proprieties in ways overlooked in feminist discussions about pornography. She argues that one reason to be interested in deliberately offensive pornography like *Hustler* magazine is that it shows just how much class has to do with sexuality and sexual norms.

Section Four, the final section of this book, brings together several articles that engage very different questions about the sex industry. Like the other articles in this collection, the articles in this section all concern questions of freedom and choice to varying degrees, but all locate their discussion within a consideration of the context in which the prostitute/client exchange occurs. The articles in this section do not share a viewpoint about the merits of prostitution so much as they share a critical approach to the way the debate is often framed in traditional feminist liberal circles. Some of the articles might be called "egalitarian" to highlight their emphasis on issues of equality and third-party effects on and of the exchange of sex for money, and to contrast them with traditional "liberal individualist" discussions of equality that emphasize the individual free agent more than the social context in which the agent's choices are to be interpreted. And some of the articles explicitly draw the reader's attention to the way traditional debates about the sex industry leave out the experiences of certain sectors of workers. What all the articles here have in common is an emphasis on the way traditional debates between radical and liberal feminists often exclude the concerns of those who are part of, or affected by, the sex industry.

In "The Name of the Pose: A Sex Worker by Any Other Name," written exclusively for this collection, Tracy Quan discusses the very words used to describe prostitution. Her article examines the different nuances of many of the terms used by various parties to debates about the sex industry. Through her discussion of words, Quan creates a snapshot of what many in the prostitutes' rights movement are talking about today. Specifically, she focuses on the growing use of the term "sex work" within certain politicized circles of the industry and academia, and she draws attention to the pros and cons of such mainstreaming terminology.

In another new piece written for this collection, "Thinking Outside the Box: Men in the Sex Industry," Julian Marlowe discusses the limitations of feminist discussions of the sex industry that focus exclusively on female sex workers, while disregarding male sex workers and clients entirely. Marlowe draws upon his own experiences to confront the conventional arguments in favor of prohibitions on prostitution and pornography, and challenges the reader to think about sexual commerce outside of the context of gender hierarchy. In addition to the point about who is left out of traditional feminist debates about the sex industry, a suggestion here is that prohibitions on prostitution rest on certain stereotypes that do more to damage women's freedom than aid it.

In "Prostitution & Sexual Autonomy: Making Sense of the Prohibition of Prostitution" Scott Anderson offers a critique of prostitution based on the philosophical idea of autonomy, or freedom, set in the context of a concern with equality and justice. He argues that sexual autonomy can be ensured for all only when sexuality is maintained as a sphere separate from economic activity for all people. In a world where sex work is fully normalized, Anderson makes the case that sex workers will lack sexual autonomy—a situation that he argues is fundamentally unjust.

The injustice of such a world is that some individuals would have more choices at the expense of some groups—namely, sex industry workers—having less freedom. As a safeguard to equality of autonomy then, Anderson thinks the prohibition of prostitution makes sense.

In "Markets in Women's Sexual Labor," Debra Satz also offers a critique of prostitution as an unjust form of labor. Like Anderson, Satz stresses the inequality outside, as well as inside, the prostitution exchange. But unlike Anderson, Satz does not think the problem here is a matter of the erosion of boundaries between workplace and sexual sphere. Rather, according to Satz, the problem lies in the social power differential between men and women that makes the realities of commerce in women's sexual labor unjust. So, although there may be nothing *inherently* demeaning about exchanging sex for money, according to Satz, the realities of women's and men's unequal economic positions in society make prostitution an unfair exchange. And by reinforcing negative stereotypes about women, prostitution not only reflects, but also causally contributes to, women's inferior social and economic status.

The collection concludes with my own "Obscene Division: Feminist Liberal Assessments of Prostitution Versus Feminist Liberal Defences of Pornography," which examines feminist liberal defenses of the sex industry in the context of the different way liberals tend to treat prostitution and pornography. I argue that, despite the fact that both prostitution and pornography involve an exchange of sex for money, there is an inconsistency between feminist liberal assessments of prostitution as a form of labor, and feminist liberal defenses of pornography as a form of expression. I offer an analysis of this inconsistency as involving differing conceptions of the self and the role that sex and sexuality play in those conceptions, and I make the case that traditional feminist liberal defenses of pornography—although they offer a more satisfying account of the self as socially "situated"—tend to ignore the very worker that is supposed to be of such primary concern in the case of prostitution.

Clearly, the intention is that readers will take away from this collection a deeper understanding of debates about the sex industry. But beyond this is also the hope that such a deeper understanding will help change the landscape of thought about the industry, particularly the relation between prostitution and other forms of sexual commerce, like pornography. This is both philosophically interesting and practically important. The differences in the way prostitution and pornography are treated highlight the ways in which we think a person's identity and freedom of choice are differently affected and implicated by different forms of commodification. The kinds of arguments made concerning the benefits/ills of restrictions on sexual commerce—and the *differences* between the types of debate surrounding prostitution and pornography in particular—are revealing for how they employ conceptions of human flourishing and ideas about the relationship between freedom, responsibility, and societal goods. And this means that the discussion here is both theoretically and practically fundamental to questions regarding personhood, the role of sex in a healthy human life, and the appropriateness or not of current societal restrictions on various kinds of commerce in sexual services.

PART ONE

Critiques of the Sex Industry

CHAPTER ONE

Duet

Prostitution, Racism and Feminist Discourse *

VEDNITA CARTER AND EVELINA GIOBBE

> and when we speak we are afraid
> our words will not be heard
> nor welcomed
> but when we are silent
> we are still afraid
> so it is better to speak
> remembering we were never meant to survive
> —Audre Lorde, "Litany for Survival"[1]

☾
.

We come to this piece from two very different backgrounds. One of us is a Black woman, the other a first-generation Italian-American. One daughter carries the familial imprint of slavery, the second, fascism. Both share a history of sexual exploitation by white men and a commitment to ending the prostitution of our sisters. We write to bear witness. We espouse an ideology of liberation rejecting any accommodation to white male supremacy.

We have written and lectured for over a decade about prostitution as a system of institutionalized violence against women. Ironically, this period approximates our collective years in the sex industry. Over the years, the

---

*Revised by Vednita Carter, 2004. Reprinted with permission from *Hastings Women's Law Journal*, Volume 10, Number 1, Winter 1999, 37–57. Copyright © 1999 by University of California, Hastings College of the Law.
    1. Audre Lorde, Litany for Survival, in The Black Unicorn (1978).

parallels between being a prostitute and organizing against prostitution as survivors has struck a discomforting chord.

This kind of activism is about giving people what they want, how they want it and asking them to let you give it to them again another time. The script always remains the same. Lawyers want to talk legal theory, sociologists want to talk occupational ideologies and postmodern feminists want to talk about sexual autonomy, free speech and choice.[2] Nobody, it appears, really wants to talk about prostitution.

Preparing for a speaking engagement is very much like turning a "talk trick." You pack your cites in your bag like condoms to protect yourself from the rhetoric spouting from the white middle-class academics while they masturbate at you. You carefully prepare your arguments to fit into the prearranged scenario. Initially, you think you can change hearts and minds by simply exposing the truth. Your early optimism begins to fade however, when you find yourself saying the same things to the same people in city after city, state after state, year after year. Part of the problem is that you are walking into a racially charged political sexual fantasy. Typically, "feminist" panels on "sex work" are mirror images of the prostitution world replete with actors assembled from central casting. There's the liberal-lefty lawyers representing the tricks, a madam representing the pimps, a prostitutes' rights activist representing the "whores," and then there is you. Conferences about prostitution are not unlike bachelor parties. The customers (conference attendees) want to watch two whores (women) mud wrestle (debate) for their sexual (intellectual) enjoyment. In the end, you get fucked (your experiences are reduced to a matter of unpopular opinion), take your money (honorarium) and go home to get ready for your next date.

The goal of these conferences is not to examine the institution of prostitution, how it functions in tandem with racism and sexism, or to find solutions to the former or the latter. To the contrary, the goal is to promote public policy that will provide more johns with more sex, more pimps with more money and prostitutes with more of the same. Prostituted women are offered two roles in these discussions: lifting one's dress with a wink and a smile or tearful, hand-wringing displays of victimization. We've never been very good at either. But then we weren't really very good at sex work.

Conference proceedings are usually published ostensibly to give a broader voice to panel participants. Central to the publication is the appearance of neutrality: the inclusion of a diversity of voices and views.

2. See generally Travis Hirschi, The Professional Prostitute, 7 Berkeley. J. Soc. 33, 44–45 (1962). See also James H. Bryan, Occupational Ideologies and Individual Attitudes of Call Girls, 13 Soc. Probs. 443 (1966).

Ironically, the parameters of the original setting and the demands of writing a journal article are exclusionary by virtue of their form. Having never read a law journal (feminist or otherwise) while waiting for the next trick to arrive or in between sets at a strip club, we question the intrinsic value of using scarce time and resources to prepare a submission. Furthermore, our primary purpose is to work towards the liberation of prostituted women, which requires the organizing of and with prostituted women. We realize it is highly unlikely that we will reach our constituents, let alone organize them, through this venue. However, considering the relatively small section of the marketplace of ideas to which our views have been relegated, we have decided to take our free speech where we can get it. At the very least, our short "duet" will provide a counterpoint to the ceaseless droning of the chorus.

If we are to design public policy that adequately addresses the issue of commercial sexual exploitation, we must retreat from the intellectual wet dream in which we have immersed ourselves. We must confront the stark reality of prostitution on its own terms, in its own language and in the social context that it exists. This is not an easy voyage. For the non-prostituted woman, it entails looking into the eyes of the men, and the all too many women whom you have allowed into your life, and daring to question the ways in which they have passed through the lives of our prostituted sisters. Men have created a society in which women occupy two opposite poles. The laws these men have created are designed to keep women apart: one in the brothel, the other in the academy—with the threat of being banished to the marriage bed as a warning to all who would question these generous options. It is long past time to cross this divide which has been built upon the silence that men have imposed on us all by exposing the reality of prostitution.[3] This Article attempts to make that leap by stripping away the metaphors which have hidden the harm of prostitution and also by examining the sex industry within the context of race, class and the gender oppression in which it is rooted.

THE NEXUS BETWEEN PROSTITUTION
AND SLAVERY

One must understand the past before one can understand the present. It is often very painful for African-Americans to look back in history.

3. See generally Margaret A. Baldwin, Split at the Root: Prostitution and Feminist Discourses of Law Reform, 5 Yale J. L. & Feminism 47 (1992) (discussing the relationship between prostitutes and other (non-prostituted) women and the way this divide is codified in law).

Most portrayals of Black women, in visual images or writing, have been negative. Black women have been depicted in ways that one would think could only be fictional or in some horror story. In truth, many of these portrayals are our reality. We have seen the Black mammy, always caring for white folks' children, even to the point of suckling milk from her breasts so she does not have enough milk for her own child.[4] We have seen her as a slave, valued only for her "breeding capacity," and we have seen her children taken from her.[5] Pornography portrays her as a wild animal that is always ready for any kind of sex, at any time, at any place, with anybody.[6] Today sex-oriented businesses are typically zoned in Black neighborhoods. Poor, Black communities have become de facto combat zones where street prostitution is highly visible and readily available.[7] The implicit message to white men is that it is all right to solicit Black women and girls for sex, that we are all prostitutes.[8] On almost any night, you can see them slowly cruising our neighborhoods, rolling down their windows, calling out to women and girls. The message to Black women is equally clear: this is how it is, this is who we are, this is what we're for. With all the negative images and labels ascribed to Black women, it is no surprise that many of us remain confused about who we really are and who we want to be.[9]

4. See Cheryl Gilkes, From Slavery to Social Welfare: Racism and the Control of Black Women, in Class, Race, and Sex: The Dynamics of Control 288–300 (Amy Swerdlow & Hanna Lessinger eds., 1983). See also bell hooks, Sisters of the Yam: Black Women and Self-Recovery 49 (1993) (arguing that over-reliance on strong Black women in the workplace cast them in the role of contemporary "mammies" who will assume the burden of all responsibilities).

5. See La Frances Rodgers-Rose, The Black Woman, in Sage Publications 18, 20 (1980).

6. See generally Patricia Hill Collins, Black Feminist Thought: Knowledge, Consciousness, and the Politics of Empowerment (1991). Patricia Collins traces the sexualized representations of African-Americans and the pornographic treatment of African-American female bodies in the 19th century, including public displays of female slaves on the auction block and the sexual objectification of Sarah Bartmann. Bartmann was put on exhibition at fashionable Parisian parties as an example of deviant sexuality. Upon her death in 1815, she was dissected and her buttocks and genitals put on display. See id. at 168–69, 171–72, 175.

7. The majority of street prostitution and illegal saunas (brothels) in Minnesota are located in pockets of urban poverty in North and South Minneapolis and to a lesser extent the Frogtown area of St. Paul.

8. See Collins, supra note 6, at 177 (arguing the myth of the Black prostitute is the justification for social control over Black women and legitimizes rape and other forms of sexual violence.

9. See generally William H. Grier & Price M. Cobbs, Black Rage (1968).

Around the late 1950s and 1960s our image was beginning to change. When our country was immersed in the civil rights movement—African-Americans banded together.[10] We had very powerful leaders, many of whom were subsequently killed.[11] For a moment in history, however, "Black Power" was our rallying cry and "Black is Beautiful" was how we identified ourselves.[12] It is what we believed about who we were and what we were capable of. When the civil rights movement waned, the identity we were beginning to create for ourselves vanished with it. Once again we became caught up in white society's denigrated image of who we are.[13]

Our ancestors did not feel this lack of self-worth. Before the invasion of Africa by the white man, Africans were a dignified people. Family was the basic unit of the nation.[14] The only way African people could survive was if the African family survived. They had but one view of women—they

10. The American civil rights movement is commonly dated from the 1954 U.S. Supreme Court ruling in Brown v. Board of Education. The banding of African-Americans occurred through events such as bus boycotts in Louisiana and Alabama, the founding of the Southern Christian Leadership Conference (SCLC) and the Student Non-violent Coordinating Committee (SNCC), voter registration drives, the freedom rides and the March on Washington. See generally Clayborne Carson et al., Eyes on the Prize Civil Rights Reader (1987).

11. We had Martin Luther King, Jr. (killed in 1968), Rosa Parks, Autherine Lucy (first Black admitted to University of Alabama), Daisy Bates (president of the NAACP in Arkansas during "Little Rock" and editor of a Black newspaper), James Farmer (CORE leader of Freedom Riders), James Meredith (first Black to attend class at the University of Mississippi, killed in 1966), Medgar Evans (head of Mississippi NAACP, killed in 1963), Herbert Lee (killed in 1961), Stokely Carmichael (chairman of SNCC) and Malcolm X (killed in 1965). See generally Carson et al., supra note 10.

12. The phrase "Black Power" was coined by SNCC field secretary Willie Ricks in June 1966. However, the slogan gained widespread movement acceptance when, frustrated by the few gains made by Blacks, Stokley Carmichael, then Chairman of SNCC, called for Black Power and the crowd of 600 passionately responded "Black Power! Black Power!" Seth Cagin & Philip Dray, We are not Afraid 440–41 (1988).

13. See bell hooks, Black Looks: Race and Representation (1992). "A culture of domination demands of all its citizens self-negation. The more marginalized, the more intense the demand. Since Black people, especially the underclass, are bombarded by messages that we have no value, are worthless, it is no wonder that we fall prey to nihilistic despair...." Id. at 19.

14. See Rodgers-Rose, supra note 5, at 16; Judy H. Katz, White Awareness 121–22 (1978) (comparing African and English culture).

were to be highly respected.[15] If a wife lost her husband, the husband's brother was obligated to take his brother's family, including the wife, into his home.[16] She was considered the queen of Africa, the giver of life, and as such was honored and adored.

Among all the jewels stripped from the Africans, when the continent was raided by whites and during their subsequent enslavement, the loss of spiritual culture and sexuality was the most devastating. During the slavery era, female slaves suffered horribly from constant and brutal sexual exploitation. Rape was a fact of life on the plantation.[17] Female slaves were continually subjected to the drunken or abusive sexual advances of a master, overseer or the master's sons.[18] Few Black women reached the age of seventeen without having been molested by a white male.[19] Many white men would deliberately impregnate Black women for the sole purpose of producing female children. They would wait until the child reached the age of eleven or twelve years old and sell them to a

15. See Rodgers-Rose, supra note 5, at 16.

16. This is not an unusual practice in family centered cultures. As late as 1933, it was a common practice in southern Italy. One of the authors' Grandfather died at the age of 33 leaving a wife and four small children in the town of Torre del Greco. His brother married his widowed sister-in-law and raised his nieces and nephews as his own children. Another widowed relative married his deceased wife's sister after her husband passed away in 1978.

17. See Rodgers-Rose, supra note 5, at 20. See also Gerda Lerner, Black Women in White America, chs. 1 & 3 (1973); Susan Brownmiller, Against Our Will: Men, Women & Rape 7 (1976) (discussing how the rape of female slaves was not punishable by law as it was impossible to rape one's own property).

18. See Testimony of Harry McMillan before the American Freedmen's Inquiry Commission (June 1863), in Freedom: Documentary History of Emancipation 1861–1867, Series I, Vol. II, The Wartime Genesis of Free Labor: The Lower South 250–54 (Ira Berlin et al. eds., 1990) (compilation of letters and testimony from the U.S. National Archives). In discussing sexual relations between female slaves and their masters McMillan states the young men did it; there was a good deal of it. They often kept one girl steady and sometimes two on different places; men who had wives did it too sometimes; if they could get it on their own place it was easier but they would go wherever they could get it. Id.

19. See Daniel A.P. Murray, The Mastership and Its Fruits: The Emancipated Slave Face to Face with His Old Master 6 (N.Y. Loyal Publication Society 1864).

The old masters usually made their selections from the house servants and young masters generally preferred for their concubines their half-sisters. It was the common custom. They were usually taken at the age of thirteen or fourteen...a chaste colored girl at the age of seventeen was almost unknown.

Id. See also Lerner, supra note 17.

"fancy house." A fancy house was a place where girls of mixed race were sold into prostitution.[20] During the period of slavery mixed-breed girls were worth a great deal of money in the prostitution business.[21] As on the plantation, the women would have to tend to the sexual needs of white men no matter how loathsome and perverted the needs.[22] In return for her submission, she was given nicer clothes, food and a decent place to stay. Because her basic needs were provided for, she was made to feel that her sexual exploitation raised her standard of life and therefore she was better than other slaves.

After their emancipation in 1863, many slaves fled from the South to the North in search of true freedom. Mistakenly believing that the northern whites' moral opposition to slavery signified their belief in racial equality, it's easy to imagine what the thoughts of Blacks might have been:[23] up North they could find work, provide for their families. There would be no more worries about mothers and daughters being raped and assaulted or sold. Little did they know the white man wasn't going to relinquish their bodies that easily. It was going to take more than the Emancipation Proclamation for this to happen. Whites continued to perpetuate the myth that all Black women were wild sex animals in an attempt to excuse and hide their continued sexual exploitation. Up until the 1960s they were still invading the homes of Black families in the South, raping mothers and daughters.[24] It wasn't until the civil rights movement that this practice appeared to stop, or at least we didn't hear about it anymore. As a result of the systematic abuse Black women have suffered in this country, the lesson sadly passed on from grandmother to daughter in our communities is that sexual exploitation by white men is inevitable.

20. See Deborah G. White, Ain't I A Woman? Female Slaves in the Antebellum South 202–03 (1979) (unpublished Ph.D. dissertation, University of Chicago) (on file with University Microfilms International). See also John D'Emilio & Estelle B. Freedman, Intimate Matters: A History of Sexuality in America 102 (1988) (discussing Black female slaves purchased for concubinage); Murray, supra note 19, at 6 ("Their own offspring ... were treated as slaves; they were frequently subjected to ferocious treatment, and sold, to be put out of their sight.").

21. See White, supra note 20.

22. Murray, supra note 19, at 6 ("I have known ... women to be severely whipped for not coming to the quarters of the overseer or master for the purpose of prostitution when ordered so to do.").

23. See Cagin & Dray, supra note 12, at 201 (discussing northern sympathies for the plight of southern whites during the mid-1870s).

24. See Lerner, supra note 17.

THE SOCIAL CONSTRUCTION OF PROSTITUTION

The function of the institution of prostitution is to allow males uncondi-
tional sexual access to females, limited solely by their ability to pay for this
privilege. Culturally supported tactics of power and control facilitate the
recruitment or coercion of women and children into prostitution and
effectively impede their escape. These tactics include economic marginalization, child sexual abuse, rape and battery, as well as racism, classism
and heterosexism.

A society that keeps women economically marginalized through educational deprivation and job discrimination[25] ensures a ready pool of
women who will be vulnerable to recruitment into, and entrapment in,
prostitution. However, poverty is only one factor that pushes women into
the sex industry. The average age of entry into prostitution in the United
States is fourteen.[26] Studies of prostituted women reveal that their initial
sexual experience occurred at a very early age,[27] most often the result
of rape.[28] The vast majority of adult prostitutes were sexually abused as
children,[29] usually by a father or step-father.[30] They commonly suffered
physical abuse and neglect in their families of origin.[31] For most, the only
way to stop the violence is to run away from home.[32] Young, frightened
and unable to find employment, these girls are easy prey for pimps who
promise them friendship, romance and riches.

Battering further facilitates the recruitment of adult women into prostitution. For example, a study conducted in New York City, found that as

25. See generally Susan Faludi, Backlash: The Undeclared War Against
American Women (1991) (discussing the status of women). See also Lerner, supra
note 17, at 83–143 (educational discrimination), 259–62 (job discrimination).

26. See Susan Kay Hunter, Prostitution is Cruelty and Abuse to Women and
Children, 1 Mich. J. Gender & L. 91 (1993).

27. See D. Kelly Weisberg, Children Of The Night: A Study Of Adolescent
Prostitution 92, 165–66 (1985) (reviewing current studies on juvenile prostitution).

28. See id.

29. See Id. at 91–93 (review of literature on childhood sexual abuse as an
antecedent to prostitution).

30. See Catharine A. Mackinnon, Prostitution and Civil Rights, 1 Mich. J.
Gender & L. 13, 28 (1993).

31. See Weisberg, supra note 27, at 93–94 (review of literature on familial
physical abuse and neglect as antecedents to prostitution).

32. See id. at 121–23, 170–71 (review of literature on runaway behavior as an
antecedent to prostitution).

many as forty percent of homeless people are battered women.[33] By the late 1980s battering had become the leading cause of injury to women.[34] Two-thirds of the women fleeing abusive relationship were turned away from battered women's shelters due to lack of space.[35] Without other resources, prostitution may be the only option available for them to feed themselves and their children.

Although individual men perpetrate child sexual abuse, rape and battery, a compelling argument can be made that these behaviors are culturally supported forms of social control. The prevalence of such occurences,[36] the fact that they differentially injure females, and the failure of male-controlled social institutions to prevent or redress such victims' injuries,[37] point to implicitly sanctioned conduct. The inordinate rate of these kinds of abuses in the lives of both women and girls as antecedents to prostitution unmasks cultural support for commercial sexual exploitation.

Racism and classism exacerbate oppressive social and economic conditions that make poor women and women of color particularly vulnerable to prostitution. African-American women are disproportionately represented among the women of color that are featured in pornography.[38]

33. See Faludi, supra note 25, at xiv.

34. See id.

35. See National Low-Income Housing Coalition: Women and Housing Task Force, Unlocking The Door: An Action For Meeting The Housing Needs Of Women 8 (1988).

36. See Phyllis Chesler, Mothers On Trial 56–57 (1987) (19% of American women (one in six) are sexually victimized as children; 2–5 million American women (one in seven) are paternally raped as children). See also Faludi, supra note 25, at xiv (battery leading cause of violence against women), xvii (reported rapes had more than doubled since 1970s; sex-related murders rose 160% between 1976 and 1984; one-third of the women murdered were killed by their spouse or male partner).

37. See National Woman Abuse Prevention Project, Understanding Domestic Violence Fact Sheets (federal funding for battered women's shelters withheld). See also Coalition On Women & The Budget, Inequality Of Sacrifice: The Impact Of The Reagan Budget On Women 23 (1986) (funding for shelters denied; Office of Domestic Violence closed); Faludi, supra note 25, at 463 (citing statistical information for 1987 from the National Center on Women and Family Law, 30 states have some form of marital rape exemption); Chesler, supra note 36, at 242–54 (fathers rarely jailed for incest; sexually abusive fathers rarely denied custody or visitation).

38. See generally Alice Mayall & Diana E.H. Russell, Racism in Porn, in Making Violence Sexy: Feminist Views On Pornography 167, 170–75 (Diana E.H. Russell ed., 1993).

Black women are portrayed as "animalistic, incapable of self-control, sexually depraved, implusive, unclean" and undeserving of human affection.[39] Pornography depicts them inviting and enjoying rape by white men.[40] These racist stereotypes promote, celebrate and perpetuate race-motivated sexual violence.[41] This created the overall environment that targets Black women for recruitment into prostitution by pimps and for harassment or solicitation by johns.[42]

Finally, heterosexism supports the male sexual imperative. Heterosexism advances the belief that men have uncontrollable sexual urges which, if not fulfilled, will drive them to rape "innocent" females.[43] Herein lies the ultimate justification for prostitution.

> The Harm Of Prostitution
> Prostitution is akin to the gardener's deliberate hand
> cutting away at the roots of a woman's soul
> pruning back the branches of her desires
> trapping her in a tiny vessel in which she cannot grow
> until her stunted, gnarled form acquiesces
> and her dwarfed, deformed spirit
> is pronounced a thing of beauty to men's eyes.[44]

The first harm of prostitution is "agreeing" to do it. A woman entering prostitution typically acquires a new name, changes her appearance and creates a fictitious past.[45] She does this not so much to protect herself from the police (although a string of aliases help), but to rearrange her persona so as to meet the market demand, and in an attempt to save something of

39. Id. at 167, 176. See also Collins, supra note 6, at 167–73.

40. See generally Mayall & Russell, supra note 38, at 171–75.

41. See id. at 176.

42. See Evelina Giobbe, Confronting Liberal Lies About Prostitution, in The Sexual Liberals And The Attack On Feminism 69 (Dorchen Leidholdt & Janice G. Raymond eds., 1990).

43. See Lars O. Ericsson, Charges Against Prostitution: An attempt at a Philosophical Assessment, 90 Ethics 335, 341 (1980) (contending that sexual satisfaction is a basic need); Kathleen Barry, Female Sexual Slavery 256 (1979) (arguing against the notion that, "the drive . . . is [believed to be] so overwhelming that the male is the one to be acted upon by it; thus the sex drive is put out of his control. At the same time it demands a fitting object for release, and thus the female role is defined.").

44. Unpublished poem by author Evelina Giobbe (on file with author).

45. See, e.g., Barry, supra note 43, at 94–95 (prostitutes commonly take on assumed names).

herself for herself.[46] Prostitutes are caricatures of women fashioned from a pastiche of pornographic films and magazines that feature prostituted women acting like prostitutes, which johns later use to teach prostitutes how to act. The process of becoming a prostitute entails the systematic destruction of an individual woman's ideas, beliefs, feelings and desires which are replaced with a compilation of values lifted from the texts of various pornographic paperbacks. A good prostitute is devoid of a unique and personal identity. She is empty space surrounded by flesh into which men deposit evidence of their masculinity. She does not exist so that he can. Prostitution done correctly begins with theft and ends with the subsequent abandonment of self. What remains is essential to the job: the mouth, the genitals, anus, breasts...and the label.

The second harm of prostitution is the prostitution itself. To be a prostitute is to be unconditionally sexually available to any male who buys the right to use your body in whatever way he chooses. Women have described prostitution as rape that is bought and paid for.[47] Prostitutes are "visited upon" by about five men per day—close to two thousand men per year. A girl who enters prostitution at fourteen will have submitted to the sexual demands of four thousand men before she is old enough to drive a car, eight thousand men before she is old enough to vote and twelve thousand men before she is deemed mature enough to buy a single beer in most states.[48] In addition to the daily mind-numbing indignity of (dis)engaging in "nonviolent" unwanted sex, prostituted women are subjected to a wide range of sexual abuse as part of the "job description."

The third harm of prostitution is a woman's accommodation to it. The repeated act of submitting to the sexual demands of strangers, with whom she wouldn't otherwise choose to engage in even the most superficial of

46. See Evelina Giobbe, Juvenile Prostitution: Profile of Recruitment, in Child Trauma I: Issues and Research 127 (Anne Wolbert Burgess ed., 1992) (interview with Karen: "When I would work the street, I wasn't 'Karen.' ... When I was on the street 'Candy' would come out.... Candy took over, or 'Randi' or 'Susie,' or how many others all took over. Those are the ones that survived that life. Karen would not have survived it.").

47. See Evelina Giobbe, Prostitution: Buying the Right to Rape, in Rape & Sexual Assault III, at 144 (Ann Wolbert Burgess ed., 1991) (interview with MD: "I don't know how else to explain it except that it felt like rape. It was rape to me.").

48. See Ruth Parriot, Health Experiences of Twin Cities Women Used in Prostitution 8 (1994) (unpublished manuscript on file with authors and WHISPER program (Women Hurt in Systems of Prostitution Engaged in Revolt) Minneapolis, MN) (reporting an average of 10,292 lifetime acts of prostitution with a high of 81,270; average number of years in prostitution was 8.6).

social interactions, necessitates that a women alienate her mind from her body. To be a prostitute is to be an object in the marketplace: a three-dimensional blank screen upon which men project and act out their sexual dominance. To be a prostitute is to witness male sexuality, stripped of any pretense of civility, and to say, "I want it." It is to withstand the unmasked fury of male supremacy pounding against your body and to say, "I want it." It is to feel the thrust of male power at the back of your throat and to choke out "I want it." To be a prostitute is to never forget: to see every man in every john and every john in any man, everywhere and always. To be a prostitute is to never be believed, unless you say, "I want it." At the very worst, prostitution is literal sexual slavery. At the very least, prostitution is an accommodation and an adaptation to white male supremacy in its most brutal incarnation.

Then there are the ancillary harms: the rapes, the robberies and the inevitable beatings punctuated by shouts of "bitch" and "whore" and "slut," gratituitously meted out by pimps, by johns and by the police.[49] These are the commonplace insults to injury that are directed at prostitutes simply because they are prostitutes.

THE HEALTH IMPLICATIONS OF SEX WORK

Prostitution has a profound effect on women's health and emotional well being. The physical and sexual abuse inherent in prostitution results in many health complications and lasting damage.[50] In a study conducted

49. Over half (52%) of prostituted women seeking services from the WHISPER program in 1995 had been physically assaulted by a john and 40% by a pimp; 48ad been raped by a customer and 29% by a pimp. Unpublished Study by CSERI, 1998 (on file with author Giobbe) [hereinafter CSERI Study A]. A second study of prostituted women conducted by CSERI revealed that 59% of prostitutes had been raped by a client and 48% were forced to commit a sexual act against their will; 27% were sexually assaulted by a police officer and half were sexually assaulted by a pimp. Unpublished Study by CSERI, 1998 (on file with author Giobbe) [hereinafter CSERI Study B]. Additionally, the women interviewed were beaten by customers (55%), the police (21%) and pimps (90%). Women also reported being robbed by customers (38%) and police officers (16%). See also Melissa Farley & Howard Barkan, Prostitution, Violence, and Posttraumatic Stress Disorder, 27(3) Women and Health 37–49 (1998) (reporting 82% of their San Francisco sample had been physically assaulted. Of these, 88% had been threatened with bodily harm and 83% had been threatened with a weapon. 68% of the respondents also reported being raped and 48% were raped more than five times.).

50. See Parriot, supra note 48, at 19.

by Melissa Farley and Howard Barkan, eight percent of the respondents reported that assaults by pimps and customers resulted in serious injury (e.g., gunshot wounds, knife wounds, etc.).[51] In a second study, conducted by Ruth Parriot, twenty-three percent of the sample who were beaten by customers suffered broken bones; two women were so severely battered that they spent time in a coma.[52] Additionally, Parriot's sample reported head injuries, knife wounds, loss of consciousness and miscarriage resulting from beatings in their personal relationships with pimps/partners.[53] In a third study conducted by CSERI (Commercial Sexual Exploitation Resource Institute) fourteen percent of the respondents reported permanent injuries, and thirteen percent disfigurement, resulting from prostitution-related violence.[54] Studies by Parriot, and those conducted by Farley and Barkan, also commented on the women's overall poor health.[55]

The emotional and psychological effects of prostitution on women's lives have been well documented. Participants in the Parriot study reported an average of six stress-related disorders, most frequently depression, insomnia, flashbacks and sexual dysfunction.[56] Sixty-eight percent of Farley and Barkan's sample of working prostitutes suffered from post-traumatic stress disorder (PTSD).[57] A study of 127 prostitutes in Puerto

51. Farley & Barkan, supra note 49, at 41.
52. Parriot, supra note 48, at 19.
53. Id.
54. CSERI Study B, supra note 49.
55. See Farley & Barkan, supra note 49, at 41 (50% of sample reported general health problems which the respondents believed were related to or exacerbated by sex work. These problems included arthritis or nonspecific joint pain (14%); cardiovascular symptoms (12%); liver disorders (11%); reproductive system symptoms (10%); respiratory symptoms (9%); neurological symptoms, such as numbness or seizures (9%); HIV infection (8%)). See also Parriot, supra note 48, at 11–14 (reporting positive pap smears (24%), colposcopy (12%), complications in pregnancy including low birth weight or premature delivery (29%), miscarriage (24%), STDs (85% reporting 4 episodes of gonorrhea, chlamydia, syphilis, genital warts or herpes) and pelvic inflammatory disease (31%)).
56. Parriot, supra note 48, at 17.
57. Farley & Barkan, supra note 49, at 42 (reporting prostitutes had an overall mean PLC (PTSD Checklist measuring severity of symptoms) of 54.9 compared to PLC scores of 30.6 in victims of child sexual abuse and 34.8 among Persian Gulf War veterans. Additionally, prostitutes scored highest on C symptoms (measuring numbing and avoidance); 79% of the sample suffered from three or more C symptoms (i.e., emotionally numb, sense of foreshortened future)).

Rico discovered a high prevalence rate of depressive symptoms.[58] In this study, researchers found that sex workers with high depression rates were more likely to report high-risk behaviors.[59] Depression contributes to a higher level of isolation.[60] Sadness and apathy associated with depression interferes with motivation.[61] PTSD causes clinically significant distress or impairment in social, occupational or other important areas of functioning and a sense of foreshortened future.[62] Prostitutes also suffer from a unique and irrational fear that could be coined "the Scarlet Letter Syndrome." They believe that people, especially men, can "tell" that they are prostitutes merely by looking at them.[63] This problem is exacerbated for Black women who have been indelibly branded as whores in the racist American consciousness. Symptoms associated with depression and PTSD, and other emotional stressors, contribute to the woman's inability to extricate themselves from the sex industry.

Considering the pervasive violence and stress in prostituted womens' lives, it is not surprising to find high levels of drug and alcohol abuse in this population. Seventy-five percent of Farley and Barkan's sample reported chemical dependency.[64] In Minnesota, one hundred percent of the CSERI Study B sample,[65] ninety-five percent of the CSERI Study A sample[66] and ninety-four percent of Parriot's sample[67] were chemically dependent. Further, fifty-five percent of Parriot's sample reported always

---

58. See Margerita Alegria et al., HIV Infection, Risk Behaviors, and Depressive Symptoms Among Puerto Rican Sex Workers, 84 (12) Am. J. Pub. Health 2000–02 (1994) (70% have a high rate of depressive symptoms).

59. Id. at 2001.

60. See Diagnostic and Statistical Manual of Mental Disorders 424 (Am. Psychiatric Ass'n. ed., 1994) (ß 309.81).

61. See id.

62. See id.

63. See CSERI Study B, supra note 49 (interview with Marlene: "I felt like I always had a big "P" on my forehead"); Giobbe, supra note 47, at 157 (interview with LV: "A man will look at me like...they just know"; interview with RM: "...people look at me...like I'm dirty...just a funny look they give you when they know you've been on the streets.").

64. Farley & Barkan, supra note 49, at 45.

65. CSERI Study B, supra note 49 (80% were poly drug users; 82% reported crack cocaine use and 39% described themselves as alcoholic as well as chemically dependent).

66. CSERI Study A, supra note 49 (reporting overall 12.2% i.v. drug use; 98f Black women surveyed were drug abusers, 92% reporting crack cocaine use).

67. Parriot, supra note 48, at 15 (reporting use of alcohol (98%), crack cocaine (96%) and heroin (38%) as well other drugs).

being high when turning a trick and thirty-four were high at least half of the time—thus further impairing judgment and further decreasing their ability to negotiate transactions with customers.[68]

The emotional impact of prostitution can be life threatening. Nineteen percent of Parriot's sample engaged in self-injurious behavior including self-mutilation. Forty-six percent attempted suicide, and within that group, sixty-five percent made subsequent attempts.[69] Fifty-three percent of the entire CSERI study A sample, and fifty-three percent of Black women surveyed attempted suicide.[70] Seventeen percent of Farley and Barkan's sample stated that they would choose immediate admission to a hospital for an acute emotional problem, drug addiction or both.[71]

THE QUESTION OF CHOICE & THE
INTERNATIONAL PROSTITUTES' RIGHTS
MOVEMENT

Probably the most disturbing aspect of the international prostitutes' rights movement is the way in which a hierarchy built on race and class privilege informs its ideology. The overwhelmingly white leadership of this well-funded movement is comprised of academics[72] and attorneys[73] who don't have to do sex work, and middle-aged former sex workers who no longer do sex work.[74] These individuals exploit third world women of color who have few viable alternatives to sex work[75] and promote the prostitution

68. Id. at 9. It is also important to note that unlike Farley and Barkan's sample of streetwalkers in San Francisco, women interviewed for Parriot's study and CSERI Studies A and B were involved in a variety of types of prostitution, including, but not limited to, street walking, working in massage parlors or saunas, escort or out call services (for madams, pimps and independently from their own book (private clientele)).

69. Parriot, supra note 48, at 17.

70. But see W. J. Fremouw et al., Suicide Risk: Assessment and Response Guidelines 25 (1990) (reporting 33% of those in the general population who attempt suicide made subsequent suicide attempts).

71. Farley & Barkan, supra 49, at 41.

72. E.g., Pricilla Alexander, Gail Pheterson.

73. E.g., American Civil Liberties Union position that prostitution should be decriminalized.

74. E.g., Margo St. James, Norma Jean Almodovar and (the younger) Carol Leigh.

75. See Debby Phillips, Sex Tourism in Thailand: A Traveler's Journal (1995) (on the Coalition Against Trafficking in Women Web Page, www.uri.edu/artsci/

of American women who are trapped in a cycle of poverty and despair.[76] The pro-prostitution lobby stands on a shaky platform of economic justice built on the false premise that prostitution is a quid pro quo commercial sexual transaction and as such should be subject to standard labor laws and protections.[77] Summarized briefly, their position holds that prostitution is a job. Therefore, prostitutes are independent businesswomen. As such, prostitutes are feminists and thus they can do what ever they choose with their bodies (sell sex) and their money (give it to pimps).[78] This view ignores the social context in which prostitution occurs, especially the race/class power differential that exists between prostitutes and their customers.[79]

wms/hughes/catw/phillips.htm.) In this village . . . young girl children were forced into prostitution. Not only to finance their community but to finance their country. For me, this experience provided a very clear example of how Third World women pay off Third World debts—yet, the men they serviced were the very culture who financed the demands and made the payments. This imbalance seemed to me, not to be with Thailand but with us. Id. (May 8 entry).

76. For a historical view of Black women and prostitution see Frank Byrd, The Private Life Of Big Bess, Social-Ethnic Studies: Life in Harlem (1938), reprinted in American Life Histories: Manuscripts from the Federal Writers' Project 1936–1940.

Women of minority races and economically bankrupt groups have always been exploited by materially stronger groups. Negro women are no exception to this rule. Many of them are forced to semi or full-time prostitution in order to have a place to sleep. This is nothing new to them. Many of their mothers before them were in the same predicament. Id. at 1. See also Farley & Barkan, supra note 49, at 46–47 (reporting 88% of the working prostitutes interviewed stated that they wanted to leave prostitution, reporting the following barriers to exiting the sex industry: lack of a home or safe place (78%); no job training (73%); absence of treatment for drug or alcohol abuse (67%); lack of childcare (34%) and the need for physical protection from pimps (28%)).

77. See Vindication of the Rights of Whores (Gail Pheterson ed., 1989) for a presentation of the positions of the national pro-prostitution lobbies, COYOTE and the National Task Force on Prostitution, as well as for the positions of the international lobbies; the International Committee for Prostitutes Rights and the Canadian Organization for the Rights of Prostitutes.

78. For an in-depth critique of these positions see Toby Summer, Women, Lesbians and Prostitution: A Working-class Dyke Speaks Out Against Buying Women for Sex, 2 Lesbian Ethics 33 (1987); Baldwin, supra note 3; Giobbe, supra note 42, at 68.

79. See, e.g., Philipa Levine, Prostitution in Florida: A Report to the Gender Bias Study Commission of the Supreme Court of Florida 9 (1988). See also id. at 95–99 (customers of prostitutes are typically suburban white, middle-class,

In a gender-stratified culture, men exert power over women when they use or manipulate sex role expectations in order to obtain their desires. Johns exert power over prostitutes by exploiting the traditional sex role expectations of women, along with the particular occupational ideology of prostitution.[80] They also exert power over prostitutes by reinforcing positive and neutralizing definitions of prostitution.[81]

Johns rigidly control the conditions under which prostitution occurs and strictly define the commercial sex transaction to meet their needs.[82] The knowledge and actual experience of customer violence reduces a woman's willingness to refuse customer demands.[83] Furthermore, a woman's willingness to risk antagonizing a potential john is further constricted by the fact that prostitution typically occurs in isolated areas and assaults against prostituted women are not treated seriously by law enforcement officials or the court.[84] Lastly, even if a woman refuses to comply with a customer demand and escapes without being harmed by the john himself, she may be beaten by her pimp or fired from the sauna or escort service who employs her, for losing a good (paying) customer.[85]

The most overt form of power used by johns to insure a prostituted woman's compliance is compensatory or economic power. Because an exchange of money occurs, the john is given license to use the woman's body in whatever manner he chooses. Any refusal on her part can result in the withdrawal of compensation. His ability to do so is enforced, directly and indirectly, by pimps and owners of prostitution businesses whose sole objective is to maximize their profits, or by the economic factors that initially put the woman at his disposal.

Racism further contributes to the power that men have over prostitutes. Racism is ubiquitous in American culture. Whites exert power over people of color by virtue of their white skin privilege. It is general knowledge that

middle-aged married men), 35–40 (prostitutes are typically teenagers or young women, poor, undereducated, homeless and drug-addicted).

80. See Charles Winick & Paul M. Kinsie, The Lively Commerce: Prostitution in the United States 50 (1971); Bryan, supra note 2, at 443.

81. For example, "prostitution is a job like any other job," "women are born with a gold mine between their legs," "prostitutes don't sell themselves, they are selling a service" etc.

82. This is not a hard concept to grasp, basically "who pays the piper, calls the tune."

83. See generally supra note 49 (prevalence of violence against prostitutes).

84. See David P. Bryden & Sonja Lengnick, Rape in the Criminal Justice System, 87 J. Crim. L. & Criminology 1194, 1304 (1997).

85. Case notes on file with authors.

white men, as a class, control the major social institutions in the United
States. They control educational institutions, the legislature, the criminal
justice system, financial institutions and major corporations in the United
States. Historically, white men as a class benefitted from the institution of
slavery, as did their wives, their families, communities and the country as
a whole. Today, all whites continue to reap the benefits of slavery and the
American system of apartheid under which Blacks currently live. Therefore, it is fair to argue that in the microcosm of prostitution, johns buy
Black women with a currency backed by a living history of domination
and oppression.

DECRIMINALIZATION/LEGALIZATION
DISCUSSION

The World Charter for Prostitutes' Rights[86] calls for the "decrimi-
naliz[ation of] all aspects of adult prostitution and [the] regulat[[[ion]
of third parties"—they mean pimps here folks, really—"according to
standard business codes."[87] The charter also demands that "prostitutes
should have the freedom to choose their place of work . . . [and] provide
their services under the conditions that are absolutely determined by themselves and no one else."[88] The charter states that "[t]here should be no law
discriminating against prostitutes associating and working collectively in
order to acquire a high degree of personal security."[89] The charter also
suggests that "prostitutes should pay regular taxes on the same basis as
other independent contractors and employees and should receive the same
benefits."[90] Finally, it calls for the creation of a committee "comprised
of prostitutes and other professionals . . . to insure the protection of the
rights of the prostitutes and to whom prostitutes can address their complaints."[91]

Proponents of prostitution advance their agenda by equating prostitutes with oppressed laborers consigned to the underground economy,
hounded by the government and deprived of the rights and benefits

---

86. World Charter for Prostitutes' Rights, International Committee for Prostitutes' Rights (ICPR), Amsterdam 1985, published in A Vindication of the Rights
of Whores, supra note 77, at 40 [hereinafter Charter].
87. Id.
88. Id.
89. Id. at 41.
90. Id.
91. Id.

afforded to workers outside of the sex industry.[92] From this perspective, decriminalization, or even the legalization of prostitution, seems logical public policy. However, when the "job" of prostitution is exposed, any similarity to legitimate work is shattered. Put simply, whether you're a "high-class" call girl or a street walkin' ho, when you're on a "date" you gotta get on your knees or lay on your back and let that man use your body any way he wants to. That's what he pays for.

Pretending prostitution is a job like any other job would be laughable if it weren't so serious. Leading marginalized prostituted women to believe that decriminalization would materially change anything substantive in their lives as prostitutes is dangerous and irresponsible. There are no liberating clauses in the World Charter. Pimps are not "third party managers."[93] Pimp/prostitute relationships are contingent on a woman engaging in prostitution and relinquishing all or part of her earnings to her man.[94] The relationship is defined and controlled by the pimp for his economic gain. What "standard business codes" are applicable to this form of economic exploitation? What regulatory body would enforce such codes? At the same time that proponents call for standard business practices to be applied to the business of prostitution, they demand that prostitutes be free of any laws that would dictate where and how they deliver their services. Why would a legitimate business enterprise be exempt from the oversight of local zoning boards? Why shouldn't the health department impose codes on an industry that can and does affect the health of its employees, customers and the public?

92. For the purpose of this section, the authors will limit their analyses to prostitution, as it is outside of the scope of this article to present a public policy perspective on the legal sex industry (i.e., pornography and stripping). Although the authors believe that the legal sex industry, like prostitution, is a form of commercial sexual exploitation, in no way do we negate the efforts of strippers, for example, to improve the immediate environmental conditions in strip clubs and bring suit against club owners if necessary for fair compensation. However, these actions do not ameliorate the inherent harms of commercial sex from our perspective.

93. For a comparison of tactics of power and control used by pimps and men who batter their partners, see Evelina Giobbe, An Analysis of Individual, Institutional, & Cultural Pimping, 1 Mich J. Gender & L. 45–50 (1993).

94. See Diana Gray Hilton, Turning-Out: A Study of Teenage Prostitution 110 (1971) (unpublished master's thesis, on file with the University of Washington) (pimps appropriate all or most of prostitutes' money). This definition may be extended to include corporate pimps or brothel owners in that a woman's "working" relationship to her pimp "employer" is contingent on her engaging in prostitution and relinquishing all or part of her earnings to him.

Finally, the charter states that "prostitutes should pay regular taxes on the same basis as other independent contractors and employees and should receive the same benefits."[95] The only person right now who does not have his hand in prostitutes' collective pockets is the government. Implementation of the Charter would change all of this. As independent contractors, prostitutes would have to pay a self-employment tax of 15.3%, plus any applicable state taxes.[96] Independent contractors do not receive benefits—because they are considered both employer and employee they must pay for their own medical insurance and retirement plan.[97]

Some advocates suggest "prostitute collectives" as a solution.[98] Would the collective be incorporated as a business? If not, what is it? If so, the corporation would be minimally responsible for paying taxes, unemployment and workers' compensation insurance for their employees. Further, the corporation would have to comply with OSHA health and safety standards, affirmative action policies and sexual harassment laws. All of this would probably require the services of an accountant, an attorney and possibly the purchase of professional liability and/or malpractice insurance. Suddenly, prostitution has become a very complex business. The likely result of these policies is a two-tier system: independent contractors and small prostitution businesses running legal operations on one hand, and "freelancers" working off the books and on the streets—at a lower rate of compensation—on the other. The Charter's most unrealistic component however, is the committee it creates "to insure the protection of the rights of the prostitutes and to whom prostitutes can address their complaints . . . comprised of prostitutes and other professionals like lawyers and supporters."[99] If prostitution were a legitimate enterprise why would prostitutes need a special committee to review workplace grievances? What entity will vest this "committee" with the legal power to arbitrate disputes? What types of "complaints" would be mediated? Is the worker unhappy with the amount of compensations negotiated with the client? Did he exceed the limit of their sexual contract? Maybe he just took too damn long. . . . Would the committee have a family law component to mediate disagreements between prostitutes and their pimps? Would this subcommittee handle domestic violence complaints? Squabbles among wife- in-laws? Maybe the complainant is unhappy because

95. Charter, supra note 86, at 41.

96. 26 USC §1401 (West 1998).

97. Id.

98. Charter, supra note 86, at 41 ("There should be no law discriminating against prostitutes associating and working collectively. . . . ") (emphasis added).

99. Charter, supra note 86, at 40.

her quota is too high or perhaps she'd like to manage her own money. Even if there were a committee, and even if they were somehow vested with the legal authority to mediate disputes, prostitution is by nature an anonymous and transitory industry—how would they actually find the person a complaint is lodged against? How would they compel him to appear before the committee, let alone comply with their findings?

Legalization and decriminalization are social experiments that have repeatedly failed.[100] They have not made a significant difference in prostituted women's lives. They have not kept all prostituted women out of jail. They have not reduced the social stigma attached to sex work. They have done nothing to ameliorate the inherent or ancillary harms of prostitution: economic exploitation by pimps, violence by johns and the trauma that results from both. Nor has it stopped the widespread use of drugs by prostitutes who can no longer separate mind from body in getting the job done. Prostitution exists in and is maintained by a male-controlled society where violence against women and children is pandemic and racism flourishes. Ultimately, decriminalization or legalization proposals merely protect some men's right to cheap, easily accessible sex and pimps' ability to earn a damn good living by getting women to do it.

CONCLUSION

In the African-American community, prostitution is rooted in that very difficult tight space where Black women attempt to survive, the space where racism and sexism intersect. A Black underclass has developed in the United States, which has at its core a culture shaped by the legacy of slavery. The Black underclass includes second and third generation welfare recipients, has gangs as social institutions, and is supported by an underground economy built on drug trafficking and prostitution. The Black underclass, along with the poor of other races, makes up the culture of poverty. As a group, they lack access to legitimate economic resources

---

100. See A Vindication of the Rights of Whores, supra note 77, at 51–102 (criticizing statutes and ordinances governing prostitution in countries where it is legal or decriminalized); Id. at 234 (Philippina women forced into prostitution in Holland); Id. at 228 (interview with "Martha" describing forced prostitution in the Netherlands); Id. at 166 (lack of police response to sexual assaults against prostitutes in England); Id. at 60 (victim blaming by Australian police responding to serial rapes of prostitutes); Id. at 73 (court refuses to prosecute johns for theft of service); Id. at 71 (criticizing compulsory medical exams of prostitutes as an invasion of privacy); Id. at 87 (criticizing registration of prostitutes as stigmatizing).

and adequate health care. They are alienated from most social institutions except those that perpetuate the cycle of poverty and despair: welfare, corrections and the underground economy.

Most Black women used in prostitution were born into the Black underclass.[101] They lost their childhood to the streets. Many came of age in juvenile detention centers and matured in adult correctional facilities.[102] They raised some and lost all too many of their children to the streets. Unless things change—unless we change them—they will raise and lose their grandchildren too.

The liberation of Black women will require a multifaceted course of action enacted on an individual, community and political playing field. White society's standards and definitions have defined our sexuality as African-American women. Although the master no longer holds us captive on the plantation, we still carry the chains of slavery by virtue of our slave mentality. For Black women to reclaim what has been stolen, we must begin to name ourselves. We must realize that we no longer have to accept the many labels that have been engraved in our minds. Instead of internalizing our oppression, we must learn the skills to transform it into political action. Only when we are able to understand and begin to de-program ourselves, will African-American women begin to understand the true meaning of self-worth. Only then, will we be able to fight and end the duel oppression of racism and sexism that collide in the sex industry.

African-Americans must recognize the shackles of slavery that still confine us. We must work together as a community to provide options for prostituted Black women. We must break the deadly silence that holds so many women and girls captive to the violence of prostitution. We must

101. See The Institute on Black Chemical Abuse, Defining the Culture of Poverty: African American Clients from the Culture of Poverty Working with African-Americans in Chemical Dependency Treatment, Recovery and Mental Health 13–16 (1992 Institute Training Manual, Minneapolis).

102. See generally U.S. Dep't Just., Off. Just. Programs, Bureau Just. Stat., Bureau of Just. Stat. Bull., NCJ-145321, Women in Prison (March 1994). See also U.S. Dep't Just., Bureau Just. Stat., Summary Findings (June 30, 1997) (reporting at year end 1996 there were 1,571 sentenced Black inmates per 100,000 Blacks in the United States (compare to 193 white inmates per 100,000 whites)); During 1997, the incarceration of women in the United States increased by 6.2% (compare to increase of male prisoners at 5.2%); U.S. Dep't Just., Advance Release, Nation's Probation and Parole Population Reached New High Last Year (August 16, 1998) (reporting Blacks represent over 1/3 of the nations probationers at year end 1997 and almost 1/2 of parolees. Number of women on probation in 1997 increased from 18% in 1990 to 21% and women parolees increased from 8% to 11% in that same period).

educate ourselves about our history and its effects on who we are now. We must understand the trickery that has been played on us since the first African was thrown on these American shores only to be forced into bondage and sexual servitude. We must understand how abolition shaped our lives and the way we see each other.

African-American churches need to recognize that women used in prostitution, pornography and stripping are victims of racism and sexism. Like other victims of sexual assault, Black women and girls used in prostitution need and deserve tangible assistance to escape and overcome the trauma of commercial sexual exploitation. Often times it is very difficult for Black women to get out of the sex industry. They must abandon their homes, flee from pimps, husbands or boyfriends who forced them to turn tricks, or at the very least benefited financially from exploiting them. Black women must receive emotional support and advocacy services in order to escape prostitution safely and establish new lives for themselves and their children.

The predominately male leaders in the Black community must commit to ending violence against women with the same vigor that they apply to ending racism. They must realize that we, as Black women, are just as vital as they are to the survival of the African-American community. Black men need to unlearn the lessons of slavery. We are not their bitches and we are not their whores, anymore than we are the bitches and whores of white men—on the plantation or in the hood.

Finally, it is time for the predominately white feminist community to take an uncompromising stand against commercial sexual exploitation. Antiracism initiatives and diversity trainings are a sham when white attendees discuss the relative merits of prostitution during a break. Affirmative action is an empty promise when the cost of a handful of Blacks begrudgingly admitted to the university is paid for on the backs of Black women in the streets. The words economic justice turn to ash in the mouth mixed with the taste of a thousand white men pounding their penises at the back of your throat. It is time, past time, for an accounting. Black women—and their white allies—will no longer be fooled by the pro-prostitution lobby's empty promises of liberation contingent on us providing sexual services to their husbands, brothers, sons and fathers, while they sit in universities and law offices planning bigger and better urban plantations for us to toil in.

The authors wish to acknowledge and thank Victoria Kelly for her administrative support and Gretchen Hansen for researching citations for this article.

CHAPTER TWO

Stripping as a System of Prostitution

CHRISTINE STARK

·

Systems of prostitution include stripping, massage parlors and brothels, saunas, prostitution rings, international and domestic trafficking, mail order bride services, street prostitution, escort services, phone sex, live sex shows, peep shows, and pornography. These systems of prostitution have a great deal of interplay in terms of both the acts and the structure in which those acts occur. For instance, stripping is an aspect of prostitution that occurs most often in strip clubs, but the act of stripping also happens in live sex shows, escort services, prostitution rings, and pornography. Prostitution rings exemplify the interlocking structure of the systems of prostitution. For example, prostitution rings may make pornography, sell women and girls in strip clubs, escort services, massage parlors, saunas, and on the street; put on live sex shows; and traffic women and girls domestically and internationally.

While it is important to analyze prostitution as an industry, a large organized, money making venture controlled by pimps, it is not by any means an "equitable business deal" for the women and girls. Prostitution must not be analyzed as a profession or occupation, but rather as organized sexual abuse. The insistence of analyzing prostitution as a business venture for the businesswoman/whore is an attempt to mainstream prostitution as work and it is not rooted in women and girls' lives. It is also a reflection of the professionalization and commercialization of U.S. society in general. Because sex is a commodity and women and girls' bodies are products for sale are reasons to fight harder against the lies and distortions, not a reason to sell out, accept and adopt the non-words and theoretical lies as sexual liberation. Prostitution is an industry of oppression; it is slavery-as-business for the slaver. What trafficking of human beings has ever not been about economics? Because men make money off of enslaving, raping, beating and otherwise degrading women does not make it an industry to be celebrated, as if whores are businesswomen out there busily choosing to perform a "service" in the free market similar to the businesswoman selecting flowers for her floral store. Naming the oppressor and analyzing oppression go hand in hand. Language is important. Pimps, academics, and other pro-prostitution people play with words to sanitize the abuse inherent to prostitution. This helps to normalize prostitution, making it easier for systems of prostitution to proliferate in the very real world.[1] Sanitized words such as sex industry, sex work, entertainment, artistic expression, businesswoman, and client are part of a broader attempt to obfuscate the reality of prostitution.[2] It is vitally important to use language that describes the reality of prostitution. The prostitution industry and their apologists are mainstreaming stripping. With the mainstreaming of strip clubs comes the acceptance of stripping as a harmless form of entertainment, separate from other systems of prostitution. But stripping is integral to other systems of prostitution, which together form an organized industry that profits from sexual violence. If there were no strip clubs, the prostitution industry would be smaller and it would not be expanding as rapidly. If stripping were recognized as the sexual exploitation of women and girls there would be less violence against women and girls, both inside and outside prostitution.[3]

I am a survivor of prostitution and incest. My father battered my mother. I was prostituted throughout my childhood, teen years and young

1. One woman in stripping said, "It's really harmful because it is so benign, so accepted." Kelly Holsopple, 'Stripclubs According the Strippers: Exposing Workplace Sexual Violence', *Making the Harm Visible: Global Sexual Exploitation of Women and Girls*. 1999.

2. It should be noted, however, that for some women and girls used in prostitution not using the term "client" or "date" resulted in beatings. It can be difficult for women to not use "client" even after they have escaped because of force of habit and the beatings they previously suffered.

3. The study conducted by Kelly Holsopple, who was in stripping and other systems of prostitution for 13 years, describes physical, sexual, and emotional abuse that occurs on a daily basis in strip clubs. In her study, women reported being called cunt, slut, whore, pussy, and bitch. Men threw ice, coins, garbage, and glasses at them and grabbed ankles, wrists, and arms. Men bit, licked, slapped, pulled hair, punched, kicked, and spit on the women. Men rubbed their penises on the women, masturbated in front of them, grabbed their genitals, breasts, and buttocks. Men penetrated women anally and vaginally with fingers and objects and forced intercourse on the women.

adulthood. I was used in many systems of prostitution, including live sex shows, pornography, domestic trafficking, and brothels. Stripping was part of the training I endured as a girl to season me to a lifetime of abuse. The sexual abuse I suffered began when I was a young girl and extended into my early twenties. The men who prostituted me-my father, his father, my father's uncles and various friends of theirs-were extremely well organized and knew exactly how to sexually torture women and girls into submission. The men who prostituted me, known as pimps and handlers in everyday parlance, were rapists and batterers who used brainwashing techniques along with sexual torture to create and maintain control over women and girls whom they then sold in systems of prostitution, especially pornography. The injustices I and others like me suffered in the 1950s, 60s, 70s, and 80s, when pornography was more covert and men needed to have Mafia and other fraternal connections to access this "underground world", can now be found in a matter of minutes on the Internet. When I pull up pornography on my computer I find the first twenty odd years of my life on display, splayed, trussed, raped, bruised, and chained. I see myself in the faces and poses of the women and girls for sale on my computer screen. I see myself when I was a sex slave, a girl child bred to be a prostitute, bred to make money for men.

Prostitution ring pimps season young girls for prostitution by teaching them to associate their bodies, and thus their self-worth with sexual objectification. This includes stripping clothes off the girls' bodies, teaching the girls how to move their bodies in sexually suggestive ways, dancing, pouting and other characteristics associated with striptease. They also teach girls to pose for pornography shots in standard pornographic poses, which often overlap with stripping postures.

My father taught me to strip and pose in a pornographic manner when I was very young. It was one of the initial steps he took to interfere with the development of my personality. Stripping made my body not mine; it made it his. He weaned me from stripping in front of him to a slightly larger audience of three or four and then an audience of ten or so in a bar. I stripped in a tavern on the bar in front of a group of men who cheered and clapped and laughed and drank their beers. It was utterly humiliating. When I passed this "test" he felt I was prepared to strip in front of a camera or to a larger audience of men, which were often live sex shows with other women and girls.

When he taught me to strip I felt humiliated and confused and afraid. I thought I did something wrong and felt like I was bad inside. When I "posed" accidentally in situations where I should not have, for example when I posed as a three-year old during an innocent picture taken in front of a pumpkin on Halloween, I felt as if I would die from the shame.

I was constantly afraid that I would accidentally expose "the secret" of the prostitution ring and that my mother, my animals or I would be hurt or killed. I thought people could see how bad I was. I thought people could see, just by looking at me, that I was a whore, which is what the men laughing and drinking beer and training me called me: little whore.

My father was obsessed with me, with making me into a product that he could sell to other men. Because my father raped me in the house there was a thin line between incest, prostitution, pornography, and being made to strip and pose for his entertainment in the house and other men's entertainment outside of the house. As a girl I so closely related doing something "bad" with being watched or filmed that I felt as if I were on camera nearly all the time. My father made money off of my rape. The men who bought me and the pornography made of me experienced sexual pleasure from the many deaths I died. My death was their business transaction.[4] I was a sexual commodity, groomed, seasoned and taught how to be raped and how to be a sexy plaything for men. This was my life and because I cannot escape the memories of it now, it is still my life.

Stripping is arguably the most socially acceptable system of prostitution. It is often not believed to be connected to other forms of prostitution and is commonly viewed by the public to be a harmless, although stigmatized, form of entertainment. However, prostitution is intimately connected to strip clubs. Prostitution occurs in the strip clubs in back rooms or upstairs. Owners set up prostitution across the street at a hotel or another location, sometimes even ordering limos. Women are forced to sell pornography in the strip club and it is common for women to be involved in another system of prostitution while stripping.

Stripping is a means by which pimps organize to make money off of the sexual abuse and second class citizenship conferred to women and girls. Strip clubs function to normalize other systems of prostitution and to coordinate the rest of the systems of prostitution by acting as a water hole, a meeting place for pimps and tricks. The strip circuit also acts as a cover for the running of sex slaves. Stripping is a portal, a revolving door into and out of other systems of prostitution. Stripping must be understood as

---

4. While bits of me died each time I was raped, each time the rapes were filmed, many women and girls in prostitution literally die. A Canadian report on prostitution and pornography found that women and girls in prostitution had a mortality rate forty times higher than the national average. Baldwin, M.A. (1992) 'Split at the Root: Prostitution and Feminist Discourses of Law Reform', Yale Journal of Law and Feminism 5:47–120.

an integral part of the prostitution industry so that prostitution in all its forms can be abolished.

Strip clubs are widely advertised and publicized through mainstream media.[5] The mainstreaming of stripping has normalized stripping and brought it into the bedrooms of many women who are not strippers or being used in other systems of prostitution. Stripping has become so normalized that young girls act out lap dancing on their boyfriends at junior high school dances.[6] Stripping as a socially acceptable system of prostitution is particularly true now as the prostitution industry has launched what amounts to a publicity campaign to recruit more young women, especially college students, into the stripping industry. The industry has undergone a face-lift in two concomitant, business savvy ways. Strip club owners and other pimps have capitalized on the anger men feel as women fight for their rights in the workforce, higher education, and in other public and private areas. The pimps, or strip club owners, are boldly pushing "high class" businessman strip clubs into markets across the United States. High-powered business deals are struck in dark strip clubs, over martinis, portfolios, stock options, women's crotches and bare breasts. This is an explosion of male power, between the negotiations, the buying of visual access of the women, and the virtual exclusion of female colleagues, it is as big a show of orchestrated cock power over pussy power as anything happening in the U.S. right now. This sends a clear message to women that the business world is a man's world. These bold new strip clubs, together with the growth of men's rights groups such as the Promise Keepers, should be an alarm signal to all women. Men are telling women loud and clear that they belong in one of two places, either the home or the whorehouse.

With the mainstreaming of strip clubs there is a need for publicity. Pimps receive free advertising through media, which include news articles, sitcoms, web sites, video games, and Hollywood movies. Media glamorization of stripping as a wonderful way to earn inordinate amounts of money while being worshipped by adoring men normalizes the prostitution industry and recruits women into the industry.[7] Media

5. Many women become involved in systems of prostitution by stripping as underage girls in strip clubs. From the author's experience and from numerous conversations with other prostituted women underage stripping even in mainstream, "above ground" strip clubs is a common practice.

6. The rise of Hooters and other titty restaurants is intricately connected with the push to mainstream stripping. See also 'Commodification of Women: Morning, Noon, and Night' by Sarah Ciriello in *Transforming A Rape Culture*. Edited by Emilie Buchwald, Pamela Fletcher, Martha Roth, Milkweed, 1993.

7. The average age of entry into prostitution in the US is 13–14 years old. Silbert, M.H. and Pines, A.M. (1982) 'Victimization of Street Prostitutes',

coverage almost always ignores the feminist analysis of prostitution as violence against women, instead covering the issue as one of Christian morality versus free speech.[8]

The idea that stripping is a career choice is promoted through media, academia, pimps, and tricks. But discussing stripping and other forms of prostitution as a career choice or a business exchange is tantamount to discussing organized rape and battery as a valid career choice. There are some prostituted women that talk about going into stripping and other forms of prostitution as a viable economic choice. They say that if everything is for sale anyway then they might as well sell their bodies. They think if they were sexually used when they were girls then why not get paid for it now? Believing that sexual exploitation is inevitable and deciding to get paid for it is a direct result of being sexually abused as a girl and it is intimately connected with being female in a sexist society. It is also a line that pimps use to season women and girls to prostitution by telling women and girls that they are smart to get paid to have sex instead of giving it away for free. Academics and media play upon the despair, limited choices and low feelings of self worth that women experience because of sexual abuse and second class citizenship and then they twist the women's reality to fit their promotion of stripping and other forms of prostitution. Pimps and tricks justify their use of women and girls in systems of prostitution by saying the women are there because they like it and because they get paid for it. The line that women might as well

Victomology: An International Journal, 7:122–33. It is not uncommon for underage girls to be stripping in clubs, especially in rural areas where there are sometimes girls as young as 12.

8. For instance, an article titled *Dirty Dancing* highlighted the Smut King of Southern Minnesota, a strip club owner, and never discussed stripping as the exploitation of women and girls. The author, Sarah Luck Pearson, said she didn't even think about how the wives of the men at a bachelor party would feel when she ordered a stripper. She said it "seemed like ordering a clown or an inflatable trampoline. A party favor" (24). Pearson did not interview the three organizations in Minnesota that help women and teens get out of prostitution. She did not cite statistics compiled by rape crisis centers, such as the one from the Wahpeton, North Dakota rape crisis center that found a "96.6% increase in domestic violence and sexual assault cases" when a second strip club opened in Wahpeton (Short). This is typical of news articles about stripping, and it is a prime example of how the arguments about stripping are constructed to make the pimps and tricks seem like rebellious heroes, while simultaneously making the harm against women and girls invisible.

The Rake, June 2003, 'Little Strip Club on the Prairie: Selling Sex in Rural Minnesota'.

be paid to be sexually abused is not something to be celebrated as self-empowerment. This ideology is rooted in the sexual objectification and rape of women, but most especially of girls.

Prostitution ring pimps break down girls, often from a very young age, through rape and other forms of torture.[9] The process of breaking girls' spirits, minds and bodies is known as seasoning for use in prostitution. It is not that much different from breaking a colt, only it is more brutal and lasts longer and the one being hurt is human. It is not that much different from being tortured as a prisoner of war except it is usually a male family member who does the torturing. And there is no reprieve, ever, and the girl will never be recognized as a prisoner of war or given any medals of honor or financial reparations and no one swoops in on a helicopter to save her. These young girls, brutalized and treated like less than animals, grow up into teenage girls and then become adult women and escape is difficult. Once these girls become legal adults society treats them as criminals, says they made the choice to be whores, and then to add insult to injury professes that they enjoy being whores.

At the center of the systems of prostitution are prostitution rings. They are involved in every kind of prostitution. This does not mean that every prostituted woman or girl is used by a prostitution ring, but rather that prostitution ring pimps make up the core of the network that loosely and sometimes not so loosely controls prostitution on a national and international scale.[10] Women and girls in prostitution rings are often used simultaneously in multiple systems of prostitution. Prostitution ring pimps use women and girls in mainstream venues such as strip clubs as well as underground prostitution venues where attendance is restricted. For instance, there are women who travel the mainstream strip circuit and they are simultaneously used as sex slaves in pornography shoots carried out by prostitution ring pimps. Other women are prostituted in a brothel during the day and used in pornography during the evenings. Pornography

---

9. The average age of entry into prostitution in the US is 13–14 years old. Silbert, M.H. and Pines, A.M. (1982) 'Victimization of Street Prostitutes', *Victomology: An International Journal*, 7:122–33. It is not uncommon for underage girls to be stripping in clubs, especially in rural areas where there are sometimes girls as young as 12.

10. A leading figure in Russian organized crime, Semion Mogilevich, runs prostitution on a massive scale throughout Eastern and Western Europe. He is also said to be involved in the traffic of nuclear materials, drugs, precious gems, stolen art and contract killings. He is thought to be behind the murder of four prostituted women. Mogilevech is described as a transnational criminal, a new kind of criminal who does not rob banks, but rather buys them.

ring pimps use these women until they are almost used up, then they back off allowing them to recover. Once the women are functional, the pimps begin using them in the pornography ring again.

This means that typically pimps sell women and girls in more than one system of prostitution.[11] Pimps coordinate the prostitution of women and girls. The strip club owners are cozy with the brothel owners and hotel managers and pornography pimps, and sometimes they are one and the same. Women and girls typically move from one system to another, and they are often involved in more than one kind of prostitution simultaneously. It is impossible to separate strip clubs from other kinds of prostitution, especially prostitution rings.

The strip club owner may also be a prostitution ring pimp or he may have connections with prostitution ring pimps. He may own or have connections with the man who owns the hotel across the street from the strip club where women turn tricks with men from the strip club. Or the strip club owner may own or know the owner of the brothel next to the state capitol where women are used interchangeably between the strip club and the brothel. The owner of the strip club may conduct the strip club business on the first floor while running prostitution ring women upstairs for men who are willing to pay big bucks to rape a woman painted in black and blue stripes.

Systems of prostitution must be stopped for two reasons. First, the women and girls in prostitution must be able to escape to have lives of dignity and worth. Second, prostitution oppresses all women by its promotion and enforcement of the belief that all women are whores by nature. A revitalization of the feminist anti-rape grassroots movement is needed, one that is inspired, committed and focused on ending prostitution as its long term goal while helping women and girls escape right now. In this revitalized movement all systems of prostitution, especially stripping, need to be recognized as the organized sexual exploitation of women and girls. Survivors should be leaders in the movement. Women who have survived prostitution understand the industry in ways that women who have not been prostituted will never be able to understand. Prostituted women and girls have insight gained from experience that is absolutely crucial when forming policy, devising curriculum, and organizing against

---

11. According to Holsopple's study "customers and pimps constantly proposition women" in the strip clubs. Almost all of the women in the study "reported that they were propositioned for prostitution every day by customers and pimps...Women said prostitution is influenced and suggested by management...management sets up tricks, says it is good for business, and obligates women to turn over money from prostitution to the club."

prostitution. In the way that rape survivors and survivors of battery founded and continue to lead the rape crisis and shelter movements, so too must prostituted women lead the work against prostitution.

The domestic violence shelters, rape crisis centers, and homeless shelters not currently accepting prostituted women must open their doors to women in systems of prostitution. Prostituted women and girls are by definition battered and raped, and many are homeless.[12] However they got where they're at, prostituted women and girls deserve services as much as any other woman or girl. To turn them away because they have been involved in prostitution is nothing less than discrimination. These organizations need to do outreach designed specifically for women in stripping and other systems of prostitution, and they need to make changes in their programs to accommodate prostituted women and girls.

Media collusion in the mainstreaming of strip clubs must be held accountable. Protests and boycotts should be organized against media establishments that promote stripping and advertise systems of prostitution. Alternative feminist media should be created to counter the promotion of stripping and prostitution. The feminist movement should be geared to the ever-evolving systems of male supremacy, such as the push to mainstream strip clubs, the growth in international trafficking, the centrality of prostitution rings, and the rise of Internet pornography.

When analyzing prostitution, the focus needs to be shifted from the women and girls and directed at the men, the pimps and johns, and how they have organized dehumanization, objectification and rape into a multi-billion dollar industry in the U.S.. The pimps and johns must be stopped. Men must be held legally accountable as perpetrators when they buy and sell women and girls for sex. The women and girls who are bought and sold in prostitution should be decriminalized. In other words, prostituted women and girls must be seen legally, socially, and politically as victims of sexual exploitation.

This does not, however, mean that the women and girls are victims in the sense that victim is the totality of who they are or ever will be. They have survived the worst of the war against women, a war that is being waged on a global scale. Prostituted women and girls must not be treated

---

12. In a study conducted in five countries with 475 prostituted people, 73% said they were physically assaulted in prostitution; 62% were raped since entering; 67% met criteria for Post Traumatic Stress Disorder, 72% had current or past homelessness.

Prostitution in Five Countries: Violence and Post-Traumatic Stress Disorder. Farley, Isin Baral, Merab Kiremire, Ufuk Sezgin. *Feminism and Psychology*, 1998, Volume 8(4):405–426.

with pity, contempt or in a way that enforces the idea they need to be saved or shown the way. They are survivors and they must be empowered to have control over their own lives. Real, viable options must be made available for them to have lives of agency and autonomy. The existing programs that help prostituted women and girls escape must multiply throughout the U.S. and the world. Women and girls need to have job training, housing, education, child care, legal and medical assistance, culturally appropriate services, and treatment for drug and alcohol abuse."

This does not exist now in any wide or effective way.

Female sexual liberation has nothing to do with stripping or other forms of prostitution; if it did women would have been free centuries ago. Stripping is sexual exploitation at best and a portal to sexual slavery at worst. If women and girls are to be free or equal or liberated prostitution in all its forms, including stripping, must end. Prostitution is the primary way that men make money off of their hatred of women. The men are organized. They are powerful. They know what they are doing. They are involved in and complicit with the largest slave running system the world has ever known. It is time to organize against the men who run women and girls in systems of prostitution. It is time to stop them.

CHAPTER THREE

What's Wrong with Prostitution?*

CAROLE PATEMAN

☾

In modern patriarchy a variety of means are available through which men can uphold the terms of the sexual contract. The marriage contract is still fundamental to patriarchal right, but marriage is now only one of the socially acceptable ways for men to have access to women's bodies. Casual sexual liaisons and 'living together' no longer carry the social sanctions of twenty or thirty years ago, and, in addition to private arrangements, there is a huge, multimillion-dollar trade in women's bodies. Prostitution is an integral part of patriarchal capitalism. Wives are no longer put up for public auction (although in Australia, the United States and Britain they can be bought by mail-order from the Philippines), but men can buy sexual access to women's bodies in the capitalist market. Patriarchal right is explicitly embodied in 'freedom of contract'.

Prostitutes are readily available at all levels of the market for any man who can afford one and they are frequently provided as part of business, political and diplomatic transactions. Yet the public character of prostitution is less obvious than it might be. Like other forms of capitalist enterprise, prostitution is seen as private enterprise, and the contract between client and prostitute is seen as a private arrangement between a buyer and a seller. Moreover, prostitution is shrouded in secrecy despite the scale of the industry. In Birmingham, a British city of about one million people, some 800 women work either as street prostitutes, or from their homes or hotels, from 'saunas', 'massage parlours', or 'escort agencies'. Nearly 14,000 men each week buy their services, i.e., about 17 men for each

*Reprinted with permssion from *The Sexual Contract* by Carole Pateman, (Stanford, CA: Stanford, 1988), pp.189–218. Originally published by Blackwell.

prostitute.[1] A similar level of demand has been recorded in the United States, and the total number of customers each week across the country has been conservatively estimated at 1,500,000 men.[2] One estimate is that $40 million per day is spent on prostitution in the United States.[3] The secrecy exists in part because, where the act of prostitution is not itself illegal, associated activities such as soliciting often are. The criminal character of much of the business of prostitution is not, however, the only reason for secrecy. Not all men wish it generally to be known that they buy this commodity. To be discovered consorting with prostitutes can, for example, still be the downfall of politicians. The empirical evidence also indicates that three-quarters of the clients of prostitutes are married men. Certainly, the prostitutes in Birmingham find that trade slackens during holiday periods when men are away from the city with their wives and children.[4]

The sexual subjection of wives has never lacked defenders, but until very recently an unqualified defence of prostitution has been hard to find. Prostitution was seen, for example, as a necessary evil that protected young women from rape and shielded marriage and the family from the ravages of men's sexual appetites; or as an unfortunate outcome of poverty and the economic constraints facing women who had to support themselves; or prostitution was seen as no worse, and as more honest, than 'legal prostitution', as Mary Wollstonecraft called marriage in 1790.[5] As prostitutes, women openly trade their bodies and, like workers (but unlike a wife), are paid in return. So, for Emma Goldman, 'it is merely a question of degree whether [a woman] sells herself to one man, in or out of marriage, or to many men'.[6] Simone de Beauvoir sees the wife as 'hired for life by one man; the prostitute has several clients who pay her by the piece. The one is protected by one male against all the others;

1. E. McLeod, *Women Working: Prostitution Now* (London and Canberra, Croom Helm, 1982), pp. 12–13; table 1.1.

2. Figure cited in M. A. Jennings, 'The Victim as Criminal: A Consideration of California's Prostitution Law', *California Law Review* 64, 5 (1976), p. 1251.

3. Cited in *San Francisco Examiner* (3 February 1985).

4. McLeod, *Women Working*, p. 43.

5. M. Wollstonecraft, 'A Vindication of the Rights of Men' in *A Mary Wollstonecraft Reader*, ed. B. H. Solomon and P. S. Berggren (New York. New American Library, 1983), p. 247. She also uses the phrase in *A Vindication of the Rights of Woman* (New York. W. W. Norton and Co., 1975) [1792]), p. 148. According to her biographer Clair Tomalin. Wollstonecraft was the first to use the phrase 'legal prostitution' to refer to marriage.

6. E. Goldman, 'The Traffic in Women', in *Anarchism and Other Essays* (New York, Dover Publications, 1969), p. 179.

the other is defended by all against the exclusive tyranny of each'.[7] Cicely Hamilton noted in 1909 that although women were prevented from bargaining freely in the only trade, marriage, legitimately open to them, they could exercise this freedom in their illegitimate trade; 'the prostitute class...has pushed to its logical conclusion the principle that woman exists by virtue of a wage paid her in return for the possession of her person'.[8]

A radical change has now taken place in arguments about prostitution. Prostitution is unequivocally defended by contractarians. The terms of the defence again illustrate the ease with which some feminist arguments occupy the contractarian terrain. Many recent feminist discussions have argued that prostitution is merely a job of work and the prostitute is a worker, like any other wage labourer. Prostitutes should, therefore, have trade union rights, and feminists often put forward proposals for workers' control of the industry. To argue in this fashion is not necessarily to defend prostitution—one can argue for trade union rights while calling for the abolition of capitalist wage labour—but, in the absence of argument to the contrary, the implicit suggestion in many feminist discussions is that, if the prostitute is merely one worker among others, the appropriate conclusion must be that there is nothing wrong with prostitution. At the very least, the argument implies that there is nothing wrong with prostitution that is not also wrong with other forms of work.

This conclusion depends on the same assumptions as the contractarian defence of prostitution. Contractarians argue that a prostitute contracts out a certain form of labour power for a given period in exchange for money. There is a free exchange between prostitute and customer, and the prostitution contract is exactly like—or is one example of—the employment contract. From the standpoint of contract, the prostitute is an owner of property in her person who contracts out part of that property in the market. A prostitute does not sell herself, as is commonly alleged, or even sell her sexual parts, but contracts out use of *sexual services*. There is no difference between a prostitute and any other worker or seller of services. The prostitute, like other 'individuals', stands in an external relation to the property in her person, Contract theory thus appears to offer a convincing reply to well-known criticisms of and objections to prostitution. For example, for contractarians, the objection that the prostitute is harmed or

7. S. de Beauvoir, *The Second Sex*, tr. H. L M. Parshley (New York, Vintage Books, 1974), p. 619.

8. C. Hamilton, *Marriage as a Trade* (London, The Women's Press, 1981), p. 37.

degraded by her trade misunderstands the nature of what is traded. The body and the self of the prostitute are not offered in the market; she can contract out use of her services without detriment to herself. Feminists who argue that the prostitute epitomizes women's subjection to men, can now also be told that such a view is a reflection of outmoded attitudes to sex, fostered by men's propaganda and the old world of women's subordination.[9] Contractarians even proclaim that 'people have a human right to engage in commercial sex'.[10]

Defenders of prostitution admit that some reforms are necessary in the industry as it exists at present in order for a properly free market in sexual services to operate. Nevertheless, they insist that 'sound prostitution' is possible (the phrase is Lars Ericsson's).[11] The idea of sound prostitution illustrates the dramatic shift that has taken place in arguments over prostitution. The new, contractarian defence is a universal argument. Prostitution is defended as a trade fit for anyone to enter. Freedom of contract and equality of opportunity require that the prostitution contract should be open to everyone and that any individual should be able to buy or sell services in the market. Anyone who needs a sexual service should have access to the market, whether male or female, young or old, black or white, ugly or beautiful, deformed or handicapped. Prostitution will then come into its own as a form of therapy—'the role of a prostitute as a kind of therapist is a natural one'[12]—or as a form of social work or nursing (taking care 'of the intimate hygiene of disabled patients').[13] No one will be left out because of inappropriate attitudes to sex. The female hunchback as well as the male hunchback will be able to find a seller of services.[14]

A universal defence of prostitution entails that a prostitute can be of either sex. Women should have the same opportunity as men to buy sexual services in the market. 'The prostitute' is conventionally pictured as a woman, and, in fact, the majority of prostitutes are women. However,

9. They are so instructed by J. Radcliffe Richards, *The Sceptical Feminist: A Philosophical Enquiry* (Harmondsworth, Penguin Books, 1980), p. 246.

10. D. A. J. Richards, *Sex, Drugs, Death, and the Law: An Essay on Human Rights and Decriminalization* (Totowa, NJ, Rowman and Littlefield, 1982), p. 121.

11. The term is used by L. Ericsson, 'Charges Against Prostitution: An Attempt at a Philosophical Assessment', *Ethics* 90 (1980), pp. 335–66.

12. D. A. J. Richards, *Sex, Drugs, Death, and the Law*, p. 115; also p. 108.

13. Ericcson, 'Charges Against Prostitution', p. 342.

14. The example comes from M. McIntosh, 'Who Needs Prostitutes? The Ideology of Male Sexual Needs', in *Women, Sexuality and Social Control*, ed. C. Smart and B. Smart (London, Routledge and Kegan Paul, 1978), p. 54.

for contractarians, this is a merely contingent fact about prostitution; if sound prostitution were established, status, or the sexually ascriptive determination of the two parties (the man as a buyer and the woman as a seller of services), will give way to contract, to a relation between two 'individuals'. A moment's contemplation of the story of the sexual contract suggests that there is a major difficulty in any attempt to universalize prostitution. Reports occasionally appear that, in large cities like Sydney, a few male heterosexual prostitutes operate (the older figure of the gigolo belongs in a very different context), but they are still rare. Male homosexual prostitutes, on the other hand, are not uncommon, and, from the standpoint of contract, they are no different from female prostitutes. The story of the sexual contract reveals that there is good reason why 'the prostitute' is a female figure.

The story is about heterosexual relations—but it also tells of the creation of a fraternity and their contractual relations. Relations between members of the fraternity lie outside the scope of my present discussion, but, as Marilyn Frye has noted, 'there is a sort of "incest taboo" built into standard masculinity'.[15] The taboo is necessary; within the bonds of fraternity there is always a temptation to make the relation more than that of fellowship. But if members of the brotherhood extended their contracts, if they contracted for sexual use of bodies among themselves, the competition could shake the foundations of the original contract. From the standpoint of contract, the prohibition against this particular exercise of the law of male sex-right is purely arbitrary, and the fervour with which it is maintained by men themselves is incomprehensible. The story of the original creation of modern patriarchy helps lessen the incomprehension.

Contractarians who defend an ostensibly sexually neutral, universal, sound prostitution have not, as far as I am aware, taken the logic of their arguments to its conclusion. The final defeat of status and the victory of contract should lead to the elimination of marriage in favour of the economical arrangement of universal prostitution, in which all individuals enter into brief contracts of sexual use when required. The only legitimate restriction upon these contracts is the willingness of another party voluntarily to make services available; the sex of the party is irrelevant. Nor does age provide a determinate limitation, but at least

15. M. Frye, *The Politics of Reality: Essays in Feminist Theory* (Trumansburg, NY, The Crossing Press, 1983), p. 143. Where men are confined together and prevented from obtaining access to women (as in prison) the 'taboo' is not observed; masculinity is then exhibited by using other men, usually young men, as if they were women.

one contractarian draws back from consistent anti-paternalism at this point.[16]

Any discussion of prostitution is replete with difficulties. Although contractarians now deny any political significance to the fact that (most) prostitutes are women, one major difficulty is that, in other discussions, prostitution is invariably seen as a problem about the prostitute, as a problem about *women*. The perception of prostitution as a problem about women is so deep-seated that any criticism of prostitution is likely to provoke the accusation that contemporary contractarians bring against feminists, that criticism of prostitution shows contempt for prostitutes. To argue that there is something wrong with prostitution does not necessarily imply any adverse judgement on the women who engage in the work. When socialists criticize capitalism and the employment contract they do not do so because they are contemptuous of workers, but because they are the workers' champions. Nevertheless, appeals to the idea of false consciousness, popular a few years ago, suggested that the problem about capitalism was a problem about workers. To reduce the question of capitalism to deficiencies in workers' consciousness diverts attention from the capitalist, the other participant in the employment contract. Similarly, the patriarchal assumption that prostitution is a problem about women ensures that the other participant in the prostitution contract escapes scrutiny. Once the story of the sexual contract has been told, prostitution can be seen as a problem about *men*. The problem of prostitution then becomes encapsulated in the question why men demand that women's bodies are sold as commodities in the capitalist market. The story of the sexual contract also supplies the answer; prostitution is part of the exercise of the law of male sex-right, one of the ways in which men are ensured access to women's bodies.

Feminist criticism of prostitution is now sometimes rejected on the grounds that prostitutes exploit or cheat their male clients; men are

16. Ericsson, 'Charges Against Prostitution', p. 363, argues (unconvincingly) that 'paternalism' does not conflict with his contractual defence of sound adult prostitution and that prostitution by minors should be prevented. He poses the problem as one of the causes (the supply) of child prostitutes, but fails to mention the problem of the *demand*. Why do men demand to have sexual relations with (sometimes very young) children? Why do resorts like Pagsanjan in the Philippines exist to cater for this demand? This question falls outside my concerns here, but a recent survey of investigations of 'incest' (father-daughter is the most common form) notes that in conjugal relations, 'many men are accustomed to the experience of sex with a weaker and unwilling partner': W. Breines and L. Gordon, 'The New Scholarship on Family Violence', *Signs* 8, 3 (1983), p. 527.

presented as the injured parties, not women. To be sure, prostitutes are often able to obtain control over the transaction with their customers by various stratagems and tricks of the trade. However, just as arguments about marriage that appeal to the example of benevolent husbands fail to distinguish between the relation of one particular husband and wife and the structure of the institution of marriage, so particular instances of the prostitution contract, in which a prostitute exploits a male customer, should be distinguished from prostitution as a social institution. Within the structure of the institution of prostitution, 'prostitutes' are subject to 'clients', just as 'wives' are subordinate to 'husbands' within the structure of marriage.

There is a huge literature on the subject of prostitution, including many official reports, and a good deal of attention has been devoted to the psychology and psychopathology of the prostitute. In 1969 a pamphlet widely read by probation officers in Britain talked of the 'proof that prostitution is a primitive and regressive manifestation'; and a Home Office report in 1974 stated that the 'way of life of a prostitute is so remarkably a rejection of the normal ways of society as to bear comparison with that of the drug addict'.[17] Much attention is also devoted to the reasons why women become prostitutes. The evidence suggests that there is nothing at all mysterious about why women enter the trade. *In extremis*, women can sell their bodies for food, like the poor unemployed young girl in nineteenth-century England who was asked the question (by the author of *My Secret Life*), 'what do you let men fuck you for? Sausage-rolls?' She replied that she would comply for 'meat-pies and pastry too'.[18] More generally, prostitution enables women to make more money than they can earn at most other jobs open to women in patriarchal capitalism. In the 1870s and 1880s, the women campaigning against the Contagious Diseases Acts in the Ladies National Association in Britain argued that prostitution was the best-paid industry for poor women. In 1980, empirical investigation showed that British prostitutes earned much more than most women workers, and were in the middle- to high-wage band compared to male workers.[19] The American film *Working Girls* illustrates

17. Cited E. McLeod, 'Man-Made Laws for Men? The Street Prostitutes' Campaign Against Control', in *Controlling Women: The Normal and the Deviant*, ed. B. Hutter and G. Williams (London, Croom Helm, 1981), p. 63.

18. Cited in E. M. Sigsworth and T. J. Wyke, 'A Study of Victorian Prostitution and Venereal Disease', in *Suffer and Be Still: Women in the Victorian Age,* ed. M Vicinus (Bloomington, Indiana University Press, 1972), p. 181. Contemporary prostitutes may still receive food from 'regulars' if, for example, he is a baker, see McLeod, *Women Working*, p. 6.

19. McLeod, *Women Working*, pp. 17, 20; tables 1.2(a), 1.2(b), 1.3.

the attraction of prostitution for young, middle-class women with college degrees who want to make relatively large sums of money in a hurry, Prostitutes also refer to the degree of independence and flexibility that the work allows, and to the relative ease with which prostitution can be combined with housework and care of children. Drug addiction is now also an important reason why women become prostitutes.

The reasons why women become prostitutes are fairly straightforward, but what counts as prostitution is less obvious. Most discussions take for granted that the meaning of 'prostitution' is self-evident; 'we seem to know pretty well what we mean by this term'.[20] To draw the line between amateurs and women engaged in the profession in our society is not always easy, but very different activities in widely differing cultures and historical periods are also lumped together. One of the most persistent claims is that prostitution (like patriarchy) is a universal feature of human social life, a claim summed up in the cliché, 'the oldest profession'. The cliché is used to refer to a wide range of cultural phenomena, from ancient times to the present, all of which are called 'prostitution'. So, for example, one contractarian defender of prostitution argues that 'commercial prostitution in the modern sense' developed from ancient temple prostitution.[21] The same social meaning is attributed to such disparate activities as, say, temple prostitution in ancient Babylonia, the sale of their bodies by destitute women for food for themselves and their children, 'white slavery', the provision of field brothels for troops, the proffering of women to white explorers, *maisons d'abattages* or *malaya* prostitution in Nairobi.[22] That all these social practices have the same significance as the prostitution contract of patriarchal capitalism is not immediately self-evident. Indeed, recent studies by feminist historians show that prostitution in the

20. Ericeson, 'Charges Against Prostitution', p. 348.

21. D. A. J. Richards, *Sex, Drugs, Death, and the Law*, p. 88. For a different view of temple prostitution, see G. Lerner, *The Creation of Patriarchy* (New York, Oxford, Oxford University Press, 1986), chapter 6.

22. On *maisons d'abbatages* see K. Barry, *Female Sexual Slavery* (Englewood Cliffs, Prentice Hall, 1979), pp. 3–4; 80–3. The *malaya* form flourished in Nairobi before the Second World War, and is discussed by L. White, 'Prostitution, Identity and Class Consciousness in Nairobi during World War II', *Signs* II, 2 (1986), pp. 255–73. Working men in Nairobi could not support their wives if they left their farms to come to the city to join their husbands, and the colonial administration did not supply sufficient accommodation for labourers. The men visited *malaya* prostitutes who 'provided bed space–cleaning, cooking, bath water, companionship, hot meals, cold meals, and tea, and . . . men who spent the night . . . received breakfast' (p. 256). How should these services be categorized; as an enlarged prostitution contract or a truncated marriage contract?

contemporary sense—the form of prostitution that makes possible the contractarian defence of 'sound' prostitution—is a distinct cultural and historical phenomenon, which developed in Britain, the United States and Australia around the end of the nineteenth and beginning of the twentieth century.[23]

There is nothing universal about prostitutes as a discrete group of wage labourers who specialize in a particular line of work, or about prostitution as a specialized occupation or profession within the patriarchal capitalist division of labour. Until the latter part of the nineteenth century in all three countries, prostitutes were part of the casual labouring poor. Women in this class drifted in and out of prostitution as they drifted in and out of other forms of work. Prostitutes were not seen as a special class of women, nor were they isolated from other workers or working-class communities; there was no specialized 'profession' of prostitution. In Britain, for example, prostitution in the contemporary sense emerged from developments precipitated by the Contagious Diseases Acts (1864, 1866, 1869). Under the Acts, women in military towns could be identified as 'common prostitutes' by plain-clothes policemen, compulsorily subjected to gynaecological examination for venereal disease and, if infected, confined to a lock hospital. An enormous political campaign, in which women were very prominent, was waged for repeal of the Acts.

Rejecting the suggestion that public hygiene required regular inspection of soldiers and sailors, as well as women, for venereal disease, the Report of a Royal Commission into the Acts stated that 'there is no comparison to be made between prostitutes and the men who consort with them. With the one sex the offence is committed as a matter of gain; with the other it is an irregular indulgence of a natural impulse'.[24] Feminist campaigners

---

23. On Britain, see J. R. Walkowitz, *Prostitution and Victorian Society: Women, Class and the State* (Cambridge, Cambridge University Press, 1980); on the United States, see R. Rosen, *The Lost Sisterhood: Prostitution in America, 1900–1918* (Baltimore and London. The Johns Hopkins University Press, 1982); on New South Wales, see J. Allen, 'The Making of a Prostitute Proletariat in Early Twentieth-Century New South Wales', in *So Much Hard Work: Women and Prostitution in Australian History*, ed. K. Daniels (Sydney, Fontana Books, 1984).

24. Cited in M. Trustram, 'Distasteful and Derogatory? Examining Victorian Soldiers for Venereal Disease', in *The Sexual Dynamics of History*, ed. The London Feminist History Group (London, Pluto Press, 1983), pp. 62–3. At present AIDS is provoking a similar response; for example a Bill has been presented to the Nevada legislature to allow murder charges to be brought against prostitutes who have the disease and continued to work. No mention is made of their male customers in the report that I read in *Washington Post* (24 April 1987).

such as Josephine Butler recognized that much more was at issue than the 'double standard' of sexual morality, the only morality compatible with the sexual contract. She argued that all women were implicated in the Acts, and they should not accept that safety and private respectability for most women depended on a 'slave class' of publicly available prostitutes. Butler wrote later to her sister that 'even if we lack the sympathy which makes us feel that the chains which bind our enslaved sisters are pressing on us also, we cannot escape the fact that we are one womanhood, *solidaire*, and that so long as they are bound, we cannot be wholly and truly free'.[25] For feminists who fought against the Acts, prostitution represented in the starkest form the sexual domination of women by men.

However, feminist questions were submerged in the social purity movement that developed in Britain in the 1880s and helped secure the passage of the Criminal Law Amendment Act in 1885 that gave the police greater summary jurisdiction over poor women. By the time that the Contagious Diseases Acts were repealed in 1886 the character of prostitution was already changing and the trade was being 'professionalized'. Women listed as common prostitutes under the Acts found it hard to have their names removed from the register, or, subsequently, to find other employment. The women had often rented rooms in boarding-house brothels, run by women with families to support who also took in other lodgers in addition to the prostitutes. The 1885 Act gave police powers to close the brothels, which were shut down systematically between 1890 and 1914, and powers against soliciting. The prostitutes turned to pimps for protection. Prostitution shifted from being female-controlled to male-controlled and, as Judith Walkowitz remarks, 'there now existed third parties with a strong interest in prolonging women's stay on the streets'.[26]

In New South Wales, Australia, the elimination of free-lance prostitution took a different path. Unlike many other British colonies, New South Wales did not enact legislation against contagious diseases, nor follow the 1885 Act. Legislation was introduced in 1908 aimed at soliciting, pimping and brothel-keeping and, according to Judith Allen, the aim of policing strategy was the abolition of the most visible aspects of prostitution. The result was that self-employed prostitutes could no longer operate; 'the work of the prostitute became structurally proletarianized'.[27] Prostitutes were forced to turn to organized criminal networks or to pimps employed by the same criminals. A similar consequence ensued from the large

25. J. E. Butler, *An Autobiographical Memoir*, 3rd edn (London, J. W. Arrowsmith, 1928), p. 215.

26. Walkowitz, *Prostitution and Victorian Society*, p. 212.

27. Allen, 'The Making of a Prostitute Proletariat', p. 213.

campaigns against prostitution in the Progressive Era in the United States. Ruth Rosen summarizes the changes, which included the shift of control of the trade 'from madams and prostitutes themselves to pimps and organized crime syndicates.... The prostitute would rarely work henceforth as a free agent. In addition, she faced increased brutality, not only from the police, but also from her new "employers".'[28] Once professionalized, prostitution developed into a major industry within patriarchal capitalism, with the same structure as other capitalist industries; prostitutes work in an occupation that is controlled by men. For example, in Birmingham, most prostitutes have ponces (pimps) and the 'saunas' and other such establishments are usually owned or managed by men. Few prostitutes become managers or 'establish some mutually beneficial business enterprise with other women'.[29]

The claim that prostitution is a universal feature of human society relies not only on the cliché of 'the oldest profession' but also on the widely held assumption that prostitution originates in men's natural sexual urge. There is a universal, natural (masculine) impulse that, it is assumed, requires, and will always require, the outlet provided by prostitution. Now that arguments that extra-marital sex is immoral have lost their social force, defenders of prostitution often present prostitution as one example of 'sex without love', as an example of the satisfaction of natural appetites.[30] The argument, however, is a *non sequitur*. Defenders of sex without love and advocates of what once was called free love, always supposed that the relationship was based on mutual sexual attraction between a man and woman and involved mutual physical satisfaction. Free love and prostitution are poles apart. Prostitution is the use of a woman's body by a man for his own satisfaction. There is no desire or satisfaction on the part of the prostitute. Prostitution is not mutual, pleasurable exchange of the use of bodies, but the unilateral use of a woman's body by a man in exchange for money. That the institution of prostitution can be presented as a natural extension of a human impulse, and that 'sex without love' can be equated with the sale of women's bodies in the capitalist market, is possible only because an important question is begged: why do men demand that satisfaction of a natural appetite must take the form of public access to women's bodies in the capitalist market in exchange for money?

28. Rosen, *Lost Sisterhood*, p. xii. Rosen (p. 172) also notes new hazards facing American prostitutes today, such as being used by the CIA to extract information or in experiments with drugs.

29. McLeod, *Women Working*, p. 51.

30. For this use of the phrase, see, e.g., J. R. Richards, The *Sceptical Feminist*, p. 244.

In arguments that prostitution is merely one expression of a natural appetite, the comparison is invariably made between prostitution and the provision of food. To claim that 'we all need food, so food should be available to us.... And since our sexual desires are just as basic, natural, and compelling as our appetite for food, this also holds for them', is neither an argument for prostitution nor for any form of sexual relations.[31] Without a minimum of food (or water, or shelter) people die, but to my knowledge no one has ever died for want of an outlet for their sexual appetites. There is also one fundamental difference between the human need for food and the need for sex. Sustenance is sometimes unavailable but everyone has the means to satisfy sexual appetites to hand. There is no natural necessity to engage in sexual *relations* to assuage sexual pangs. Of course, there may be cultural inhibition against use of this means, but what counts as food is also culturally variable. In no society does the form of food production and consumption, or the form of relations between the sexes, follow directly, without cultural mediation, from the natural fact that all humans feel hunger and sexual impulses. The consequences of sexual inhibitions and prohibitions are likely to be less disastrous than prohibitions on what counts as food.

Another difficulty in discussing prostitution in late twentieth-century patriarchy is that it is also usually assumed to be obvious which activities fall under the heading of 'prostitution'. Prostitution is now part of an international sex industry that includes mass-marketing of pornographic books and films, widespread supply of strip-clubs, peep-shows and the like and marketing of sex-tours for men to poor Third World countries. The general display of women's bodies and sexual parts, either in representation or as live bodies, is central to the sex industry and continually reminds men—and women—that men exercise the law of male sex-right, that they have patriarchal right of access to women's bodies. The story of the original sexual contract helps sort out which of the plethora of activities in the sex industry are appropriately called 'prostitution'. For example, satisfaction of a mere natural appetite does not require a man to have access to a woman's body; what then, is the significance of the fact that 15 to 25 per cent of the customers of the Birmingham prostitutes demand what is known in the trade as 'hand relief'?[32]

The story of the sexual contract suggests that the latter demand is part of the construction of what it means to be a man, part of the contemporary

31. Ericcson, 'Charges Against Prostitution', p. 341. Compare D. A. J. Richards, *Sex, Drugs, Death, and the Law*, p. 49.

32. McLeod, *Women Working*, p. 69. The men give a variety of reasons, all of which beg the question of the capitalist virtue of self-help.

expression of masculine sexuality. The satisfaction of men's natural sexual urges must be achieved through access to a woman, even if her body is not directly used sexually. Whether or not any man is able and willing to find release in other ways, he can exhibit his masculinity by contracting for use of a woman's body. The prostitution contract is another example of an actual 'original' sexual contract. The exemplary display of masculinity is to engage in 'the sex act'. (Hence, sale of men's bodies for homosexual use does not have the same social meaning.) The institution of prostitution ensures that men can buy 'the sex act' and so exercise their patriarchal right. The activities that, above all else, can appropriately be called prostitution are 'the sex act', and associated activities such as 'hand relief' and oral sex (fellatio), for which there is now a very large demand.[33] Some of the most prevalent confusions in discussions of prostitution might be avoided if other activities were seen as part of the wider sex industry. The market includes a vigorous demand for 'bondage and discipline' or fantasy slave contracts. The mass commercial replication of the most potent relations and symbols of domination is a testament to the power and genius of contract, which proclaims that a contract of subordination is (sexual) freedom.

Since the 1970s prostitutes have been organizing in the United States, Britain and Australia—and the International Committee for Prostitutes' Rights held the second World Whores' Congress in 1986—to improve their working conditions, to combat hostility and violence and to press for the decriminalization of prostitution. In short, prostitutes are endeavouring to be acknowledged as workers in an occupation that lacks trade union safeguards and protection. The prostitute is a woman and thus shares with all women in paid employment an uncertain status as a 'worker'. But the prostitute is not quite like other women workers; her status is even more uncertain. Prostitution is seen as different from other forms of women's work and, especially at the lower end of the market, prostitutes are set apart from other women workers (almost everyone can picture 'the prostitute' soliciting in the street, with her typical costume, stance and heart of gold). Contractarian defences of prostitution attribute the lack of acceptance of the prostitute as a worker, or purveyor of services, to the hypocrisy and distorted attitudes surrounding sexual activity. To be sure,

---

33. In the 1930s in the United States, only 10 per cent of customers demanded oral sex; by the 1960s nearly 90 per cent did so, either instead of or in addition to intercourse (figures cited by R. Rosen, *The Lost Sisterhood*), p. 97. Could it be conjectured that men's current widespread demand to buy women's bodies to penetrate their mouths is connected to the revitalization of the feminist movement and women's demand to speak?

hypocrisy is rife and irrational attitudes abound around the question of prostitution, as George Bernard Shaw's *Mrs. Warren's Profession* laid bare some time ago. However, reference to hypocrisy hardly seems to capture the emotions with which some men regard prostitutes.

Prostitutes are murdered because they are seen as fonts of pollution and their murderer's names can become household words, like Jack the Ripper. Less dramatically, prostitutes run considerable risk of physical injury every day from their male customers, especially if they work on the streets. Eileen McLeod found that, in Birmingham, 'almost without exception, prostitutes I have had contact with have experienced some form of serious physical violence from their clients'.[34] Prostitutes are not, of course, the only workers who face physical hazards in their work. Little publicity is given to the large numbers of workers killed or injured each year in the workplace through lack of, or inadequate, or unenforced safety precautions, or through genuine accidents. These injuries, though, do not occur because the worker is a *woman*. Contractarians are not alone in denying significance to the fact that prostitutes are women. Apart from some feminist analyses, it is hard to find discussions that acknowledge that prostitution is part of the patriarchal structure of civil society. The Left and Right, as well as some feminists, share the assumption that the prostitute's work is of exactly the same kind as any other paid employment. The prostitute merely works in a different profession and offers a different service (form of labour power) from that of a miner or electrician, secretary or assembler of electronic goods. Not surprisingly, criticism of prostitution is then usually couched in economic terms. For example, the argument that prostitutes are forced by economic necessity to enter the trade has been heard for a very long time. The conditions of entry into the prostitution contract have received as much attention as entry into the employment or marriage contracts, and involuntary entry is often presented as the problem about prostitution. Thus, Alison Jaggar has stated that 'it is the economic coercion underlying prostitution, . . . that provides the basic feminist objection to prostitution'.[35]

Another common argument, now made by the religious Right as well as by the Left, is that what is wrong with prostitution is that, once a woman has entered the trade, she is exploited and degraded like many other workers under capitalism. Once again, the question of subordination is ignored. In arguments about economic coercion and exploitation the comparison is often turned round; instead of prostitutes being seen

34. McLeod, *Women Working*, p. 53.

35. A. Jaggar, 'Prostitution', in *The Philosophy of Sex: Contemporary Readings*, ed. A. Soble (Totowa, NJ, Rowman and Littlefield, 1980), p. 360.

as exploited workers, workers are held to be in the same position as prostitutes. Marxist critics of prostitution take their lead from Marx's statement that 'prostitution is only a *specific* expression of the *general* prostitution of the *laborer*'.[36] Prostitution then represents the economic coercion, exploitation and alienation of wage labour. As one critic has stated, 'prostitution is the incarnation of the degradation of the modern citizen as producer'.[37] The prostitution contract is not merely one example of the employment contract; rather, the employment contract becomes a contract of prostitution. The figure of the prostitute can, therefore, symbolize everything that is wrong with wage labour.

To see prostitutes as epitomizing exploitation under capitalism, and to represent the worker by the figure of the prostitute, is not without irony. 'The worker' is masculine—yet his degradation is symbolized by a female emblem, and patriarchal capitalism is pictured as a system of universal prostitution. The fact that the prostitute seems to be such an obvious symbol of the degradation of wage labour, raises the suspicion that what she sells is not quite the same as the labour power contracted out by other workers. If prostitution is work in exactly the same sense as any other paid employment, then the present status of the prostitute can only be attributed, as contractarians insist, to legal prohibition, hypocrisy and outdated ideas about sex. The story of the sexual contract provides another explanation for the difference between prostitution and other paid employment in which women predominate. The prostitution contract is a contract with a woman and, therefore, cannot be the same as the employment contract, a contract between men. Even though the prostitution contract is sealed in the capitalist market, it still differs in some significant respects from the employment contract. For example, a worker always enters into an employment contract with a capitalist. If a prostitute were merely another worker the prostitution contract, too, would always involve a capitalist; yet very frequently the man who enters into the contract is a worker.

Supposing, the objection might be raised, that the prostitute works in a 'massage parlour'. She will then be a paid employee and have entered into an employment contract. True; but the prostitution contract is not an employment contract. The prostitution contract is entered into with the male customer, not with an employer. The prostitute may or may not be a paid employee (worker); some prostitutes are 'more adequately described

36. K. Marx, *Economic and Philosophic Manuscripts of 1844*, ed. D. J. Struik (New York, International Publishers, 1964), p. 133, footnote.

37. J. H. Reiman, 'Prostitution, Addiction and the Ideology of Liberalism', *Contemporary Crises* 3 (1979), p. 66.

as small-scale private entrepreneurs'.[38] The difference is, however, irrelevant to the question of how prostitution is to be characterized; is it free work and a free exchange, or exploitation, or a specific kind of subordination? Whether the prostitute is a worker or petty entrepreneur she must be seen as contracting out labour power or services if the prostitution contract is also to be seen as an employment contract. From the standpoint of contract, the employment contract is infinitely elastic, stretching from the lifetime of the civil slave to the brief period of the prostitution contract in a brothel for troops or immigrant workers. No matter whether the prostitute is an exploited or free worker or a petty entrepreneur, labour power or services are assumed to be contracted out. As Ericsson asserts, a prostitute must necessarily sell 'not her body or vagina, but sexual *services*. If she actually did sell herself she would no longer be a prostitute but a sexual slave'.[39]

More accurately, she would resemble a slave in something of the same fashion that a worker, a wage slave, resembles a slave. Labour power is a political fiction. The capitalist does not and cannot contract to use the proletarian's services or labour power. The employment contract gives the employer right of command over the use of the worker's labour, that is to say, over the self, person and body of the worker during the period set down in the employment contract. Similarly, the services of the prostitute cannot be provided unless she is present; property in the person, unlike material property, cannot be separated from its owner. The 'john', the 'punter', the man who contracts to use the services of the prostitute, like the employer, gains command over the use of her person and body for the duration of the prostitution contract—but at this point the comparison between the wage slave and the prostitute, the employment contract and the prostitution contract, breaks down.

The capitalist has no intrinsic interest in the body and self of the worker, or, at least, not the same kind of interest as the man who enters into the prostitution contract. The employer is primarily interested in the commodities produced by the worker; that is to say, in profits. The peculiar character of the relation between the owner of labour power and his property means that the employer must organize (embodied) workers, and compel or induce them to labour, in order to produce commodities with his machinery and other means of production. But the employer can and often does replace the worker with machines or, in the 1980s, robots and other computerized machines. Indeed, employers prefer machines to workers because machines are like absolutely faithful slaves; they cannot

38. Ericcson, 'Charges Against Prostitution', p. 351.
39. Ibid., p. 341.

be insubordinate, resist the employer's commands or combine together in trades unions or revolutionary associations. On the other hand, if the employer replaces all his workers by machines, he becomes merely a proprietor. The employer has an interest in workers as selves in that, without them, he ceases to be a master and loses the enjoyment of command over subordinates.

In contrast to employers, the men who enter into the prostitution contract have only one interest; the prostitute and her body. A market exists for substitutes for women's bodies in the form of inflatable dolls, but, unlike the machines that replace the worker, the dolls are advertised as 'lifelike'. The dolls are a literal substitute for women, not a functional substitute like the machine installed instead of the worker. Even a plastic substitute for a woman can give a man the sensation of being a patriarchal master. In prostitution, the body of the woman, and sexual access to that body, is the subject of the contract. To have bodies for sale in the market, as bodies, looks very like slavery. To symbolize wage slavery by the figure of the prostitute rather than that of the masculine worker is thus not entirely inappropriate. But prostitution differs from wage slavery. No form of labour power can be separated from the body, but only through the prostitution contract does the buyer obtain unilateral right of direct sexual use of a woman's body.

A contractarian might respond at this point that far too much weight is being placed on the body. Even if reference is made to the body rather than (as it should be) to services, moral freedom can be retained when use of the body, or part of the body, is being contracted out. The self or person is not identical to the body, so that the self is not injured if property in the body is used. David Richards has taken issue with Kant, and with Marxists and feminists whom he assumes are following Kant, on this question. Kant condemned prostitution as a *pactum turpe*; to contract out a bodily part for sexual use is to turn oneself into property, a *res*, because of the 'inseparable unity of the members of a Person'.[40] Kant writes that man cannot dispose of himself as he wills:

He is not his own property; to say that he is would be self-contradictory; for in so far as he is a person he is a Subject in whom the ownership of things can be vested, and if he were his own property, he would be a thing over which he could have ownership . . . it is impossible to be a person and a thing, the proprietor and the property.[41]

40. I. Kant, *The Philosophy of Law*, tr. W. Hastie (Edinburgh, T. and T. Clark, 1887), third section, §26, p. 112; cf. I. Kant, *Lectures on Ethics*, tr. L. Infield (New York, Harper and Row, 1963), p. 166.

41. Kant, *Lectures on Ethics*, p. 165.

Richards argues that Kant's condemnation of prostitution is inconsistent with his general view of autonomy. I shall not attempt to ascertain whether it is more inconsistent than his view of wage labour or, in particular, the marriage contract, since Richards fails to mention that Kant upholds patriarchal right and so has to deny that women are persons and, hence, autonomous. Kant's inconsistency is that he wants to confine fulfillment of the terms of the sexual contract to conjugal relations; women's bodies may be used as property by men as husbands, but women must not sell this commodity in the market and be paid for sexual use. Richards claims that to argue against prostitution is arbitrarily to limit sexual freedom. The embodiment of the self places no constraints on an individual's moral autonomy. Richards' argument is based on a version of the disembodied, rational entities who inhabit (one aspect of) Kant's contract theory and Rawls' original position. Autonomy is merely 'persons' self-critical capacities to assess their present wants and lives.... Autonomy occurs in a certain body, occasioning a person self-critically to take into account that body and its capacities in deciding on the form of his or her life'.[42] In short, freedom is the unconstrained capacity of an owner (rational entity), externally related to property in its person (body), to judge how to contract out that property.

Human beings certainly possess the capacity for critical self-reflection—and that capacity can be understood as if it encompassed nothing more than individual rational calculation of how property can be used to the maximum advantage. If a complex, multifaceted capacity could not be reduced to this bleak, culturally and historically specific achievement, patriarchal civil society could not have developed. Richards' 'autonomy' was summed up more economically in Richard Lovelace's lines:

> Stone walls do not a prison make,
> Nor iron bars a cage.

Nor is this very partial and socially tangential (though in some circumstances, heroic) notion of moral—or spiritual—freedom at issue in prostitution or other forms of civil subordination. Civil subordination is a *political* problem not a matter of morality, although moral issues are involved. To try to answer the question of what is wrong with prostitution is to engage in argument about political right in the form of patriarchal right, or the law of male sex-right. Subordinates of all kinds exercise their capacity for critical self-reflection every day—that is why masters are thwarted, frustrated and, sometimes, overthrown. But unless masters

---

42. D. A. J. Richards, *Sex, Drugs, Death, and the Law*, p. 109.

are overthrown, unless subordinates engage in political action, no amount of critical reflection will end their subjection and bring them freedom.

To grant that human embodiment is of more than merely contingent or incidental significance for freedom and subordination, may not seem sufficient to distinguish the profession of prostitution from some other forms of work, or sufficient to establish that there is something wrong with prostitution that is not also wrong with wage labour. A prostitute's body is for sale in the market, but there are also other professions in which bodies are up for sale and in which employers have an intrinsic interest in their workers' bodies. For example, now that sport is part of patriarchal capitalism, the bodies of professional sportsmen and sportswomen are also available to be contracted out. Orlando Patterson discusses the case of baseball in the United States where, until 1975, players could be bought and sold like any material property at the will and for the profit of the owners of their teams. Patterson emphasizes that the baseball players were not and are not slaves, they are juridically free citizens, and they now have some voice in their disposition—but their bodies are still bought and sold. Patterson comments that employers do not now demand that workers

stand naked on an auction block being prodded and inspected by the employers and their physicians. But when an employer requires a medical certificate from a worker or professional athlete before hiring him, he is not only soliciting the same kind of information as a slavemaster inspecting his latest cargo of bodies, he is betraying the inherent absurdity of the distinction between 'raw bodies' and the services produced by such bodies.[43]

However, there is a difference in the uses to which bodies are put when they are sold. Owners of baseball teams have command over the use of their players' bodies, but the bodies are not directly used sexually by those who have contracted for them.

There is an integral relationship between the body and self. The body and the self are not identical, but selves are inseparable from bodies. The idea of property in the person has the merit of drawing attention to the importance of the body in social relations. Civil mastery, like the mastery of the slave-owner, is not exercised over mere biological entities that can be used like material (animal) property, nor exercised over purely rational entities. Masters are not interested in the disembodied fiction of labour power or services. They contract for the use of human embodied selves. Precisely because subordinates are embodied selves they can perform the required labour, be subject to discipline, give the recognition and offer

43. O. Patterson, *Slavery and Social Death: A Comparative Study* (Cambridge, MA and London, Harvard University Press, 1982), p. 25.

the faithful service that makes a man a master. Human bodies and selves are also sexually differentiated, the self is a masculine or feminine self. One illustration of the integral connection between the body and the self is the widespread use of vulgar terms for women's sexual organs to refer to women themselves, or the use of a slang term for the penis is make disparaging reference to men.

Masculinity and femininity are sexual identities; the self is not completely subsumed in its sexuality, but identity is inseparable from the sexual construction of the self. In modern patriarchy, sale of women's bodies in the capitalist market involves sale of a self in a different manner, and in a more profound sense, than sale of the body of a male baseball player or sale of command over the use of the labour (body) of a wage slave. The story of the sexual contract reveals that the patriarchal construction of the difference between masculinity and femininity is the political difference between freedom and subjection, and that sexual mastery is the major means through which men affirm their manhood. When a man enters into the prostitution contract he is not interested in sexually indifferent, disembodied services; he contracts to buy sexual use of a *woman* for a given period. Why else are men willing to enter the market and pay for 'hand relief'? Of course, men can also affirm their masculinity in other ways, but, in relations between the sexes, unequivocal affirmation is obtained by engaging in 'the sex act'. Womanhood, too, is confirmed in sexual activity, and when a prostitute contracts out use of her body she is thus selling *herself* in a very real sense. Women's selves are involved in prostitution in a different manner from the involvement of the self in other occupations. Workers of all kinds may be more or less 'bound up in their work', but the integral connection between sexuality and sense of the self means that, for self-protection, a prostitute must distance herself from her sexual use.

Women engaged in the trade have developed a variety of distancing strategies, or a professional approach, in dealing with their clients. Such distancing creates a problem for men, a problem that can be seen as another variant on the contradiction of mastery and slavery. The prostitution contract enables men to constitute themselves as civil masters for a time, and, like other masters, they wish to obtain acknowledgment of their status. Eileen McLeod talked to clients as well as prostitutes in Birmingham and, noting that her findings are in keeping with similar investigations in Britain and the United States, she states that 'nearly all the men I interviewed complained about the emotional coldness and mercenary approach of many prostitutes they had had contact with'.[44] A master

44. McLeod, *Women Working*, p. 84.

requires a service, but he also requires that the service is delivered by a person, a self, not merely a piece of (disembodied) property. John Stuart Mill remarked of the subordination of wives that, 'their masters require something more from them than actual service. Men do not want solely the obedience of women, they want their sentiments. All men, except the most brutish, desire to have, not a forced slave but a willing one, not a slave merely, but a favourite'.[45]

An employer or a husband can more easily obtain faithful service and acknowledgment of his mastery than a man who enters into the prostitution contract. The civil slave contract and employment and marriage contracts create long-term relationships of subordination. The prostitution contract is of short duration and the client is not concerned with daily problems of the extraction of labour power. The prostitution contract is, one might say, a contract of specific performance, rather than open-ended like the employment contract and, in some of its aspects, the marriage contract. There are also other differences between the employment and prostitution contracts. For example, the prostitute is always at a singular disadvantage in the 'exchange'. The client makes direct use of the prostitute's body and there are no 'objective' criteria through which to judge whether the service has been satisfactorily performed. Trades unions bargain over pay and conditions for workers, and the products of their labours are 'quality controlled'. Prostitutes, in contrast, can always be refused payment by men who claim (and who can gainsay their subjective assessment?) that their demands have not been met.[46]

The character of the employment contract also provides scope for mastery to be recognized in numerous subtle ways as well as in an open, direct fashion. The worker is masculine, and men must mutually acknowledge their civil equality and fraternity (or the social contract cannot be upheld) at the same time as they create relations of subordination. The brief duration of the prostitution contract gives less room for subtlety; but, then, perhaps it is not so necessary. There need be no such ambiguities in relations between men and women, least of all when a man has bought a woman's body for his use as if it were like any other commodity. In such a context, 'the sex act' itself provides acknowledgment of patriarchal right. When women's bodies are on sale as commodities in the capitalist market, the terms of the original contract cannot be forgotten; the law of male sex-right is publicly affirmed, and men gain public acknowledgment as women's sexual masters—that is what is wrong with prostitution.

---

45. J. S. Mill, The Subjection of Women', in *Essays on Sex Equality*, ed. A. S. Rossi (Chicago and London, University of Chicago Press, 1970), p. 141.

46. I owe thanks to Mary Douglas for drawing my attention to this point.

Another difference between the prostitution contract and the other contracts with which I am concerned is also worn noting. I have argued that contracts about property in persons take the form of an exchange of obedience for protection. A civil slave and wives (in principle) receive lifelong protection, the family wage includes protection and the organizational complexities of extracting labour power for use in capitalist production have led to provision of protection over and above the wage. But where is the protection in the prostitution contract? The pimp stands outside the contract between client and prostitute, just as the state stands outside, but regulates and enforces, the marriage and employment contracts. The short-term prostitution contract cannot include the protection available in long-term relations. In this respect, the prostitution contract mirrors the contractarian ideal. The individual as owner will never commit himself far into the future; to do so is to give himself up as hostage to the self-interest of other individuals. The individual will make simultaneous exchanges, an impossible exchange if use is to be made of property in persons. The exchange of money for use of a woman's body comes as close as is feasible in actual contracts to a simultaneous exchange. For Marx, prostitution was a metaphor for wage labour. The more appropriate analogy is also more amusing. The contractarian idea of universal sale of property (services), is a vision of unimpeded mutual use or universal prostitution.

The feminist argument that prostitutes are workers in exactly the same sense as other wage labourers, and the contractarian defence of prostitution, both depend on the assumption that women are 'individuals', with full ownership of the property in their persons. Women are still prohibited from contracting out their property in their sexual parts in some legal jurisdictions in the three countries with which I am concerned. Nevertheless, while I was completing this chapter, a judge in New Jersey, in the leading case of Baby M, ruled that women could contract out another piece of property, their wombs, and that they must be held to this contract. This contract of so-called surrogate motherhood is new, and it provides a dramatic example of the contradictions surrounding women and contract. The surrogacy contract also indicates that a further transformation of modern patriarchy may be underway. Father-right is reappearing in a new, contractual form.

My argument, as I have emphasized, is not about women as mothers, but the significantly named 'surrogate' motherhood has little to do with motherhood as generally understood. The political implications of the surrogacy contract can only be appreciated when surrogacy is seen as another provision in the sexual contract, as a new form of access to and use of women's bodies by men. A 'surrogate' mother contracts to be artificially inseminated with the sperm of a man (usually the sperm belongs

to a husband whose wife is infertile), to bear a child, and to relinquish
the child to the genetic father. In exchange for use of her services the 'surrogate' receives monetary payment; the market rate at present appears to
be US$10,000.

Artificial insemination is far from new—the first human pregnancy was
achieved by this means in 1799—but 'surrogate' motherhood is frequently
and confusingly discussed together with a range of developments, such
as *in vitro* fertilization, which have resulted from new technologies.[47]
(*In vitro* fertilization is now sold on the capitalist market; in the United
States the market is estimated at $30–40 million per year, even though the
success rate of the technology is very low). New technology also makes
other forms of 'surrogacy' possible. For instance, the ovum and sperm of
a married couple may be joined and grown *in vitro*, and the embryo then
inserted into the uterus of a 'surrogate'. In this case, the baby is the genetic
offspring of husband and wife and such a surrogacy contract differs significantly from a contract involving artificial insemination. I shall concentrate
on the latter to draw out a point about paternity and patriarchy, but tech-
nological developments and *in vitro* surrogacy also raise some general,
profoundly important issues about contract and use of women's bodies.

In mid-1987, there is no legal consensus about the legitimacy or status
of surrogacy contracts. In the United States, the judgement in the case of
Baby M—which arose from a dispute over a contract when the 'surrogate'
mother refused to relinquish the baby—unequivocally confirmed the bind-
ing legal status of such contracts (the case is currently under appeal to the
New Jersey Supreme Court). Long before this, however, surrogacy agencies had been set up and press reports state that some 600 contracts have
been made, at least one woman having entered and fulfilled two contracts.
The agencies are profitable; one is reported to have made $600,000 gross
in 1986. In Australia, only Victoria has legislated on the question and has
prohibited commercial surrogacy and denied legal enforcement to informal arrangements. In Britain, the 1985 Surrogacy Arrangements Act has
effectively prohibited commercial surrogacy contracts. For third parties to
benefit from a surrogacy contract is a criminal offence, and to pay a 'surrogate' mother or for her to receive payment may be an offence under the
Adoption Act. Non-commercial surrogacy arrangements are not illegal.[48]

47. See V. Stolcke, 'Old Values, New Technologies: Who Is the Father?', paper
presented to the Kolloquium am Wissenschaftskolleg zu Berlin, March 1987, p. 6.
(My thanks to Verena Stolcke for sending me a copy of the paper.)
48. Information from D. Brahams, 'The Hasty British Ban on Commercial
Surrogacy', *Hastings Center Report*, February 1987, pp. 16–19. (Lionel Cossman
kindly supplied me with a copy of this paper.)

At this point, the old argument about prostitution and legal prostitution (marriage) immediately presents itself. Is not a contract in which money is exchanged for services more honest about the position of the woman involved than marriage or informal surrogacy? The Report of the Waller Committee which led to the Victorian legislation (and which considered 'surrogate' motherhood in the context of *in vitro* fertilization) recommended that neither commercial nor non-commercial surrogacy should form part of *in vitro* programmes.[49] But is a *gift* of the 'surrogate's' services more acceptable than an exchange of her services for money? The British legislation clearly implies that this is the case. To see surrogacy as a gift relation is, however, to beg the question of to whom it is that the service is rendered. Is surrogacy an example of one woman donating a service to another woman, or is it an example of a woman being inseminated with the sperm of a man to bear his child in exchange for money? Prostitution is often defended as a type of social work or therapy, and, similarly, 'surrogate' motherhood is defended as a service offered in the market from compassion for the plight of infertile women. To ask questions about the surrogacy contract is not to deny that women who enter the surrogacy contract may feel compassion for infertile women, nor to deny that women can be made miserable by infertility (although in current debates it is frequently forgotten, or even implicitly ruled out, that infertile women, and their husbands, can come to terms with the condition and lead satisfying lives). As in so many discussions of prostitution, the argument from compassion assumes that any problem about 'surrogate' motherhood is a problem about women, and about the supply of a service. The character of men's participation in the surrogacy contract and the character of the demand for this service is treated as unproblematic.

In the controversy over 'surrogate' motherhood, the comparison with prostitution is often made. As the eminent historian, Lawrence Stone, commented about the case of Baby M, 'contracts should be fulfilled. This is a rather bizarre contract, I agree. You're renting out your body. But one expects a prostitute to fulfill a contract'.[50] Most of the arguments used to defend or condemn prostitution have reappeared in the controversy over 'surrogate' motherhood. Obviously, surrogacy contracts raise questions about the conditions of entry into the contract and economic coercion.

---

49. The Committee to Consider the Social, Ethical and Legal Issues Arising from In Vitro Fertilization, *Report on the Disposition of Embryos Produced by In Vitro Fertilization* (Victoria, August 1984), §4.17. (I am grateful to Rebecca Albury for sending me a copy of the relevant part of the *Report*.)

50. *The New York Times* (5 April 1987).

The sexual division of labour in patriarchal capitalism and the 'feminiza-
tion of poverty' ensure that a surrogacy contract will appear financially
attractive to working-class women, although the payment is very meagre
for the time involved and nature of the service. Class questions are also
clearly raised. In the Baby M case, for instance, the 'surrogate' mother
dropped out of high school and was married aged sixteen to a man who
is now a sanitation worker earning $28,000 per year. The income of the
man who entered into the contract, together with that of his wife, both
professionals with doctoral degrees, is about $91,500 per year.[51] How-
ever, emphasis on class inequality and economic coercion to enter the
contract, draws attention away from the question of what exactly is being contracted for and how the surrogacy contract resembles or differs
from other contracts about property in the person.

In Victoria, 'surrogate' motherhood was rejected on the grounds that
'arrangements where fees are paid are, in reality, agreements for the purchase of a child, and should not be countenanced . . . The buying and selling of children has been condemned and proscribed for generations. It
should not be allowed to reappear'.[52] Adoption is strictly regulated to
avoid poor women—or, at least, poor white women—being offered incentives to sell their babies. The problem with this line of argument is not
that common sense is a poor guide here, but that references to baby-selling
completely fail to meet the defence of surrogacy contracts derived from
contract theory. From the standpoint of contract, talk of baby-selling reveals that surrogacy is misunderstood in exactly the same way that prostitution is misunderstood. A prostitute does not sell her body, she sells
sexual services. In the surrogacy contract there is no question of a baby
being sold, merely a service.

The qualifier 'surrogate' indicates that the point of the contract is to
render motherhood irrelevant and to deny that the 'surrogate' is a mother.
A woman who enters a surrogacy contract is not being paid for (bearing)
a child; to make a contract of that kind *would* be tantamount to baby-
selling. The 'surrogate' mother is receiving payment in return for entering
into a contract which enables a man to make use of her services. In this
case the contract is for use of the property a woman owns in her uterus.

From the standpoint of contract, the tact that provision of a service
involves motherhood is purely incidental. The womb has no special status
as property. A woman could just as well contract out use of a different
piece of property in her person. Furthermore, the fact that disposition of a

51. Information from *The New York Times* (12 January 1987).
52. Committee to Consider In Vitro Fertilization, *Report on the Disposition
of Embryos*, §4.6; §4.11.

baby is at issue is of no special significance. Contracts for the use of other forms of service, notably that provided through the employment contract, also result in property over which one party alone has jurisdiction. The worker has no claim to the commodities produced through use of his labour; they belong to the capitalist. In a similar fashion, the baby that is produced through use of a 'surrogate' mother's services is the property of the man who contracts to use the service. The judge in the case of Baby M made this point very clearly. In his decision he stated that:

the money to be paid to the surrogate is not being paid for the surrender of the child to the father.... The biological father pays the surrogate for her willingness to be impregnated and carry his child to term. At birth, the father does not purchase the child. It is his own biologically genetically related child. He cannot purchase what is already his.[53]

Appeal is often made in discussions of 'surrogate' motherhood to two biblical precedents in the book of *Genesis*. In the first story, Sarai, unable to have a child, says to her husband Abram, 'I pray thee, go in unto my maid; it may be that I obtain children by her'. Then Sarai 'took Hagar her maid the Egyptian, . . . and gave her to her husband Abram to be his wife'. In the second story, Rachel, another infertile wife, gives Jacob 'Bilhah her handmaid to wife: and Jacob went in unto her'.[54] In the biblical stories, the 'surrogate' mother is a maid, a servant, a subordinate—and she is the *wife's* servant. The stories will thus seem to reinforce an objection that will be made to my characterization of 'surrogate' motherhood as a contract in which the services of the 'surrogate' mother are used by a man. On the contrary, the objection will be pressed, the biblical stories show that the surrogacy contract has been misrepresented; the service is used by women. The contract is made by a husband and a wife for use of the 'surrogate's' services. The man's infertile wife, not the man himself, is the true user of the service. She is the mother for whom the 'surrogate's' services are contracted. A woman enters a surrogacy contract with another woman (although male sperm is needed for insemination).

Ironies never cease in the matter of women and contract. After the long history of exclusion of women from contract, the surrogacy contract is presented as a woman's contract; women are now seen as the parties to the contract. The question of men's demand for the service is thus obscured, together with the character of the 'exchange' that takes place. The question of who exactly uses the services of a 'surrogate' mother is

53. Cited in excerpts from the decision by Judge Harvey R. Sorkow, printed in *The New York Times* (1 April 1987).
54. *Genesis* 16:2, 3; *Genesis* 30:4.

confused by the strong social pressures in Britain, Australia and the United States to restrict surrogacy contracts (and access to the new reproductive technologies) to married couples. But there is no need at all for a wife to be involved. The comparison with prostitution is revealing here (though not quite in the way that is always intended). From the standpoint of contract, the demand for use of prostitutes is sexually indifferent, and so is the demand for 'surrogate' motherhood; men can contract for the use of a 'surrogate' without the mediation of another woman. All that is taking place is that one individual is contracting to use another's property. A wife is superfluous to the contract (though, socially, her presence legitimizes the transaction). A wife may be a formal party to the surrogacy contract but the substance of her position is quite different from that of her husband. A wife contributes no property to the contract; she merely awaits its outcome.

The exchange in the surrogacy contract is between part of the property of a man, namely his sperm or seed, and part of the property of the 'surrogate', her uterus. A surrogacy contract differs from a prostitution contract in that a man does not make direct sexual use of a woman's body; rather, his use is indirect via artificial insemination. The man's seed, to use Locke's language, is mixed with the woman's uterus, and, if she performs her service faithfully, he can claim the property thereby produced as his own. Locke's language brings out the way in which contract is now taking a new turn. Contract transformed classic into modern patriarchy, but, with the invention of the surrogacy contract, one aspect of classic patriarchy has returned. If a woman's uterus is nothing more than a piece of property to which she is externally related, she is analogous to Sir Robert Filmer's empty vessel. But now the empty vessel can be contracted out for use by a man who fills it with his seed and, in another example of masculine creativity, thereby creates a new piece of property. Perhaps the man who enters into the surrogacy contract might be compared to the employer who, in contract doctrine, is the creative principle who transforms labour power into commodities. But he can now also do much more; in a spectacular twist of the patriarchal screw, the surrogacy contract enables a man to present his wife with the ultimate gift—a child.

Labour power is a political fiction, but the service performed by the 'surrogate' mother is a greater fiction. The worker contracts out right of command over the use of his body, and the prostitute contracts out right of direct sexual use of her body. The selves of the worker and the prostitute are, in their different ways, both put out for hire. The self of the 'surrogate' mother is at stake in a more profound sense still. The 'surrogate' mother contracts out right over the unique physiological, emotional and creative capacity of her body, that is to say, of herself as a woman. For nine months she has the most intimate possible relation with another developing being; the being is part of herself. The baby, once born, is a separate being, but the mother's relation to her infant is qualitatively different from that of workers to the other products that ensue from contracts about the property in their persons. The example of a smoothly completed surrogacy contract and an unconcerned 'surrogate' mother, like examples of husbands who have renounced patriarchal right or prostitutes who exploit clients, reveals little about the *institution* of marriage, prostitution, or 'surrogate' motherhood. The surrogacy contract is another medium through which patriarchal subordination is secured. In one respect, a surrogacy contract is rather like an employment contract. The employer obtains right of command over the use of the bodies of workers in order, unilaterally, to have power over the process through which his commodities are produced. There is no reason why a surrogacy contract should not enable a man to ensure that the service for which he has contracted is faithfully performed by restricting the use to which the 'surrogate' may put her body until the service is fulfilled.

That women are willing to be parties to contracts that constitute other women as patriarchal subordinates is not surprising. Women are still treated as less than women if we do not have children. Contract doctrine entails that there are no limits to the uses that may legitimately be made of property in persons, providing only that access to use is established through contract. Why, then, in a period when contract holds sway, should childless women not take advantage of this new contract? Using the services of a 'surrogate' mother to provide an infertile married couple with a child is often compared to adoption, previously their only legitimate recourse if they were not prepared to accept their condition, but there is a crucial difference between the two practices. An adopting couple are not, except in rare circumstances, genetically related to the child. But the child of the 'surrogate' is also the child of the husband. The wife is more accurately called the surrogate mother, just as, in cases of adoption, the couple are surrogate mother and father. The wife will, of course, like adopting parents, bring up the child 'as if it were her own' but, irrespective of the happiness of the marriage and how well the child flourishes and *is* their own, in the last analysis, the child is the father's.

The story of the original contract tells of the political defeat of the father and how his sons, the brothers, establish a specifically modern nonpaternal form of patriarchy. The emergence of 'surrogate' motherhood suggests that contract is helping to bring about another transformation. Men are now beginning to exert patriarchal right as paternal right again, but in new forms. The logic of contract as exhibited in 'surrogate' motherhood shows very starkly how extension of the standing of 'individual' to women can reinforce and transform patriarchy as well as challenge patriarchal institutions. To extend to women the masculine conception of the individual as owner, and the conception of freedom as the capacity to do what you will with your own, is to sweep away any intrinsic relation between the female owner, her body and reproductive capacities. She stands to her property in exactly the same external relation as the male owner stands to his labour power or sperm; there is nothing distinctive about womanhood.

From the standpoint of contract, not only is sexual difference irrelevant to sexual relations, but sexual difference becomes irrelevant to physical reproduction. The former status of 'mother' and 'father' is thus rendered inoperative by contract and must be replaced by the (ostensibly sex-neutral) 'parent'. At least in the case of the surrogacy contract, the term 'parent' is far from sexually indifferent. The shade of Sir Robert Filmer hangs over 'surrogate' motherhood. In classic patriarchalism, the father is *the* parent. When the property of the 'surrogate' mother, her empty vessel, is filled is with the seed of the man who has contracted with her, he, too, becomes the parent, the creative force that brings new life (property) into the world. Men have denied significance to women's unique bodily capacity, have appropriated it and transmuted it into masculine political genesis. The story of the social contract is the greatest story of men giving political birth, but, with the surrogacy contract, modern patriarchy has taken a new turn. Thanks to the power of the creative political medium of contract, men can appropriate physical genesis too. The creative force of the male seed turns the empty property contracted out by an 'individual' into new human life. Patriarchy in its literal meaning has returned in a new guise.

Until the present, womanhood has been seen as inseparable from, even subsumed in, maternity. For at least three centuries, feminists have spent enormous efforts endeavouring to show that women, like men, have a range of capacities that could be exercised in addition to their unique capacity to create physical life. Now motherhood has been separated from womanhood—and the separation expands patriarchal right. Here is another variant of the contradiction of slavery. A woman can be a 'surrogate' mother only because her womanhood is deemed irrelevant and she is declared an 'individual' performing a service. At the same time, she can be a 'surrogate' mother only because she is a *woman*. Similarly, the relevant property of the man in the surrogacy contract can only be that of a *man*; it is the property that can make him a father. Appropriately, sperm is the only example of property in the person that is not a political fiction. Unlike labour power, sexual parts, the uterus, or any other property that is contracted out for use by another, sperm *can* be separated from the body.

Indeed, sperm can be used in artificial insemination, and the sperm of men deemed genetically superior can be stored away until a suitable woman is located, only because it can be separated from the person.

Until the surrogacy contract was invented, this peculiarity of the male seed rendered genetic paternity inherently problematic; paternity always hinged on a woman's testimony. Maternity, however, was always certain and, according to Hobbes, in the natural condition the mother was the lord, with political right over her child; a man had to contract with a mother to obtain mastery as a father. Thanks to the power of contract, genetic paternity can now be made secure and brought together with masculine political creativity. Through contract, men can at last be certain of paternity. A momentous change has thus occurred in (one aspect of) the meaning of 'fatherhood' and the power of fatherhood—or patriarchy in the traditional sense.

It is far too soon to say exactly how important 'surrogate' motherhood will be in the future development of patriarchal domination. In 1979, when (with Teresa Brennan) I published my first examination of social contract theory from a feminist perspective, the term was unknown to us. There are other straws in the wind that point in the same direction as 'surrogate' motherhood—for instance, men have taken legal action as fathers in Britain, Australia and the United States to try to prevent women obtaining abortions and to keep women's bodies artificially alive in order to sustain a foetus. Fathers are also fighting for custody of children. In recent years, in a reversal of the practice in the mid-nineteenth century, the mother has usually been awarded custody of any children if a marriage breaks down. Indeed, the practice of awarding custody to mothers led Christine Delphy to argue that divorce is merely an extension of marriage in which men, once again, are exempted from responsibility for children. Now that feminists have succeeded in winning some much-needed legal reforms, and now that, in many matters, women and men are being placed on the same civil footing, mothers can no longer assume that they will attain custody. Nor can unmarried mothers be sure that the father will not be awarded access to and rights over the child. Some winds, though, blow in a different direction. For example, artificial insemination enables women to become mothers without sexual relations with men.

The contractual subjection of women is full of contradictions, paradoxes and ironies. Perhaps the greatest irony of all is yet to come. Contract is conventionally believed to have defeated the old patriarchal order, but, in eliminating the final remnants of the old world of status, contract may yet usher in a new form of paternal right.

CHAPTER FOUR

Equality and Speech*

CATHARINE MacKINNON

The law of equality and the law of freedom of speech are on a collision course in this country. Until this moment, the constitutional doctrine of free speech has developed without taking equality seriously—either the problem of social inequality or the mandate of substantive legal equality. Originally, of course, the Constitution contained no equality guarantee to serve as context, expansion joint, handmaiden, counterbalance, or co-equal goal to the speech guarantee. Yet the modern doctrine of speech dates from considerably after the entrenchment of equality in the Four-teenth Amendment,[1] and still the First Amendment has been interpreted, with a few exceptions, as if it were not there.

More precisely, the First Amendment has grown as if a commitment to speech were no part of a commitment to equality and as if a commitment to equality had no implications for the law of speech—as if the upheaval that produced the Reconstruction Amendments did not move the ground under the expressive freedom, setting new limits and mandating new ex-tensions, perhaps even demanding reconstruction of the speech right itself. The version of equality that *has* become part of First Amendment law has

---

*Reprinted by permission from *Only Words* by Catharine MacKinnon, Cambridge, MA: Harvard University Press, Copyright © 1993 by Catharine MacKinnon.

1. Of course, the modern doctrine of free speech technically relies on the Fourteenth Amendment to apply its prohibition of government censorship to the states, without involving the equality guarantee at all. Modern speech doctrine dates from *Masses Pub. Co. v. Patten*, 244 F. 535 (S.D.N.Y. 1917), rev'd, 246 F. 24 (2d Cir. 1917); *Schenck v. United States*, 249 U.S. 47 (1919); and *Abrams v. United States*, 250 U.S. 616 (1919) (especially the dissent of Justice Holmes).

been negative—equally keeping law from regulating one forum or view as another—and formal—speech protected for one group or interest is equally protected for others.[2] It is, in other words, largely redundant. The subprovince of the First Amendment that resonates in equal protection is simply an unbiased extension of precedent and the rule of law—a narrow equality supporting a shallow speech. Fourteenth Amendment equality, for its part, has grown as if equality could be achieved while the First Amendment protected the speech of inequality, meaning whenever inequality takes an expressive form, and without considering equal access to speech as central to any equality agenda.

Both bodies of law accordingly show virtually total insensitivity to the damage done to social equality by expressive means and a substantial lack of recognition that some people get a lot more speech than others.[3] In the absence of these recognitions, the power of those who have speech has become more and more exclusive, coercive, and violent as it has become more and more legally protected. Understanding that there is a relationship between these two issues—the less speech you have, the more the speech of those who have it keeps you unequal; the more the speech of the dominant is protected, the more dominant they become and the less

2. As the Court put it, "necessarily...under the Equal Protection Clause, not to mention the First Amendment itself, government may not grant the use of a forum to people whose views it finds acceptable, but deny it to those wishing to express less favored or more controversial views." *Police Department v. Mosley*, 408 U.S. 92, 96 (1972). Some possible implications of these cases are discussed in a seminal article by Kenneth L. Karst, "Equality as a Central Principle in the First Amendment," 43 *University of Chicago Law Review* 20 (1975). While the article notes that "the relation between formal and substantive equality" is raised by these speech cases decided on equal protection grounds (p. 22), it does not discuss this issue in any depth, nor does it see any tension between existing First Amendment approaches and the trajectory of the equality principle.

3. Access problems are better recognized, for example, in the broadcast area than are the damage issues anywhere. On access, see Karst, "Equality as a Central Principle" note 2 above; Thomas I. Emerson, "The Affirmative Side of the First Amendment," 15 *Georgia Law Review* 795 (1981); *Red Lion Broadcasting Co. v. FCC*, 395 U.S. 367 (1969). A particularly pertinent discussion is *Metro Broadcasting, Inc. v. FCC*, 497 U.S. 547 (1990), in which a narrow Supreme Court majority upheld minority preferences in "distress sales" of radio or television broadcast licenses, in part on a rationale of promoting greater programming diversity. But cf. *Lamprecht v. FCC*, 958 F.2d 382 (D.C. Cir. 1992) (preferences for women owners of radio station violate equal protection). See also the perceptive opinion of justice O'Connor on the implications of expressive association in *Roberts v. United States Jaycees*, 468 U.S. 609, 631 (1984) (O'Connor, J., concurring).

the subordinated are heard from—is virtually nonexistent. Issues at the equality-speech interface are not framed as problems of balance between two cherished constitutional goals, or as problems of meaningful access to either right in the absence of the other, but as whether the right to free speech is infringed acceptably or unacceptably. Equality-promoting provisions on hate crimes, campus harassment, and pornography,[4] for example, tend to be attacked and defended solely in terms of the damage they do, or do not do, to speech. At the same time, issues such as racial segregation in education, with its accompanying illiteracy and silence, are framed solely in equality terms, rather than also as official barriers to speech and therefore as violations of the First Amendment.[5]

First Amendment speech and Fourteenth Amendment equality have never contended on constitutional terrain. The reason is largely that both have been interpreted more negatively than positively, prohibiting violations by government more than chartering legal intervention for social change, even as governmental inaction and the more extended consequences of governmental action undermine this distinction in both areas. It is also relevant that federal equality statutes have not been seen to arise under the Fourteenth Amendment, although it expressly authorizes them,[6] and action by states against social inequalities needs no constitutional authority, so invokes the Constitution only when said to violate it.

This mutual one-sidedness in the law has made it virtually impossible to create a community of comprehension that there is a relation, for example, between the use of the epithet "nigger" and the fact that a disproportionate number of children who go to bed hungry every night in this country are African-American; or the use of the word "cunt" and the fact that most prostitutes are women. It creates no room to see that slave codes that made it a crime to teach a slave to read, or schools in which Black children cannot learn to write, deny them freedom of speech; or that judicially eliminating grievance procedures that recognize racist or homophobic vilification as barriers to education officially denies students

---

4. See 11, notes 31 and 32; and *R.A.V. v. City of St. Paul*, 112 S. Ct. 2538 (1992); *Doe v. University of Michigan*, 721 F. Supp. 852 (E.D. Mich. 1989); *UMW Post, Inc.v. Board of Regents*, 774 F. Supp. 1163 (E.D. Wis. 1991).

5. Thus Kalven treating problems raised by "the Negro" for the First Amendment in 1965 does not mention education. Harry Kalven, Jr., *The Negro and the First Amendment* (1965).

6. "The Congress shall have power to enforce, by appropriate legislation, the provisions of this article." U.S. Const. amend. XIV, §5. See also Catharine A. MacKinnon, "Reflections on Sex Equality under Law," 100, *Yale Law Journal* 1281, 1283 n.12 (1991).

equality in education.[7] The tensions and intersections between the deeper principles and wider orbits of equality and speech remain unmapped, equality unspeaking and speech unequal.

The official history of speech in the United States is not a history of inequality—unlike in Europe, where the role of hate propaganda in the Holocaust has not been forgotten. In America, the examples that provide the life resonance of the expressive freedom, the backdrop of atrocities for the ringing declarations, derive mostly from attempts to restrict the political speech of communists during the McCarthy era. Through this trauma, the country relearned its founding lesson: not to stifle political dissent. Horrible consequences to careers, families, privacy, and security resulted from attempts that now look paranoid to shut up what mostly good and creative people could think and say, from academic theory to street advocacy, about the form of government and economic system we should have. The story of the First Amendment is an epic story of overcoming that, of progress, of making sure it never happens again.

The litany predicated on this experience goes like this. The evil to be avoided is government restricting ideas because it disagrees with the content of their political point of view. The terrain of struggle is the mind; the dynamic at work is intellectual persuasion; the risk is that marginal, powerless, and relatively voiceless dissenters, with ideas we will never hear, will be crushed by governmental power. This has become the "speech you hate" test: the more you disagree with content, the more important it becomes to protect it. You can tell you are being principled by the degree to which you abhor what you allow. The worse the speech protected, the more principled the result. There is a faith that truth will prevail if left alone, often expressed in an openly competitive laissez-faire model taken from bourgeois economics and applied to the expressive marketplace: the "marketplace of ideas" metaphor.[8] The marketplace becomes the battlefield when we are assured that truth will prevail while grappling

---

7. A further possible result is that escalations of hate propaganda and pornography, as for example in Eastern Europe, will be met with indifference or embraced as freedom under U.S.-style speech theory. As pornography and its defense as "speech" take over more of the world, pervading law and consciousness, desensitizing populations to inhumanity, and sexualizing inequality, there are grounds for concern that legal attempts to reverse rising racial, ethnic, and religious discrimination, harassment, and aggression will be disabled.

8. The origin of this notion appears to be "The best test of truth is the power of the thought to get itself accepted in the competition of the market." *Abrams*, 250 U.S. 616 at 630 (Holmes, J., dissenting).

in open encounter with falsehood, to paraphrase Milton, as he so often is.[9]

In this faith, restricting some speech can only eventuate in restricting more or all speech: the "slippery slope" hazard.[10] Restricting speech is seen to be tempting, to have a seductive power that draws governments to its totalitarian—also regarded as principled—logic: if we restrict this bad thing now, we will not be able to stop ourselves from restricting this good thing later. One corollary is that everyone has an interest in everyone else's speech being free, because restriction will get around to you eventually; the less power you have, the sooner it will get around to you. Crucial is that speech cannot be restricted because you fear its consequences: the "bad tendency" or "witch-hunt" doctrine. If some speech is conceded to be risky, more speech to the contrary will eliminate that risk. Most of all, government can make no judgment as to content.[11] For constitutional purposes, there is no such thing as a false idea,[12] there are only more or less "offensive" ones,[13] to remedy which, love of liberty recommends averting the eyes[14] or growing a thicker skin.

9. John Milton, *Areopagitica* 58 (Richard Jebb ed., 1918): "Let [Truth] and falsehood grapple; who ever knew Truth put to the worse, in a free and open encounter?"

10. See a wonderful critical article by Fred Schauer, "Slippery Slopes," 99 *Harvard Law Review* 361 (1985).

11. This, of course, is not the real law of the First Amendment, which makes judgments as to content all the time.

12. The authoritative articulation of this notion is in a defamation case, *Gertz v. Robert Welch*, Inc., 418 U.S. 323, 339–340 (1974): "Under the First Amendment there is no such thing as a false idea. However pernicious an opinion may seem, we depend for its correction not on the conscience of judges and juries but on the competition of other ideas." While the second sentence suggests that the marketplace of ideas, not courts, is the forum for rectifying false opinions, the Court has refused to recognize a special exemption from defamation actions "for anything that might be labeled 'opinion . . .'" *Milkovich v. Lorain Journal Co.*, 497 U.S. 1, 18 (1990). The Court also stated that "the fair meaning of the [*Gertz*] passage is to equate the word 'opinion' in the second sentence with the word 'idea' in the first sentence," suggesting that while ideas should be corrected by other ideas, there is no blanket protection from libel actions based on "anything that might be labeled 'opinion.'" *Milkovich*, 497 U.S. at 18.

13. *Cohen v. California*, 403 U.S. 15 (1971). "Offensive" is a word used to describe obscenity. *Paris Adult Theatre I v. Slaton*, 413 U.S. 49, 71 (1973) (Douglas, J., dissenting) ("'Obscenity' at most is the expression of offensive ideas"). Indeed, "patently offensive" is an element of the obscenity test. *Miller v. California*, 413 U.S. 15, 24 (1973).

14. *Erznoznik v. City of Jacksonville*, 422 U.S. 205, 212 (1975).

Americans are taught this view by about the fourth grade[15] and continue to absorb it through osmosis from everything around them for the rest of their lives, including law school, to the point that those who embrace it think it is their own personal faith, their own original view, and trot it out like something learned from their own personal lives every time a problem is denominated one of "speech," whether it really fits or not. Any issue that strikes this chord, however faintly, gets played this tune, even if the consequences are more like a replay of McCarthyism than resistance to it. This approach is adhered to with a fundamentalist zeal even when it serves to protect lies, silence dissent, destroy careers, intrude on associations, and retard change. At least as ironic is the fact that the substance of the left's forbidden theories, which were a kind of argument for class equality, made no impression on the law of speech at all.

Has this doctrinal edifice guaranteed free and equal speech? These days, censorship occurs less through explicit state policy than through official and unofficial privileging of powerful groups and viewpoints. This is accomplished through silencing in many forms and enforced by the refusal of publishers and editors to publish, or publish well, uncompromised expressions of dissent that make them uncomfortable by challenging the distribution of power, including sexual power. Such publishing decisions, no matter how one-sided and cumulative and exclusionary, are regarded as the way the system of freedom of expression is supposed to work. Legal accountability for these decisions is regarded as fascism; social accountability for them is regarded as creeping fascism; the decisions themselves are regarded as freedom of speech. Speech theory does not disclose or even consider how to deal with power vanquishing powerlessness; it tends to transmute this into truth vanquishing falsehood, meaning what power wins becomes considered true. Speech, hence the lines within which much of life can be lived, belongs to those who own it, mainly big corporations.

Refusals to publish works that criticize the sexual distribution of power in particular are often, in my experience, supported by reference to the law of libel. Libel law, just one subdivision of the law of speech which lacks sensitivity to the substance of social inequality, has become a tool for justifying refusals to publish attacks on those with power, even as

15. It is my observation that anyone who attended primary school anywhere but in the United States tends to regard this approach, and the passion with which it is defended, as an American cultural peculiarity or fetish to be tolerated. That the United States fails to ratify various international treaties because of this oddity is viewed with somewhat less affection. Mari J. Matsuda, "Public Response to Racist Speech: Considering the Victim's Story," 87 *Michigan Law Review* 2320, 2341–46 (1989).

it targets the powerless for liability. Its equality-blindness goes back at least to the formative *New York Times v. Sullivan*,[16] in which the law of libel was first recognized as coming under the First Amendment. The *New York Times* ran a civil rights fundraising ad for Black leaders that described racist misbehavior by white police in the South. On the basis of minor inaccuracies in the ad, the *Times* was successfully sued for libel under state law by the police commissioner of Montgomery, Alabama. The newspaper argued that more than minor inaccuracies should be required to sue for a form of speech. When the *Times* won this argument before the Supreme Court, a new First Amendment doctrine was born.

In reality, *Sullivan* was animated by issues of substantive equality as powerful as they were submerged; indeed, they were perceptible only in the facts. The case lined up an equality interest—that of the civil rights activists in the content of the ad—*with* the First Amendment interest of the newspaper. This aligned sentiment in favor of racial equality with holding libel law to standards of speech protection higher than state law would likely enforce on racists. In other words, *Sullivan* used support for civil rights to make it easier for newspapers to publish defamatory falsehoods without being sued.[17] This brigading of support for racial equality with enhanced power for the media to be less careful about what they publish was utterly tacit. The argument for the *Times* by Herbert Wechsler—originator of the broadside attack on *Brown v. Board of Education*, which prohibited racial segregation in the public schools, as unprincipled constitutional adjudication—did not mention equality at all, while benefiting from the pro-equality wind at its back.[18]

16. *New York Times Co. v. Sullivan*, 376 U.S. 254 (1964).

17. It is fascinating that Kalven's treatment of the then one-month-old *Sullivan*, discussing First Amendment issues raised by "the Negro," has not a glimmer of the role of racial politics in the decision. Kalven, *The Negro and the First Amendment*.

18. *Brown v. Board of Educ.*, 349 U.S. 294 (1955). *Brown*'s invalidation of "separate but equal" education was unprincipled, according to Wechsler, because it was a new fact-driven doctrinal leap addressing a problem that was not really about inequality, but about a deprivation of freedom of association. Herbert Wechsler, "Toward Neutral Principles of Constitutional Law," 73 *Harvard Law Review* 1, 31–34 (1959). From a doctrinal perspective; the *Sullivan* argument that libel could raise First Amendment speech issues was *totally* new. Is libel more obviously speech than segregation is inequality? In the companion case to *Sullivan*, *Abernathy v. Sullivan*, 376 U.S. at 254, brought against the civil rights leaders themselves, those leaders did complain of the racism and denial of equal protection of aspects of their trial, but not of inequality problems in the speech arguments of the libel claim. *Abernathy* was not chosen by the Supreme Court as the flagship case for its First Amendment decision. For Wechsler's argument in

Because the *Times* won without any acknowledgment that concern for substantive equality powered this extension of the First Amendment, the decision did not consider whether the standard of care for truth might have been drawn higher if, for example, southern racist police had been accused of libeling prominent leaders of the nascent civil rights movement in an ad with a few inaccuracies. The extent to which publishers had to know the truth before they could recklessly disregard it, as *Sullivan* newly required for libel of public figures, might have appeared especially problematic if the submerged equality issues had been exposed. Bigotry as often produces unconscious lies as knowing ones, indeed often precludes the dominant from seeing the truth of inequality being lived out beneath their station, hence vision. The implications for subordinated groups of a relaxed standard of truth for publishers—perhaps the stake of the subordinated in having publishers substantiate what they print might be as often on the other side? perhaps media are owned and run by dominant groups who sincerely see a dominant way of seeing as the truth?—was not discussed. Nor was social inequality considered when, in the same case, the constitutional status of laws against group defamation was undermined in advance of a real case on the subject.[19]

The resulting law of libel has had the effect of licensing the dominant to say virtually anything about subordinated groups with impunity while supporting the media's power to refuse access to speech to the powerless, as it can always cite fear of a libel suit by an offended powerful individual. This situation is exacerbated by the facts that it is subordinated groups who are damaged by group defamation and mostly the privileged who can make credible threats to sue even for true statements that make them look bad. Because the *Sullivan* holding made it easier for media to get away with false and damaging statements about public figures, individuals from subordinated groups who take on dominant interests in public are left especially exposed—sexually libeled feminists who oppose pornography, for example.[20] The assumption seems to be that anyone who stands up in public has the same power that government and its officials do, and possesses access to speech equal to that of socially privileged or unscrupulous operatives of the status quo, like pornographers.

Sullivan, see Brief for the Petitioner, *New York Times Co. v. Sullivan*, 376 U.S. 254 (1964) (No. 39).

19. *Sullivan*, 376 U.S. at 268–269 (discussing *Beauharnais v. Illinois*, 343 U.S. 250 (1952)).

20. *Dworkin v. Hustler Magazine Inc.*, 867 F.2d 1188 (9th Cir. 1988), cert. denied, 493 U.S. 812 (1989); *Leidholdt v. L.F.P. Inc.*, 860 F.2d 890 (9th Cir. 1988), cert. denied, 489 U.S. 1080 (1989).

The *Sullivan* dictum on group libel substantially undermined the vitality of an earlier case, *Beauharnais v. Illinois*,[21] which had held that group defamation, including publications that expose the citizens of any race, color, creed, or religion to contempt, could be made criminal, without violating the First Amendment. *Sullivan* tilted First Amendment law in the direction of the conclusion that individual libel is actionable but group libel is not, making injury to the reputation of individuals legally real and consigning injury to the reputation of groups to legal limbo. Reputational harm to those who are allowed to be individuals—mostly white men—is legal harm. Those who are defined by, and most often falsely maligned through, their membership in groups—namely almost everyone else—have no legal claim. Indeed, those who harm them have something of a speech right to do that harm. This arrangement avoids the rather obvious reality that groups are made up of individuals. It also looks a lot like discrimination against harms done through discrimination, in favor of what are regarded by distinction as individual harms. In reality, libel of groups multiplies rather than avoids the very same damage through reputation which the law of individual libel recognizes when done one at a time, as well as inflicting some of its own.

The effectiveness of *Sullivan*'s undermining of *Beauharnais* became vividly clear in the later case that arose out of the Nazis' proposed march in Skokie, Illinois, a site chosen because it was largely populated by Jewish survivors of the Holocaust. The march was found to be protected speech, invalidating a group defamation law that would have stopped it, by judges who had never faced a pogrom piously intoning how much they abhorred what the Nazis had to say, but how legally their hands were tied and how principled they were in allowing it. You can tell how principled they were because of how much they hated the speech.

Over a notable dissent by Justice Blackmun, the U.S. Supreme Court denied review,[22] leaving this result standing and leaving unvindicated a perception on fascist speech by Justice Jackson in a dissent of a decade before: "These terse epithets come down to our generation weighted with hatreds accumulated through centuries of bloodshed. They are recognized words of art in the profession of defamation.... They are always, and in every context, insults which do not spring from reason and can be answered by none. Their historical associations with violence are well understood, both by those who hurl and those who are struck by these

---

21. Wechsler said in oral argument in *Sullivan* that *Beauharnais* was not correctly decided. 32 U.S.L.W. 3250 (Jan. 14, 1964).

22. *Smith v. Collin*, 439 U.S. 916 (1978).

missiles."[23] Justice Jackson was later to dissent in *Beauharnais*, but when he wrote this, he had just returned from the Nuremberg trials, facing what those who became the residents of Skokie had survived.

Nobody mentioned that to be liquidated because of one's group membership is the ultimate inequality. Constitutional equality has never been the interest that hate speech prohibitions are seen to promote.[24] No one to my knowledge has proposed that Congress prohibit hate propaganda to effectuate the Fourteenth Amendment. Instead, when hate speech regulations are assessed, the question has been: does a given law trench too far, or not too far, on the right of free speech? The political speech litany is invoked: nasty ideas that may or may not cause harm, depending on whether they are acted upon (we are supposed to wait); truth outing; more speech solving the problem; swallowing your gorge and adjusting your dignitary standards if you want to be part of the big bad real world. This, under a document that accepts balancing among constitutional interests as method.

The closest the Court has come to recognizing substantive equality in the hate speech area occurred in *Beauharnais*. Writing for the majority, Justice Frankfurter said: "[A] man's job and his educational opportunities and the dignity accorded him may depend as much on the reputation of the racial and religious group to which he willy-nilly belongs, as on his own merits."[25] Employment, education, and human dignity are all on equality territory but went unmarked as such. Civil unrest—otherwise known as oppressed people agitating for their equality or expressing frustration at their inequality—was also noted as a possible consequence of allowing group defamation to go unchecked.

Justice Douglas, in his dissent in *Beauharnais*, came almost as close: "Hitler and his Nazis showed how evil a conspiracy could be which was aimed at destroying a race by exposing it to contempt, derision, and obloquy. I would be willing to concede that such conduct directed at a race or group in this country could be made an indictable offense. For such a

---

23. *Kunz v. New York*, 340 U.S. 290, 299 (1951) (Jackson, J., dissenting).

24. Usually, they sound in tort. See the creative, audacious, and foundational article by Richard Delgado, "Words That Wound: A Tort Action for Racial Insults, Epithets, and Name-Calling," 17 *Harvard Civil Rights–Civil Liberties Law Review* 133 (1982). Sometimes, in international law or in other countries, hate propaganda laws are rendered as "antidiscrimination" provisions, but this is little discussed. The major exception, of course, is Canada. See text accompanying note 55 below and Catharine A. MacKinnon, "Pornography as Defamation and Discrimination," 71 *Boston University Law Review* 793, 806 n.33 (1991).

25. *Beauharnais*, 343 U.S. at 263.

project would be more than the exercise of free speech."[26] He does not say what that more would be an exercise in. Kalven writes of this passage, "There is a germ of a powerful idea here," but he does not call that idea by its name either.[27] The statute in *Beauharnais* was not defended as an equality law, and no argument in the case located group defamation as part of social inequality.[28] Legal equality under the Fourteenth Amendment, in effect for almost a hundred years, was not mentioned.

So there never has been a fair fight in the United States between equality and speech as two constitutional values, equality supporting a statute or practice, speech challenging it. Courts have balanced *statutory* equality interests against the constitutional speech protection. Equality always won these fights until pornography, statutorily framed as sex inequality, lost to the First Amendment, and now equality is losing to speech-based attacks on hate provisions as well.[29] In other words, pornography ordinances and hate crime provisions fail constitutional scrutiny that they might, with constitutional equality support, survive. Moreover, speech is not extended that might be, as in the broadcasting or campaign financing areas.[30] If speech were seen through an equality lens, nude dancing regulations might be tailored to ending the sex inequality of prostitution, at the same time undermining the social credibility of the pimp's lie that

26. Ibid. at 284.

27. Kalven, *The Negro and the First Amendment* at 35.

28. However, in defense of its statute, Illinois did argue that the speech of *Beauharnais* was unprotected because it led to discrimination in violation of Illinois's state Civil Rights Act. Respondent's Brief, *Beauharnais v. Illinois*, 343 U.S. 250 (1952) (No. 118) at 4. Such discrimination was argued to be a "substantive evil" that petitioner's publications may "directly tend to incite." Ibid. at 5–6. Illinois also argued that prevention of riots and lynchings is a duty of government and the history of Illinois was "stained with blood spilled from Negroes simply because they were Negroes." Ibid. at 6. "Every riot has its incitement in words." Ibid. Further worth noting, the ACLU argued for *Beauharnais* that since racial segregation did not violate the federal Civil Rights Act, and "we attorneys for the ACLU' have never been so bold to make that invalid suggestion ourselves in our efforts to combat segregation," advocacy of segregation cannot violate the law either. Petitioner's Reply Brief, *Beauharnais*, 343 U.S. 250 (1952)(No. 118) at 5–6.

29. The most notable victory of this kind is *Pittsburgh Press Co. v. Pittsburgh Comm'n on Human Relations*, 413 U.S. 376 (1973). Pornography regulation lost in *American Booksellers Ass'n, Inc. v. Hudnut*, 771 F.2d 323 (7th Cir. 1985), aff'd, 475 U.S. 1001 (1986). See also *State v. Mitchell*, 485 N.W.2d 807 (Wis. 1992) (invalidating sentence enhancements on protected grounds under First Amendment), cert. granted, 113 S. Ct. 810 (1992).

30. On campaign financing as speech, see *Buckley v. Valeo*, 424 U.S. 1 (1976).

public sex is how women express themselves. Crossburning prohibitions would be seen as the civil rights protections they are. Women might be seen to have a sex equality right to the speech of abortion counseling.[31] Poverty might even be seen as the inequality underlying street begging, at once supporting the speech interest in such solicitations and suggesting that equal access to speech might begin before all one can say is "spare change?"[32]

Since this perspective does not yet animate case law, speech cases that consider words as triggers to violent action instead submerge inequality issues further. In *Brandenburg v. Ohio*, a case that set the standard on speech and consequent conduct with regard to inflammatory advocacy, the words were Ku Klux Klan racism.[33] *Claiborne Hardware*, a further ruling on instigating speech, questioned whether the arm-twisting rhetoric of leaders of a civil rights boycott was protected or whether the activists could be held responsible for the lost business in money damages.[34] *Brandenburg's* concern was whether the "ideas" of the Klan were a sufficient "incitement" to restrict the speech, meaning were they immediate enough to the assaults. *Claiborne Hardware* explored the parameters of holding public speakers responsible for the consequences of their persuasive advocacy. Suppressed entirely in the piously evenhanded treatment of the Klan and the boycotters—the studied inability to tell the difference between oppressor and oppressed that passes for principled neutrality in this area as well as others—was the fact that the Klan was promoting inequality and the civil rights leaders were resisting it, in a country that is supposedly not constitutionally neutral on the subject.

If this was expectable, the virtual absence of discussion of equality in recent litigation over discrimination policies that prohibit group-based harassment and bigotry on campuses was astounding. Denominated "campus speech codes" by their opponents, these regulations are formally predicated on federal laws that require equal access to an education on the basis of race and sex.[35] In challenges to these regulations under the First Amendment, which have been successful so far, the statutory equality interest is barely mentioned. That these procedures might vindicate

---

31. Cf. *Rust v. Sullivan*, 111 S. Ct. 1759 (1991).

32. *Young v. New York City Transit Authority*, 903 F.2d 146 (2d Cir. 1990), cert. denied, 111 S. Ct. 516 (restriction on begging and panhandling in some public transit does not violate First Amendment).

33. *Brandenburg v. Ohio*, 395 U.S. 444 (1969).

34. *NAACP v. Claiborne Hardware Co.*, 458 U.S. 886 (1982).

35. 42 U.S.C. §2000 (d) et seq. (1988) (Title VI, requiring racial equality in education); 20 U.S.C. §1681 (1988) (Title IX, requiring sex equality in education).

a constitutional interest in equality which is as important as, or part of, the speech interest used to demolish them is not considered. What can one say about the failure to take seriously the educational equality these provisions exist to serve?

Nor is equality recognized as legally relevant to the problem of pornography, which is addressed instead under the First Amendment doctrine of obscenity. Obscenity law started with the "deprave and corrupt the morals of consumers" test (*they're* being hurt); moved through the censorship of literature from Joyce through Radclyffe Hall to Henry Miller, making them all bestsellers (*they're* being hurt); winding up with the Supreme Court devising its own obscenity test,[36] which is so effective that, under it, the pornography industry has quadrupled in size (*they're* being hurt?). The ineffectuality of obscenity law is due in some part to exempting materials of literary, political, artistic, or scientific value. Value can be found in anything, depending, I have come to think, not only on one's adherence to postmodernism, but on how much one is being paid. And never underestimate the power of an erection, these days termed "entertainment," to give a thing value.[37] Adding to the unworkability of the obscenity test is the requirement that the state prove "prurient interest": is the average person turned on? The more violent pornography is, the less willing juries and police are to say it is arousing, and more and more pornography is more and more violent, and arousing.

Equally difficult in practice has been the requirement in the obscenity test that community standards be proven violated. The more pornography there is, the more it sets de facto community standards, conforming views of what is acceptable to what is arousing, even as the stimulus to arousal must be more and more violating to work. In other words, inequality is allowed to set community standards for the treatment of women. What is wrong with pornography is that it hurts women and their equality. What is wrong with obscenity law is that this reality has no role in it. This irrelevant and unworkable tool is then placed in the hands of the state, most of whose actors have little interest in stopping this abuse but a substantial interest in avoiding prosecutions they cannot win. The American law of obscenity, as a result, is only words.

The pornography issue, far more than the political speech cases, has provided the setting for the definitive development of the absolutist

36. *Miller*, 413 U.S. at 15.

37. Edward DeGrazia appears to support the view that the capacity of a work to produce sexual arousal should be considered a "value" for legal purposes, *Girls Lean Back Everywhere: The Law of Obscenity and the Assault on Genius* 518 (1991).

approach to speech. First Amendment absolutism did not begin in obscenity cases, but it is in explaining why obscenity should be protected speech, and how it cannot be distinguished from art and literature, that much of the work of absolutism has been done, taking as its point of departure and arrival the position that whatever is expressive should be constitutionally protected. In pornography, absolutism found, gained, and consolidated its ground and hit its emotional nerve. It began as a dissenting position of intellectual extremists and ended by reducing the regulation of obscenity to window dressing on violence against women.[38]

Concretely, observe that it was the prospect of losing access to pornography that impelled the social and legal development of absolutism as a bottom line for the First Amendment, as well as occasioned bursts of passionate eloquence on behalf of speech per se: if we can't have this, they seem to say, what can we have? During the same twenty-year period of struggle over obscenity standards, the Court was watching more and more pornography as its mass-marketed forms became more and more intrusive and aggressive. Observing this process from its end point of state protection of pornography, I have come to think that the main principle at work here is that, once pornography becomes pervasive, speech *will* be defined so that men can have their pornography. American obscenity law merely illustrates one adaptation of this principle: some men ineffectually prohibit it while others vaunt it openly as the standard for speech as such.

Consider the picture. The law against pornography was not designed to see harm to women in the first place. It is further weakened as pornography spreads, expanding into new markets (such as video and computers) and more legitimate forums and making abuse of women more and more invisible as abuse, as that abuse becomes more and more visible as sex. So the Court becomes increasingly *unable to tell* what is pornography and what is not, a failing it laments not as a consequence of the saturation of society by pornography, but as a specifically judicial failure, then finally as an impossibility of line-drawing. The stage is thus set for the transformation of pornography into political speech: the excluded and stigmatized "ideas" we love to hate. Obscured is the way this protects what pornography says and ignores what it does, or, alternatively,

38. This history, with a different moral to the story, is traced by DeGrazia, ibid. See especially *Ginzburg v. United States*, 383 U.S. 463, 476 (1966) (Black, J., dissenting) and 482 (Douglas, J., dissenting); *Jacobellis v. Ohio*, 378 U.S. 184, 196 (1964) (Black, J., concurring); *Roth v. United States*, 354 U.S. 476, 508 (1957) (Douglas, J., dissenting); *Paris Adult Theatre I v. Slaton*, 413 U.S. at 70 (Douglas, J., dissenting) and 73 (Brennan, J., joined by Stewart and Marshall, JJs., dissenting).

protects what pornography says as a means of protecting what it does. Thus can a law develop which prohibits restricting a film because it advocates adultery,[39] but does not even notice a film that is made from a rape.[40]

Nothing in the American law of obscenity is designed to perceive the rape, sexual abuse of children, battering, sexual harassment, prostitution, or sexual murder in pornography. This becomes insulting upon encountering obscenity law's search for harm and failure to find any. The law of child pornography, by contrast—based as it is on the assumption that children are harmed by having sex pictures made of them—applies a test developed in areas of speech other than the sexual: if the harm of speech outweighs its value,[41] it can be restricted by properly targeted means. Given the history of the law of pornography of adult women, it is tempting to regard this as a miracle. Child pornography is not considered the speech of a sexually dissident minority, which it is, advocating "ideas" about children and sex, which it does. Perhaps the fact that boys were used in the film in the test case has something to do with it. The ability to see that child pornography is harmful has everything to do with a visceral sense of the inequality in power between children and adults, yet inequality is never mentioned.

Now, in this context of speech and equality concerns, consider again the judicial opinion on the law Andrea Dworkin and I wrote and Indianapolis passed. This law defines the documented harms pornography does as violations of equality rights and makes them actionable as practices of discrimination, of second-class citizenship. This ordinance allows anyone hurt through pornography to prove its role in their abuse, to recover for the deprivation of their civil rights, and to stop it from continuing. Judicially, this was rendered as censorship of ideas.

In *American Booksellers v. Hudnut*, the Court of Appeals for the Seventh Circuit found that this law violated the First Amendment. It began by recognizing that the harm pornography does is real, conceding that the legislative finding of a causal link was judicially adequate: ". . . we accept the premises of this legislation. Depictions of subordination tend to perpetuate subordination. The subordinate status of women in turn leads to affront and lower pay at work, insult and injury at home, battery and rape

---

39. *Kingsley Int'l Pictures Corp. v. Regents of the University of. New York*, 360 U.S. 684 (1959).

40. The litigation on Deep Throat is a clear example. See citations in Catharine A. MacKinnon, *Feminism Unmodified: Discourses on Life and Law* 34 n.30 (1987).

41. *New York v. Ferber*, 458 U.S. 747, 762 (1982).

on the streets. In the language of the legislature, '[p]ornography is central in creating and maintaining sex as a basis of discrimination.'"[42] Writing for the panel, Judge Easterbrook got, off and on, that "subordination" is something pornography does, not something it just says, and that its active role had to be proven in each case brought under the ordinance. But he kept losing his mental bearings and referring to pornography as an "idea,"[43] finally concluding that the harm it does "demonstrates the power of pornography as speech."[44] This is like saying that the more a libel destroys a reputation, the greater is its power as speech. To say that the more harm speech does, the more protected it is, is legally wrong, even in this country.

Implicitly applying the political speech model, Judge Easterbrook said that the law restricted the marketplace of ideas, the speech of outcast dissenters—referring presumably to those poor heads of organized crime families making ten billion dollars a year trafficking women. He said the law discriminated on the basis of point of view, establishing an approved view of what could be said and thought about women and sex. He failed to note at this point that the invalidated causes of action included coercion, force, and assault, rather a far cry from saying and thinking. He reminded us of *Sullivan*, whose most famous dictum is that to flourish, debate must be "uninhibited, robust, and wide-open."[45] Behind his First Amendment facade, women were being transformed into ideas, sexual traffic in whom was protected as if it were a discussion, the men uninhibited and robust, the women wide-open.

Judge Easterbrook did not say this law was not a sex discrimination law, but he gave the state interest it therefore served—opposition to sex inequality—no constitutional weight. He did this by treating it as if it were a group defamation law, holding that no amount of harm of discrimination can outweigh the speech interests of bigots, so long as they say something while doing it. Besides, if we restrict this, who knows where it will end. He is sure it will end with "Leda and the Swan." He did

42. *Hudnut*, 771 F.2d at 328–329.

43. ". . . above all else, the First Amendment means that government has no power to restrict expression because of its message [or] ideas . . ." Ibid. at 328 (quoting *Police Department v. Mosley*, 408 U.S. at 95). Similar construction of nude dancing, as public discourse opinion in *Miller v. Civil City of South Bend*, 904 F.2d 1081, 1088 (7th Cir. 1990), invalidating a provision restricting nude dancing. The Supreme Court upheld the provision, reversing the Seventh Circuit in *Barnes v. Glen Theatre, Inc.*, 111 S. Ct. 2456 (1991). See I, pages 31–33.

44. *Hudnut*, 771 F.2d at 329.

45. *Sullivan*, 376 U.S. at 270.

not suggest that bestiality statutes also had to go, along with obscenity's restrictions on depictions of sex between humans and animals. Both restrict a disapproved sexuality, that, no doubt, contains an element of "mental intermediation."[46] Nothing in *Hudnut* explains why, if pornography is protected speech based on its mental elements, rape and sexual murder, which have mental elements, are not as well.

A dissent in a recent case invalidating sentence enhancements for crimes of bias could have been a dissent here: "The majority rationalizes their conclusion [that the statute violates the First Amendment] by insisting that this statute punishes bigoted thought. Not so. The statute does not impede or punish the right of persons to have bigoted thoughts or to express themselves in a bigoted fashion or otherwise, regarding the race, religion, or other status of a person. It does attempt to limit the effects of bigotry. What the statute does punish is acting upon those thoughts. It punishes the act of [discrimination] not the thought or expression of bigotry."[47]

Perhaps it is the nature of legal inequality that was missed by the Seventh Circuit. Discrimination has always been illegal because it is based on a prohibited motive: "an evil eye and an unequal hand,"[48] what the perpetrator is thinking while doing, what the acts mean. Racial classifications are thought illegal because they "supply a reason to infer antipathy."[49] A showing of discriminatory intent is required under the Fourteenth Amendment. Now we are told that this same motive, this same participation in a context of meaning, this same hatred and bigotry, these same purposes and thoughts, presumably this same intent, *protect* this same activity under the First Amendment. The courts cannot have it both ways, protecting discriminatory activity under the First Amendment on the same ground they make a requirement for its illegality under the Fourteenth. To put it another way, it is the "idea" of discrimination in the perpetrator's mind that courts have required be proven before the acts that effectuate it will be considered discriminatory. Surely, if acts that are otherwise legal, like hiring employees or renting rooms or admitting students, are made illegal

46. *Hudnut*, 771 F.2d at 329.
47. *State v. Mitchell*, 485 N.W.2d at 820 (Bablitch, J., dissenting). The Supreme Court of Oregon, siding with this dissent, upheld an Oregon hate crime statute against First Amendment attack, *Oregon v. Plowman*, 838 P.2d 558 (Or. 1992). The U.S. Supreme Court upheld the Wisconsin statute, *Wisconsin v. Mitchell*, 1993 U.S. LEXIS 4024 (June 11, 1993).
48. *Yick Wo v. Hopkins*, 118 U.S. 356 (1886).
49. *Personnel Administrator v. Feeney*, 442 U.S. 256, 272 (1979); *Vance v. Bradley*, 440 U.S. 93, 97 (1979).

under the Constitution by being based on race or sex because of what those who engage in them think about race or sex, acts that are otherwise illegal, like coercion, force, and assault, do not become constitutionally protected because they are done with the same thoughts in mind.

Seventh Circuit cases after *Hudnut* show that court attempting to straddle the fault lines beneath that decision without falling into an abyss. Some fancy footwork was required in a death penalty cases[50] in which a sex murderer claimed he could not be held responsible for his actions because he was a lifelong pornography consumer. To receive the death penalty, a defendant must be capable of appreciating the wrongfulness of his actions, but that is exactly what pornography was proven to destroy in the consumer by evidence in this case. Noting that the *Hudnut* court had accepted the view that pornography perpetuates "subordination of women and violence against women" yet is protected because its harm depends on "mental intermediation," this panel, which included Judge Easterbrook, faced the dilemma *Hudnut* placed them in: "It would be impossible to hold both that pornography does not directly cause violence but criminal actors do, and that criminals do not cause violence, pornography does. The result would be to tell Indiana that it can neither ban pornography nor hold criminally responsible persons who are encouraged to commit violent acts because of pornography!"[51]

To get out of this, the court imagined that Indiana must have decided that rapists who are aware that a woman does not consent are not then excused by the rapists' belief that they have a right to proceed anyway. This is unsatisfying, as pornography makes rapists unaware that their victims are not consenting. As this record showed, it creates "a person who no longer distinguishes between violence and rape, or violence and sex."[52] There will, ultimately, be no way of addressing this problem short of changing the rape law so that it turns on what the perpetrator did rather than on what he thought *and* holding the pornographers jointly responsible for rapes they can be proven to have caused. Meantime, we kill a man rather than let his victims stop the pornography that produced him—leaving the pornographers completely off the hook. If anyone knows what they are doing, it is the pornographers.[53]

---

50. This was discussed in I. *Schiro v. Clark*, 963 F.2d 962 (7th Cir. 1992), cert. granted, May 17, 1993 (No. 92-7549).

51. *Schiro*, 963 F.2d at 972–973.

52. Arguments of counsel relying on experts Osanka and Donnerstein, *Schiro*, 963 F.2d at 971–972.

53. The Seventh Circuit affirmed the penalty of death for Schiro on the legally unsatisfying conclusion that although pornographers could be held responsible

The nude dancing case the Supreme Court ultimately resolved came from the Seventh Circuit, where it produced eight separate opinions, the majority invalidating the regulation on First Amendment grounds. Judge Posner's concurrence turned Judge Easterbrook's protected "ideas" into protected "emotions," explaining that "[m]ost pornography is expressive, indeed expressive of the same emotions that a striptease expresses."[54] Since a videotape of nude dancing would be covered under the ordinance in *Hudnut*, and the ordinance in *Hudnut* restricted protected speech, he reasoned that nude dancing had to be protected speech as well: ". . . if this analysis is wrong, our decision in *Hudnut* is wrong."[55] The Supreme Court found the analysis was wrong. The regulation of nude dancing was valid under the First Amendment, even though striptease was not obscene. But Judge Posner was right about the connection between that case and protecting pornography as speech: their decision in *Hudnut* is wrong.

That these tortured consequences result from the lack of an equality context in which to interpret expressive freedoms is clear from the fact that the same issues produced exactly the opposite results in Canada. Canada's new constitution, the Charter of Rights and Freedoms,[56] includes an expansive equality guarantee and a serious entrenchment of freedom of expression. The Supreme Court of Canada's first move was to define equality in a meaningful way—one more substantive than formal, directed toward changing unequal social relations rather than monitoring their equal positioning before the law. The United States, by contrast, remains in the grip of what I affectionately call the stupid theory of equality. Inequality here is defined as distinction, as differentiation, indifferent to whether dominant or subordinated groups are hurt or helped. Canada, by contrast, following the argument of the Women's Legal Education and Action Fund (LEAF), repudiated this view in so many words, taking as its touchstone the treatment of historically disadvantaged groups and aiming to alter their status. The positive spin of the Canadian interpretation holds the law to promoting equality,[57] projecting the law into a

---

for some rapes(!), *Hudnut* does not say "the rapist is not also culpable for his own conduct." *Schiro*, 963 F.2d at 973.

54. *Miller*, 904 F.2d at 1092 (Posner, J., concurring).

55. Ibid.

56. The Charter came into effect in 1982, the equality provision in 1985.

57. Compare *Law Society v. Andrews* [1989] 1 S.C.R. 143 (Can.) with *Regents of the University of California v. Bakke*, 438 U.S. 265 (1978), and *City of Richmond v. J. A. Croson Corp.*, 488 U.S. 469 (1989). The closest the United States has come to approximating the Canadian standard is in *California Federal Savings and Loan Ass'n v. Guerra*, 479 U.S. 272 (1987), a Title VII case recognizing that legislation to help pregnant women at work promotes sex equality, therefore does not discriminate on the basis of sex.

more equal future, rather than remaining rigidly neutral in ways that either reinforce existing social inequality or prohibit changing it, as the American constitutional perspective has increasingly done in recent years.

The first case to confront expressive guarantees with equality requirements under the new constitution came in the case of James Keegstra, an anti-Semite who taught Holocaust revisionism to schoolchildren in Alberta. Prosecuted and convicted under Canada's hate propaganda provision, Keegstra challenged the statute as a violation of the new freedom of expression guarantee. LEAF intervened to argue that the hate propaganda law promoted equality. We argued that group libel, most of it concededly expression, promotes the disadvantage of unequal groups; that group-based enmity, ill will, intolerance, and prejudice are the attitudinal engines of the exclusion, denigration, and subordination that make up and propel social inequality; that without bigotry, social systems of enforced separation, ghettoization, and apartheid would be unnecessary, impossible, and unthinkable; that stereotyping and stigmatization of historically disadvantaged groups through group hate propaganda shape their social image and reputation, which controls their access to opportunities more powerfully than their individual abilities ever do; and that it is impossible for an individual to receive equality of opportunity when surrounded by an atmosphere of group hate.

We argued that group defamation is a verbal form inequality takes, that just as white supremacy promotes inequality on the basis of race, color, and sometimes ethnic or national origin, anti-Semitism promotes the inequality of Jews on the basis of religion and ethnicity. We argued that group defamation in this sense is not a mere expression of opinion but a practice of discrimination in verbal form, a link in systemic discrimination that keeps target groups in subordinated positions through the promotion of terror, intolerance, degradation, segregation, exclusion, vilification, violence, and genocide. We said that the nature of the practice can be understood and its impact measured from the damage it causes, from immediate psychic wounding to consequent physical aggression. Where advocacy of genocide is included in group defamation, we said an equality approach to such speech would observe that to be liquidated because of the group you belong to is the ultimate inequality.

The Supreme Court of Canada agreed with this approach, a majority upholding the hate propaganda provision, substantially on equality grounds. The Court recognized the provision as a content restriction—content that had to be stopped because of its antiegalitarian meaning and devastating consequences.[58]

58. *Regina v. Keegstra* [1991] 2 W.W.R. 1 (1990) (Can.).

Subsequently, the Winnipeg authorities arrested a whole pornography store and prosecuted the owner, Donald Victor Butler, for obscenity. Butler was convicted but said the obscenity law was an unconstitutional restriction on his Charter-based right of freedom of expression. LEAF argued that if Canada's obscenity statute, substantially different from U.S. obscenity law in prohibiting "undue exploitation of sex, or sex and violence, cruelty, horror, or crime," was interpreted to institutionalize some people's views about women and sex over others, it would be unconstitutional. But if the community standards applied were interpreted to prohibit harm to women as harm to the community, it was constitutional because it promoted sex equality.

The Supreme Court of Canada essentially agreed, upholding the obscenity provision on sex equality grounds.[59] It said that harm to women—which the Court was careful to make "contextually sensitive" and found could include humiliation, degradation, and subordination—*was* harm to society as a whole. The evidence on the harm of pornography was sufficient for a law against it. Violent materials always present this risk of harm, the Court said; explicit sexual materials that are degrading or dehumanizing (but not violent) could also unduly exploit sex under the obscenity provision if the risk of harm was substantial. Harm in this context was defined as "predispos[ing] persons to act in an anti-social manner, as, for example, the physical or mental mistreatment of women by men, or, what is perhaps debatable, the reverse." The unanimous Court noted that "if true equality between male and female persons is to be achieved, we cannot ignore the threat to equality resulting from exposure to audiences of certain types of degrading material." The result rested in part on *Keegstra* but also observed that the harms attendant to the production of pornography situated the problem of pornography differently, such that the appearance of consent by women in such materials could exacerbate its injury. Recognizing that education could be helpful in combating this harm, the court held that that fact did not make the provision unconstitutional.[60]

Although the Canadians considered the U.S. experience on these issues closely in both cases, the striking absence of a U.S.-style political speech litany suggests that taking equality seriously precludes it, or makes it look like the excuse for enforcing inequality that it has become. The decision did not mention the marketplace of ideas. Maybe in Canada, people talk to each other, rather than buy and sell each other as ideas. In an equality context, it becomes obvious that those with the most power buy the most

---

59. *Butler v. Regina* [1992] 2 W.W.R. 577 (Can.).
60. Ibid. at 594–597, 601, 609.

speech, and that the marketplace rewards the powerful, whose views then become established as truth. We were not subjected to "Let [Truth] and falsehood grapple; who ever knew Truth put to the worse, in a free and open encounter." Milton had not been around for the success of the Big Lie technique, but this Court had.

Nor did the Canadian Court even consider the "slippery slope," a largely phony scruple impossible to sustain under a contextually sensitive equality rule. With inequality, the problem is not where intervention will end, but when it will ever begin. Equality is the law; if the slippery slope worked, the ineluctable logic of principle would have slid us into equality by now. Also, perhaps, because the Canadian law of equality is moored in the world, and knows the difference between disadvantaged groups and advantaged ones, it is less worried about the misfiring of restrictions against the powerless and more concerned about having nothing to fire against abuses of power by the powerful.

Fundamentally, the Supreme Court of Canada recognized the reality of inequality in the issues before it: this was not big bad state power jumping on poor powerless individual citizen, but a law passed to stand behind a comparatively powerless group in its social fight for equality against socially powerful and exploitative groups. This positioning of forces—which makes the hate propaganda prohibition and the obscenity law of Canada (properly interpreted) into equality laws, although neither was called such by Parliament—made the invocation of a tradition designed to keep government off the backs of people totally inappropriate. The Court also did not say that Parliament had to limit its efforts to stop the harm of inequality by talking to it. What it did was make more space for the unequal to find voice.

Nor did the Canadians intone, with Brandeis and nearly every American court that has ruled on a seriously contested speech issue since, that "[f]ear of serious injury cannot alone justify suppression of free speech. . . . Men feared witches and burnt women."[61] I have never understood this argument, other than as a way of saying that zealots misidentify the causes of their woes and hurt the wrong people. What has to be added, to fear of serious injury to justify doing something about the speech that causes it? *Proof* of serious injury? If we, can't restrict it then, when can we? Isn't fear of serious injury the concern behind restricting publication of the dates on which troop ships sail? Is it mere "fear" of injury to children that supports the law against the use of children to make pornography? If that isn't enough, why isn't proof of injury required? "Men feared witches and burnt women." Where is the speech here? Promoting the

61. *Whitney v. California*, 274 U.S. 357, 376 (1927) (Brandeis, J., concurring).

fear? Nobody tried to suppress tracts against witches. If somebody had, would some women not have been burnt? Or was it the witches' writings? Did they write? So burning their writings is part of the witch-hunt aspect of the fear? The women who are being burned as witches these days are the women in the pornography, and their burning is sex and entertainment and protected as speech. Those who are hunted down, stigmatized, excluded, and unpublished are the women who oppose their burning.

Neither Canadian decision reduces the harm of hate propaganda or pornography to its "offensiveness." When you hear the woman next door screaming as she is bounced off the walls by a man she lives with, are you "offended"? Hate speech and pornography do the same thing: enact the abuse. Women's reactions to the presentation of other women being sexually abused in pornography, and the reactions of Jews living in Skokie to having Nazis march through their town, are routinely trivialized in the United States as "being offended." The position of those with less power is equated with the position of those with more power, as if sexual epithets against straight white men were equivalent to sexual epithets against women, as if breaking the window of a Jewish-owned business in the world after Kristallnacht were just so much breaking glass.

In the cases both of pornography and of the Nazi march in Skokie, it is striking how the so-called speech reenacts the original experience of the abuse, and how its defense as speech does as well.[62] It is not only that both groups, through the so-called speech, are forcibly subjected to the spectacle of their abuse, legally legitimized. Both have their response to it trivialized as "being offended," that response then used to support its speech value, hence its legal protection.[63] Both are also told that what

62. This connection was made by Anne E. Simon in a letter to me.

63. First Amendment law has long taken the position that the "sensibilities of readers" must be ignored in deciding whether a state has an interest in suppression of expression. *Simon & Schuster, Inc. v. Members of the New York Crime Victims Bd.*, 112 S. Ct. 501, 509 (1991). As the Court sees it, the offensiveness of an opinion goes to establishing its protection: "The fact that society may find speech offensive is not a sufficient reason for suppressing it. Indeed, if it is the speaker's opinion that gives offense, *that consequence* is a reason for according it constitutional protection." *FCC v. Pacifica Foundation*, 438 U.S. 726, 745 (1978) (emphasis added), quoted with approval in *Hustler Magazine, Inc. v. Falwell*, 485 U.S. 46, 55 (1988). See also *Texas v. Johnson*, 491 U.S. 397, 414 (1989): "If there is a bedrock principle underlying the First Amendment it is that the Government may not prohibit the expression of an idea simply because society finds the idea itself offensive or disagreeable." These authorities were found to support the view in *Simon & Schuster* that the Crime Board "does not assert any interest in limiting whatever anguish Henry Hill's victims may suffer from reliving their

they can do about it is avert their eyes, lock their doors, stay home, stay silent, and hope the assault, and the animus it makes tangible, end when the film or the march ends. This is exactly what perpetrators of rape and child sexual abuse tell their victims and what the Jews in Germany were told by the Nazis (and the rest of the world) in the 1930s. Accept the freedom of your abusers. This best protects you in the end. Let it happen.

You are not really being hurt. When sexually abused women are told to let the system work and tolerate the pornography, this is what they are being told. The Jews in Germany, and the Jews in Skokie, were told to let the system work. At least this time around, the Jews of Canada were not, nor were sexually abused women.

The final absence in the Canadian decisions, perhaps the most startling, is the failure to mention any equivalent to the notion that, under the First Amendment, there is no such thing as a false idea. Perhaps under equality law, in some sense there is. When equality is recognized as a constitutional value and mandate, the idea that some people are inferior to others on the basis of group membership is authoritatively rejected as the basis for public policy. This does not mean that ideas to the contrary cannot be debated or expressed. It should mean, however, that social inferiority cannot be imposed through any means, including expressive ones.

Because society is made of language, distinguishing talk about inferiority from verbal imposition of inferiority may be complicated at the edges, but it is clear enough at the center with sexual and racial harassment, pornography, and hate propaganda. At the very least, when equality is taken seriously in expressive settings, such practices are not constitutionally insulated from regulation on the ground that the ideas they express cannot be regarded as false. Attempts to address them would not be prohibited—as they were in rejecting the Indianapolis pornography ordinance, for example—on the ground that, in taking a position in favor of equality, such attempts assume that the idea of human equality is true. The legal equality guarantee has already decided that. There is no requirement that the state remain neutral as between equality

---

victimization," 112 S. Ct. at 509. *Hudnut* states that the role of pornography in perpetuating subordination "simply demonstrates the power of pornography as speech." 777 F.2d at 329. As distinguished from *Hudnut*, in *Simon & Schuster* it was not asserted that the crimes were committed to produce the accounts of the crimes, as women coerced into pornography assert; nor does *Simon & Schuster* bar civil recovery for damages either for mental anguish or to reputational or privacy interests. There was also no claim in that case that the portrayals of the crime victims were false, defamatory, placed them in a false light, or discriminated against them.

and inequality—quite the contrary. Equality is a "compelling state interest" that can already outweigh First Amendment rights in certain settings.[64] In other words, expressive means of practicing inequality can be prohibited.

This is not the place to spell out in detail all the policy implications of such a view. Suffice it to say that those who wish to keep materials that promote inequality from being imposed on students—such as academic books purporting to document women's biological inferiority to men, or arguing that slavery of Africans should return, or that Fourteenth Amendment equality should be repealed, or that reports of rape are routinely fabricated—especially without critical commentary, should not be legally precluded from trying on the grounds that the ideas contained in them cannot be assumed false. No teacher should be forced to teach falsehoods as if they must be considered provisionally true, just because bigots who have managed to get published have made their lies part of a debate. Teachers who wish to teach such materials should be prepared to explain what they are doing to avoid creating a hostile learning environment and to provide all students the equal benefit of an education. Wherever equality is mandated, racial and sexual epithets, vilification, and abuse should be able to be prohibited, unprotected by the First Amendment. The current legal distinction between screaming "go kill the nigger" and advocating the view that African-Americans should be eliminated from parts of the United States needs to be seriously reconsidered, if real equality is ever to be achieved. So, too, the current line separating pornography from hate speech and what is done to make pornography from the materials themselves.

Pornography, under current conditions, *is* largely its own context. Many believe that in settings that encourage critical distance, its showing does not damage women as much as it sensitizes viewers to the damage it does to women. My experience, as well as all the information available, makes me think that it is naive to believe that anything other words can do is as powerful what pornography itself does. At the

---

64. *Roberts v. U.S. Jaycees*, 468 U.S. 609, 623 (1984), holds that states have a "compelling interest in eradicating discrimination" on the basis of sex, which can outweigh the First Amendment right of association, as it did here. In ruling against the First Amendment challenge, and in favor of statutory sex equality, *Roberts* states that "acts of invidious discrimination in the distribution of goods, services, and other advantages cause unique evils that government has a compelling interest to prevent–wholly apart from the point of view such conduct may transmit. . . . Accordingly . . . such practices are entitled to no constitutional protection." Ibid. at 628.

very least, pornography should never be imposed on a viewer who do not choose—then and there, without pressure of any kind—to be exposed to it. Tom Emerson said a long time ago that imposing what he called "erotic material" on individuals against their will is a form of action that "has all the characteristics of a physical assault."[65] Equality on campuses, in workplaces, everywhere, would be promoted if such assaults were actionable. Why any woman should have to attend school in a setting stacked against her equality by the showing of pornography—especially when authoritatively permitted by those who are legally obligated to take her equality seriously—is a question that those who support its showing should have to answer. The answer is not that she should have to wait for the resulting abuse or leave.

Where is all this leading? To a new model for freedom of expression in which the free speech position no longer supports social dominance, as it does now; in which free speech does not most readily protect the activities of Nazis, Klansmen, and pornographers, while doing nothing for their victims, as it does now; in which defending free speech is not speaking on behalf of a large pile of money in the hands of a small group of people, as it is now. In this new model, principle will be defined in terms of specific experiences, the particularity of history, substantively rather than abstractly. It will notice who is being hurt and never forget who they are. The state will have as great a role in providing relief from injury to equality through speech and in giving equal access to speech as it now has in disciplining its power to intervene in that speech that manages to get expressed.

In a society in which equality is a fact, not merely a word, words of racial or sexual assault and humiliation will be nonsense syllables. Sex between people and things, human beings and pieces of paper, real men and unreal women, will be a turn-off. Artifacts of these abuses will reside in a glass case next to the dinosaur skeletons in the Smithsonian. When this day comes, silence will be neither an act of power, as it is now for those who hide behind it, nor an experience of imposed powerlessness, as it is now for those who are submerged in it, but a context of repose into which thought can expand, an invitation that gives speech its shape, an opening to a new conversation.

65. Thomas I. Emerson, *The System of Freedom of Expression* 496 (1970): "A communication of this [erotic] nature, imposed upon a person contrary to his wishes, has all the characteristics of a physical assault" and "can therefore realistically be classified as action." A comparison with his preliminary formulation in *Toward a General Theory of the First Amendment* 91 (1963) suggests that his view on this subject became stronger by his 1970 revisiting of the issue.

CHAPTER FIVE

Split at the Root

Prostitution and Feminist Discourses of Law Reform[*]

Margaret A. Baldwin

Evelina Giobbe, an anti-prostitution activist and educator, inspired this paper. At a radical feminist conference in 1987, she said: "Prostitution isn't like anything else. Rather, everything else is like prostitution because it is the model for women's condition."[1] This paper attempts a response to Giobbe's insight. The fundamental inquiry I pursue is how the relationship between "prostitutes" and "other women" is given meaning—in the sexual abuse of women and girls, in the legal response to that abuse, and in feminist reform strategies. To be deemed a "prostitute," whether by the state, by a john, or by any other man for that matter, targets a girl or woman for arrest, for sexual assault, for murder, or at the very least, for dismissive scorn. Victims of rape, of incest, of domestic battery, of sexual harassment, are only too familiar with this guilt by association. Declared to be "whores" and "sluts" by the men who abuse them, women then

[*]Thank you to the prostitute advocates who have so kindly supported this piece since an earlier version was published over a decade ago (*Yale Journal of Law and Feminism* 5:47 (1992), pp. 47–120), especially Evelina Giobbe, Susan Hunter, K.C. Reed, Melissa Farley, and Susan Mooney, and to Lily McCarty and Jessica Spector for editorial assistance. Jonquil Livingston and Christine Senne provided able help in preparing this manuscript.

1. Evelina Giobbe, *Confronting the Liberal Lies about Prostitution, in* The Sexual Liberals and the Attack on Feminism 67, 76 (Dorchen Leidholdt & Janice Raymond eds., 1990). Evelina Giobbe is a survivor of prostitution.

confront a legal system which puts the same issue in the form of a question: was she in fact a "slut" who deserved it, as the perpetrator claims, or not-a-slut, deserving of some redress? (The outcome of this interrogation is commonly referred to as "justice.")

I am not alone in this analysis. Feminist legal reformers have long challenged the legal relegation of "other women" to the status of prostitutes, in rape law reform, in representation of battered women in court, and in anti-sexual harassment advocacy. However, as I further contend, these strategies have not undermined the dichotomy between "prostitutes" and other women," but have further entrenched it. The core assertion advanced by this work has been the claim that "other women" are not *really* prostitutes, after all, and are, therefore, denied justice by evidentiary standards and uneducated inferences yielding the contrary conclusion. Abusers, judges, and legal feminists thus seem agreed on the significance of the distinction between prostitutes and other women, but disagree on the finer points of identification and definition.

In the second part of this paper, I discuss where this approach leaves women who *are* prostitutes. In short, in some difficulty. Lacking an alternative, feminist advocates for prostitutes have attempted to establish that prostitutes, too, are "other women," just as "other women" have sought to distance themselves from prostitutes. Needless to say, these assimilation attempts have not proceeded smoothly. In part three, I argue that distancing oneself from prostitution, while representing oneself as an "other women," the political position adopted by all of these advocates, is both the sexual demand made of women *in* prostitution, and the political demand made of all women *vis-á-vis* the state. I conclude that we must squarely face, examine, and challenge these demands that women split themselves—from prostitutes, and within themselves—so that we can more fruitfully advance our feminist work together.

That is the analytic agenda of this paper. Here, a word about analysis, and the subject matter of prostitution. After reading about, documenting, and classifying the murders, disappearances, tortures, fast or slow suicides of women in prostitution, I have often thought that the only ethical stance toward prostitution is the confrontational: This must end. To render this slaughter of women as analytic argument has, at times, seemed to me an act of barbarism. This work of mine, then, is intended not solely as argument, but as a meditation upon witnessing brutality: the scale of it, the dailiness of it, the seeming inevitability of it; the torture, the rapes the murders, the beatings, the despair, the hollowing out of the personality, the near extinction of hope commonly suffered by women in prostitution. And what I ask of you is simple: where my logic fails, please remember these women and do better than I have done.

There is a further complication. Brutality, written about, is different from brutality, lived. Writing, especially theoretical writing, is a practice which requires and maintains a certain distance from its subject matter. The attempt to render women's pain into words, cast to the kindness of strangers, has caused me great anguish and frustration. I had been both warned of and instructed about this trouble by feminist theorists, pedagogically though the feminist legal critique of objectivity, and more immediately by the examples of scholars who have expressed similar anxieties about their own work. More than once I read Kathleen Barry's description of her heartbreak, "an emotion men condemn as a failure of objectivity,"[2] while writing her landmark book on sexual slavery:

And yet I realize that it is the stifling of such emotion that creates conditions of violence and slavery. I've come to recognize in a way I've never before known so deeply and powerfully the extent to which emotionless objectivity leads directly to objectification—the starting point of violence, particularly sexual violence.[3]

I finally came to understand that one cannot write objectively from the victim's point of view; she must be abandoned as one pulls chair to table. The urgent collaboration, rather, is between the author and the reader. And in that collaboration, the sufferings of the victims are too often "used to create something, works of art, that are thrown to the consumption of a world which destroyed them."[4]

In a paper about prostitution, it is difficult to avoid the inference that this collaboration shares certain features with that between pimp and john: the "prostitute" shaped by the author into a representation suitable and desirable for the anonymous reader's temporary, fleeting engagement. Again, the "prostitute" is but a species of exchange in a transaction through which her value is debated, quarreled over, but to which she remains a stranger. This dilemma—the revictimization of the sufferer in the very act of the writing that tries to render her visible—can perhaps only finally be overcome by the eradication of the suffering such writing seeks to disclose. Thus, the very themes of this essay I may describe, but I cannot yet enact. It is with said irony, then, that I here turn to the first question I would like to explore; that is, the political significance of the dichotomy drawn between "prostitutes" and "other women," in life and then again in law, a dichotomy exactly founded on the assumption that "prostitution isn't like anything else." I begin with a story.

2. KATHLEEN BARRY, FEMALE SEXUAL SLAVERY 215 (1979).
3. *Id.*
4. Theodor Adorno, *Commitment, in* THE ESSENTIAL FRANKFURT SCHOOL READER 300, 312 (Andrew Arato & Eike Gebhardt eds., 1982).

1. A TWICE TOLD TALE

My activist colleague, K.C. Reed, is a strong woman. She was raped by her father, and then sexually abused by her grandfather, from the age of two. She was prostituted for over 20 years, first at age 13.[5] She is now trying to remember her life as a way of beginning to live it in her own self. She needs to remember where she has lived, whether she did or did not attend a community college sometime in the 1970's, when and where she was in prison. This is difficult work. Her life's witnesses—family, friends, lovers, children, even the shreds of paper we rely on to remind us who we are and who we have been—number few. Many of the men are dangerous to her. Her children are far away. One of them, a daughter, is dead. K.C. believes she was murdered by a trick. Her sons are in the care of others. K.C. hopes for them, but has no direct contact with them. Other family members know little. The facts have faded. The feelings were always wrapped tightly, or foregone by numbness, or dreamed in hard drugs that can make you feel a tenderness inside. Her memory is complex, kaleidoscoped, fluid. She is smart and vivid and full of dedication. She organizes on behalf of herself and other women in prostitution for help in ending prostitution.

K.C. recently wrote down what happened to her during one night in prostitution when she was 15 years old. She and two other women had run away from a state hospital. They were picked up by some men and taken to a hotel room where about 25 other men had assembled. She describes how the men talked and acted, how many men penetrated her (15), in what positions, and with what objects after the penises gave out, how the men insisted that the women have sex with each other when the men wanted to watch, how the pictures were taken, how she moved to the next gang of men, the next road. She mailed her testimony to the newsletter of a feminist anti-rape organization for publication. One of the editors questioned whether her piece was suitable for publication: "It just goes on and on and there's no point to it." The author's response was simple. "Yes, that's right. It went on and on and there was no point to it."[6]

K.C. Reed told a story that another woman, a feminist, could not hear. She heard words, "on and on," but not a proper "story." She heard

5. See K.C. Reed, *There Isn't No Easy Way* 1–2 (July 6, 1990) (unpublished pamphlet on file with author).

6. Thankfully, with the support of other editors, Reed's piece was ultimately published. See K.C. Reed, *A Former Prostitute Speaks*, NCASA 24 (Fall/Winter 1990).

some representational version of nagging, signifying nothing. These are the charges we conventionally associate with the suppression of women's voices within masculinist systems of meaning: less that we do not or cannot *talk*, than that we do not make *sense*. The editor is a fine woman, clear-headed, smart, dedicated; she is neither cruel nor insensitive. But what K.C. had to say about one night of prostitution didn't yield meaning to her on its own terms.

I am compelled by this story, and wanted to tell it to you, for a number of reasons in addition to witnessing to the anguish of my friend. I am haunted by the fear that this story is less anecdote that synecdoche, characteristic of a profound incomprehensibility of prostitution to feminism. Certainly I need search neither long nor hard to discover myself in K.C.'s editor. For a long time in my life, not one woman ever talked to me about being prostituted. That was a deafening silence, given that, during the same period, many women spoke to me about rapes, incest, abuse-related substance dependency, and beatings, and given that, as Catharine MacKinnon reports, some 20% of women engage in prostitution at some time in their lives.[7] Then, a 20% estimate would have seemed impossibly high. Now, it seems low. It seems plain to me now that, however trustworthy I seemed to listen respectfully to what women had to say about other violence and shame and fear in their lives, they did not feel safe talking to me about prostitution.

A few years later, something shifted. Some women with whom I worked closely and whom I love began to tell me of their histories in prostitution, carefully and from a distance. Sometimes in writing, sometimes by unexpected announcement in a public place, sometimes as if they had already told me, and nothing more needed to be said. I had to force myself to listen; they knew it and I knew it. It was a brutal time, much more for them than for me. I was part of the brutality. I didn't know how to hear, and I resisted learning. My friends seemed disoriented, too. Uncertain, it appeared, of what to say, how to say it; why, even, to continue to speak. "On and on." Usually, the first conversation was about the johns, about the men. Tucked behind a corner, in the next conversation perhaps, a slightly different theme: how she betrayed another woman as a way to get out, or to placate a pimp, or to keep a john quiet. Sometimes, too, a resolve not to give over her own daughter to be prostituted as she had been.

Now I believe I hear better. More women talk to me. I work on issues of prostitution in the feminist movement. Women call. I feel, perhaps

----

7. CATHARINE A. MACKINNON, TOWARD A FEMINIST THEORY OF THE STATE 143 (1989).

wrongly, that when the woman begins to speak I already know some of it: about the tricks, the drugs, the cops, the welfare, how things come to be after 3 weeks, after 3 months, after 3 years, after 30 years. In these conversations I hear a quality of uncontained contempt for men, for johns in particular, that is new to me in its conviction. Sometimes I think to ask about women she may have betrayed, if she seems to want to talk about it. There is great grief there. I wonder if *she* is that other woman, to me: the one I will renounce. I pray that it isn't true, but know it has been. "There is no point to it."

I begin, too, to wonder if these women are telling me something about all the *other* "other" women, the women who haven't been prostituted, and the stories we tell. These days, we more readily tell each other all kinds of stories about how we have lived our women's lives. Those stories, too, now seem familiar, yet they are shapelier than the prostitution stories, more formally precise, more modulated. I wonder where the ease comes from , where the "form" comes from. I wonder if it comes from leaving out the "pointless" parts, the parts *about* prostitution. Could we be suppressing stories about johns, or about contempt, or about money? Are we suppressing the stories in which we renounce a woman more vulnerable than ourselves, in our own defense? Do our stories *participate* in prostitution, operating as rehearsals for telling men the stories they want to hear from us, so that we can use them as best we can while we renounce prostitutes as part of the bargain? I am not sure, any more, about many tales I believed in once. What is the point to *them?*

One of feminism's stories, entrenched deeply in the history and political landscape of the contemporary movement, is that prostitution is indeed not "like anything else." The theme was often sounded in the early movement that prostitution is *only* a story, a slanderous fiction masking real abuse and sex-based inequality suffered by (other?) women. For example, for Jackie MacMillian, "[p]rostitution is an important issue for feminists because prostitutes most clearly express the cultural valuation and image of women as primarily sexual beings."[8] Patricia Hill Collins emphasizes the same theme in her analysis of the import of prostitution for Black women. With Angela Davis, Collins argues that "the myth of the Black prostitute" constitutes an ideological vehicle used to legitimate rape and other sexual violence against all Black women.[9] The problem of prostitution to feminist reform, in consequence, was posed as the problem the *idea*

---

8. Jackie MacMillian, *Prostitution as Sexual Politics*, 4 QUEST 41 (no. 1, 1977).
9. PATRICIA HILL COLLINS, BLACK FEMINIST THOUGHT: KNOWLEDGE, CONSCIOUSNESS, AND THE POLITICS OF EMPOWERMENT 177 (1991). *See also* ANGELA DAVIS, WOMEN, RACE, AND CLASS (1981).

of prostitution creates for women's authority to tell our own, authentic stories of our own experiences.

At least for women who are not publicly identified as "real prostitutes," this understanding of prostitution as a false and dangerous idea seems well enough supported in the experience of many women. In one collection of thirty-three women's accounts of being battered, for example, nearly one third had been accused of prostitution or labeled as "whores" during beatings and rapes. Exemplary are the following:

After my mom died we went East for the funeral. . . . At the funeral home everyone was hugging and kissing. Gerry went off mad and came back drunk, saying, "You want your uncle's in you." He grabs me and calls me a slut. "I'm going to tell your uncles you're out here waiting with your legs wide open."[10]

He also humiliated her by telling her that other men thought she was a prostitute, and occasionally they did make that assumption and offered Matthew money for her sexual services. "Slowly," she says, "everything edged away from me."[11]

Batterers who kill their wives and girlfriends make the same charge. As one defendant put the point, the murdered victim was "just a slut" and he "had to kill her."[12] The same theme arises repeatedly in divorce actions,

10. Gina NiCarthy, The Ones Who Got Away: Women Who Left Abusive Partners 290 (1987).

11. *Id.* at 120. These accounts corroborate Andrea Dworkin's conclusion that:

[T]he reality is that you can do everything in the world to be a good woman in this society, but when you are in the private house with the private husband whom you've attracted through your conformity to being what is on the surface a good woman, when the man starts hitting you, he hits you because you are bad.

Andrea Dworkin, *Woman-Hating Right and Left, in* The Sexual Liberals and the Attack on Feminism, *supra* note 1, at 28, 33. Margo St. James, the founder of COYOTE, a pro-prostitution organization, on this point uncharacteristically agrees with Dworkin. "[W]hen a man slugs his wife, he precedes the abuse with, 'You slut! You whore!'" Margo St. James *(Comment) From the Floor, in* Good Girls/Bad Girls: Feminists and Sex Trade Workers Face to Face 114, 130 (Laurie Bell ed., 1987).

12. People v. Carroll, 180 Cal. Rptr. 327 (Cal. Ct. App. 1983). *See also* People v. District Court, 595 P.2d 1945 (Col. 1979) (defendant, who lived with pregnant victim, called her a "bitch, whore, and a slut," while he beat her to death); People v. Cooley, 27 Cal. Rptr. 543 (Cal. Ct. App. 1963) (Defendant was convicted of first-degree murder in the beating and torture death of his wife. Over 15 years of marriage, defendant had inflicted numerous severe beatings on her, resulting in many broken bones, choked her, threatened to kill her and the children, accused her of having extramarital affairs with two homosexual men, burned her nipples with cigarettes while she was semi-conscious, ripped out clumps of her hair, told

often when the husband had beaten and tortured his wife during the course of the marriage, complaining of her whorish behavior.[13] Then, having labeled a victim a "whore," a batterer may go on to act like a pimp. Ann Jones explains:

[I] meet more and more battered women—severely battered women and women who have struck back—who were not being supported by the men who were their abusers. Rather, the economic arrangement is often the other way around: The man lives off the woman, off her wages or her welfare check or off the proceeds of her prostitution. He dominates and exploits her economically, just as he does physically and sexually. The parties may be husband and wife or a cohabiting couple, but the arrangement is the classic one of pimp and prostitute.[14]

Nor is the prostitution charge limited to victimized wives and girl-friends. It is by now a sad therapeutic commonplace that female victims of incest tend to identify as prostitutes as adult women, and to feel irrevo-cably separated from other, "normal" women. Judith Herman explains: "Many women felt that what set them apart from others was their own evilness. With depressing regularity, these women referred to themselves as bitches, witches and whores."[15] Child sexual abuse researchers David Finkelhor's and Angela Browne's analysis of the "traumatic sexualization" caused by childhood sexual abuse suggests the social dynamic underly-ing this self-identification. "Traumatic sexualization occurs through the exchange of affection, attention, privileges, and gifts for sexual behavior, so that a child learns sexual behavior as a strategy for manipulating [sic]

his daughter that her mother was a "whore" and a "slut", and kicked her mother in the stomach, saying to the daughter, "See, she only cries when you hit her, she doesn't care what's happening.").

13. *See, e.g., In re* the Marriage of Ruby Elizabeth Walls, 743 S.W. 2d 137 (Mo. Ct. App. 1988) (Wife testified that defendant struck and kicked her on numerous occasions, called her a "fuckin' slut and a whore," and threatened: "[J]ust tell your mother you're sick and I'll tie you up in the basement and just kill you a little each day."); Rollyson v. Rollyson, 294 S.E.2d 131 (W. Va. 1982) (wife testified that her husband had struck her on several occasions during their marriage, frequently called her a slut and a whore, accused her of "slutting around," and threatened her on several occasions, saying if he "caught her down on the street slutting around with those sluts and whores that they would be picking her up off the street, dead).

14. Ann Jones, *Family Matters, in* THE SEXUAL LIBERALS AND THE ATTACK ON FEMINISM, *supra* note 1, at 61, 63.

15. JUDITH HERMAN, FATHER-DAUGHTER INCEST 96–98 (1981).

others to get his or her other developmentally appropriate needs met."[16] Abusers may directly label their victims as "sluts" to enforce girls' silence, to stigmatize compliance, and to reinforce the girls' sense of complicity.[17] Those who learn of the abuse may do the same, excusing the father's behavior and punishing the girl as sexually provocative.[18] Girls may engage in bargains with their fathers for food, clothing, or some regulation of their father's sexual access to them.[19]

Similar patterns emerge in less intimate, non-familial abuse, like sexual harassment and stranger rape. As Catharine MacKinnon points out, "a great many instances of sexual harassment in essence amount to solicitation for prostitution."[20] In many hostile work environment claims, harassers seem to presume that their female coworkers are "asking for it"

16. David Finkelhor & Angela Browne, *Initial and Long-Term Effects: A Conceptual Framework, in* A SOURCEBOOK ON CHILD SEXUAL ABUSE 180 (David Finkelhor ed., 1986).

17. *See* Lazarowicz v. State, 51 So.2d 392 (Fla. 3d Dist. Ct. App. 1990) (New trial ordered for defendant convicted of sexual battery of his seventeen-year-old daughter. The daughter testified that her father forced her to engage in sexual intercourse and fellatio with him in 1985. When he began to suspect that she was having sexual relations with her boyfriend, he "punched me, knocked my head into the wall, threw me around the room, took me into the bedroom and laid me on the bed and punched me in the face, kicked me, and gave me a black eye," put bruises over her other eye, called her a "slut" and a "whore," and every time he walked by her he would punch her in the face.); Commonwealth v. LaSota, 557 N.E. 2d 34 (Mass. App. Ct. 1990) (Defendant denied allegations by his sixteen-year-old daughter that he had sexually abused her continuously since she was in kindergarten, and claimed that when he discovered pornographic photographs of her in her closet, he slapped he and called her a "slut".).

18. For example, Herman reports that mothers sometimes react to daughters' reports of abuse by fathers by sending their daughters away from home. One woman reported: "[My mother] was afraid I would become a lesbian or a whore. So she put me in a mental hospital. It was a good excuse to get rid of me." HERMAN, *supra* note 15, at 90.

19. *See, e.g.,* LOUISE ARMSTRONG, KISS DADDY GOODNIGHT 74, 75 (1978) (father agreed that he wouldn't touch her anymore, provided she went along with any decisions he made whenever she asked for anything; daughter could stay out until 8:30 at the Homecoming Parade if she had sex with father); KATHLEEN BRADY, FATHER'S DAYS 87 (1979) (among many examples of "bargaining" between father and daughter, Brady reports that when she wanted to get a job at age 16, her father agreed to sign her application form, but only if she would "be nicer" to him, threatening to make her quit if she didn't "keep her end").

20. CATHARINE A. MACKINNON, SEXUAL HARASSMENT OF WORKING WOMEN: A CASE OF SEX DISCRIMINATION 159 (1979).

sexually and economically, either because the women are perceived to be working in the "wrong" workplace (that is, in male dominated trades and professions, where she can make a living wage), or because harassers believe that sexual availability *is* her work (that is, in female dominated jobs, where she cannot.)[21] A similar presumption, that men commit sexual assault because of women's exploitative, "sluttish" sexual enticements, summed up by one rape defendant's view that "all women were whores and sluts and they all deserved what the victim was getting,"[22] persists *ad nauseum.*[23] In discussing this paper with women around the country, I have been told repeatedly by women rape victims that rapists threw $20, or $50, at them after the attack, conduct which at the time confused them. Is the ploy now, like the old rape consent rule, that a woman can be made a whore "before or after the act"?

Given the enormous prevalence rates of each of these forms of sexual violence, it must be the rare woman who has not heard herself described as a prostitute, or heard a justification for abusive behavior couched in related terms. The "prostitute" charge is hurled at women whenever we are punished for sexual behavior, fantasized or real, or for simply occupying the body of a woman, for which the punishment takes the form of sexualized terrorism. At least where a victim can show she is "not a prostitute," the problem of prostitution seems to abide in the falsity of the man's belief about her, and in the over-pervasiveness generally of the "whore" stigma.

And much feminist legal reform work against sexual violence has explicitly or implicitly promoted strategies aimed at strengthening the distinction between "prostitutes" and "other women." The political

21. *See, e.g.,* Hansel v. Public Service Co. of Colorado, 778 F. Supp. 1126 (D. Col. 1991) (harassment included graffiti like "VH sucks all cocks," rape, co-worker facing her with a hangman's noose and suggesting she commit suicide; court believed conduct designed to drive her out of an all-male plant); Jew v. Univ. of Iowa, 749 F. Supp. 946 (S.D. Iowa 1990) (woman professor called "slut" and "whore" by another faculty member in front of students).

22. Fuget v. State. 522 A.2d 1371 (Md. App. 1987).

23. Diana Scully reports that, among her sample of 114 convicted rapists, 69% of those who denied having committed a "real" rape justified their behavior "by claiming that the victim was known to be a prostitute, or a 'loose' woman, or to have had a lot of affairs, or to have had child out of wedlock." DIANA SCULLY, UNDERSTANDING SEXUAL VIOLENCE: A STUDY OF CONVICTED RAPISTS 108 (1990). *See also* Justice v. State, 1986 WL 1505 (Ark. App.) (defendant convicted of raping an eight-year-old girl claimed she tried to seduce him on many occasions, characterizing her as a "wanton libertine"; prosecuting attorney stated in closing argument that defendant was trying to "make out the victim to be a slut").

rescue of "real womanhood" from the stigma of prostitution, within the spheres of life believed occupied by "normal women," has been the mainstream feminist tactic advanced within many of our campaigns. Each promotes a predictable theme about prostitution: emphatically, that we are *not* prostitutes. A mistake has been made—a grievous failure to contour the proper distinctions between the prostitution with which we are charged and our own conduct, and a consequent failure to treat us with justice.

The success of these distancing strategies relies on an initial agreement among all concerned that we can identify who a genuine prostitute actually *is*. Existing law offers a conveniently unambiguous definition of the type. Among statutory definitions, the New York law is typical, defining a woman as culpable of prostitution if she "engages or agrees or offers to engage in sexual conduct with another person in return for a fee."[24] A "prostitute" is a woman who has indiscriminate sex with many men, who are strangers to her, who pay her for it (or who promise to pay, and if not her, someone). Each of our counter-representations, our "true" stories, seeks to disidentify a sexual violence victim from the status of prostitute by distinguishing her behavior from at least one of the legal elements of prostitution.

In rape law reform, for example, feminist lawyers have long labored to establish a victim's "discriminateness" in her choice of sexual partners, both in articulating the injury rape entails, and in the representation of the victim at trial. Our most significant work focuses on the habilitation of a woman's "no" as probative of her lack of consent. This commitment in turn locates the injury of rape in the disregard of a woman's sexual selectiveness.[25] Rape shield evidentiary rules, and the articulation of women's injury through testimony of rape trauma syndrome, continue this theme. Rape shield rules limit the admissibility of a woman's prior sexual history for the purpose of proving consent, at least when the defendant has not had sex with the victim before.[26] These rules are intended to sever the inference a jury might otherwise draw between a woman's past sexual "promiscuity," and her consent on a particular occasion. Less politely, these rules are designed to defeat the whore status her prior activity might

---

24. N.Y. PENAL LAW § 230.00 (McKinney?s 1991). *See also* TEX. PENAL CODE ANN. § 43.02(a)(1) (West 1984) (same language).

25. *See, e.g.,* SUSAN ESTRICH, REAL RAPE 102 (1987) ("'Consent'? should be defined so that no means no.").

26. For discussion of the rationales for rape shield rules, see Harriet Galvin, *Shielding Rape Victims in the State and Federal Courts: A Proposal for the Second Decade,* 70 MINN. L. REV. 763 (1983).

ascribe to her.[27] The admissibility of evidence of rape trauma syndrome, describing the crippling physical, psychological, and behavioral effects of sexual assault, has also been advocated by feminist reformers, both to corroborate a woman's testimony that she did not consent to the act, and to dispel juror misunderstanding that women "ask for it," by rendering plain the profound, complex, and enduring suffering that unwanted sex causes.[28]

Prostitutes, of course, say "yes" a great deal. Our threshold commitment to the disregard of a woman's "no" as the talismanic violation of rape renders prostitution beyond the pale of our rape reforms, and segregates prostitutes as the women we are not. The courts have clearly understood the intended limits of these reforms, consistently holding that rape shield rules should give way when the defendant can prove that the victim "really was" a prostitute, or that financial arrangements were involved in the contested act.[29] This conclusion is echoed in the avoidance of the question whether prostitutes endure some form, perhaps extreme, of rape trauma syndrome.[30] Are we afraid to explore what it means that prostituted women engage in otherwise nonconsensual sex for twenty dollars, apparently accepting what amounts to a pittance in liquidated damages for rape, while "other women" assert deep and lasting trauma as a result of unwanted sex? Our strategy of differentiating prostitutes from ourselves, begun by categorically distinguishing between "yes" and "no" sex, here seems elevated to an ontological divide between nice women who are hurt by sex they don't want, and not so nice women presumptively calloused or insensible to selling themselves for the equivalent of a parking fine.

Feminist explanations for why women stay in abusive relationships also marginalize prostituted women. These accounts explain how battered

27. The point is put bluntly in the Florida case law predating the enactment of the Florida shield statute. Evidence of prior sexual history was admissible in Florida to prove "promiscuous intercourse with men, or common prostitution." Rice v. State, 17 So. 286, 287 (Fla. 1895).

28. On the rationales for admissibility, see Patricia Frazier & Eugene Borgida, *Juror Common Understanding and the Admissibility of Rape Trauma Syndrome Evidence in Court*, 12 LAW & HUM. BEHAV. 101 (1988).

29. *See, e.g.*, People v. Varona, 143 Cal. App. 2d 566 (1983) (abuse of discretion to exclude evidence that the complaining witness was a prostitute); People v. Randle, 130 Cal. App. 3d 286 (1982) (exclusion of evidence that complaining witness had solicited public sex for money, drugs and alcohol reversible error even though there was evidence of physical injury to the woman).

30. In recent years, some researchers and activists have begun to examine the trauma impact of prostitution. *See, e.g.*, PROSTITUTION, TRAFFICKING, AND TRAUMATIC STRESS (Melissa Farley ed., 2004).

women become increasingly enmeshed with men who abuse them. A battered woman clings to hope for the batterer's eventual reform, within a downward spiral of collapsing self-esteem extinguishing her feeling that she is entitled to better treatment. In this account, the complexities of love, intimacy, and commitment to a man over time are stressed as crucial to women's decisions to remain in abusive relationships.[31] Social science researchers frame these decisions within the broader context of women's sex role socialization. Women are culturally oriented toward a value system that endorses the view that "their expected role is to be the wife and mother and that keeping the family together is their responsibility and obligation,"[32] the passing of love, and its spectacularized publicity in divorce, the most bitter of diminishments.[33] On each of these accounts, the woman's "problem," if she has one, abides in an overcommitment to monogamous fidelity, even at the risk of her own life.

Self-defense strategies urge a similar framework for explaining the validity of a battered woman's perception of imminent danger from an abuser, in circumstances that might be seen by a jury as less than immediate. Her *familiarity* with the particular man's habits and patterns of violence, it is argued, yields her a special understanding of the risks he threatens.[34] Further, women's economic motives for staying in abusive relationships are rarely emphasized, either by courts or by feminist critics. At most, we maternalize the economic dimension, attending to the special economic pressures placed on battered mothers to remain in abusive marriages. Avoidance of the economic question also distances the "good woman" from the taint of prostitution, while more deeply stigmatizing prostituted women themselves. Whatever the reasons we stay in abusive

31. *See* LENORE WALKER, THE BATTERED WOMAN 55–70 (1979) (outlining the three stages of the cycle of violence, rotating from "tension-building" to violent attack to "loving . . . contrite behavior").

32. Lynne Bravo Rosewater, *The Clinical and Courtroom Application of Battered Womens Personality Assessments, in* DOMESTIC VIOLENCE ON TRIAL: PSYCHOLOGICAL AND LEGAL DIMENSIONS OF FAMILY VIOLENCE 86, 91 (Daniel Jay Sonkin ed., 1987).

33. Phyllis Crocker summarizes this view as follows: "A battered woman who does not leave her husband, seek help, or fight back is behaving according to societal expectations: the cultural perception of marriage as a lifelong bond and commitment instructs a woman to stay and work to improve—not abandon the marriage." Phyllis Crocker, *The Meaning of Equality for Battered Women Who Kill in Self Defense*, 8 HARV. WOM. L. J. 121, 135 (1986).

34. *See, e.g.*, State v. Hundley, 693 P.2d 475, 475–76 (Kan. 1985) (degree of imminence to be evaluated from perspective of a "prudent battered woman").

relationships, a good woman isn't there for the money. If he is no trick, she is no whore.

This representation, like that drawn of rape victims under the rape shield laws, benefits women little in encounters with real johns, or toward explaining why a woman "stays" in prostitution, even if, like most women in the life, she is raped, assaulted, and threatened with murder on a regular basis. The ties and insights of persistent affection are not often present between a prostitute and a john. "Loving contrition" is not a common behavior pattern in men who buy women for sex. Nor does the prostitute enjoy the status of an otherwise socially conforming victim. The "good woman" sex role of loyalty to intimate monogamous fidelity, while perhaps of tactical assistance in garnering sympathy for women battered by husbands, only serves to punish women in prostitution. A prostitute who kills a john cannot argue a specialized understanding of a particular john's habits of violence, at least so long as johns are not understood to pose predictable risks to prostituted women. Nor are these theoretical distancing strategies only of academic significance. The inapplicability, even structural hostility, of battered women's defenses to women in prostitution contributed strongly to Aileen Carol Wuornos's first degree murder conviction for killing a john, for which she was executed by the State of Florida on October 9, 2002.[35]

Legitimate work is, after all, how women are supposed to make money, an assumption fueling anti-sexual harassment legal initiatives and education efforts. Here, our advocacy stresses the *distinction* between a woman's willingness to work, and her willingness to have sex as part of the bargain: "real women" do not combine sex and money. As Chief Justice Rehnquist has acknowledged, sexual harassment prohibitions stand at the ready to sanction any "requirement that a man or a woman run a gauntlet of sexual abuse in return for the privilege of being allowed to work and earn a living."[36] By "sexual abuse," Justice Rehnquist seems here to mean any unwelcome sex imposed on a woman as a condition or entailment of her job.

Thus, it would seem but a small step conceptually to hold all prostitution to be *per se* actionable as sexual harassment. The demand for money in the transaction shows that a woman's sexual compliance in the acts were otherwise unwanted. Indeed, Catharine MacKinnon acknowledges that prostitution represents in pure form the model of *quid pro quo* sex

35. *See* Florida Department of Corrections, *Execution List 1976-present*, *http://www.dc.dtate.fl.us/oth/deathros/execlist.html*.

36. Meritor Savings Bank v. Vinson, 477 U.S. 57, 67 (1986) (holding that sexual harassment constitutes sex discrimination prohibited under Title VII).

for money exchange, prohibited in sexual harassment law. She nevertheless retreats from the conclusion that prostitution should be actionable as
such, apparently even when "unwelcome." Her hesitation seems driven
by the belief that, for women materially supported in the practice, prostitution may be better than nothing at all,[37] and more rewarding than
"romantic" sexual compliance promising little by way of material benefits.[38] While prostitution may represent the "fundamental" economic and
sexual "condition of woman,"[39] it is, itself, deemed here by MacKinnon
a condition too fundamental for redress.[40]

Taken together, these boundary defenses form a solid wall against the
imputation of prostitution to "other" women: she is not sexually promiscuous, does not subject herself to random treatment by strangers, and
doesn't do it for cash. Beyond these defenses, is but silence. The recent
legal scholarship on prostitution is largely limited in vision to the rather
narrow question of whether prostitution should or should not be decriminalized.[41] Anti-discrimination litigation strategies have been confined to
challenges to statutory schemes which criminalize the behavior of prostitutes, but not the behavior of johns, or which impose sanctions at different severity levels, and to enforcement practices having the same effect.
Conceptually, these strategies exclude consideration of the experience of
women in prostitution beyond the rather abstract injury of being jailed,

---

37. MacKinnon argues:

In these situations, more than is impermissibly the case for most womens jobs, without
the sexual harassment, there *is* no job. Until all women *need* no longer sell their physical
attractiveness, there is no point in the law prohibiting all such behavior in these contexts.

MacKinnon, Sexual Harassment, *supra* note 20, at 209.

38. MacKinnon quotes Roberta Victor, a woman with a history in prostitution,
to the point:

What I did was no different from what ninety-nine percent of American women are taught
to do. I took the money from under the lamp instead of in Arpege. What would I do with
150 bottles of Arpege a week?

MacKinnon, Sexual Harassment, *supra* note 20, at 217.

39. MacKinnon, Toward a Feminist Theory of the State, *supra* note 7,
at 243.

40. MacKinnon does declare in her later work that, under a legal theory of
equality sufficient for redress of women's subordination, "prostitution would become actionable." *Id.* at 248.

41. *See, e.g.*, Deborah L. Rhode, Justice and Gender: Sex Discrimination and the Law 259 (1989).

while her john goes free.[42] That insult, I would propose, pales in comparison to other relevant comparisons in life circumstances that might be made between them.

Our activism in providing support services, and in progressive organizing, has done little better than our legal initiatives. Domestic violence shelters remain in practical fact inaccessible to women and girls prostitution. As a matter of policy, most shelters exclude drug and alcohol dependent women, and deny program assistance to women who engage in illegal activities of any kind. The resulting invisibility of prostitution to service providers limits their awareness of prostituted women's access and safety needs, the urgency of maintaining confidentiality of the identities of minor girls when sought by police and social service agencies, and the urgent need for long-term support for prostituted women and girls. From my observation, once women are admitted to shelters, they often feel constrained to lie about their circumstances, reducing the possible benefits of proffered support to painful farce. Prostituted women in shelters shape their stories to the perceived tolerance of shelter staff: her pimp becomes her husband, the cigarette burns on her thighs the outcome of a jealous outburst over her "seeing" other men, she is sexually harassed on the job, and on and on. Anti-pornography activism, which has mobilized the most visible contemporary feminist challenge to prostitution in the United States, has been largely pushed "underground," unlike pornography or prostitution. Women's health agendas, to the extent that work has comprehended prostitution as health issue at all, have limited the scope of their consideration of prostitution to the risk of AIDS transmission to and by prostitutes. This emphasis obscures the significance of research indicating that chronic poor health among juvenile prostitutes is often a consequence of inadequate clothing,[43] that injuries from beatings and sexual assaults most commonly immobilize

42. It is also not altogether clear to me that these strategies, aimed at reducing the risk of arrest for women in prostitution, serve womens immediate interests. At present, jail is the closest thing many women in prostitution have to a battered womens shelter. Among the reasons women have recited to me as why sometimes they seek "voluntary arrest" include: trying to get a nights sleep, to escape a violent pimp or john, to detox, to get AZT therapy, to not have to turn tricks, and to eat a hot meal. I beg the civil libertarians among my readers who represent women in prostitution to please interview a woman carefully on these issues before deciding unilaterally what is best for her when she is jailed.

43. D. KELLY WEISBERG, CHILDREN OF THE NIGHT: A STUDY OF ADOLESCENT PROSTITUTION 116 (1985) (citing DOROTHY H. BRACEY, BABY-PROS: PRELIMINARY PROFILES OF JUVENILE PROSTITUTES 62–63 (1979)).

women in prostitution,[44] and the fact that all prostitutes are targets for murder.[45]

Prostitution, indeed, is not like "anything else," especially anything that we might be. The most brutal rendition of this theme may be Kate Millett's account, as recounted by Alice Echols, of an episode at a radical feminist conference on prostitution in 1971:

> The place finally erupted when a member of The Feminists declared herself an "honorable woman" because she lived in a tenement, worked as a secretary, and yet refused to sell her body. As Millett noted, "the accusation, so long buried in liberal good-will and radical rhetoric—'You're selling it, I could too, but I won't'—was finally heard. Said out loud at last."[46]

As Andrea Dworkin puts the point, "The woman's effort to stay innocent, her efforts to prove innocence, her effort to prove that she was used against her will is always and unequivocally an effort to prove she is not a whore."[47]

II. THE GREATEST STORY NEVER TOLD

Some women find such proof hard to come by. Prostitutes, for example. Some notice has been taken of this, inspiring feminist prostitution activists—including prostituted women and girls, and their allies—to begin to organize on their own behalf. This work has relied on the most significant method for feminist investigation devised in the modern movement: consciousness-raising, this time among prostituted women themselves. Prostituted women began to tell their own stories of the

---

44. Eleanor Miller reports of her research on health conditions of "street women":

> Health-related [concerns]...even more frequently mentioned as occasions for temporary withdrawal from street life than disease or pregnancy included the bruises, broken bones, cuts and abrasions that were the result of the ever-present risk of violence on the streets. The beatings and sexual assaults female street hustlers received at the hands of their "men," their dates, their wives-in-law, former "women" of their "men," and other street people as well as the police were numerous and often brutal.

ELEANOR MILLER, STREET WOMAN 138 (1986).

45. See Jane Caputi, The Sexual Politics of Murder, 3 GENDER & SOCIETY 437 (1989). See also infra notes 52–67 and accompanying text.

46. ALICE ECHOLS, DARING TO BE BAD: RADICAL FEMINISM IN AMERICA 1967–1975, 194 (1989).

47. ANDREA DWORKIN, PORNOGRAPHY: MEN POSSESSING WOMEN 204 (1989).

experience of prostitution, to devise political responses to that experience, and to express their own views of the relationship between themselves and "other women."[48] While these efforts have yielded some magnificent results, women in prostitution and their allies have still encountered significant difficulties in organizing among themselves, and in efforts to progress the feminist agenda beyond the prostitute/other women impasse I just described. In this section, I detail three fundamental difficulties that, I think, have contributed to this frustration of forward movement on behalf of prostituted women.

The first is the difficulty of including those prostituted women who are most profoundly in peril, in the conversation of consciousness-raising. As I explain below, those women and girls cannot participate in the discourse, because they are dead, or disappeared, or broken. The tragic silence of these women already tends to create a split at the core of prostitution activism: between the silenced women who are the most hurt, and the women, less harmed or threatened, who can speak. The second difficulty is the confusion women feel as individuals whether they are *really* prostitutes, or not, voicing a split *within* women about the meaning of their own lives, to themselves and to others. These confusions are often richly suggestive of both the continuities women discern linking prostitution with other ways women act or are treated as women, and the discontinuities, where women actually see the "line" between prostitution and everything else. However, the way these confusions are resolved in part generates the third difficulty I discuss here. Politically, the confusions voiced by individual women tend to be resolved by emphasizing the continuities between

---

48. On the practice of consciousness-raising within feminism generally, see MacKinnon, Toward a Feminist Theory of the State, *supra*, note 7, at 83–105. A central premise of feminist consciousness-raising is that, by encouraging women to address issues usually wrapped in shame and secrecy with other women, we can begin to develop political critiques of those issues from a standpoint of genuine dignity and strength. I have been truly astounded by the different things my own law students talk to me about, since I have been publicly identified with prostitute support work. Before "coming out" as a prostitution activist, not one student ever told me about her own history in prostitution, her present involvement in prostitution, her self-identification as a prostitute, her "fucking everybody" periods, about behaviors associated with prostitution like excessive drug and alcohol use as a way of "getting over" in the sex, "consenting" to oral and anal sex as a tactic to avoid vaginal intercourse, cutting herself with knives and razor blades in the crotch and thighs, and performing sex with men or women to please a husband or lover. Now, these are commonplace discussions, enabled, I believe, by students' trust that I do not find these disclosures abnormal, but all too ordinary occasions for grief.

prostitutes and "other women," repressing what might distinguish them. On the face of it, this strategy appears to deeply challenge the sharp polarity between prostitutes and other women that mainstream feminism has tended to reinforce. If prostitutes *are* other women, what could be left of the opposition between them? I argue here, though, that this strategy has less empowered prostituted women, than it has colonized them yet again to the agendas and aims of "other women." The distinctive experience of prostitution must be split off, as the price of political inclusion in the larger movement, continually thwarting the possibility of genuine solidarity among prostituted women. These difficulties have proven complex and enduring in prostitution activism. Let me take up each in turn.

The first difficulty—the silence of the most victimized prostituted women in feminist consciousness-raising—is perhaps obvious, but profoundly underappreciated. The dead, the deeply incoherent, and those presently living in conditions of grave danger, are not participants in consciousness-raising. Consciousness-raising is necessarily a practice for survivors, not casualties. As a method relying on *participation* for its political analysis, consciousness-raising excludes the testimony of women who did not survive. Reliable rates of prostitute murders are not available, in part due to statistical reporting methods,[49] but also, and more importantly, because of the "disappeared" status of women and girls involved in the practice. They are "unaccounted for," are often runaways or "throwaways" from families,[50] sometimes pimped by them.[51] Family members likely have no knowledge of or interest in a girl's whereabouts. Those more immediately present in a girl's life may readily assume she merely "moved on," fear compromising themselves to the police, be the killer,

---

49. For a critique of the statistical reporting of homicide as it pertains to women, see William Wilbanks, *Murdered Women and Women Who Murder: A Critique of the Literature, in* JUDGE, LAWYER, VICTIM, THIEF: WOMEN, GENDER ROLES, AND CRIMINAL JUSTICE 157 (Nicole Hahn Rafter & Elizabeth A. Stanko eds., 1982).

50. Running away from and being "shoved out" of families are the most common predicates for juvenile entry into prostitution. *See, e.g.,* MILLER, *supra* note 44, at 87–108 (approximately half of her sample are either runaways or "pushouts"); WEISBERG, *supra* note 43 (summarizing research to date).

51. Two major studies of juvenile prostitution report that 4% of girls interviewed were either with a family member at the time of their first act of prostitution, or reported that a family member turned them out. *See* WEISBERG, *supra* note 43 *(citing* MIMI SILBERT, SEXUAL ASSAULT OF PROSTITUTES: PHASE ONE 40 (1980), and JENNIFER JAMES, ENTRANCE INTO JUVENILE PROSTITUTION 77 (1980)).

or simply not care.[52] Police may make similar assumptions,[53] while the vagaries of a prostituted woman's legal identity[54] render reports, listing a woman under a possibly false name and a cursory description, of little assistance in linking a corpse to an identifiable woman's life. One team of researchers has hypothesized that many "missing persons" may be serial murder victims,[55] and even the number of victims reported by apprehended perpetrators may never adequately be established. "We will never know for certain, because the majority of the [victims] would have been prostitutes whose disappearance may not have been reported. Some may have ended up among the many 'Jane Does' in the Los Angeles County morgue."[56] Pornographic "snuff" films eroticize this ambiguity.

When the bodies are found, and even tagged with names, the women even in death are still not "real women." The murdered spirits of women are contested, in doubt, tainted, interrogated. Were they good women or bad? Deserving dead or undeserving bystanders? During the investigation of the "Yorkshire Ripper" murders, Jim Hobson, police investigator, issued the following statement:

He has made it clear that he hates prostitutes. Many people do. We, as police force, will continue to arrest prostitutes. But the Ripper is now killing innocent girls. That indicates your mental state and that you are in urgent need of medical

---

52. Robert Keppel, chief investigator for the Washington State Attorney General?s Office and consultant to the Green River investigation, stated, "Nobody keeps track of these women, monitors where they are going to be day by day. Often, by the time the police get involved, it?s a historical research project." Michael Hedges, *Prostitutes, Psychopaths Too Often a Deadly Match,* WASH. TIMES, June 12, 1998, at A10. Retired Los Angeles Police Department Captain Pierce Brooks deems prostitutes the "easiest victims to kill. All you have to do is drive up, wave a $5 or $20 bill. [She] hops in the car and off you go. No muss, no fuss." Lisa Faye Kaplan, *Someone is Killing U.S. Hookers,* GANNETT NEWS SERVICE, June 7, 1990.

53. Robert DePue, former administrator of the FBI National Center for the Analysis of Violent Crime, asserts that prostitutes are "easier" to murder than children. "Prostitutes can disappear, and there won't even be a missing person report filed. They're expendable people, unfortunately, in our society." Kaplan, *supra* note 52.

54. Women and girls commonly take on a series of assumed names, sometimes in the course of being seasoned for prostitution by pimps, *see* BARRY, *supra* note 2, at 94–95, and in an attempt to avoid an extensive police record under any one name.

55. JACK LEVIN & JAMES ALAN FOX, MASS MURDER: AMERICA'S GROWING MENACE 19 (1985).

56. *Id.* at 75.

attention. You have made your point. Give yourself up before another innocent women dies.[57]

According to one reporter: "It is the main grief work for the families of [the Ripper's] non-professional victims to try to understand how their girls came under this man's hand. By having the same killer as the prostitutes, their daughters have somehow been tainted."[58]

It thus seems prudent that the murder data that do exist be evaluated in light of whatever multiplier might fairly comprehend prostitutes' social invisibility, compounded yet again by the gendered specificity of their status as "safe" objects of eroticized violence and misogynist hatred.[59] Some numbers are available. Up to thirty-one women murdered in Miami over a three year period, most of them prostitutes;[60] fourteen in Denver; twenty-nine in Los Angeles;[61] seven in Oakland.[62] Forty-three in San Diego;[63] fourteen in Rochester;[64] eight in Arlington, Virginia; nine in New Bedford, Massachusetts; seventeen in Alaska, ten in Tampa.[65] Three

57. Jane Caputi, The Age of Sex Crime 93 (1987) (quoting Joan Smith, *Getting Away with Murder,* New Socialist 10, 12 (May/June 1982)).

58. *Id.* at 95.

59. The director of a support program for women in prostitution estimates that 23 women a year *she knows of* disappear from the streets of Portland, Oregon; she assumes they have been murdered. Interview with Susan Kay Hunter (July 13, 1990).

60. See Hedges, *supra* note 52. Hedges estimates a "low-end" figure of eighteen. *Id. See also* Barry Bearak, *Eerie Deaths of 17 Women Baffle Miami,* L.A. Times, May 14, 1989, Part 1, at 1.

61. *See* Nieson Himmel & Edward J. Boyer, *2nd South-Central Wave of Prostitute Slayings Probed,* L.A. Times, Feb. 17, 1989, Part 2, at 3.

62. *See Seventh Victim lied to Serial Killer,* L.A. Times, Oct. 8, 1989, Part 1, at 2. Describing the circumstances of six of the women?'s deaths, the reporter recites that three were shot to death on the street, two were beaten to death, and one hung from a tree.

63. *See Suspect in 2 Oakland Killings Probed in 42 San Diego County Murders,* L.A. Times, Oct. 13, 1989, at A34. Two of the victims were police informants suspected to have been murdered by police officers. *See* Seth Mydans, *Police Criticized in San Diego Killings,* N.Y. Times, September 22, 1990, at A7.

64. *See Serial Killer Convicted of Second Degree Murder,* Rochester Times Union, Dec. 13, 1990 (9 prostitutes of 10 female victims, all strangled); Mills, *5 Killings Stir Talk of New Serial Killer,* Rochester Democrat, July 12, 1991 (all 5 women prostitutes).

65. *See* Hedges, *supra* note 54, at A10. Regional distinctions fleetingly surface; the women in Alaska were allegedly killed after being taken into wilderness areas, stripped, and hunted with a high-powered rifle.

girls, ages 3, 4, and 6, sold in Suffolk, New York.[66] Three prostitutes were reported dead in Spokane, Washington in 1990, leading some to speculate that the "Green River" murderer of 48 women and girls had once again become active.[67]

Evaluating the cause of death poses its own complications.[68] By whatever means, women in prostitution are dying quickly. One authority cited in the 1985 Canadian government report on prostitution and pornography concluded that women and girls in prostitution suffer a mortality rate 40 times the national average.[69]

These women are not telling their "prostitution stories." Nor do a great many survivors. For storytelling, especially of past sexual abuse and

66. *See* Carolyn Colwell, *4 Arraigned on Sexual Abuse of 3 Girls*, NEWSDAY (Suffolk Home Edition), May 31, 1991, at 33.

67. *See Suspected Serial Killer Grips Seattle for 2nd Time in Six Years*, DURHAM MORNING HERALD, May 28, 1990, at B4.

68. On the complexities of determining causation in this context, Robin Morgan is illuminating:

[Lisa McElhaney's] seventeen year old body was found in a plastic bag in Columbus, Ohio in April 1987. Her father was an alcoholic, her mother had tried to get an abortion when pregnant with Lisa, but couldn't afford it. Lisa was raped as a child, became pregnant and miscarried at age fifteen, was thrown out by her family, became addicted to drugs, and worked in pornography and prostitution to support her habit. Each time she ran afoul of the law and was incarcerated in a home for delinquents, social workers noted on her file that she displayed an eagerness for relationships and was "starved for affection." But the system was set up to rehabilitate, not to provide relationships or affection, so Lisa withdrew and "would sit for hours and hours, staring into space." When photographs of her performing sexual acts were discovered by the police, she was subpoenaed to testify in a child pornography case against Larry Miller, the pornographer. Although Miller was a suspect in her murder, police believed the killer was a client of hers, Rob Roy Baker, a thirty-four-year-old truck driver who had been linked to similar attacks on other prostitutes. When police came to question him, Baker shot himself to death in a house filled with pictures of nude women cut from pornographic magazines. So I would ask myself, did Lisa die of assault? Which assault? The lack of affordable abortion for her mother? The beating from her john? Did she die of the disease called "family" or the disease called "rehabilitation," of poverty or drugs or pornography, of economic or sexual slavery or a broken body? Or a broken spirit? Perhaps she died of unknown causes.

ROBIN MORGAN, THE DEMON LOVER: ON THE SEXUALITY OF TERRORISM 316 (1989). Commenting on the death of Ingeborg Bachmann by burns sustained in a fire in her apartment, Karen Achberger finds the circumstances, in common with the deaths of other women, to "elude our customary distinctions between accident, murder, and suicide." Karen Achberger, *Introduction, in* INGEBORG BACHMANN, THE THIRTIETH YEAR (Michael Bullock trans., 1987).

69. *See* SPECIAL COMMITTEE ON PORNOGRAPHY AND PROSTITUTION, PORNOGRAPHY AND PROSTITUTION IN CANADA 350 (1985).

humiliation, has a particular sexual significance to women in prostitution. Often a john's "tell me about yourself" gambit operates as a bid for verbal arousal in a prostitution transaction, a dynamic too often mirrored in conversation with self-proclaimed "sympathetic" others.[70] The recollection and articulation of a history in prostitution may bring with it the reliving of profound pain and anguish, experience which may seem better left abandoned. The "acting" theme of the prostitution transaction itself is too closely echoed in the "self-performance" of disclosure; the proximity of persuasion to pleasing an audience, erotically and otherwise, verging on the too familiar dynamics of hooking, this time, of feminists. Storytelling also requires the ability to remember, to draw connections, to reflect. Among women in prostitution, researchers report a disproportionately high incidence of psychogenic amnesia, multiple personality disorder, clinical depression, and borderline personality disorder inhibiting those powers.[71] Care-givers trace the origin of such disintegration of the self to an attempted defense against shattering and repetitive trauma, entailing the collapse of memory and profound fragmentation of linguistic cognition.[72] As Andrea Dworkin put the problem:

The formal writing problem, frankly, is that the bait can't write the story.... I barely know any words for what happened to me yesterday, which doesn't make tomorrow something I can conceive of in my own mind; I mean words I say to

70. Similar dynamics have been depressingly detected by incest survivors seeking help from male therapists. *See* HERMAN, *supra* note 15, at 186–187. Herman reports the account of one survivor:

When I began trying to find help, it was the beginning of a bitter education in human failings. As I went from therapist to therapist, it became terribly clear that the supposedly dispassionate professionals seemed just as titillated by my story of incestuous involvement with my father as my father had been excited by the actual experience with me.

Id. at 186 (quoting SANDRA BUTLER, THE CONSPIRACY OF SILENCE: THE TRAUMA OF INCEST 170 (1978)).

71. *See* Colin A. Ross et al., *Dissociation and Abuse Among Multiple-Personality Patients, Prostitutes, and Exotic Dancers*, 41 HOSP. & COMM. PSYCHIATRY 328 (1990) (significant incidence of psychogenic amnesia, multiple personality disorder, clinical depression and borderline personality disorder among prostituted women and "dancers." Nineteen percent of sample of persons affected by multiple personality disorder had been prostituted).

72. *See* James A. Chu & Diana L. Dill, *Dissociative Symptoms in Relation to Childhood Physical and Sexual Abuse*, 147 AMER. J. OF PSYCHIATRY 887 (1990); Frank Putnam et al., *The Clinical Phenomenology of Multiple Personality Disorder: Review of 100 Recent Cases*, 47 J. CLIN. PSYCHIATRY 285 (1986). *See generally* JUDITH LEWIS HERMAN, TRAUMA AND RECOVERY (1992).

myself in own head; not social words you use to explain to someone else. I barely know anything and if I deviate I am lost; I have to be literal, if I can remember, which mostly I cannot.73

For those women able to speak, whether a woman feels she is entitled to speak "as a prostitute" is also a complex question. Some women take on the label as a shield, so that other people can't use it as a weapon. A woman who had for a period of time performed in pornographic films and as stripper reports: "Within a month, I did my first job as a whore... It was quicker, it was more money, and it was definite. I felt like: 'Okay, now, I am a whore and if anyone calls me that they are right.'"74 Or one is not a "real prostitute" if the men don't seem like strangers, or if the financial arrangement is indefinite, or if the woman doesn't care for the sex:

I never called myself a prostitute; I never called myself a porno actress either. I was a filmmaker. I didn't work the streets, I didn't work every day, my customers were repeats, referrals. I called them my friends... it was an easy lie. They didn't pay me, I would tell myself; they helped me out with my rent and bills and they would land me film jobs. And I liked them; you're never a prostitute when you like them. Besides, I was a lesbian, and I was experimenting, and it was safe. I could get out or stop anytime I wanted. . . . I was on top.75

73. ANDREA DWORKIN, MERCY 229, 231 (1990). Primo Levi counts among the silences, at the core of our knowledge of the conditions of torture in the Nazi concentration camps, the accounts of the most deeply victimized. "At a distance of years one can today definitely affirm that the history of the Lagers has been written almost exclusively by those who, like myself, never fathomed them to the bottom. Those who did so did not return, or their capacity for observation was paralyzed by suffering and incomprehension." PRIMO LEVI, THE DROWNED AND THE SAVED 17 (1986).

74. Eva Rosta, *Comment, in* A VINDICATION OF THE RIGHTS OF WHORES 144, 145 (Gail Pheterson ed., 1989).

75. Sharon Kaiser, *Coming Out of Denial, in* SEX WORK: WRITINGS BY WOMEN IN THE SEX INDUSTRY 104, 105 (Frederique Delacoste & Priscilla Alexander eds., 1987). Another woman who had worked as a topless dancer expressed similar ambivalence, doubting her credentials to submit a piece for publication in the same anthology:

Maybe my experiences weren't really "sex industry." I couldn't waste people's time with my writing because what I had done was too "tame" to be legitimate. And anyway, my experience didn't really count because I was a college student; I wasn't tied to it; I was really above it all, not part of it.

Judy Helfand, *Silence Again, in id.* at 99.

Or as one woman, addicted to heroin, states:

Yeah, I've turned tricks, but I don't consider myself a prostitute. I always got pretty embarrassed about it. I'd tell the guy, "Hey man, I'm not really into this, but I really do need the money."[76]

Complying to the sex may be, for the woman, only a last ditch method of getting money, or only one of many strategies for survival.[77] Or the distinction between prostitution and any other "work" may seem, at least at the beginning, wholly artificial and illusory. One isn't a prostitute if everyone else is, too. "When I was nineteen years old I made what seemed like a conscious decision to become a prostitute. Having experienced sexual harassment on the job, in the streets, and in virtually every area of life, it was not a particularly fantastic leap to take."[78] "No trick ever broke my ribs like my husband did."[79] This ordeal of self-definition, though, is also avoidable by anticipatory defense: "I had considered myself a whore from the time I had become sexually active, even before I became sexually active. From that time on, I had thought of myself as a whore, and it was like well, I'm gonna make money at it."[80]

In our political critiques of prostitution, we have less acknowledged these equivocations than reified them, within an array of contending advocacy positions. The tones of doubt, reflection, bravado, defensiveness, and inevitability these women express about "being prostitutes" have been dispersed and frozen politically, in the competing terms of a political debate over what the experience of prostitution really is. Uniting the visions of these advocates is a shared assumption that the particular case of prostitution can be assimilated into the general case of "women's oppression" as feminism has heretofore elaborated that condition. Each coalition of advocates has seized a different version of our "other woman" representations, and claims it as the salient description of *prostitution*, as well. If "other women" seek to split from prostitution by disidentifying

76. Marsha Rosenbaum, *Work and the Addicted Prostitute, in* JUDGE, LAWYER, VICTIM, THIEF, *supra* note 49, at 131, 148.

77. As one woman told me: "I didn't think I would ever have to actually fuck them. I thought I could just rob them."

78. Donna Marie Niles, *Confessions of a Priestesstute, in* SEX WORK, *supra* note 75, at 148. Niles ultimately left prostitution, stating that "I simply no longer could justify working in an industry that profited from the sexual objectification of women." *Id.* at 149.

79. Phyllis Luman Metal, *One for Ripley's, in* SEX WORK, *supra* note 75, at 119, 120.

80. Priscilla Alexander, *Interview with Nell, in* SEX WORK, *supra* note 75, at 53, 55.

from one element of it, prostitute advocates have sought to identify *as* "other women" by identifying *with* one of the "not a prostitute" stories. Prostitutes thereby can "become" other women; prostitution is positioned as but one variant of a condition shared in common with those others. If other women aren't prostitutes, neither are prostitutes. On *all* of the contending perspectives, prostitution *is* "like everything else." The dispute turns on what the "else" is characterized to be.

The most publicly visible of these positions is that advanced by prostitutes' rights organizations, who promote political demands for affirmative legal and social rights for women to practice prostitution.[81] These advocates advance this view under principles familiar from mainstream liberal feminism: the fostering of women's individual autonomy and sexual self-expression. In this normative emphasis, these campaigns follow themes familiar in mainstream feminist anti-rape work. The manifesto of the International Committee on Prostitutes' Rights, for example, states that it *"affirms the right of all women to determine their own sexual behavior, including commercial exchange, without stigmatization or punishment."*[82] The strong version of this argument asserts that prostitution is a sexually progressive practice for women, yielding women both useful rewards in return for the sex we otherwise forfeit for no discernible benefit, and, for some women, a context for the felt exercise of control and power in sexual transactions. The weaker version, less committed to wholesale endorsement of prostitution as a practice of sexual freedom for women, urges the decriminalization and social acceptance of prostitution consistent with the feminist program of state deregulation of women's sexual behavior: If no means no, yes should mean yes under whatever conditions a woman chooses. Voluntariness may be inferred from ordinary indicia of age and capacity, confirmed in the receipt of cash.

Challenging this account, that frames prostitution as no different from other forms of private, consensual sex, are the data suggesting that prostitution entails significantly greater risks to prostituted women than those faced by sexually active, "other women." Those risks include contracting

---

81. Those organizations include Call Off Your Old Tired Ethics (COYOTE), founded in 1973 by Margo St. James, the National Task Force on Prostitution (NTFP), and the International Committee for Prostitutes' Rights (ICPR). *See* A VINDICATION OF THE RIGHTS OF WHORES, *supra* note 74, at 33–51 (on the organization of the ICPR); *COYOTE/National Task Force on Prostitution, in* SEX WORK , *supra* note 75, *at* 290 (organizing and policy statement of COYOTE); *id.* at 305 (charter of ICPR and statements from conferences).

82. *International Committee for Prostitutes' Rights World Chapter and World Whores' Congress Statements, in* SEX WORK, *supra* note 75, at 305, 310.

venereal disease, drug abuse, and being targeted for criminal victimization by sexual assault, battery, and incest. Pro-prostitution advocates, in response, question whether these risks are not similarly posed for or by "other women." For example, data on the incidence of venereal diseases among prostitutes does not support the inference that prostitution contributes substantially to the spread of those diseases in the general population.[83] Consequently, it is no more medically risky to have sex with a prostituted woman than with an "other woman." More problematic is the link between prostitution and criminal victimization. As the statistics on the incidence of violence against prostitutes continues to mount, it seems incontrovertible that prostituted women are disproportionately targeted for violent crime. The most detailed of those investigations is Mimi Silberts's analysis of victimization rates among 200 street prostitutes in San Francisco. Silbert summarizes her findings on the incidence of prostitute victimization by johns:

Of the subjects, 78% reported being victimized by forced perversion an average of 16.6 times each woman. Also, 70% were victimized by customer rape or clients similarly going beyond the prostitution contract, an average of 31.3 times. Of the subjects, 41% were victimized in some other way, and average of 2.6 times (e.g., forced into sex for no pay with police, being beaten by police, being beaten by other prostitutes). Additionally, 65% of the prostitutes were physically abused and beaten by customers, an average of 4.3 times. More than three-fourths of the victims stated there was nothing they could do about customer abuse; only 1% mentioned reporting to the police.[84]

These data are consistent with other studies finding high sexual and physical victimization rates among woman engaged in prostitution in its various milieus, inflicted by pimps, other women, and strangers other than johns.[85]

83. *See, e.g.*, Pasqua Scibelli, *Empowering Prostitutes: A Proposal for International Reform*, 10 HARV. WOMEN'S L. J. 117, 129–131 (1987) (assembling data on incidence of AIDS, syphilis, and gonorrhea among prostitutes).

84. Mimi H. Silbert & Ayala M. Pines, *Occupational Hazards of Street Prostitutes*, 8 CRIM. JUST. & BEHAV. 395, 397 (1981).

85. *See supra* notes 55–69 and accompanying text (on murder); ENABLERS, JUVENILE PROSTITUTION IN MINNESOTA: THE REPORT OF A RESEARCH PROJECT 70, 75 (1978) [hereinafter ENABLERS] (more than half of girls beaten by pimps; 20% report constant or regular beatings); (40% beaten by johns; 28% three or more times); MILLER, *supra* note 44, at 138; ROBERTA PERKINS & GARRY BENNETT, BEING A PROSTITUTE: PROSTITUTE WOMEN AND PROSTITUTE MEN 238–41, 295–96 (1985) (33.99% of women raped while engaging in prostitution); A VINDICATION OF THE RIGHTS OF WHORES, *supra* note 74, at 161–68 (routine violence reported

Prostitution proponents contend, however, that these data show merely that prostitutes face the same risks of sexual violence that other women do. For example, Barbara Milman queries: "The prostitute who is regularly beaten by her pimp is, like a battered wife, certainly the victim of violent crime. But is she a victim of prostitution?"[86] The astronomical incidence of drug dependency among women in prostitution[87] is similarly dispatched as accidental to the woman's situation as a prostitute.[88] The correlation between childhood sexual abuse, especially incest, and prostitution is less readily suppressed. The prevalence statistics suggest very high rates of incestuous sexual abuse, physical harm, and emotional brutalization in prostituted women's childhood histories.[89] These data are typically addressed, however, only in analyses of juvenile prostitution. Eleanor Miller's otherwise astute and detailed interviews with a sample of Milwaukee "street women" failed to include questions related to incest until she began to note the high rates of unsolicited disclosure of incestuous sexual abuse from her subjects.[90] The empirical assumption appears to be that the effects of child abuse simply wither away when a girl turns eighteen. In sum, insofar as women in prostitution share the

by ICPR conference attendants); WEISBERG, *supra* note 43, at 108–110 (with few exceptions, girls reported that any pimp would beat a prostitute given "provocation;" more than half of girls and women beaten regularly or constantly by pimps; rape by "non-customers" common and extremely violent).

86. Barbara Milman, *New Rules for the Oldest Profession: Should We Change Our Prostitution Laws?* 3 HARV. WOM. L. J. 1, 33 (1980).

87. For incidence rates of drug use and addiction, *see* Mimi H. Silbert et al., *Substance Abuse and Prostitution*, 14 J. PSYCHOACTIVE DRUGS 193 (1982); WEISBERG, *supra* note 43, at 99–100; PERKINS & BENNETT, *supra* note 85, at 241–42 (estimating 70–75% of women drug users).

88. *See* Milman, *supra* note 86, at 25 ("[T]he literature suggests that drug addiction and prostitution are probably not causally related to each other."); Scibelli, *supra* note 83, at 128; MILLER, *supra* note 44, at 108 (few women in her study "describe substance abuse as the thing that caused them to be involved in deviant street networks").

89. For rates of incest, *see* ENABLERS, *supra* note 85, at 22–23 (31% of respondents reported incestuous abuse); WEISBERG, *supra* note 43, at 91–92 (66% of women sexually abused by fathers or father figures, including stepfathers, foster fathers, or mothers' common law husbands) (citing SILBERT, *supra* note 51, at 85 (1980)). For sexual abuse by others, see Jennifer James & Jane Meyerding, *Early Sexual Experience and Prostitution*, 134 AMER. J. PSYCHOL. 38 (65% of respondents had been raped; 85% of those occurred when victim was under 15); Mimi Silbert & Ayala Pines, *Entrance Into Prostitution*, 13 YOUTH & SOC'Y 471, 479 (1982) (60–70% of women in prostitution sexually abused as children).

90. MILLER, *supra* note 44, at 114–15.

wounds of all women, by disease, by rape, by battery, by drug abuse, by incest, prostitution is effaced as a cause or consequence of them.

A second group of prostitute advocates, who identify with the socialist feminist tradition, take strong issue with the assimilation of the sex of prostitution, with non-commercial consensual sex, as urged by the liberal faction. For what woman and girls are enacting in prostitution is not their "self determining sexuality," but paid sexual compliance to the demands of a consumer. Accordingly, prostitution is reconceptualized by socialist feminist advocates as a form of work, rather than as sexual self-expression. Thus, Rachel West, a spokeswomen for the United States Prostitutes Collective, emphatically severs the connection drawn by prostitutes rights organizations between prostitution, and a woman's experience of sexuality. "Prostitution is about money, not about sex."[91] This account seeks to place prostitution squarely in the public realm of commerce and exchange as organized under capitalism, split conceptually and experientially from sex as an expression of personal, emotional, private identity.

The institutional, economic organization of prostitution reinforces this claim. One report asserts that 40 million dollars *per day* is spent on prostitution in the United States,[92] while in 1978, the French Ministry of the Interior reported that pimping and procuring constituted that country's third largest business, generating seven billion dollars in annual profit.[93] A 1986 report on prostitution commissioned by the United Nations Educational, Scientific and Cultural Organization concluded that some nations foster prostitution as a fruitful development strategy, elevating private economic incentive to the level of state fiscal policy. Distinguishing such "promotional" governments, from those states which benefit from prostitution more passively, the report explains:

In certain parts of the world, however, prostitution is not a consequence of the national income but a 'planned' and 'institutionalized' part of it. In certain countries in South-East Asia and Europe, the existence of mass prostitution and the structure of the market, which makes use of the media, airlines, hotel chains, international communications and the banks, mean that it

---

91. Rachel West, *U.S. PROStitutes Collective, in* SEX WORK, *supra* note 75, at 279, 283.

92. *See* CAROLE PATEMAN, THE SEXUAL CONTRACT 190 (1988) (citing SAN FRANCISCO EXAMINER (Feb. 3, 1985)).

93. This figure is reported in SISTERHOOD IS GLOBAL 226–27 (Robin Morgan ed., 1984). *See also* Kathleen Barry, *The Underground Economic System of Pimping,* 35 J. INT'L AFF. 117 (1981).

could neither exist nor develop without the tacit or implicit agreement of the institutions.[94]

Despite the magnitude of the demand for prostitution, most prostituted women and girls are poor. D. Kelly Weisberg's study of adolescent prostitution concludes that "[m]ost street walkers are constantly on the edge of financial crisis."[95] The 1990 annual report of one prostitute support program states that 90% of the women in the program had been transient for an average of six years,[96] while 88% of the women who participated in Mimi Silbert's study "described themselves as poor."[97] Kim Romanesko and Eleanor Miller's study of street women in Milwaukee found: "[A]lthough women do make a great deal of money from their work as street hustlers, they personally derive little benefit from the wealth they create."[98] The authors conclude generally that women and girls in prostitution suffer even greater economic marginalization as a consequence of their involvement in prostitution than in the "licit" market where they were already marginalized as workers.[99]

The reform agenda advanced by advocates committed to the "prostitution as work" position accordingly gives priority to placing "ownership" control over prostitution in the women themselves, to the ends of greater economic empowerment and improved working conditions. Women's economic disempowerment in prostitution, it is argued, is a consequence of the pervasiveness of economic exploitation of women in the practice by "third party" pimps, massage parlors, brothels and outcall services. Like other "owners," these actors appropriate percentages of 50–100% of the cash taken in by the women, either in exchange for facilities, promises of protection, displays of affection, or through simple brutality or its threat.[100]

94. UNESCO, DIVISION OF HUMAN RIGHTS AND PEACE, *Final Report: International Meeting of Experts on the Social and Cultural Causes of Prostitution and Strategies for the Struggle Against Procuring and the Sexual Exploitation of Women*, SHS-85/Conf. 608/14, 7 (1986).

95. WEISBERG, *supra* note 43, at 112–113.

96. COUNCIL FOR PROSTITUTION ALTERNATIVES (PORTLAND, OREGON), ANNUAL REPORT 2 (1990) (data based on case histories of 72 women).

97. Silbert & Pines, *Occupational Hazards*, *supra* note 84, at 396.

98. Kim Romanesko & Eleanor Miller, *The Second Step in Double Jeopardy: Appropriating the Labor of Female Hustlers*, 35 CRIME AND DELINQUENCY 109, 131 (1989).

99. *Id.* at 109–10.

100. *Id.* at 116–19, 123–128

Further, the economic interest of these actors in rationalizing the prostitution transaction itself has increasingly proletarianized prostitution as a labor practice over the last century. As Rachel West points out, especially in highly regulated, stated licensed prostitution, the practice is organized both for the john and for the woman into "assembly line" systems, each behavior sought by the john broken down into commodified units, each with a predetermined value.[101] From the point of view of the john, the woman so "assembled" as product is apotheosized in pornography.

Fundamentally, though, the "money not sex" critique avoids the questions of *what* the woman is selling, and the john buying, in the prostitution transaction. The particular social interaction between prostitute and john, that produces prostitution as a commodity, is never addressed. The issue of gender is also suppressed, in regard to both the pimp/prostitute relationship and the john/prostitute relationship. The fact that both are typically male/female arrangements, both economizing the prostitute's identity as a "sexed female," huddles silently, inarticulable within an analysis rigorously distinguishing "sex" from "work." And, for the woman used in this transaction, neither the money nor the sex may translate readily as anything genuinely her own. With respect to both, she remains a stranger, neither worker nor erotic partner. As K.C. Reed once said to me, "I could never make it feel like a job, not once. I would go to COYOTE meetings; they would tell me it was a job. I would try to make it feel like a job. I felt like a failure, again. I couldn't make it feel like a job, when they were telling me it was." Evelina Giobbe reports, based on her oral history research among women with histories in prostitution, survivors have "testified repeatedly that they did not experience prostitution as a career."[102]

Devoted to making visible that experience is a third group of advocates, comprised of a loose collective of prostitute advocacy groups, prostitution survivors and academic activists, commonly umbrellaed under the label "radical feminist."[103] These advocates, including myself, have pursued an analysis of prostitution that severs, not the sex from the money, but the john from the prostitute. This analysis

101. *See* Rachel West, *U.S. PROStitutes Collectives, in* Sex Work, *supra* note 75, at 279.

102. Giobbe, *supra* note 1, at 68.

103. For a rough-cut sampling of the organizations and individuals who have aligned themselves with this position, see Margaret A.Baldwin, *Pornography and the Traffic in Women,* 1 Yale J. L. & Feminism 111, 116 (1989) (listing amici supporting radical feminist position on prostitution in pornography litigation).

conceives of the prostitution transaction as one in which, even if both parties are present, they are not to each other. Rather, each is viewed as experiencing the transaction fundamentally differently, and that difference is the focus of description and critique. On this account, the prostitute is present to the john literally and solely as a thing that produces an experience of sex for him, as he wishes it. As both "owner" and "consumer" of the transaction, the john dominates both economically and sexually.[104]

Basic to the john's sexual experience is eroticized disregard of the woman. Developing Hanna Olsen's description of the sex of prostitution as "masturbation in a woman's body," Kathleen Barry details the john's sexual agenda as the reduction of a woman to "body parts separated from the self and the woman's sexual experience. . . . This experience constitutes an essentially noninteractive, non-mutual sexual experience which establishes the basis for further demands of perversions and violence in the exchange."[105] Timothy Beneke refers to this sexual process as "pornographizing," whereby "one anonymizes the woman and fails to acknowledge her moral, spiritual or emotional being. One relates to her as a thing without a soul. The woman as a locus of experience is denied."[106] The transfer of money from the john to the prostitute, on this view of his sexual interest, confirms and celebrates his entitlement to treat the woman this way (any way his wishes). As Susanne Kappeler has observed, the transfer confirms his dominance, his power to control the value, the meaning, the script of the "exchange": "It is the one with the surplus (capital) who decides what is 'like for like,' who fixes the price according to his demand. He decides what to buy, and what is a commodity. He writes the possible scenarios, and determines how they are viewed."[107] Among those possible scenarios are the rapes, the lacerations, the murders prostituted women face in every encounter—whatever a john might have in mind for a woman whose status as human is for him to determine. That is the sexual authority men buy in prostitution: to fix the meaning of who or what a woman *is*. "This woman wants nothing,

---

104. *See* Kathleen Barry, *Social Etiology of Crimes Against Women*, 10 VICTIMOLOGY 164, 171 (1985) (quoting Hanna Olsen).

105. *Id.* at 172.

106. TIMOTHY BENEKE, MEN ON RAPE 23–24 (1982). *See also* Steven Katz, *Desire and Expectation in the Law of Forcible Rape*, 26 San Diego L. Rev. 21, 620 (1989) ("pornographizing" of women predicates men's felt entitlement to rape).

107. SUSANNE KAPPELER, THE PORNOGRAPHY OF REPRESENTATION 159 (1986).

asks nothing, needs nothing. I don't need to please her or be concerned about whether she's enjoying it. I can do what I want and please myself."[108]

For the woman, much different meanings accrue to the money, and the sex, in the prostitution transaction. Women may experience deep ambivalence regarding their right to benefit from money received in prostitution which they nominally control, even absent direct economic exploitation by third parties.[109] Eleanor Miller's study of street woman in Milwaukee indicates that, for many women, the cash has a particular meaning as "fast money": as dead, as useless , as phony, as demeaning to hold, as the trick.[110] Moreover, life in prostitution is simply expensive: the cost of transience is very high in lodging, food, and the need for constant replacement of necessities. If the cash is never quite hers, neither, exactly, is the sex. The sex is done to her, on her, in her; certainly never *with* her. Renditions of women's experience of the sex of prostitution, on these advocates' accounts, commonly proceed by way of flat, objective description of the acts performed by the woman at the man's express or implied behest. Andrea Dworkin's narrative summaries of the content of pornography capture the tone;[111] K.C. Reed's story of one night in prostitution speaks in the same voice. This narrative style conveys the woman's utter irrelevance to what happens, how it happens, why it happens, much less her subjective response to the encounter.

Yet for these advocates, too, who have devoted the closest attention of all prostitution advocates to comprehending the process and consequences of the transaction to the woman, the point lies principally elsewhere. The principal explanatory emphasis urged by radical feminist advocates goes to the "why did she stay" question applied to prostitution. In common with the representational strategies advanced on behalf of battered women, these advocates stress the significance of the incest, seasoning by pimps, battery, rape, humiliation, and torture conceded by all as the preconditions and conditions of life for vast numbers of women and girls involved in the practice. The direction of this work was charted by Kathleen Barry's groundbreaking investigations of domestic and international trafficking in women for prostitution, which she theorizes as practices of

---

108. LEWIS DIANA, THE PROSTITUTE AND HER CLIENTS: YOUR PLEASURE IS HER BUSINESS 191 (1985).

109. *See* BARRY, *supra* note 2, at 135–36.

110. MILLER, *supra* note 44, at 139–40 ("The women always corrected me when I asked if there was 'good money to be made on the streets. They said that there was, rather, fast money.").

111. *See* DWORKIN, *supra* note 47, *passim*.

female sexual slavery.[112] Barry identifies as a key feature of forced prostitution the dynamics of traumatic intimacy, now familiar from feminist accounts of domestic battery.[113] Here, the pimp stands in the role of the controlling, battering, cajoling husband, a continuity, as I noted earlier, often seized upon by (non-pimping) husbands as they shout "you slut" at their bewildered wives. The woman's prostitution adds but another means by which he can humiliate and injure her, with the added boot of a profit.

The overwhelming incidence of incest in the life histories of women in prostitution expands this basic framework for understanding "why she stayed." Among radical prostitution advocates, incest is understood as a way of seasoning a girl to prostitution, a practice of a father pimping his daughter to himself: isolating her in silence, from recognition or help, imposing as a condition of survival her sexual compliance, and delivering the deal in the names of love and protection. On this view, incest is less a precondition of prostitution, than a practice of it. The common self-identification of incest victims as "whores" noted by Judith Herman,[114] and the "traumatic sexualization" suffered by them theorized by David Finkelhor,[115] traces the continuity symptomatically. Like the battering husband, the father rapist who calls his daughter a "slut" is missing the obvious point: that he is a pimp, turning his daughter out first to himself and later, if passively, to others. For the girl, "[o]nce in prostitution, both pimps and johns replicate the abuse these girls endured in their families."[116] Johns purport to "turn child sexual abuse and rape into a job by throwing money at their victims."[117]

I honor this story, because it acknowledges and respects women's pain. It knows the murdered women are out there, stuffed in garbage cans, floating in rivers, tossed by the roadside, because a john chose not to believe she was alive in the first place, or because killing her was his idea of a good time. It knows that the incest, the neglect, the beatings, the betrayals, have real and deep consequences. It knows, too, that these women are the least likely to be recognized as injured, ever, because everyone is too busy fantasizing them, beyond the pale of suffering or empathy.

The argumentative rejoinder is obvious, and, as I have already explored, often lodged by advocates of the opposing positions: all of this

---

112. *See* BARRY, *supra* note 2, at 77–79.
113. *See supra* notes 31–34 and accompanying text.
114. *See* HERMAN, *supra* note 15.
115. *See* Finkelhor et al., *supra* note 16.
116. Evelina Giobbe, *The Vox Fights*, VOX MAGAZINE 29, 33 (Winter 1991).
117. Giobbe, *supra* note 1, at 3.

torture, humiliation, exploitation may happen, and be truly terrible, but what does it have to do with prostitution? Are not the incest, the beatings, the rapes (on and on) but "ancillary" to prostitution, itself? Doesn't the radical feminist critique merely restate, if rather more grimly, the point made by all of these advocates: that prostitutes *are* "other women," and prostitution, *per se*, therefore unremarkable? And they would be right, as right as each of the advocacy groups is in making the identical criticism of each of the others. *For the purpose of each of these positions is to erase prostitution as a distinctive experience in women's lives, and to merge it with a pre-existing account of other forms of oppression.* Each of us more apt to savor this point in criticism of our opponents, than reflect on its implications for ourselves, or for what it means for advancing this debate. The measure of success we each set for our own accounts of prostitution is the ease with which our "other woman" story can swallow it whole. This same measure of success is, in turn, the measure of failure we use to castigate the failings of our opponents. The more persuasively we argue the continuity of our accounts of prostitution with our renditions of "other women's" life conditions, the more vulnerable we are to the charge that we have failed to grasp the specificity, the "reality," of "prostitution itself."

The genuine rejoinder to the entire debate is this: why is it that none of us—prostituted women or women like me who have worked for years with women in prostitution—can speak very long or clearly about what *does* make prostitution different from what "other women" experience? Among prostituted women, that difference is felt as real, as crucial, and as nearly inexpressible. Part of the difference is the totality of the abuse that comes from nearly everyone in the woman's life. Not one man, or three, but thousands; and not only johns, but dads, brothers, pimps, police, boyfriends; also women, including moms, other prostitutes, straight women. And it goes on and on: beginning in childhood, ending too often in prison, disability, early death. The intensity of the humiliation is nearly unendurable for many women; no one wants to talk about what actually goes on during those hundreds of blow jobs in cars. Would you? And each of the advocacy positions at least gives prostitutes ground for dignity. Pro-prostitution advocates insist that prostituted women no longer need to justify themselves to anyone; "worker" advocates distinguish who prostitutes are from the "work" they perform; radical advocates give voice to what came before prostitution in their lives. For many women, there is more comfort here, than in telling women who may not even want to hear, what really happens.

And in the larger movement, the "true" question in contest in the prostitution debate is also not really prostitution at all. The struggle over prostitution, as it is presently argued, is a bid by each tendency in feminism for territory largely ceded to the others by each before prostitution entered the scene: a bid for a story of money by liberals, for a story of sex by socialists, and for a story of strange men by radicals. Some factions within liberal feminism, for example, express enthusiasm for the liberal and socialist advocates' position on prostitution, because those advocates help shore liberal defenses of choice and privacy against radical feminist critique. Those of us who identify as radical feminists, in turn, look for leverage in our critiques of liberal theories of consent in the display of our prostitutes, whose stories we consume with satisfaction until we move on to the next workshop. Feminists of post-modern sensibility may marvel at the complexities, how "prostitution" can mean so many things, and, as they would argue, the more prolific the discursive possibilities, the freer we know we are. In all of this, we cast ourselves in the role of the john: It could be any way. This is how I want it. (And if we can have it lots of ways, so much the better.)

The real struggle, most days, seems far from these debates—getting some money together for prostitution support programs; calling to see if there is one more space at the "good" juvenile detention center for another 15 year-old; seeing the look on a woman's face which says that she will be calling tomorrow, or next year, to tell you about the prostitution; overcoming in myself again and again the flicker of despair just before I hear what I will hear when she calls. (Will it be *worse*? How *can* it be worse?). Afterwards, losing some of the women and knowing it may be permanent. The "larger movement" at these times seems scarcely to exist, the "prostitution debate" of little aid in meeting these women's needs or in gaining further clarity for myself or them or how, ever, to get them met.

Sometimes these moments occur at feminist meetings. These are moments with "other women" who don't believe in the stories we tell about them, either: the woman whose father gave her money, maybe a lot of it; the woman who "stayed" because she wanted to prove she could beat him back; the woman who cuts herself after a couple of drinks; all the stories that don't quite fit the "other woman" stories we tell. There are "other women," too, who see how close they were, or are, to being prostituted; who were prostituted, and could never talk about it to anyone. All the "you whore! you slut!" stories wanting to be told. The pressure to speak, the pressure not to speak, is enormous. There is a fear of the boundaries eroding, and a fear of the boundaries not eroding.

What is lost in the prostitution debate, as we are all asked to justify the lives of prostitutes as just like those of other women, is what other women need to learn and know and appreciate and politicize about the conditions of their own existence *from* women in prostitution. That is the fundamental condition of consciousness-raising that has been forfeited by the larger movement: that women in prostitution have insight and knowledge that other women need to make sense of their *own* lives. The continued silence, the shame, the elevation of theorizing over action stifling the participation of woman in prostitution in our movement is supported by a political climate that wants prostitutes only to ask permission to join, not authority to direct. "Other women" don't want to hear, perhaps, that our boyfriends and husbands are buying sex from women in prostitution. "Other women" don't want hear, perhaps, that the "straight" jobs we have are sexualized top to bottom. "Other women" don't want to hear, perhaps, that we are each one man from the street. But if our stories are to gain in boldness and integrity, we all need to be able to hear all of that, and to find the "point to it."

I am not about to say, as you may think I am about to say, that "all women are prostitutes." That is a glib and silly, nearly insulting, thing to say (I mean, insulting to women in prostitution). There is a theme, though, that obviously links all of these stories. That is the story that *no one is a prostitute*, recited with the utmost conviction, or with the passion of a final plea for help and justice. And perhaps *that* is the story that is the prostitution story itself: a woman declaring, with equal parts conviction and resignation, that she is not a prostitute, to please somebody else upon whom her survival depends.

[III. UNTITLED]

There is one more prostitution story I want to tell you. This is it:

There you are, in a dump that's more or less clean, holding a towel in you hand, looking at somebody you've never seen before. The more you retreat, the more he advances; since the room is fairly cramped, you soon find yourself with your back against the wall. The guy's arms are around you, they're all over your body like slimy tentacles that grope you, strip you, and drag you down as he pulls you over the bed . . .

For an instant, you escape from the nightmare:

you are back in the church playground, playing hopscotch. It seems like yesterday. You almost feel good, and you shut your eyes to make the dream last. When you reopen them, after a split second, reality blinds you.
 Reality has take the form of a cock, a real family man's wiener, a little soft but still enterprising.[118]

118. JEANNE CORDELIER, THE LIFE: MEMOIRS OF A FRENCH HOOKER 69–70 (1978), *quoted in* Kathleen Barry, *Prostitution, Sexual Violence, and*

This is not an isolated incident. It is a commonplace observation within prostitution support and advocacy circles that dissociative strategies of distancing the act, herself, and the john are routine tactics practiced by women in prostitution, described by Kathleen Barry as constructing a split self, between "that" woman performing an act of prostitution and her "other" self.[119] "Disengagement," Barry explains, "is the up-front strategy of women in prostitution."[120] Nor is this a costless tactic. The terrible psychic injury absorbed as a consequence of these survival tactics is recorded in the litany of "splitting" disturbances suffered by prostitutes.[121] As is becoming better known, similar strategies of disengagement, of "not being there," are also commonly employed by women and girls to avoid trauma in incest and rape.[122] The term "denial," I think, but weakly and perhaps misleadingly convey this experience. From the inside, the feeling is less one of repression than of being released to someplace *else*, anywhere else, where it feels better, or doesn't feel at all. "It's not happening, no, this *other* thing is happening." For women in prostitution, these other things may occur very frequently. Estimates of the frequency of sale of women in prostitution range from three or four to 80 tricks *a day*, over a course of days, months, or years.[123] These disengagement strategies, though, as Barry further points out, are not only

Victimization: Feminist Perspectives on Women's Human Rights 7–8 (1991) (unpublished manuscript).

119. Barry, *supra* note 104, at 171.

120. Barry, *supra* note 104, at 5. In the words of women Barry quotes:

Dia says: "I have to be a little stoned to go through with it. I have to shove my emotions completely to the side. I get talkative and don't give a shit." Elizabeth reports: "You switch off your feelings, you have to do it." Brita reports "I've taught myself to switch off, to shove my feelings away. I don't give a damn, as long as there's money. It doesn't have anything to do with feelings."

Id. Former prostitute Rosie Summers describes the sexual experiences of prostitution as "a [woman] turning off her emotions, being psychically someplace else while someone who despises her is making love to her." Rosie Summers, *Prostitution, in* SEX WORK, *supra* note 75, at 117–18.

121. *See supra* notes 71–73 and accompanying text.

122. *See, e.g.,* WOMEN'S RESEARCH CENTRE, RECOLLECTING OUR LIVES: WOMEN'S EXPERIENCE OF CHILDHOOD SEXUAL ABUSE (1989); ELIZABETH A. STANKO, INTIMATE INTRUSIONS: WOMEN'S EXPERIENCE OF MALE VIOLENCE (1985).

123. *See, e.g,* PERKINS & BENNETT, *supra* note 85, at 16 (Sydney, Australia sample averaged 40 to 50 johns per week); Matthew Freund et al., *Sexual Behavior of Resident Street Prostitutes with Their Clients in Camden, New Jersey,* 26 J. SEX RESEARCH 460, 465 (1989) (average of 4.13 johns per workday; 553 johns over a seven month period).

the last defenses of the used. "Disengagement" from her "real self" is the fundamental demand made of woman in prostitution, the essential term of the transaction itself. What a john wants is for the woman to *act* like the woman he wants, and for the woman to maintain a credible performance as part of the bargain. She is to act as if she *is* the role he wants her to play.[124] This dynamic plainly exceeds in complexity the description of prostitution as "objectified sex," understood as a wholly unselfconscious, unilateral act of sexual consumption. Rather, the demand made of the woman is to demonstrate a happy complicity, to whatever role is demanded.[125]

I would suggest that a similar demand, and a similar defensive strategy in the face of it, drives the design of our feminist advocacy. The disengagement tactic step, has, I hope, been demonstrated throughout this paper: whatever we are, wherever we are, it is not prostitution. It is love, or freedom, or work, or force, or fear; anything by prostitution. We can prove it by our arguments, over and over, from every possible angle that might be mustered in opposition. It is all a great mistake, and if no one else is convinced, we can at least convince ourselves. "I was never really into it." How many times a day do we turn this trick? How many years has feminism told this story, been "somewhere else" as a strategy of resisting what we are told we are?

And who are we talking to? Who is it, who cares so much, that we should care to convince? The men, it seems: the men who feel license to destroy us if we fail to convince them, the johns we hope at the risk of our lives will remember that we are human beings. We are not prostitutes, and hope we can act well enough to fit the part of not being one. The law, too, we hope to convince. Our stories of "consent," of "intimacy," have been crafted with the law in mind, placating its demand that we not "really" be sluts. We deliver the goods, compliantly, now in the name of a self-determining, liberated feminism. "It was good for me, too, honest."

My further intuition is that this is a structural political requirement, not only a problem of bad men, silly laws, or shortsighted feminism. My belief, also my fear, is that within the existing political and legal order, and the possibilities for change afforded some women, is embedded a profound bargain: take what you can, but it will always be at the price of abandoning prostitutes, of gaining your advantage of her expense. There is a term for

124. BARRY, *supra* note 104, at 6–7.
125. *See* Harold R. Holzman & Sharon Pines, *Buying Sex: The Phenomenology of Being a John*, DEVIANT BEHAVIOR 89, 108–109 (Oct.–Dec. 1982) (reporting that johns hope that prostitute will become an energetic participant in the john's fantasy).

women who accept bargains like that. It's called being pimp's "bottom woman," the one who treasures his highest regard, and sometimes gets off the street herself, but only if she helps run the less lucky girls. There is also a term for the arrangement that makes this bargain compelling. It's called pimping, period. If my intuition is correct, this is the arrangement women presently have with the state, motivating the "not a prostitute" content of our legal stories as a condition of our legal citizenship. My question for all of us, in love and struggle, is this: if I am right, in this intuition, do we love our pimp so much, after all? What stories would we tell, if not for him?

PART TWO

Liberalism and Prostitution

CHAPTER SIX

Porn Stars, Radical Feminists, Cops, and Outlaw Whores

The Battle Between Feminist Theory and Reality, Free Speech, and Free Spirits

NORMA JEAN ALMODOVAR

On a very warm summer evening in the San Fernando Valley, the golden California sun is about to dip below the horizon, leaving long spiraling trails of drifting orange and pink clouds to cover the darkening western sky. A slight breeze can be felt as the outside temperature drops to a more comfortable 89°, a welcome indication that darkness will bring even more relief from the day's record high of 104° in the shade.

Inside a one-story, four-bedroom, canary-yellow, California Ranch-style house on a nondescript street in the upper middle-class Los Angeles suburb designated "Encino," a slightly built but very busty blonde female is taking a shower. She's had a long day and the sweat from the heat and her sex partners has taken its toll on her and all she wants to do is collect her pay and get into her air-conditioned BMW, drive to Gelsons on Van Nuys to pick up a pint of Ben and Jerry's "Cherry Garcia" ice cream before driving to her upscale West Los Angeles apartment. The cool water erases the memories of the day's intense labor as it trickles down between her famous silicone-enhanced breasts, down her flat abs, between her legs, and on to her well-pedicured feet. In another bathroom on the other side of the house, one of her sex partners is also showering. He, too, is exhausted from the daylong session, which required a number of "money shots." For him, the end of the day promises a relaxing evening in the pool with his girlfriend and their three-year-old son, a T-bone steak grilled to perfection, and a few cold beers to unwind.

Now dressed and feeling much refreshed, he and the blonde, hereafter called Blonde A, enter the living room where they pick up their respective envelopes on the coffee table—containing their pay for the day's sexual activities.

Inside the one-story, four-bedroom, adobe-colored California Ranch-style house next door, a slightly built but very busty blonde female, hereafter called Blonde B, is taking a shower. She, also, had a long day and the sweat from the heat and her sex partners has taken its toll on her and all she wants to do is collect her pay and get into her air-conditioned BMW, drive to Gelsons on Van Nuys to pick up a pint of Ben and Jerry's "Cherry Garcia" ice cream and drive back to her Encino home. The cool water erases the memories of the day's intense labor as it trickles down between her silicone-enhanced breasts, down her flat abs, between her legs and on to her well-pedicured feet. In another bathroom on the other side of the house, one of her sex partners is also showering. He, too, is exhausted from the hour-long session. For him, the end of the day promises a T-bone steak grilled to perfection, a relaxing evening in the pool with his girlfriend and their three-year-old son, and a few cold beers to unwind.

Blonde B has already dressed and enters the living room as her partner joins her and places an envelope on the coffee table—containing her pay for the hour's sexual activities.

Suddenly the thunderous roar of a police helicopter directly overhead disturbs the quiet neighborhood, and the blare of sirens approaching pierces the serenity of the early evening calm. The first patrol car screeches to a stop in front of house B, just as Blonde A and her sex partner step outside to go to their cars. The other patrol cars pull up alongside the first until a caravan of black and white units completely block the street. Armed officers swarm out of the cars and surround house B, shotguns poised and ready for action. The powerful beam of light from the helicopter, focused on house B, turns the growing twilight into day. Inside, Blonde B and her male companion face each other, looking extremely perplexed. They go to the window to see what all the commotion is about—not knowing that they are the targets of the police activity outside.

The front door bursts open as it yields under the collective force of the cops and their weapons. The lead officer barks commands at the two to put their hands in the air. A female officer comes up behind the blonde and forces her to the floor with her baton. The lead officer again barks at the male and demands his name. Once given, the officer nods his head and signals that the man can leave. His hands nervously flailing about in midair, the man quickly runs out of the front door and flees into the night.

On the floor, Blonde B's hands are behind her back. She is not offering any resistance, but the female officer nevertheless has a gun drawn on the "suspect." Blonde B looks up at the lead officer and demands to know what she has done that she is being treated thus. The officer grabs the envelope stuffed with cash lying on the coffee table and waves it at her; his voice trembles with scorn, "You're under arrest for prostitution, you whore!"

Outside, Blonde A and her companion ask one of the armed officers milling about the yard of house B what is happening. "Got a whore living in there, ma'am. She was entertaining one of her 'johns' when we got a call from a neighbor telling us that there was an act of prostitution in progress!" The rest of the crew from house A gather outside to watch the action. The cameraman tightly clutches his video camera under his arm— after all, it is the only thing that differentiates the earlier sexual activity in house A from the criminal sexual activity in house B.

As the handcuffed Blonde B is escorted out of her house and shoved into the first patrol car parked in her driveway, Blonde A sighs. She is, of course, distressed to see her neighbor dragged off to jail—but at least *she* never has to worry about being arrested for prostitution, because she is exercising her First Amendment rights when she performs her sex acts for money— the Supreme Court of the United States said so.

Even though the incident above is fictional, the legal situation it describes is real. The 1988 California "People versus Freeman" decision,[1] which ostensibly legalized prostitution on camera, produced a division in the sex industry as it left outside the law those sex workers who did not have a camera and crew present to document their paid sexual performances.

The Freeman decision ostensibly disconnected prostitution and its ancillary activities, pandering and pimping, from making any adult material that was not obscene. Specifically, the court held, "[E]ven if Defendant's conduct could somehow be found to come within the definition of 'prostitution' literally, the application of the pandering statute to the hiring of actors to perform in the production of a non-obscene motion picture would impinge unconstitutionally on First Amendment values." According to P.J. Huffstutter, Times Staff Writer in an *LA Times* article, "To the California Supreme Court, ruling in Freeman's case, that definition meant that an adult filmmaker could hire actors and actresses to perform sexual acts as long as they were being recorded on film. In its 1988 decision, the California court said there is no evidence that Freeman paid the acting fees 'for the purpose of sexual arousal or gratification, his own or the

1. *People vs. Freeman*, 46 Cal.3d 419, 250 *Cal.Rptr.* 598, 758 p.2d 1128 (1988).

actors'.' Instead, he hired them simply to make a non-obscene movie—an act protected by the *First Amendment.*"[2]

To someone who does not know or understand the fine variances of the law,[3] paid acts of sex all look alike; if it looks like a duck, walks like a duck, and quacks like a duck, it must be a duck. It must be very puzzling

---

2. *Los Angeles Times,* January 12, 2003, *See No Evil* By P.J. Huffstutter, Times Staff.

3. Prostitution defined: "in that there is much disagreement on all sides on what constitutes prostitution, I will use the legal definitions from the California Penal Code; other states' legal definitions are similar although may be worded differently.

"CALIFORNIA PENAL CODE SECTION 647. Every person who commits any of the following acts is guilty of disorderly conduct (a) misdemeanor (b) who solicits or who agrees to engage in or who engages in any act of prostitution. A person agrees to engage in an act of prostitution *when, with specific intent to so engage, he or she manifests an acceptance of an offer or solicitation to so engage, regardless of whether the offer or solicitation was made by a person who also possessed the specific intent to engage in prostitution.* No agreement to engage in an act of prostitution shall constitute a violation of this subdivision unless some act, in addition to the agreement, is done within this state in furtherance of the commission of an act of prostitution by the person agreeing to engage in that act. As used in this subdivision, *"prostitution" includes any lewd [the touching of breasts, buttocks or genitals for the purpose of sexual gratification or arousal]? act between persons for money or other consideration.*653.20 (a) "Commit prostitution" means to engage in sexual conduct for money or other consideration, but does not include sexual conduct engaged in as a part of any stage performance, play, or other entertainment open to the public. (b) "Public place" means an area open to the public, or an alley, plaza, park, driveway, or parking lot, *or an automobile, whether moving or not,* or a building open to the general public. (c) "Loiter" means to delay or linger without a lawful purpose for being on the property and for the purpose of committing a crime as opportunity may be discovered. 653.22. (a) It is unlawful for any person to loiter in any public place *with the intent to commit prostitution.* This intent is evidenced by acting in a manner and under circumstances which openly demonstrate the purpose of inducing, enticing, or soliciting prostitution, or procuring another to commit prostitution.

PIMPING: 266h. (a) Except as provided in subdivision (b), any person who, knowing another person is a prostitute, lives or derives support or maintenance in whole or in part from the earnings or proceeds of the person's prostitution, or from money loaned or advanced to or charged against that person by any keeper or manager or inmate of a house or other place where prostitution is practiced or allowed, or who solicits or receives compensation for soliciting for the person, is guilty of pimping, a felony, and shall be punished by imprisonment in the state prison for three, four, or six years.

PANDERING: 266i. (a) Except as provided in subdivision (b) any person who does any of the following is guilty of pandering, a felony, and shall be punished by

to discover that our courts consider that the only thing that separates a crime from protected free speech is the intent or purpose of the individual orchestrating the acts of sex. In this case, if you can prove that *you* did not intend to get turned on, and that the sole purpose of paying for the acts of sex is to make money through the sale of your produced film, from others who ultimately will (hopefully) get turned on, then you are not exploiting the persons who are being paid to have sex.

However, to be protected speech, not only must there be a lack of intent to get turned on, but in most states there must also be a separation of time and space between those who are performing paid acts of sex and those who pay to get turned on. In its determination that regarding a [live] theatrical performance in Arizona,4 where two women fondled each other's breasts on stage, "the State could prosecute for prostitution a woman who, in the setting of a sexual theater, performed sexual acts upon other women for the gratification of customers who paid to watch, without having to prove obscenity;" STATE of Arizona versus TAYLOR [No. 1 CA-CR 88-927. November 6, 1990], the court said in reference to the California Freeman decision, "While the film [produced by Hal Freeman] might ultimately have induced sexual arousal or gratification in the hands of remote consumers, the performers were separated from such consumers by time and the distancing medium of film. Any question of illegal sexual arousal or gratification thus required a judgment concerning the nature of the film—a judgment indistinguishable from the question of obscenity".

And by reason of this intent, time and distance separation, paid sexual performers are transformed from prostitutes into actors, and all the

---

imprisonment in the state prison for three, four, or six years: (1) Procures another person for the purpose of prostitution.

(2) By promises, threats, violence, or by any device or scheme, causes, induces, persuades or *encourages* another person to become a prostitute.

4. STATE of Arizona, Appellee, vs. Laure TAYLOR, Appellant. No. 1 CA-CR 88-927. November 6, 1990. Defendant was convicted of four prostitution-related crimes before the Superior Court of Maricopa County, Cause No. CR-87-06582, Gregory H. Martin, J., and she appealed. The Court of Appeals, Fidel, J., held that State could prosecute the defendant for prostitution and avoid burden of proving obscenity, even though the defendant had, in the setting of a sexual theater, performed sexual acts upon other women for the gratification of customers who paid to watch. Affirmed.

A defendant's engaging in the fondling of another woman's breasts under a fee arrangement whereby undercover police detectives paid to watch the defendant and the other woman constituted "prostitution." A.R.S. 13-3211, subds. 5, 8, 9. Hmm...the detectives got to watch the show—and although they "paid" (the tax payers did the "paying") the money was confiscated as evidence and so the performance was free for the cops.

adjuvant State rationales cited in prohibiting prostitution become irrelevant. Again from the State of Arizona versus Taylor, "[the] State has legitimate interests in regulating prostitution unrelated to suppressing free speech; supporting rationales include preventing communicable disease, preventing sexual exploitation, and reducing assorted criminal misconduct that tends to cluster with prostitution. USCA Const.Amend. 1." The problem with these legislative/government rationales is that they are often intentionally vague and subjectively worded and don't appear to need facts or logic to support them. Surely the State realizes that regardless of *when* the induced sexual arousal or gratification occurs with the "remote consumers," the persons (performers, actors, etc.) engaging in multiple sex acts with a variety of partners are at risk of catching and spreading communicable diseases, particularly if they do not engage in safe sex practices. If preventing communicable diseases is truly a legitimate rationale for regulating [prohibiting] prostitution, it must also be for those who engage in the same type of sexual behavior in front of a camera. It does not seem to matter that in all the many, many reports from the health studies conducted on prostitutes, time and time again it is concluded that the amount of attributable STDs to prostitutes is negligible in proportion to the number of acts of sex involved.[5] If noone pays any attention to these reports, many written by the Centers for Disease Control, it is a waste of the taxpayer's money for the government to continue to pay for the research conducted by these health institutions.

The word "exploitation" is a subjective and condescending term, which when combined with "sexual" becomes a politically explosive concept promoted by radical feminists, legislators, and religious conservatives to denote what they consider to be the infantile mental capacity of those whom these groups have deemed to be the "exploited." Logically, it is not possible for a consenting adult who engages in the exact same behavior to be considered "exploited" in one situation and not the other. At least the radical feminists and religious conservatives are consistent in their argument that *all* porn and prostitution are "sexual exploitation," even if their argument is fallacious. If exploitation is inherent in prostitution, as is frequently claimed by state governments in their prohibition

5. *Oregon Law Review,* Vol. 55, 1976, p. 556: "The reporter's first argument for continued penal sanctions that prostitution is a significant factor in the spread of venereal disease, is contradicted by recent studies which show that prostitutes account for a very small percentage of those infected with gonorrhea or syphilis.... Dr. Charles Winnick... has stated 'We know from many different studies that the amount of VD attributable to prostitution is remaining fairly constant at a little under 5 percent, which is a negligible proportion compared to the amount of VD that we have...' "

rationales, how does this exploitation disappear in the presence of a camera? And what are these acts of "assorted criminal misconduct that tend to cluster with prostitution" and why do they disappear when time and distance separate the "remote consumer" from the performers? As we have learned from our prohibition experiment, almost all of the alleged acts of assorted criminal misconduct are a direct result of the criminalization of prostitution rather than the work itself, and such misconduct and ancillary crimes would disappear if consenting adult prostitution weren't against the law.

If the average person who looks at the behavior of a prostitute and a porn actor and cannot distinguish one from the other, believe me, the average prostitute cannot distinguish it either. It is incomprehensible that identical behavior is, in one set of circumstances, protected by the constitution, but in another set of circumstances can result in arrest, criminal prosecution and incarceration if those present at the scene of the paid sexual performance, whether or not participants, are sexually gratified or even *merely* aroused. All because it is spuriously alleged by those who make and enforce the law that the latter activity will always result in "sexual exploitation" regardless of the age, intellect, educational background, or consent of those who are "exploited."

As I mentioned previously, there are many radical feminists and others whose worldview allows no distinction between prostitution and pornography. These feminists, however, are not champions or defenders of decriminalizing prostitution for consenting adults—rather they make the astonishing claim that *all* pornography and prostitution are *"...incompatible with the dignity and worth of the human person and must be eliminated."*[6] What a terrifying thought for anyone who knows how draconian the current sentencing laws are for prostitution and its related activities and the dramatic increases in these penalties that would have to be legislated and enforced to accomplish this!

---

6. (From the 1995 United Nations Women's Conference in Beijing, China: Platform for Action, paragraph 225 [Violence against women both violates and impairs or nullifies the enjoyment by women of human rights and fundamental freedoms. There has been a long-standing failure to protect and promote these rights and freedoms in relation to violence against women. Gender-based violence and *all forms of* sexual harassment, *prostitution, pornography,* sexual slavery and exploitation, including those violations resulting from cultural prejudice, racism and racial discrimination, xenophobia, ethnic cleansing, religious and anti-religious extremism and international trafficking in women and children, *are incompatible with the dignity and worth of the human person and must be eliminated....*)

On their web site and in the literature distributed by the Amherst, MA-based Coalition Against Trafficking, it is stated:

"... We agree that pornography is violence against women, a mainstay of male power and female subjugation, and a practice of sex discrimination. ... It is important to make the connections, additionally, between pornography and prostitution. Pornography is actually a practice of prostitution. It is the sex of prostitution made public. Pornography can only be manufactured through the prostitution of women and children, i.e., through the buying and selling of the women and children who perform the sex of prostitution before cameras. The sex of pornography is the real sex of prostitution, only it is bought for public display and distribution. ... Sexual exploitation is a practice by which person(s) achieve sexual gratification or financial gain or advancement through the abuse of a person's sexuality by abrogating that person's human right to dignity, equality, autonomy, and physical and mental well-being. Sexual exploitation includes sexual harassment, rape, incest, battering, pornography and prostitution. ... All prostitution exploits women, regardless of women's consent."7

These patently subjective statements are the worst form of patronization there is, and it is clear that they lump together more than pornography and prostitution. In their minds, there is no difference between an

7. "China Executes a Woman for Running Prostitutes," March 2, 1999 (*Reuters*). Beijing: "China has executed a woman for running a prostitution racket in Beijing, the China News Service said on Tuesday. It said Ma Yulan, 41, ran 10 prostitutes from her restaurant and a hotel in 1996 and 1997 and was executed on Monday. All of Ma's assets were confiscated by the Beijing No.1 People's Intermediate Court, it said. It gave no more details. China handed down its first death sentence for prostitution in November under new criminal statutes approved by the National People's Congress, or parliament, last March." Prostitutes are beheaded in Iraq and other Muslim countries in an effort to stamp out or "eliminate" prostitution. Is this what these feminists have in mind for the rest of the world to achieve their goals?

"Cops Hit Suspected Valley Prostitution Dens," *Los Angeles Daily News*, June 25, 2003, By Ryan Oliver, Staff Writer: "In one of the LAPD's largest prostitution stings in several years, vice detectives fanned out across the San Fernando Valley on Wednesday and simultaneously raided seven suspected prostitution dens fronting as legitimate businesses. Approximately 100 officers took part in 'Operation Silver Bullet,' netting 14 arrests," said Detective Rick McElroy. "Because of the influx of locations, it's been necessary to do unconventional means of enforcement to keep a lid on this type of activity," McElroy said. If you can do the math—that it takes seven officers to arrest one suspected prostitute— you won't get even half that many cops to respond if you call for help while you are being robbed—or if you are the victim of a rape or spousal abuse!

adult woman and a child, excluding themselves and their feminist or academic peers. The rest of us women, particularly those of us in sex work, might as well accept our lot as the poor, feeble-minded creatures we were considered at the turn of the twentieth century,[8] because as far as these feminists are concerned, we are just not capable of self- determination when it comes to sex in general, and commercial sex specifically.

There is a new approach being taken by some of these paternalistic feminists in that they are now pressing for the decriminalization of prostitution for the prostitute, but demanding increased laws and penalties for our clients. "We don't want *you* to go to jail," they say as they pat us on the head, "just the men who make it possible for you to pay your bills." These feminists and the legislators they influence don't have a clue how the real world works and don't seem to understand that there are simply not enough law enforcement resources in the world to arrest all the men who are our clients. This means that the police who enforce the law will simply shift their emphasis from "if you don't give me the sex, money or information you're going to jail tonight, Honey" to "if you don't give

---

8. *The Lost Sisterhood—Prostitution in America*, 1900–1918, Ruth Rosen, John Hopkins University Press, 1982. "A surprisingly high percentage of prostitutes were described as feeble-minded and gradually the belief in feeble-mindedness as a cause of prostitution received widespread acceptance. The Massachusetts White Slave Commission found that only 154 out of 300 interviewed prostitutes could be described as "normal." The 'mental defects' of the others, they asserted 'were so pronounced and evident to warrant the legal commitment of each one as a feeble-minded person or as a defective delinquent.'..."

"What was feeble-mindedness? ...Another writer noted that two kinds of feeble-mindedness existed among prostitutes: those 'whose sexual inclinations are abnormally strong or whose power of self-control over natural impulses is abnormally weak' and those 'who are passive, non-resistant, and will yield to anyone.' The Massachusetts investigation into white slavery further explained that the 'well known immoral tendencies and suggestibility and social incapacity of the feeble-minded cause them to drift naturally into prostitution. The feeble-minded need only opportunity to express their immoral tendencies.'"

"It appears, then that feeble-mindedness had little to do with women's mental capacities; rather, the term 'explained' both 'inherited strains of degeneracy'—for which the prostitute could not really be blamed—and willful immoral behavior. That many prostitutes expressed contempt for middle-class niceties and values was offered as strong evidence of their feeble-mindedness. ...Rather than indicating mental deficiency, the label feeble-minded instead referred to prostitutes' refusal to conform to middle-class values and behavioral patterns. Using the scientific language of the day, reformers could both excuse and blame prostitutes at the same time, thus expressing their deep ambivalence about the nature of prostitution and female sexuality."

me the sex, money or information, I am going to arrest YOUR clients tonight, Honey." How does it make life better for prostitutes to have the police threaten to arrest our clients so we can't earn a living? Later in this chapter I will address what I hope are the unintended consequences of the enforcement of these laws at length.

It is irrational and illogical to declare that any human activity that *may* lead to abuse or exploitation *"must be eliminated,"* and to condemn through legislation adults who, with full knowledge of their actions, freely choose to engage in commercial sexual activity that may offend moral or feminist sensibilities. As a woman and a retired sex worker (prostitute) I am deeply offended by their assertion that regardless of my consent, I was sexually exploited. However, I do agree with these feminists that pornography and prostitution are one and the same.

The word "pornography" [9] literally means the [erotic] writings of [10] prostitutes. When filmed, pornography becomes the re-enactment of the type of sexual activities in which prostitutes typically engage, with 'actors' playing the role of prostitutes. These actors are not themselves prostitutes, anymore more than an actor playing the role of a lawyer on TV is really a lawyer, right? Not exactly. When I refer to the "actors playing the role of prostitutes" I don't mean the script actually defines the role

9. "Pornography is easily recognized but is often difficult to define concisely. The word pornography originates from the Greeks who defined it as writing *about* prostitutes." (Easton, 1998, p.605). http://www.slais.ubc.ca/courses/libr500/fall1999/www_presentations/ c_hogg/define.htm.

"ETYMOLOGY: 19th Century: from Greek pornographos writing *of* harlots, from porne a harlot + graphein to write." http://www.wordreference. com/English definition.asp?en=pornography.

"'Pornography' derives from the Greek (harlot, and graphos, writing). The word now means (1) a description of prostitutes or prostitution (2) a depiction (as in a writing or painting) of licentiousness or lewdness: a portrayal of erotic behavior designed to cause sexual excitement. *Webster's Third New International Dictionary* [Unabridged 1969])."

10. It is interesting to note that a number of sources interpret the original Greek language words as meaning "writings *about* prostitutes/harlots" but others as meaning "writings *of* prostitutes/harlots." There is a significant difference between the two—as one indicates that prostitutes were merely the subject of erotic stories and the other indicates that the prostitutes themselves may have generated erotic stories or literature—possibly for the reading pleasure of their clients at a later time, or as a method of advertising by describing their particular skills and services to entice potential clients. In today's world, phone sex would be the equivalent of erotic story telling, where women (or men) spin exciting sexual tales for the caller, with the sole purpose of inducing orgasm orally.

being played as that of a prostitute, rather that the various, explicit, clearly non-monogamous, recreational sexual activities being depicted are not the type of activities commonly practiced by so-called "good girls" or "good women," wives, girlfriends, radical feminists (that whore-Madonna conundrum thing), and that to engage in such promiscuous conduct for pay, one is taking on the attributes of a prostitute in both the literal and metaphorical sense.

The goal of the prostitute is to excite, turn on, and give pleasure to his or her clients, for which the prostitute is paid, either in cash or "other consideration"; the goal of the porn actor is to excite, turn on, and give pleasure to the consumer, for which the porn actor is paid—either in cash or "other consideration." In addition, whereas the prostitute is only seeking to sexually stimulate and gratify his or her clients, the porn actor must also sexually stimulate and gratify the partner porn actor (particularly where the partner is male and an erection and ejaculation cannot be faked), or the goal of a satisfied consumer will not be achieved. In this sense, the porn actor 'out-prostitutes' the prostitute because the porn actor is responsible for the sexual gratification of more persons for the same pay.

If the average person, radical feminists and prostitutes can see that the work done by porn actors and prostitutes is fundamentally the same, why don't most porn actors and producers of porn view it the same way? Because producing and acting in porn is legal and prostitution is not, and that is the point. There should be no legal distinction between the two groups of sex workers, and all those who work in the adult sex industry should join together to make their industry legal and safer for everyone. Where there is abuse, coercion, or underage persons employed by unscrupulous individuals or companies, the entire sex industry must take appropriate action to rid itself of these truly criminal elements.

The sex workers who had been involved in porn when it was still considered prostitution, and many of them had been arrested on prostitution charges, continue to be activists in the sex worker rights' movement. Most of these old-school porn actors have always considered themselves to be whores[11] and understood we were all in the same boat morally, regardless of our work's legality. However, the new crop of porn actors seem not to know anything of their legal history and care not to involve themselves

11. Ancient whore culture where the sacred prostitute was honored and revered has made a resurgence among its present-day adherents—sex-positive females who embrace their sexuality and find joy and inner peace in their work in the sex industry— strong women who have reclaimed whoredom from its negative connotation created by Judeo- Christian religions.

in the continuing battle fought by those still outside the law. And despite the fact that many of them have private paid sexual encounters with their fans, they do not consider themselves prostitutes.

If one can make no fundamental distinction in the work done by porn actors and prostitutes, other than that one group is protected by the First Amendment and the other is not, are there perhaps emotional or temperamental differences between porn actors and prostitutes themselves? I would have to say absolutely that there are.

One might ask why doesn't someone who works outside the law "change professions" so they can do the same work legally? If one type of work were the same as the other, wouldn't it be wise to go with the work that won't send one to jail? Although there are as many reasons for men and women seeking employment in the sex industry as there are for men and women seeking employment anywhere else, the way in which sex workers prefer to work[12] underscores differences in personality types and their general perception of themselves. It is not just a simple matter of changing careers so one can steer clear of laws that can send one to jail.

To get work, porn actors generally need to be young and attractive, particularly the females. It helps if one is an exhibitionist, as one will be displaying one's body for many to view. With luck, one's videos will be on the market for years to come. As one begins to age, the available roles decline, and making the transition from adult films into mainstream movies is a feat accomplished by very few.

In prostitution, it may help to be young and attractive, but it isn't necessary—despite all the claims to the contrary, which insist that the majority of prostitutes are fourteen years or younger when they enter prostitution. One can be older, heavy set, and a prude and still be successful as a prostitute, allowing sex workers to remain in their careers much longer than in porn. This alone may be a determining factor for those adults considering their options in the sex industry. Other very important factors for me, at age thirty-two when I chose prostitution over porn work, were that I did not have to put up with multiple "retakes" on a daylong film shoot, there was no crew to drool over me, no casting couch, no fellow actors' egos to step on, and so forth. That's not to say these working conditions are overly demanding or intolerable, just that

---

12. I am writing only about adult sex workers who consent to the work they do—not underage children or women who were forced into sexual labor against their will. Having been a sex worker for a number of years before retiring to become a full-time activist and writer, I feel qualified to speak from this perspective. I was thirty-two years of age when I chose the profession of prostitution after leaving a ten-year career with the Los Angeles Police Department.

they were not palatable to me. These are just some of the many significant reasons to prefer prostitution as a profession.

There are so many more work options in prostitution that don't exist in making porn. For example, a sex worker may not like to have intercourse or intimate body contact with his or her clients and prefer to perform a full body massage to bring their clients to orgasm. This can be done in the sex worker's home, at the client's home or hotel room, or at a massage parlor, depending upon where a sex worker feels most comfortable working.

Another option for sex workers who may not want intimate body contact with clients is to specialize as a dominatrix or fantasy fulfillment expert. When one is performing some types of fantasy fulfillment with a client, it may not even be necessary to remove one's clothing much less have sexual contact. I had a client whose fantasy was cross dressing— and all I did to earn my pay was to apply cosmetics to his face, help him select a sexy ensemble, tell him how beautiful he was, and create fantastic stories for him about sexual encounters with non-existent women that took place in a non-existent apartment. For these encounters, I didn't get undressed and he masturbated to orgasm while I talked to him.

Often, when a session does include sexual intercourse of any sort, the sex might last a mere five minutes or less, while stimulating conversation is the primary activity that occurs during the time one spends with a client. The reason for this is that many clients just don't fit the public concept of a horny married man out to cheat on his wife. Clients of prostitutes are often men who are widowed, newly divorced or disabled, either physically or socially. It is comforting to them to know that sex is available if they want it, but sex isn't necessarily the reason for making a date with a sex care provider. There is certainly much less wear and tear on one's body working this way than a porn actor would encounter in a day's work.

Other employment alternatives[13] for prostitutes include working in a brothel, legal or otherwise; working for an escort service; working for

---

13. For this discussion I am deliberately leaving out street workers, although there are places around the world where working on the street is not only safe, but also legal, and where it is a desirable method of working. Street prostitution in the United States carries such a negative connotation, in part because it is the most visible form of prostitution, which is constantly presented by the media as representing all prostitution and it is seen as the last stop for desperate men and women who may or may not be diseased and drug- addicted. According to some government statistics, research and general knowledge of the other forms of prostitution, street workers may in fact only represent between ten and fifteen percent of Prostitution. In any other profession, this percentage of workers would not be touted as a representative "majority" and the media would be taken to task for suggesting that it was.

a madam or madams (male or female); advertising on the internet or in newspapers and magazines and being self-employed; working out of bars, strip clubs or other semi-public places where one might find eager clients, having a same-sex partner to perform private "shows" for clients (the client only watches but does not participate); working as an in-house prostitute for a hotel or casino (where clients are referred by the concierge or bellman); working as an in-house prostitute for a corporation (VIP guests of the company are sent to the company apartment where the sex workers entertain them, and the company, rather than the client, pays the sex worker); and working the circuit (this means the sex worker travels from one city to the next and remains in that city long enough to entertain all the interested clients of the host madam, who generally provides an apartment or hotel room where the sex worker stays and entertains the clients).

A sex worker can work in as many areas of the industry as one wants, choosing to work in all areas or only one, as time allows and financial needs require. Some choose to work as employees in places such as brothels or massage parlors, which create a more traditional work environment for the sex worker. By "traditional" I mean that they are required to show up for work a certain number of days per week and work a set number of hours, and they are probably paid in much the way other employees are, at the end of a work week or a daily shift rather than per encounter. Employees of an escort service might also be required to be "on-duty" a certain number of days or evenings a week, although they might not have to go to a physical location to report for work before they are given an assignment. In the Nevada brothels, which are legal, the women are required to live on the premises during their tour of duty. They may only work a particular shift, such as days, afternoons, evenings, or nights, but they must remain in the house even when they are off duty unless accompanied by an escort from the management team to go shopping, to do their errands, or go out to dinner. From my perspective, the only advantage of working in a legal brothel is that one doesn't have to contend with the daily fear of arrest and incarceration.

Sex workers who are self-employed and work through advertisements in newspapers, magazines, and on the internet are the most likely to possess the "Outlaw Whore" free spirit personality. As long as one is employed by someone else, one is less likely to be outspoken and by necessity be more cautious in one's speech, attitude, and actions. This "Outlaw Whore" or "bad girl" mindset is a positive trait that often gets short shrift by society in general and feminists in particular. Only true "bad girls" can say outrageous things that need not be retracted for propriety's sake. Only "bad girls" can point fingers at society's moral hypocrisy *and* flaunt their sexuality—something that both radical feminists and society seem to find threatening. "Whores" upset the social order because they refuse to be controlled and don't buy into the "woman as victim by consequence of her birth" rhetoric that these feminists embrace and are determined to impose on all women. "Whores" don't need the emotional crutches offered by those benevolent feminists who wish to save women from men. Who can blame these feminists for not wanting to debate the issues with outspoken whores?[14] They know their fatuous arguments won't stand up against a woman who knows who she is and what she wants.

I am not claiming that "outlaw whores" wish to remain outside the law. On the contrary, most of the "outlaw whores" I know have been fighting for the decriminalization of prostitution, loudly and frequently, vocalizing their opinions to whoever will listen. Unfortunately their (our) voices have been subjugated by the chronic babble from the radical feminists who have the ear of the legislators and the media. Only the victimized prostitute is allowed to be heard—the poor, sad, pathetic creatures that they are—periodically trotted out of their dismal habitats for the public display of their cliche-driven lives by the MacKinnon/ Barry/ Dworkin gang, and by the religious conservatives who have adopted the radical feminist rhetoric.

Unlike the virulently anti-porn, anti-prostitution academics, feminists and religious conservatives who disallow the very existence of a "happy hooker," outlaw whore activists know and freely acknowledge that there are women and children *and* men for whom sex work is wholly inappropriate. We know that abuse exists in every area of human life—domestic abuse, child abuse, elderly abuse, labor abuse, police abuse—and we condemn these abuses. Many of us have come from abused lives (does anyone know of any human being anywhere who hasn't suffered some form of abuse at some time in their life?) but found a way to overcome the abuse and heal ourselves by taking back our sexuality and declaring ourselves independent, free agents who will do with our lives what we want, and will say what we think, and to hell with social convention. And we have paid dearly for our attitude.

14. Despite repeated attempts to engage feminists such as Andrea Dworkin, Catharine McKinnon, and Kathleen Barry in academically sponsored debates with sex workers and other pro-decriminalization feminists, they refused these opportunities. Kathleen Barry was invited to present at the 1997 International Conference on Prostitution sponsored by Cal State University, Northridge, and COYOTE, but declined the invitation because she could not have a general session where she was the sole presenter.

Many were the atrocities committed against prostitutes by the reformers and moral crusaders of the late nineteenth and early twentieth
century[15] who claimed to "love the sinner, but hate the sin."[16] They
wanted to save our souls,[17] they said, and reform us to be good girls who
married and raised many children for our husbands/owners. Of course
once we had become "soiled," we weren't really fit to become wives or
to be accepted by the community, so the reformation actually worked to
force us into low-paying employment or to become wards of the state.

Anti-sex feminists have replaced these moral "reformers" and their
creed is "love the prostitute, but hate her work and her clients", . . . which
is not that different from the creed of their spiritual ancestors. These feminists wish to "rescue" us from "male aggression" rather than "reform"
us. And along with this protectionist "for your own good" philosophy,
which has been incorporated into current laws, have come the atrocities
committed against us by law enforcement and other government agents.
In today's world, if we have an arrest record, we are "soiled" and unfit for

15. *Police Corruption—A Sociological Perspective*, Edited by Lawrence
W. Sherman, 1974: "*prostitution was a particularly vexing legal and police problem and most reform movements in* New York City developed out of revelations
of police protection of organized prostitution" pp. 56–57.

16. "Love the sinner, hate the sin" a phrase that came to be associated with
the anti-gay and lesbian Christians of the late twentieth century—was the concept
behind most of the reformers' work with prostitutes.

17. *Uneasy Virtue* by Barbara Meil Hobson, 1987: "Female Reformers ideal-
istically believed that the vulnerability of all women, regardless of class, to male
sexual aggression would create a Christian sisterhood able to transcend class differences in their mutual struggle. The New England Female Reform Society had
two strategies for eliminating the sexual double standard. One strategy was to
press for legal remedies that would punish men who violated chastity codes. The
other, more important strategy was to use social ostracism—informal sanctions—
against the seducer. The society knew that prejudice against the fallen woman was
so strong that a virtuous woman who had any contact with her would become
morally contaminated, loss of reputation was assumed."

More than a century-old campaign: "The anti-pornography campaign dates
back to the Victorian period in the late nineteenth century in Great Britain."
Past generations of feminists attacked prostitution, pornography, white slavery, and homosexuality as manifestations of undifferentiated male lust," said
Judith Walkowitz in her article: "The Politics of Prostitution." But these earlier moral campaigns, she says, frequently "failed to achieve their goals." Feminists who started a discourse on sex "lost control of the movement as it
diversified." This "resulted from contradictions in their attitudes; in part, it
reflected feminists' impotence to reshape the world according to their own
image."

other high-paying employment opportunities that require licenses, which our arrest records preclude us from obtaining. Thus we are forced into low-paying jobs—if we can find employment at all—or we must become wards of the state. But thank goodness, the *"abrogating"* of our *"human right to dignity, equality, autonomy, and physical and mental well-being"* has been thwarted.

Earlier I expressed hope that the inexcusable but inevitable consequences of enforcing these laws are not what those who support anti-prostitution, anti-pornography legislation intended. However, that is presupposing that none of these feminists or legislators have read account after account of police corruption and abuse relating to the enforcement of prostitution laws, accounts often written by police themselves.[18] In the real world, where prostitutes live, "protectionist" feminist and academic theories collide with human nature. Laws prohibiting consensual commercial sex are enforced by fallible human beings, and sting operations to arrest female prostitutes are carried out by men—aggressive men who also possess sexual appetites, greed, and little concern for achieving the lofty goals of those who write the laws. Some courts have ruled that these police officers may have sex with those suspected of being prostitutes in order to arrest them.[19] Since these cops are paid to have sex as part of their job, doesn't that make the cops "prostitutes" as well? Shall we include them in the class of victims whose work is "incompatible with the dignity and worth of the human person" and must be eliminated?

In other horror stories, some judges have refused to prosecute men who have forced sex upon a woman who was a prostitute, noting that women

18. *LA Secret Police Inside the LAPD Elite Spy Network* by Mike Rothmiller and Ivan G. Goldman. "Detectives would lure the sucker into a trap with a call girl... and lots of cops had a list of call girls with whom they traded information and other favors." p.91 "There was the time a black pimp by the name of Willy Cunningjam complained to [officer]? Skrah that a certain deputy chief was shaking down one of his hookers for free sex..." p. 133. "In the old days—going back to Prohibition and into the thirties and forties—the LAPD had been a typically corrupt urban police force, probably even more corrupt than most. The town was brimming with brothels..." p. 143.

19. Spokane WA(AP) "Prostitution investigators may have sex." "Police agents may engage in sex to carry out prostitution investigations as long as they don't try to trap anyone into the crime," a Spokane County District Court judge has ruled. A two-month investigation last fall, which reportedly involved spending $2,000 for two agents to engage in sex acts for evidence, did not constitute entrapment, Judge Daniel Maggs ruled. ... "It may violate public morals, but personal beliefs can't be substituted for the law," Maggs said.

who make whores out of themselves are not afforded the protection of the law against rape or sodomy.[20]

Prostitutes are frequently targets of other police and judicial abuse as well, and when the cops are caught, they seldom get arrested or go to jail. In a classic example of what really happens when these laws are enforced, this 1984 incident in San Francisco is far from being an isolated case.

"Prostitute at Cop Party to Testify Today," May 17, 1984, *San Francisco Chronicle*, by Robert Popp and Randy Shilts: "... *The San Francisco criminal grand jury has so far subpoenaed two women in the case, including the woman allegedly hired by two vice officers to orally copulate a recruit during the rowdy Police Academy graduation party....*"

Notice the date? Let's see what happens to her the following day:

"Police Party Prostitute Arrested," May 18, 1984, *San Francisco Chronicle*: "The woman reputed to have performed a sex act on a San Francisco police cadet was arrested early yesterday on prostitution charges... [the day after she testified before a grand jury about police misconduct]... This is the woman who allegedly performed oral sex on a cadet at a police graduation party.... She was apparently taken to the party by police officers and paid for her services. As a result the entire graduation class was ordered to be retrained on police ethics and conduct and five police officers were suspended... "

And how was this situation finally resolved? Were the vice cops who hired the prostitute charged with pandering and sent to prison for years and years under the mandatory sentencing law? No. According to the *San Francisco Chronicle*, August 2, 1984, by Robert Popp: "No Indictments due in S.F. Cops Sex Party." No cops lost their job, and no one went to jail except the prostitute. A very typical outcome for those charged with

---

20. *Los Angeles Times*, April 24, 1986, by Mark Arax:" 'Judge Says Law Doesn't Protect Prostitutes, Drops Rape Count.' ... Pasadena Superior Court Judge Gilbert C. Alston granted his own motion last week for a finding of not guilty in the case against Daniel Zabuski, a former South Gate police jailer. In granting the motion [to dismiss]... Alston made a general statement that a working prostitute could not be the victim of a rape, even if she was forced to engage in sexual intercourse. ... In an interview, Alston repeated his belief that the law did not afford prostitutes protection against rape or sodomy. ... 'A woman who goes out on the street and makes a whore out of herself opens herself up to anybody,' Alston said. 'She steps outside the protection of the law. That's a basic and fundamental legal concept. ...' " (It should be noted that Judge Alston was a former police officer, according to the article.)

protecting women from "sexual exploitation" who do the real exploiting. Unfortunately such cases are common.[21]

It seems that police have always had a difficult time keeping their pants up around prostitutes. Whether it was the turn of the nineteenth century, the middle or the late twentieth century, cops and judges[22] just can't be

21. In Sacramento, California, Superior Court Judge Benjamin Diaz was fined $265 and placed on three years probation for soliciting a prostitute, which he said he did for laughs (*Sacramento Bee*, November 5, 1984, UPI). The judge was cited for soliciting a prostitute and engaging in a lewd public act. A police report said that a woman named Kasandra Daniels was seen getting into a car driven by Diaz, who had been drinking with friends at a nearby bar. A police officer said that upon following the couple into a nearby alley he saw the woman performing oral sex on Diaz. The prostitute was arrested and released on $2,000 bail. Judge Diaz was cited and released on his promise to appear at his arraignment. He pleaded no contest to the charges, and remained in his own courtroom and attended to his regular calendar. Daniels went to jail, which I am sure she didn't find one bit amusing.

22. "Hookers: Cops Made Us Squad-car Sirens," by Murray Weiss, Criminal Justice Editor, *New York Post*. New York, September 29, 1998, p. 14: "Prosecutors for the Manhattan district attorney and internal police probers heard numerous accounts of cops in uniform being serviced inside [Ramos] brothel on West 39th Street, in apparent exchange for not busting the 60-hooker operation. Ramos claimed she provided cops with sex for up to 15 years, but only one of the six cooperating cops has admitted ongoing sexual dalliances."

"Five Brothel-case Cops Face Arrest—Indicted In Sex-for-protection Scandal" by Murray Weiss Criminal Justice Editor, *New York Post*. New York, April 27, 1999, p. 16: "*As many as six cops implicated in the scandal have been cooperating with authorities since last summer when cops arrested [Helena Ramos] and her prostitutes—who then complained that officers in uniform routinely visited her West 39th Street brothel for sex.... Ramos identified the officers who protected her operation in exchange for leniency on the prostitution charges, officials said....*"

"Cops Spilling Their Guts In Brothel Probe," by Murray Weiss, *New York Post*. New York, September 27, 1998, p. 4: "The sources say reputed Midtown Madam Helena Ramos identified cops who frequented her West 39th Street brothel from NYPD personnel file photos.... In addition to turncoat cops and Ramos' confessions, investigators won the cooperation of a number of hookers who work for Ramos or who ply their trade on Manhattan's West Side streets...."

"Vice Squad Nails Cop On John Rap" by Philip Messing, *New York Post*. New York, July 13, 2002. p.008: "Officer John Brower, 35, an NYPD cop for 11 years who had been assigned to the 111th Precinct in Bayside, Queens, was off-duty when he allegedly approached a woman at 4 a.m. at the intersection of Ingraham Street and Porter Avenue..."

"Vice Cop Nabbed In Hooker Assault" by Erika Martinez. *New York Post*. New York, January 28, 2001, p. 030: "Detective Anthony Downing, 27, a

trusted to behave in a manner ostensibly envisioned by the feminists whose philosophical ideals are inscribed into law. Surely the following incidents are the *unintended* consequences of the enforcement of the law and were not what the legislators, religious conservatives, or radical feminists had in mind to protect women from sexual exploitation!

Los Angeles Daily News, September 25, 1994, Dennis McCarthy, "Donut Shop Smells Good, Public Nuisance label reeks": The woman behind the counter filling an order of a dozen assorted doughnuts at Orvilles Originals didn't look or sound like a public nuisance. She looked and sounded like a woman working hard to make a living. But in the eyes of the Los Angeles City Office of Zoning Administration, Zuita Contador was public enemy No.1. ... "I don't understand it. The police say I should not sell doughnuts to prostitutes. I say 'Fine, tell me who is and who is not a prostitute.' They say I should know one when I see one. OK, but I ask them to please sign a paper so that if I am sued for not serving someone because I think they are a prostitute, the police will be responsible, not me. They won't sign any paper. I am a doughnut maker not a policeman,' Zuita says."

Perhaps the police didn't want Zuita Contador to sell doughnuts to prostitutes because the cops were concerned about the prostitutes' health and well-being. No one knows better than cops how detrimental to one's health eating all those sugar-laden, cholesterol-filled doughnuts can be! But is it "protecting women from sexual exploitation" by pressuring mom-and-pop doughnut stores not to sell doughnuts to prostitutes? What's next? Why should doughnut shops be the only stores verbally prohibited from selling to prostitutes? Why shouldn't the police be able to insist that clothing stores not sell clothes or shoes to prostitutes? And if the police insisted that no one could rent apartments or houses to prostitutes, which they already do by applying the red-light abatement laws that many states have enacted, prostitutes would all be homeless and naked. This would certainly make them very easy to identify! Why not a scarlet letter tattooed on their forehead? Or perhaps if all prostitutes were forced to wear an unflattering paper jump suit, they could be persuaded to stop exploiting themselves![23]

six-year vet who works in the Manhattan South Vice Squad, allegedly picked up an 18-year-old Manhattan woman in the Hunts Point section of the Bronx at around 4:30 a.m. ... "

Los Angeles Times, Orange County Edition, October 11, 1988, by Terry Pristin and Mark Landsbaum: "Two Orange County municipal judges are being investigated by the state Commission on Judicial Performance for allegedly offering lenient treatment to prostitutes in exchange for sex... "

23. "Police Seize Clothes to Collar Prostitution" *Los Angeles Times,* February 20, 1996, by Lee Romney: "Officials say taking garments can be an effective

Of course, this treatment is only applied to uncooperative prostitutes. Madams and prostitutes who provide information, money,[24] and sex to cops are lauded as being helpful and are allowed to continue to practice their trades.[25] When the notorious Hollywood Madam Heidi Fleiss'

tool... the practice of seizing the clothes of suspected prostitutes is just one in an arsenal of enforcement tools that frustrated officers hope will put a halt to the revolving door of misdemeanor prostitution arrests.... Critics denounce the paper clothing (jump suits given to the prostitutes) as sexist and possibly unconstitutional, noting that no other criminal suspects are treated this way. ... But vice detectives say the jump suit gimmick... is a legal and effective way to make the arrest process as unpleasant as possible. .... "The more we can cost a hooker—as far as the time out of service—and do it within the legal framework that's what we're trying to do," Costa Mesa (CA) Police Sgt. Loren Wyrick said: "We're trying to make them as uncomfortable as possible. ... " (No doubt to prevent the further "abrogating [of] that person's human right to dignity, equality, autonomy, and physical and mental well-being... ")

24. *Police Corruption–A Sociological Perspective*, Edited by Lawrence W. Sherman, 1974: "...A precinct could be rated by the number of establishments featuring gambling and prostitution, which could be systematically assessed by the police. When Captain Alexander S. 'Clubber' Williams... was transferred to the Twenty-ninth Precinct, the city's most fashionable red-light district, he rubbed his hands together and spoke of moving up from 'salt-chuck' to 'tenderloin'. Thus the district was christened 'the Tenderloin.' " pp. 50–51

25. *San Diego Union*, September 30, 1990, by Joe Cantelupe and Dayna Lynn Fried: "Continuing allegations of relationships between San Diego police officers and prostitutes have raised troubling questions about how the department polices itself against such improper ties. ... Did police officials turn a blind eye toward such relationships between its officers and prostitutes? ... Police officers getting involved and having sex with prostitutes is hardly a new problem... Police Chief Bob Burgreen said last week that the department is reviewing its policies to determine whether it was careful enough in ensuring that officers do not become involved [sexually] with the prostitutes they work with... However, Burgreen said dealing with prostitutes—especially on an informant basis—is 'a very large part of our business' and that perhaps citizens in a largely conservative community like San Diego may have a hard time understanding that. ... " I know I have a hard time understanding how this helps reduce the "sexual exploitation" of women!

Los Angeles Times, March 1987, by Kim Murphy: "Ruling that it is 'unrealistic to expect law enforcement officers to ferret out criminals without the help of unsavory characters, a federal appeals court has reinstated criminal charges against a suspected heroin dealer caught with the help of a prostitute acting as a government informant."

San Diego Union Tribune, 1988, by Joe Cantlupe: "Trial Could Uncover Way Police Operate Vista, CA." As the trial of Oceanside police officer Rex Nemeyer—a 36-year old patrolman accused of supplying drugs to a prostitute—unfolds, it

procuring predecessor Madam Alex, was arrested by one officer who was upset that she no longer provided information to *him*, another officer, veteran Los Angeles Police Detective, Daniel Lott, testified on her behalf, stating "... The information we gleaned from her far surpassed what she was doing..."[26]

What Elizabeth Adams, aka Madam Alex, was "doing" was "pandering and pimping," which according to former Los Angeles District Attorney, Ira Reiner, are worse crimes than rape or robbery.[27] I doubt if robbers or rapists would be allowed to continue to engage in their criminal pursuits even if they provided extremely valuable information to the cops, and yet feminists and legislators don't seem to be the least bit troubled by the selective enforcement practices of cops, which are engendered by the protectionist legislation they advocate.

The sexual abuses committed by law enforcement agents are not limited to prostitutes.[28] If law enforcement cannot be trusted to protect

promises to give the public glimpses into the inside politics and hidden mechanics of the police department itself... 'Prostitutes have been specifically targeted' by the Oceanside police, [defense attorney Craig] Griswold said, because officials believe that vice activities are linked to illegal drug sales and theft downtown.'The goal of the night shift was to find, interrogate, and gain information from prostitutes. There was intense competition and pride among the police in striving to meet department goals,' the lawyer said."

26. *Los Angeles Times*, May 19, 1990, Lois Timnick: "'Beverly Hills madam, Elizabeth Adams, was lauded for her undercover police work Friday by the same agency that arrested her on suspicion of pandering in 1988. 'She was the best informant I ever met,' veteran Los Angeles Police Detective Daniel Lott testified... 'Adams had enough class not to flaunt her brothel activities and the department looked the other way because of the help she provided on numerous criminal cases. ...We considered Betty as an undercover agent. ...The information we gleaned from her far surpassed what she was doing..."

27. *People vs. Almodovar*, December 9, 1985, L.A.S.C. No. A-394853 p. 19, l; pp.29–38, "Nevertheless, in terms of impact upon the victim, whereas a robbery may have a traumatic effect on the victim lasting weeks or months, pandering can lead its victim to a lifetime of shame and degradation, robbing her of her bodily integrity, personal privacy, self-respect and reputation. Whereas rape is accomplished by one act of force, pandering can cause a woman to be pressured into an endless series of acts of indiscriminate sexual intercourse, which progressively rape her spirit, character, and self-image. Unlike rape, pandering is a cold-blooded, calculating, profit-seeking criminal enterprise. It is clearly a 'vicious practice.' "

28. http://www.policeaccountability.org/drivingfemale.htm. "In April, 2002, a Virginia state trooper was indicted for soliciting sex from female drivers in return for dropping traffic charges against them. Just one week earlier, a San Bernardino,

"good women," how can radical feminists, courts, and legislators trust law enforcement agents with proper enforcement of laws that regulate (prohibit) prostitution or pornography, as these feminists include in their long-term goals to eliminate? These abuses are not going to go away, as any honest politician or cop will concede. Historically, this has frequently

California, police officer was charged with sexually assaulting or raping 11 women while on duty. Also in March 2002, a suburban Philadelphia police officer was convicted of raping an intoxicated woman while on duty and in uniform. "

"These and numerous other cases highlight a national problem of 'driving while female' where police officers use their authority, often in traffic stops, to harass or assault women drivers, or to take advantage of women who have been stopped for legitimate violations."

"The 'driving while female' problem became apparent in early 2001 in a series of cases on Long Island, New York. On New Year's Day, 2001, a Suffolk County (NY)? police officer stopped a female driver for an alleged traffic violation and instead of issuing her a traffic ticket forced her to strip and walk home wearing only her underpants." Reports of 'driving while female' abuses are found in every part of the country, and the level of abuse runs the gamut from harassment to sexual assault and even murder:

- In 2000, a Houston, Texas, police officer was convicted and sentenced to twenty years in prison for the sexual assault of a female driver.
- A Milwaukee police officer was sentenced to eight years in prison in 1998 for sexually assaulting a female driver.
- In 1996, a Chicago police officer was sentenced to four years in prison for fondling women during traffic stops.
- And in perhaps the most grotesque case of all, Cara Knott was murdered in 1986 by a predatory California Highway Patrol officer who stopped her for a traffic violation. "These are not isolated incidents. A review of national print media from 1990 to 2001 revealed literally hundreds of allegations of 'driving while female' abuses, and an average of over a dozen substantiated cases each year."

The estimate cited in this report is conservative in two ways. First, it only includes abuses that were substantiated by the criminal justice system (i.e., the officer was indicted, found guilty, etc.). Second, it defines "cases" by the number of victims. Many officers were charged with several criminal counts associated with each victim.

Additionally, there is good reason to believe that these cases represent only the tip of the iceberg. Many victims do not come forward because of humiliation and fear of reprisal. And some police departments do not accept and investigate complaints from many victims who do come forward." ... And when the victim is a prostitute, she is even less likely to be believed and will not file a complaint because she will never get any justice from the cops or the courts.

been the case.[29] Feminists, legislators, religious conservatives or any others are far too nescient to be allowed to inspire, influence, author, or enact legislation if they believe that human nature has changed significantly to make one postulate that the integrity of the police officer of the twenty-first century will no longer be compromised when pitted against these unenforceable laws and the temptations that confront them!

The credibility of radical feminists must be called into question if they continue to support legislation as a means of achieving their goal to eliminate all pornography and prostitution. If they refuse to recognize the vast and fundamental difference between forced prostitution and sex work in which some (many) women and men willingly engage, they do not have the best interests of prostitutes or any other women at heart. If they will not acknowledge the horrible damage and destruction of lives caused not by the work itself but by the laws which prohibit voluntary, adult commercial sexual activity, they cannot continue to claim moral high ground for their position of the "elimination" of all forms of violence against women, if it was ever theirs to claim.

The state rationales for prohibiting prostitution must also be exposed as the irrational, irresponsible, histrionic, balderdash arguments that they are, and as well, expose the law-makers who continue to use such rationales to "control prostitution."

The recent 2003 Supreme Court decision, in Lawrence versus Texas, which overturned state sodomy laws was ballyhooed by conservative justices and law-makers as being the harbinger for the repeal of all sorts of

29. In the book *Police Corruption—A Sociological Perspective*, edited by Lawrence W. Sherman (1974): "Introduction toward a sociological theory of police corruption," Sherman writes, "Part of the dilemma may be resolved by considering those universal aspects of police work that make corruption possible or likely...Discretion. The most important constant is the extraordinary discretion inherent in police work. The officer's exercise of the discretion to arrest someone or not and his choice of the specific charge has numerous bases, both legitimate and illegitimate. It is the legitimate bases that allow an officer to cover up any illegitimate basis for his discretion, particularly the choice not to make an arrest." (p. 12). And what "crime" but prostitution could offer an officer more latitude in discretion of whether or not to arrest a woman who is willingly plying her trade?

In "The Integrity of the European Police in 1914," Raymond P. Fosdick describes how "...wherever the control of prostitution by regulation has been attempted it has been accompanied, if not by open corruption, at least by grave suspicions that such corruption exists..." (pp. 64–65). And from a high official of Scotland Yard, "we cannot guarantee the integrity of the police against the vicious influences arising from unenforceable laws" (pp. 68).

"morality" laws. "This effectively decrees the end of all morals legislation," wrote Justice Antonin Scalia in his dissenting opinion. "State laws against bigamy, same-sex marriage, adult incest, prostitution, masturbation, adultery, fornication, bestiality, and obscenity are likewise sustainable only in light of Bowers' validation of laws based on moral choices," wrote Justice Scalia. "Every single one of these laws is called in to question by today's decision." And repealed they should, no,*must* be. The Texas state prosecutor acknowledged that the sodomy law wasn't really enforced, but he maintained that the law served to keep some people from committing homosexual acts. ...And this serves a free society in what way? Is there anything moral or defensible about the police corruption that results from the arbitrary enforcement of laws, which have the sole purpose of controlling a group of women whose sexual activities some people find offensive?

Thankfully, the majority of the Supreme Justices disagreed with Texas' discrimination policy. "The petitioners are entitled to respect for their private lives," Justice Anthony Kennedy wrote for the court's majority. "The state cannot demean their existence or control their destiny by making their private sexual conduct a crime." And although he voted against overturning the Texas sodomy law, Justice Clarence Thomas said that if he were a Texas legislator and not a judge, he would vote to repeal the law: "Punishing someone for expressing his sexual preference through non-commercial consensual conduct with another adult does not appear to be a worthy way to expend valuable law enforcement resources." Thomas does not mention why he believes that punishing *commercial* consensual adult conduct is a worthy way to expend valuable law enforcement resources.

Well then, how shall those of us who wish to eliminate the real source of violence against prostitutes proceed? Do we petition the courts to overturn the prostitution laws on the grounds that the laws are and can only be arbitrarily enforced and thus do not and will never provide equal protection under the law? Are there truly any constitutional "free speech" grounds for separating pornography and prostitution if the acts are one and the same? And if there are fundamental personality differences between porn actors and prostitutes, do these differences justify the criminalization of one group and the liberation of the other? Further, if the end result of both commercial activities is the "sexual arousal and gratification" of someone at some time, is the state justified in criminalizing the sexual behavior of those who provide or are the recipients of immediate gratification *because* it is immediate and not delayed?

A battle must be fought—in public, in court, and in the legislature—to change the minds and hearts of those who control the laws. The myth that is perpetuated by the radical feminists through the media that all prostitution and pornography equals violence against women must be countered by the reality of the lives of sex workers. Yes, there is violence against women, and men, and children, in so many areas of life, but promoting irresponsible laws that are arbitrarily enforced causes the greatest violence against us.

This battle must be fought by all those who gain from the sex industry—the sex workers and the consumers, the porn producers, and the legal teams who support them. Sadly, it has been my experience that much of legal adult industry does everything it can to distance itself from outlaw prostitutes because they have already won their freedom and now wish to acquire the respect of the community. Being associated in any way with outspoken outlaw whores is not good for their image.

However, if radical feminists and religious conservatives had their way, the state governments, indeed all governments everywhere in the world, would criminalize any commercial behavior between men and women that resulted in sexual arousal or gratification of anyone at any time, whether or not it was considered "free speech." Radical feminists are using the United Nations Platform for Action to accomplish their goals. By labeling pornography as "an act of violence against women," by equating consenting adult sex work with coerced prostitution and stating that both are "incompatible with the dignity and worth of the human person and must be eliminated," and by demanding that member countries enact legislation that reflects their philosophy, the radical feminists may accomplish what the religious conservatives could not, and porn stars and producers may end up as outlaws once again.

Perhaps before that happens, porn stars and porn producers will catch the "outlaw whore" spirit and speak up to demand rights for all of us. The issues that divide us, as sex workers, should only relate to our personal employment preferences and not to prison bars.

CHAPTER SEVEN

"Whether from Reason or Prejudice"

Taking Money for Bodily Services*

MARTHA NUSSBAUM

Taking leave of Binod, Durga slowly, deliberately walks towards the
shack of Sukhlal the contractor, who stared at her even yesterday
and flashed ten-rupee notes.
   What else can one do, she argues to herself, except fight for
survival? The survival of oneself, one's loved ones, and the hopes
that really matter.
                    —Manik Bandyopadhyay,
           "A Female Problem at a Low Level" (1963)

If the story is about the peasant wife selling her body, then one must
look for the meaning of that in the reality of peasant life. One can't
look at it as a crisis of morality, in the sense one would in the case of
a middle-class wife.
                    —Manik Bandyopadhyay,
                About This Author's Perspective

☾

I. BODY SELLERS

All of us, with the exception of the independently wealthy and the unemployed, take money for the use of our body. Professors, factory workers,
lawyers, opera singers, prostitutes, doctors, legislators–we all do things

with parts of our bodies, for which we receive a wage in return.[1] Some people get good wages and some do not; some have a relatively high degree of control over their working conditions and some have little control; some have many employment options and some have very few. And, some are socially stigmatized and some are not.

The stigmatization of certain occupations may be well founded, based on convincing, well-reasoned arguments. But it may also be based on class prejudice, or stereotypes of race or gender. Stigma may also change rapidly, as these background beliefs and prejudices change. Adam Smith, in *The Wealth of Nations*, tells us that there are "some very agreeable and beautiful talents" that are admirable as long is no pay is taken for them, "but of which the exercise for the sake of gain is considered, whether from reason or prejudice, as a sort of publick prostitution." For this reason, he continues, opera singers, actors, and dancers must be paid an "exorbitant" wage, to compensate them for them for the stigma involved in using their talents "as the means of subsistence." "Should the publick opinion or prejudice ever alter with regard to such occupations," he concludes, "their pecuniary recompense would quickly diminish."[2] Smith was not altogether right about the opera market,[3] but his discussion is revealing for what it shows us about stigma. Today few professions are more honored than that of opera singer, and yet only two hundred years ago, that public use of one's body for pay was taken to be a kind of prostitution. Looking back at that time, we now think that the judgments and emotions underlying the stigmatization of singers were irrational and objectionable, like prejudices against members of different classes and races. (I shall shortly be saying more about what I think those reasons were.) Nor do we see the slightest reason to suppose that the unpaid artist is a purer and truer artist than the paid artist. We think it entirely right and reasonable that high art should receive a high salary. If a producer of opera should take the position that singers should not be paid, on the grounds

---

1. Even if one is a Cartesian dualist, as I am not, one must grant that the human exercise of mental abilities standardly requires the deployment of bodily skills. Most traditional Christian positions on the soul go still further: Aquinas, for example, holds that souls separated from the body have only a confused cognition and cannot recognize particulars. So my statements about professors can be accepted even by believers in the separable soul.

2. Smith, The *Nature and Causes of the Wealth of Nations*, I.x.b.25. Elsewhere, Smith points out that in ancient Greece acting was "as creditable . . . as it is discreditable now" (LRBL ii.230).

3. He expresses the view that the relevant talents are not so rare, and that when stigma is removed, many more people will compete for the jobs, driving down wages; this is certainly true today of acting, but far less so of opera, where "the rarity and beauty of the talents" remains at least one dominant factor.

that receiving money for the use of their talents involves an illegitimate form of commodification and even market alienation of those talents, we would think that this producer was a slick exploiter, out to make a profit from the ill treatment of vulnerable and impressionable artists.[4] On the whole we think that far from cheapening or ruining talents, the presence of a contract guarantees conditions within which the artist can develop her art with sufficient leisure and confidence to reach the highest level of artistic production.[5]

It is widely believed, however, that taking money or entering into contracts in connection with the use of one's sexual and/or reproductive capacities is genuinely bad. Feminist arguments about prostitution, surrogate motherhood, and even marriage contracts standardly portray financial transactions in the area of female sexuality as demeaning to women and as involving a damaging commodification and market alienation of women's sexual and reproductive capacities.[6] The social meaning of these transactions is said to be both that these capacities are turned into objects

---

4. Such arguments have often been used in the theater; they were used, for example, in one acting company of which I was a member, in order to persuade actors to kick back their (union-mandatory) salaries to the owners. This is fairly common in theater, where the union is weak and actors are so eager for employment that they are vulnerable to such arguments.

5. The typical contract between major U.S. symphony orchestras and the musicians' union, for example, guarantees year-round employment to symphony musicians, even though they do not play all year; this enables them to use summer months to play in low-paying or experimental settings in which they can perform contemporary music and chamber music, do solo and concerto work, and so forth. It also restricts hours of both rehearsal and performance during the performing season, leaving musicians free to teach students, attend classes, work on chamber music with friends, and in other ways to enrich their work. It also mandates blind auditions (i.e., players play behind a curtain)—with the result that the employment of female musicians has risen dramatically over the past twenty or so years since the practice was instituted.

6. See Elizabeth Anderson, *Value in Ethics and Economics* (Cambridge, MA: Harvard University Press, 1993), and Anderson, "Is Women's Labor a Commodity?" *Philosophy and Public Affairs* 19 (1990), 71–92; Margaret Jane Radin, *Contested Commodities: The Trouble with the Trade in Sex, Children, Bodily Parts, and Other Things* (Cambridge, MA: Harvard University Press, 1996); and Radin, "Market-Inalienability," *Harvard Law Review* 100 (1987), 1849–1937; Cass R. Sunstein, "Neutrality in Constitutional Law (With Special Reference to Pornography, Abortion, and Surrogacy)," *Columbia Law Review* 92 (1992), 1–52; and Sunstein, *The Partial Constitution* (Cambridge, MA: Harvard University Press, 1993), 257–90. For contrasting feminist perspectives on the general issue of contract, see Jean Hampton, "Feminist Contractarianism," in *A Mind of One's Own: Feminist Essay on Reason and Objectivity* (Boulder, CO: Westview, 1993),

for the use and control of men and also that the activities themselves are being turned into commodities, and thereby robbed of the type of value they have at their best.

One question we shall have to face is whether these descriptions of our current judgments and intuitions are correct. But even if they are, what does this tell us? Many things and people have been stigmatized in our nation's history, often for very bad reasons. An account of the actual social meaning of a practice is therefore just a door that opens onto the large arena of moral and legal evaluation. It invites us to raise Adam Smith's question: Are these current beliefs the result of reason or prejudice? Can they be defended by compelling moral arguments? And, even if they can, are these the type of moral argument that can properly be a basis for a legal restriction? Smith, like his Greek and Roman Stoic forebears, understood that the evaluations that ground emotional responses and ascriptions of social meaning in a society are frequently corrupt—deformed by self-interest, resentment, and mere unthinking habit. The task he undertook, in *The Theory of Moral Sentiments*, was to devise procedures and strategies of argument through which one might separate the rationally defensible emotions from the irrational and prejudiced. In so proceeding, Smith and the Stoics were correct. Social meaning does no work on its own: It offers an invitation to normative moral and political philosophy.

My aim in this essay will be to investigate the question of sexual "commodification" by focusing on the example of prostitution.[7] I argue that a fruitful debate about the morality and legality of prostitution should begin from a twofold starting point: from a broader analysis of our beliefs and practices with regard to taking pay for the use of the body, and from a broader awareness of the options and choices available to poor working women. The former inquiry suggests that at least some of our beliefs about prostitution are as irrational as the beliefs Smith reports about singers; it will therefore help us to identify the elements in prostitution

227–55; Susan Moller Okin, *Justice, Gender, and the Family* (New York: Basic Books, 1989).

7. I use this term throughout because of its familiarity, although a number of international women's organizations now avoid it for reasons connected to those in this essay, preferring the term "commercial sex worker" instead. For one recent example, see Report of the Panel on Reproductive Health, National Research Council, *Reproductive Health in Developing Countries: Expanding Dimensions, Building Solutions*, ed. Amy O. Tsui, Judith N. Wasserheit, and John G. Haaga (Washington, DC: National Academy Press, 1997), 30, stressing the wide variety of practices denoted by the term "commercial sex" and arguing that some studies show economic hardship as a major factor but some do not.

that are genuinely problematic. Most, though not all, of the genuinely problematic elements turn out to be common to a wide range of activities engaged in by poor working women, and the second inquiry suggests that many of women's employment choices are so heavily constrained by poor options that they are hardly choices at all. I think that this should bother us—and that the fact that a woman with plenty of choices becomes a prostitute should not bother us provided there are sufficient safeguards against abuse and disease, safeguards of a type that legalization would make possible.

It is therefore my conclusion that the most urgent issue raised by prostitution is that of employment opportunities for working women and their control over the conditions of their employment. The legalization of prostitution, far from promoting the demise of love, is likely to make things a little better for women who have too few options to begin with.[8] The really helpful thing for feminists to ponder, if they deplore the nature of these options, will be how to promote expansion in the option set, through education, skills training, and job creation. These unsexy topics are not common themes in U.S. feminist philosophy, but they are inevitable in any practical project dealing with prostitutes and their female children.[9] This suggests that at least some of our feminist theory may be insufficiently grounded in the reality of working-class lives and too focused on sexuality as an issue in its own right, as if it could be extricated from the fabric of poor people's attempts to survive.

II. STIGMA AND WAGE LABOR

Why were opera singers stigmatized? If we begin with this question, we can move on to prostitution with expanded insight. Although we can hardly provide more than a sketch of the background here, we can confidently say that two common cultural beliefs played a role. First, throughout much of the history of modern Europe—as, indeed, in ancient

8. Among feminist discussions of prostitution, my approach is close to that of Sibyl Schwarzenbach, "Contractarians and Feminists Debate Prostitution," *New York University Review of Law and Social Change* 18 (1990–1), 103–29, and to Laurie Shrage, "Prostitution and the Case for Decriminalization," *Dissent* (Spring 1996), 41–5 (in which Shrage criticizes her earlier view expressed in "Should Feminists Oppose Prostitution?," *Ethics* 99 [1989]: 347–61).

9. To give just one example, the Annapurna Mahila Mandel project in Bombay offers job training and education to the daughters of prostitutes, in a residential school setting; they report that in five years they have managed to arrange reputable marriages for 1,000 such girls.

Greece—there was a common aristocratic prejudice against earning wages. The ancient Greek gentleman was characterized by "leisure"—meaning that he did not have to work for a living. Aristotle reproved the Athenian democracy for allowing such base types as farmers and craftsmen to vote, because, in his view, the unleisured character of their daily activities and their inevitable preoccupation with gain would pervert their political judgment, making them grasping and small-minded.[10] The fact that the Sophists typically took money for their rhetorical and philosophical teaching made them deeply suspect in the eyes of such aristocrats.[11] Much the same view played a role in the medieval Church, where it was controversial whether one ought to offer philosophical instruction for pay.[12] Bernard of Clairvaux, for example, held that taking fees for education is a "base occupation" (*turpis quaestus*). (Apparently he did not think this true of all wage labor but only where it involved deep spiritual things.)

Such views about wage labor remained closely linked to class privilege in modern Europe and exercised great power well into the twentieth century. Any reader of English novels will be able to produce many examples of the view that a gentleman does not earn wages, and that someone who does is too preoccupied with the baser things in life, and therefore base himself. Such views were a prominent source of prejudice against Jews, who, not having the same land rights as Christians, had no choice but to earn their living. Even in this century, in the United States, Edith Wharton shows that these attitudes were still firmly entrenched. Lily Bart, impoverished heroine of *The House of Mirth* (1905), is discussing her situation with her friend Gus Trenor. He praises the investment tips he has gotten from Rosedale, a Jewish Wall Street investments expert whose wealth has given him entry into the world of impoverished aristocrats who both use and despise him. Trenor urges Lily to encourage Rosedale's advances: "The man is mad to know the people who don't want to know him, and when a fellow's in that state, there is nothing he won't do for the first woman who takes him up." Lily dismisses the idea, calling Rosedale "impossible" and thinking silently of his "intrusive personality." Trenor replies: "Oh, hang it—because he's fat and shiny and has a shoppy manner!... A few years from now he'll be in it whether we want him or not, and then he won't be giving away a half-a-million tip for a dinner!" In the telling phrase "a shoppy manner," we see the age-old aristocratic

10. Aristotle, *Politics*, III.5 and VII.9–10.

11. See Plato, *Apology* 19D–20C, *Protagoras* passim, *Gorgias* passim.

12. I have profited here from reading an unpublished paper by Dan Klerman, "Slavery, Simony and Sex: An Intellectual History of the Limits of Monetary Relations."

prejudice against wage work, so deeply implicated in stereotypes of Jews as pushy, intrusive, and lacking in grace.

To this example we may add a moment in the film *Chariots of Fire* when the Jewish sprinter hires a professional coach to help him win. This introduction of money into the gentlemanly domain of sport shocks the head of his college, who suggests to him that as a Jew he does not understand the true spirit of English athletics. Genteel amateurism is the mark of the gentleman, and amateurism demands, above all, not earning or dealing in money. It may also imply not trying too hard, as if it were really one's main concern in life, but this attitude appears to be closely related to the idea that the gentleman does not *need* the activity because he has his living provided already; so the rejection of hard work is a corollary of the rejection of the tradesman. (Even today in Britain, such attitudes have not totally disappeared; people from aristocratic backgrounds frequently frown on working too hard at one's scholarly or athletic pursuits, as if this betrays a kind of base tradesmanly mentality.)

What is worth noting about these prejudices is that they do not attach to activities themselves, as such, but, rather, to the use of these activities to make money. To be a scholar, to be a musician, to be a fine athlete, to be an actor even, is fine—so long as one does it as an amateur. But what does this mean? It means that those with inherited wealth[13] can perform these activities without stigma and others cannot. In England in the nineteenth century, it meant that the gentry could perform those activities, and Jews could not. This informs us that we need to scrutinize all our social views about money making and alleged commodification with extra care, for they are likely to embed class prejudices that are unjust to working people.

Intersecting with this belief, in the opera singer example, is another: that is shameful to display one's body to strangers in public, especially in the expression of passionate emotion. The anxiety about actors, dancers, and singers reported by Smith is surely of a piece with the more general anxiety about the body, especially the female body, that has been a large part of the history of quite a few cultures. Thus, in much of India until very recently (and in some parts, still), it is considered inappropriate for a woman of good family to dance in public; when Rabindranath Tagore included middle-class women in his theatrical productions early in this century, it was a surprising and somewhat shocking move. Similarly in the West: The female body should be covered and not displayed, although in some respects these conditions could be relaxed among friends and acquaintances. Female singers were considered unacceptable during the early history of opera; indeed, they were just displacing the *castrati* during

13. Or those supported by religious orders.

Smith's lifetime, and they were widely perceived as immoral women.[14] Male actors, singers, and dancers suffered too; and clearly Smith means to include both sexes. Until very recently such performers were considered to be a kind of gypsy, too fleshy and physical, unsuited for polite company. The distaste was compounded by a distaste for, or at least a profound ambivalence about, the emotions that it was, and is, the business of these performers to portray. In short, such attitudes betray an anxiety about the body, and about strong passion, that we are now likely to think irrational, even though we may continue to share there at times; certainly we are not likely to think them a good basis for public policy.

When we consider our views about sexual and reproductive services, then, we must be on our guard against two types of irrationality: aristocratic class prejudice and fear of the body and its passions.

III. SIX TYPES OF BODILY SERVICE

Prostitution is not a single thing. It can only be well understood in its social and historical context. Ancient Greek *hetairai*, such as Pericles's mistress Aspasia, have very little in common with a modern call girl.[15] Even more

14. Mrs. Elizabeth Billington, who sang in Arne's *Artaxerxes* in London in 1762, was forced to leave England because of criticisms of her morals; she ended her career in Italy. Another early *diva* was Maria Catalani, who sang for Handel (d. 1759), for example, in *Samson*. By the time of the publication of *The Wealth of Nations*, female singers had made great headway in displacing the *castrati*, who ceased to be produced shortly thereafter. For Smith's own attitudes to the female body, see *The Theory of Moral Sentiments* I.ii.1.3, where he states that as soon as sexual passion is gratified it gives rise to "disgust," and leads us to wish to get rid of the person who is their object, unless some higher moral sentiment preserves our regard for (certain aspects of) this person. "When we have dined, we order the covers to be removed; and we should treat in the same manner the objects of the most ardent and passionate desires, if they were the objects of no other passions but those which take their origin from the body." Smith was a bachelor who lived much of his life with his mother and did not have any lasting relationships with women.

15. Aspasia was a learned and accomplished woman who apparently had philosophical and political views; she is said to have taught rhetoric and to have conversed with Socrates. On the other hand, she could not perform any of the functions of a citizen, both because of her sex and because of her foreign birth. On the other hand, her son Pericles was subsequently legitimated and became a general. More recently, it has been doubted whether Aspasia was in fact a *hetaira*, and some scholars now think her a well-born foreign woman. But other *hietairai* in Greece had good education and substantial financial assets; the two women

important, within a given culture there are always many different types and levels of prostitution: In ancient Greece, the *hetaira*, the brothel prostitute, the streetwalker; in modern America, the self-employed call girl, the brothel prostitute, the streetwalker (and each of these at various levels of independence and economic success). It is also evident that most cultures contain a continuum of relations between women and men (or between same-sex pairs) that have a commercial aspect—ranging from the admitted case of prostitution to cases of marriage for money, going on an expensive date when it is evident that sexual favors are expected at the other end, and so forth. In most cultures, marriage itself has a prominent commercial aspect: The prominence of dowry murder in contemporary Indian culture, for example, testifies to the degree to which a woman is valued, above all, for the financial benefits one can extract from her family.[16] Let us, however, focus for the time being on contemporary America (with some digressions on India), on female prostitution only, and on explicitly commercial relations of the sort that are illegal under current law.

It will be illuminating to consider the prostitute by situating her in relation to several other women who take money for bodily services:

1. A factory worker in the Perdue chicken factory, who plucks feathers from nearly frozen chickens.

2. A domestic servant in a prosperous upper-middle-class house.

3. A nightclub singer in middle-range clubs, who sings (often) songs requested by the patrons.

4. A professor of philosophy, who gets paid for lecturing and writing.

5. A skilled masseuse, employed by a health club (with no sexual services on the side).

6. A person whom I'll call the "colonoscopy artist": She gets paid for having her colon examined with the latest instruments, in order to test out their range and capability.[17]

By considering similarities and differences between the prostitute and these other bodily actors, we will make progress in identifying the distinctive features of prostitution as a form of bodily service.

---

recorded as students in Plato's Academy were both *hetairai*, as were most of the women attested as students of Epicurus, including one who was apparently a wealthy donor.

16. See chapter 3.

17. As far as I know, this profession is entirely hypothetical, though not by any means far-fetched. It is clear, at any rate, that individuals' abilities to endure colonoscopy without anesthesia and without moving vary considerably, so one might well develop (or discover) expertise in this area.

Note that nowhere in this comparison am I addressing the issue of child prostitution or nonconsensual prostitution (e.g., young women sold into prostitution by their parents, forcible drugging and abduction, etc). Insofar as these features appear to be involved in the international prostitution market, I do not address them here, although I shall comment on them later. I address only the type of choice to be a prostitute that is made by a woman over the age of consent, frequently in a situation of great economic duress.

THE PROSTITUTE AND THE FACTORY WORKER

Both prostitution and factory work are usually low-paid jobs, but in many instances a woman faced with the choice can (at least over the short haul) make more money in prostitution than in this sort of factory work. (This would probably be even more true if prostitution were legalized and the role of pimps thereby restricted, though the removal of risk and some stigma might at the same time depress wages, to some extent offsetting that advantage for the prostitute.) Both face health risks, but the health risk in prostitution can be very much reduced by legalization and regulation, whereas the particular type of work the factory worker is performing carries a high risk of nerve damage in the hands, a fact about it that appears unlikely to change. The prostitute may well have better working hours and conditions than the factory worker; especially in a legalized regime, she may have much more control over her working conditions. She has a degree of choice about which clients she accepts and what activities she performs, whereas the factory worker has no choices but must perform the same motions again and again for years. The prostitute also performs a service that requires skill and responsiveness to new situations, whereas the factory worker's repetitive motion exercises relatively little human skill[18] and contains no variety.

On the other side, the factory worker is unlikely to be the target of violence, whereas the prostitute needs—and does not always get—protection against violent customers. (Again, this situation can be improved by legalization: Prostitutes in the Netherlands have a call button wired up to the police.) This factory worker's occupation, moreover, has no clear connection with stereotypes of gender—though this might not have been the case. In many parts of the world, manual labor is strictly segmented

18. It is probably, however, a developed skill to come to work regularly and to work regular hours each day.

by sex, and more routinized, low-skill tasks are given to women.[19] The prostitute's activity does rely on stereotypes of women as sluttish and immoral, and it may in turn perpetuate such stereotypes. The factory worker suffers no invasion of her internal private space, whereas the prostitute's activity involves such (consensual) invasion. Finally, the prostitute suffers from social stigma, whereas the factory worker does not—at least among people of her own social class. (I shall return to this issue, asking whether stigma too can be addressed by legalization.) For all these reasons, many women, faced with the choice between factory work and prostitution, choose factory work, despite its other disadvantages.

THE PROSTITUTE AND THE DOMESTIC SERVANT

In domestic service as in prostitution, one is hired by a client and one must do what that client wants, or fail at the job. In both, one hay; a limited degree of latitude to exercise skills as one sees fit, and both jobs require exercise of some developed bodily skills. In both, one is at risk of enduring bad behavior from one's client, although the prostitute is more likely to encounter physical violence. Certainly both are traditionally professions that enjoy low respect, both in society generally and from the client. Domestic service on the whole is likely to have worse hours and lower pay than (at least many types of) prostitution, but it probably contains fewer health risks. It also involves no invasion of intimate bodily space, as prostitution (consensually) does.

Both prostitution and domestic service are associated with a type of social stigma. In the case of domestic service, the stigma is, first, related to class: It is socially coded as an occupation only for the lowest classes.[20] Domestic servants are in a vast majority of cases female, so it becomes

19. Consider, for example, the case of Jayamma, a brick worker in Trivandrum, Kerala, India, discussed by Leela Gulati, *Profiles of Female Poverty* (Delhi: Hindustan Publishing Corp., 1981) and whom I met on March 21,1997, when she was approximately sixty-five years old. For approximately forty years, Jayamma worked as a brick carrier in the brick-making establishment, carrying heavy loads of bricks on her head all day from one place to another. Despite her strength, fitness, and reliability, she could never advance beyond that job because of her sex, whereas men were quickly promoted to the less physically demanding and higher-paying tasks of brick molding and truck loading.

20. Indeed, this appears to be a ubiquitous feature: In India, the mark of "untouchability" is the performance of certain types of cleaning, especially those dealing with bathroom areas. Mahatma Gandhi's defiance of caste manifested itself in the performance of these menial services.

coded by sex. In the United States, domestic service is very often racially coded as well. Not only in the South, but also in many parts of rile urban North, the labor market has frequently produced a clustering of African-American women in these low-paying occupations. In my home in suburban Philadelphia in the 1950s and 1960s, the only African Americans we saw were domestic servants, and the only domestic servants we saw were African American. The perception of the occupation as associated with racial stigma ran very deep, producing difficult tensions and resentments that made domestic service seem to be incompatible with dignity and self-respect. (It need not be, clearly, and I shall return to this.)

THE PROSTITUTE AND THE NIGHTCLUB SINGER

Both of these people use their bodies to provide pleasure, and the customer's pleasure is the primary goal of what they do.[21] This does not mean that a good deal of skill and art is not involved, and in both cases it usually is. Both have to respond to requests from the customer, although (in varying degrees depending on the case) both may also be free to improvise or to make suggestions. Both may be paid more or less and have better or worse working conditions, more or less control over what they do.

How do they differ? The prostitute faces health risks and risks of violence not faced by the singer. She also allows her bodily space to be invaded, as the singer does not. It may also be that prostitution is always a cheap form of an activity that has a higher better form, whereas this need not be the case in popular vocal performance (though of course it might be).[22] The nightclub singer, furthermore, does not appear to be participating in, or perpetuating, any type of gender hierarchy—although in former times this would not have been the case, singers being seen as "a type of publick prostitute" and their activity associated, often, with anxiety about the control of female sexuality. Finally, there is no (great)

---

21. This does not imply that there is some one thing, pleasure, varying only by quantity, that they produce. With Mill (and Plato and Aristotle), I think that pleasures differ in quality, not only in quantity.

22. This point was suggested to me by Elizabeth Schreiber. I am not sure whether I endorse it: It all depends on whether we really want to say that sex has one highest goal. Just as it would have been right, in an earlier era, to be skeptical about the suggestion that the sex involved in prostitution is "low" because it is nonreproductive, so too it might be good to be skeptical about the idea that prostitution sex is "low" because it is nonintimate. Certainly nonintimacy is involved in many noncommercial sexual relationships and is sometimes desired as such.

moral stigma attached to being a nightclub singer, although at one time there certainly was.

THE PROSTITUTE AND THE PROFESSOR OF PHILOSOPHY

These two figures have a very interesting similarity: Both provide bodily services in areas that are generally thought to be especially intimate and definitive of selfhood. Just as the prostitute takes money for sex, which is commonly thought to be an area of intimate self-expression, so the professor takes money for thinking and writing about what she thinks—about morality, emotion, the nature of knowledge, whatever—all parts of a human being's intimate search for understanding of the world and oneself. It was precisely for this reason that the medieval thinkers I have mentioned saw such a moral problem about philosophizing for money: It should be a pure spiritual gift, and it is degraded by the receipt of a wage. The fact that we do not think that the professor (even one who regularly holds out for the highest salary offered) thereby alienates her mind, or turns her thoughts into commodities—even when she writes a paper for a specific conference or volume—should put us on our guard about making similar conclusions in the case of the prostitute.

There are other similarities: In both cases, the performance involves interaction with others, and the form of the interaction is not altogether controlled by the person. In both cases there is at least an element of producing pleasure or satisfaction (note the prominent role of teaching evaluations in the employment and promotion of professors), although in philosophy there is also a countervailing tradition of thinking that the goal of the interaction is to produce dissatisfaction and unease. (Socrates would not have received tenure in a modern university.) It may appear at first that the intimate bodily space of the professor is not invaded—but we should ask about this. When someone's unanticipated argument goes into one's mind, isn't this both intimate and bodily (and far less consensual, often, than the penetration of prostitute by customer)? Both performances involve skill. It might plausibly be argued that the professor's involves a more developed skill, or at least a more expensive training—but we should be cautious here. Our culture is all too ready to think that sex involves no skill and is simply "natural," a view that is surely false and is not even seriously entertained by many cultures.[23]

23. Thus the *Kama Sutra*, with its detailed instructions for elaborately skilled performances, strikes most Western readers as slightly comic, because the prevailing romantic ideal of "natural" sex makes such contrivance seem quite unsexy.

The salary of the professor, and her working conditions, are usually a great deal better than those of (all but the most elite) prostitutes. The professor has a fair amount of control over the structure of her day and her working environment, although she also has fixed mandatory duties, as the prostitute, when self-employed, does not. If the professor is in a nation that protects academic freedom, she has considerable control over what she thinks and writes, although fads, trends, and peer pressure surely constrain her to some extent. The prostitute's need to please her customer is usually more exigent and permits less choice. In this way, she is more like the professor of philosophy in Cuba than like the U.S. counterpart[24]—but the Cuban professor appears to be worse off, because she cannot say what she really thinks even when off the job. Finally, the professor of philosophy, if a female, both enjoys reasonably high respect in the community and also might be thought to bring credit to all women in that she succeeds at an activity commonly thought to be the preserve only of males. She thus subverts traditional gender hierarchy, whereas the prostitute, while suffering stigma herself, may be thought to perpetuate gender hierarchy.

THE PROSTITUTE AND THE MASSEUSE

These two bodily actors seem very closely related. Both use a skill to produce bodily satisfaction in the client. Unlike the nightclub singer, both do this through a type of bodily contact with the client. Both need to be responsive to what the client wants, and to a large degree take direction from the client as to how to handle his or her body. The bodily contact involved is rather intimate, although the internal space of the masseuse is not invaded. The type of bodily pleasure produced by the masseuse may certainly have an erotic element, although in the type of "respectable" masseuse I am considering, it is not directly sexual.

The difference is primarily one of respectability. Practitioners of massage have fought for, and have to a large extent won, the right to be considered dignified professionals who exercise a skill. Their trade is legal; it is not stigmatized. And people generally do not believe that they degrade their bodies or turn their bodies into commodities by using their bodies to give pleasure to customers. They have positioned themselves alongside physical therapists and medical practitioners, dissociating themselves from the erotic dimension of their activity. As a consequence of this successful self-positioning, they enjoy better working hours, better pay,

---

24. We might also consider the example of a skilled writer who writes advertising copy.

and more respect than most prostitutes. What is the difference, we might ask? One is having sex, and the other is not. But what sort of difference is this? Is it a difference we want to defend? Are our reasons for thinking it so crucial really reasons, or vestiges of moral prejudice? A number of distinct beliefs enter in at this point: the belief that women should not have sex with strangers; the belief that commercial sex is inherently degrading and makes a woman a degraded woman; the belief that women should not have to have sex with strangers if they do not want to, and in general should have the option to refuse sex with anyone they do not really choose. Some of these beliefs are worth defending and some are not. (I shall argue that the issue of choice is the really important one.) We need to sort them out and to make sure that our policies are not motivated by views we are not really willing to defend.

THE PROSTITUTE AND THE COLONOSCOPY ARTIST

I have included this hypothetical occupation for a reason that should by now be evident: It involves the consensual invasion of one's bodily space. (The example is not so hypothetical, either: Medical students need models when they are learning to perform internal exams, and young actors do earn a living playing such roles.[25]) The colonoscopy artist uses her skill at tolerating the fiber-optic probe without anesthesia to make a living. In the process, she permits an aperture of her body to be penetrated by another person's activity—and, we might add, far more deeply penetrated than is generally the case in sex. She runs some bodily risk, because she is being used to test untested instruments, and she will probably have to fast and empty her colon regularly enough to incur some malnutrition and some damage to her excretory function. Her wages may not be very good—for this is probably not a profession characterized by what Smith called "the beauty and rarity of talents," and it may also involve some stigma given that people are inclined to be disgusted by the thought of intestines.

And yet, on the whole, we do not think that this is a base trade, or one that makes the woman who does it a fallen woman. We might want to ban or regulate it if we thought it was too dangerous, but we would not be moved to ban it for moral reasons. Why not? Some people would point

25. See Terri Kapsalis, *Public Privates: Performing Gynecology front Both Ends of the Speculum* (Durham: Duke University Press, 1997); and Kapsalis, "In Print: Backstage at the Pelvic Theater," *Chicago Reader*, April 18, 1997, 46. While a graduate student in performance studies at Northwestern, Kapsalis made a living as a "gynecology teaching associate," serving as the model patient for medical students learning to perform pelvic and breast examinations.

to the fact that it does not either reflect or perpetuate gender hierarchy, and this is certainly true. (Even if her being a woman is crucial to her selection for the job—they need to study, for example, both male and female colons—it will not be for reasons that seem connected with the subordination of women.) But surely a far greater part of the difference is made by the fact that most people do not think anal penetration by a doctor in the context of a medical procedure is immoral,[26] whereas lots of people do think that vaginal or anal penetration in the context of sexual relations is (except under very special circumstances) immoral, and that a woman who goes in for that is therefore an immoral and base woman.

IV. SEX AND STIGMA

Prostitution, we now see, has many features that link it with other forms of bodily service. It differs from these other activities in many subtle ways, but the biggest difference consists in the fact that it is, today, more widely stigmatized. Professors no longer get told that selling their teaching is a *turpis quaestus*. Opera singers no longer get told that they are unacceptable in polite society. Even the masseuse has won respect as a skilled professional. What is different about prostitution? Two factors stand out as sources of stigma. One is that prostitution is widely held to be immoral; the other is that prostitution (frequently at least) is bound up with gender hierarchy, with ideas that women and their sexuality are in need of male domination and control, and the related idea that women should be available to men to provide an outlet for their sexual desires. The immorality view would be hard to defend today as a justification for the legal regulation of prostitution, and perhaps even for its moral denunciation. People thought prostitution was immoral because they thought nonreproductive and especially extramarital sex was immoral; the prostitute was seen, typically, as a dangerous figure whose whole career was given over to lust. But female lust was (and still often is) commonly seen as bad and dangerous, so prostitution was seen as bad and dangerous. Some people would still defend these views today, but it seems inconsistent to do so if one is not prepared to repudiate other forms of nonmarital sexual activity on an equal basis. We have to grant, I think, that the most common reason for the stigma attaching to prostitution is a weak reason, at least as a public reason: a moralistic view about female sexuality that is rarely

---

26. The same goes for vaginal penetration, according to Kapsalis: She says that the clinical nature of the procedure more than compensates for "society's queasiness with female sexuality."

consistently applied (to premarital sex, for example), and that seems unable to justify restriction on the activities of citizens who have different views of what is good and proper. At any rate, it seems hard to use the stigma so incurred to justify perpetuating stigma through criminalization unless one is prepared to accept a wide range of morals laws that interfere with chosen consensual activities, something that most feminist attackers of prostitution rarely wish to do.

More promising as a source of good moral arguments might be the stigma incurred by the connection of prostitution with gender hierarchy. But what is the connection, and how exactly does gender hierarchy explain pervasive stigma? It is only a small minority of people for whom prostitution is viewed in a negative light because of its collaboration with male supremacy; for only a small minority of people at any time have been reflective feminists, concerned with the eradication of inequality. Such people will view the prostitute as they view veiled women, or women in *purdah*: with sympathetic anger, as victims of an unjust system. This reflective feminist critique, then, does not explain why prostitutes are actually stigmatized and held in disdain—both because it is not pervasive enough and because it leads to sympathy rather than to disdain.

The way that gender hierarchy actually explains stigma is a very different way, a way that turns out in the end to be just another form of the immorality charge. People committed to gender hierarchy, and determined to ensure that the dangerous sexuality of women is controlled by men, frequently have viewed the prostitute as a sexually active woman, as a threat to male control of women. They therefore become determined either to repress the occupation itself by criminalization or, if they also think that male sexuality needs such an outlet and that this outlet ultimately defends marriage by giving male desire a safely debased outlet, to keep it within bounds by close regulation. (Criminalization and regulation are not straightforwardly opposed; they can be closely related strategies. Similarly, prostitution is generally conceived as not the enemy but the ally of marriage: The two are complementary ways of controlling women's sexuality.) The result is that social meaning is deployed in order that female sexuality will be kept in bounds carefully set by men. The stigma attached to the prostitute is an integral part of such bounding.

A valuable illustration of this thesis is given by Alain Corbin's valuable and careful study of prostitutes in France in the late nineteenth century.[27] Corbin shows that the interest in legal regulation of prostitution was justified by the alleged public interest in reining in and making submissive

27. *Women for Hire: Prostitution and Sexuality in France After 1850*, trans. Alan Sheridan (Cambridge, MA: Harvard University Press, 1990).

a dangerous female sexuality that was always potentially dangerous to marriage and social order. Kept in carefully supervised houses known as *maisons de tolérance*, prostitutes were known by the revealing name of *filles soumises*, a phrase that most obviously designated them as registered, "subjugated" to the law, but that also connoted their controlled and confined status. What this meant was that they were controlled and confined so that they themselves could provide a safe outlet for desires that threatened to disrupt the social order. The underlying aim of the regulationist project, argues Corbin (with ample documentation), was "the total repression of sexuality."[28] Regulationists tirelessly cited St. Augustine's dictum: "Abolish the prostitutes and the passions will overthrow the world; give them the rank of honest women and infamy and dishonor will blacken the universe" (*De ordine* 2.4.12). In other words, stigma has to be attached to prostitutes because of the necessary hierarchy that requires morality to subjugate vice, and the male the female, seen as an occasion and cause of vice. Bounding the prostitute off from the "good woman," the wife whose sexuality is monogamous and aimed at reproduction, creates a system that maintains male control over female desire.[29]

This attitude to prostitution has modern parallels. One instructive example is from Thailand in the 1950s, when Field Marshal Sarit Thanarat began a campaign of social purification, holding that "uncleanliness and social impropriety . . . led to the erosion of social orderliness. . . ."[30] In theory, Thanarat's aim was to criminalize prostitution by the imposition of prison terms and stiff fines; in practice, the result was a system of medical examination and "moral rehabilitation" that shifted the focus of public blame from the procurers and traffickers to prostitutes themselves. Unlike the French system, the Thai system did not encourage registered prostitution, but it was similar in its public message that the problem of prostitution is a problem of "bad" women, and in its reinforcement of the message that female sexuality is a cause of social disruption unless tightly controlled.

28. Ibid., 29. Representative views of the authors of regulationism include the view that "[d]ebauchery is a fever of the senses carried to the point of delirium; it leads to prostitution (or to early death) . . . " and that "[t]here are two natural sisters in the world: prostitution and riot." Ibid., 373.

29. For a more general discussion of the relationship between prostitution and various forms of marriage, see Richard Posner, *Sex and Reason* (Cambridge, MA: Harvard University Press, 1992), 130–3.

30. Sukanya Hantrakul, "Thai Women: Male Chauvinism à la Thai," *The Nation*, November 16, 1992, cited with further discussion in Asia Watch Women's Rights Project, *A Modern Form of Slavery: Trafficking of Burmese Women and Girls into Brothels in Thailand* (New York: Human Rights Watch, 1993).

In short, sex hierarchy causes stigma, commonly, not through feminist critique but through a far more questionable set of social meanings, meanings that anyone concerned with justice for women should call into question. For it is these same meanings that are also used to justify the seclusion of women, the veiling of women, the genital mutilation of women. The view boils down to the view that women are essentially immoral and dangerous and will be kept in control by men only if men carefully engineer things so that they do not get out of bounds. The prostitute, being seen as the uncontrolled and sexually free woman, is in this picture seen as particularly dangerous, both necessary to society and in need of constant subjugation. As an honest woman, a woman of dignity, she will wreck society. As a *fille soumise*, her reputation in the dirt, she may be tolerated for the service she provides (or, in the Thai case, she may provide an engrossing public spectacle of "moral rehabilitation").

All this diverts attention from some very serious crimes, such as the use of kidnapping, coercion, and fraud to entice women into prostitution. For these reasons, international human rights organizations, such as Human Rights Watch and Amnesty International, have avoided taking a stand against prostitution as such and have focused their energies on the issue of trafficking and financial coercion.[31]

It appears, then, that the stigma associated with prostitution has an origin that feminists have good reason to connect with unjust background conditions and to decry as both unequal and irrational, based on a hysterical fear of women's unfettered sexuality. There may be other good arguments against the legality of prostitution, but the existence of widespread stigma all by itself does not appear to be among them. As long as prostitution is stigmatized, people are injured by that stigmatization, and it is a real injury to a person not to have dignity and self-respect in her own society. But that real injury (as with the comparable real injury to the dignity and self-respect of interracial couples, or of lesbians and gay men) is not best handled by continued legal strictures against the prostitute and can be better dealt with in other ways (e.g., by fighting discrimination against these people and taking measures to promote their dignity). As the Supreme Court said in a mixed-race custody case, "Private biases may

31. See *A Modern Form of Slavery; the Human Rights Watch Global Report on Women's Human Rights* (New York: Human Rights Watch, 1995), 196–273, esp. 270–3. The pertinent international human rights instruments take the same approach, including the International Covenant on Civil and Political Rights, the Convention on the Elimination of All forms of Discrimination against Women, and the Convention for the Suppression of Traffic in Persons and the Exploitation of the Prostitution of Others.

be outside the reach of the law, but the law cannot, directly or indirectly, give them effect."[32]

V. CRIMINALIZATION: SEVEN ARGUMENTS

Pervasive stigma itself, then, does not appear to provide a good reason for the continued criminalization of prostitution, any more than it does for the illegality of interracial marriage. Nor does the stigma in question even appear to ground a sound *moral* argument against prostitution. This is not, however, the end of the issue. There aw a number of other significant arguments that have been made to support criminalization. With our six related cases in mind, let us now turn to those arguments.

(1) *Prostitution involves health risks and risks of violence.* To this we can make two replies. First, insofar as this is true, as it clearly is, the problem is made much worse by the illegality of prostitution, which prevents adequate supervision, encourages the control of pimps, and discourages health checking. As Corbin shows, regimes of legal but regulated prostitution have not always done well by women: The health checkups of the *filles soumises* were ludicrously brief and inadequate.[33] But there is no reason why one cannot focus on the goal of adequate health checks, and some European nations have done reasonably well in this area.[34] The legal brothels in Nevada have had no reported cases of AIDS.[35] Certainly risks of violence can be far better controlled when the police are the prostitute's ally rather than her oppressor.

To the extent to which risks remain an inevitable part of the way of life, we must now ask what general view of the legality of risky undertakings we wish to defend. Do we ever want to rule out risky bargains simply because they harm the agent? Or do we require a showing of harm to others (as might be possible in the case of gambling, for example)?

32. *Palmore v. Sidoti*, 466 U.S. 429 (1984).

33. See Corbin, 90: In Paris, Dr. Clerc boasted that he could examine a woman every thirty seconds, and estimated that a single practitioner saw 400 women in a single twenty-four-hour period. Another practitioner estimated that the average number of patients per hour was fifty-two.

34. For a more pessimistic view of health checks, see Posner, *Sex and Reason*, 209, pointing out that they frequently have had the effect of driving prostitutes into the illegal market.

35. See Richard Posner, *Private Choices and Public Health: The AIDS Epidemic in an Economic Perspective* (Cambridge, MA: Harvard University Press, 1993), 149, with references.

Whatever position we take on this complicated question, we will almost certainly be led to conclude that prostitution lies well within the domain of the legally acceptable, for it is certainly far less risky than boxing, another activity in which working-class people try to survive and flourish by subjecting their bodies to some risk of harm. There is a stronger case for paternalistic regulation of boxing than of prostitution, and externalities (the glorification of violence as example to the young) make boxing at least as morally problematic and probably more so. And yet I would not defend the criminalization of boxing, and I doubt that very many Americans would either. Sensible regulation of both prostitution and boxing, by contrast, seems reasonable and compatible with personal liberty.

In the international arena, many problems of this type stem from the use of force and fraud to induce women to enter prostitution, frequently at a very young age and in a strange country where they have no civil rights. An especially common destination, for example, is Thailand, and an especially common source is Burma, where the devastation of the rural economy has left many young women an easy mark for promises of domestic service elsewhere. Driven by customers' fears of HIV, the trade has focused on increasingly young girls from increasingly remote regions. Human rights interviewers have concluded that large numbers of these women were unaware of what they would be doing when they left their country and are kept there through both economic and physical coercion. (In many cases, family members have received payments, which then become a "debt" that the girl has to pay off.)[36] These circumstances, terrible in themselves, set the stage for other forms of risk and/or violence. Fifty to seventy percent of the women and girls interviewed by Human Rights Watch were HIV positive; discriminatory arrests and deportations are frequently accompanied by abuse in police custody. All these problems are magnified by the punitive attitude of the police and government toward these women as prostitutes or illegal aliens or both, although under both national and international law trafficking victims are exempt from legal penalty and are guaranteed safe repatriation to their country of origin. This situation clearly deserves both moral condemnation and international legal pressure, but it is made worse by the illegality of prostitution itself.

(2) *The prostitute has no autonomy; her activities are controlled by others.* This argument[37] does not distinguish prostitution from very many

36. See *Human Rights Watch Global Report*, 1–7.
37. See Anderson, *Value in Ethics and Economics*, 156: "Her actions under contract express not her own valuations but the will of her customer."

types of bodily service performed by working-class women. The factory worker does far worse on the scale of autonomy, and the domestic servant no better. I think this point expresses a legitimate moral concern: A person's life seems deficient in flourishing if it consists only of a form of work that is totally out of the control and direction of the person herself. Marx rightly associated that kind of labor with a deficient realization of full humanity and (invoking Aristotle) persuasively argued that a flourishing human life probably requires some kind of use of one's own reasoning in the planning and execution of one's own work.[38] But that is a pervasive problem of labor in the modern world, not a problem peculiar to prostitution as such. It certainly does not help the problem to criminalize prostitution—any more than it would be to criminalize factory work or domestic service. A woman will not exactly achieve more control and "truly human functioning" by becoming unemployed. What we should instead think about are ways to promote more control over choice of activities, more variety, and more general humanity in the types of work that are actually available to people with little education and few options. That would be a lot more helpful than removing one of the options they actually have.

(3) *Prostitution involves the invasion of one's intimate bodily space.* This argument[39] does not seem to support legal regulation of prostitution, provided that as the invasion in question is consensual; that is, that the prostitute is not kidnapped, or fraudulently enticed, or a child beneath the age of consent, or under duress against leaving if she should choose to leave. In this sense prostitution is quite unlike sexual harassment and rape, and far more like the activity of the colonoscopy artist—not to everyone's taste, and involving a surrender of bodily privacy that some will find repellant—but not for that reason necessarily bad, either for self or others. The argument does not even appear to support a moral criticism of prostitution unless one is prepared to make a moral criticism of all sexual contact that does not involve love or marriage.

(4) *Prostitution makes it harder for people to form relationships of intimacy.* This argument is prominently made by Elizabeth Anderson, in

---

38. This is crucial in the thinking behind the "capabilities approach" to which I have contributed in *Women, Culture, and Development* and other publications. For the connection between this approach and Marx's use of Aristotle, see Martha C. Nussbaum, "Aristotle on Human Nature and the Foundations of Ethics," in *World, Mind, and Ethics: Essays on the Philosophy of Bernard Williams*, ed. J. E. J. Altham and R. Harrison (Cambridge: Cambridge University Press, 1993).

39. Made frequently by my students, not necessarily to support criminalization.

defense of the criminalization of prostitution.[40] The first question we should ask is, Is this true? People still appear to fall in love in the Netherlands and Germany and Sweden; they also fell in love in ancient Athens, where prostitution was not only legal but also, probably, publicly subsidized.[41] One type of relationship does not, in fact, appear to remove the need for the other—any more than a Jackie Collins novel removes the desire to read Proust. Proust has a specific type of value that is by no means found in Jackie Collins, so people who want that value will continue to seek out Proust, and there is no reason to think that the presence of Jackie Collins on the bookstand will confuse Proust lovers and make them think that Proust is really like Jackie Collins. So, too, one supposes, with love in the Netherlands: People who want relationships of intimacy and commitment continue to seek them out for the special value they provide, and they do not have much trouble telling the difference between one sort of relationship and another, despite the availability of both.

Second, one should ask which women Anderson has in mind. Is she saying that the criminalization of prostitution would facilitate the formation of love relationships on the part of the women who were (or would have been) prostitutes? Or, is she saying that the unavailability of prostitution as an option for working-class women would make it easier for romantic middle-class women to have the relationships they desire? The former claim is implausible, because it has hard to see how reinforcing the stigma against prostitutes, or preventing some poor women from taking one of the few employment options they might have, would be likely to improve their human relations.[42] The latter claim might possibly be true (though it is hardly obvious), but it seems a repugnant idea, which I am sure Anderson would not endorse, that we should make poor women

40. *Value in Ethics and Economics*, 150–8; Anderson pulls back from an outright call for criminalization, concluding that her arguments "establish the legitimacy of a state interest in prohibiting prostitution, but not a conclusive case for prohibition," given the paucity of opportunities for working women.

41. See K. J. Dover, *Greek Homosexuality*, 2nd ed. (Cambridge, MA: Harvard University Press, 1978); and David Halperin, "The Democratic Body," in *One Hundred Years of Homosexuality and Other Essays on Greek Love* (New York: Routledge, 1990). Customers were all males, but prostitutes were both male and female. The evidence that prostitution was publicly funded is uncertain because it derives from comic drama, but it is clear that both male and female prostitution enjoyed broad public support and approval.

42. For a similar point, see M. J. Radin, "Market-Inalienability," 1921–25; and *Contested Commodities*, 132–6; Anderson refers to this claim of Radin's, apparently as the source of her reluctance to call outright for criminalization.

poorer so that middle-class women can find love. Third, one should ask Anderson whether she is prepared to endorse the large number of arguments of this form that might plausibly be made in the realm of popular culture—and, if not, whether she has any way of showing how she could reject those as involving an unacceptable infringement of liberty and yet allowing the argument about prostitution that she endorses. For it seems plausible that making rock music illegal would increase the likelihood that people would listen to Mozart and Beethoven; that making Jackie Collins illegal would make it more likely that people would turn to Joyce Carol Oates; that making commercial advertising illegal would make it more likely that we would appraise products with high-minded ideas of value in our minds; that making television illegal would improve children's reading skills. What is certain, however, is that we would and do utterly reject those ideas (we do not even seriously entertain them) because we do not want to live in Plato's *Republic*, with our cultural options dictated by a group of wise guardians, however genuinely sound their judgments may be.[43]

(5) *The prostitute alienates her sexuality on the market; she turns her sexual organs and acts into commodities.*[44] Is this true? It seems implausible to claim that the prostitute alienates her sexuality just on the grounds that she provides sexual services to a client for a fee. Does the singer alienate her voice, or the professor her mind? The prostitute still has her sexuality; she can use it on her own, apart from the relationship with the client, just as the domestic servant may cook for her family and clean her own house.[45] She can also cease to be a prostitute, and her sexuality will still be with her, and hers, if she does. So she has not even given anyone a monopoly on those services, far less given them over into someone else's hands. The real issue that separates her from the professor and the singer seems to be the degree of choice she exercises over the acts she performs.

43. I would not go quite as far as John Rawls, however, in the direction of letting the market determine our cultural options. He opposes any state subsidy to opera companies, symphony orchestras, museums, and so on, on the grounds that this would back a particular conception of the good against others. I think, however, that we could defend such subsidies, within limits, as valuable because they preserve a cultural option that is among the valuable ones, and that might otherwise cease to exist. Obviously much more argument is needed on this entire question.

44. See Radin, "Market-Inalienability"; and Anderson, 156: "The prostitute, in selling her sexuality to a man, alienates a good necessarily embodied in her person to him and thereby subjects herself to his commands."

45. On this point, see also Schwarzenbach, with discussion of Marx's account of alienation.

But is even this a special issue for the prostitute, any more than it is for the factory worker or the domestic servant or the colonoscopy artist—all of whom choose to enter trades in which they will not have a great deal of say over what they do or (within limits) how they do it? Freedom to choose how one works is a luxury, highly desirable indeed, but a feature of few jobs that nonaffluent people perform.

As for the claim that the prostitute turns her sexuality into a commodity, we must ask what that means. If it means only that she accepts a fee for sexual services, then that is obvious, but nothing further has been said that would show us why this is a bad thing. The professor, the singer, the symphony musician—all accept a fee, and it seems plausible that this is a good state of affairs, creating spheres of freedom. Professors are more free to pursue their own thoughts now, as money makers, than they were in the days when they were supported by monastic orders; symphony musicians playing under the contract secured by the musicians' union have more free time than nonunionized musicians, and more opportunities to engage in experimental and solo work that will enhance their art. In neither case should we conclude that the existence of a contract has converted the abilities into things to be exchanged and traded separately from the body of the producer; they remain human creative abilities, securely housed in their possessor. So, if to "commodify" means merely to accept a fee, we have been given no reason to think that this is bad.

If, on the other hand, we try to interpret the claim of "commodification" using the narrow technical definition of "commodity" used by the Uniform Commercial Code,[46] the claim is plainly false. For that definition stresses the "fungible" nature of the goods in question, and "fungible" goods are, in turn, defined as goods "of which any unit is, by nature or usage of trade, the equivalent of any other like unit." Although we may not think that the soul or inner world of a prostitute is of deep concern to the customer, she is usually not regarded as simply a set of units fully interchangeable with other units.[47] Prostitutes are probably somewhat more fungible than bassoon players but not totally so. (Corbin reports that all *maisons de tolérance* standardly had a repertory of different types of women, to suit different tastes, and this should not surprise us.) What seems to be the real issue is that the woman is not attended to as an individual, not considered a special, unique being. But that is true of many ways people treat one another in many areas of life, and it seems implausible

46. See Richard Epstein, "Surrogacy: The Case for Full Contractual Enforcement," *Virginia Law Review* 81 (1995), 2327.

47. Moreover, the UCC does not cover the sale of services, and prostitution should be classified as a service rather than a good.

that we should use that kind of disregard as a basis for criminalization. It may not even be immoral, for surely we cannot deeply know all the people with whom we have dealings in life, and many of those dealings are just fine without deep knowledge. So our moral question boils down to the question: Is sex without deep personal knowledge always immoral? It seems to me officious and presuming to use one's own experience to give an affirmative answer to this question, given that people have such varied experiences of sexuality.

In general, then, there appears to be nothing baneful or value debasing about taking money for a service, even when that service expresses something intimate about the self. Professors take a salary, artists work on commission under contract—frequently producing works of high intellectual and spiritual value. To take money for a production does not turn either the activity or the product (e.g., the article or the painting) into a commodity in the baneful sense in which that implies fungibility. If this is so, there is no reason to think that a prostitute's acceptance of money for her services necessarily involves a baneful conversion of an intimate act into a commodity in that sense. If the prostitute's acts are, as they are, less intimate than many other sexual acts people perform, that does not seem to have a great deal to do with the fact that she receives money, given that people engage in many intimate activities (painting, singing, writing) for money all the time without loss of expressive value. Her activity is less intimate because that is its whole point; it is problematic, to the extent that it is, neither because of the money involved nor because of the nonintimacy (which, as I have said, it seems officious to declare bad in all cases) but because of features of her working conditions and the way she is treated by others.

Here we are left with an interesting puzzle. My argument about professors and painters certainly seems to imply that there is no reason, in principle, why the most committed and intimate sex cannot involve a contract and a financial exchange. So why doesn't it, in our culture? One reply is that it quite frequently does, when people form committed relationships that include an element of economic dependence, whether one-sided or mutual; marriage has frequently had that feature, not always for the worse. But to the extent that we do not exchange money for sex, why don't we? In a number of other cultures, courtesans, both male and female, have been somewhat more common as primary sexual partners than they are here. Unlike quite a few cultures, we do not tend to view sex in intimate personal relationships the way we view an artist's creation of a painting, namely, as an intimate act that can nonetheless be deliberately undertaken as the result of an antecedent contract-like agreement. Why not? I think there is a mystery here, but we can begin to grapple with it by mentioning two features. First, there is the fact that sex, however prolonged, still takes up much less time than writing an article or producing a painting. Furthermore, it also cannot be done too often; its natural structure is that it will not very often fill up the entire day. One may therefore conduct an intimate sexual relationship in the way one would wish, not feeling that one is slighting it, while pursuing another line of work as one's way of making a living. Artists and scholars sometimes have to pursue another line of work, but they prefer not to. They characteristically feel that to do their work in the way they would wish, they ought to spend the whole day doing it. So they naturally gravitate to the view that their characteristic mode of creative production fits very well with contract and a regular wage.

This, however, still fails to explain cultural differences. To begin to grapple with these we need to mention the influence of our heritage of romanticism, which makes us feel that sex is not authentic if not spontaneous, "natural," and to some degree unplanned. Romanticism has exercised a far greater sway over our ideas of sex than over our ideas of artistic or intellectual production, making us think that any deal or antecedent arrangement somehow diminishes that characteristic form of expression.

Are our romantic ideas about the difference between sex and art good, or are they bad? Some of each, I suspect. They are problematic to the extent that they make people think that sex happens naturally, does not require complicated adjustment and skill, and flares up (and down) uncontrollably.[48] Insofar as they make us think that sex fits badly with reliability, promise keeping, and so forth, these ideas are certainly subversive of Anderson's goals of "intimacy and commitment," which would be better served, probably, by an attitude that moves sex in intimate personal relationships (and especially marriages) closer to the activity of the artist or the professor. On the other hand, romantic views also promote Anderson's goals to some degree, insofar as they lead people to connect sex with self-revelation and self-expression rather than prudent concealment of self. Many current dilemmas concerning marriage in our culture stem from an uneasy struggle to preserve the good in romanticism while avoiding the dangers it poses to commitment. As we know, the struggle is not always successful. There is much more to be said about this fascinating topic. But since (as I've argued) it leads us quite far from the topic of prostitution, we must now return to our primary line of argument.

(6) *The prostitute's activity is shaped by, and in turn perpetuates, male dominance of women.*[49] The institution of prostitution as it has most

---

48. It is well-known that these ideas are heavily implicated in the difficulty of getting young people, especially young women, to use contraception.

49. See Shrage's earlier article; Andrea Dworkin, "Prostitution and Male Supremacy," *Life and Death* (New York: The Free Press, 1997).

existed is certainly shaped by aspects of male domination of women. As I have argued, it is shaped by the perception that female sexuality is dangerous and needs careful regulation; that male sexuality is rapacious and needs a "safe" outlet; that sex is dirty and degrading, and that only a degraded woman is an appropriate sexual object.[50] Nor have prostitutes standardly been treated with respect, or given the dignity one might think proper to a fellow human being. They share this with working-class people of many types in many ages, but there is no doubt that there are particular features of the disrespect that derive from male supremacy and the desire to lord it over women, as well as a tendency to link sex to (female) defilement that is common in the history of Western European culture. The physical abuse of prostitutes and the control of their earnings by pimps—as well as the pervasive use of force and fraud in international markets—are features of male dominance that are extremely harmful and do not have direct parallels in other types of low-paid work. Some of these forms of conduct may be largely an outgrowth of the illegality of the industry and closely comparable to the threatening behavior of drug wholesalers to their—usually male—retailers. So there remains a question how far male dominance as such explains the violence involved. But in the international arena where regulations against these forms of misconduct are usually treated as a joke, illegality is not a sufficient explanation for them.

Prostitution is hardly alone in being shaped by, and reinforcing, male dominance. Systems of patrilineal property and exogamous marriage, for example, almost certainly do more to perpetuate not only male dominance but also female mistreatment and even death. There probably is a strong case for making the giving of dowry illegal, as has been done since 1961 in India and since 1980 in Bangladesh[51] (though with little success), for it can be convincingly shown that the institution of dowry is directly linked with extortion and threats of bodily harm, and ultimately with the deaths of large numbers of women.[52] It is also obvious that the dowry system pervasively conditions the perception of the worth of girl

50. An eloquent examination of the last view, with reference to Freud's account (which endorses it) is in William Miller, *The Anatomy of Disgust* (Cambridge, MA: Harvard University Press, 1997), chap. 6.

51. The Dowry Prohibition Act of 1961 both makes both taking and giving of dowry illegal; in Bangladesh, demanding, taking, and giving dowry are all criminal offenses. See chapter 3 (in this volume).

52. It is extremely difficult to estimate how many women are damaged and killed as a result of this practice; it is certainly clear that criminal offenses are vastly underreported, as is domestic violence in India generally, but that very problem makes it difficult to form any reliable idea of the numbers involved. See

children: They are a big expense, and they will not be around to protect one in one's old age. This structure is directly linked with female malnutrition, neglect, noneducation, even infanticide, harms that have caused the deaths of many millions of women in the world.[53] It is perfectly understandable that the governments of India, Bangladesh, and Pakistan are very concerned about the dowry system, because it seems very difficult to improve the very bad economic and physical condition of women without some structural changes. (Pakistan has recently adopted a somewhat quixotic remedy, making it illegal to serve food at weddings—thus driving many caterers into poverty.) Dowry is an institution affecting millions of women, determining the course of almost all girl children's lives pervasively and from the start. Prostitution as such usually does not have either such dire or such widespread implication: (Indeed, it is frequently the product of the dowry system, when parents take payment for prostituting a female child for whom they would otherwise have to pay dowry.) The case for making it illegal on grounds of subordination seems weaker than the case for making dowry, or even wedding feasts, illegal, and yet these laws are themselves of dubious merit and would probably be rightly regarded as involving undue infringement of liberty under our constitutional tradition. (It is significant that Human Rights Watch, which has so aggressively pursued the issue of forced prostitution, takes no stand one way or the other on the legality of prostitution itself.)

More generally, one might argue that the institution of marriage as most frequently practiced both expresses and reinforces male dominance. It would be right to use law to change the most inequitable features of that institution—protecting women from domestic violence and marital rape, giving women equal property and custody rights and improving their exit options by intelligent shaping of the divorce law. But to rule that marriage as such should be illegal on the grounds that it reinforces male dominance would be an excessive intrusion upon liberty, even if one should believe marriage irredeemably unequal. So, too, I think, with prostitution: What seems right is to use law to protect the bodily safety of prostitutes from assault, to protect their rights to their incomes against the extortionate behavior of pimps, to protect poor women in developing countries from

Indira Jaising, *Justice for Women* (Bombay: The Lawyers' Collective, 1996); and chapter 3 (in this volume).

53. See Amartya Sen and Jean Drèze, *Hunger and Public Action* (Oxford: Clarendon Press, 1989), 52; and chapter 1 (in this volume). Kerala, the only Indian state to have a matrilineal property tradition, also has an equal number of men and women (contrasted with a 94/100 sex ratio elsewhere), and 97 percent both male and female literacy, as contrasted with 32 percent female literacy elsewhere.

forced trafficking and fraudulent offers, and to guarantee their full civil rights in the countries where they end up—to make them, in general, equals under the law, both civil and criminal. But the criminalization of prostitution seems to pose a major obstacle to that equality.

Efforts on behalf of the dignity and self-respect of prostitutes have tended to push in exactly the opposite direction. In the United States, prostitutes have long been organized to demand greater respect, though their efforts are hampered by prostitution's continued illegality. In India, the National Federation of Women has adopted various strategies to give prostitutes more dignity in the public eye. For example, on National Women's Day, they selected a prostitute to put a garland on the head of the prime minister. Similarly, UNICEF in India's Andhra Pradesh has been fighting to get prostitutes officially classified as "working women" so that they can enjoy the child-care benefits local government extends to that class. As with domestic service, so here: Giving workers greater dignity and control can gradually change both the perception and the fact of dominance.

(7) *Prostitution is a trade that people do not enter by choice; therefore the bargains people make within it should not be regarded as real bargains.* Here we must distinguish three cases. First is the case in which the woman's entry into prostitution is caused by some type of conduct that would otherwise be criminal: kidnapping, assault, drugging, rape, statutory rape, blackmail, a fraudulent offer. Here we may certainly judge that the woman's choice is not a real choice, and that the law should take a hand in punishing her coercer. This is a terrible problem currently in developing countries; international human rights organizations are right to make it a major focus.[54]

Closely related is the case of child prostitution. Child prostitution is frequently accompanied by kidnapping and forcible detention; even when children are not stolen from home, their parents have frequently sold them without their own consent. But even where they have not, we should judge that there is an impermissible infringement of autonomy and liberty. A child (and, because of clients' fears of HIV, brothels now often focus on girls as young as ten[55]) cannot give consent to a life in prostitution; not only lack of information and of economic options (if parents collude in the deal) but also absence of adult political rights, makes such a "choice" no choice at all.

---

54. See, for example, *A Modern Form of Slavery: Trafficking of Burmese Women; Human Rights Watch Global Report*, 1296–373; Amnesty International, *Human Rights Are Women's Right* (London: Amnesty International, 1995), 53–6.
55. See *Human Rights Watch Global Report*, 197, on Thailand.

Different is the case of an adult woman who enters prostitution because of bad economic options: because it seems a better alternative than the chicken factory, because there is no other employment available to her, and so on. This too, we should insist, is a case in which autonomy has been infringed but in a different way. Consider Joseph Raz's vivid example of "the hounded woman," a woman on a desert island who is constantly pursued by a man-eating animal.[56] In one sense, this woman is free to go anywhere on the island and do anything she likes. In another sense, of course, she is quite unfree. If she wants not to be eaten, she has to spend all her time and calculate all her movements in order to avoid the beast. Raz's point is that many poor people's lives are nonautonomous in just this way. They may fulfill internal conditions of autonomy, being capable of making bargains, reflecting about what to do, and so on. But none of this counts for a great deal, if in fact the struggle for survival gives them just one unpleasant option, or a small set of (in various ways) unpleasant options.

This seems to me the truly important issue raised by prostitution. Like work in the chicken factory, it is not an option many women choose with alacrity, when many other options are on their plate.[57] This might not be so in some hypothetical culture, in which prostitutes have legal protection, dignity and respect, and the status of skilled practitioner, rather like the masscuse.[58] But it is true now in most societies, given the reality of the (albeit irrational) stigma attaching to prostitution. But the important thing to realize is that this is not an issue that permits us to focus on prostitution in isolation from the economic situation of women in a society generally. Certainly it will not be ameliorated by the criminalization of prostitution, which reduces poor women's options still further. We may grant that poor women do not have enough options, and that society has been unjust to them in not extending more options while nonetheless respecting and honoring the choices they actually make in reduced circumstances.

How could it possibly be ameliorated? Here are some things that have actually been done in India, where prostitution is a common last-ditch option for women who lack other employment opportunities. First, both government and private groups have focused on the provision of education to women, to equip them with skills that will enhance their options.

56. Joseph Raz, *The Morality of Freedom* (Oxford: Clarendon Press, 1986), 374.
57. See Posner. *Sex and Reason*, 132 n. 43 on the low incidence of prostitution in Sweden, even though it is not illegal; his explanation is that "women's opportunities in the job market are probably better there than in any other country."
58. See Schwarzenbach.

One group I recently visited in Bombay focuses in particular on skills training for the children of prostitutes, who are at especially high risk of becoming prostitutes themselves unless some action increases their option. Second, nongovernmental organizations have increasingly focused on the provision of credit to women, in order to enhance their employment options and give them a chance to "upgrade" in the domain of their employment. One such project that has justly won international renown is the Self-Employed Women's Association (SEWA), centered in Ahmedabad in Gujerat, which provides loans to women pursuing a variety of informal-sector occupations,[59] from tailoring to hawking and vending to cigarette rolling to agricultural labor.[60] With these loans, they can get wholesale rather than retail supplies, upgrade their animals or equipment, and so forth. They also get skills training and, frequently, the chance to move into leadership roles in the organization itself. Such women are far less likely to need to turn to prostitution to supplement their income. Third, they can form labor organizations to protect women employed in low-income jobs and to bargain for better working conditions—once again making this work a better source of income and diminishing the likelihood that prostitution will need to be selected. (This is the other primary objective of SEWA, which is now organizing hawkers and vendors internationally.) Fourth, they can form groups to diminish the isolation and enhance the self-respect of working women in low-paying jobs; this was a ubiquitous feature of both government and nongovernment programs I visited in India, and a crucial element of helping women deliberate about their options if they wish to avoid prostitution for themselves or their daughters.

These four steps are the real issue, I think, in addressing the problem of prostitution. Feminist philosophers in the United States do not write many articles about credit and employment;[61] they should do so far more.

59. An extremely high proportion of the labor force in India is in the informal sector.

60. SEWA was first directed by Ela Bhatt, who is now involved in international work to improve the employment options of informal-sector workers. For a valuable description of the movement, see Kalima Rose, *Where Women Are Leaders: The SEWA Movement in India* (Delhi: Sage Publications, 1995).

61. But see, here, Schwarzenbach and Shrage (op. cit.). I have also been very much influenced by the work of Martha Chen, *A Quiet Revolution: Women in Transition in Rural Bangladesh* (Cambridge, MA: Schenkman, 1983); Chen, "A Matter of Survival: Women's Right to Work in India and Bangladesh," in *Women, Culture, and Development*, ed. M. Nussbaum and J. Glover (Oxford: Clarendon Press, 1995); and Bina Agarwal, *A Field of One's Own: Gender and Land Rights in South Asia* (Cambridge: Cambridge University Press, 1994); and also

Indeed, it seems a dead end to consider prostitution in isolation from the other realities of working life of which it is a part, and one suspects that this has happened because prostitution is a sexy issue and getting a loan for a sewing machine appears not to be. But feminists had better talk more about getting loans, learning to read, and so forth if they want to be relevant to the choices that are actually faced by working women, and to the programs that are actually doing a lot to improve such women's options.

VI. TRULY HUMAN FUNCTIONING

The stigma traditionally attached to prostitution is based on a collage of beliefs most of which are not rationally defensible, and which should be especially vehemently rejected by feminists: beliefs about the evil character of female sexuality, the rapacious character of male sexuality, and the essentially marital and reproductive character of "good" women and "good" sex. Worries about subordination more recently raised by feminists are much more serious concerns, but they apply to many types of work poor women do. Concerns about force and fraud should be extremely urgent concerns of the international women's movement. Where these conditions do not obtain, feminists should view prostitutes as (usually) poor working women with few options, not as threats to the intimacy and commitment that many women and men (including, no doubt, many prostitutes) seek. This does not mean that we should not be concerned about ways in which prostitution as currently practiced, even in the absence of force and fraud, undermines the dignity of women, just as domestic service in the past undermined the dignity of members of a given race or class. But the correct response to this problem seems to be to work to enhance the economic autonomy and the personal dignity of members of that class, not to rule off limits an option that may be the only livelihood for many poor women and to further stigmatize women who already make their living this way.

In grappling further with these issues, we should begin from the realization there is nothing per se wrong with taking money for the use of one's body. That's the way most of us live, and formal recognition of that fact through contract is usually a good thing for people, protecting their security and their employment conditions. What seems wrong is that

"'Bargaining' and Gender Relations: Within and Beyond the Household," FCND Discussion Paper No. 27, Food Consumption and Nutrition Division, International Food Policy Research Institute, Washington, DC.

relatively few people in the world have the option to use their body, in their work, in what Marx would call a "truly human" manner of functioning, by which he meant (among other things) having some choices about the work to be performed, some reasonable measure of control over its conditions and outcome, and also the chance to use thought and skill rather than just to function as a cog in a machine. Women in many parts of the world are especially likely to be stuck at a low level of mechanical functioning, whether as agricultural laborers or as factory workers or as prostitutes. The real question to be faced is how to expand the options and opportunities such workers face, how to increase the humanity inherent in their work, and how to guarantee that workers of all sorts are treated with dignity. In the further pursuit of these questions, we need, on balance, more studies of women's credit unions and fewer studies of prostitution.

NOTE AT BEGINNING OF PUBLISHED

FOOTNOTES:

Both epigraphs to this chapter are translated from the Bangali by Kalpana Bardhan, in *Women, Outcastes, Peasants, and Rebels: A Selection of Bengali Short Stories* (Berkeley: University of California Press, 1990). Bandyopadhyay (1908–56) was a leading Bengali writer who focused on peasant life and issues of class conflict.

CHAPTER EIGHT

Contractarians and Feminists Debate Prostitution*

SIBYL SCHWARZENBACH

Much of the recent debate regarding prostitution, between liberal contractarians and feminists, only seems to confirm the hypothesis that there are significantly more than two sides to any story. In particular, the present article will focus on the debate between Lars Ericsson and Carole Pateman—between a representative contractarian defense of "sound prostitution" and a self-proclaimed and influential "feminist criticism" of the same.[1] Its aim will be to reveal the limits of both analyses. Not only might the complex phenomenon of prostitution thereby gain a further degree of clarity, but the growing disagreement *within* the feminist stance shall be revealed and highlighted. The hope is that a subtler and more refined philosophical, feminist position on prostitution may arise from the ashes of the old debate.

*Reprinted with permission from *NYU Review of Law and Social Change*, (1991), pp. 103–130.
  1. See Lars Ericsson "Charges against Prostitution: An Attempt at a Philosophical Assessment", *Ethics* 90 (April 1980): 335–66, and Carole Pateman "Defending Prostitution: Charges against Ericsson" *Ethics* 93 (April 1983): 561–565. We shall also be dealing with Pateman's new book *The Sexual Contract* (California: Stanford University Press, 1988), especially Chapter 7 entitled "What's Wrong with Prostitution?" pp. 189–218.

In general, feminists are in a bit of a bind when it comes to prostitution. Although they often concede they are not opposed to decriminalization (prostitutes themselves, of course, argue for this[2]), feminists at the same time offer such scathing critiques exposing the domination, exploitation or violence which they argue is essential to the phenomenon, that one is left with no clear-cut reason to decriminalize, much less any motive to help bring it about.[3] Pateman, as we shall see, argues in her analysis that the prostitute in fact sells not her sexual services, but her very "self" or "body" in the prostitute-client relation. But if this is indeed the case, if the activity in question entails the sale of bodies and selves, how could we possibly *not* be opposed to decriminalization? Slavery, after all, has long been illegal in this country. Something is amiss here.

It is perfectly consistent, of course, to argue that prostitution is morally wrong and that it should not be legalized under any circumstances; this is in fact the *status quo* view in the United States of America today (unlike in most European countries). What I shall be concerned with in the following paper, however, are arguments which might facilitate the move towards decriminalization; arguments which must entail showing (unlike so much of the feminist literature) where there is something "right" in prostitution, something which the present state of affairs, in criminalizing the activity, violates. And the paper tries to locate this "something" itself from an explicitly feminist point of view. If we are to take decriminalization seriously, we must come up with weighty arguments in its favor, and not merely pay lip service to it.

2. See the collected papers in the volume *A Vindication of the Rights of Whore's* edited by G. Pheterson (Seattle: Seal Press, 1989) where prostitute's speak for themselves. This volumne also includes summaries of the First and Second World Whore's Congresses in Amersterdam (1985) and Brussels (1986) respectively.

3. Laurie Shrage's recent "Should Feminist's Oppose Prostitution?" *Ethics* 99 (Jan.1989): 347–361, is a good example of this ambivalent tendency in recent feminist writing. Although Shrage claims her position is "consistent with decriminalization" the whole thrust of her work ends with the conclusion that since "commercial sex, unlike marriage, is not reformable" feminists should "outwardly oppose prostitution itself" (p. 360). I think it is fair to ask how, in this case, decriminalization could *ever* come about. (In private conversation, Shrage has admitted that she does not believe prostitution should be legalized.) For a feminist position, by contrast, that comes close to the view defended here, see Margaret Radin's "Market-Inalienability", *Harvard Law Review* 100 (June 1987), especially pp. 1907ff.

I. THE CONTRACTARIAN DEFENSE OF
"SOUND" PROSTITUTION

I shall only briefly summarize the liberal contractarian position on prostitution for its major tenets, I believe, are by now familiar.[4] The contractarian argues that our opposition to commercial sex lies primarily in our outmoded attitudes towards sexuality. Once we acknowledge our Puritan heritage in general, and our critical attitude toward female promiscuity in particular, for what they in fact are—lingering prejudices—, and once we recognize that the need for sexual gratification is as basic a need as that for food and fresh air (and hence should be readily available), our opposition to commercial sex will vanish.[5] We shall begin to recognize that a person's right to sell their sexual services is no more nor less of a right than that of selling their labor-power in any other of its multifaceted forms.[6]

As typified by Ericsson, liberal contractualism, of course, does not condone prostitution as it is now practiced. Ericsson puts forth a model of "sound prostitution" in which numerous reforms are necessarily incorporated.[7] Specifically, sound prostitution must entail first of all decriminalization; the prostitute should be given the same legal rights as anyone else, including the right to rent or own a suitable location of practice, legal protection from the exploitation by pimps and landlords, from possible abuse by customers, and so forth.[8] Secondly, the phenomenon must be cleansed of child and teen prostitution (on paternalistic grounds) and perhaps combined with anti-drug programs.[9] Third, the profession must become "freely chosen", or at least no more forced than a number of other legal trade choices.[10] Fourth, it must be equally available to both sexes; as it now stands most prostitutes are women and their clients are men, but this is only a contingent aspect of the phenomenon.[11] Finally, and perhaps most importantly, prostitution must be practiced in a social climate freed

---

4. I shall primarily be referring to Ericsson (1980), but see also D. Richards' *Sex, Drugs, Death and the Law* (Rowman and Littlefield: Toronto, 1982), especially Chapter 3 entitled "Commercial Sex and the Rights of the Person", pp. 84–153.
5. Ericsson (1980); 338, 341, 355.
6. Ericsson (1980); 342ff.
7. Ericsson (1980); 362ff.
8. Ericsson (1980); 362, 366.
9. Ericsson (1980); 363.
10. Ericsson (1980); 366.
11. Ericsson (1980); 366.

from emotional prejudice and stigma.[12] "In order to improve prostitution, we must first and foremost improve our attitudes towards it" writes Ericsson.[13] As Pateman notes, the contractarian extends the liberal ideas of the free market, of individual freedom and equality of opportunity, to sexual life.[14] Ericsson does not argue that commercial sex is ultimately desirable, only that it is acceptable given certain "ubiquitous and permanent imperfections of actual human societies."[15] These imperfections include, presumably, the inevitable frustration of sexual needs produced by any society, the general human propensity for not only variety, but even for mysterious and perverse gratification, as well as for intercourse free from entangling cares and civilized pretenses.[16]

2. THE FEMINIST CRITIQUE

According to Carole Pateman, on the other hand, "the central feminist argument" against liberal contractualism is "that prostitution remains morally undesirable, no matter what reforms are made, because it is one of the most graphic examples of men's domination of women."[17] Pateman argues that liberal contractualism in general, and Ericsson's position in particular, "systematically excludes the patriarchal dimension of our society from philosophical scrutiny."[18] That is, both neglect what Pateman (following Adrienne Rich) calls "the law of male-sex right": the traditional right possessed by men guaranteeing them access to, and power over, women's bodies.[19] Historically, this right has been justified by various arguments and myths, the most powerful one perhaps still being that men have a "natural and uncontrollable" sexual urge which it would be dangerous for society in general not to recognize.[20] Pateman shows, moreover, how conceptions of "masculinity" still today are closely intertwined with this presumed capacity to dominate a (some) woman. Echoing Marx's famous analysis of the domination of wage-labor by capital, Pateman claims that behind all talk of "free contractual relations"

12. Ericsson (1980); 365.
13. Ericsson (1980); 366.
14. Pateman (1983); 561.
15. Ericsson (1980); 366.
16. Ericsson (1980); 360.
17. Pateman (1983); 561.
18. Pateman (1983); 561.
19. Pateman (1988); 2.
20. See Shrage (1989); 353.

between the sexes, the problem of the continued social domination and subjugation of women by men is being both hidden and denied.[21]

Now in regard to this last point—that liberalism's methodological individualism essentially renders invisible the problem of the continued social domination of women—feminists of late are surprisingly united, and it is a point they have argued elsewhere at length.[22] But one may well accept this first premise of Pateman's line of attack, while simultaneously denying her conclusion: that commercial sex remains morally undesirable "no matter what reforms are made". And it is in fact such a position which will be argued in this paper.

To begin with, even the most cursory glance at our social and political history confirms Pateman's general thesis that men have traditionally enjoyed a "sex-right" due simply to their being born of a particular gender; men have had access to, and a control over, women's bodies (a control which has hardly been reciprocated by women). It is well known, for instance, that at one point in Roman Law the *Paterfamilias* outright "owned" his wife, children and slaves; he could essentially do with them what he willed and the law did not protect them from physical harm or even death.[23] In late feudal times, we still find a form of ownership of wife, children and servant—reflected, for instance, in Kant's category of rights *in rem* over persons—which grants the male household head an assortment of legal rights over family members falling short now of maiming or killing them.[24] And, of course, the principle of "unity of person" (advertised so well by William Blackstone in his commentaries on English law in 1765–69) meant that many married women in England and America, well into the nineteenth century, could still not divorce nor hold private property on their own; even the wage they earned in the factories legally belonged to their husband.[25] And so history, it seems, tends to confirm

---

21. Pateman (1983); 561–562.

22. See, for instance, M. Vadas' "A First Look at the Pornography/Civil Rights Ordinance: Could Pornography be the Subordination of Women?" *Journal of Philosophy* (Fall 1987): 487–511. See also Shrage (1989).

23. See, for instance, Sir Henry Maine's discussion of the Roman *Patria Potestas* in his *Ancient Law* (London, Holt and Co., 1884), p. 129ff.

24. See I. Kant's *Metaphysik der Sitten*, Paras. 22–36 where. J. Ladd does not even translate these paragraphs because he believes they are "of little interest except to the specialist"; See Kant's *The Metaphysical Elements of Justice*, translation and notes by J. Ladd (Indianapolis: Bobbs-Merrill 1965), p. 67.

25. As Blackstone expresses the doctrine of "union of person" between man and wife, "By marriage, the husband and wife are one person in law: that is, the very being or legal existence of the woman is suspended during the marriage, or at least is incorporated and consolidated into that of the husband: under whose

Pateman's thesis; it is difficult not to view it as a struggle by women to gain "autonomy"—defined here as the capacity of persons to direct their own lives, limbs and actions. What is of particular interest in this context, however, is the relation between our history of patriarchy and the growing commercialization of society. That is, as will hopefully become clear, with the phenomenon of prostitution we find ourselves at a "crossroads". On the one hand, women are just beginning to obtain a full right over their own bodies and actions (we often forget how recent it is that they can divorce, hold property, etc.).[26] And this development is no doubt due *in part* to commercialization—to the right slowly being granted everyone to control their own limbs and actions, as well as to sell their labor-power on the market. But by extension of *this* particular trend (reflected in the contractualist position) one would think the prostitute too should be allowed to enter the market with her brothers and sisters.

The commercialization of traditional female roles, on the other hand, understandably causes consternation. Women have, after all, traditionally performed sexual services, cared for children, cleaned their own homes and so forth, all without pay.[27] The recent controversies surrounding surrogate motherhood and pornography also reflect the invasion of capitalist market relations into the home, family and most intimate domains.[28]

wing, protection, and *cover*, she performs every thing." *Commentaries on the Laws of England*, 4 Vol. (Oxford, 1765–69), I, 430. In more practical terms, this meant that after marriage, all of the personal property brought to the marriage by a wife came under the exclusive control of her husband; he could spend her money, including wages, sell her slaves or stocks, appropriate her clothing and jewelry, and with regard to real property his rights were almost as extensive. See M.Salmon's discussion in *Women and the Law of Property in Early America* (Chapel Hill: University of North Carolina Press, 1986) p. 14ff. It was not until well into the mid-19th century—with the passage of the various Married Women Property Acts—that most women in America obtained the right to divorce, as well as the right to hold private property on their own. See E. Flexner's *Century of Struggle* (Cambridge: Harvard University Press, 1979), especially Ch.IV.

26. See Supra. Note 25. The right of a woman to terminate an unwanted pregnancy, of course, was constitutionally granted to women in the United States only in 1973, with the Supreme Court Decision on *Row v. Wade*, and this right even now is still in danger of being revoked.

27. See N. Cott, *The Bonds of Womanhood* (1977) pp. 19–63; see also B. Harris, *Beyond Her Sphere: Women and the Professions in American History* (1978) 32–72.

28. On surrogate motherhood, see for instance, the 1987 New Jersey Supreme Court decision on *Baby M*. Regarding pornography see the Indianapolis, Ind., City County General Ordinance No.35 against pronography (which was signed

And, if my reading is correct, Carole Pateman's concern is that the commercialization of sex—rather than breaking patriarchy—is in fact a further extension of it. For, she argues, the prostitute's presumed contract with her customer is not the usual employment contract at all. Unlike the wage-laborer, the prostitute does not sell her "labor-power", but in fact "her body" which cannot be separated from her person.[29] In contrast to the case of the capitalist who is interested only in the *products* of the wage-worker's labor, the client of the prostitute is interested in the prostitute's actual *body* itself.[30] Prostitution is fundamentally different from wage-labor, Pateman claims, because it violates the intimate relation between personality and physical embodiment.[31]

This point is central to Pateman's feminist critique; she not only reiterates it numerous times, but it is found over and again in the feminist literature.[32] "When sex becomes a commodity on the market so, necessarily, do bodies and selves."[33] Prostitution, in Pateman's eyes, is one of the last vestiges of the male sex-right; if a man can no longer "own" a female body outright, he can yet still possess one for a limited period of time, and thereby gain public acknowledgement as woman's sexual master.[34] I shall argue, however, that Pateman here commits a critical error; there is a legitimate sense to the contractualist's claim that the prostitute does *not* sell her body, but in fact a "service". Before I try to show this, however, we must clarify what it means to have "property in one's person" or "in one's body" in the first place. Not only is there much confusion on this point, but I wish to suggest that if one looks both to our philosophical tradition, as well to common sense, at least two different conceptions of "ownership" operate, and these two are not being kept distinct.

June 11, 1984 by the Marion County major) and which was followed immediately by a suit in federal court, see American Booksellers, Inc. v. Hudnut, 598 F.Supp. 1316 (S.D.Ind.1984). See also the *Public Hearings on Ordinances to Add Pornography as Discrimination against Women*, Committee on Government Operations, City Council, Mineapolis, Minn. (Dec. 12–13, 1983). For a discussion of these ordinance's see C. MacKinnon's *Feminism Unmodified* (Cambridge: Harvard University Press, 1987) especially Ch.13 entitled "Not a Moral Issue".

    29. Pateman (1983); 562.

    30. Pateman (1988); 203.

    31. Pateman (1988); 206–207.

    32. Pateman (1983) at 362, 363, 364; (1988); 202–208. See also, for instance, Susan Brownmiller's *Making Out on Prostitution* (1971) where the author repeatedly speaks of the prostitute's "selling her body" or, conversely, describes the male client as "buying another human being's body" (p. 37).

    33. Pateman (1983); 562.

    34. Pateman (1988); 208.

3. PROPERTY IN ONE'S PERSON

Of two distinct and important conceptions of ownership which may be found (I am claiming) in the modern Western tradition,[35] the first is the more familiar one to us all. It is what is usually understood by the notion of "private property" and—as originally set forth by John Locke—such property entails a number of characteristics. First, private property is typically something I obtain by my own efforts or an act of will; it is something I have "mixed my labor with", for instance, or contracted with another for. If I own something in this private form it entails, first, that I can use, manage, and enjoy the property *exclusively* as I will (provided, of course, I do not harm others or infringe on their similar property rights). But the full-fledged or "mature" conception of private property entails something further; it entails the right to *alienate* (sell) the thing and even *destroy* it if I should so wish.[36] In purchasing an automobile, for example, I cannot only use it as I will (provided I do not harm others), but I even have the right to destroy it (dissemble it, say, and sell it for scrap). Now some, namely Robert Nozick, actually seem to think that this is the form in which we possess our own bodies; Nozick advocates the right of the individual to suicide and even self-sale into slavery.[37] But the vast majority of modern Western thinkers,[38] as well as common sense, appears to disagree.

I now introduce a second, less well recognized (but equally fundamental) form of property which I shall call property *qua gift*. Unlike private property, the genuine gift is an unearned value which is "bestowed" upon us by another (a donor) for our benefit (in contrast, say, to a bribe) and our individual will here plays a far smaller role. As one author has shown,

35. See my *Towards a New Conception of Ownership* (Unpublished Dissertation, Harvard 1985) as well as my "Locke's Two Conceptions of Property" *Social Theory and Practice*, Vol.14, No.2 (Fall 1988) pp. 141–172.

36. A.M. Honore has given perhaps the most careful account of what is entailed by the modern conception of private ownership. Honore explicitly states that the right to use as one pleases, the right to exclude others, the power of alienating, and an immunity from expropriation are "cardinal features" of the institution. See his "Ownership", in *Oxford Essays in Jurisprudence*, ed. A.Guest (Oxford: Oxford University Press, 1961) pp. 111ff.

37. See Nozick's *Anarchy, State and Utopia* (Basic Books, 1978), p. 331. See also J. Philmore's illuminating discussion in "The Libertarian Case for Slavery", *The Philosophical Forum*, Vol.XIV, No.1, (Fall 1982).

38. See Schwarzenbach (1985) where the author argues that not only in Locke, but in the works of nearly all the modern thinkers (for instance, in Kant, Hegel, Marx, Rousseau, Rawls and others) "personality" and limb are essentially inalienable.

the authentic gift (unlike private property or the commodity) tends to be far more than a simple transfer of value; insofar as the gift brings into being a new moral relation between persons, it is a reality laden with subtle but very real "oughts".[39] And thus "owning", in this instance, comes closer to being a form of guardian- or *stewardship*. In Locke's thought, for example, our life, limb, natural freedom and equal political jurisdiction are original gifts granted us all by God in the state of nature. We did not "earn" such values; they were freely and generously given. Nor, he goes on, can we do with such property what we will; we can neither injure nor destroy our life and limb, because ultimately both belong to God whose "servants" we are.[40]

I wish to suggest that Locke's intuition regarding the fundamental stewardship of our bodies is very much alive today even if the surrounding theological justification has been dropped.[41] That is, in nearly all modern societies, I may not cut off my hand and sell it, nor may I alienate myself (or my life) to another (as in slavery). The point is that we *still today* continue to treat our bodies and lives as, in large part, "gifts"—not as private property, but as objects of our stewardship. (We did not, after all, create these original values; my freedom to direct my life, limb, etc. may be viewed as a "gift" from the rational community at large, and so forth.) Moreover, the notion of our lives as primarily a "stewardship" of our bodies accounts for why many think we may have a right to suicide at the age of seventy, but that something is terribly wrong when teenagers

39. See Camenisch's "Gift and Gratitude in Ethics", *The Journal of Religious Ethics*, Vol.IX, No.1, (Spring 1981): 1–34.

40. See J. Locke *Second Treatise of Government*, Ch.II, Para.6; also Ch.IV, para.32. See also Schwarzenbach (1988).

41. Locke's justification of our basic rights to life and limb is essentially theological (a point often not recognized in the Lockean secondary literature); see his *Second Treatise of Government* para.6 where Locke derives man's natural right to life, independence and to equal political jurisdiction, from the fact that we are all equally God's "workmanship" (his "servants" "sent into the world by his order") and thus not subject to another man's authority without our consent, etc. More recent attempts at justification, however, include interpreting these basic rights as self-evident to our reason (as in Kant where the basic right to freedom can rest on no appeal to God, see the *Groundwork of the Metaphysic of Morals*, Ch.1 and 3), or, as in the thought of Hegel and the later Rawls, where our basic rights are viewed as an historical given from the "free and rational community" at large [see Schwarzenbach (1985), (1988) and my recent "Rawls, Hegel and Communitarianism" in *Political Theory*, vol. 19 (1999), pp. 62–95]. Whichever interpretation one takes, these rights are viewed as an unearned gift or "given" with which each begins life.

do it. The teenager, it can be argued, has not been around long enough to fully appropriate and make his or her life their own "private" possession.

My claim is that when most people speak today of our "owning" our bodies, they in fact have *both* these concepts confusedly in mind. I wish to claim further that true self-possession of one's life, limb and actions entails the capacity to consider them under *both* property descriptions. That is, as I grow older my early stewardship of my body and acts (although normally never abandoned) does become more fully "mine" as it were. But this is not to say that we ever condone treating our bodies and lives as private property—as mere alienable and destructible things.

We need not go further into this distinction here.[42] Suffice it to note that the debate between Pateman and the liberal contractarian may perhaps be clarified by revealing the extent to which each side fixes on aspects of one of these conceptions of property precisely because, it seems, the other position is in danger of ignoring it. Pateman, for instance, can be shown to have operating in the background of her criticism something like the notion of an inalienable stewardship (although she does not, of course, use this terminology). Contracting out one's body, whether in prostitution or in slavery, violates moral personality's necessary, physical embodiment in the world.[43] Our lives and limbs are "not ours" to sell, and society must set limits in the case of prostitution as it does in the case of slavery.

The contractarian, on the other hand, will think Pateman misses a crucial point. The contractarian argues that the prostitute—in what is called "sound prostitution"—does not sell her body to another *in the sense of private property* even temporarily. The prostitute is not, for instance, granting the customer rights of destruction over her body, but only circumscribed "use" for a very limited period of time. The contractarian wants to argue that selling such "limited use", or restricted aspects of oneself, is no different from selling one's labor-power in a number of other fully legitimate forms.[44]

4. THE SALE OF LABOR-POWER

The issue between Pateman and the contractarian thus comes down to the question of whether it is possible that I can alienate an aspect of my concrete self (my physical body for use, say, for half an hour) and yet

---

42. For a more extended account, see my *Locke's Two Conceptions of Property* (1988) pp. 141ff.

43. Pateman (1988): 206–208.

44. Ericsson (1980); 343, 366.

not at the same time be alienating *myself*. At this point it is important to look more closely at the concept of labor-power, a notion which was first introduced by Hegel in his *Philosophy of Right*.[45] I turn to Hegel at this point, not only because Pateman and other feminists refer to him, but because his analysis of wage-labor remains, I believe, one of the most careful and trenchant.[46]

In unison with the whole of the modern tradition, Hegel argues that our "substantial personalities" are not for sale; we are each but the first steward of them. Under "substantial personality" Hegel includes our life and limb (our bodies) and also our reason, freedom of will, ethical life and religion.[47] And we may presume that he also includes our sexuality. The fact that these aspects of our substantive personalities are not for sale, Hegel claims, is already universally recognized in the modern system of rational law.[48] However, in his careful account of (political) personality, Hegel stresses a *dual aspect*; he distinguishes between the concrete empirical self, on the one hand, and the self as rational agency which is able to "abstract" or "distance" itself from any *particular* state of mind or action, on the other.[49] Hegel writes,

Single products of my particular physical and mental skill, and of my power to act, I can alienate to someone else and can give him the use of my abilities for a restricted period, because *on the strength of this restriction*, my abilities acquire an external relation to the [totality] of my being.[50]

45. Hegel, *The Philosophy of Right*, tr.T.M.Knox (Oxford: Oxford University Press; 19). All further references to this work will be indicated by (*PHR:*) followed by paragraph number.

46. Pateman (1988): 146ff. See also Radin (1987) who makes use of Hegel's account (although I believe with some incorrectness) in her analysis of market-alienability. It is also important to note here that Pateman views the concept of "labor-power" *in general* as nothing but a "political fiction", and she claims that to sell one's labor-power in *any* form is really only to enter into, as a subordinate, a domination relation (1988: 146ff.). I shall not decide here whether this is in fact the case (or whether it is an accurate portrayal of Marx's theory); our society in general (right or wrong) does not treat it as such. My point thus relates only to the distinction *between* prostitution (which is criminalized in our society) and other widespread and perfectly legal forms of wage-labor. My question is whether this distinction has any valid basis, and for this purpose Hegel's analysis is helpful.

47. Hegel, *PHR:* #66.

48. *PHR:* 36, 40, 43, 57. See also Hegel's Preface, p. 3.

49. *PHR;* 67.

50. *PHR;* 67, emphasis added.

That is, the human personality is distinguished precisely by its capacity for "expression" (*Entausserung*), by its ability to "distance itself" from particular products, actions or aspects of its physical being. Nor need this distancing ability be interpreted (as Pateman interprets it, and as Marx sometimes seems to)[51] as a necessarily *alienated* activity. Hegel is simply pointing to a capacity which underlies, not only our political personalities, but much of everyday human life; we all have the ability to obtain critical distance regarding not only others, but regarding many aspects of our particular selves, actions, or products. Hegel cites examples of art works, lectures, but also sermons and even prayers (aspects of our substantive personalities) which may be distanced or relinquished to the will of another.[52] Definite restrictions, however, always apply; by alienating a) too wide a range of one's abilities, or b) too much of one's time, moral personality, self and ultimate stewardship are clearly violated.[53]

Allow me to illustrate this important point by way of an example which parallels quite closely, I believe, the case of prostitution. I am a dancer and my body is *not separable* from the dance I perform. Those who come to see me dance, therefore, are interested—not in some product separable from my body—but in *my body itself*. If I have freely decided to dance for a wage, however, we do not (today) consider it a transgression of moral personality that I do so. My autonomy has not been infringed because others make visual use (as it were) of my body's activities temporarily; it has been my decision to make public and for hire certain particular expressions of my physical being for a restricted period of time. If, however, there are no limits on the time I must dance (if I must dance non-stop all evening, for example), or if I must relinquish the wider range of my abilities (such as my reason, or my religion, etc.) personality will clearly be violated.

5. THE CASE OF SEXUALITY

I will now try to show that there is in the end no relevant legal difference between the case of the dancer and that of (at least a version of) "sound prostitution". First, let us distinguish clear cases of "unsound"

51. See Supra. Note 46 above and Pateman (1988); 146ff. For Marx's views on alienation, see his *Economic and Philosophical Manuscripts of 1844* (especially the first manuscript on "estranged labor") in *Marx-Engels Collected Works* Vol.3 (New York: International Publishers) pp. 270ff.

52. *PHR*: 66–69.

53. *PHR*: 67.

prostitution. If the prostitute is under-aged, if she is tricked or forced (in any reasonable sense of the term) into the profession, if she must perform sex for hours (or continually all day, etc), if she must, in doing so, alienate a wider range of her abilities (such as her reason, or her personal morality, etc.), if her life or limb are at risk in any way and so on, then moral personality is clearly being infringed. But if, on the other hand, a mature woman decides when and where to offer a particular expression of her being (use of her body for a stipulated period of time) to a particular man (or to another woman) for touch, if the surroundings are safe and healthful, if she always retains the right not to have to perform any act which is distasteful to her, etc., why—we are obliged to ask—should moral personality be violated? The woman has in no way relinquished her general stewardship, but only treated various circumscribed expressions of herself as alienable property. She has in no way sold "her body"—in the sense of private property—to another even temporarily; she has only granted limited use.

A natural response here is that sexuality is surely of a different order than most other forms of wage-labor such as dancing or acting on stage. I agree, but it is not so easy to get at what this different order is. One might argue that "visual touch" by strangers is surely far less intimate and distasteful than "physical touch" by a strange man, especially "physical sexual touch". Many women, at the *mere thought* of being in the prostitute's position, begin to experience sensations of horror, repulsion, humiliation or disgust. But can these sensations (or responses) *at the mere thought* of another's being touched be sufficient grounds for rendering that other activity illegal? It seems they cannot for a number of reasons.

Most importantly, as was even argued in the British 1979 Report of the Committee on Obscenity and Film Censorship, "[i]f one accepted, as a basis for coercing one person's actions, the fact that others would be upset even by the thought of [his] performing those actions, one would be denying any substantive liberty at all."[54] So too, many activities cause near universal experiences of revulsion, at least at first—the internal organs spewing forth from the butcher's knife, the cold touch of the cadaver to the undertaker's hand, its putrid smell, etc.—but these activities are not (and certainly not for that reason) illegitimate. (It goes without saying

54. Report of the Committee on Obscenity and Film Censorship (also known as the "Williams Report") Cmnd 7772, (HMSO, London, 1979), p. 100. That is, one can imagine almost *any* activity causing *someone* upset under *some* circumstances. See R. Dworkin's discussion of this point (and his criticism of other aspects of the Williams Report) in "Do we have a Right to Pornography?", in *A Matter of Principle* (Harvard University Press; Cambridge, MA 1985) pp. 335–372.

that no one should be forced to have to perform them.) And here it is of critical importance to stress that sexual responses are hardly uniform across particular women. Many, perhaps most, women are repulsed and humiliated by (even the thought of) the physical touch of a strange man, but others obviously mind it far less (and this will depend in part on each's cultural and sexual history).[55] The surrounding background conditions (the degree of choice or coercion, the level of health and safety, etc.) are here of foremost importance.

Similarly, just as responses among individual women vary significantly, so does the delineation of acceptable moral and social behavior between cultures. Western women, for example, freely expose their faces in public (and frequently their whole bodies, say, on a nude beach), but a traditional Arab women will often experience shock, embarrassment and severe humiliation if only her veil happens to slip from her face.[56] And it is important to remember that our own culture—but a short time ago—forbade women entry into the acting profession and dancing on a theatrical stage, not only spelled social ruination, but prompted public outcries of "whore!".[57]

Despite the above considerations, however, a natural objection at this point runs: but what about the possibility that serious work as a prostitute cannot really be "limited" in time, in the sense that such activity tends to have a "numbing" effect on general sexual responsiveness? Does it not incapacitate one for normal sexual relations? And if so, by hiring out for sex one might be doing something analogous to selling a bodily organ, where the result is (a greater risk of) impairment of some bodily function. To this frequent objection I believe the most adequate response is: there does not appear to be any empirical evidence to support the above

55. This point does not mean to overlook the fact that the sexual history of many prostitutes is often one of sexual molestation, incest and child-abuse—a state of affairs which must be battled on its own grounds. Nonetheless, this unpleasant fact not withstanding, it still remains the case that prostitutes frequently have a different relationship to their own bodies than many of the rest of us do, and surely women in different times, places and cultures have. I elaborate upon this point below.

56. For discussions regarding the veil (or chador), largely limited to Muslim women of the urban upper and middle classes, see the collection of essays in *Women in the Muslim World*, ed. by L. Beck and N. Keddie (Cambridge, Mass: Havard University Press, 1978).

57. For a discussion of the Victorian stance on the actress as Fallen Woman—where the phrase "public woman" was still used interchangeably for performer and prostitute—see N. Auerbach's *Women and the Demon* (Cambridge: Harvard University Press, 1982) Ch.5: 182.

concern. On the contrary, prostitutes not only appear as capable as the rest of us of forming long-term, intimate sexual relationships, but there is even some evidence that the prostitute's level of sexual satisfaction could be higher than the average women's.[58] This objection is based on but one of the many myths surrounding the phenomenon of prostitution.

I wish to make it clear that I am not saying that there is not a fine line between selling one's abilities and selling one's self. I am only suggesting that where the line is drawn at present in the United States—where all forms of commercial sex among consenting adults are illegal (excluding, of course, various counties in Nevada where there is a limited amount of state-regulated prostitution), and yet working as a butcher or body guard, in a dark factory day in and out, or at many other highly distasteful, dangerous or unhealthy activities—this line begins to crumble under careful scrutiny. And I am suggesting that from a legal standpoint, there begins to be good justification for claiming that the activity of a mature woman (or man) who decides at some point in their life to sell their sexual services, limited in time, and who retains the right not to perform any act distasteful to them (as well as the right to interrupt the whole process at will), such a mature person should not be stigmatized and forbidden to do so, however much one's personal morality may rebel. For what is at issue here touches on one of the most fundamental individual rights of all: a person's right to direct their own life and limb as they think fit.[59] And this is a right which is only just beginning to obtain for women. Finally, as we have tried to show, the prostitute strictly speaking no more sells "her body"—as a physical entity, and in the sense of private property—than the dancer for hire does. In both cases the individual remains the ultimate steward of their physical being and each relinquishes only particular, restricted expressions of themselves for limited periods of time. And this fact alone is enough to distinguish sound prostitution from slavery: from the practice where bodies and selves are literally being "bought and sold".[60]

58. See Richards (1982) Ch.3; p. And we should note that even if such evidence turns out to be spurious (which only further empirical studies can reveal), this result would not automatically support continued criminalization; it might only require more stringent restrictions on type and hours of work, say, as in many other forms of employment.

59. See Locke's *Second Treatise* para.22. See also Richards (1982), Ch.3 entitled "Commercial Sex and Rights of the Person" where the author gives one of the most careful accounts in the literature of an individual "right to sexual autonomy" (pp. 84ff). Such a right, if recognized, also protects other practices still considered illegal and "abnormal" such as homosexual or lesbian sex.

60. This is not to deny, of course, that there exists *de facto* a worldwide practice of *forced* prostitution, which must be condemned. See K. Barry's

But although we have tried to show that Pateman's claim that the prostitute "sells her body" entails a confusion, and although we have emphasized certain similarities between prostitution and other kinds of wage-labor, we have not yet understood prostitution's *differentia specifica*; we have not reached what it is that distinguishes prostitution and makes it *appear as if* bodies and selves were in fact for sale. I believe it emerges quite clearly at this point that what is in fact being alienated or violated, even in sound prostitution, is not some physical or bodily entity, but rather a delicately constructed social identity.

Female Sexual Slavery (New York University Press: New York, 1984). But it seems important—precisely *because* there is such an extensive black market—that we distinquish legitimate or sound cases of prostitution from forced and altogether unacceptable forms, thereby allowing us to concentrate our energies on halting the latter.

I might also here note, in regard to another worry that many have expressed, that the legalization of the sale of certain forms of sexual activity on the market *need not* extend the overall power of the market in our lives. On the contrary, decriminalization could work to limit and regulate the activities (place and type of work, say) and protect the persons involved in (set health and safety standards for, etc.) the various types of sexual services which we all know are *de facto* being sold at this very moment. Nor is there any evidence (considering the cases of various European countries) that *decriminalization* causes an increase in the phenomenon of prostitution.

So too, we might note, that allowing certain traditional female activities legitimacy on the market (sexual services being one, but also surrogate motherhood, say) could well be combined with efforts to *limit* the overall effect the market has on our lives in other areas. It could be combined, for instance, with greater efforts at establishing unions, reducing the working day in general, raising minimum wage, etc. as well as with attempts to rescue other items (our major natural resources, for instance) from the open market and subject them to democratic control, and so forth. Thus the effect of decriminalizing prostitution need not be to expand the market, but may simply allow women a greater legitimate share of it. For the fact remains that "the market" as it now stands is deeply "sexist"; it tends to remunerate the labor of men, while it devalues traditional women's activity (pregnancy, housework, child-care, the servicing of needs, sexual and otherwise, and so forth). See J. Scales "A Tort of Feminist Jurisprudence" Again, the move to recognize certain limited expressions of women's traditional role as legitimate objects of market transactions (if combined with general efforts to restrict the overall power of the market) could work, not to expand the market, but simply to right the present imbalance within it with regard to gender. Of course, the idea of women becoming economically strong and powerful—of capitalizing on their traditional training and roles—strikes horror in the heart of many.

6. CULTURAL CONSTRUCTIONS OF SEXUALITY

The question must now be addressed as to why the prostitute's services *appear* to be a selling of her very body and self? Why is it that we distinguish so sharply between prostitution and, say, the dancer's profession? It is important to stress again the fact that little over a century ago people did *not* so clearly distinguish the two; a Victorian woman performing either activity was considered a "harlot" and socially ostracized.[61] And this suggests again, that what is being violated in both cases is not some "natural" relation between a woman and her body, but a culturally constructed norm of female personality.

There is little doubt that our society reifies persons in terms of their sexual practices.[62] Most of us consider our sexuality to lie at the "heart" of our being rather than, say, at the periphery. This may be attested to by the hostility with which persons of known different sexual practices are often treated (not just prostitutes, but homosexuals, practitioners of other cultures, or subcultures, etc.);[63] the *whole* of that person tends to be considered untrustworthy, threatening or morally suspect. And yet it appears that we reify persons in terms of their sexual practices less so today than we did one hundred years ago.

Let us take the instance of the 19th century upper-class Victorian woman. Her general respectability rested upon a tightly circumscribed sexual behavior indeed. She was not only not to have sex for money, but she was not to have it with more than one man (her husband), nor for more than one purpose (reproduction), and preferably with no sexual desire or satisfaction expressed on her part, and so forth.[64] In this case, her (Victorian) self—a social construct identifying the whole of her personality with her role of wife, attendant and mother—was violated by the simple activities of acting on a stage or of speaking out in public; such activities lay on the hitherside of her circumscribed role and performance of them was enough to lead to severe censorship if not to her social ruin.[65] And yet presumably *today* we consider such an infringement of her old

---

61. See footnote 57.

62. See Shrage's discussion (1989): 356.

63. *Bowers v. Hardwick.*

64. See N. Cott, *The Bonds of Womanhood* (1977); and Nina Auerbach, "The Rise of the Fallen Women" in *Women and the Demon*, pp. 182–83 (1982).

65. See Flexner's discussion of the early attempts by women in the 19th century to win the right to speak in public, to petition and to hold public meetings in *Century of Struggle* Ch.III, p. 41ff.

self—a woman pursuing an acting career, for instance—as fundamentally "liberating".

By the same token, may it not be that the prostitute's sale of services simply violates a contemporary social norm of female activity—a norm which still, to an extraordinary degree, identifies her legitimate personality with, and restricts her legitimate activities to, the role of wife and mother? After all, many woman are still called "sluts" or "whore" (by someone or other) if they simply have multiple sexual partners. Quite clearly we have not freed ourselves entirely from our Victorian legacy and generally from the sexual double standard; good women in particular are still expected to be virtuous, chaste, receptive, and their sexuality is often perceived as far less powerful than that of a man's. Luckily these myths are in a state of disintegration, but they are *only* in a state of disintegration and not yet gone. Might not a further violation of this social construct of female personality in fact be liberating for women in general, just as dancing on stage or speaking in public, was in the context of the 19th century?

As both Pateman (1988) and Shrage's (1989) accounts indicate, however, the matter is not so simple. For although the prostitute's activity flies in the face of restrictive social conceptions of woman as primarily wife and mother, there is an even deeper and more oppressive norm of female activity which it in fact upholds: the norm, deeply grounded in our tradition, which identifies woman's ultimate purpose as lying in her dedicated service to a man or master.[66] With the phenomenon of prostitution, that is, the myth is perpetuated that there is something "right" or "natural" about women devoting their entire lives to the well-being and pleasure of the male sex. And indeed, as we shall now see, Ericsson's contractualist account may be shown to rest implicitly on numerous assumptions about "our natural" sexuality and its fulfillment which are far from innocent.

The inability to recognize our current sexual practices as but one cultural construction among others is undoubtedly, as Pateman and Shrage have pointed out, the weak point behind Ericsson's contractualist account of "sound" prostitution. That is, Ericsson employs in his defense of decriminalization premises in regard to sexuality which are far from uncontroversial. Specifically, Ericsson takes what is often pereived to be characteristics of male sexuality in our society—an unrelenting desire for sex and an undiscriminating selection of sexual partners—as the human norm which, he claims, will survive all attempts at abolishing

---

66. Pateman (1988); 208–209, and Shrage (1989); p. 354.

prostitution.[67] Rather than trying to end prostitution, Ericsson argues, we should acknowledge and decriminalize it "for it is after all less difficult to alter our views, attitudes, and values than to alter our physiological nature."[68]

The positing of "our physiological nature" in this manner rightly outrages feminists; the claim ignores the by now vast literature which has not only revealed the astonishing diversity and complexity of sexual behavior between cultures (Foucault's work here comes to mind),[69] but significantly also the differences in our own culture between what may be called typical male and female responses.[70] Scholars continue to reveal how, for instance, in our society a woman's eroticism is differently constituted than that of the predominant male image of urgency and philandering; a woman's sexual satisfaction remains far more closely tied to the rest of her emotional life, to a need for security, long-term relationships, intimacy, and so on (and this is hardly surprising considering the primary social role of women over the centuries has been to be wife and mother.)[71] If such recent literature is correct, Ericsson's positing of

67. Ericisson (1980); 360. The positing of what is emerging as almost exclusively "male" sexual behavior (and an extreme form of it at that) as the human norm is found over and again in the literature on sexuality. See, for instance, W.Earle's "Depersonalized Sex and Moral Perfection" *International Journal of Moral and Social Studies*, Vol.2, No.3 (1987): 203–210 where the author claims "Sexual desires never have whole or integral persons as their objects" (p. 204). To put this forth as a truth about human sexuality in general is dubious, to say the least.

68. Ericsson (1980); 362.

69. M. Foucault *The History of Sexuality*, Vol.1&2 (New York: Vintage Books, 1980).

70. For just some of the literature pointing out such differences, see S. Hite, *The Hite Report: A Nationwide Study of Female Sexuality* (New York: Macmillian, 1976): M.J. Sherfey, *The Nature and Evolution of Female Sexuality* (New York: Random House, 1966); and *Philosophy and Sex*, ed.R.Baker & F.Elliston (New York: Prometheus Books 1984). See also the impressive collection of essays entitled *The Sexuality of Men*, ed.Andy Metcalf and Martin Humphries, (New York: Pluto Press, 1985).

71. T. Eardley has recently stressed how 19th century Darwinian theory gave a powerful scientific rational to the sexual double standard: to the model of male sexual urgency and promiscuity on the one hand, and female chastity and receptivity on the other, which standard still persists today despite growing awareness of women's sexual needs and pleasures. Significantly, Charles Darwin himself believed that the "evolutionary role" of the female sex was none other than to restrain the "animal urges" of men. See Eardley's "Violence and Sexuality" in *The Sexuality of men* (1985).

"our physiological nature" takes on a sinister quality; it is by no means an innocent commission of the "myth of the given". By positing characteristic male sexuality as at base "physiological" (and hence the need for an indiscriminate, quick trick becomes grounded in nature), Ericsson, unwittingly at best, removes much of contemporary male sexual practice from the possibility of all criticism. The following passage of Ericsson's brings this out clearly.

> It is also naive to think that an open, honest, and equal relationship between partners would do away with the demand for prostitution. Sexual attraction and the lack of it are largely irrational phenomena and as such are only marginally influenceable (thank heaven!) by open, honest discussions between men and women.[72]

Thank heaven! for the irrational, male sex urge forever closed to human reason! Ericsson's argument here (if one may call it that) is a paradigm of self-congratulatory, ideological intelligence; it is typical of those who do not wish to reflect deeply on, nor introduce reason into, the domain of their own crude habits and impulses. Instead they proclaim the present state of their own passions, urges and obsessions as somehow fixed in the nature of the universe. Much recent feminist discussion of sexuality, by contrast, can be viewed as the express attempt to "bring reason" to the situation; to unveil the brutality, violence and degradation (primarily against women, but which keeps men enthralled as well) that goes hand and hand with so much contemporary sexual practice (as well as the multibillion dollar a year U.S. sex industry, etc.). But I shall not dwell longer on this point—despite its importance—for it has been argued extensively elsewhere.[73] I turn instead to another version of the naturalistic fallacy, this time committed, surprisingly enough, by acutely aware and astute feminists.

In her article *Should Feminists Oppose Prostitution?*[74] Laurie Shrage is fully aware of the degree to which different practices of sexuality are indeed cultural constructions, and she notes that in other times and places the selling of sex did not spell oppression, nor induce loss of social recognition, as it does in our society today. Shrage cites, for instance, Gerda Lerner's study of Babylonian temple prostitution,

---

72. Ericsson, (1980); 360.
73. For instance, Pateman (1983), Eardley (1985), or Shrage (1989). See also C.McKinnon *Feminism Unmodified* (Cambridge: Harvard University Press 1987), A.Dworkin *Pornography: Men Possessing Women* (1981), and K. Barry *Female Sexual Slavery* (1984).
74. *Ethics*, Vol.99, No.2, (Jan.1989); 347–362.

For people who regarded fertility as sacred and essential to their own survival, the caring for the gods included, in some cases, offering them sexual services. Thus, a separate class of temple prostitutes developed. What seems to have happened was that sexual activity for and in behalf of the god or goddesses was considered beneficial to the people and sacred.[75]

Shrage admits that in a society where the rationale for the impersonal provision of sex is conceived in terms, say, of the promotion of nature's sacred fecundity—in contrast to our society where the rationale is in terms of the last-gap "restraint" of male sexual urges, or the release of repressed natural needs, etc.—"the social meaning this activity has may differ substantially."[76]

Shrage claims to have adopted a "relativist approach" which is justified in part by looking to the different consequences for prostitutes in Babylonian and other societies *vis* a *vis* their position in our society today; prostitutes in these other times and places were often appreciated, even respected and revered.[77] But despite this new approach, Shrage concludes (in accordance with Pateman's view) that in our society—where the social meaning of commercial sex is supported by cultural principles oppressive to women—to engage in , or to tolerate prostitution is "politically reactionary" and feminists should "outwardly oppose prostitution itself."[78]

Once again, from sound premises the conclusion by no means follows. Shrage's position, in the end, differs little from that of Pateman; it has only incorporated the realization that sexual practices and their "social meanings" may differ within different societies. Both thinkers nevertheless conclude that, since the practice is generally one of domination in our own society, its institutionalization (at least here) "degrades all women".[79] Interestingly enough, despite the recognition that "social meanings" in regard to the same physical, sexual act may differ in different societies, Shrage apparently denies that the "individual meaning" of the same sexual act *within* the same society can differ at all, i.e. her position is forced to deny the possibility that what one person experiences as degrading and humiliating *need not* necessarily be so experienced by another.

And yet if this were not possible—if the dominant "social meaning" of a phenomenon remains monolithic and closed to all competing interpretations (which would mean it amounts in the end to nothing less than

75. Shrage (1989): 349. See G. Lerner, "The Origin of Prostitution in Ancient Mesopotamia", *Signs: Journal of Women in Culture and Society* 1, (1976): 239.
76. Shrage (1989): 352.
77. Shrage (1989): 349–350.
78. Shrage (1989); 360.
79. Pateman (1988): 19.

a definition), or if this "meaning" were not capable consciously of being called into question and modified by particular individuals—then it is difficult to see how such "social meanings" could ever change over time, which they clearly do. (One might propound, of course, some crude materialist model of social change, which I would reject on other grounds.) For instance, how did it ever come about that women broke through the strict Victorian morality and began dancing on stage? Surely a *part* of the change was brought about by the actions of many particular women who simply refused to consider themselves "harlots" or "whores" despite their public dancing or speaking activity.[80] These women refused, that is, to go along with the dominant social meaning and their public actions surely contributed to the alteration of that social meaning over time.

But it is a further difficulty with Shrage's position which I wish to stress. The position taken here is not denying that despite variations in "individual meaning" regarding particular actions, there may be such a thing as a general "social meaning" of a phenomenon—a general backdrop, as it were, against which individual actions gain their particular significance. Nor does it deny that the predominant "social meaning" of prostitution at this time in our society is based on cultural principles oppressive to women: on principles which view women as subservient, as essentially subordinate to male needs and desires, as a repository for the release of male tension, and so forth. But as with most arguments from "social meaning" (Michael Walzer's included),[81] the proponent here fails to recognize that such "meanings" are not only rather "loose" and "unstable", but subject to change from *various* directions. That is, "social meanings" are expressly not natural, self-evident first principles which presume to determine a unique conclusion (in this case continued criminalization). Where the contractualist all too frequently interprets present male sexuality as an unchanging physiological given, the feminist here regards women's present oppression as inextricable from the phenomenon of any form of impersonal sex. But why, we must ask, do the present circumstances—granting the social meaning of prostitution is still predominantly one of male domination—why do these circumstances dictate "opposition", rather than decriminalization and reform?

To this question Shrage gives a most cursory dismissal. She claims that legitimate commercial sex would have to be predicated on principles other than the need to satisfy the presumed uncontrollable and socially

---

80. See Auerbach's discussion of the social "transforming power" of the Fallen Women in the Victorian Literary Imagination in *Woman and Demon's* (1982) Ch.V:180.

81. See M. Walzer's *Spheres of Justice* (New York: Basic Books, 1983) Ch.I. .

destabilizing sexual appetite of men.[82] And this seems true enough. If our critique of Ericsson above is correct, we need alternative principles to the "irrational but ubiquitous urge" of men which it would be dangerous for society to suppress, in order to support decriminalization and reform; such principles go hand in hand with woman's inferior and servile position. Shrage herself, however, fails to uncover any other possible set of principles which might support decriminalization. Regarding the case of prostitution she writes,

"However, I am unable to imagine nonpernicious principles which would legitimate the commercial provision of sex and which would not substantially alter or eliminate the industry as it now exists. Since commercial sex, unlike marriage, is not reformable, feminists should seek to undermine the beliefs and values which underlie our acceptance of it."[83]

As I argued in the first half of this paper, however, the newly emerging right of women to dispose over their own body, limbs and actions as *they* think fit is no right to scoff at; it is a right only recently being granted them and central to their new found and developing freedom.[84] Hence, for one, the principle of individual (sexual) autonomy underlies the call for decriminalization and reform of prostitution, a right not even considered by Shrage (or Pateman). Shrage's conclusion, moreover, that "(...) prostitution needs no unique remedy, legal or otherwise; it will be remedied as feminists make progress in altering patterns of belief and practice that oppress women in all aspects of their lives... "[85] begins to emerge, on my reading, as highly irresponsible. The claim that we should first work to change the "social meaning" of a phenomenon, and then the institution will "wither away" on its own, overlooks the fact that in the meantime the woman on the street corner is not only continually being exposed to a host of hazards and dangers (and hence needs protection), but that she is also being denied many of the rights routinely granted the rest of us (for instance, legally enforced protection against bodily harm, fraud, rape and racism, the right to sell one's labor-power in non-harmful ways, the right to rent a safe and healthful place of work, the right to travel and to freedom of association, etc.).[86] When this principle of the political

82. Shrage (1989): 359–360.
83. Shrage (1989); 360.
84. See Supra Notes 25, 26.
85. Shrage (1989): 360–61.
86. See the full list of grievances and violations of rights against prostitutes spelled out in the World Charter For Prostitutes' Rights (International Committee for Prostitutes' Rights, Amsterdam, February 1985) in *Vindication of the Rights of Whores'*, ed. Pherterson (1989) pp. 40–42.

integrity of the person (the principle which underlies equal enforcement of the law) is taken together with the principle of personal (sexual) autonomy, and when both are combined with various other principles sometimes suggested by those who argue for decriminalization—commercial sex allows sexual experimentation and even therapy—a powerful case for decriminalization in this country begins to emerge and this, I insist, from a feminist point of view.[87]

7. PROSTITUTION AS SEXUAL THERAPY

In particular, let us focus on what a scattered voice here and there has begun to argue: that commercial sex be perceived as providing skilled sexual therapy.[88] Now, by "sexual therapy" I do not here have in mind such hackneyed old defenses of prostitution which claim, for instance, that the prostitute plays a valuable social role insofar as her activity can "save" a dying marriage, or insofar as it provides release for pent up and otherwise dangerous male urges, etc.; such "therapy" would only work to maintain the *status quo*. By contrast, the expression "sexual therapy", or better "erotic therapy", will here be used as a term of art; it refers to that therapeutic process whereby sexual gratification—and erotic desire itself—is freed from their present fascination with domination and subservience.

87. I may here just note that the form of my argument is clearly not that of a deduction from self-evident first principles to a set of necessary conclusions. The model of practical reasoning here employed comes closer to a "balancing" or "weighing" of various principles [the search for which has come to be called the method of "reflective equilibrium". Cf. Rawls *A Theory of Justice* (Cambridge: Harvard University Press, 1971): 20ff]. The premises from which it begins are not strictly speaking self-evident, but rather deeply held and widely shared beliefs concerning the importance of individual freedom, sexual autonomy, and of the political integrity of the person—and this despite the fact that such freedom and integrity have long been denied to women. The aim of the argument is thus to seek a "deeper congruence" between such deeply held general principles and our individual, conflicting judgments regarding a particularly problematic case such as prostitution.

88. For instance, Margo St. James, Speech to the San Diego County National Organization for Women, La Jolla, California, February 27, 1982 as noted in Shrage (1989): 357. Whereas St.James also emphasizes the possible aesthetic opportunities of impersonal sex, I am here concerned mainly with its therapeutic possibilities.

Taking this line for a moment, one can well imagine a society which valued the physical and psychical well-being of *all* its members (including the infirm, retarded, the ugly and very old, etc.). And such a society generally regarded frequent and satisfying sexual experiences between persons free of domination as a healthy, even necessary, component of the good life. In such a society it is generally believed, moreover, that there is a direct correlation between healthy, mutually satisfying, erotic relations and a decrease in violent crime and anti-social behavior.[89] Surely here commercial sex could exist but it would not have, in Shrage's language, the "same social meaning"; the prostitute could now be respected because of, and turned to for, the wealth of her emotional and sexual knowledge. Now my question is: why could not such an ideal of impersonal sex help guide our legal reform of the institution of prostitution?

To Margo St. James's attempt to represent the commercial sex provider as a skilled sexual therapist,[90] Shrage quips "The fact that prostitutes have such low social status in our society indicates that the society in which we live is not congruent with this imaginary one."[91] But this is to reverse the order of cart and horse. We all know that our society is not congruent with this imaginary one; the issue is whether such an ideal may not provide further support and guidance for decriminalization and reform. Shrage's real complaint, however, is that one cannot simply supply a different rationale for the prostitute's services "on an *ad hoc* basis", and on her view prostitute *qua* therapist would be such an *ad hoc* rational. But is it? Again, Shrage runs the danger of regarding the present "social meaning" of prostitution as monolithic and unyielding.

Perhaps it is not widely enough known, for instance, that many male clients seek out a prostitute not even primarily with the aim of sex, but in her role of providing traditional female comfort and refuge.[92] Further, many psychiatrists at this very moment (at least in New York City) frequently employ an experienced prostitute in order to help client's overcome severe sexual problems (a phenomenon more politely referred to as "sexual surrogacy"). Should this role of prostitute as skilled emotional and sexual therapist—a role which is just emerging into the light of day—be driven underground again? Or should we not, conversely,

---

89. William Reich was the first, I believe, seriously to argue this point. See, for instance, *The Mass Psychology of Fascism*, tr. V. Carfango (new York: Farrar, Straus & Giroux 1970). See also Eardley (1985).

90. *Supra* note 88.

91. Shrage (1989); 358.

92. See D. Richards (1982); 123.

begin to encourage its humaner aspects, recognize the wealth of sexual knowledge the prostitute often possesses, while seeking to remove the phenomenon's surrounding male bias, brutality and exploitation? Nor should we forget that moves to de-stigmatize (at least certain forms of) impersonal sex may well allow more women in the future to seek out male (or lesbian) prostitutes (or sex-therapy clinics) themselves, and thus afford to women new avenues for coming to terms with their own long-neglected, sexual fears and frustrations. And should such activity begin to approach what we have called "erotic therapy"—should the attempt to alleviate sexual sorrow and suffering be consciously wedded to the project of overcoming domination and learning respect for personhood— we then not only have ample grounds for decriminalization of impersonal sex, but we have a model of "sound prostitution" which is positively *moral*.

At this point I anticipate a natural objection which could run: but is it realistic to believe that the role of prostitute could *ever* be "therapeutic"— particularly with regard to dominance and submission? Whatever plausibility there is to the idea of prostitute *qua* therapist seems to stem from the notion of women in general, and prostitutes in particular, as being "useful" in the "servicing" of male needs and in the soothing of their bruised egos—in short, from women's traditional position of dependency and submission. It surely requires a leap of the imagination to view the prostitutes' activity as even potentially undercutting dominance and submission, especially when the relation is set up in buyer/seller terms. Is the soothing of bruised male egos supposed somehow to deflate them?

To this last (rhetorical) question I answer a qualified "Why not?". How else are we going to successfully, and over the long run, deflate male egos other than through "therapy"—whatever other moral and legal means we use at the same time? If sexual therapy could be consciously wedded to a general insistence on respect for personhood, the result of such decriminalization may well just be a tendency to deflate the traditional male ego. If women work together (and not isolated one by one) they could (and I believe they eventually *will*) bring about a general restructuring of our dominant modes of culturally constructed sexual practices. And I do not see why such an ideal cannot lie at the very heart of attempts at decriminalizing prostitution: among the goals seeking full legal rights and protection for the prostitute, by encouraging her to unionize and fight for better working conditions (in terms of place, hours, and safety of work), by demanding a greater respect for the nature and art of her activity, as well as for a general recognition of sexual suffering and unhappiness, etc.[93] On the contrary, it is the *criminalization* of prostitution which continues to keep such women vulnerable and isolated, dependent on pimps and on criminal elements of society, as well as *separated from*, and unable to depend fully on, *each other*. On the view presented here, criminalization plays a major role in perpetuating the subservient and degrading role of the prostitute in our society. And I believe this the most cursory comparison between the status of prostitutes in the United States, and in those countries where her activities are legal (such as in the Netherlands, West Germany, Switzerland, Austria and Canada)[94] reveals.

Nor does the fact that the relation between the prostitute and client is "essentially" a relation in buyer-seller terms *necessitate* a relationship of

93. See the summaries of the First World Whores' Conference (Amsterdam, February 14, 1985) and the Second World Whores' Conference at the European Parliament (Brussels, October 1–3, 1986) in *A Vindication of the Rights of Whores*, ed. Pheterson (1989).

94. Being a prostitute is not even illegal in England and Italy, although the many state regulations and restrictions surrounding prostitution make it almost impossible to practice it legally. See the comparison between the status of prostitutes in various European Countries in contrast to their position in the United States and in Third World Countries in *Vindication of the Rights of Whores'* pp. 52–102.

To take but one aspect, whereas prostitutes in the United States (due to criminalization of their activity) are forced to live "under ground"—to combine with other criminal elements in society in order to protect themselves from violence and abuse by customers, in order to battle police, avoid prison, fight the discrimination of landlords, furtively seek safe places of work, adequate health care, etc.—prostitutes in the Netherlands and West Germany are struggling to have their activity not simply legalized (which is already the case), but fully recognized as a profession on a par with other forms of work; the latter would entail contributing to, and inclusion in, the National Health System and The Government Pension Scheme, as well as eligibility for Unemployment Benefits. See *The Vindication of the Rights of Whores* pp. 70–73, 78–82, 85–88. It seems the major further complaints of prostitute's in these European countries concerns an all pervading racism against women of color, and an unreasonable "state interference" in the women's lives: in particular, strict zoning laws and compulsory V.D. checks by doctors not of their own choosing (p. 72). Such concerns appear (at least to me) of an entirely different order (even a different order of racism) than those experienced by most American prostitutes many of which live in simple fear of their lives. In short, the the position taken by the United States on the issue of prostitution approaches more closely that of countries of the Third World with their routine violations of individual rights.

"dominance and submission" as Pateman would have it.[95] It seems to me one of the lingering fantasies of the most infantile, left-wing Marxism that all market transactions are meant to vanish completely, and particularly that they should do so all at once. By contrast, a more realistic, practical goal would entail isolating the most serious forms of economic and social injustices in the background circumstances of our society, and then moving to rectify these injustices first. Again, it seems appropriate that reform and decriminalization of prostitution discriminate between "sound" and "unsound cases" and our position not entail a blanket rejection of all impersonal sex.

In sum, if the view propounded here is correct, feminists such as Shrage and Pateman commit a surprisingly similar error to that of Ericsson. Where the latter posits a culturally based, specifically male sexual practice as "natural" and fixed in human nature, the former take the present "social meaning" of prostitution *qua* domination to be uniform and unyielding. The only way to proceed according to Ericsson is to allow things to stand pretty much as they are now (with a few minor adjustments here and there), while in the case of Pateman and Shrage, the proposals tend towards intolerance of each and every act of impersonal sex. But thereby the possibility of any deep and fundamental transformation, as well as evolution, in our culturally constructed sexual practices eludes both positions.

8. CONCLUSION

As I suggested at the beginning of this paper, with the phenomenon of prostitution American women are at a "crossroads" and can take either road. They can continue to downgrade their own sexuality, limit their eroticism to their role of spouse or parent (as has traditionally been the case) and now demand the same from men. Or, conversely, they can begin fully to acknowledge their sexuality, as well as how powerful and differently constituted (how much gentler, say, and more integrated with the whole personality) it traditionally has been. But one way of taking the latter road, it can be argued, is by the explicit call for decriminalization—by standing behind the prostitute and demanding her legal rights and safety, by attempting to better her working conditions as well as the profession's general self-conception through the formation of unions, by creating alternative avenues for work if the woman should so desire, and so forth.[96]

95. See Supra Notes 46 & 51 above.
96. This is the tact taken by Margo St. James in forming the prostitute's union in California entitled COYOTE (Call Off Your Old Tired Ethics). Richards also

At the same time, however, we must acknowledge how valuable such "erotic therapy" can actually *be*.

And thus to distinguish my position, first, from contractarian defenses of decriminalization, the portrait of "sound prostitution" here put forth is essentially a "feminist" one. The rationale in defense of "sound prostitution" cannot be that society must accommodate itself to some dangerous and ubiquitous male sex urge; such a rationale is increasingly being revealed as ideological since it continues to view women as natural servants to a fickle and arbitrary master. The rationale I am proposing in fact comes closer to being the reverse; the sexual autonomy of women must finally be granted at the same time as dominant male sexual practice is publicly acknowledged as being in dire need of therapy. Dominant practice is in need of a therapy which works to free sexual fascination and satisfaction once and for all from its present connection with violence, domination and subservience—a connection established through long custom and habit. But who, may I ask, is in a better position to perform such sexual therapy on men than women united together and working as a group? Who is in a better position to put forth alternative models of erotic gratification? In contrast to Ericsson's position, it does not suffice that our Puritan hangover (with its Christian denial of sensuous bodily pleasure, etc.) be rubbed away; we must simultaneously rid ourselves of our traditional male-tainted visions of sex. And there is no question here of positing some "physiological sexual urge" which always seems, in the end, to find fulfillment in the same crude way. The position here urged, by contrast, stresses the profound complexity of human sexuality. The account posits in general only a deep need in persons for equality, freedom and respect, as well as for emotional and physical closeness. But these are needs which, in our increasingly complex society, appear to demand ever new and creative methods of expression and fulfillment.

In contrast to the work of Pateman and Shrage, on the other hand, I am suggesting that a "feminist" account can no longer rest content with a depiction of woman's mere exploited and victim status; a feminist account today must work from, and play towards, female strengths as well. As I have argued, both Pateman and Shrage simply ignore in their discussions of prostitution, the important right a mature woman possesses to

notes that "Probably the best way to aid prostitutes to protect themselves from unfair business dealings with customers and pimps would be to provide legal facilities in the form of unions of prostitutes, which would bring the force of collective organizational self-protection to this atomistic profession (1982): 123. Again, such "organization" has to some extent already been achieved in many European countries.

determine and to control her own body and actions, and this in a manner that others (including other women) personally may find objectionable. The stewardship, however, is hers, not theirs.[97] Contemporary feminists, I believe, should be as wary of falling into a paternalism (or "maternalism") as we might have wished Marxists had been of the idea of a "party elite". Further, by not distinguishing between the many different forms of impersonal sex—by viewing them all as one monolithic domination of men by women—Pateman and Shrage's accounts, not only oversimplify the phenomenon, but actually tend to render invisible much of the *de facto* power women at this moment possess: a power which grows out of their traditional roles as nurturers and healers, as care-takers not only of the soul, but of the body too. And this is a role (irrespective of gender) which is being increasingly acknowledged today as critical to the health of any social order.

Finally, I wish to make it clear that my argument in no way depends on my putting forth sexual promiscuity as an ideal (and there is no evidence that decriminalization of prostitution leads to this). Nor am I claiming that commercial sex is particularly good sex or ultimately very satisfying. On the contrary, I am arguing that it need not be in order for us to legitimize it, and, under less than ideal circumstances, even consider it positively valuable. And it should be clear by now that I am not taking the stance (as Ericsson does) that the institution of prostitution as it is now practiced, or even as it may be practiced in the near future, is some "inevitable state of affairs" due, presumably, to some irrational and dark side of our natures. On the contrary, my suggestion has been that decriminalization of prostitution may be an important, even necessary step, to the institution's ultimate demise. That is, if the decriminalization process is wedded to a general and public acknowledgement not only that i) women have long been denied autonomy over their own limbs and action, but also importantly that ii) dominant male sexual practice is in desperate need of therapy—both points could be made explicit in the actual wording of the new legislation—such decriminalization may well allow prostitution as we know it to "wither away", or at least to transform itself into something else.

---

97. As one prostitute herself remarked in response to an International Abolitionist (of prostitution) Federation Congress (as quoted in Pheterson 1989:14):
"They get hysterical about us! I am tired of all these people who lie all the time. It is not right to call prostitution a threat to humanity. It is ridiculous to mix up forced prostitution and child prostitution and slavery and exploitation with *us*: I am a free and conscious adult."

In slightly different words, the position defended here is one which claims that if we not only aim for the general alleviation of poverty, as well as for women's equal participation in the full range of economic, social and political power, but importantly also work to reconstruct the fundamentals of received doctrine regarding male and female sexuality, then we can quite legitimately ask: what *need* will there be in the future for the phenomenon we *now* call prostitution? There may well be a continued need for intimate, long-term and mutually satisfying erotic unions between persons. But this is a need which, paradoxically, we might better come to understand, appreciate and even satisfy, if we at present stop stigmatizing all forms of impersonal sex.[98]

98. I would still like to note that I am well aware that this paper contains few, if any, concrete suggestions regarding how decriminalization might proceed in practice (whether there should be state licensing of erotic therapists, for instance, or to what degree there should be reasonable public regulation of the obtrusive solicitation of sexual relations, or of the health conditions of prostitutes, and so on). (For a discussion of such issues, see the Pheterson 1989 volumne). My aim in this essay, however, has been slightly different; I have tried to lay bare a theoretical foundation for decriminalization, and this from a distinctively *feminist* point of view. Nothing I have said thus far is meant to deny that the practical details of the legalization process are of the utmost importance and need still to be worked out. To the contrary, I have tried to shift the terms of the original debate in this direction: from the question of *whether* we should decriminalize prostitution, to the question of *what form* such decriminalization should take.

CHAPTER NINE

Prostitution and the Case for Decriminalization*

Laurie Shrage

☾.

Responses to prostitution from the left have been radically contradictory. Marxist thinkers, for example, are committed to study social phenomena in terms of systems of production and their related labor forms. But they rarely treat prostitution as a kind of work; instead they treat it as a side effect of the moral decay, corruption, or cultural collapse that occurs under particular social conditions. Why? Leftists generally respect working-class people and their political and economic struggles. Yet they rarely exhibit respect toward prostitute organizations or their political activists and intellectuals. For the most part, such groups and individuals are ignored.[1] Again, why?

Many on the left want to believe that prostitution would not exist or would not be common or tolerated in a world free of economic, gender, and sexual exploitation. The problem of prostitution would solve itself once other problems are solved. Yet speculative judgments like this one are abstract and academic. Prostitution isn't any single thing—a unitary social phenomenon with a particular origin—and so it doesn't make sense to argue about whether it would or wouldn't be present in this or that type of society. Working from crosscultural and historical studies, I have examined institutionalized and commodified exchanges of sexual services between women providers and their male customers in many different

*Reprinted with permission from *Dissent*, (Spring 1996), pp. 41–45.
  1. One recent notable exception to this is Shannon Bell's *Reading, Writing, and Rewriting the Prostitute Body* (Bloomington: Indiana University Press, 1994).

social contexts.[2] I conclude that there are (or have been) places and times where exchanges of sexual services between women and men are (or were) relatively free of gender and class domination. How then should leftists respond to the varieties of prostitution in the contemporary United States, where the labor practices involved are shaped by pernicious class and gender asymmetries?

I want to argue that we should include in our political agendas the dismantling of the legal and social structures that criminalize prostitution and stigmatize prostitutes. In conjunction with this project, we will need to invent regulatory alternatives to the current punitive systems of control. These are the primary aims of numerous prostitute civil rights and labor groups, and I think both feminists and socialists should support them, though not for the libertarian reasons many representatives of these groups give. Arguments for decriminalizing prostitution can be made by appealing to notions of workers' rights and the dignity of low-status work; they need not appeal to the libertarian ideal of total freedom from governmental intrusion into the lives of presumably independent individuals. These arguments can also be strengthened by accepting a robust pluralism with regard to sexual customs and practices. I don't mean that we cannot criticize sexual practices, only that the criticism must take into account different cultural conceptions of human sexuality and not dismiss out of hand those that are unfamiliar. Again, this desire to understand alien customs should not be confused with a libertarian laissez-faire morality. The libertarian sees sexual desires as a natural force that society should respect; the pluralist understands that desire, including the desire for noncommodified sex, is shaped by cultural and social forces.

Feminist theorists have argued that prostitution involves the sexual and economic subordination, degradation, and exploitation of women and girls. Many forms of prostitution are indeed brutal and oppressive: the near slave conditions that have been reported recently in brothels in Thailand, the use of "comfort women" by the Japanese during the Second World War, the prostitution that exists around U.S. military bases and in many contemporary urban spaces ("streetwalking," "massage parlors," "escort services," and so on). Women and girls have been tricked, or physically and economically coerced, into the prostitution business and then kept in it against their will. Women have contracted fatal diseases; they have been beaten and raped. These are common aspects of contemporary prostitution that anyone concerned with social justice must address.

2. *Moral Dilemmas of Feminism: Prostitution, Adultery, and Abortion* (New York: Routledge, 1994).

But we must also ask whether the legal structures that have been set up to control and discourage prostitution—including voluntary prostitution where it exists—also oppress women. Both women who work as prostitutes and women who are suspected of doing so (usually poor women of color) are frequently harassed, manipulated, and exploited by police officers and others who have power over them. Criminalization contributes to the stigma that prostitutes bear, making them more vulnerable to hate crimes, housing and employment discrimination, and other violations of their basic rights.

Because both the operation of prostitution businesses and their legal suppression typically sacrifice women's interests, feminists generally oppose both prostitution and its criminalization. Many feminists aim to devise nonpunitive, extralegal responses, such as providing other work opportunities. Yet there has been no concerted feminist attempt to undo the laws that define acts of prostitution as criminal offenses and impose penalties on participants—more often the female vendors than the male customers. Certainly feminist groups have not given the decriminalization of prostitution the same priority they have given to other issues, such as ensuring the legality of abortion, reforming rape and sexual harassment laws, and desegregating corporate management and the professions. Moreover, feminists have been more vocal in opposing sex businesses than the laws that criminalize the activities of commercial providers, and thus have contributed to creating a climate conducive to the continued degradation of prostitutes.

Feminists have not mobilized around the decriminalization of prostitution because of our lingering ambivalence about the subject. Some question whether commodified exchanges of sexual services are ever voluntary and regard prostitutes always as manipulated victims rather than autonomous agents—a view that requires us to second guess the motives, desires, and values of all prostitutes. Other feminists argue for decriminalizing only the prostitute's work while maintaining the criminal status of pimping, pandering, and so on. But this requires the state to determine which of the prostitute's partners are exploiting her and which are not—unless we wish to punish all the prostitute's possible business partners, including her spouse, boyfriend or girlfriend, parents and siblings, and other comrades.

Although feminists are fully aware of the varieties of abuse prostitutes suffer, many of them fear that decriminalization will lead to more prostitution and thus more exploitation of women and children. So they are willing to tolerate the often brutal enforcement of laws against it. Yet realistically, we are more likely to discourage the exploitation of women and children by regulating the labor practices followed by sex businesses.

If businesses that provide customers with personal sexual services could operate legally, then they would be subject to the same labor regulations that apply to other businesses (given the nature of the work, additional regulations might be necessary).[3] Such businesses would not be allowed to treat workers like slaves, hire underage workers, deprive them of compensation for which they contracted, or expose them to unnecessary risks. The businesses could be required to enforce health and safety codes, provide workers with a minimum income and health insurance, and allow them to form collectives to negotiate for improved working conditions, compensation, and benefits.

Many feminists find it frightening to imagine a society where sex can be purchased as easily as soap, where selling sex is an occupational option like selling shoes, and where businesses that profit from commercial sex are as legitimate as Ben and Jerry's. Such imaginings usually lead to the question, "What next?" This is the slippery-slope argument, which is elaborated as follows: "Are we now going to allow the sale of *x*?"— where *x* is your favorite tabooed object (babies, vital organs, bombs, and so on). The answer to this question is "No—not unless by tolerating the commercial distribution of *x* we can better protect the rights of particular people or better realize some moral ideal." By tolerating the commercial distribution of sexual services within certain limits, we can better protect the rights and interests of those who seek these services and, importantly, those who choose to earn income by providing them.

Though it is useful to ask what social forces lead some people to seek the relatively *impersonal* provision of *personal* sexual services, we should be equally critical of the cultural assumptions embedded in this question and in our various answers. At best, such excursions may help us understand how prostitution is shaped by large and small capital interests, as well as dominant gender, racial, and sexual ideologies, and thus how to devise regulatory instruments that discourage the recognizable forms of abuse, exploitation, and humiliation.

The argument I am making is simply this: that the forms of exploitation and abuse suffered by prostitutes are similar to those suffered by other workers (though they are often more intense because of the illegal status of this work). Therefore these abuses should be addressed by mechanisms that improve the condition of workers generally. Sweatshop conditions

---

3. Roger Matthews proposes some general guidelines for regulating prostitution informed by radical rather than liberal principles in "Beyond Wolfenden?: Prostitution, Politics and the Law," in R. Matthews and J. Young, eds., *Confronting Crime* (London: Sage, 1986). See also my discussion of his proposals in *Moral Dilemmas of Feminism*, pp. 83–87 and 158–161.

should not be tolerated, violations of workers' constitutionally protected rights should not be tolerated, customers should not be permitted to engage in behaviors that endanger the workers' health or well being, care should be taken to avoid harm to noninvolved third parties, contracts for compensation and services should be voluntary and take into account the interests of all affected, and when these conditions are met such contracts should be respected (though not necessarily enforced by outside authorities). If the sex trade were regulated like other businesses, we would not have a perfect world—labor would still be underpaid and exploited and needs would still go unmet—but the world would be modestly improved.

The prostitute has often served as a symbol for the degraded status of the worker in capitalist societies, and prostitution itself has been evoked as a metaphor for the general relationship between workers and owners under capitalism. It is also used to represent other often exploitative social relationships, between husbands and wives, for example. But the metaphor works only if we assume that prostitution is universally exploitative and degrading, so that activities likened to it are cast as illegitimate. Rather than make the Marxist point that exchanges of sex or labor for money in a capitalist market are necessarily exploitative, the point of the metaphor is that the exchange of labor for money under capitalism is like the exchange of sex for money in *any* circumstances. But the assumption that all sex commerce is inherently exploitative fails to take into account the diversity of actual and possible practices. The degradation of the worker under capitalism is more like the degradation of someone who is forced to sell his/her labor—sexual or nonsexual—but it seems redundant to point this out. By insisting on the inherent and unqualified degradation of sex commerce, those who use the metaphor only add to the degradation they presumably oppose.

Prostitutes—like gays, lesbians, and other sexual dissidents—are commonly viewed as threatening to families. But those who see them in this light often have a very narrow notion of what constitutes a family. In her book *The Comforts of Home: Prostitution in Colonial Nairobi*, Luise White describes relationships between prostitutes and their customers that might be compared to informal polyandrous unions, where a variety of physical and social needs are met—needs that more conventional families also serve.[4] In the United States and elsewhere, many prostitutes have children, partners, and parents that they support through their work. Prostitutes and those with whom they are socially intimate and interdependent, and with whom they share households, are in fact families, and they

4. Luise White, *The Comforts of Home: Prostitution in Colonial Nairobi* (Chicago: University of Chicago Press, 1990).

deserve the same social supports as other families. Laws that criminalize prostitution tear families apart, separate parents and children, and render sex workers and their intimate partners criminals.

All this said, some may feel that there is still something immoral or objectionable about the prostitute's work, and that we would be better off suppressing the practice and finding other livelihoods for the people involved. At least three articles appearing in academic journals and books in recent years bear the title "What's Wrong With Prostitution?" Each attempts to locate just what it is that distinguishes prostitution from other human activities, although one concludes contrary to the others that nothing is deeply wrong with waged sex work.[5] Perhaps one way to approach the intuition that there *is* something inherently wrong is to compare commercial sex to other work that is very similar to it. For example, many prostitutes like to compare themselves to sex therapists, educators, and entertainers. Annie Sprinkle likens her work to both bodily and spiritual forms of guidance and help. Either we must show that there is something wrong with these activities or we must show that the analogy between prostitution and sex therapy/education/entertainment doesn't hold. Frankly, I can't see how to show either.

One fear that many feminists have about legalizing prostitution is that this would create just one more female job ghetto where women are coerced into stereotypical and subordinate roles, and low-paying, low-status, dead-end work. Furthermore, the industry's "products" would very likely reproduce status hierarchies among people based on age, race, class, gender, physical ability, and so on. Subordinate service roles would be filled—as they already are in the illegally run sex industry—by age, class, race, and gender subordinates, and their commercial sexual availability would perpetuate myths about the inferiority of persons from the subordinated groups. These are legitimate fears, and supporters of decriminalization have to consider how such outcomes might be avoided.

One of the first things to be said is that although the overwhelming majority of customers for prostitution are male, not all prostitutes are women. It's important to notice that some prostitutes serve customers of the same gender as themselves, the same economic class, and the same socially defined racial category. Though a great deal of contemporary prostitution involves heterosexual white, bourgeois males exploiting

5. See Christine Overall, "What's Wrong With Prostitution?: Evaluating Sex Work" in *Signs* 17 (Summer 1992), pp. 705–724; Carole Pateman, "What's Wrong With Prostitution?" in *The Sexual Contract* (Stanford: Stanford University Press, 1988), pp. 189–218; and Igor Primoratz, "What's Wrong With Prostitution?" in *Philosophy* 68 (1993), pp. 159–182.

working-class or underclass women (especially women of color), keeping prostitution illegal will not affect this situation. Instead, by developing programs and policies that address poverty, racism, and sexism, and by regulating a legal sex industry, we can hope to make those who are socially oppressed less vulnerable to exploitation from those who aren't.

Anyone who advocates the legalization of prostitution needs to address the "But would you want your daughter . . . ?" argument. I suppose the only way to answer this question/objection is to take it personally—I happen to have a daughter who is now eight. This argument is meant to expose the hypocrisy of anyone who has made the assertions I've made. For, not surprisingly, my answer is "No, I wouldn't want my daughter to be a prostitute." So how can I accept this occupation for others? Well, first of all, this isn't all of my answer. The more nuanced answer is that, although I would prefer my daughter to be a mathematician, pianist, or labor organizer, were she to seek employment in the sex trade, I would still want the best for her. Her choice would be less heartbreaking to me if the work were legal, safe, reasonably well paid, and moderately respectable. In arguing for the decriminalization of prostitution, we need not go from the extreme of deploring it to the other extreme of romanticizing it. This objection works only if these are our only alternatives.

If prostitution remains criminalized, what can we expect? In Hollywood, some prostitutes will continue to profit from the instant celebrity status that being arrested at the right time and with the right customer can bring. But the average prostitute will continue to be abused by her (or his) clients and co-workers, exposed unnecessarily to disease, socially marginalized and demonized, harassed by public officials, and separated from her children and other family members; her children will suffer from neglect and poverty. And underage workers will continue to be used, with or without their or their family's consent. Perhaps, a large and coordinated effort to decriminalize prostitution for the sake of workers and their families is one more battle we need to wage with the radical religious right.

PART THREE

Liberalism and Pornography

CHAPTER TEN

Private Acts versus Public Art

Where Prostitution Ends and Pornography Begins

Theresa A. Reed aka "Darklady"

☽

Conventional anti-sex work feminist wisdom has encouraged several generations of men and women to believe that the commercialization of sexuality is inherently demeaning, dehumanizing, oppressive, exploitive, morally offensive, and contrary to fundamental human rights. Based on my professional experiences in the adult entertainment industry as a writer, photographer, and event coordinator, as well as friend to many sex workers, the only thing truly accurate about this statement is that it is "conventional," by which I mean "lacking originality or individuality," to quote my Merriam-Webster Dictionary. It certainly lacks wisdom and, frankly, hardly seems truly feminist in any positive sense.

I was raised in a family where any use of the word "feminist" was given as much respect as "Communist," "atheist," or "hippy." With a neurotically Roman Catholic mother and a hot-tempered Vietnam-era Army-drill sergeant father, the rules were pretty simple: obedience to a higher authority, a greater cause. I wore dresses to grade school every day because that's what the school dress code required. As a girl, for me to have done otherwise would have resulted in my being immediately sent home. Once home, I played with trucks as well as dolls, had both male and female early childhood companions, was held to nearly impossibly high standards of self-sufficiency, and played hard, whether in pants or in skirts. Before I was old enough to have any idea what sex or sexuality was, I knew that it was something that a good girl must avoid at all costs. I slept in the same bedroom as my mother until I was twenty-one—and the harsh words exchanged during her rare and grudging visits to my father's bed reinforced my decision to remain silent about my own sexual experiences once they began. So, I began to search for role models that had endured trials and tribulations, while remaining true to their beliefs and values.

To my surprise, some of the most powerful women I encountered had lived highly sexual lives, sometimes as prostitutes, sometimes as "fallen" or "immoral" women whose romantic, sexual, or intellectual pursuits had placed them outside the bounds of so-called polite society. Compared to the often stern, disapproving, and frequently angry women I was told were feminists, these women seemed to be more in line with what I considered to be true feminism: literary women including Aspasia of Miletus, Victoria Woodhull, George Sand, and Mary Wollstonecraft. Early sex workers like Mary Magdalene, the Greek Hetaerae, the Japanese Geisha, Renaissance Venetian courtesans, and frontier brothel workers of the United States. All of these ladies populated my landscape of strong, brave, independent, intelligent, self-reliant, and hard-loving females. These women were some of those that exemplified values I came to identify with my developing personal vision of feminism. They were sexual horizon walkers who were ready, willing, and able to accept responsibility for the results of their actions—and not take the low road, attempting to use their gender as a sympathy card or claim victim status. Socially transgressive women often pay a high price in social stigma for their pioneer spirit, although some are fortunate enough to live within circumstances that allow them to be reasonably free and unmolested despite their unorthodox lifestyles, be that accepting financial or material compensation for their time and attentions, or speaking their minds on issues or in venues traditionally deemed the exclusive domain of men.

Ironically, although I associated strength and independence with early free love advocates and prostitutes, my exposure to the feminist rhetoric of the 1980s and my developing work as an activist on size acceptance and body issues did not result in the development of a similar perception regarding women involved in video pornography or erotic photographs. While a university student, I attended a feminist presentation that included a careful explanation of how women are exploited in sexy photos of all kinds. According to the speaker, women are often intentionally posed in mainstream advertisements, photo art, and pornography to appear vulnerable, submissive, exposed, or even dead. Throats bared, bodies recumbent—these were alleged to be visible expressions of female helplessness that presumably inspire men to spend money and develop potentially threatening erections. That lecture left me conflicted because, although I found the ideas presented intriguing, I found some of the images highly arousing, artistically appealing, and both intellectually and emotionally evocative.

So, I began to scour the pages of my boyfriend's *Playboy Magazine* in search of offensive imagery. The photo spreads didn't necessarily support the speaker's claims, but they certainly aggravated my own insecurities. The absence of pubic hair and the relentlessly youthful appearance of most models disturbed me. Although unwilling to discount the entire industry based on my own body issues, I nonetheless developed and nurtured an uncomfortable prejudice against it for several years. I never adopted the popular fiction that pornography is inherently demeaning or abusive, but I did assume that it was a form of employment that women did not actually enjoy. This was based largely upon the opinions of anti-sex work feminists I had encountered and my own extremely limited exposure to substandard hard- and soft-core pornographic materials.

That all changed during the early 1990s when I had the unexpected opportunity to write professionally—about the sex industry. Suddenly, I was watching pornographic videos, spending time in strip clubs, and meeting dancers, magazine models, escorts, and professional dominants on a regular basis. Within a year I became the editor and chief writer for Portland, Oregon's biggest adult publication. During that time, the number of male and female sex workers I came into contact with increased considerably. The vast majority were intelligent, pleasant individuals who enjoyed their work and made a decent living by it, sometimes putting themselves through college or supporting a family with the income. Even those with emotional or chemical dependency issues were able to earn money and thus remain independent by working in one of the few industries that could accommodate their special scheduling needs.

At the same time, I also had the decidedly unpleasant experience of encountering fanatically motivated anti-sex work activists from both the "Right" and "Left" side of the ideological fence. Each time that I appeared as an official representative of the adult industry on "Town Hall," a televised group interview/discussion program, I was followed to my car by angry protestors. Those offended by sex work due to their religious views and personal misconceptions about its impact on neighborhoods threatened to cause trouble with my employment—and those that identified as anti-prostitution or "prostitution alternative" feminists screamed angrily that I was a "traitor to women." Clearly, there was no room for discussion or debate with either group.

Now, I readily admit that sex work as practiced in the United States includes unsavory elements. Like any other profession, it is not the best career decision for every person who gives it a try. Sometimes it attracts emotionally unstable or chemically dependent individuals. But those who choose to see me as an enemy of women or of God's morality absolutely refuse to consider the possibility that sex work could be an appropriate form of alternative employment for anyone—especially women—or that adjustments to the current system could make it safer. I've been told that it would be better to work as a migrant worker, at a minimum wage job, or accept public assistance than turn to sex work of any kind for any reason. This strikes me as being an incredibly offensive way to justify marginalizing a population, disempowering individuals, and limiting personal, artistic, and political speech and expression.

A number of fundamental messages communicated by many of those in the "prostitution alternatives" camp are deeply disturbing in other ways, as well. Whether they have come to their conclusions independently or been influenced by philosophical extremists such as theorist Andrea Dworkin, attorney Catharine MacKinnon, or anti-porn social psychologist Diana Russell—they make it crystal clear that they consider all sex workers to be prostitutes, regardless of whether or not their work actually involves sexual contact. Phone sex operator, peep show exhibitionist, exotic dancer, lingerie modeling salon performer, escort, porn star, streetwalker, call girl, bordello worker: every one of them is a prostitute in their eyes. Especially troubling is the prevalent belief that sex work universally victimizes all women and that any woman who doesn't identify as a victim proves the point; and that these ivory tower feminists and their allies are somehow wiser and more capable of making lifestyle, employment, and artistic decisions than those who consider or are involved in sex work. Regrettably, this line of thinking is not a local phenomenon but permeates much of the anti-sex work movement on an international level, making meaningful dialogue or the identification of common areas for joint activism nearly impossible.

Fortunately, sex workers throughout the United States are becoming increasingly visible and organized in their own defense, which strikes me as being a truly feminist form of social activism and self-determination. Organizations such as Call Off Your Old Tired Ethics (COYOTE), Prostitutes of New York (PONY), Danzine, the Exotic Dancers Alliance, and successful efforts by San Franciscan exotic dancers to save the Lusty Lady by cooperatively purchasing it, prove that sex workers can and do value their work, take it seriously, and believe that it can be a satisfying—or even empowering—form of employment. Such self reliance and activism show that sex workers as a group do not need to be told how to live by others, including feminist academics who are more in tune with the agenda of the supposedly moral right wing than with the realities of working women's lives. Dworkin claimed that pornography inherently and invariably harms women, including those utterly uninvolved in the industry.[1] Yet, an increasing number of women are consumers of pornography—and those involved in it for employment are playing a greater role in its development and presentation. Women such as Annie Sprinkle, PhD., Carol Queen, PhD., Marianna Beck, PhD., Carol Leigh, Shar Rednaur, Veronica Hart, Candida Royalle, Mason, Jill Kelly, and Belladonna have become directors and producers of adult video. Additionally, an increasing number of past and present prostitutes are speaking up in defense of their craft and developing ways to implement innovative ways to improve working conditions and overall community livability. This is far preferable and more empowering than legislating the industry out of existence.

The sad truth is that most anti-sex work feminists are woefully uninformed about the material and activities that they oppose. Even more regrettably, many have allowed themselves to be duped by arguments proposed by forces hostile to women's rights and individuals such as Professor Dolf Zillman, an anti-pornography researcher. Zillman, whose essay, "Effects of Prolonged Exposure to Pornography," was presented as testimony before the Meese Commission, concludes that pornography causes men to treat women callously, to lose sexual interest in their partners, and to become "desensitized" to sexual violence. However, what feminists swayed by these arguments have failed to notice is that FBI statistics indicate that violent crimes against women have actually decreased since the 1970s, although the willingness of women to report such crime has increased. According to Avedon Carol,[2] founder of Feminists Against Censorship, Zillman's evidence in support of his sensational claims includes behavior that has traditionally been near and dear to feminist hearts: greater acceptance of homosexuality and of non-traditional roles for women. Carol further points out that inconsistencies with Zillman's methodology have also been overlooked, including the fact that his control group was representative of the men in the general population as a whole (including both younger, single men and older men in more stable relationships), those actively watching pornography were predominantly younger and single. Hence, the study group and control group were not comparable. In other words, the study's conclusions are simply not useful from a scientific standard, although its twisted results clearly serve to further the agendas of

1. Dworkin Andrea and Catharine A. MacKinnon, 1988. *Pornography and Civil Rights: A New Day for Women's Equality.* Minneapolis: Organizing Against Pornography.

2. Carol, Avedon. 1999. *The Harm of Porn: Just Another Excuse to Censor.*

anti-sex work groups desperately looking for "proof" to support their claims.

Another popular and equally unreliable source for anti-pornography opinions is Dr. Diana Russell, a feminist researcher once arrested while leading a porn magazine tearing party outside an adult bookstore. She demonstrates her resistance to exposing herself to differing opinions when she admits that she dislikes discussing the topic with anyone who does not already agree with her conclusions.[3] So lost is she in moral outrage that she complains about the need to pay to reproduce copyrighted photos and illustrations she wanted to use as vilifying examples. Unable to retain a third party publisher, she self-published her book[4] and claims that the need to do so proves that anti-porn activists are being "censored in this misogynist porn-saturated society."[5] Not content to merely direct her hostility at pornographers, she also directs her baleful glare at ACLU president, Nadine Strossen, for defending pornography.

Well-researched information and opinions regarding sex work by academics and theorists are important for understanding the impact of sex work on people's lives. But the experiences and opinions of those who willingly engage in sex work must be part of that process. In order to contribute to this collection of insider insights, I have interviewed numerous people employed in the sex industry, discussed pornography and prostitution, differences and similarities between the two, and the question of why pornography enjoys legal protection, while prostitution is illegal in nearly all states. I include here the observations of two people who articulate particularly well some important points regarding these issues: writer/director David Aaron Clark, a stocky, soft-spoken, heavily tattooed man with a keen intellect and a journalism degree from Rutgers, whose video work specializes in darkly stylish titles featuring Asian women; and Lena Ramon, an articulate, intelligent, feminist-identified bisexual fetish and mainstream video performer who recently worked as a prostitute at Miss Kitty's, a bordello in Nevada.

Clark offers a paradigm that I believe has great merit—and which was echoed by many of the prostitutes and pornographers I spoke with. In his opinion, pornography is a form of public artistic and sexual expression protected by laws that should be further extended to include prostitution,

3. Russell, Diana. 1999. *The Trials & Tribulations Of Publishing A Book Attacking Porn.* August 2003, http://www.mergemag.org/1999/russell.html.

4. Russell, Diana. 1993. *Against Pornography: The Evidence of Harm.* Berkeley:Russell Publications.

5. Russell, Diana. 1999. *The Trials & Tribulations Of Publishing A Book Attacking Porn.* August 2003, http://www.mergemag.org/1999/russell.html.

which has the potential to be a private form of artistic sexual expression. According to Clark, although there was a time when many porn stars saw their work as being fundamentally different from prostitution, that perception has changed over the past few years. Evidence of that is the increasing number of adult performers who also work as escorts or in legal bordellos. Clark expresses a certain feeling of moral outrage at the legal distinction between the two professions and the marginalization of those who choose the more personal, one-on-one profession. As he so aptly puts it: "It's not anybody's business if anybody takes money for sex. Non-harmful, consenting behavior between adults should not be subject to government interventions. That just seems like common sense. When you start legislating private behavior strictly on a moral base and not based on something like public health safety or an actual injury to another party it's ridiculous."

Indeed it is ridiculous, for it relies upon prejudice disguised as common sense to anticipate harm without bothering to learn if any harm exists. In fact, the ultimate result of such legislation is more likely to be harm than its relief. Transgression of a religious/social boundary does not justify suppression by a secular government. Other sex workers I have spoken with emphatically agree about the value of considering the importance of mutual consent and safety when developing policy regarding pornography and prostitution. Lena Ramon, a petite brunette who entered the adult industry five years ago, in cautious stages, sees mutual consent as a vital part of any debate concerning the combined topic of sex, morality, career choices, artistic expression, and the legal system. She confesses that had she known "how much fun" it was to work in the adult industry she'd have started earlier instead of accepting the boredom she felt in a meaningless conventional job, while simultaneously enduring a "horrible relationship." Although she lacked the courage to work as an escort during her senior year in college, she did make some money posing as an erotic model. Upon graduation she entered porn. Her reasons for doing so relate to Clark's earlier observations about the primary difference between porn and prostitution: "It seemed safer than other parts of the sex industry. It was very public and I'd always been a lot more comfortable with public sex than being stuck in a room with one person. I also liked that it was a product that you were creating. It wasn't like you were just having sex. You were making something. I liked that it was an art form."

While she was pleased and surprised to find that she enjoyed her work in porn, Ramon continued to hold negative opinions about prostitution and the kind of women employed in it. These preconceived ideas continued even after she made the decision to work in a bordello herself. Like so many of us who move from abstract assumptions about various aspects of the sex industry to concrete experiences within it, once at Miss Kitty's Ramon's views changed radically: "Oh, my god. I was blown away. Every possible kind of person you can imagine works there and goes there. The sheer diversity of background and interest and education and life experience...It was just astounding." She was equally impressed by the kind of men who frequented the bordello. Initially expecting hoards of "scumbags" and "creepy" men, what she found was a diverse collection of lonely, open-minded individuals who had overcome the stigma of procuring the sexual services of a prostitute. Far from being depraved scumbags, she found that most of her clients made exceptionally tame requests, either wanting "fast sex, blowjobs, or talking"—things they often were unable to experience in their private lives or receive from their primary partners.

The common bond that prostitution and pornography share that attracts the most attention is sexual contact. People are especially concerned about who is participating and why they are doing so. Ultimately, the primary difference between being a porn star and being a whore is the presence of the camera and its associated artistic realities. Having sex in a discrete room alone with a businessman from out of town is prostitution. Having sex in front of a digital camera with a gonzo porn director in order to create a product for mass distribution is pornography. In a Capitalist society that at least claims to prize freedom of speech, it's hardly a surprise that pornography would be afforded more rights—however grudgingly—than the far more private activities of prostitutes. Although recent Supreme Court decisions have supported individual rights to privacy, the issue continues to generate controversy, particularly in this post-9/11 world where the Federal government regularly proposes ways and justifications for non-consensually peeking into the private lives of its citizens and visitors.

Yet, an argument can easily be made that both pornography and prostitution are capable of being forms of artistic expression, although the latter is directed at a private consumer, a limited audience. Video and photography perfectly accommodate the creative exhibitionism requirement for the resulting product. With its talent agencies, portfolios, and auditions, it clearly qualifies as a form of art, expression, and speech. Its professionals receive compensation for acting out roles and performing in scenes with one another. Prostitutes, on the other hand, engage in more intimate forms of therapy and performance art, directing their message in a targeted manner, directly to a single consumer. In each case, those involved negotiate boundaries, although those employed within pornography are often limited by the product's structure as a commodity. Clearly, an all-anal video will require that its performers engage in anal activity, for instance. Just as a mainstream film about dancing will likely require at least some scenes of dancing, thus requiring the hire of performers who can either dance already or learn to do so. Prostitutes, however, retain the right to negotiate their services individually, retaining the greater autonomy enjoyed by most freelancers, regardless of industry. The right to choose which form of employment or creative expression one wishes to participate in seems a valid right for any adult—and extremely feminist.

Ramon, whose favorite feminist writers are Audre Lorde and Alice Walker, speaks for me and many other sex workers when she expands the dialogue from the artistic realm into the social and economic: "As long as I've been around people who talk about feminism there's always been this debate about the privileged white upper class women versus the rest of women." Given that the goals of feminism are to work toward political, economic, and social equality of the sexes, it seems illogical to remove options. If women and men want to truly achieve sexual equality, society must expand the economic and lifestyle options available to everyone, as well as allow access to the vital informational tools necessary for responsible decision-making. In order to accomplish that, pro- and anti-sex work forces need to set aside personal moral agendas, identify genuine workplace issues unique to those who consensually engage in sex work and then—with the assistance of those within the industry—resolve those issues. Thus empowered, those who wish to consider such employment— be they male, female, or transgender—will be better able to select the economic alternative best suited to their individual circumstances without the worry of social stigma, threat of legal penalty, or incarceration. Until then, equality will remain illusory, artistic and political speech will remain constrained, and our solutions will continue to lack Merriam-Webster's "originality or individuality." The most inherently demeaning, dehumanizing, oppressive, exploitive, morally offensive action contrary to fundamental human rights that one can take is to limit or restrict people from consensually using their bodies to communicate or interact with others as they see fit. Such is the lot of slaves and prisoners—not free men and women.

CHAPTER ELEVEN

Freedom, Equality, Pornography*

JOSHUA COHEN

☽
.

EQUALITY AND EXPRESSIVE LIBERTY

According to Andrea Dworkin, "The left—ever visionary—continues to
caretake the pornography industry, making the whole wide world—street,
workplace, supermarket—repellent to women."[1] Dworkin is right that
many people who locate themselves on the political Left oppose restrictive pornography regulations.[2] Her explanation of this opposition is uncertain, however, because she does not explain what she means by "the

*Reprinted with permission from *Justice and Injustice in Law and Legal The-
ory*, ed. by Sarat and Kearns (Ann Arbor: The University of Michigan Press, 1996),
pp. 99–137. Copyright © 1996 by The University of Michigan.

1. "Women in the Public Domain: Sexual Harassment and Date Rape," in
Sexual Harassment: Women Speak Out, ed. Amber Coverdale Sumrall and Dena
Taylor (Freedom, Calif.: Crossing Press, 1992), 3. This passage restates a central
message of Dworkin's earlier writing on pornography: that the Right's celebration
of domesticity and the Left's celebration of sexual liberation represent two variations on the same malign themes—a practice of male dominance, an ideology of
male supremacy, and a metaphysics of women as whores. See Andrea Dworkin,
Pornography: Men Possessing Women (New York: Penguin, 1981), 203–09.

2. The American conflict over pornography regulation has parallels elsewhere,
for example in British debate in the early 1990s. For debate among British femi-
nists, see Catherine Itzin, ed., *Pornography: Women, Violence, and Civil Liberties*
(Oxford: Oxford University Press, 1992); Feminists Against Censorship, *Pornog-
raphy and Feminism: The Case Against Censorship*, ed. Gillian Rodgerson and
Elizabeth Wilson (London: Lawrence and Wishart, 1991); Lynne Segal and Mary
MacIntosh, eds., *Sex Exposed: Sexuality and the Pornography Debate*. (London:
Virago Press, 1992).

left." Let's assume, then, that it refers to people whose conceptions of justice give a large place to social equality—everyone who accepts, at a minimum, the following propositions:

1. Substantive equality of opportunity is a basic element of social justice. Substantive equality of opportunity—as distinct from the formal equality of opportunity associated with the ideals of equality before the law and careers open to talents[3]—requires that people not be disadvantaged in life because they were, for example, born with few resources, with dark skin, or female.

2. Existing inequalities of wealth and power thwart substantive equality of opportunity.

3. Achieving substantive equality of opportunity requires an affirmative role for the state—for example, in regulating market choices. For "if inequality is socially pervasive and enforced, equality will require intervention, not abdication, to be meaningful."[4]

This understanding of the Left is quite comprehensive, encompassing virtually all egalitarians. Precisely for this reason it highlights the interest and polemical thrust of Dworkin's point. For more than a decade now, one group of feminists has urged pornography regulations as a strategy for combating the eroticization of sexual subordination, arguably an important factor in reproducing sexual inequality.[5] Egalitarians embrace regulations of "market choices" in the name of economic equality, and commonly accept certain regulations of political expression—the content-neutral regulation of political expenditures—in the name of political equality.[6] In short, they emphasize the importance of liberty and equality as political values, accept regulations of choice in the name of equality,

---

3. On the distinction, see John Rawls, *A Theory of Justice* (Cambridge: Harvard University Press, 1971), sec. 12; Brian Barry, *Theories of Justice* (Berkeley: University of California Press, 1989), secs. 26–28.

4. Catharine MacKinnon, "Privacy v. Equality: Beyond Roe v. Wade," in her *Feminism Unmodified: Discourses on Life and Law* (Cambridge: Harvard University Press, 1983), 100.

5. On equality as the basis for pornography regulation, see Catherine MacKinnon, *Only Words* (Cambridge: Harvard University Press, 1993), part 3. On feminist opposition to pornography regulation, see Nadine Strossen, *Defending Pornography: Free Speech, Sex, and the Fight for Women's Rights* (New York: Scribner, 1995), 31–5.

6. See John Rawls, "The Basic Liberties and Their Priority," in *Political Liberalism* (New York: Columbia University Press, 1993), lecture 8, secs. 7, 12; Charles Beitz, *Political Equality* (Princeton: Princeton University Press, 1989), chap. 9.

and in some areas (say, the economy) think that justice requires such regulation. If substantive equality of opportunity is an important aspect of justice, and if there are background inequalities of power between men and women, then why, apart from reflex appeals to freedom of speech, resist the regulation of "sexual choices" in the name of sexual equality?[7]

One answer is that the regulations are divisive and diversionary, and probably ineffective cures for subordination. Although such pragmatic objections carry some weight, they fail to account for the special energy that has surrounded the debate about regulation—a debate that has focused on rights of expression. Moreover, for reasons I will discuss later, the Left—as I have interpreted Dworkin's use of the term—cannot rely exclusively on such objections. According to a second line of argument, stringent regulations of pornography are wrong, and not just unlikely to be effective.[8] I think these criticisms have some force, and propose to explore its scope and limits.

More specifically, I make three principal points:

1. The debate about pornography regulation, like much American political debate, is excessively legal.[9] We are invited, for example, to assume that the MacKinnon-Dworkin account of pornography is correct, and then asked to consider what can we do about it, consistent with taking

7. "The law of equality and the law of freedom of speech are on a collision course in this country." MacKinnon, *Only Words*, 71.
8. The regulations favored by MacKinnon and Dworkin are civil, not criminal, and it might therefore be said that they are not "stringent." But stringency should not be settled by reference to regulatory form; it depends on the extent of a regulation's coverage, and the sanctions attached to violating it. Restrictions on political speech prior to *New York Times v. Sullivan* were stringent, though they derived from tort law.
9. For a striking and interesting exception, see Susan E. Keller, "Viewing and Doing: Complicating Pornography's Meaning," *Georgetown Law Journal* 81: 2195–2228. See also Nadine Strossen, *Defending Pornography*. Strossen's book, published after I completed the penultimate draft of this chapter, argues that pornography regulations conflict with settled First Amendment doctrine, and that they would be bad for women's rights and equality, both because their enforcement would likely be damaging to women, and because they rest on distorted views of women (as victims), sex (as degrading to women), and pornography (as uniformly negative about women). Although I dislike the book's polemical tone and cartoonishly simple picture of the First Amendment, I agree with much of its content, and with Strossen's effort to engage the substance of sexual expression and not simply its doctrinal status.

the First Amendment seriously.[10] As a matter of method, I suggest that the argument—even the legal argument—ought to be more about pornography. The proper resolution of issues about regulation depends on what pornography is and whether it merits the strong protections properly extended to political and artistic expression or rather the reduced levels of protection appropriate to commercial speech or personal libel.[11] An assessment of pornography regulation can no more avoid a discussion of the interests implicated in sexually explicit expression than an account of commercial speech regulation can proceed without reference to the interests implicated in it.

2. Because sexual expression serves basic interests, regulations of the sort advanced by MacKinnon and Dworkin are unacceptably broad and intrusive. Egalitarians ought not to treat the ideas of sexual choice and sexual liberation simply as ideologies that reflect, mask, and sustain practices of sexual subordination. I sketch a more limited form of pornography regulation—targeted on constitutionally obscene materials that sexualize violence (the pornographically obscene)—that is less vulnerable to objection than more restrictive regulations. But its restricted range is bound to limit its impact.

3. People committed to an ideal of justice that embraces substantive equality and expressive liberty ought not simply notice the lack of substantive equality, express opposition to restrictions on expression, and conclude with hand-wringing about the shame of sexual inequality, and how sadly tragic it is that a commitment to liberty stands as a bar to its remedy. We need to find a way to accommodate both commitments. So I conclude by sketching some proposals that might accommodate commitments to equality and free expression.

To put the main idea in broader terms: From Emma Goldman to Noam Chomsky, an important strand of the egalitarian tradition has urged that expressive liberty is an intrinsic element of human liberation and a precondition for popular democratic politics. I endorse that strand of free-speech egalitarianism and explore its implications for the case of pornography.

10. The classic version of this strategy of argument is Judge Easterbrook's opinion in *American Booksellers Ass'n. v. Hudnut*, 771 F.2d 323 (7th Cir. 1985), affirmed without opinion, 475 U.S. 1001 (1986).

11. On reduced protection of commercial speech, see C. Edwin Baker, *Human Liberty and Freedom of Speech* (Oxford: Oxford University Press, 1989), chap. 9; Rawls, "The Basic Liberties," 363–68.

A RATIONALE FOR REGULATION

In this section, I sketch one style of argument for regulation, drawn largely from Catharine MacKinnon. So there is nothing original in the substance of my presentation, though I have tried to make the argument's assumptions and logic fully explicit.[12]

1. As a general matter, women suffer systematic social disadvantage by comparison with men. They are economically subordinate, required to bear the double burdens of production and reproduction, and physically insecure and subject to abuse.[13]

2. Such systematic disadvantage—that is, sexism—is a fundamental injustice. Like racism, it makes a difference into a source of disadvantage, violating the requirement of substantive equality of opportunity.

3. The reproduction of unjust, systematic disadvantage—whether the distinction underlying the disadvantage is sex, race, or class—is always a complicated causal story, featuring the internalization of dominant norms, social formation of desires that fit with existing opportunities, and rational calculations of advantage under constraints. But force, and threats of force, are also part of the answer. In the case of gender, women are subject to abuse by men, to rape, incest, harassment on the street and at work, physical abuse at home. Such violence and pervasive threats of violence have a social function. Not merely the sick behavior of individual men, they serve as enforcement mechanisms, as disciplinary devices that contribute to the reproduction of a system in which sex is a basis

12. For an especially clear statement of these themes and their connections, see Catharine MacKinnon, "Pornography as Defamation and Discrimination," *Boston University Law Review* 71 (1991), 795–802. She emphasizes (at 796): (1) that women are "used, abused, bought, sold, and silenced," (2) that "this condition is imposed by force," and (3) that "pornography has a central role in actualizing this system of subordination in the contemporary West." My presentation in the text aims to fill out these three points and make the connections more explicit. Also, see Catherine Itzin, "Pornography and the Social Construction of Sexual Inequality," in Itzin, *Pornography*, chap. 2; Wendy E. Stock, "Feminist Explanations: Male Power, Hostility, and Sexual Coercion," in *Sexual Coercion: A Sourcebook on its Nature, Causes, and Prevention*, ed. Elizabeth Grauerholz and Mary A. Koralewski (Lexington, Mass.: Lexington Books, 1991), 61–73.

13. On abuse, see MacKinnon, *Only Words*, 7. More generally, see, for example, Susan Faludi, *Backlash: The Undeclared War Against American Women* (New York: Crown, 1991); Susan Okin, *Justice, Gender, and the Family* (New York: Basic Books, 1989), chap. 7.

for disadvantage by increasing the costs to women of violating gendered norms of proper behavior.[14]

In short, force and threats of force function as enforcement mechanisms for gender norms, thus helping to maintain a system that disadvantages women because of their sex, and benefits men because of theirs.[15]

4. Many people—and not only men[16]—find subordination and the force that helps to sustain it sexually exciting: they find sexism and its disciplinary armature sexy.[17]

5. An important part of the explanation for the reproduction of sexual subordination is that many people—and not only men—find subordination and the force that helps to sustain it sexually exciting.[18] Because they

14. On sexual abuse as a disciplinary device, see Duncan Kennedy, "Sexual Abuse, Sexy Dressing, and the Eroticization of Domination," in *Sexy Dressing*: (Cambridge: Harvard University Press, 1993), 147–62. Wendy Stock summarizes some of the empirical literature linking fear of assault (rape, in particular) with ("self-imposed") behavioral restrictions in her "Feminist Explanations," 67.

15. Of course the fact of disadvantage—the imbalance of power—also explains vulnerability to the imposition of sanctions. Coercion, then, reflects the vulnerability that it helps to sustain. For an interesting and subtle discussion of the issue of male benefit, see Kennedy, "Sexual Abuse," 138–47.

16. "Some [women] eroticize dominance and submission; it beats feeling forced. Sexual intercourse may be deeply unwanted—the woman would never have initiated it—yet no force may be present. Catharine MacKinnon, "Feminism, Marxism, Method, and the State," *Signs* 8 (1983), 650; also MacKinnon, "Does Sexuality Have a History?" in *Discourses of Sexuality*, ed. Domna C. Stanton (Ann Arbor: University of Michigan Press, 1992), 134.

17. Affirming and linking the third and fourth points, Jane Caputi says that rape, like femicide, "is a social expression of sexual politics, an institutionalized and ritual enactment of male domination, and a form of terror that functions to maintain the power of the patriarchal order [point three]. Femicide, moreover, is not only a socially necessary act; it also is experienced as pleasurable and erotic [point four]." Caputi assumes—though she does not say here—that its being experienced as pleasurable and erotic helps to explain why it is done, that is, why acts that are "socially [i.e., functionally] necessary" are actually performed (see point 5 in the text). See Caputi, "Advertising Femicide: Lethal Violence Against Women in Pornography and Gorenography," in *Femicide: The Politics of Women Killing*, ed. Jill Radford and Diana E.H. Russell (New York: Twain Publishers, 1992), 205.

18. Whereas point 4 alleges a fact about sources of sexual excitement, point 5 gives prominent place to that fact—as distinct from, say, the sexual division of household labor, or early patterns of socialization, or strategies of human capital investment—in explaining sexual inequality.

find sexism sexy, they tolerate—or actively embrace—subordination and violence. In short, sexism is reproduced because it is sexy.

6. It is not original or intrinsic to human nature that people find sexism sexy. Although sexual desire, abstractly understood, may be intrinsic and original,[19] the particular forms of sexual desire dominating our lives are a product of politics—in particular, the power of men and a culture dominated by that power.[20]

7. Pornography plays a central role in defining what sexuality is for us, in particular in sexualizing—and so making permissible and attractive—subordination and the force that helps to sustain it. It "works by making sexism sexy;"[21] it "makes hierarchy sexy."[22] More strongly put: pornography "is *a major way* [my emphasis] in which sexism is enjoyed and practiced as well as learned."[23]

Pornography, a subset of sexually explicit expression (see the later section "The Regulations" for the legal definition), sexualizes subordination in two ways. First, its content fuses sex and subordination. It presents

19. Nothing in the argument requires affirming (or denying) the naturalness of some form of sexual desire. The distinction between a natural and socially constructed form of sexual desire traces at least to Rousseau. See his *Discourse on the Origin and Foundations of Inequality Among Men*, trans. Victor Gourevitch (New York: Harper and Row, 1986), 163–66.

20. Strossen badly misunderstands MacKinnon's views on this point. She says that "procensorship feminists," including MacKinnon, believe that men are "essentially bestial" (*Defending Pornography*, 113). It is difficult to understand how a reader of MacKinnon's work could think that MacKinnon believes that men or women are *essentially* anything. For example: "Sometimes people ask me, 'Does that mean you think there's no difference between men and women?' The only way I know how to answer that is: of course there is; the difference is that men have power and women do not. I mean simply that men are not socially supreme and women subordinate by nature; the fact that socially they are, constructs the sex difference as we know it. I mean to suggest that the social meaning of difference—in this I include *différance* [sic]—is gender-based" ("Desire and Power," in *Feminism Unmodified*, 51). Strossen offers a misinterpretation of a passage from *Only Words* as supporting evidence.

21. MacKinnon, "Pornography as Defamation and Discrimination," 802.

22. MacKinnon, "Pornography, Civil Rights, and Speech," *Harvard Civil Rights—Civil Liberties Law Review* (1985), 17.

23. MacKinnon, "Pornography as Defamation and Discrimination," 796. John Stoltenberg puts the point still more strongly: "Pornography is what makes subordination sexy" [my emphasis]. See his "Gays and the Pornography Movement: Having the Hots for Sex Discrimination," in *Men Confronting Pornography*, ed., Michael Kimmel (New York: Crown Publishers, 1990), 260.

women as enjoying subordination and as willing subjects of it: resistance as desire; fear and horror as enjoyment; "no" as "yes."[24] By presenting subordination and the abuse that serves to sustain it as consensual, pornography presents them as acceptable: "the victim must look free, appear to be freely acting. Choice is how she got there."[25] Moreover, by presenting them as sexually exciting—as what sex is—it has the effect of fusing sexual desire with the desire for relations of subordination and domination: it accounts for the distinctive, politically constructed content of sexual desire. "In the subordination of women, inequality itself is sexualized: made into the experience of sexual pleasure, essential to sexual desire. Pornography is the material means of sexualizing inequality; and that is why pornography is a central practice in the subordination of women."[26] Pornography produces a psychology perfectly suited to a social structure of sexual inequality, and in so doing provides the linchpin for the reproduction of such inequality.[27]

How precisely does pornography produce such a psychology? How, in Dworkin's words, does it sexualize "inequality itself," and serve as the "material means of sexualizing inequality?" Two mechanisms—one cognitive, the other behavioral—have been proposed to account for this fusion. The cognitive mechanism reflects the fusion of sexuality and subordination in pornographic images, the background fact of male dominance, and two psychological facts—that we grasp concepts in part by mastering their paradigmatic instances, and that our desires are, as a general matter,

---

24. The experimental literature on the effects of exposure to violent pornography in particular appears to bear out this claim about the importance of presenting women as "willing victims." In experimental settings, men who are not antecedently angry at a woman (the confederate in the experiments) are then exposed to a rape video in which the victim expresses pleasure at the end. They are more likely to be aggressive with the confederate in subsequent stages of the experiment than men who are exposed to a rape video in which the woman is said to find the experience humiliating and degrading. See Edward Donnerstein, Daniel Linz, and Steven Penrod, *The Question of Pornography: Research Findings and Policy Implications* (New York: Free Press, 1987), 98.

25. Catharine MacKinnon, "Frances Biddle's Sister," in *Feminism Unmodified*, 172.

26. Andrea Dworkin, "Against the Male Flood," in *Pornography*, 527.

27. I suspect that adherents of the view sketched in the text implicitly assume that such a close fit between structure and psychology is required for the reproduction of sexual inequality. But there are many reasons, short of full endorsement, for compliance with, or consent to, system of inequality. For one discussion of such reasons, see Joshua Cohen and Joel Rogers, *On Democracy* (New York: Penguin, 1983), chap. 3.

concept dependent. According to this proposal, men master the concept of sex (and related concepts, including sexual pleasure, enjoyment, satisfaction, gratification) in part by recognizing the enjoyment of force and subordination as sexual enjoyment. Given a background of male power, these pornographic paradigms of sexuality are generalized: "Men treat women as who they see women as being. Pornography constructs who that is. Men's power over women means that the way men see women defines who women can be. Pornography is that way."[28] Suppose, now, that desires are concept dependent, that we cannot specify the content of desires independently from the concepts available to the person whose desires they are—that, as applied to the case of sex, our sexual desires are desires for sex as we socially cognize it. As a result, sexual desires themselves are desires for sexual subordination; what counts as and what is experienced as sexual enjoyment reflects the pornographic conception of sexuality: "feminism exposes desire as socially relational, internally necessary to unequal social orders but historically contingent."[29] The problem in short is not that guys are animals, or that they never grow up; the trouble lies in the perfection of their (our) socialization under conditions of sexual inequality.

According to the behavioral mechanism, pornography works by "conditioning men's orgasm to sexual inequality."[30] Pornography depicts subordination and force; men watch (or read, or listen to) pornography; they masturbate; that reinforces an association between sexual excitement and subordination (alternatively, men and women together watch, read, or listen to pornography; they have sex; that reinforces a link between male sexual excitement and subordination). MacKinnon suggests an important role for this behavioral mechanism when she distinguishes the contribution of pornography to sexual inequality from the contribution of racial hate speech to racial subordination. Whereas pornography "manipulates the perpetrator's socialized body relatively primitively and directly," and

28. Catharine MacKinnon, "Not a Moral Issue," in *Feminism Unmodified*, 148.

29. Catharine A. MacKinnon, *Toward a Feminist Theory of the State* (Cambridge: Harvard University Press, 1990).

30. MacKinnon, "Pornography as Defamation and Discrimination," 802. It is not clear in this article whether MacKinnon endorses the behavioral mechanism described in the text; it is more strongly suggested in *Only Words*, 16. Diana E.H. Russell provides the clearest statement in "Pornography and Rape: A Causal Model," in *Pornography: Women, Violence, and Civil Liberties*, ed. Catherine Itzin (Oxford: Oxford University Press 1992), 324. Also, see Stoltenberg, "Pornography, Homophobia, and Male Supremacy," in ibid., 148.

works "by circumventing conscious processes,"[31] "[n]othing analogous to the sexual response has been located as the mechanism of racism, or as the mechanism of response to sexist material that is not sexual."[32] These claims are puzzling. If the distinction ("nothing analogous") is simply that racist hate speech does not work through sex, then it seems uncontroversial, but irrelevant. If the distinction assumes that racist hate speech works through conscious processes, then it is of clear relevance, but highly implausible, and at odds with common understandings of categorization and stereotyping.[33] In any case, the behavioral mechanism is less plausible because it applies only to men whose orgasms are associated sufficiently frequently with consuming pornography for the reinforcement to work its effects.

AN EXCURSUS

This account of pornography derives its force from its apparent fit with certain illustrative cases of pornography. Consider, for example, *Shackled*, a quarterly magazine published by London Enterprises Limited "in the interest of informing and educating the adult public on the various forms and means of sexual expression."[34]

Shackled is, as the name indicates, a bondage and discipline magazine, one of roughly thirty-five such magazines distributed by Lyndon Distributors. More precisely, it is a bondage and discipline magazine depicting women bound and disciplined (men are presented through their words, not in pictures). The work of "informing and educating the adult public" starts with the cover: one issue features a naked woman lying on her back with her legs spread, eyes closed, a ball-gag in her mouth, and wrists in leather cuffs, which are strapped to the metal bed she is lying on. Another woman stands behind her, checking the strap that holds the ball-gag in place. The cover line reads "Girls Who Love Heavy Restraint! See 'Em

31. Several proponents of pornography regulation have argued that its direct effects on the body, unmediated by cognition, remove it from the category of protected expression. For discussion and criticism, see David Coles, "Playing by Pornography's Rules: The Regulation of Sexual Expression," *University of Pennsylvania Law Review*, 143, no. 1 (November 1994): 124–27.

32. See MacKinnon, *Only Words*, 61–62.

33. See, for example Henri Tajfel, *Differentiation Between Social Groups: Studies in the Social Psychology of Intergroup Relations* (London: Academic Press, 1978).

34. Editorial, *Shackled* no. 9 (May 1993): 2.

Stripped Naked and Chained." A page 2 editorial—which includes the
language about "informing and educating"—tells us that "Finding girls
who love heavy restraint is easier than folks imagine. The censors who seek
to ban bondage magazines—like this one—should understand that these
are girls who enjoy shackles." The first photo layout ("Bi-Babe Bondage")
features two women, "One who thrives on suffering and tight restraint,
the other on dishing out pain." Another shows a woman (the girlfriend of
a "brilliant young barrister" who has brought her to the "bar of justice")
with her wrists attached to a metal bar (said bar), eyes blindfolded, and
mouth taped. According to the caption: "The tighter the rope—and the
bigger the dick—the better she likes it." Another: "Sure it hurts my tits,
but I enjoy every pang." Another: "Steel cuts into her tit, a gag into her
mouth, but does she complain? Hell, yes!" The last layout: "Heavy chain
and padlocks are her special thing. The weight really turns her on." And
it concludes: "After an hour of bondage, she's screaming for hard cock."

It does not add up to much of a narrative, but it covers the major points.
Sexualize subordination ("girls stripped naked and chained"). Emphasize
the moment of consent: that these women love enforced subordination
(that it is easier to find bondage lovers than you might have thought,
that they "love heavy restraint," "enjoy shackles," "thrive on suffering
and restraint," and "thrill to that constricting feeling, whether from rope
or metal"). Depict pain and resistance as part of the pleasure, and so as
constituting no objection to subordination ("thrives on suffering," "Sure
it hurts my tits, but I enjoy every pang.") Finally, link subordination, the
bondage that enforces it, and the consent that legitimates bondage (the
pleasures of the accompanying pain), with intercourse and male orgasm.
("The tighter the rope—and the bigger the dick—the better she likes it.")
Thus the slogan: "pornography makes sexism sexy."

NO OTHER EXIT

I return later to *Shackled*. For now, let's consider the argument for regulation, which falls out more or less directly from the analysis I sketched
above. Not simply an argument about the "themes" or "ideas" present in
pornography, the case turns principally on claims about what pornography does: "Men treat women as who they see women as being. Pornography constructs who that is. Men's power over women means that the
way men see women defines who women can be. Pornography is that
way."[35] Operating through the cognitive and behavioral mechanisms,

35. MacKinnon, "Not a Moral Issue," 148.

pornography makes subordination and the force that contributes to its reproduction sexually exciting and definitive of women's nature: it gives sexual desire and the experience of sexual satisfaction—which are not intrinsically attracted to subordination—their determinate content;[36] it gives subordination a central role in our self-definition as men and women ("Gender is sexual"[37]); and it makes the harm of enforced subordination "invisible as harm" by presenting women at consenting to and enjoying their own subordination and abuse.[38]

Suppose all of this is right. Then, pornography is *key to making sexual subordination into a system*—to "creating and maintaining sex as a basis for discrimination."[39] Pornography serves as a linchpin not simply because of what it says, but because of what it does.[40] It takes our sexuality, a deep fact about our lives, and enlists it—as idea, identity, desire, and practice—in support of subordination. Pornography is not a treatise that justifies subordination, but a device that makes it seem right, look natural, and feel good. By producing a psychocultural setting that makes us experience sexism as irresistible, it closes off all avenues of exit from subordination, except the avenue of regulating pornography itself.

This account of pornography's role is sometimes summarized in the claim that pornography subordinates—and not simply that its graphic, sexually explicit depictions of subordination *cause* subordination to be sexualized. A pornography ordinance adopted in Indianapolis in 1984 defines pornography in part as "the graphic sexually explicit subordination of women, whether in pictures or in words" (for the full definition, see the next section, "The Regulations"). "What pornography *does* goes beyond its content: it eroticizes hierarchy, it sexualizes inequality. It makes dominance and submission into sex."[41] The claim that pornography subordinates should be understood in three ways.

---

36. MacKinnon, "Pornography as Defamation and Discrimination," 802.

37. MacKinnon, "Not a Moral Issue," 148.

38. MacKinnon, "Francis Biddle's Sister," 178; also MacKinnon, *Feminist Theory of the State*, 204.

39. Minneapolis Public Hearings, cited in Donnerstein, Linz, and Penrod, *The Question of Pornography*, 139.

40. MacKinnon, *Only Words*, 22.

41. MacKinnon, "Francis Biddle's Sister," 172; *Only Words*, 11, 22. For proposals about how to interpret the claims that pornography subordinates and silences, see Rae Langton, "Speech Acts and Unspeakable Acts," *Philosophy and Public Affairs* 22, no. 4 (fall 1993): 293–330; Andrew Altman, "Liberalism and Campus Hate Speech: A Philosophical Examination," *Ethics* 103 (January 1993): 302–17.

1. The production of pornography regularly uses force.[42]
2. Sexual force against women sometimes involves the use of pornography as a model: men force women to view pornography and to do what the pornography shows women doing.
3. Pornography reproduces sexual inequality by shaping gender identities and sexual desires in ways that make force attractive, subordination natural, and their injuries invisible. Given male power, pornography has those effects; and once those effects are in place, the reproduction of sexual inequality is the inevitable result.

I offer these three points as explication of the claim that pornography *is* "the graphic, sexually explicit subordination of women." But do they really explain the "*is*"? I have two responses: "yes" and "wrong question."

As to "yes": what I have described is *how*—according to defenders of regulation—pornography subordinates: by depicting subordination and force as sexy, thereby giving sexual desires and gender identities their content. Consider an analogous case. Suppose I say to you, "I didn't incite the people demonstrating in front of the building to burn the building down; I simply urged them to do it, and by urging them caused them to be incited to burn it down." To which the right response is: "You are telling me *how* you incited them, not that you didn't."

Similarly with subordinating: if someone says, "I know there is subordination, that pornography depicts subordination and violence as sex, that it thereby makes subordination and violence sexually exciting, and that subordination is reproduced because it is experienced as gender identity and sexual desire. But the pornography does not subordinate." It is perfectly fair for the critic to respond: "You have told me how it subordinates; not that it doesn't."

As to "wrong question": I think it is a mistake to suppose that the issue of regulation can or ought to be settled by first determining whether pornography is expression that *says* something objectionable and thereby

---

42. As MacKinnon emphasizes, the claim that some pornography is made using coercion is not the "legal basis for restricting all of it (*Only Words*, 20). Still, the pornography industry appears especially sensitive to the charge that coercion and abuse are central to the production of pornography. This sensitivity is highlighted in the Code of Ethics adopted by the Free Speech Coalition (an Industry association). Five of eight items in the Code address issues about the consensual nature of the production of pornography (including one that condemns the use of drugs and alcohol in production, and another that requires performers to be old enough to give their consent). See *Adult Video News* 8, no. 7 (June 1993), 24. On the extent of force in production, see Strossen, *Defending Pornography*, chap. 9.

causes injury or instead *is* injurious conduct (perhaps an illocutionary speech act)—put otherwise, by first determining whether it causes subordination or subordinates.[43] This supposition reflects a general approach to freedom of expression that exaggerates the importance of a prior expression-action distinction in settling issues of regulation.[44] An answer to the expression-or-action question is, I think, not best understood as a premise in argument about the regulation of expression. We do not first decide "expression or action" and then decide whether to regulate. Rather, the distinction reports a conclusion: when we have decided that regulation is permissible, we say that expression is conduct—we say that when we have decided to assign responsibility to the speech (think of blackmail and extortion). When we think regulation is inappropriate—when we are reluctant to assign responsibility to the use of words, rather than to events downstream—we say that the words are speech. But it is wrong to think that we settle "speech or action?" "saying or doing?" antecedent to argument about the assignment of responsibility and the permissibility of regulation, and then use that resolution in deciding the regulatory issue.

As applied to the issue at hand: the disagreement about whether pornography is subordinating conduct or is instead speech that may cause subordination is best understood as a disagreement about whether regulation is appropriate. It is best understood as a disagreement about where to assign responsibility, not as a claim about causation or constitution that might resolve an argument about such assignment.

THE REGULATIONS

Pornography regulations—for example, the ordinance adopted in Indianapolis in 1984 and overturned in 1986—reflect this analysis. The Indianapolis ordinance defines pornography as: The graphic sexually explicit

43. For discussion of speech act theory and pornography, see Langton, "Speech Acts." According to Langton, pornography subordinates (and silences) only if pornographers' speech is authoritative about matters of sex (p. 311). I cannot see how this could settle the issue, because their speech may be authoritative because people regard them as "in the know" and so listen to them. Or it might be that men who think that women enjoy subordination go to pornography to learn how to do it (not because a producer of pornography is in authority, but because he or she is an authority). No amount of speech act theory is going to shift the debate away from causal argument and questions about the assignment of responsibility.

44. For criticism of the project of founding an account of freedom of expression on a prior expression-action distinction, see Thomas J. Scanlon, "A Theory of Freedom of Expression," *Philosophy and Public Affairs* 1 (1972), 205–08.

subordination of women, whether in pictures or in words, that also includes one or more of the following:

- Women are presented as sexual objects who enjoy pain or humiliation;
- Women are presented as sexual objects who experience sexual pleasure in being raped;
- Women are presented as sexual objects tied up or cut up or mutilated or bruised or physically hurt;
- Women are presented being penetrated by objects or animals;
- Women are presented in scenarios of degradation, injury, torture, shown as filthy or inferior, bleeding, bruised or hurt in a context that makes these conditions sexual;
- Women are presented as sexual objects for domination, conquest, violation, exploitation, possession, or use, or through postures or positions of servility or submission or display.[45]

The regulations establish four offenses: coercing someone into pornographic performance; forcing pornography on a person; assault caused by "specific pornography," and trafficking in pornography. They empower an administrative agency to issue cease-and-desist orders against those who commit these offenses, and award damages to victims. And, whereas offenses under the coercion, forced viewing, and assault provisions cover materials in each of the six categories described in the regulation, the trafficking provision covers only the first five. The intent of this limits is to confine the trafficking provision to more violent and hard-core pornography.[46] But not all materials that fall into the first five categories are violent or brutal. Susie Bright's anatomically precise discussion of the many varieties of dildo in her "Shiny Plastic Dildos Holding Hands" appears to fall into the fourth category, because women in it are penetrated by objects. But the depiction is neither violent nor brutal.[47] For now, though, let's put such details to the side.

45. Indianapolis, Ind., City-Council General Ordinance No. 35 (June 11, 1984). The full text is cited in MacKinnon, *Feminism Unmodified*, 274, n. 1. The regulation was overturned in *American Booksellers Ass'n. v. Hudnut*.

46. Owen Fiss, for example, describes the materials covered by the trafficking provision as "the most violent and brutal forms of pornography." See his "Freedom and Feminism," *Georgetown Law Review* 80, no. 6 (August 1992), 2051.

47. See *Susie's Bright's Sexual Reality: A Virtual Sex World Reader* (Pittsburgh and San Francisco: Cleis Press, 1992), 27–36. Consider, too, the sexual fantasies

To see the connection with the analysis of the injuries of pornography, consider the contrast with obscenity regulations. In the 1973 case of *Miller v. California*, the Supreme Court held that expression is obscene and so has a reduced level of First Amendment protection only if it is offensive, prurient, and of no serious literary, artistic, political, or scientific value: in short, offensive, sexually preoccupied, crap.[48] Pornography regulations differ from obscenity regulations on each of these three dimensions.

1. Pornography regulations do not go after the prurient.[49] Their target is not sexual explicitness, preoccupation, or perversion but graphic materials that sexualize subordination. The concern is not—or at least is asserted not to be—pornography's sexual content, but its role in discrimination.

2. The regulations are not justified by reference to the *offensiveness* of graphic subordination[50]—nor because it insults, damages reputations of women as a class,[51] or inspires disgust, guilt, or fear[52]—but by the harms of such representations, their role in reproducing a system of discrimination that turns the fact of sexual difference into a basis for social inequality.

The concern with the harm of sexual subordination is less immediately in evidence with the coercing, forcing, and assault provisions, which target either uncontroversially harmful consequences (assault), or coercive means (coercion and forced viewing). Such injuries are substantial, quite apart from their implications for discrimination. But even in these

---

involving animals reported in Nancy Friday, *Women on Top* (New York: Simon and Schuster, 1991), 106–11, 444–45. The passages reporting these fantasies appear also to fall into the fourth category.

48. See *Miller v. California* 413 U.S. 15 (1973).

49. On the problems of showing prurience, see MacKinnon, *Only Words*, 88.

50. Ibid., 100.

51. MacKinnon criticizes the reputational injury view of pornography in "Pornography as Defamation and Discrimination"; see also MacKinnon, *Only Words*, 11.

52. It does seem to inspire such reactions in some women: a survey published in *Cosmopolitan* in March 1990 reported that 66 percent of respondents (all women) did not enjoy seeing pornography, 32 percent felt disgusted, 32 percent felt offended, 31 percent felt guilty, and 18 percent felt frightened. See Catherine Itzin and Corinne Sweet, "Women's Experience of Pornography," in *Pornography: Women, Violence, and Civil Liberties*, ed. Catherine Itzin (Oxford, Oxford University Press, 1992), 228.

cases, the regulations reflect a concern with subordination: why target, for example, the forced viewing of pornography rather than all forced viewing, or coerced performances in pornography rather than all coerced performances? The natural explanation is that the aim is to remove, or at least to chill the production and distribution of, materials that fall into these six categories—materials that subordinate. Although the trafficking provision, then, is the most controversial element of the regulations, it reveals their overall aim, which is to target materials that sexualize subordination, and not simply those that produce specific injuries associated with particular uses of pornography.

3. They allow no exception for materials with serious literary, artistic, scientific, or political value.[53] This distinction connects with an important difference: the natural objection to obscenity regulations is that offensiveness is not a sufficient basis for state regulation. The exemption for materials with serious value provides the basis for a reply: "because this stuff has little value, the normal presumption against regulating offensive expression is suspended."[54] The issue with pornography is different. Harm, unlike offense, does conventionally establish a case for legal regulation—at least outside the context of expression. So, here the question is: given the harms, why does it matter if the stuff is not worthless?

POLICY CASE AGAINST REGULATION

Thus the case for regulation. Why doesn't it settle the matter—at least for people who endorse a conception of justice in which equality is an important political value? Equality is a fundamental political value; some uses of state power are justified because they promote that value. So why not in this case? Because pornography regulations violate the right to free expression? Maybe so. But let's put aside reflex appeals to rights of expression—the issue is why we should think those rights are at stake here, and sufficiently so to cause troubles for the regulations.

53. "The ineffectualness of obscenity law is due in some part to exempting materials of literary, political, artistic, or scientific value. Value can be found in anything, depending, I have come to think, not only on one's adherence to postmodernism, but on how much one is being paid. And never underestimate the power of an erection, these days termed 'entertainment,' to give a thing value." MacKinnon, *Only Words*, 87–88.
54. On the presumption, see *Cohen v. California* 403 U.S. 15 (1971).

THE LAWYER'S BATTERY

What are the alternatives to a reflex appeal? One is to offer a familiar lawyer's battery of arguments against the regulations:

- The Case for Regulation is Too Speculative: "I agree that there is subordination [point 1]; that it is a basic injustice [point 2]; that it is maintained in part through force [point 3], which I hasten to add is already illegal; and that some people get off on it [point 4]. But is it so clear that the sexualization of subordination explains much about the reproduction of subordination [doubting point 5]? And if it does—and even acknowledging that sexuality is socially constructed [accepting point 6]—how compelling is the evidence that pornography lies at the heart of that construction [doubting point 7]? Even if I grant that the sexualization of subordination is important to sex discrimination, I still have real doubts about whether pornography is the right target.

"Labor market segregation, economic inequality, and the unequal division of the labor of reproduction and socialization are far more important than the sexualization of subordination in explaining the reproduction of subordination. Or if you prefer to concentrate on cultural sources of gender inequality, consider conventional representations of women in commercial advertising. If you want to understand the legitimization of force, consider the pervasiveness of violence in popular culture and *Texas Chainsaw Massacre* and Brian de Palma-style slasher movies. Or if you want to focus on the sexualization of subordination, try the endless sexualization of movies and commercial advertising. Consider, in short, sexism without sex or violence; or violence without sexism or sex; or violent sexism without sex; or sexually suggestive sexism without violence or vivid subordination.

"With so much to consider, why pick on pornography as the basis of sex discrimination? Pornography is, after all, less pervasive than other cultural images, and less believable because it is so highly ritualized, badly written, and poorly acted.[55] Isn't it really because pornography is *sexually explicit*?[56] Isn't the political motive to build an alliance between people

55. See Carlin Meyer, "Sex, Censorship, and Women's Liberation," *Texas Law Review* 72 (1994): 1097–1201.

56. In a discussion of pornography and advertising, Jane Caputi lumps together sexism without sex or violence (an Yves Saint Laurent stocking ad), sexism and violence without explicit sex (Brian de Palma movies), sexism and sex without violence (*Penthouse Magazine*), and the combination of sexism, sex, and

who are antisexism and people who are antisex? And so isn't the line between pornography and obscenity regulation really, in the end, not so sharp?"[57]

This last set of polemical questions is meant to suggest that the diagnosis set out earlier is not what drives the focus on pornography. But the more fundamental objection fueling those political suspicions is that the diagnosis is too speculative to sustain the case for regulation.[58]

• Besides, The Regulations Themselves Are too Vague: "Assume, arguendo, that pornography is the linchpin of the system of sexual inequality. Still, the ordinances are hopelessly vague: 'sexual objects who enjoy...humiliation'; 'postures or positions of servility or submission or display.' Who could possibly tell whether their work was actionable under such a regulation?"[59]

Consider, for example, Susie Bright's "Story of O Birthday Party." Susie Bright's girlfriend Honey Lee arranges a thirtieth birthday celebration modeled on Pauline Reage's *Story of O*. She dresses Susie Bright in a tight leather corset, has her shine the boots of a policewoman, and arranges for a "gourmet sadomasochist" friend to whip her.[60] Is this pornography, as the regulation defines it?

The story does, to be sure, include humiliation. And while "enjoyment" does not fully capture Susie Bright's response to the humiliation, she does at least partly enjoy it. But it is hard to see Susie Bright as a "sexual *object* who enjoys humiliation," rather than a sexual subject who sometimes enjoys humiliation, or at least who enjoys playing at enjoying humiliation, or enjoys playing at wondering (and getting other people to wonder) whether she enjoys humiliation.

And there are plenty of postures and positions of servility, submission, and display. But do these postures, set within the "Story of O Birthday Party," subordinate? Perhaps not, given the author. Of course they might

---

violence (the movie *Cunt Torture*). According to Caputi, they all have the effect of "reflecting, normalizing, and legitimating violence against women." She does not indicate the regulatory implications of this conclusion. See Caputi, "Advertising Femicide," 203–221. For MacKinnon's response to the question in the text, see her *Only Words*, 61–2.

57. See, for example, Feminists Against Censorship, *Pornography and Feminism*, 28–9. The suggestion there is that the focus on sexual explicitness reflects a strategy of political alliance aimed at winning conservative, antisex allies.

58. See Strossen, *Defending Pornography*, 39.

59. Feminists Against Censorship, *Pornography and Feminism*, 69; Strossen, *Defending Pornography*, 75.

60. *Susie's Bright's Sexual Reality*, 17–26.

be said to subordinate *women as a class*, even though they do not subordinate Susie Bright. But why not think instead that because they do not subordinate Susie Bright, they do not subordinate *women as a class*.

Consider, for example, this interchange between Susie Bright and Coral—the gourmet sadomasochist.[61]

> *SB:* How am I supposed to take this pain? It is so intense. I don't know where to go with it.
>
> *C:* When I get hit, I like to think about deserving it, needing to be punished.
>
> *SB:* I can't do that. I was just thinking the very opposite . . all I can think of is that I don't deserve this. I didn't do anything wrong.
>
> *C:* Well, you can do it for Honey Lee. I know that's what she'd like.
>
> *SB:* Yes, that's what O would do, but I'm too selfish for that.
>
> *C:* You can be selfish as well. A lot of people like to take the pain, and connect the intensity to their clit or their nipples.
>
> *SB:* Maybe. When you stroke my clit and fuck me, I appreciate the whip a little, because my cunt sucks the sensation right up.
> [Coral hits her twice with the bamboo cane.]
>
> *SB:* SB: Coral, please, please, I can't do it, please, Jesus, I can't.

After begging Coral to stop, "She complied instantly." And then, as Bright leaves, she says "Coral, you're going to suffer terribly for what you did to me today."

Is this "graphic subordination"? Or graphic insubordination? Does it sexualize subordination? Or make a compelling case that sadomasochistic "herotica" is not for everyone? Perhaps it is and does all these things, depending on the audience. But to introduce this dependence on the audience is precisely to underscore the uncertainty about what the regulations cover.

• Moreover, More Narrowly Drawn Regulations Would Be Pointless: "Assume that the regulations were tightened up—as in the restriction of the trafficking provision to more hard-core and violent materials. As they become narrower and more precise, they become less objectionable. But the less restrictive regulatory means are also less likely to be effective in achieving the stated aim of sexual equality. Moreover, the likelihood grows that other remedies—still less restrictive of expression—will do just as well. So the dangers grow of diverting attention and resources from real cures by focusing on pornography."

• And, Anyway, The State is Patriarchal: "Who can trust the state to regulate speech—in particular to regulate it in ways that serve the interests

---

61. Ibid., 24. I have edited out inessential details, and omitted ellipses.

of women?[62] Consider the parallel with race: a Two Live Crew song was the first target of an obscenity prosecution for a piece of music. Give the state power to regulate expression, and it will inevitably use that power on less-powerful citizens.

"Put this well-founded mistrust together with the point about the vagueness in the regulatory language. Do we want—do women want—the state (say, the state of Utah) deciding whether oral sex is a posture of sexual submission?[63] Suppose the man is standing up, and the woman is kneeling. Suppose she is sitting on a chair. What about anal sex? Suppose the woman is on her hands and knees. Suppose she is lying on her back. Suppose she is on her hands and knees, but the anal sex is part of a safe sex video.

"Many distinctions can be drawn, and exploring their nuances makes attractive fare for conferences on cutting-edge film theory.[64] But this is not a role for courts, or for the administrative bodies empowered to hear civil rights complaints under the proposed ordinances, especially given that 'the law sees and treats women the way men see and treat women. The liberal state coercively and authoritatively constitutes the social order in the interest of men as a gender—through its legitimating norms, forms, relation to society, and substantive policies.'"[65]

LIMITS OF THE LAWYER'S BATTERY

These considerations all have some force, and I will say later just what that force is. But it is, I believe, commonly exaggerated. Taken on their own, these four points are not especially damaging to pornography regulations, for parallel objections apply to acceptable regulations in other areas (acceptable at least to those who endorse equality as an important political value).

Start with the first claim about speculativeness—that pornography has not been shown to be the problem, so regulations of it may not really

62. See Burstyn, "Beyond Despair," 158, and Strossen, *Defending Pornography*, 217–46, particularly her discussion of Canadian regulation in the wake of *Butler v. the Queen*, 1 S.C.R. 452 (1992, Canada).

63. See Feminists Against Censorship, *Pornography and Feminism*, 69.

64. For an interesting discussion of pornography and safe sex videos—delivered at such a conference—see Cindy Patton, "Safe Sex and the Pornographic Vernacular," in *How Do I Look: Queer Film and Video*, ed. Bad Object-Choices (Seattle: Bay Press, 1991), 31–51, and the discussion at 51–63.

65. MacKinnon, *Feminist Theory of the State*, 161–2.

get at the harms that they are alleged to address. This point is surely correct. Experimental evidence and cross-national studies fail to establish a compelling case for connections between pornography and rape and subordination. Indeed, most studies find no connection between nonviolent pornography—sexually explicit and sexist—and increased aggression or a heightened disposition toward sexual coercion and violence. There is some evidence for a connection between violent pornography and hostility towards women. Taken together with studies about the effects of graphic, nonsexual violence, however, that evidence suggests that the problem is the violence, not the sex.[66]

But none of these doubts settles anything. The problem with this first objection is that many regulations—for example, regulations of economic activity—are not supported by demonstrative reasoning, but only by considerations that do not offend common sense. Maybe the demand for labor really is highly elastic and minimum-wage laws hurt the poor by shrinking the pool of low-wage jobs. Maybe they do not force firms to enhance productivity by training workers and upgrading technology. Maybe the principal effects of rent control are to limit the supply of housing and generate a secondary market for sublets from long-term renters, worsening the situation for low-income people. People disagree about these issues. But egalitarians believe that democratically elected bodies have the authority to decide how best to ensure substantive equality, and to employ strategies based in some measure on speculation.[67] Why, then, prevent democratically elected bodies—like the Indianapolis City Council—from going after abuse and subordination by regulating what they judge to be an essential link in the chain?[68]

We'll get to the second point momentarily, but turn now to the third point—that narrower regulations are less objectionable, but also less likely to succeed. That observation is certainly true. But it is difficult to see how it amounts to a deep objection to the regulations, rather than a familiar policy disagreement.[69]

Or take the final consideration: about mistrust in the state's capacity to regulate speech. Generic mistrust of the state cannot be the reason for

66. For a review of the literature, see Donnerstein, Linz, and Penrod, *Question of Pornography*, esp. chap. 6.
67. It is not up to them whether to ensure substantive equality: justice demands that.
68. Frank Michelman, "Conceptions of Democracy in American Constitutional Argument: The Case of Pornography Regulations," *Tennessee Law Review* 56 (1989): 291–322.
69. See Fiss, "Freedom and Feminism," 2052.

opposing the regulation of pornography, at least not for egalitarians. Generic mistrust would reject the affirmative state that, at least in the context of a market economy, is necessary to economic egalitarianism. Whatever the favored methods of ensuring distributive fairness—progressive taxation, support for public schools, programs of training and retraining, regulations on concentrations of wealth—the state has an important role to play in achieving it.

Suppose we narrow the scope of the mistrust, focusing it on the state's capacity to regulate expression. That will not do either. I take it to be common ground among egalitarians that commercial speech ought not to receive the strong protection appropriate to political advocacy: for example, false and misleading commercial representations should not get the same protection as false and misleading political speech.[70] But the state enacts and enforces regulations of false and misleading commercial speech.

It is equally implausible to make the case rest on the refined distinctions that the state would need to draw in order to regulate sexually explicit expression—or, as in the second objection, the vague language of the regulations. Courts must constantly make extremely fine distinctions and interpret vague language. Courts decide if capital punishment is cruel, whether animal slaughter is a legitimate part of a religious practice, which imbalanced agreements are unconscionable, whether twenty-four-hour waiting periods are unduly burdensome on rights of reproductive choice, and which persons are public figures for the purposes of libel law. Why can't they, in the fullness of time, develop ways to determine which postures are servile, for the purposes of adjudication?

But don't all of these replies to the objections neglect the fact that what pornography regulations regulate is *expression*? And isn't it appropriate to impose a higher burden of proof on such regulations? It is not the replies that neglect this fact; it is the objections themselves that do. Indeed, that is the point of the replies, which, generically speaking, underscore that the arguments in the lawyer's battery *assume* what needs to be shown: that regulations of pornography must meet a very high burden of justification, a higher burden for example than regulations of economic activity or commercial speech or personal libel. Much of the debate about pornography that pretends to assess the evidence for its harmful effects is rather about the proper burden of proof: about how compelling the evidence

70. For an argument based more fundamentally on mistrust, see Richard Epstein, *University of Chicago Law Review* 59 (1992): 41–90. For criticisms, see Frank Michelman, "Liberties, Fair Values, and Constitutional Method," *University of Chicago Law Review* 59 (1992): 91–114.

needs to be. More specifically, criticisms commonly assume a very high burden of justification. Of course, setting the burden very high is almost certain to defeat the regulations (scrutiny of them will be "strict in theory, fatal in fact"): they will be overtaken by concerns about speculativeness, vagueness, the availability of less restrictive alternatives, and mistrust.

But the prior question is whether the burden ought to be pushed so high. Why protect pornography so stringently that the objections in the lawyer's battery suffice to defeat regulations? That is the question. And the arguments considered thus far do not answer it. To say this is not to dismiss the four objections, and later I will come back to them, indicating the role that they should play in the rejection of stringent regulations. But first we need to address the more fundamental question.

STRONGER CASE AGAINST REGULATIONS

What, then, is the problem with pornography regulations? To answer this question, I start with some general background on the basic expressive and deliberative interests that underlie the case for stringently protecting expressive liberty.[71] Then, I develop the following two theses:

1. The same reasons that support stringent protections of, for example, artistic and political expression apply to expression that would be restricted by Indianapolis-style regulations (the same basic interests are at stake here as well).

2. Because those reasons apply, the lawyer's battery does have some force, and therefore it is important to offer other means for addressing the harms of subordination.

BASIC INTERESTS

Strong protections of expressive liberty serve three basic interests—expressive, deliberative, and informational—and the weight of those interests explains the importance of especially stringent protections.[72] I have

71. This discussion of the fundamental interests draws on my "Freedom of Expression," *Philosophy and Public Affairs* 22, no. 3 (Summer 1993), sec. 3.
72. Freedom of expression is commonly associated with such values as the discovery of the truth, individual self-expression, a well-functioning democracy, and a balance of social stability and social change. See Thomas Emerson, *The System of Freedom of Expression* (New York: Random House, Vintage, 1971). Lee C. Bollinger emphasizes as well the importance of encouraging tolerance in

argued for this view elsewhere (see note 71), and will confine my remarks here to a sketch of the expressive and deliberative interests.

The *expressive* interest is a direct interest in articulating thoughts, attitudes, and feelings on matters of personal or broader human concern, and perhaps through that articulation influencing the thought and conduct of others. Some examples will clarify the nature of the interest and the bases of its importance.

A common feature of different evaluative conceptions is that they single out certain forms of expression as especially important or urgent; the conception implies that an agent has weighty reasons for expression in certain cases or about certain issues. Consider two central cases in which agents hold views that assign them very strong, perhaps compelling, reasons for expression:

1. In a range of cases, the limiting instance of which is a concern to "bear witness," an agent endorses a view that places her under an *obligation* to articulate that view, and perhaps urge on others a different course of thought, feeling, or conduct. Restricting expression would prevent the agent's fulfilling what she takes to be an obligation; it would impose conditions that the agent reasonably takes to be unacceptable. Here, expressive liberty is on a footing with liberty of conscience, regulations are similarly burdensome, and the magnitude of the burden reflects the weight of the reasons.

2. In a second class of cases, expression addresses a matter of political justice. Here, the importance of the issue—indicated by its being a matter of justice—provides a substantial reason for addressing it. The precise content and weight of the reason are matters of controversy. According to some views, public engagement is the highest good, and Brandeis urged that "public discussion is a political duty."[73] But even if political expression is neither the highest good nor a matter of duty, still, it is a requisite for being a good citizen, sometimes a matter of sheer decency. Characteristically, then, it has support from substantial reasons within different moral-political conceptions.

The Tolerant Society (Oxford: Oxford University Press, 1986); and Vincent Blasi examines the role of freedom of expression as a check on official misconduct in "The Checking Value in First Amendment Theory," *American Bar Foundation Research Journal* 3 (1977): 521–649. I think that the tie to the basic interests provides a more fundamental explanation for the protections. For discussion, see Cohen, "Freedom of Expression," secs. 3, 4.

73. *Whitney v. California*, 274 U.S. 357, 375 (1927) (Brandeis, J., concurring).

Other important cases include an interest in creating things of beauty. But the two I have mentioned suffice to underscore the importance of the expressive interest. They work outward from the case of fully conscientious expression, the paradigm of expression supported by substantial reasons from the agent's point of view. To be sure, different evaluative conceptions have different implications for what is reasonable to say and do. But all conceptions assign to those who hold them substantial reasons for expression, quite apart from the value of the expression to the audience, and even if there is no audience at all.

My emphasis on the expressive interest may suggest that the conception of expressive liberty I sketch here is more sectarian than I claim, in particular that it depends on a general philosophy of life according to which self-expression is the fundamental human good. But no such expressivist philosophy is at work.[74] The characterization of the expressive interest focuses on the role of reasons, and that distinguishes it from conventional discussion of the value of self-expression and self-fulfillment. When, for example, people aim to comply with the moral obligations assigned to them by their moral views (whatever the content of those views), it may be misleading to treat their action as a matter of self-expression or self-fulfillment: from the inside, the conduct is mandatory, and the agent may think that conduct important because it fulfills an obligation disconnected from the self's inner nature.[75]

The *deliberative* interest has two principal aspects. The first is rooted in the abstract idea—shared by different evaluative conceptions—that it is important is to do what is genuinely worthwhile, not simply what one now believes to be worthwhile. For this reason, we have an interest in circumstances favorable to finding what is worthwhile: that is, to finding out which way(s) of life are supported by substantial reasons.

The second aspect of the deliberative interest is rooted in the idea that it is important that one's evaluative views not be affirmed out of ignorance or out of a lack of awareness of alternatives. Alongside the interest in doing what the strongest reasons support, then, there is also an interest in understanding what those reasons are and the kind of support they give. This, too, leads to an interest in circumstances favorable to such understanding.

---

74. On expressivism, see Charles Taylor, *Sources of the Self: The Making of Modern Identity* (Cambridge: Harvard University Press, 1989), chaps. 21, 24, 25.
75. Kantians will identify acting from the moral law with revealing our nature as free, reasonable beings. Although I do not wish to dispute the truth of that view, I think that a conception of free expression should not depend upon it. For discussion, see Cohen, "Freedom of Expression,", 223–4.

These two aspects of the deliberative interest are connected to expression because reflection on matters of human concern characteristically requires others to advance alternative views. So the deliberative interest calls for circumstances suited to understanding what is worth doing and what the reasons are that support it—for example, circumstances featuring a diversity of messages, forcefully articulated.

Finally, the *informational interest* is an interest in securing reliable information about the conditions required for pursuing one's aims and aspirations. Although sexual expression does advance this interest, it is also less weighty than the others and so I will put it to the side.[76]

INTERESTS AND PORNOGRAPHY

I want now to suggest that the problems with stringent regulations lie in their capaciousness. More particularly, they are—both in the underlying principles and in their details—designedly inattentive to the expressive and deliberative interests in the sexually explicit materials that are, by the lights of the regulations, pornographic.

Let's start with the expressive interest. Earlier I mentioned cases of bearing witness and of expression on matters of political justice. In a third class of cases, concerns about human welfare and the quality of human life prompt expression; the evident importance of those concerns provides substantial reasons for the expression.

A paradigm is expression about sex and sexuality—say, artistic expression (whether with propositional content or not) that displays an antipathy to existing sexual conventions, to the limited sensibilities revealed in those conventions, and the harms they impose. In a culture that is, as Kathy Acker says, "horrendously moralistic," it is understandable that such writers as Acker challenge understandings of sexuality "under the aegis of art, [where] you're allowed to actually deal with matters of sexuality."[77] Again in an interview, Kathy Acker says: "I think you'd agree there are various things in us—not all of which are kind, gentle, and tender—readers of de Sade and Genet would probably agree on this point! But I think you can explore these things without becoming a mass murderer...without causing *real* damage, without turning to *real* crime. One way of exploring these things is through *art*; there are various ways

76. On pornography's informational role, see Strossen, *Defending Pornography*, 165–67.

77. See Kathy Acker, "Devoured by Myths: An Interview with Sylvere Lotringer," in *Hannibal Lecter, My Father* (New York: Semiotext(e), 1991).

of doing this. We have ... to find out what it is to be human—and yet not wreak total havoc on the society."[78]

The human significance of sexuality lends special urgency to the explorations Acker describes. Moreover, that urgency does not decline when sexuality mixes with power and subordination—when it is not "kind, gentle, and tender." On the contrary, a writer may reasonably think—as Acker apparently does—that coming to terms with such mixing is especially important, precisely because, in the world as it is, power is so deeply implicated in sexual identity and desire. To stay away from the erotcization of dominance and submission is to avoid sexuality as it, to some indeterminate degree, is. But because the proposed regulations address what pornography (allegedly) does, they make no provision for the importance of the expressive interest—for the weight of the reasons that move at least some people to produce sexually explicit materials that conflict with the regulations.

At this point, a proponent of the regulations may wish to concede the point about the expressive interest, but wonder why anyone would think that this interest outweighs the harms of pornography. I reply to this concern after first discussing the deliberative interest.

An essay by several members of the Feminist Anti-Censorship Task Force (FACT) suggests the connections between deliberative interests and pornography:

[The existence of pornography] serves some social functions which benefit women. Pornographic speech has many, often anomalous, characteristics. One is certainly that it magnifies the misogyny present in the culture and exaggerates the fantasy of male power. Another, however, is that the existence of pornography has served to flout conventional sexual mores, to ridicule sexual hypocrisy and to underscore the importance of sexual needs. Pornography carries many messages other than woman-hating: it advocates sexual adventure, sex outside of marriage, sex for no other reason than pleasure, casual sex, anonymous sex, group sex, voyeuristic sex, illegal sex, public sex.[79]

They describe the importance of sexually explicit materials from the audience's point of view, not—as with the expressive interest—from the speaker's, and claim that such materials enable audiences to understand

78. Kathy Archer interview by Andrea Juno in *Angry Women*, ed. Andrea Juno and V. Vale (San Francisco: Re/Search Publications, 1991), 184–85.

79. Lisa Duggan, Nan Hunter, and Carole Vance, "False Promises: Feminist Antipornography Legislation," in *Caught Looking: Feminism, Pornography, and Censorship*, ed. Kate Ellis, Beth Jaker, Nan D. Hunter, Barbara O'Dair, Abby Tallmer (East Haven, Conn.: Long River Books, 1992), 82.

sexual possibilities, perhaps to reconceive their own sexual commitments. And—though the passage just cited does not say this—that enabling is not confined to more kind and gentle erotica; it cuts across the lines drawn in the regulations.

Three features of sexually explicit expression—its diversity, interpretability, and uncertain connections with sexual practice—are important to the connections between sexually explicit materials (including materials covered by pornography regulations) and the deliberative interest.[80]

By "diversity," I mean the sheer variety of pornography. Earlier, I mentioned *Shackled*, which is illustrative but not representative. There are also many Fem-Dom magazines and videos, featuring dominant women and submissive men (or a mixture of submissive men and submissive women). In fact, one study shows Fem-Dom magazines outpacing Male-Dom.[81] Moreover, bondage and discipline is only one of many themes in contemporary pornography. With easy desktop publishing, low-cost VCRs, and sexual materials all over the Internet, XXX-cinemas are in decline and the pornography market is not confined to men in trench coats. The shifting technologies and markets have apparently had important implications for content. There is more bisexual, gay male, lesbian, soft X (no erection, no penetration), and sadomasochism (downplaying genital sexuality), and more heterosexual pornography that is not organized around a culminating cum shot.[82] The fact of diversity baffles efforts to identify a single message of pornography, underscores the "many messages" described in the FACT passage, and suggests that pornography is more than a device that triggers erections and orgasms.

By interpretability, I mean that different viewers/listeners/readers will respond to pornography differently in part because of the wide-ranging

---

80. These points are common in what Judith Butler calls the "pro-sexuality movement within feminist theory and practice." See her *Gender Trouble: Feminism and the Subversion of Identity* (New York: Routledge, 1990), 30–31; see also Susan Keller, "Viewing and Doing: Complicating Pornography's Meaning," *Georgetown Law Review* 81 (1993): 2195–2228; Duncan Kennedy, *Sexy Dressing*, 126–213.

81. See Lynne Segal's Introduction to *Sex Exposed*, 6.

82. On the many varieties of pornography, see Linda Williams, "Pornographies on/scene," in *Sex Exposed: Sexuality and the Pornography Debate*, ed. Lynne Segal and May McIntosh (London: Virago, 1972), ibid., 233–65; Cindy Patton, "Safe Sex," 31–51; and the interview with "Kay," in Robert Stoller, *Porn: Myths for the Twentieth Century* (New Haven: Yale University Press, 1991), 120–25. For a striking illustration of market fragmentation, see the list of alt.* newsgroups on Internet.

sexual beliefs, feelings, sensibilities, desires, and imaginations they bring to it. There appears to be no hope of establishing a common conception of sexuality or a shared understanding of sexual pleasure and its role in a good human life—for example, of the relative importance of love and release from conventional inhibition in making for good sex. Lacking any basis in a shared, public view about sexuality, interpretations of pornography (and reactions to it) vary widely. Like the fact of diversity, this variation makes it tendentious to suppose that hard-core, sexually explicit expression contains a single message of sexual subordination, or has a determinate effect. And the absence of a single message or determinate effect underscores the connections with the deliberative interest.

Let's return to the case of *Shackled*. Earlier, I presented a flat interpretation of it, presenting it as a paradigm of sexualized subordination. But other readings of its message and effect are available. For example, no men appear in the pictures: does this show that phallic absence enhances phallic power, or suggest that men are irrelevant to women's sexual pleasure? Moreover, we have a magazine evidently intended for male pleasure, which emphasizes throughout the pleasures of the shackled women. In one interpretation, this emphasis is what erotizing subordination is all about; but perhaps *Shackled* is a gender-bender magazine, whose intent or effect is to encourage a male audience to identify with the shackled women who are experiencing pleasure; and perhaps the pictorial absence of men is a precondition for fully identifying with the women. Or maybe *Shackled* is about transgression and resistance: after all, is "screaming for hard cock" a matter of begging, or commanding? To raise these questions is not to deny the obvious: photographs of women in chains, loving their bondage, and screaming for sex are not likely to do much to reduce sexual subordination, or men's apparently inexhaustible reserves of misogyny. But I doubt that a world without *Shackled* will be created by more stringent regulations of pornography, or by denying its human complexity.

Finally, the uncertain connections of pornography and practice also weaken the link between pornography and subordination, and suggest connections with the deliberative interest. Pornography is as much an ingredient of sexual fantasy as it is a guide to sexual practice. Though some may see it as reflecting or guiding practice, others will see that it provides pleasures in part precisely because it enables viewers/readers/listeners to explore in fantasy (or play) aspects of desire and identity that they do not wish to pursue in practice (the pleasure of pretending to do the forbidden). Moreover, pornography does not simply "advocate" alternatives to conventional sexual practice, but instead it shows—as Duncan Kennedy has argued about sexy dressing—the erotic possibilities that lie in the transgression of conventions: the transgression itself is important to the erotic power.[83]

Commenting on the complex connections of pornography and practice, Susie Bright, for example, reminds us that our fantasies are not "some kind of *McGuffey's Reader* on how to live."[84] And, speaking to the issue of transgression, she adds that the "sexual liberation" message goes further than feminism "in not just *criticizing* the fact that sex roles were restricting, but advocating that sex roles had erotic possibilities if you *subverted* them."[85]

But as this last point underscores, pornography can play a role in advancing the deliberative interest in a world of unequal power in part by engaging our sexual desires, categories, identities, and fantasies as they are—even if our aim is to transform them. On this point, Judy Butler makes an essential observation: "[S]exuality is always constructed within the terms of discourse and power, where power is partially understood in terms of heterosexual and phallic conventions.... If sexuality is culturally constructed within existing power relations, then the postulation of a normative sexuality that is 'before,' 'outside,' or 'beyond' power is a cultural impossibility and a politically impracticable dream, one that postpones the concrete and contemporary task of rethinking subversive possibilities for sexuality and identity within the terms of power itself."[86] As applied to the issue of pornography, this proposed "rethinking... within the terms of power" suggests that regulations targeted particularly on the fusion of sexuality and subordination—on the apparent extremes of heterosexual and phallic conventions—will cover too much. For it may be in part by working with that fusion and acknowledging its force, rather than by simply depicting a world of erotic possibilities beyond power, that we establish the basis for transforming existing forms of sexuality.

It may be objected, however, that if reflection proceeds *within the terms of power*, then it does not advance the deliberative interest, which is an interest in following the promptings of reason, not the dictates of power.[87] This objection raises large issues about practical reason that I am not able to address within the confines of this article. I will, however, make a few remarks aimed at dispelling the air of inconsistency.

---

83. "Sexual expression... subverts every taboo by making it a fetish. The forbidden is simultaneously eroticized." Cole, "Playing By Pornography's Rules," 116.

84. See the interview of Susie Bright by Andrea Juno in *Angry Women*, 201.

85. Ibid., 202.

86. Butler, *Gender Trouble*, 30.

87. I am indebted to Susan Dwyer for raising this objection.

The force of the objection depends on how we understand "rethinking within the terms of power." If it is interpreted to mean that we must accept existing gender norms and relations of power as circumscribing reflection, then the rethinking is, as the objection complains, disconnected from the deliberative interest. But "within the terms of power" should not be understood to imply such acceptance.[88] I take it to stand for the less controversial thesis that practical reflection must use as a point of departure norms (of gender, for example) and categories (of sexual orientation and conduct, for example), as well as images and desires, shaped by relations of power. Even on this interpretation of the phrase, however, the objection would still raise serious troubles *if* acknowledging the role of power-laden norms, categories, images, and desires in practical reflection required us to give up the idea that some patterns of conduct are better supported by reasons than others or the interest in pursuing those patterns. But no such nihilism about practical reason follows. Even if reflection uses power-laden norms and categories, we still have a reason to go to the store if we are hungry and know we can get food there; we still have a reason to believe that $2 + 2 = 4$, not to poison two-year-old children, and to be open to relevant evidence. To give such examples is not, of course, to answer the question: What is a reason (whether theoretical or practical)? That question lacks a simple answer. But whatever the correct explication, the intuitive force of claims about reasons of the kind just noted stands as an obstacle to any straightforward route from power-ladenness to nihilism.

A DIGRESSION ON METHOD

I want to digress for a moment to comment on a feature of my argument that may not have gone unnoticed. I have principally cited women in my discussion of the connections between pornography and the expressive and deliberative interests. There may be some temptation to dismiss their remarks as collaboration, yet further evidence that pornography constructs women as the "agents" of their own subordination—that all they "do" is collaborate. After all, "[i]t would be surprising if men eroticized

---

88. "[T]o operate within the matrix of power is not the same as to replicate uncritically relations of domination." Butler, *Gender Troubles*, 30. More generally, *Gender Trouble* is about displacing gender norms (p. 148) by understanding identity generally and gender identities in particular as performances, grasping the diversity of those performances, and developing a vocabulary suited to that diversity (as distinct from the binary oppositions that dominate current discourse).

dominance, practiced it, and enforced it over women, and there were no women who eroticized subordination. The surprise is that so many of us don't...."[89] And there is a temptation as well to treat my citations of women as "hiding behind skirts."[90]

Both complaints have some force. But in the end I find it difficult simply to dismiss as collaboration considerations about the expressive and deliberative values of sexual expression. Those claims seem very plausible, and I see no *independent* evidence of collaboration.

As to hiding behind skirts: what else can I do to make the case for the expressive and deliberative interests? Refer to men who think pornography is great?[91]

INTERESTS AND PORNOGRAPHY, REDUX

Let's return, then, to the interests and the regulations. Suppose one accepts the connections with expressive and deliberative interests, and agrees about the importance of those interests. That may suffice to establish the first thesis I stated at the beginning of this section: that the same reasons that support stringent protections of, for example, artistic and political expression apply to expression that Indianapolis-style regulations would restrict. Still, the trouble for the regulations may not be obvious, for it might be thought that we now simply have a stand-off. On the one hand, we have a case that pornography is seriously injurious; on the other, a case for connections with important human interests. Indeed, given the importance of substantive equality, appealing to the idea that it advances weighty interests will strike some as applauding rank self-indulgence, or as worrying more about artists and male orgasms than about women's lives.

This objection misstates the argumentative situation. In my earlier discussion of the "Policy Case Against Regulation," I did not dismiss the conventional criticisms, but complained that they assume what needs showing—that the regulations must satisfy a very high burden of justification. The weight of the considerations in the lawyer's battery—about the speculativeness of arguments supporting regulation and the importance

89. MacKinnon, "Does Sexuality Have a History?" 134, and MacKinnon, "On Collaboration," in *Feminism Unmodified*, 198–205.

90. I borrow the phrase from Catharine MacKinnon. She used it at the Brown conference mentioned at the beginning of these notes in connection with the phenomenon of citing women in arguments against pornography regulations.

91. But for some thoughtful remarks, see Kennedy, "Sexual Abuse," 210–11.

of exploring less restrictive alternatives for addressing abuse and subordination—is not freestanding; instead, it reflects the importance of the regulated target.[92] Thus, more speculative arguments will suffice when basic interests are not at stake. But given the importance of expressive and deliberative interests, and the connections between sexual expression and those interests, the high burden of justification is appropriate, and each of the four criticisms raises a serious objection to stringent regulations. Thus the second thesis: because the reasons for supporting stringent protections of, for example, artistic and political expression carry over to expression that Indianapolis-style regulations restrict, the lawyer's battery has some force; so we need to find other means to address the harms of subordination.

ALTERNATIVE STRATEGIES

Proposals to regulate pornography are animated by the damage pornography (allegedly) does to the cause of substantive sexual equality. I have criticized the remedies. But because substantive equality is a fundamental political value, critics need to say something about alternative remedies. What might some alternative strategies be for addressing the problems of subordination that pornography regulations aim to address? Here I want to make three suggestions.

Before getting to the suggestions though, I emphasize that I offer them as supplements to, not substitutes for, familiar economic initiatives for achieving sexual equality and undermining the vulnerability that comes with inequality: say, policies of comparable worth to reduce unequal compensation within segregated labor markets, and a range of policies—including quality day care, flextime, parental leaves, mandatory support from absent fathers, equal legal entitlements to wage and salary income in the case of single-earner households, and a new framework of divorce law designed to equalize standards of living for post-divorce households—to address the unequal division of household labor.[93]
More immediately, then:

1. If the problem with pornography is that it legitimates sexual abuse and force by sexualizing it, then a first natural step would be to target sexual abuse—the abuse of women as women—more directly. Such

92. This is the point of the familiar idea in constitutional law, that the level of scrutiny depends on the regulated target.
93. See, for example, Okin, *Justice, Gender, and the Family*, chap. 8.

targeting might, for example, include a tort of domestic sexual harassment modeled on workplace sexual harassment—including elements of quid pro quo and hostile environment harassment.[94] To be sure, the modeling would need to be very loose: sex is supposed to play some role in the lives of married couples; it is not supposed to play a role in the lives of people who happen to be working in the same office. But extreme sexual demands coupled with threats, or public sexual humiliation, might be forms of domestic sexual harassment. And such a tort could be a natural setting for actions against forcing pornography on a person, one element in the pornography ordinance I discussed earlier.

2. My second suggestion emerges from a claim commonly stated in debate about issues of expression: that the way to combat the injuries of speech is, as Justice Brandeis said, with more speech.[95] Brandeis's point is tirelessly repeated in discussions of freedom of expression. But the context of his remark is important. Brandeis was writing about a case of "subversive advocacy." He did not, however, address his remarks to the advocates: Anna Whitney, a 1920s leftist, was trying to speak; the state was shutting her up. Brandeis was reminding political elites of their vast resources for responding to arguments for revolutionary change: they might, for example, try to cure the social ills that prompt them or to argue the case against a revolutionary solution.

Addressed to less powerful groups, with restricted access to means of expression or whose voice is in other ways excluded or silenced, the easy injunction "More speech!" loses its force. Recommending "more speech" carries with it an obligation to ensure fair access to facilities of expression. It is unacceptable to impose a high burden on justifying restrictions on expression, justify that burden in part by the possibilities of combating the harms of expression with more speech, and then not endorse the requirement of ensuring such facilities.

The implications of this observation in the area of conventional political speech are easy to see. In that setting, fair access means: ensuring open public forums for expression; affirming the importance of diverse broadcast messages and the role of fair access in contributing to such diversity; financing political campaigns through public resources; and regulating private political contributions and expenditures.

Applied to the case of subordination, the implications are less clear because the mechanisms of exclusion—or "silencing"—do not have principally to do with the distribution of material resources, but—it is

94. I take the proposal from Kennedy, "Sexual Abuse," 135.
95. *Whitney v. California*, 274 U.S. 357 (1927). This and subsequent paragraphs on fair access draw on Cohen, "Freedom of Expression."

argued—precisely with what is said. So here there may be serious tensions between a commitment to fair access and an opposition to regulating the content of expression.

But we should resist jumping too quickly to this conclusion. For other measures of empowerment that are more affirmative than regulations of expression may show real promise in combating silencing and exclusion. Among the possibilities are regular public hearings on sexual abuse— perhaps subsidies for women's organizations to hold such hearings[96]— or easier access of women to broadcast licenses. Moreover, insofar as silencing has economic foundations, efforts to ensure fair compensation and to address the traditional division of household labor would help.

3. Some regulations of violent pornography are not so vulnerable to the criticisms leveled earlier against the Indianapolis-style regulation. The central idea would be to define regulable pornography as a subcategory of the obscene expression that the Court now treats as having lower value. Consider an illustrative proposal.

Take obscenity, as currently understood. As I mentioned earlier, this category is defined so that material falls into it only if it is prurient, offensive, and lacking an intimate connection with First Amendment values. Putting to the side the puzzling role of prurience in the rationale for the category,[97] the idea is straightforward: low value reduces the case for protection and thereby permits regulation in the name of otherwise insufficient concerns about offensiveness. Accepting for the sake of argument that obscenity does not have First Amendment protection, one natural strategy would be to regulate the subcategory of obscene materials that sexualize subordination, or, more narrowly, that sexualize violence. The strong presumption against regulation would be reduced because none of the obscene has a strong claim to protection—that is how the category has been defined. Assuming that reduced presumption, it ought to be permissible to regulate obscenity where there is a case for harm—in particular, violent pornography.[98] Indeed, that case ought to carry some weight even if one rejects offensiveness altogether as a basis for regulation, and so rejects obscenity regulations as currently understood.

96. For a more general discussion of associative approaches to reconciling egalitarian and liberal commitment, see Joshua Cohen and Joel Rogers, "Secondary Associations and Democratic Governance," *Politics and Society*, 20, no. 4 (December 1992): 393–472.

97. If material is low-value and offensive, what does prurience add to the case for regulation?

98. On the evidence that violent pornography is harmful, see Donnerstein, Linz, and Penrod, *Question of Pornography*.

If the principal reason for opposing Indianapolis-style pornography regulations is that the capacious category of the pornographic includes much that has substantial value, then a proposal along these lines may be workable. But the U.S. Supreme Court's decision in *R.A.V. v. St. Paul*—striking down a hate speech regulation—appears to block this subcategorization strategy.[99] In *R.A.V.*, the Court majority held that it was impermissible to target a regulation on the hate speech that falls into the regulable category of fighting words. According to the Court, it *is* permissible to target a regulation on all fighting words, or on the especially provocative fighting words, because the provocativeness of fighting words underlies the permission to regulate them. But it is not permissible to target the hateful or racially insulting subcategory of fighting words: that is content regulation, as it would be content regulation to target violent pornography in which Republican men are the perpetrators.

By analogy, my guess is that the Court might accept regulations confined to obscene material that is grossly offensive—say, sex with animals or golden shower movies—for the offensiveness of obscenity is the reason for permitting its regulation. But they would not accept regulations targeted on the subcategory of obscene material that sexualizes violence: that would be content or viewpoint regulation. Here I disagree with Owen Fiss.[100] Fiss argues that regulations of pornographic obscenity would be acceptable because they would regulate the subset of obscene material that is especially extreme from the point of view of the very considerations that initially justify regulating obscenity: "to protect women from violence and sexual abuse."[101] But this seems wrong. The rationale for obscenity regulations lies in offensiveness, not in protecting women from violence and sexual abuse. For that reason, the court's position suggests a willingness to accept regulations of the grossly offensive, but not the pornographically obscene.

I think this is an indefensible position. And perhaps I am wrong about the Court's response to the subcategorization strategy in this area. But even if I am, I do not think that pressing for such regulations would be a very wise political investment; the third point in the lawyer's battery strikes me as relevant here. I doubt that regulations focused on sexually violent obscenity would do much work in addressing the harms of subordination. Suppose we agree that pornography, through cognitive or behavioral means, fuses sexual desire with the desire for subordination. Still, it seems very implausible that such fusion occurs through the consumption

99. *R.A.V. v. St. Paul*, 122 S. Ct. 2538 (1992).
100. See Fiss, "Freedom and Feminism," 2056, and n. 50.
101. Fiss, "Freedom and Feminism," 2056.

of violent pornography, which is not especially prominent, even in outlets dedicated entirely to hard-core, sexually explicit magazines, videos, and paraphernalia.[102]

Here, however, we arrive at a familiar disagreement about effectiveness. It is not a disagreement of political principle—not a division on the importance of values of free expression and substantive equality—and treating it as one serves only to weaken support for those values.

CONCLUSION

Replying to a question put to her after a lecture several years ago, Catharine MacKinnon said that "equality is important but pleasure is too." And she criticized those who do not accept that "equality matters on any level approximate to pleasure."[103] The criticism is well taken. That's why we need to attack the injustice of inequality and subordination while accommodating the importance of pleasure. Perhaps there is no way to do both. But without a compelling case for its impossibility, such pessimism seems unwarranted.

This chapter began as a reply to a talk at Brown University by Catharine MacKinnon on "Pornography: Left and Right" (March 1993). I presented a draft in my fall 1993 Political Philosophy seminar at MIT, and later versions at Wesleyan University, McGill University Law School, and the Central Division meeting of the American Philosophical Association (spring 1995). I am grateful to those audiences, and to Cass Sunstein and Pam Spritzer, for helpful criticisms, and to Karen Rothkin for research assistance.

---

102. So it seems from outlets in Boston and New York, where sadomasochism (not always violent) is simply one among many niches—hetero, gay, bi, anal, oral, coeds, TV/TS, group, enema, and so on. More systematic surveys confirm the results of my causal inspection. For a discussion of some of the evidence on low and *declining* rates of violent imagery, see Lynn Segal's introduction to *Sex Exposed*, 6 (and the studies cited in notes 12 and 13).

103. MacKinnon, "Does Sexuality Have a History," 134.

CHAPTER TWELVE

Women and Pornography*

RONALD DWORKIN

•

I

People once defended free speech to protect the rights of firebrands attacking government, or dissenters resisting an established church, or radicals campaigning for unpopular political causes. Free speech was plainly worth fighting for, and it still is in many parts of the world where these rights hardly exist. But in America now, free-speech partisans find themselves defending mainly racists shouting "nigger" or Nazis carrying swastikas or—most often—men looking at pictures of naked women with their legs spread open.

Conservatives have fought to outlaw pornography in the United States for a long time: for decades the Supreme Court has tried, though without much success, to define a limited category of "obscenity" that the Constitution allows to be banned. But the campaign for outlawing all forms of pornography has been given new and fiercer form, in recent years, by the feminist movement. It might seem odd that feminists have devoted such energy to that campaign: other issues, including abortion and the fight for women's equality in employment and politics, seem so much more important. No doubt mass culture is in various ways an obstacle to sexual equality, but the most popular forms of that culture—the view of women presented in soap operas and commercials, for example—are much greater obstacles to that equality than the dirty films watched by a small minority.

*Reprinted with permission from *The New York Review of Books*, Copyright © 1993 NYREV, Inc.

But feminists' concentration on pornography nevertheless seems easy to explain. Pornographic photographs, films, and videos are the starkest possible expression of the idea feminists most loathe: that women exist principally to provide sexual service to men. Advertisements, soap operas, and popular fiction may actually do more to spread that idea in our culture, but pornography is the rawest, most explicit symbol of it. Like swastikas and burning crosses, pornography is deeply offensive in itself, whether or not it causes any other injustice or harm. It is also particularly vulnerable politically: the religious right supports feminists on this issue, though on few others, so feminists have a much greater chance to win political campaigns for censorship than any of the other campaigns they fight.

And pornography seems vulnerable on principle as well. The conventional explanation of why freedom of speech is important is Mill's theory that truth is most likely to emerge from a "marketplace" of ideas freely exchanged and debated. But most pornography makes no contribution at all to political or intellectual debate: it is preposterous to think that we are more likely to reach truth about anything at all because pornographic videos are available. So liberals defending a right to pornography find themselves triply on the defensive: their view is politically weak, deeply offensive to many women, and intellectually doubtful. Why, then, should we defend pornography? Why should we care if people can no longer watch films of people copulating for the camera, or of women being whipped and enjoying it? What would we lose, except a repellent industry?

Professor Catherine MacKinnon's new book of three short essays, *Only Words*, offers a sharp answer to the last of these questions: society would lose nothing if all pornography were banned, she says, except that women would lose their chains. MacKinnon is the most prominent of the feminists against pornography. She believes that men want to subordinate women, to turn them into sexual devices, and that pornography is the weapon they use to achieve that result. In a series of highly charged articles and speeches, she has tried to talk or shock other women into that view. In 1986, she wrote that

Pornography constructs what a woman is as what men want from sex. This is what pornography means. . . . It institutionalizes the sexuality of male supremacy, fusing the eroticization of dominance and submission with the social construction of male and female. . . . Pornography is a harm of male supremacy made difficult to see because of its pervasiveness, potency, and principally, because of its success in making the world a pornographic place.[1]

1. Catharine MacKinnon, "Pornography, Civil Rights and Speech," reprinted in Catherine Itzin, editor, *Pornography: Women, Violence and Civil Liberties, A*

Only Words is full of language apparently intended to shock. It refers repeatedly to "penises slamming into vaginas," offers page after page of horrifying descriptions of women being whipped, tortured, and raped, and begins with this startling passage:

> You grow up with your father holding you down and covering your mouth so that another man can make a horrible, searing pain between your legs. When you are older, your husband ties you to the bed and drips hot wax on your nipples and brings in other men to watch and makes you smile through it. Your doctor will not give you drugs he has addicted you to unless you suck his penis.

The book offers arguments as well as images, however, and these are presented as a kind of appeal, to the general public, from a judicial decision MacKinnon lost. In 1983, she and a feminist colleague, Andrea Dworkin, drafted an ordinance that outlawed or attached civil penalties to all pornography, defined as the "graphic sexually explicit subordination of women through pictures and/or words" that meet one or more of a series of tests (some of which are impossibly vague) including: "women are presented dehumanized as sexual object, things, or commodities"; or "women are presented as sexual objects experiencing sexual pleasure in rape, incest, or other sexual assaults"; or "in positions of sexual submission, servility, or display"; or "women's body parts—including but not limited to vaginas, breasts, or buttocks—are exhibited such that women are reduced to those parts."

In 1984, largely through their efforts, a similar ordinance was adopted by the Indianapolis legislature. The ordinance included no exception for literary or artistic value, and it could plausibly be interpreted to outlaw not only classic pornography like John Cleland's *Memoirs of a Woman of Pleasure*, but a great deal else, including, for example, D. H. Lawrence's novels and Titian's *Danae*. In 1985, the Seventh Circuit Court of Appeals held the ordinance unconstitutional on the grounds that it violated the First Amendment's guarantees of free speech and press, and in 1986, the Supreme Court declined to overrule the Seventh Circuit's decision.[2]

Only Words offers several arguments in favor of the Indianapolis ordinance and against the Seventh Circuit's ruling, though some of these

Radical View (Oxford University Press, 1992), page 456. (Quotations are from 461–463.)

2. *American Booksellers Ass'n v. Hudnut*, 771 F.2d 323 (1985), aff'd 475 US 1001 (1986). In a decision that MacKinnon discusses at length, a Canadian court upheld a similar Canadian statute as consistent with that nation's Charter of Rights and Freedoms. I discuss that decision in "The Coming Battle over Free Speech," *The New York Review*, June 11, 1992.

are run together and must be disentangled to make sense. Some of MacKinnon's arguments are old ones that I have already considered in these pages.[3] But she devotes most of the book to a different and striking claim. She argues that even if the publication of literature degrading to women is protected by the First Amendment, as the Seventh Circuit declared, such material offends another, competing constitutional value: the ideal of equality embedded in the equal protection clause of the Fourteenth Amendment, which declares that no state may deprive any person of the equal protection of the laws. If so, she says, then the courts must balance the two constitutional values, and since pornography contributes nothing of any importance to political debate, they should resolve the conflict in favor of equality and censorship.

Unlike MacKinnon's other arguments, this claim has application far beyond the issue of pornography. If her analysis is right, national and state governments have much broader constitutional powers than most lawyers think to prohibit or censor any "politically incorrect" expression that might reasonably be thought to sustain or exacerbate the unequal positions of women or of racial, ethnic, or other minorities. I shall therefore concentrate on this new argument, but I shall first comment briefly on MacKinnon's more conventional points.

2

In *Only Words*, she repeats the now familiar claim that pornography significantly increases the number of rapes and other sexual crimes. If that claim could be shown to be even probable, through reliable research, it would provide a very strong though not necessarily decisive argument for censorship. But in spite of MacKinnon's fervent declarations, no reputable study has concluded that pornography is a significant cause of sexual crime: many of them conclude, on the contrary, that the causes of violent personality lie mainly in childhood, before exposure to pornography can have had any effect, and that desire for pornography is a symptom rather than a cause of deviance.[4] MacKinnon tries to refute these studies, and

3. "Two Concepts of Liberty," in *Isaiah Berlin: A Celebration*, edited by Edna and Avishai Margalit (University of Chicago Press, 1991), and printed in *The New York Review of Books*, August 15, 1991.
4. Among the prestigious studies denying the causal link MacKinnon claims are the 1970 report of the National Commission on Obscenity and Pornography, appointed by Lyndon Johnson to consider the issue, the 1979 report of the Williams Commission in Britain, and a recent year-long British study which

it is important to see how weak her arguments are. One of them, though repeated several times, is only a metaphysical sleight-of-hand. She several times insists that pornography is not "only words" because it is a "reality." She says that because it is used to stimulate a sexual act—masturbation— it is sex, which seems to suggest that a film or description of rape is itself a kind of rape. But obviously that does not help to show that pornography causes rape in the criminal sense, and it is only the latter claim that can count as a reason for outlawing it.

Sometimes MacKinnon relies on breathtaking hyperbole disguised as common sense. "Sooner or later," she declares, "in one way or another, the consumers want to live out the pornography further in three dimensions. Sooner or later, in one way or another, they do. *It* does make them want to; when they believe they can, when they feel they can get away, *they* do." (Confronted with the fact that many men who read pornography commit no rapes, she suggests that their rapes are unreported.)[5] Elsewhere she appeals to doubtful and unexamined correlations: In a recent article, for example, she declares that "pornography saturated Yugoslavia before the war," and suggests that pornography is therefore responsible for the

concluded that "the evidence does not point to pornography as a cause of de- viant sexual orientation in offenders. Rather it seems to be used as part of that deviant sexual orientation." MacKinnon and other feminists cite the voluminous, two-volume report of the infamous Meese Commission, which was appointed by Reagan to contradict the findings of the earlier Johnson-appointed group and was headed by people who had made a career of opposing pornography. The Meese Commission duly declared that although the scientific evidence was inconclusive, it believed that pornography (vast tracts of which were faithfully reprinted in its report) did indeed cause crime. But the scientists on whose work the report relied protested, immediately after its publication, that the commission had misunder- stood and misused their work. (For a thorough analysis of all these and other stud- ies, see Marcia Pally, *Sense and Censorship: The Vanity of Bonfires* (Americans for Constitutional Freedom, 1991). MacKinnon also appeals to legal authority: she says, citing the Seventh Circuit opinion holding her antipornography statute unconstitutional, that "not even courts equivocate over [pornography's] carnage anymore." But this is disingenuous: that opinion assumed that pornography is a significant cause of sexual crime only for the sake of the argument it made, and it cited, among other material, the Williams Commission report, as support for the Court's own denial of any such demonstrated causal connection.

5. In "Pornography, Civil Rights and Speech," MacKinnon said, "It does not make sense to assume that pornography has no role in rape simply because little about its use or effects distinguishes convicted rapists from other men, when we know that a lot of those other men *do* rape women; they just never get caught." (p. 475).

horrifying and widely reported rapes of Croatian and Muslim women by Serbian soldiers.[6] But, as George Kennan has noted in these pages, rape was also "ubiquitous" in the Balkan wars of 1913, well before any "saturation" by pornography had begun.[7]

Her main arguments, however, are anecdotal: she cites examples of rapists and murderers who report themselves as having been consumers of pornography, like Thomas Shiro, who was sentenced to death in 1981 in Indiana for raping and then killing a young woman (and copulating with her corpse) and who pleaded that he was not responsible because he was a lifelong pornography reader. Such evidence is plainly unreliable, however, not just because it is so often self-serving, but because, as the feminists Deborah Cameron and Elizabeth Fraser have pointed out, criminals are likely to take their views about their own motives from the folklore of their community, whether it is sound or not, rather than from serious analysis of their motives. (Cameron and Fraser, who favor banning pornography on other grounds, concede that "arguments that pornography 'causes' violent acts are, indeed, inadequate.")[8]

MacKinnon's second argument for censorship is a radically different one: that pornography should be banned because it "silences" women by making it more difficult for them to speak and less likely that others will understand what they say. Because of pornography, she says,

You learn that language does not belong to you.... You learn that speech is not what you say but what your abusers do to you.... You develop a self

6. "Turning Rape into Pornography: Postmodern Genocide," *Ms.*, July/August 1993, p. 28.

7. "The Balkan Crisis: 1913 and 1993," *The New York Review*, July 15, 1993.

8. Catherine Itzin, editor, *Pornography: Women, Violence and Civil Liberties*, p. 359. At one point MacKinnon offers a surprisingly timid formulation of her causal thesis: she says that "there is no evidence that pornography does no harm." The same negative claim can be made, of course, about any genre of literature. Ted Bundy, the serial murderer who said he had read pornography since his youth, and whom feminists often cite for that remark, also said that he had studied Dostoevsky's *Crime and Punishment*. Even MacKinnon's weak statement is controversial, moreover. Some psychologists have argued that pornography, by providing a harmless outlet for violent tendencies, may actually reduce the amount of such crime. See Patricia Gillian, "Therapeutic Uses of Obscenity," and other articles reprinted and cited in *Censorship and Obscenity*, edited by Rajeev Dhavan and Christie Davies (Rowman and Littlefield, 1978). And it is at least relevant that nations with the most permissive laws about pornography are among those with the least sexual crime, though of course that fact might be explained in other ways. (See Marjorie Heins, *Sex, Sin, and Blasphemy*, New Press, 1993, p. 152.)

who is ingratiating and obsequious and imitative and aggressively passive and silent.[9]

In an earlier work she put the point even more graphically:

> Who listens to a woman with a penis in her mouth? ... Anyone who cannot walk down the street or even lie down in her own bed without keeping her eyes cast down and her body clenched against assault is unlikely to have much to say about the issues of the day. ... Any system of freedom of expression that does not address a problem where the free speech of men silences the free speech of women ... is not serious about securing freedom of expression."[10]

On this view, which has been argued more elaborately by others,[11] it is women not pornographers who need First Amendment protection, because pornography humiliates or frightens them into silence and conditions men to misunderstand what they say. (It conditions them to think, for example—as some stupid judges have instructed juries in rape trials—that when a woman says no she sometimes means yes.) Because this argument cites the First Amendment as a reason for banning, not for protecting, pornography, it has the appeal of paradox. But it is premised on an unacceptable proposition: that the right to free speech includes a right to circumstances that encourage one to speak, and a right that others grasp and respect what one means to say.

These are obviously not rights that any society can recognize or enforce. Creationists, flat-earthers, and bigots, for example, are ridiculed in many parts of America now; that ridicule undoubtedly dampens the enthusiasm many of them have for speaking out and limits the attention others pay to what they say. Many political and constitutional theorists, it is true, insist that if freedom of speech is to have any value, it must include some right to the opportunity to speak: they say that a society in which only the rich enjoy access to newspapers, television, or other public media does not accord a genuine right to free speech. But it goes far beyond that to insist that freedom of speech includes not only opportunity to speak to the

9. MacKinnon's frequent rhetorical use of "you" and "your," embracing all female readers, invites every woman to see herself as a victim of the appalling sexual crimes and the abuses she describes, and reinforces an implicit suggestion that women are, in pertinent ways, all alike: all passive, innocent, and subjugated.

10. Reprinted in Catherine Itzin, editor, *Pornography: Women, Violence and Civil Liberties*, p. 483–484.

11. See Frank I. Michelman, "Conceptions of Democracy in American Constitutional Argument: The Case of Pornography Regulation," *Tennessee Law Review* Vol. 56, No. 2 (1989), pp. 303–304.

public but a guarantee of a sympathetic or even competent understanding of what one says.

MacKinnon's third argument centers on the production rather than the distribution or consumption of pornography: she argues that women who act in pornographic films suffer actual, direct sexual subordination, compounded by the fact that their degradation is recorded for posterity. She points out that some women are coerced or tricked into making pornographic films, and mentions the notorious "snuff" films which are said to record the actual murder of women. But of course all these crimes can be prosecuted without banning pornography, and, as MacKinnon herself concedes, it would be wrong to "rely on the fact that some pornography is made through coercion as a legal basis for restricting all of it." Laws banning child pornography are indeed justified on the grounds that children may be damaged by appearing in pornographic films. But these laws, like many others that treat children differently, suppose that they are not competent to understand and consent to acts that may well be against their present and future interests.

It would plainly be a mistake to assume that women (or men) who appear in pornographic films do so unwillingly. Our economic system does, it is true, make it difficult for many women to find satisfactory, fulfilling employment, and may well encourage some of them to accept roles in pornographic films they would otherwise reject. The system, as MacKinnon grimly notes, works to the benefit of the pornographers. But it also works to the benefit of many other employers—fast-food chains, for example—who are able to employ women at low wages. There is great economic injustice in America, but that is no reason for depriving poor women of an economic opportunity some of them may prefer to the available alternatives.

I should mention a fourth consideration that MacKinnon puts forward, though it is difficult to find an argument in it. She says that much pornography is not just speech—it is not "only words"—because it produces erections in men and provides them with masturbatory fantasies. (She warns her readers never to "underestimate the power of an erection.") Her view of the psychology of sexual arousal is mechanical—she thinks men who read pornography "are sexually habituated to its kick, a process that is largely unconscious and works as primitive conditioning, with pictures and words as sexual stimuli." In any case, she thinks that pornography's physiological power deprives it of First Amendment protection: "An orgasm is not an argument," she says, "and cannot be argued with. Compared with a thought, it raises far less difficult speech issues, if it raises any at all." But that seems a plain non sequitur: a piece of music or a work of art or poetry does not lose whatever protection the First

Amendment affords it when some people find it sexually arousing, even if that effect does not depend on its argumentative or aesthetic merits, or whether it has any such merits at all.

3

The continued popularity of bad arguments such as those in *Only Words* testifies to the strength of the real but hidden reason why so many people despise pornography and want to ban it. The sado-masochistic genre of pornography, particularly, is so comprehensibly degrading that we are appalled and shamed by its existence. Contrary to MacKinnon's view, almost all men, I think, are as disgusted by it as almost all women. Because those who want to forbid pornography know that offensiveness alone does not justify censorship, however, they disguise their repulsion as concern that pornography will cause rape, or silence women, or harm the women who make it.

In the most interesting parts of *Only Words*, MacKinnon offers a new argument that is also designed to transcend mere repulsion. She says that the way in which pornography is offensive—that it portrays women as submissive victims who enjoy torture and mutilation—contributes to the unequal opportunities of women in American society, and therefore contradicts the values meant to be protected by the equal protection clause. She concedes, for the sake of this argument, that in spite of its minimal contribution to intellectual or political debate, pornography is protected under the First Amendment. But that First Amendment protection must be balanced, she says, against the Fourteenth Amendment's requirement that people be treated equally. "The law of equality and the law of freedom of speech are on a collision course in this country," she says, and she argues that the balance, which has swung too far toward liberty, must now be redressed.

The censorship of pornography, she says, should be regarded as like other kinds of government action designed to create genuine equality of opportunity. It is now accepted by almost everyone that government may properly prohibit discrimination against blacks and women in employment and education, for example. But such discrimination may take the form, not merely of refusing them jobs or university places, but of subjecting those who do manage to find jobs or places to an environment of insult and prejudice that makes work or education less attractive or even impossible. Government prohibits racial or sexual harassment at work—it punishes employers who subject blacks to racial insult or women to sexual pressures, in spite of the fact that these objectionable practices are carried out through speech—and many universities have adopted "speech codes" that prohibit racial insults in classrooms or on campus. Banning or punishing pornography, MacKinnon suggests, should be regarded as a more general remedy of the same kind. If pornography contributes to the general subordination of women by picturing them as sexual or servile objects, as she believes it does, then eliminating pornography can also be defended as serving equality of opportunity even though it restricts liberty.[12] The "egalitarian" argument for censorship is in many ways like the "silencing" argument I described earlier: it supposes not that pornography significantly increases sexual crimes of violence, but that it works more insidiously to damage the standing and power of women within the community. But the "egalitarian" argument is in two ways different and apparently more cogent.

First, it claims not a new and paradoxical conflict within the idea of liberty, as the silencing argument does, but a conflict between liberty and equality, two ideals that many political philosophers think are often in conflict. Second, it is more limited in its scope. The "silencing" argument supposes that everyone—the bigot and the creationist as well the social reformer—has a right to whatever respectful attention on the part of others is necessary to encourage him to speak his mind and to guarantee that he will be correctly understood; and that is absurd. The "egalitarian" argument, on the contrary, supposes only that certain groups—those that are victims of persisting disadvantage in our society—should not be subjected to the kind of insult, harassment, or abuse that has contributed to that disadvantage.

But the "egalitarian" argument is nevertheless much broader and more dangerous in its scope than might first appear. The analogies MacKinnon proposes—to sexual harassment laws and university speech codes—are revealing, because though each of these forms of regulation might be said to serve a general egalitarian purpose, they are usually defended on much more limited and special grounds. Laws against sexual harassment are designed to protect women not from the diffuse effects of whatever derogatory opinions about them are part of the general culture, but from

12. Not all feminists agree that pornography contributes to the economic or social subordination of women. Linda Williams, for example, in the Fall, 1993 issue of the *Threepenny Review*, claims that "the very fact that today a variety of different pornographies are now on the scene in mass market videos is good for feminism, and that to return to the time of repressing pornographic sexual representations would mean the resurgence of at least some elements of an underground tradition . . . of misogyny."

direct sexual taunts and other degrading language in the workplace.[13] University speech codes are defended on a different ground: they are said to serve an educational purpose by preserving the calm and reflective atmosphere of mutual respect and of appreciation for a diversity of cultures and opinions that is essential for effective teaching and research. I do not mean that such regulations raise no problems about free speech. They do. Even if university speech codes, for example, are enforced fairly and scrupulously (and in the charged atmosphere of university politics they often are not) they sometimes force teachers and students to compromise or suppress their opinions by erring on the side of safety, and some speech codes may actually be unconstitutional. I mean only that constraints on speech at work and on the campus can be defended without appealing to the frightening principle that considerations of equality require that some people not be free to express their tastes or convictions or preferences anywhere. MacKinnon's argument for banning pornography from the community as a whole does presuppose this principle, however, and accepting her argument would therefore have devastating consequences.

Government could then forbid the graphic or visceral or emotionally charged expression of any opinion or conviction that might reasonably offend a disadvantaged group. It could outlaw performances of *The Merchant of Venice*, or films about professional women who neglect their children, or caricatures or parodies of homosexuals in nightclub routines. Courts would have to balance the value of such expression, as a contribution to public debate or learning, against the damage it might cause to the standing or sensibilities of its targets. MacKinnon thinks that pornography is different from other forms of discriminatory or hostile speech. But the argument she makes for banning it would apply to much else. She pointedly declares that freedom of speech is respected too much by Americans and that the Supreme Court was right in 1952 when it sustained a prosecution of anti-Semitic literature—a decision it has since abandoned[14]—and wrong in 1978 when it struck down an ordinance banning a Nazi march in Illinois.[15]

So if we must make the choice between liberty and equality that MacKinnon envisages—if the two constitutional values really are on a collision course—we should have to choose liberty because the alternative would be the despotism of thought-police.

13. See Barbara Presley Noble, "New Reminders on Harassment," *The New York Times*, August 15, 1993, p. 25.

14. *Beauharnais v. Illinois*, 343 US 250 (1952), abandoned in *New York Times v. Sullivan*, 376 US 254 (1964) at 268–269.

15. See *Smith v. Collins*, 439 US 916 (1978).

But is she right that the two values do conflict in this way? Can we escape despotism only by cheating on the equality the Constitution also guarantees? The most fundamental egalitarian command of the Constitution is for equality throughout the political process. We can imagine some compromises of political equality that would plainly aid disadvantaged groups—it would undoubtedly aid blacks and women, for example, if citizens who have repeatedly expressed racist or sexist or bigoted views were denied the vote altogether. That would be unconstitutional, of course; the Constitution demands that everyone be permitted to play an equal part in the formal process of choosing a president, a Congress, and other officials, that no one be excluded on the ground that his opinions or tastes are too offensive or unreasonable or despicable to count.

Elections are not all there is to politics, however. Citizens play a continuing part in politics between elections, because informal public debate and argument influences what responsible officials—and officials anxious for re-election—will do. So the First Amendment contributes a great deal to political equality: it insists that just as no one may be excluded from the vote because his opinions are despicable, so no one may be denied the right to speak or write or broadcast because what he will say is too offensive to be heard.

That amendment serves other goals as well, of course: free speech helps to expose official stupidity and corruption, and it allows vigorous public debate that sometimes generates new ideas and refutes old ones. But the First Amendment's egalitarian role is independent of these other goals: it forbids censoring cranks or neo-Nazis not because anyone thinks that their contributions will prevent corruption or improve public debate, but just because equality demands that everyone, no matter how eccentric or despicable, have a chance to influence policies as well as elections. Of course it does not follow that government will in the end respect everyone's opinion equally, or that official decisions will be equally congenial to all groups. Equality demands that everyone's opinion be given a chance for influence, not that anyone's opinion will triumph or even be represented in what government eventually does.

The First Amendment's egalitarian role is not confined, however, to political speech. People's lives are affected not just by their political environment—not just by what their presidents and legislators and other public officials do—but even more comprehensively by what we might call their moral environment. How others treat me—and my own sense of identity and self-respect—are determined in part by the mix of social conventions, opinions, tastes, convictions, prejudices, life styles, and cultures that flourish in the community in which I live. Liberals are sometimes accused of thinking that what people say or do or think in private has no impact on anyone except themselves, and that is plainly wrong. Someone to whom religion is of fundamental importance, for example, will obviously lead a very different and perhaps more satisfying life in a community in which most other people share his convictions than in a dominantly secular society of atheists for whom his beliefs are laughable superstitions. A woman who believes that explicit sexual material degrades her will likely lead a very different, and no doubt more satisfying, life among people who also despise pornography than in a community where others, including other women, think it liberating and fun.

Exactly because the moral environment in which we all live is in good part created by others, however, the question of who shall have the power to help shape that environment, and how, is of fundamental importance, though it is often neglected in political theory. Only one answer is consistent with the ideals of political equality: that no one may be prevented from influencing the shared moral environment, through his own private choices, tastes, opinions, and example, just because these tastes or opinions disgust those who have the power to shut him up or lock him up. Of course, the ways in which anyone may exercise that influence must be limited in order to protect the security and interests of others. People may not try to mold the moral climate by intimidating women with sexual demands or by burning a cross on a black family's lawn, or by refusing to hire women or blacks at all, or by making their working conditions so humiliating as to be intolerable.

But we cannot count, among the kinds of interests that may be protected in this way, a right not to be insulted or damaged just by the fact that others have hostile or uncongenial tastes, or that they are free to express or indulge them in private. Recognizing that right would mean denying that some people—those whose tastes these are—have any right to participate in forming the moral environment at all. Of course it should go without saying that no one has a right to *succeed* in influencing others through his own private choices and tastes. Sexists and bigots have no right to live in a community whose ideology or culture is even partially sexist or bigoted: they have no right to any proportional representation for their odious views. In a genuinely egalitarian society, however, those views cannot be locked out, in advance, by criminal or civil law: they must instead be discredited by the disgust, outrage, and ridicule of other people.

MacKinnon's "egalitarian" argument for censorship is important mainly because it reveals the most important reason for resisting her suggestions, and also because it allows us to answer her charge that liberals who oppose her are crypto-pornographers themselves. She thinks that people who defend the right to pornography are acting out of self-interest, not principle—she says she has been driven to the conclusion that "speech *will* be defined so that men can have their pornography." That charge is based on the inadequacy of the conventional explanation, deriving from John Stuart Mill, that pornography must be protected so that truth may emerge. What is actually at stake in the argument about pornography, however, is not society's chance to discover truth, but its commitment to the very ideal of equality that MacKinnon thinks underrated in the American community. Liberals defend pornography, though most of them despise it, in order to defend a conception of the First Amendment that includes, as at least one of its purposes, protecting equality in the processes through which the moral as well as the political environment is formed. First Amendment liberty is not equality's enemy, but the other side of equality's coin.

MacKinnon is right to emphasize the connection between the fight over pornography and the larger, more general and important, argument about the freedom of Americans to say and teach what others think politically incorrect. She and her followers regard freedom of speech and thought as an elitist, inegalitarian ideal that has been of almost no value to women, blacks, and others without power; they say America would be better off if it demoted that ideal as many other nations have. But most of her constituents would be appalled if this denigration of freedom should escape from universities and other communities where their own values about political correctness are now popular and take root in the more general political culture. Local majorities may find homosexual art or feminist theater just as degrading to women as the kind of pornography MacKinnon hates, or radical or separatist black opinion just as inimical to racial justice as crude racist epithets.

That is an old liberal warning—as old as Voltaire—and many people have grown impatient with it. They are willing to take that chance, they say, to advance a program that seems overwhelmingly important now. Their impatience may prove fatal for that program rather than essential to it, however. If we abandon our traditional understanding of equality for a different one that allows a majority to define some people as too corrupt or offensive or radical to join in the informal moral life of the nation, we will have begun a process that ends, as it has in so many other parts of the world, in making equality something to be feared rather than celebrated, a mocking, "correct" euphemism for tyranny.

CHAPTER THIRTEEN

Desire and Disgust
Hustler *Magazine**

LAURA KIPNIS

☽

When *Hustler* publisher Larry Flynt was shot outside a Georgia court-room in 1978 in an assassination attempt that left him paralyzed from the waist down, the nation hardly mourned. News reports of the shooting took an ironic tone (*Time* billed it "The Bloody Fall of a Hustler"). There were no candlelight vigils outside his hospital room or impassioned calls for the nation's prayers, even though when a similar fate befell Alabama governor George Wallace six years earlier, Wallace was instantly converted from Southern racist to elder statesman in the national consciousness (and actually went on to win substantial support from black voters in his 1982 gubernatorial race after renouncing his segregationist ways). An avowed white supremacist named Joseph Paul Franklin was indicted for the Flynt shooting, but never tried.[1]

Flynt's spinal nerves were severed, leaving him both paralyzed and in constant pain. He became a paranoid recluse, barricading himself behind a steel door to the bedroom of his Bel Air mansion, surrounded by thuggish bodyguards. Wife Althea Leasure, then twenty-seven and a former go-go dancer, took control of the multi-million dollar Flynt empire, comparing herself to a rogue version of *Washington Post* publisher Katherine

*Reprinted with permission from *Bound and Gagged*, Grove/Atlantic Press, 1992. Copyright © 1992 by Laura Kipnis.
1. Officials said they were troubled by inconsistencies in the evidence and didn't take the case to trial. Franklin has been convicted of killing interracial couples in Utah and Wisconsin, and linked to thirteen racially motivated killings across the country, including the shooting of civil rights leader Vernon Jordan.

Graham, a woman whose publishing career also followed her husband's demise. Although Flynt is now a wheelchair-bound paraplegic, it seems impossible to muster sympathy for his plight. He'd made a national nuisance of himself, like some attention-grabbing overgrown adolescent boy mooning the guests at a church social, and the attitude of the nation appeared to be that he pretty much got what he deserved.

Maybe the roadblock to a Wallace-like sentimental rehabilitation of Flynt was that his career as a pornographer spilled out into the political arena rather than being confined to the pages of his smut sheet (and the only thing he renounced was his weird, highly publicized preshooting conversion to Christianity). Flynt had fashioned himself into a one-man bug up the nation's ass, single-mindedly dedicating himself to his self-appointed role as loudmouthed whistle-blower on what he regarded as our national hypocrisy. His favored tactic was to violate, systematically and extravagantly, in the most profoundly offensive way possible, each and every deeply held social taboo, norm and propriety he could identify. The nation responded with its kneejerk response to any perceived insult or injury: the lawsuit.

As with transvestite porn and fat porn, pornography can provide a home for those narratives exiled from sanctioned speech and mainstream political discourse, making pornography, in essence, an oppositional political form. If this seems to attribute too much credit or too much intelligence to mere smut, recall that most recently it has, in fact, been pornography—via Larry Flynt—that has had a decisive effect on expanding the perimeters of political speech in this country. Not the mainstream press, the political left, or the avant-garde. The 1988 Rehnquist Supreme Court decision against Moral Majoritarian Jerry Falwell's $45-million suit against Flynt and *Hustler* (for a mercilessly pornographic antireligious parody), was the biggest victory for freedom of the press in years; its sweeping protection of pornographic political satire also, perhaps unwittingly, reconfirmed pornography's historic role *as* political speech.

Since the democratizing invention of print and the birth of a print culture, pornography has been a favored strategy of social criticism, slinging muddy handfuls of obscenity and blasphemy at the power of political and religious authorities. Who responded, of course, by doing everything possible to eliminate it. *Hustler's* fusion of nudity and vulgarity with attacks on established political power, organized religion, and class privilege, places it squarely within this five-century-long rabble-rousing tradition. Its commitment to disobedience and insubordination, to truth-telling—as it sees truth, anyway—and exposing social hypocrisy, prompts the question of whether it's *Hustler's political* project (fueled by Flynt's longstanding grudge match with the state) that makes it the most reviled instance of mass-circulation porn. In other words, maybe it's not just those naked women. Historically, pornography was defined as what the state was determined to suppress.[2] *Hustler*'s entire publishing history, in line with tradition, has also been punctuated by extraordinarily numerous attempts at regulation and suppression, both public and private.

Larry Flynt was born in Appalachia, in Magoffin County, Kentucky (then the poorest county in America), the son of a pipe welder, making him very much a product of the white trash demographic his magazine appears to address. He quit school after the eighth grade, joined the navy at fourteen with a forged birth certificate, got out, worked in a General Motors auto assembly plant, and foresightedly parlayed $1,500 in savings into a chain of go-go bars in Ohio called the Hustler Clubs. The magazine originated as a two-page newsletter for the bars, and the rest was rags to riches: Flynt's income was as high as $30 million a year when *Hustler* was at its peak circulation of over 2 million. At this point he built, in the basement of his mansion, a scale replica of the cabin in which he grew up. Its purpose: to remind him of his roots. The model is said to be replete with chickenwire, hay, and a three-foot lifelike statue of the chicken he claims to have lost his virginity to at age eight. Who says he's an unsentimental guy? (When Flynt started his magazine *Chic*, having little facility with a French accent, he insisted his staff pronounce it "Chick"—another homage, maybe.)[3]

Since *Hustler*'s inception, Flynt has probably been hauled through the civil and criminal courtrooms of the nation more often than anyone in recent memory, on an astonishing array of obscenity, libel and criminal charges. (These, in turn spawned assorted contempt charges—fines and jail time—given his propensity for indecorous courtroom behavior.) In no particular order: Flynt was sued by rival *Penthouse* publisher Bob Guccione for invasion of privacy over a number of venomous cartoons chronicling his sexual exploits (and in a separate suit, by a female *Penthouse* executive who thought *Hustler* had libeled her by printing that she'd contracted VD from Guccione). He was sued by socialite-novelist Jackie Collins, after the magazine published nude photos it incorrectly identified as the nude authoress (she wound up having to pay court costs after an initial $40 million verdict in her favor was thrown out on appeal).

2. Hunt, *The Invention of Pornography*, 10–30.

3. For biographical information on Flynt I've drawn on Robert Ward, "Grossing out with Publishing's Hottest Hustler," *New Times* (January 9, 1976); Rudy Maxa, "Behind the Steel Door," *California Magazine* (June 1983); Jeffrey Klein, "Born Again Porn," *Mother Jones* (February/March 1987); Tom Johnson, "The Hustler," *Los Angeles* (April 1987). Flynt's life and his legal travails have also been widely covered in the national press.

Antipornography feminist Andrea Dworkin brought a $150 million lawsuit for invasion of her privacy, which was thrown out by the Supreme Court; her lawyer, the not particularly publicity-shy Gerry Spence, then filed suit when *Hustler* named him its "Asshole of the Month" for representing Dworkin.

Flynt was fined $10,000 a day—upped to $20,000 a day—when he refused to turn over to the feds tapes he claimed he possessed documenting a government frame of the dashing and bankrupt automaker John DeLorean on drug charges. Flynt, who didn't actually know DeLorean, but had apparently formed an imaginative identification with him as a victim of the same "repressive establishment," managed to place himself at the center of the high-profile DeLorean trial by presenting CBS News with audiotapes of mysterious origin revealing a key FBI informant threatening DeLorean's daughter when DeLorean tried to back out of the drug frame. No charges were brought against columnist Jack Anderson, who also claimed to have copies of the tapes (and also refused to divulge their source). Flynt, however, not commanding the journalistic legitimacy of a Jack Anderson in the eyes of the court, served over six months in a federal penitentiary on contempt charges, which were eventually dismissed.

Following the assassination attempt, which took place outside yet another courtroom where he was being tried, again, for obscenity, Flynt's public behavior became increasingly bizarre. (In constant pain, he had become addicted to morphine and Dilaudid, finally detoxing to methadone.) He appeared in court sporting an American flag as a diaper and was arrested. At a 1984 Los Angeles trial, described by the *Los Angeles Times* as "legal surrealism," his own attorney requested permission to gag his unruly client; after an "obscene outburst," Flynt, like Black Panther and Chicago Seven coconspirator Bobby Seale before him, was bound and gagged at his own trial.[4]

The same year the FCC was compelled to issue an opinion on Flynt's threat to force television stations to show his X-rated presidential campaign commercials. In a new bid for the nation's love and attention, he was running for president, as a Republican, with Native American activist Russell Means as his vice-presidential candidate. Or because, as he eloquently put it, "I am wealthy, white, pornographic, and, like the nuclear-mad cowboy Ronnie Reagan, I have been shot for what I believe in." Flynt's new compulsion was to find loopholes in the nation's obscenity laws, and with typical monomania vowed to use his presidential campaign to test those laws by insisting TV stations show campaign commercials

4. The Supreme Court's 1973 ruling on obscenity allowing communities to set their own standards for offensiveness meant that separate suits could be brought against pornographers for obscenity by any locality around the country.

featuring hard-core sex acts. (The equal time provision of Federal Communications Act prohibits censorship of any ad in which a candidate's voice or picture appears.⁵)

Then there was his stormy, anxiety-ridden love affair with the First Amendment, with Flynt, like one half of some inseparable codependent couple, forever testing, demanding, entreating its fidelity. Would it betray him, or bestow its favors once more? In 1986, a federal judge ruled that the U.S. Postal Service couldn't constitutionally prohibit Flynt from sending copies of *Hustler* to members of Congress, a ruling stemming from Flynt's beneficent decision to confer free copies upon elected officials so they could be "well informed on all social issues and trends." (More than 260 complained, ungraciously, to the postal service.)

But Flynt's most renowned First Amendment contretemps was the $45 million federal libel suit brought by an unamused Jerry Falwell over the notorious Campari "first time" ad parody which suggested that Falwell's "first time" had occurred with his mother behind an outhouse. Flynt turned up in court ensconced in a gold-plated wheelchair: A Virginia jury dismissed the libel charge but awarded Falwell $200,000 for intentional infliction of emotional distress. A federal district court upheld the verdict, but when it landed in the Rehnquist Supreme Court the judgment was reversed by a unanimous Rehnquist-written decision that the Falwell parody was not reasonably believable, and thus fell into the category of satire, an art form often "slashing and one-sided."

This Supreme Court decision significantly extended the freedom of the press won in the 1964 *New York Times vs. Sullivan* ruling, which ruled that libel could be found in cases of "reckless disregard." For the press, this was one of the most significant legal triumphs in recent years, and they unanimously hailed the decision as "an endorsement of robust political debate," which promised to end the influx of what they regarded as "pseudo-libel suits" brought by money-grubbing celebrities with hurt feelings. A grateful national press grappled with the contradiction between its relief at the outcome and its profound desire to distance itself from Flynt and *Hustler*, generally concluding that the existence of excrescences like *Hustler* are the price of freedom of the press, with frequent recourse to platitudes about "strange bedfellows." As political cartoonist Pat Oliphant put it, with morning-after pensiveness: "You're forced into bed with very strange people when you believe in the right of free expression . . . we all had to go to bat for Larry Flynt—not that we wanted to, and you felt like taking a shower afterward."

5. Interestingly, the FCC's decision in Flynt's case is now being employed as a precedent by antiabortion candidates who want to run campaign ads featuring graphic footage of bloody, aborted fetuses.

In the last analysis, however squeamish those who value the First Amendment are about that one-night stand with *Hustler*, it's been Larry Flynt's apparently compulsive need to pit himself against the state's enforcement of bodily proprieties, and against its desire to regulate how sex and the body can be represented, that betrays to what extent these *are* political issues. Otherwise, why the state's compelling interest in the matter? For Flynt, and within the pages of *Hustler*, sex has always been a political, not a private matter. The *Hustler* body is a battleground of opposing social and cultural forces: religious morality, class pretensions, and feminist censoriousness duke it out with the armies of bodily vulgarity, kinky fantasy, and unromanticized fucking. Although often lumped together in the popular imagination into an unholy trinity with *Penthouse* and *Playboy*, the other two top-circulation men's magazines, *Hustler* is actually quite a different beast in any number of respects, setting itself apart, from its inception, with its antiestablishment, anarchist-libertarian politics. But it also outstripped the other two in its unprecedented explicitness and raunch (unprecedented for a mass-circulation, as opposed to hard-core, magazine), and through its crusade *for* explicitness, shrilly accusing the other two of not really delivering the goods. The strategy paid off: *Hustler* captured a third of the men's market with its entrée into the field in 1974 by being the first of the torrid trio to reveal pubic hair. *Penthouse* swiftly following suit, in response to which a *Hustler* pictorial presented its model shaved; *Hustler* then further upped the explicitness ante and created a publishing scandal by displaying a glimpse of pubic hair on its cover in July 1976. This was *Hustler*'s unique commemoration of our nation's bicentennial: the model wore stars and stripes, although far too few of them.

Throughout these early years *Hustler*'s pictorials persisted in showing more and more of what had previously been the forbidden zone (the "pink" in *Hustler*-speak), with *Penthouse* struggling to keep up and *Playboy*, whose focus had always been above the waist anyway, keeping a discreet distance. In *Hustler*'s ideology, *Playboy* and *Penthouse*'s relative discretion about the female body makes them collaborationists in the forces of repression and social hypocrisy that *Hustler* had set itself the task of exposing. It continually railed against their lack of explicitness, their coyness and veiling of the body—by *Hustler*'s standards—which smacks of all the forms of social hypocrisy that depend on decorum and civility, on not naming names or saying it how it really is, on docility in the face of secret abuses of power and privilege. The veiled "private" body is analogous to the hidden government (the Iran-Contra scandal was a shining moment for *Hustler*), analogous to the hidden sources of wealth of the ruling classes, which secretly the rest of us are paying for through our labor, and to the hidden abuses of power and privilege that make the social engine chug so smoothly along, benefiting the few, but not the *Hustler* reader.

Not for *Hustler* are the upwardly mobile professional-class fantasies that fuel the *Playboy* and *Penthouse* imaginations, or the celebrity interviews that cozy up to the power elite and rich media bigshots. *Hustler* addresses itself to what it describes as a working-class audience, ranting madly against all forms of power—whether state sanctioned or criminally insane—by making them indistinguishable from one another. (*"Hustler* has taken readers into the twisted minds of Hillside Strangler Kenneth Bianchi, the Republican National Committee and Los Angeles' hitmen cops" as it put it in a typical piece of self-promotion.) The catalogue of social resentments *Hustler* trumpets, particularly against class privilege, makes it by far the most openly class-antagonistic, mass-circulation periodical of any genre. (And after all, class privilege is the dirty little secret of all national and electoral politics: face it, no welfare moms, homeless, unemployed, no blue-collar workers represent the nation in those hallowed legislative halls of our "representative" democracy.)

Hustler was, from the beginning, determined to violate all the taboos observed by its more classy men's-rag brethren. It began by introducing penises. This was a sight so verboten in traditional men's magazines that its strict prohibition impels you to wonder about just what traumas the sight of a penis might provoke in the male viewer. (And of course, the focus on "female objectification" in critiques of hard-core pornography also symptomatically ignores the truth of heterosexual hard-core, which is that, by definition, it features both women *and* men, which allows men *and* women to view male *and* female bodies in sexual contexts.)

From its inception, *Hustler* made it its mission to disturb and unsettle its readers, both psychosexually and sociosexually, by interrogating the typical men's magazine conventions of sexuality. *Hustler*'s early pictorials included pregnant women, middle-aged women (horrified news commentaries referred to "geriatric pictorials"), hugely fat women, hermaphrodites, amputees, and in a moment of true *frisson* for your typical heterosexual male, a photo spread of a preoperative transsexual, doubly well-endowed. *Hustler* continued to provoke reader outrage with a 1975 interracial pictorial (black male, white female), which according to *Hustler* was protested by both the KKK and the NAACP. It enraged readers with explicit photo spreads of the consequences of venereal disease, graphic war carnage, and other in-your-face pictorials. You looked to *Hustler* for what you wouldn't get the chance to see elsewhere, for the kind of visual materials the rest of society devotes itself to not portraying and not thinking about. (And *Hustler*'s influence on the genre has been such that by 1991, *Playboy* was willing to scandalize its somewhat less adventuresome readers by running a photo spread of a beautiful *post*operative transsexual, unintentionally reminding readers that the requirement to become a *Playboy* centerfold is, as usual, simply vast amounts of cosmetic surgery and silicone, whether you're born male *or* female.)

Even beyond its explicitness, *Hustler*'s difference from *Playboy* and *Penthouse* is in the sort of female body it imagines. The *Hustler* body is an unromanticized body: no Vaselined lenses or soft focus here. This is neither the airbrushed top-heavy fantasy body of *Playboy*, nor the slightly cheesy opulence of *Penthouse*, whose lingeried and sensitive crotch shots manage to transform female genitalia into ersatz *objets d'art*. The sexuality *Hustler* delivers is far from normative, with the most polymorphous array of sexual preferences regarded as equivalent to "normal sex," whether they adhere to the standard heterosexual teleology of penetration or not. Male-male sexuality is even raised as a possibility. And in stark distinction to the *Playboy/Penthouse* body, the *Hustler* body has an interior, not just a suntanned surface. It's insistently material, defiantly vulgar, corporeal. In fact, the *Hustler* body is often a gaseous, fluid emitting, *embarrassing* body, one continually defying the strictures of social manners and mores and instead governed by its lower intestinal tract: a body threatening to erupt at any moment. *Hustler*'s favorite joke is someone accidentally defecating in church.

Particularly in its cartoons, but also in its editorials and political humor, *Hustler* devotes itself to what we might call "grossness": an obsessive focus on the lower half of the body, and on the processes (and products) of elimination. Its joke techniques are based on exaggeration and inversion, which has long been a staple of pornographic political satire. In fact, the *Hustler* worldview is quite similar to that of Rabelais, the sixteenth-century French social satirist, whose emphasis was also was on the bodily and the grotesque.[6] And although Rabelais has now taken up his place in the canon of classics, he was, in his own day, forced to flee France when his work was condemned for heresy (and placed on the *Index of Forbidden Books* by the Council of Trent) in something of a prequel to Larry Flynt's run-ins with current obscenity law.

Hustler's quite Rabelaisian exaggeration of everything improper is apparent in even a partial inventory of the subjects it finds of fascination. Fat women, assholes, monstrous and gigantic sexual organs, body odors (the notorious scratch-and-sniff centerfold, which due to "the limits of the technology," Flynt apologized, strongly reeked of lilacs), anal sex, and anything that exudes from the body: piss, shit, semen, menstrual blood,

---

6. Mikhail Bakhtin, *Rabelais and His World* (Bloomington: University of Indiana Press, 1984). My reading of *Hustler* owes much to Bakhtin's dazzling analysis of the politics of the grotesque.

particularly when they sully public, sanitary, or sanctified sites. And especially farts: farting in public, farting loudly, Barbara Bush farting, priests
and nuns farting, politicians farting, the professional classes farting, the
rich farting. All of this is certainly a far remove from the sleek, laminated
Playboy/Penthouse body. As *Newsweek* once complained of *Hustler*,
"The contents of an average issue read like something Krafft-Ebing
might have whispered to the Marquis de Sade.... *Hustler* is into erotic
fantasies involving excrement, dismemberment, and the sexual longings
of rodents... where other skin slicks are merely kinky, *Hustler* can be
downright frightful.... The net effect is to transform the erotic into the
emetic."[7]

It's not clear if what sets *Newsweek* to crabbing is that *Hustler* trans-
gresses proper social mores or that *Hustler* violates men's magazine conventions of sexuality. On both fronts it's transgressive. In fact, on *every*
front *Hustler* devotes itself to producing generalized Rabelaisian transgression. According to Larry Flynt in a reflective moment, "Tastelessness
is a necessary tool in challenging preconceived notions in an uptight world
where people are afraid to discuss their attitudes, prejudices and misconceptions." This too, is not so far from Rabelais, who also used the lower
body as a symbolic attack on the pompous false seriousness of high culture, church and state.[8]

Hustler's insistent, repetitive return to the imagery of the body out
of control, rampantly transgressing social norms and sullying property
and proprieties, can't fail to raise certain political questions. Anthropol-
ogists have observed that the human body is universally employed as
a symbol for human society, and that control over the body is always
a symbolic expression of social control.[9] The body and the social are
both split into higher and lower strata, with images or symbols of the
upper half of the body making symbolic reference to the society's upper
echelons—the socially powerful—while the lower half of the body and
its symbols (*Hustler*'s métier) makes reference to the lower tiers—those
without social power. Given this reading, the meaning of the symbolic
inversion *Hustler* performs—in which the lower stratum dominates and
indeed triumphs over the forces of reason, power and privilege—starts to
have some political resonance.[10]

7. *Newsweek* (February 16, 1976): 69.
8. Bahktin, 376.
9. Mary Douglas, *Natural Symbols: Explorations in Cosmology* (London: Bar-
rie & Rockliff, 1970): 70.
10. Peter Stallybrass and Allon White, *The Politics and Poetics of Transgression*
(Ithaca: Cornell University Press, 1986). Stallybrass and White don't write on

Symbolically deploying the improper body as a mode of social sedition also follows logically from the fact that the body is the very thing those forms of power under attack—government, religion, bourgeois manners and mores—devote themselves to keeping "in its place." Control over the body has long been considered essential to producing an orderly work force, a docile populace, a passive law-abiding citizenry. Just consider how many actual laws are on the books regulating *how* bodies may be seen and what parts may not, *what* you may do with your body in public *and* in private, and it begins to make more sense that the out-of-control, unmannerly body is precisely what threatens the orderly operation of the status quo. Historically, local carnivals were something of a release valve from the shackles of social control: seasonal or yearly festivals of improprieties, where drunkenness, low humor, and grotesque, out-of-control bodies rampaged and reigned.[11] As carnivals too became increasingly regulated and sanitized (and in our own day, expropriated by big business: carnivals were the predecessors of today's sterile corporate-owned theme parks), other cultural expressions of the out-of-control body appear and are subject to regulation. Like pornography. But the tethers of bodily propriety have become so increasingly internalized, so much a cornerstone of the modern self, that the grotesqueries of the sixteenth-century carnival would no doubt seem extraordinarily unnerving and unpleasurable to the contemporary citizen.

What we consider gross and disgusting is hardly some permanent facet of the human psyche: it's historically specific and relatively recent. According to social historian Norbert Elias, disgust only fully emerges in the course of the sixteenth century rise of individualism, during which time we see the invention of the concept of privacy as well: our various requirements about closed (and locked) bathroom doors, our own plates to eat from, and delicacy around sexual and bodily matters are all aspects of this same social process. Disgust is something precariously acquired in the course of the civilizing process (and a process that has to be recapitulated in the socialization of each individual modern child). During this social transformation, once communal activities—sleeping, sex, elimination, eating—became subject to new sets of rules of conduct and privatization. An increasingly heightened sense of disgust at the bodies and body functions of others emerged, and simultaneous with this process of privatization came a corresponding sense of shame about one's own body and its functions. Certain once-common behaviors become

pornography specifically, but the influence of their work very much shapes this chapter, as it does my general understanding of pornography throughout the book.

11. Stallybrass and White, chapters 1 and 5.

socially frowned on: spitting, scratching, farting, wiping your mouth on the tablecloth, or blowing your nose into your sleeve were replaced by increasingly detailed rules devoted to restraining the conduct of the body (and even how it might be spoken of) in public.

Historically speaking, manners have a complicated history as a mechanism of class distinction, that is, of separating the high from the low. Implements we now take for granted, like the fork and the handkerchief, were initially seen as upper-class affectations (you both blew your nose into and ate with your hands, and from communal dishes). Only gradually did they filter down through the social hierarchy. But as money rather than aristocratic origins became the basis for social distinctions, manners took on an increasing sense of importance, and they too started disseminating down throughout the population. Although originally mechanisms of social distinction, these behavior reforms and increasingly refined manners were also progressively restructuring *internal* standards of privacy, disgust, shame and embarrassment throughout the population, thus transforming both daily *and* inner life. Although as with any massive social transformation, though this was a gradual and incomplete process.

It was also a social transformation with the most profound consequences on individual psychology and subjectivity. As far more attention came to be paid to proprieties around elimination, to hygiene, to bodily odors, and to not offending others, thresholds of sensitivity and refinement in the individual psyche became correspondingly heightened. It wasn't just behavior being reformed, it was the entire structure of the psyche, with the most shameful and prohibited behaviors and impulses (those around sex and elimination) propelled into the realm of the unconscious. This split, which Freud would later describe with the terms "ego" and "id," is what would become the very substance of the modern individual. The experience of disgust at what was once an ordinary part of daily life has become so completely part of our "nature" that defiance of bodily proprieties can result in actual physical revulsion. When we say of something disgusting: "It made me sick," this can be a physical fact, revealing just how very deeply these codes have become embedded in who we are. And how threatening to our very *beings* transgressions of manners can be. (This is far from only an individual issue, as these codes of conduct became part of the implicit rationale of the imperial project as well: the lack of "civilization" of the inhabitants of other parts of the globe was always part of the justification for invading, colonizing or enslaving them.[12])

Here's a clue about why *Newsweek* should get so crabby about *Hustler*, and why *Hustler*, with its anarchistic, antiestablishment, working-class politics, should seize on grossness as the perfect blunt instrument with

---

12. See Norbert Elias, *History of Manners* (New York: Pantheon, 1978).

which to register its protests. Here also is a way to think about why the state would be so interested in matters of the body and its symbols. The power of grossness is very simply its opposition to high culture and official culture, which feels the continual need to protect itself against the debasements of the low (the lower classes, low culture, the lower body...).

When the social and the bodily are put side by side, it becomes apparent how grossness and erupting bodies manage to suggest the ongoing jeopardy (to those in power) and ongoing uncertainty of a social hierarchy only tenuously held in place through symbolic (and real) policing of the threats posed by rebellious bodies: by the unruly classes, by angry mobs. And apparently by at least some forms of pornography.

The history of disgust as a mechanism of class distinction is another reason the feminist antipornography movement is so politically problematic. There's a telling moment in the early antiporn documentary *Not a Love Story*, in which feminist author-poet (and former *Ms.* magazine editor) Robin Morgan turns up to register a genteel protest against pornography. Posed in her large book-lined living room, poet-husband Kenneth Pitchford (who appears to be wearing an ascot) at her side, she inveighs against a range of sexual practices: not only masturbation—on the grounds that it promotes political passivity—but also, "superficial sex, kinky sex, appurtenances and [sex] toys" for, as she puts it "benumbing... normal human sensuality." She then breaks into tears as she describes the experience of living in a society where pornographic media thrives.

Keep this scene in mind as you imagine the following, slightly less proper one, described in a letter to *Hustler* from "E.C," a reader who introduces an account of an erotic experience involving a cruel-eyed, high-heeled dominatrix with this vivid self-description: "One night, trudging home from work—I gut chickens, put their guts in a plastic bag and stuff them back in the chicken's asshole—I varied my routine by stopping at a small pub...."[13]

Let's allow these two scenes—one filmed, one literary—to stand in for the combative and mutually uncomprehending relation of *Hustler* and its critics. The stark differences in tone, setting, affect, and even accessories, ushers in a generally off-limits topic: the relation between sexuality and class (or modes of representing them). In one corner we have a tearful Morgan, laboring for the filmmakers and their audience as a feminist intellectual, constructing, from a relatively privileged social position, a

13. Several writers who have visited the *Hustler* offices testify that (to their surprise) these sorts of letters *are* sent by actual readers, and at its peak circulation *Hustler* received well over a thousand letters a month. As to whether this particular letter was written by a reader or a staff writer, I have no way of knowing, but it's typical of the *Hustler* worldview.

normative theory of sexuality which she endeavors to impose on the rest of the population. While "feminist intellectual" is not necessarily the highest-paying job category these days, it's quite a few steps up the social hierarchy from that of "E.C.," whose work is of a character that tends to be relegated to the lower rungs within a society (and a social division of labor) which categorizes jobs dealing with things that smell, or that for other reasons we prefer to hide from view—garbage, sewerage, dirt, animal corpses—as of low status, both monetarily and socially.

E.C.'s letter, carefully (a lot more carefully than Morgan) framing his sexuality in relation to his material circumstances and with a keen awareness of how social distinctions operate in our culture, is typical of *Hustler*, in its vulgarity, its explicitness about "kinky" sex, and in the insistent association between sexuality and class. *Hustler* consistently frames sex acts as occurring within historically and economically specific contexts, in distinction to the set of *universal* norms feminist Morgan attempts to disseminate downward. Morgan's vision of "normal human sensuality" neither comprehend nor includes E.C.'s night of bliss with his Mistress, who incidentally, "mans" herself with just the kind of appurtenances Morgan seems to be referring to. (And can Morgan seriously mean to so blast "appurtenances" like the dildo, that distinguished emblem of feminist self-reliance?)

Hustler too offers its readers a "theory of sexuality," although unlike Morgan's feminism, *Hustler* isn't disseminating universal pronouncements. It offers an explicitly political analysis of power and the body, in addition to being explicit about its own class location. Comparing these two scenes—Morgan's living room versus E.C's night of kinky sex—it begins to appear that Morgan's tears, her sentiment, are performed *against* E.C.'s vulgarity, and that the desire to banish from one's existence the cause of one's distress has something of an historical imperative. Social distinctions are maintained through the expression of taste, disgust, and exclusion. Historically, the upper classes defined themselves against what they defined as dirty, low, repulsive, noisy, and contaminating: acts of exclusion that precisely maintained their identity as a class.[14] Disgust has a long and complicated history, central to which is the tendency of the emerging bourgeoisie to want to remove the distasteful from the sight of society (including, of course, dead animals, which might interest E.C., degutter of chickens), because as Norbert Elias puts it, "People in the course of the civilizing process seek to suppress in themselves every characteristic they feel to be animal."[15]

14. Stallybrass and White, 191.
15. Elias, 120.

These gestures of disgust are crucial to the regulations surrounding the body, which has become so rigidly split into higher and lower stratum that tears—as Morgan so well demonstrates—become the only publicly permissible display of body fluids. The products of the body start to stack up into a set of neat oppositions: on the one side upper bodily productions, a heightened sense of delicacy, sentiment, refinement, and the social project of removing the distasteful from sight (and sight, of course, is at the top of the hierarchy of the senses central to Enlightenment identity and rationality); and on the other side, the lower body and *its* productions (shit, farts, semen—*Hustler*'s staple joke materials), the insistence on vulgarity and violations of the "proper" body. From this vantage point, Morgan's antipornography project, not to mention those tears—devoted as they are to concealing the unruly, unregulated body from view—can be seen as part of a centuries-long sociohistorical process, and one that plays an ongoing role in maintaining social hierarchies.

It's difficult to see feminist disgust in isolation and disgust at pornography as strictly a gender issue if you take into account the historic function of these sorts of gestures. Western feminism has often been accused of wearing blinders: of formulating itself strictly in relation to the experiences of white, upper-class women. Insofar as the feminist antiporn movement devotes itself to rehearsing the experience of disgust and attempting to regulate sexual imagery, the class issue will continue to be one of its formative blind spots. One might want to interpret feminist disgust as expressing *symbolically* the very real dangers that exist for women in the world. But the net effect is to displace those dangers onto a generalized disgust with sex and the body (or more specifically, onto heterosexual sex and the male body). Andrea Dworkin, for example, writes extensively about her disgust at semen, a lower bodily production which, she tells us, she regards as a form of "pollution."[16] Her disgust is her prerogative (as long as she doesn't attempt to enact legislation on the basis of it[17]), but even as mobilized against a perception of violation to the female body, it's more than problematic in a political movement devoted to achieving liberation and social equity.

As a feminist (not to mention a petit bourgeois and denizen of the academic classes), I too find myself often disgusted by *Hustler*. This is *Hustler* hitting its target, like some heat-seeking offense missile, because it's someone like me who's precisely *Hustler*'s ideal sitting duck. *Hustler*

16. Andrea Dworkin, *Intercourse* (New York: Free Press, 1987): 187.
17. Dworkin, along with Catharine MacKinnon, is the author of antipornography legislation that a number of municipalities around the country have attempted to enact.

pits itself against not just the proper body, that holdover of the bourgeois revolution, but against all the current paraphernalia of yuppie professionalism. At its most obvious, *Hustler* is simply allergic to any form of social or intellectual affectation, squaring off like some maddened pit bull against the pretensions and the earning power of the professional classes: doctors, optometrists, dentists and lawyers are favored targets. It's pissed off by liberals, and particularly nasty to academics, who are invariably prissy and uptight. (An academic to his wife: "Eat your pussy? You forget Gladys, I have a Ph.D.") It rants against the power of government, which is by definition corrupt, as are elected officials, the permanent government, even foreign governments. Of course it smears the rich against the wall, particularly rich women, and dedicates many, many pages to the hypocrisy of organized religion, with a nonstop parade of jokes on the sexual instincts of the clergy, the sexual possibilities of the crucifixion, the scam of the virgin birth, and the bodily functions of nuns, priests, and ministers.

These are just *Hustler*'s more manifest targets. Reading a bit deeper, its offenses create a detailed blueprint of the national cultural psyche. *Hustler*'s favored tactic is to zero in on a subject, an issue, an "unsaid" that the bourgeois imagination prefers to be unknowing about—those very problematic materials a protectively tight-assed culture has founded itself upon suppressing, and prohibits irreverent speech about. Things we would call "tasteless" at best, or might even become physically revulsed by: the physical detritus of aborted fetuses, how and where the homeless manage to relieve themselves (not much social attention devoted to this little problem), amputation, the proximity of sexual organs to those of elimination, the various uses to which liposuctioned fat might be put—any aspect of how the material body fares in our current society.[18]

A case in point, and one that subjected *Hustler* to national outrage: its two cartoons about former first lady Betty Ford's mastectomy. If we can distance ourselves from our automatic indignation for a moment, *Hustler* might be seen as posing, through the strategy of transgression, an interesting cultural question: Which subjects are taboo ones for even sick humor? It wasn't uncommon, following the *Challenger* explosion, to hear the sickest jokes about scattered body parts, while jokes about amputees

---

18. There are ongoing attempts to regulate this sort of imagery. During the controversies over National Endowment for the Arts funding for artists, a Republican representative attempted to introduce a bill in Congress that would prohibit public funding of art that depicts aborted fetuses. This was something of a shortsighted strategy, as the aborted fetus has been, of course, a favored incendiary image of antiabortion forces. *New York Times* (October 10, 1990): 6.

and paraplegics are not unknown even on broadcast TV (and of course abound on the pages of *Hustler*); jokes about blindness are considered so benign that one involving blind bluesman Ray Charles featured in a long-running "blind taste test" soda pop commercial. Yet mastectomy is one subject that appears to be completely off limits as a humorous topic. But back to amputees, perhaps a better comparison: apparently a man without a limb is considered less tragic by the culture at large, less mutilated, and less of a cultural problem than a woman without a breast. A mastectomy more of a tragedy that the deaths of the seven astronauts.

This offers some clues about the deep structure of a cultural psyche, as does our deeply felt outrage at *Hustler*'s transgression. After all, what *is* a woman without a breast in a culture that measures breasts as the measure of the woman? Not a fit subject for comment. It's a subject so veiled that it's not even available to the "working through" of the joke. (And a case once again, where *Hustler* seems to be deconstructing the codes of the typical men's magazine: where *Playboy* creates a fetish of the breast, and whose very *raison d'être* is the cultural obsession with them, *Hustler* perversely points out that materially speaking, they're merely tissue—another limb.)

One way to thing about *Hustler*'s knack for locating and attacking the jugular of a culture's sensitivity is as intellectual work not unlike those classic anthropological studies that translate a culture into a set of structural oppositions (obsession with the breast/prohibition of mastectomy jokes), laying bare the structure of its taboos and arcane superstitions. (It's not only "primitive" cultures that have irrational taboos, after all.) In fact *Hustler* performs a similar cultural mapping to Mary Douglas's classic anthropological study *Purity and Danger*, which produces a comparable social blueprint. The vast majority of *Hustler* humor seems animated by the desire to violate what Douglas describes as "pollution" taboos and rituals. These are a society's set of beliefs, rituals and practices having to with dirt, order, and hygiene (and by extension, the pornographic), which vary from culture to culture. Douglas points out that such violations aren't entirely unpleasurable: confronting ambiguity, even revulsion and shock, isn't unrelated to the kinds of transgressions that make us laugh and give us pleasure in the realm of comedy and humor.[19]

That sense of pleasure and danger that violation of pollution taboos invokes in us clearly depends on the existence, within every culture, of symbolic maps or codes. These are, for the most part, only semi-conscious. *Hustler*'s defilement isn't some isolated event: it can only engage our

19. Mary Douglas, *Purity and Danger: An Analysis of the Concepts of Pollution and Taboo* (London: Routledge, 1966): 37.

interest or provoke our anxiety or our disgust to the extent that our ideas about these things form a cultural system, and that this system matters enormously—to our society, and in our very beings. As Freud remarks in his study of humor, *Jokes and Their Relation to the Unconscious*, "Only jokes that have a purpose run the risk of meeting with people who do not want to listen to them." Given that so much of the *Hustler* idiom is couched in the joke form (as is much pornography), the pleasures and displeasures of jokes—jokes are often a coded way of saying something slightly transgressive—are probably not unrelated to the transgressive pleasures and displeasures of pornography.

Although Mary Douglas highlights the ambivalent pleasures of purity violations, confronting transgression and violation can be profoundly displeasurable, too, as *Hustler's* many opponents so vehemently attest. For Freud, interestingly, this displeasure has mostly to do with gender and class. Freud first undertakes to categorize jokes according to their gender effects: for example, regarding excremental jokes (a staple of *Hustler* humor), Freud tells us that these jokes are targeted to both men and women, as we all experience a common sense of shame surrounding bodily functions. And it's true that *Hustler's* numerous jokes on the proximity of the sexual organs to those of elimination, the confusion of assholes and vaginas, turds and penises, shit and sex (a typical example: a couple is fucking in a hospital room while someone in the next bed is getting an enema, all get covered with shit), aren't targeted to a particular gender. Unless, that is, we women put ourselves, more so than men, in the position of upholders of good taste.

But *obscene* humor, whose purpose is to expose sexual facts and relations verbally, is, for Freud, the result of male and female sexual discordances, and the dirty joke is something like a seduction gone awry. The motive for (men's) dirty jokes is that women are incapable of tolerating undisguised sexuality, and this incapacity increases correspondingly as your educational and social level rise. Both men and women are subject to sexual inhibition or repression, but women, and especially, upper-class women, are the most seriously afflicted in the Freudian world. So dirty jokes function as a sign for both sexual difference ("smut is like an exposure of the sexually different person to whom it is directed ... it compels the person who is assailed to imagine the part of the body or the procedure in question") and class difference. If it weren't for women's lack of sexual willingness and uptight class refinement, the joke wouldn't be a joke, but a proposition: "If the woman's readiness emerges quickly the obscene speech has a short life; it yields at once to a sexual action," hypothesizes Freud hopefully.

This might all sound a bit Victorian, but it's also still true that pornographic images and jokes are aggressive to women because they're capable of causing discomfort. And they're capable of causing discomfort insofar as there are differing levels of sexual inhibition between at least some men and some women. And upper-classness or upper-class identification exacerbates this difference. (For Freud, even the form of the joke is classed, with a focus on joke "technique" associated with higher social classes and education levels, which explains something about how really stupid *Hustler*'s jokes are—even to find a pun is rare.) It's also still true that obscene jokes and pornographic images are only perceived by *some* women as an act of aggression against women, not by all, and individual "properness"—one index of class identification—is certainly a factor in how offended you get at a dirty joke or image.

This displeasure over pornography regularly gets expressed by feminists in the argument that pornography is dangerous to women. Or in statements like Andrea Dworkin's that "any violation of a woman's body can become sex for men; this is the essential truth of pornography."[20] But consider just how close these "danger arguments" are to what Mary Douglas calls "danger beliefs." These are all the ways that members of a society exhort each other into good citizenship by deploying predictions of disaster to enforce certain moral codes and social rules. In this kind of cosmology, centered on threats and fear, physical disasters or dangerous diseases are said to result from bad moral conduct—one sort of disease is caused by adultery, another by incest, and so on. Sexual dangers are a crucial part of this cosmology, with pollution fears, as we'll see, never very far away. According to Douglas's fieldwork, gender plays an important symbolic role in the realm of purity rituals and pollution violations: what it means is a way of symbolizing issues of social hierarchy.

I believe that some pollutions are used as analogies for expressing a general view of the social order. For example, there are beliefs that each sex is a danger to the other through *contact with sexual fluids* [my emphasis].... Such patterns of sexual danger can be seen to express symmetry or hierarchy. It is implausible to interpret them as expressing something about the actual relation of the sexes. I suggest that many ideas about sexual dangers are better interpreted as symbols of the relation between parts of society, as mirroring designs of hierarchy or symmetry which apply in the larger social system.[21]

Compare Douglas's comments on danger beliefs focused on "sexual fluids" to another passage by Andrea Dworkin: "In literary pornography, to ejaculate is to *pollute* the woman" (her emphasis). Dworkin goes on to discuss, in a lengthy excursus on semen, the collaboration between women-hating women's magazines, which "sometimes recommend

20. Dworkin, 138.
21. Douglas, *Purity and Danger*, 3.

spreading semen on the face to enhance the complexion" and pornography, where ejaculation often occurs on the woman's body or face: both, she writes, force women to accept semen and eroticize it. Her point seems to be is that men *prefer* that semen be seen as disgusting, because the only way they can get sexual pleasure is through violation. Thus semen is "driven into [the woman] to dirty her or make her more dirty or make her dirty by him"; at the same time semen has to be eroticized to get the woman to comply in her own violation.[22] That Dworkin sees contact with male "sexual fluids" as harmful to women is clear, as is the relation between pollution (again, it's Dworkin's own word), and ways of symbolizing danger beliefs.

For while it's true that *some* men *sometimes* pose sexual danger to women, the content of pollution beliefs, like Dworkin's analysis of pornography, expresses that danger symbolically at best: as anthropologist Douglas tells us, it's simply not plausible to take the content of these beliefs literally. In the Dworkin cosmology, there's a magical leap from the fact that "some men are violent," to "semen is dangerous," paralleling the equally problematic magical leap from the possibility that some rapists may look at pornography to the conclusion that pornography causes rape. A real fear, rape, finds expression in a symbolic and imaginary cause: pornography.

Historically, female reformism aimed at bettering the position of women has often had an unfortunately conservative social thrust. The temperance movement is a prime example, with the local interests of women in reforming rowdy or irresponsible male behavior too easily dovetailing with the interests of capital and officialdom in maintaining a passive, sober and obedient workforce. Although *Hustler*'s attacks on feminism might be seen simply as backlash against the feminist second wave, they can also be seen as a political response to the conservatism of feminist calls for reform of the male imagination. There's no doubt that *Hustler* sees itself as doing battle with feminists: Gloria Steinem makes frequent appearances in the pages of the magazine as an uptight, and predictably upper-class, bitch. From *Hustler*'s point of view, feminism is an upper-class movement dedicating to annihilating the low-rent *Hustler* male and his pleasures. Resisting is a nascent form of class consciousness. To acquiesce to feminist insistence on the reform of the male imagination would be to identify upward along the social hierarchy—anathema to *Hustler*'s politics and ideology.

What precisely does it mean to be offended by pornography? And what it means to be offended as *women* by pornography?

22. Dworkin, 187.

Freud's view of the difference between the sexes is that little boys and girls are, at an early stage, both just as "interested" in sex. As each mature, part of the process of sexual differentiation is the increasing level of inhibition that girls and women inherit as part of the acquisition of femininity. Women end up, generally speaking, the more afflicted by sexual repression, according to Freud. This is actually pretty similar to *Hustler*'s view: repression is a social process that produces differing levels of inhibition, displeasure, or sexual interest between at least some men and some women. Antipornography feminists (along with the Christian right) tend to take the opposite position, rejecting a social-constructionist argument like Freud's, in favor of a description of female sexuality as inborn and biologically based—something akin to the "normal human sensuality" Robin Morgan referred to.[23]

So a woman's discomfort at the dirty joke, and by extension, at pornography, is actually twofold. There's her discomfort at the intended violation, at being assailed, as Freud puts it, "with the part of the body or the procedure in question." But at the same time, what she's assailed with is the fact of her own repression (which isn't inborn or natural, according to Freud and *Hustler*, but acquired). Pornography's net effect (and perhaps its intent) is to unsettle a woman in her subjectivity, to point out that any "naturalness" of female sexuality and subjectivity of the sort that Morgan and many other feminists propagate isn't nature at all, but culture: part of the woman's own long-buried prehistory. A Freudian might add that what intensifies women's disgust at pornography is the unconscious renunciation of any residue of that early, pre-Oedipal "interest" in sex that little boys and little girls once shared. The classic Freudian example of a reaction-formation is a housewife whose obsession with cleanliness stems from a repressed interest in what's not "clean" (that is, sex), an obsession which actually allows her to focus all her attention on dust and dirt, thus affecting virtue and purity while coming close to satisfying the opposing, unacceptable instinct.[24] An antipornography crusader might be another such example: waging a fight against pornography means, in effect, spending most of your time looking at it and talking about it, while projecting the dirty interest onto others.

In addition, there's certainly a level of discomfort, for women, with the social fact of differences *between* women—that is, with other women's

---

23. As for Catharine MacKinnon and Andrea Dworkin, even if they don't strictly reject social constructionism, their social descriptions, particularly of male sexuality, have a tendency to fall back on what sound like biologically based and essentialist notions of masculinity and femininity.

24. Laplanche and Pontalis, *The Language of Psychoanalysis*, 376–78.

sexuality. After all, not all women *do* feel violated by male pornography, a fact which argues pretty convincingly against any account of female sexuality as uniform and natural. The antiporn rejoinder to these very real difference is to label those sisters "coerced," "brainwashed," or "male-identified," and resolutely attempting to force onto all of us this singular version of inborn femininity, which is somehow less inborn in some of us than in others.

So pornography sets up a force field of disturbances around the thorny question of female subjectivity, and the even thornier question of the origins of sexual differences between men and women. After all, what does *Hustler*-variety porn consist of but some sort of male fantasy of women whose sexual desires are in perfect unison with men's? The male fantasy of female sexual willingness is perceived by some women as doing violence to their very beings. But the violence here is that of being misidentified, of having one's desire misfigured as "male desire." I can easily feel offended at (my fantasy of) some disgusting, hairy, belching *Hustler* male imagining me or some other hapless woman panting lustfully after his bloated body, and imagining that our greatest goal in life is to play geisha girl to his kinky and bizarre pleasures. On the other hand, maybe if men read more Harlequin Romances, they'd be similarly offended to find *their* desires so misfigured—romance novels having been aptly been referred to as "pornography for women." Pornography forces social differences in our faces: not only class differences, not only differences between male and female sexuality, but the range of differences between *women*. Calling one version of sexuality "nature" and assigning it to all women is false in many ways, not least of which involves turning an historically specific class and educational position—coincidentally, that of the feminist antiporn intellectual—into a universal that tramples over the existence of very real divisions between women.

Any automatic assumptions about *Hustler*-variety porn aiding and abetting the entrenchment of male power will be put into question by reading the magazine, which few of its critics manage to do. *Hustler* itself often seems quite dubious about the status of men, wry and frequently perplexed about male and female sexual incompatibility. On the one hand it offers the standard men's magazine fantasy bimbette: always ready, always horny, willing to do anything, and who inexplicably finds the *Hustler* male simply irresistible. But just as often there's her flip side: the woman disgusted by the *Hustler* male's desires and sexuality, a haughty, superior, rejecting, upper-class bitch-goddess. Class resentment is modulated through resentment of women's power to humiliate and reject: "Beauty isn't everything, except to the bitch who's got it. You see her stalking the aisles of Cartier, stuffing her perfect face at exorbitant cuisineries, tooling her Jag along private-access coastline roads...."

Doesn't this reek of disenfranchisement rather than any certainty about male power over women? The fantasy life here is animated by cultural disempowerment in relation to a sexual caste system and a social class system. This magazine is tinged with frustrated desire and rejection: *Hustler* gives vent to a vision of sex in which sex is an arena for failure and humiliation, rather than domination and power. Numerous ads play off male anxieties and feelings of inadequacy: various sorts of penis enlargers ("Here is your chance to overcome the problems and insecurities of a penis that is too small. Gain self-confidence and your ability to satisfy women will sky rocket" reads a typical ad), penis extenders, and erection aids (Stay-Up, Sta-Hard, etc.).[25] One of the problems with most porn is that men arrogate the power and privilege of having public fantasies about women's bodies without any risk or comparable exposure of the male body, which is invariably produced as powerful and inviolable. But *Hustler* does put the male body at risk, rehearsing and never completely alleviating male anxiety. And there's a surprising amount of castration humor in *Hustler*, as well.

Rejecting the compensatory fantasy life mobilized by *Playboy* and *Penthouse*, in which all women are willing and all men are studs—as long as its readers fantasize and identify upward, with money, power, good looks, and consumer durables—*Hustler* pulls the window dressing off the market/exchange nature of sexual romance: the market in attractiveness, the exchange basis of male-female relations in a society where men typically have more social and earning power than women. Sexual exchange is a frequent joke topic: women students are coerced into having sex with professors for grades, women are fooled into having sex by various ruses, lies, or barters engineered by males in power positions—bosses, doctors, and the like. All this is probably truer than not, but problematic from the standpoint of male fantasy. Power, deep pockets and social prestige are represented as essential to sexual success, but the magazine works to disparage and oppose identification with these attributes on every front. The ways in which sex, gender, class and power intersect in *Hustler* are complex, contradictory, unpredictable, and ambivalent, making it impossible to maintain that this is a simple exercise in male domination.

25. *Hustler*'s advertising consists almost entirely of ads for sex toys, sex aids, porn movies, and phone sex services, as the automobile makers, liquor companies and manufacturers of other upscale items that constitute the financial backbone of *Playboy* and *Penthouse* refuse to hawk their wares in the pages of *Hustler*. Flynt also early on rejected cigarette ads, both because he's adamantly antismoking, and probably because numerous *Hustler* cartoons consist of grisly cancer jokes. In order to survive financially, *Hustler* began, among other enterprises, its now hugely successful magazine distribution company.

Much of *Hustler*'s humor is also manifestly political, devoted to dismantling abuses of political power and official privilege. A 1989 satirical photo feature titled "Farewell to Reagan: Ronnie's Last Bash" highlights just how the magazine's standard repertoire of aesthetic techniques—nudity, grossness and offense to the conventions of polite society—can be directly translated into scathingly effective political language. The pornographic idiom is quite explicitly deployed as a form of political speech, one that refuses to buy into the pompously serious and high-minded language that high culture considers appropriate to political discourse. Here *Hustler* thumbs its nose at both dominant culture's politics *and* its language.

The photo spread, laid out like a series of black and white surveillance photos, begins with this no-words-minced introduction:

It's been a great eight years—for the power elite, that is. You can bet Nancy planned long and hard how to celebrate Ron Reagan's successful term of filling special-interest coffers while fucking John Q. Citizen right up the yazoo. A radical tax plan that more than halved taxes for the rich while doubling the working man's load; detaxation of industries, who trickled down their windfalls into mergers, takeovers, and investments in foreign lands; crooked deals with enemies of U.S. allies in return for dirty money for right wing killers to reclaim former U.S. business territories overseas; more than 100 appointees who resigned in disgrace over ethics or outright criminal charges . . . are all the legacies of the Reagan years . . . and we'll still get whiffs of bullyboy Ed Meese's sexual intimidation policies for years to come, particularly with conservative whores posing as Supreme Court justices.

The photos that follow are of an elaborately staged orgiastic White House farewell party, with the appropriate motley faces of the eighties political elite photomontaged onto naked and semi-naked bodies doing obscene things to each other. (The warning "Parody: Not to be taken seriously. Celebrity heads stripped onto our model's bodies" accompanies each and every photo, a concession to *Hustler*'s legal travails.) That more of the naked bodies are female and that many are in what might be described as a service relation to male bodies opens up the possibility of misogyny charges. But what becomes problematic for such a singular reading is that within the parody, the imaginary staging of the rituals of male sexual power functions in favor of an overtly political critique.

The style is like a *Mad* magazine cartoon come to life with a multiplication of detail in every shot: the Ted Kennedy dartboard in one corner; in another, stickers that exhort "Invest in South Africa"; the plaque over Reagan's bed announcing "Joseph McCarthy slept here." In the main room of the party, various half-naked women cavort, Edwin Meese is glimpsed filching a candelabra. Reagan greets a hooded Ku Klux Klanner at the door, and a helpful caption translates the action: "Ron tells an embarrassed Jesse Helms it wasn't a come-as-you-are party." In the background the corpse of deceased CIA chief Bill Casey watches benignly over the proceedings (his gaping mouth doubles as an ashtray), as does former press secretary James Brady—the victim of John Hinkley's attempted assassination and Reagan's no-gun control policy—who, propped in a wheelchair, wears a sign bluntly announcing "Vegetable Dip" around his neck.

In the next room Oliver North, cast as a muscle-bound male stripper, gyrates on top of a table, while the fawning figures of Iran-Contra co-conspirators Poindexter, Secord, and Weinberger are gathered at his feet, stuffing dollar bills into his G-string holster in homoerotic reverie. Next we come upon Jerry Falwell, masturbating to a copy of *Hustler* concealed in his Bible, a bottle of Campari at his bedside and an "I love Mom" button pinned to his jacket (this a triumphant post-libel suit *Hustler* pouring salt on the wound). In yet another bedroom, "former Democrat and supreme skagbait Jeanne Kirkpatrick demonstrates why she switched to the Republican Party," as, grinning and topless, we find her on the verge of anally penetrating a bespectacled George Bush with the dildo attached to her ammunition belt. A whiny Elliott Abrams, pants around his ankles and dick in hand, tries unsuccessfully to pay off a prostitute who won't have him; and the naked Pat Robertson, doggie style on the bed, is being disciplined by a naked angel with a cat-o'-nine tails. And on the last page the invoice to the American citizen: $283 million.

While the antiestablishment politics of this photo spread are pretty clear, *Hustler* can also be maddeningly incoherent, marauding all over what we usually think of as the political spectrum. *Hustler*'s development of the pornographic idiom as a political form may make it politically troublesome if you're coming from the old world of traditional political alliances and oppositions: right-left, misogynist-feminist. And it may be just these traditional political meanings that *Hustler* throws into question, along with the whole question of what misogyny means.

It's true that many women feel assaulted and affronted by *Hustler*'s images. But it's also true that *Hustler*'s use of nudity is often political: it's clear in "Reagan's Farewell Party" that nudity is deployed as a leveling device, a deflating technique following a long tradition of political satire. This puts another of *Hustler*'s scandals—its notorious nude photo spread of Jackie Onassis, captured sunbathing on her Greek island, Skorpios, by telephoto lens—in a different and perhaps more subversive light.

Feminists regarded this as simply another case of *Hustler*'s misogyny, but the strategic uses of nudity we've seen elsewhere in the magazine indicate something else entirely: not Onassis as unwilling sexual object, but Onassis as political target. Nudity is used throughout the magazine as an attack on the life-styles of the rich, famous, and politically powerful—Reagan, North, Falwell, Abrams, Kirkpatrick, and in another feature, Thatcher, all (unfortunately for the squeamish) *sans* clothes. This makes it difficult to argue that Onassis's nudity functions strictly in relation to her sex, exploiting women's vulnerability as a class, or that its message can be reduced to a genericizing one like "You may be rich but you're just a cunt like any other cunt." Rather, Jackie Onassis's appearance on the pages of *Hustler* forces to our attention what might be called the sexual caste system, and these connections between sex and caste make it difficult to come to easy moral conclusions about *Hustler*'s violation of Onassis's privacy.

As various pulp biographies inform us, the Bouvier sisters, Jacqueline and Princess Lee, were more or less bred to take up positions as consorts of rich and powerful men—to use their femininity in a professional way, to put it bluntly. This isn't so very unlike the case of *Hustler*'s somewhat less privileged, consenting models, who while engaged in a similar activity, are confined to very different social locales and addresses. Some of these are portrayed in a regular *Hustler* feature, "The Beaver Hunt," a photo gallery of snapshots of nonprofessional models sent in by readers.[26]

Posed in paneled rec rooms, on plaid Sears sofas or cheap chenille bedspreads, draped amidst the kind of matching bedroom suites seen on late-night easy-credit furniture ads, nude or in polyester lingerie, they're identified as secretaries, waitresses, housewives, nurses, bank tellers, cosmetology students, cashiers, factory workers, saleswomen, data processors, and nurse's aides. Without generalizing from this insufficient data about any kind of *typical* class differences about appropriate or inappropriate displays of the body, we might simply ask, so where are all the doctors, lawyers, corporate execs, and college professors? Or moving up the social hierarchy, where are the socialites, the jet setters, the wives of CEOs? Absent because of their fervent feminism? Probably not. Isn't it because they've struck—or were born into—a better deal?[27]

26. After yet another legal entanglement, *Hustler* began threatening in its model release form to prosecute anyone who sent in a photo without the model's consent. They now demand photocopies of two forms of ID for both age and identity purposes; they also stopped paying the photographer and began paying only the model.

27. Because *Hustler* doesn't subsist on advertising, its readership demographics aren't made public, making speculation about the actual class position of its readers unreliable at best. *Mother Jones* magazine did obtain and publish *Hustler*'s 1976 demographics, which were made available to them because Larry Flynt was courting *Mother Jones* for his distribution stable Jeffrey Klein writes, "Originally it was thought that *Hustler* appealed to a blue-collar audience yet . . . demographics indicate that except for their gender (85 percent male), *Hustler* readers can't be so easily categorized. About 40 percent attended college; 23 percent are

By placing the snapshots of Onassis in the place of the cashier, the secretary, and the waitress, *Hustler* performs another upheaval, violating all the rigid social distinctions that our classless society claims it doesn't make, and violating those spatial boundaries (like private islands) that the rich are able to purchase to protect themselves from the hordes. These are precisely the kinds of unconscious distinctions we *all* make that allow us to regard the deployment of femininity that achieves marriage to a billionaire shipping magnate as a very different thing from the one that lands you an honorary spot in this month's "Beaver Hunt."

The political implications of the Onassis photo spread demonstrate the need for a vastly more complex approach to the question of misogyny than those currently circulating. If any symbolic exposure or violation of *any* woman's body is regarded by feminists as simply a byproduct of the misogynistic male imagination, we overlook the fact that not all women, simply by virtue of being women, are allies. Women can both symbolize and exercise class power and privilege, not to mention oppressive political power. (And thanks to equal opportunity employment, even wage pointless neoimperialist wars.)

Hustler's "violations" are *symbolic*. Treating images of staged sex or violence as equivalent to real sex or violence, or cynically trying to convince us that it's a direct line from sexual imagery to rape—as if merely looking at images of sex magically brainwashes any man into becoming a robotic sexual plunderer—will clearly restrict political expression and narrow the forms of political discourse. Given the pervasiveness of real violence against women, it's understandable to want to pin it on something so easily at hand as sexual representation. But this mistakes being offended for being endangered, and they're not the same thing. Pornography makes an easy target for all manner of social anxieties, but the bad consequences for both feminism and democracy make this a dangerously insufficient tactic.

On the other hand, *Hustler* is certainly not politically unproblematic. While it may be radical in its refusal of bourgeois proprieties, its transgressiveness has limits, and its refusal of polite speech in areas of social sensitivity—AIDS or race, for example—doesn't automatically guarantee any kind of counter-cultural force. Although frequently accused of racism, *Hustler* basically just wants to offend anyone, of any race, any ethnic group. Not content to offend only the Right, it makes doubly sure

professionals, 59 percent have households incomes of $15,000 or more a year [about $38,000 in 1993 dollars], which is above the national mean, given the median reader age of 30." His analysis of these figures is, "Probably it's more accurate to say that *Hustler* appeals to what people would like to label a blue-collar urge, an urge most American men seem to share." Klein, "Born Again Porn."

to offend liberals; not content merely to taunt whites, it hectors blacks and other minorities. Its favored tactic with regard to race is simply to reproduce every stereotype it can think of: the subject of most *Hustler* cartoons featuring blacks will invariably be huge sexual organs that every woman lusts after, alternating with black watermelon-eating lawbreakers. *Hustler*'s letter columns carry out a raging debate on the subject of race, with black readers writing variously that they find *Hustler*'s irreverence funny or resent its stereotypes, whites either applauding or protesting. (And it's clear that the most explicitly political forms of popular culture these days—rap music, for example—are ones, that also refuse polite speech.)

If publisher Larry Flynt, who has been regularly accused of racism, was indeed shot by white supremacist Joseph Paul Franklin, who is serving two life sentences for racially motivated killings (and who has claimed responsibility for the shooting), this is yet another twist in the strange and contradictory tale of *Hustler*'s curious impact on American culture. Larry Flynt's swaggering determination to parade the contents of his private obsessions as public psychodrama in the courtrooms and headlines of the nation—not so unlike other "larger-than-life" figures who sporadically capture the public imagination—is just one element in a life story replete with all the elements of epic drama. (So it comes as no surprise that the equally swaggering director Oliver Stone is producing a bio-pic on Flynt's life.) The Flynt biography is nothing short of a morality tale for our times: a late-twentieth-century pornographic Horatio Alger who comes to suffer horribly for his ambitions, despite his frantic, futile gestures of repentance.

Shortly before the 1978 shooting, at the height of both *Hustler*'s circulation and his own near-universal excoriation, Flynt undertook one of those elaborate acts of self-reinvention that are so deeply American, given our national legacy of Puritan conversion narratives and self-refashioning: he underwent a highly publicized conversion to evangelical Christianity at the hands of presidential sister Ruth Carter Stapleton. The two were pictured chastely hand in hand as Flynt announced plans to turn *Hustler* into a *religious* skin magazine and told a Pentecostal congregation in Houston (where he was attending the National Women's Conference), "I owe every woman in America an apology." He was apparently sincere, and announced plans to reincarnate the "Asshole of the Month" as "Turkey of the Month," and to convert the unsavory cartoon character "Chester the Molester" into the more benign "Chester the Protector," whose mission would be protecting young girls from corruption. Flynt became celibate (he claimed) and a vegetarian, in an attempt to "purify himself." Ironically, it was this very religious conversion that led to the notorious *Hustler* cover of a woman being ground up in a meat grinder, which was, according to insiders, a sheepish and flat-footed attempt at an another public apology by Flynt to women at large. ("We will no longer hang women up as pieces of meat" was the widely ignored caption to the photo. Recall here Freud's observation on the sophistication of the joke form as a class trait.[28]) Flynt proclaimed, "It's not a publicity stunt. I have asked God for forgiveness for anything I have done to hurt anyone. I've been all the way to the bottom. There's only one way to go now, and that's up. I'm going to be hustling for the Lord." (Wife Althea, the practical half of the couple, commented, "God may have walked into your life, but twenty million dollars just walked out.")

But it was not to be. There was another fate in store for Larry Flynt, and one less convert for the Lord: Flynt renounced religion shortly after the shooting. In one of the many ironies of this all-too ironic story, one which would seem absurd in the most hackneyed piece of fiction, the man who raked in millions on the fantasy of endlessly available fucking is now left impotent. And in 1982, after four years of constant pain, the nerves leading to his legs were cauterized to stop all sensation. Flynt, who built an empire offending bourgeois sensibilities with their horror of errant bodily functions, is left with no bowel or urinary control. Some God with a cruel and over-developed sense of irony seems to have authored the second act. And while the Flynt empire is now a hugely profitable conglomerate, publishing mainstream rags like *Maternity Fashion and Beauty* (and distributing numerous others, including the intellectually tony *New York Review of Books*),Larry Flynt lately devotes his days to collecting antiques, finally adopting the pastimes of the leisure classes into which his talent for vulgarity allowed him entree.[29]

Flynt's obsessional one-man war against all public and private constraints on the body made him evil personified to the government, the church, and feminists. Yet willingly or not, Flynt's own body has been on the line as well. In this case the pornographer's body has borne, full force, the violent reprisals aimed at those who transgress our most deeply venerated social boundaries and bodily proprieties.

28. The story of the cover was related by Paul Krassner, who worked for *Hustler* in 1978, in "Is This the Real Message of Pornography?" *Harpers* (November 1984): 35. This cover was instrumental in the founding, the following year, of Women Against Pornography (WAP), the first feminist antipornography group. *Hustler's* lack of joke sophistication seems to be its downfall, and if there's any truth to the cliché about feminists lacking a sense of humor, it may be that it's a class attribute as opposed to something inherent to feminism.

29. LFP Enterprises is a $100-million business, publishing about thirty different magazines and distributing over eighty more. Michael Kaplan, "The Resurrection of Larry Flynt; Owner of Larry Flynt Publications, Inc.," *Folio: The Magazine for Magazine Management* (June 15, 1993): 36.

PART FOUR

The Limits of Liberalism

CHAPTER FOURTEEN

The Name of the Pose

A Sex Worker by Any Other Name?

TRACY QUAN

"Sex work" has become so fashionable that, in some circles, "sex work" is mandatory and "prostitution" frowned upon.

I'm talking about language, of course—not the work itself —for I move in circles where prostitution is taken for granted as a normal human activity. We refuse to debate whether prostitution is politically or morally acceptable. If you think that means we're shutting down the dialogue, you're mistaken. The sex workers' movement is enmeshed in dialogue, some of it rather heated, and much of it fueled by a desire to control the words we use—or reject—when describing prostitution.

Leslie Bull, Ariel Lighteningchild, and Penny Arcade have provoked new dialogue with a recent video, *on being a junkie ho in sex worker world*. Packed into that saucy title is a lot of conflict, history, discomfort— and a sense of what the future holds.[1] *Ho* might be to *sex worker* what *queer* has been to *gay*—a generational marker that makes some people cringe, and not by accident.

English is thought to be a unifying language but that isn't always the case. A feisty American prostitute can argue that *ho* trumps *sex worker* because it conveys street cred. Elsewhere, an ex-pat Australian, Cheryl Overs, has challenged "all the big AIDS agencies to stop calling sex

---

1. "on being a junkie ho in sex worker world" (USA, 2003) is a fifteen-minute documentary-style video, conceived by Leslie Bull, which sets out to address "issues of class, race, and marginalization" in the prostitutes' rights movement. It was shown at the San Francisco Sex Worker Film and Video Festival (May, 2003) and continues to generate heated discussions in classrooms and other venues.

workers CSWs." This acronym for "commercial sex worker" infuriates some activists—who prefer Sex Worker—because "commercial sex work" is a term invented by researchers and bureaucrats.

I have been part of this international conversation for more than fifteen years. Recently, Andrew Sorfleet of the Network of Sex Work Projects, brought to my attention a curious new trend. On a well-known e-mail discussion list, a newspaper story about prostitution at the US-Mexico border was circulating, with every reference to "prostitution" replaced and bracketed as [sex work.] Similar cosmetic surgery had been performed on "prostitute," which became ["sex worker."] Sorfleet was alarmed. Concerned about protecting archival integrity, he also noted: "When you decide that the word 'prostitute' is so dirty that you attempt to make it disappear, what does that say to those of us who *are* prostitutes?"

Those who follow the politics of the prostitutes' movement might be surprised. After all, Sorfleet is a member of the Network of Sex Work Projects, an international NGO, which has worked hard since 1991 to represent prostitutes in many forums, especially the United Nations. In 1997, the NSWP persuaded the World Bank to abandon "commercial sex worker" for the more politically elegant "sex worker." Sorfleet is a founder of the Sex Workers' Alliance of Toronto and was for five years co-ordinator of the Sex Workers Alliance of Vancouver. Clearly, "sex work" has both currency and support in Sorfleet's world. But, he pointed out, "The terms 'sex worker' and 'sex work' were initially adopted... because we were seeking a broader category... to ally with, so we could all improve our collective bargaining position. It wasn't because we were ashamed to be prostitutes."

Carol Leigh, the COYOTE member who coined the term "sex work" while attending a feminist conference in the late 1970s, basically agrees. When asked why her new book, *Unrepentant Whore*,[2] was not entitled "Unrepentant Sex Worker", she said, "I never imagined it would be the *only* term we could use to refer to prostitutes. As a matter of fact, *sex worker* describes the entire range. It helps unify peep show dancers, strippers, and prostitutes. Prior to this, other workers in the sex industry would not identify with prostitutes. This is a term invented so we could have some solidarity."

In her one-woman show, "The Adventures of Scarlot Harlot," Leigh—as Scarlot Harlot—introduced the English-speaking world to a new way of

---

2. *Unrepentant Whore: The Collected Works of Scarlot Harlot* by Carol Leigh (Last Gasp, USA, 2003). This collection of articles, photos, and essays documents over twenty years of Leigh's "prostitute radicalism."

talking about prostitution. It was 1981. During the last two decades, *sex worker* has taken on a life of its own. For one thing, it has been translated into numerous languages. Some aspects of the term have not changed. "I was also using it in a jocular way," Leigh recently told me. "The tinge of political correctness was funny to me." There has always been an easy interplay between whimsy and political purpose in Leigh's work—in her writing, performing, and conversational style—and the fate of *sex work* reflects the personality of its parent. There is a serious side to *sex work* and a comical one—as witnessed by the Orwellian disappearance of *prostitute* from a news clipping, and the ensuing dialogue between Sorfleet and the moderators of the SEX-WORK list.3

A former sex worker myself, I am skeptical about a trend that puts more picturesque language out of business. During my career in the New York sex trade, the prostitutes I worked with used words like *working girl, call girl, hooker, hustler,* and *pro.* We spoke about "the life" when feeling clannish, sentimental, or philosophical—"the business" when we were being practical. (In Britain, where I briefly worked, we were "on the game.") Rarely was the word *prostitute* employed—perhaps because it sounds clinical or formal—and I've only heard *sex worker* in activist and media circles, never on the job. We routinely called each other "girls"—and I was routinely challenged when I repeated the habit in meetings with feminist allies of the hookers' movement. Our authentic language was not politically viable.

"Why can't you call them 'women'?" one disgruntled activist inquired. "This is how we normally talk," I explained. "It's the vernacular of the sex trade." I had the sense that I was being asked to "clean up" my language and make myself more presentable for the feminist ear.

Is the spread of *sex worker*—the brave new thing we are encouraged to call ourselves—part of a similar clean-up campaign? Despite my reservations, I find myself using the term a great deal, mostly in my writing or in public situations. *Sex work* makes it possible to talk about prostitution in a relaxed, confident way because it's a little detached, perhaps even bureaucratic. As I get farther away from actually turning tricks, I hear myself calling it *sex work* more often. That's because I am talking, not only to my fellow prostitutes, but also to the public and the press. To always speak the vernacular of the trade, using insider slang, would be precious

3. The SEX-WORK discussion list, moderated by the Health & Development Networks Moderation Team (HDN, http://www.hdnet.org) is described as "the international forum looking at links between sex-work and HIV/AIDS." Discussions about legal and political issues are a natural outgrowth of this mission and the forum is archived at: http://archives.healthdev.net/sex-work.

or awkward. It's necessary to find words that fit my new situation, and *sex work* fits.

Recently, somebody suggested to me that *sex worker* is a euphemism for *prostitute*, but Leigh argues that *prostitute* has euphemistic origins, too. The Latin root of *prostitute* did not necessarily refer to sex, she points out. Although *sex work* speaks more bluntly about what prostitutes actually do, it has a euphemistic reputation because it ignores or undercuts the emotions that surround prostitution—and prostitutes.

Does *sex work* cut us off from our history? Or allow us to have more control over the future by helping us to shape the way we're perceived? Will bureaucrats, health researchers, and police officers treat us more fairly if we're called sex workers? Can words really have that much power, influence, and utility? We certainly behave as if they do.

"Prostitute" is often used to describe professional cynicism—to describe, say, an artist catering to the highest bidder or the largest audience. "Whore" is an angry insult during a marital row or, in bed, a spicy term evoking erotic abandon. It's hard to imagine a man calling his unfaithful wife a "sex worker" in a moment of violence or anger. Try to imagine a passionate lover replacing "whore" with "sex worker" during an exchange of erotic sweet-nothings. In moments of anger and intimacy, men and women resort to the old-fashioned and well-established words that signify "prostitute"—not the polite, newly adopted terms.

In the 1980s, *sex work* was adopted by many in the prostitutes' movement to describe and include, not only prostitution, but also the work done by porn actors, erotic dancers, peep show performers and others in the sex trade. As the prostitutes' rights movement was coming of age, our language began to reflect an inclusive, genderless mood. *Sex work* was also code. In two words, selling sex is just another occupation. *Sex work* sidesteps pejorative meanings associated with 'to prostitute' (the verb) and 'prostitute' (the person). Its blandness suggests that morality is no longer an issue.

As an activist hooker, I have helped to promote the fashionable status of the term *sex work*. But when I got involved with reviving PONY (Prostitutes of New York) in 1989, I balked at changing the name. PONY had been dormant for many years and, one Australian activist suggested, this could be the right moment for linguistic reform. "Many people in prostitution don't call themselves prostitutes," he pointed out, "They might just say 'I'm out here working'." The possibility of calling ourselves a Sex Workers' Alliance came up. Ultimately, we fell back on tradition. I saw it as a way to pay tribute to the history of this movement, for PONY had originally been formed in the 1970s, before the invention of "sex work." Others, who were equally part of the decision, had their own reasons for choosing *prostitute* over *sex worker*.

Sex worker is to *prostitute* what gender is to sex: a usage (with some practical value) that is identified with political rectitude. *Sex worker* is gender-free. It's true that males, females, and transsexuals can sell sex. But genderless lingo enables some feminists to ignore the way differences between men and women are accepted in our industry—rather than being neurotically denied, as is often the case in more respectable jobs. Many indoor hookers complain that the word *prostitute* conjures up the image of a street hussy. But I am alarmed because *sex worker* conjures up no image at all. Prostitutes, nude dancers, porn stars and other erotic workers are very attached to their images. The erotic image is a sex worker's bread and butter—the thing that makes us different from people in more prosaic occupations.

Sex work connotes that prostitutes are engaged in labor rather than business or frivolous entertainment, making us a bit more acceptable to the Left. At one time, prostitutes were viewed as insufficiently proletarian—too entrepreneurial—and some Marxists debated whether prostitutes who came from working class backgrounds were authentically working class. This now seems moot. We have been calling ourselves sex workers for more than a decade. If our new terminology was a political mating call to the Left, it worked. We have become the kind of cause you can take home to Marx. At this point, the enemies of "sex work" are more likely to be found on the Religious Right.

There was a time when some of us worried about whether *sex work* would make the purveyor of erotic pleasure so ordinary that he or she would lose that special erotic aura. Some, including Andrew Sorfleet—and myself—still wonder about this.

A more urgent question today is a pernicious movement against the use of "sex work" by government agencies in the United States. Recently, a number of American scientists reported that they had been warned by federal health officials not to use certain key words in their applications for grants. According to *The New York Times*, [April 18, 2003], Dr. Alfred Sommer, dean of the Bloomberg School of Public Health at Johns Hopkins University, "said a researcher at his institution had been advised by a project officer at NIH [National Institutes of Health] to change the term 'sex worker' to something more euphemistic in a grant proposal for a study of HIV prevention among prostitutes." Other AIDS researchers chose to remain anonymous in their discussions with the *Times*, but they reported that "sex workers" and "men who sleep with men" were among the key phrases now considered impolitic.[4] "Sex work" is forbidden in these quarters for the same reason that "commercial sex work" is disliked

---

4. *The New York Times*, April 18, 2003, p. A-10, Erica Goode, "Certain Words Can Trip Up AIDS Grants, Scientists Say".

in others. It's the language of the opponent. "Sex work" is associated with acceptance of the prostitute and with prostitute power. Although this ban might seem to originate in the United States, sex workers in other countries are following the story because anti-prostitution forces within the United States have global ambitions.

On both sides of the prostitution issue—for and against—words have been embraced, tweaked, and employed to send a message about sex work. In the mid-1970s, some Marxist-feminists began referring to "prostitute women," rather than "prostitutes." In the 1980s, we began to hear the term "prostituted women." To a casual listener these may sound alike, but they are different terms because they are used by different factions. True, both were designed to generate sympathy for the prostitute by refusing to reduce the person to the job, but there are differences worth taking into account.

The organizers who called us "prostitute women" were seeking to humanize prostitutes by feminizing the issue. Their terminology suggests we're part of a sisterhood—but this creates other problems because many sex workers aren't women, they're men. Or something more nuanced: transgender. The term *prostitute woman* did not stick to us the way *sex worker* does.

The anti-prostitution organizers who embrace the concept of the "prostituted" woman are, of course, highlighting the victimization or passivity of prostitutes. Those who employed the term *prostitute women* have always been for the abolition of prostitution laws. In the case of *prostituted* women, the activists using that term have often been in favor of enforcement, claiming that prostitution laws can protect people from abuse. These terms are like uniforms—an activist can tell quickly whether she's talking to someone who wants to reform the law or reform the prostitute.

In some parts of the American anti-prostitution movement, the use of *sex worker* is virtually forbidden. This taboo extends to outreach projects and services for young prostitutes who are down on their luck. An ex-prostitute I know has been teaching writing workshops for "young women who are still in the Life and some who've just gotten out." He has been told, "several times in no uncertain terms by the powers-that-be that the term 'Sex Worker' was NOT to be used with these young women" because, he says, "their contention is that these girls were slaves." Several of the young women who were still working on the streets "called themselves ho's," and many had heard the term *sex worker*, but "didn't understand it." He adds that when he explained it to them, "they really liked it, and I heard them using it later."

For quite some time, the prostitutes' movement has talked about reclaiming and using "whore" as an expression of pride. In 1985, the First

World Whores' Congress was held in Amsterdam, the seat of legalized prostitution. In more recent years, though, "First World Whores" has taken on a new resonance. European racism has become a hot issue in the hookers' movement. The movement is, in fact, showing signs of a schism, with some activists intensely focused on the concerns of the southern hemisphere or the developing world—and others seemingly oblivious. One criticism of the 1985 conference was, indeed, its Eurocentric atmosphere. This raises a question in my mind about the use of *whore* in public situations. It has shock value and guerilla theatre appeal but it's not a word we can use at a United Nations conference or when challenging state violence. Many prostitutes shy away from it. *Whore* is a word we can use if we're engaged in identity politics, in artistic expression, but this implies a level of privilege or comfort. It is not generally a useful word when bringing attention to a serious human rights abuse.

In Bangladesh, during the summer of 1999, prostitutes were being violently evicted from the brothel areas of Tanbazar and Nimtoli where they had been living, working, and paying rent. Water and electricity had been cut off by the local police department. Beatings, abductions, imprisonment, and sexual assault were part of the campaign to "rehabilitate" prostitutes who had been living in a traditional brothel district, reputed to be 200 years old. Here is a situation where reclaiming the word "whore" would be counter-productive or irrelevant. The statements issued by Shonghoti, an alliance of groups protesting the violence, referred throughout to the women as *sex workers*. The word *whore* may be a more viable tool in the so-called First World.

In many parts of the English-speaking world, *sex worker* is only used by activist hookers and by other people who are not, themselves, sex workers: researchers, academics, artists, government officials, United Nations bureaucrats, and newspaper reporters. In the United States, it's so rarely used by working prostitutes—and so often used by others—that you could argue for its objectifying status. But *sex work* has a certain currency, in part because it is one of the most unemotional terms we have for describing a job that people are emotionally conflicted about.

Political language becomes a sitting duck for ridicule when it becomes obligatory. However, when the *New York Times* began to call us sex workers, we knew our movement had come of age. Getting people to use this very nonjudgmental term has been a challenge and the widespread use of "sex work" represents a cultural victory for the prostitutes' movement— but the tensions continue.

In the United States, some indoor prostitutes feel that *sex work* sounds too much like labor or drudgery—they see themselves as business owners. They may prefer to call themselves working girls, escorts, or "providers"—vague terms that don't incriminate. Some street-based prostitutes argue that "sex worker" is imposed on them by middle class call girls who use their bland lingo to erase the "street ho" and deny the realities of street life. In a recent essay that echoes the title of her video, Leslie Bull writes: "I can't help wondering where the tricks, pimps, hos, and dope men are in sex worker world."[5] Bull insists, "The term sex worker has nothing to do with what I did off and on for twelve years on the street, out of hotel bars, and through escort services (briefly), mostly I was a street ho."

Sex work has been translated so widely and is used in so many countries that we have to ask: is it typically isolationist for Americans to reject or ban the term? This may be a shortsighted reading of the situation. I recently met an AIDS educator from Russia who works primarily in Moscow with the local sex industry. He explained that all prostitutes are *seks rabotniki*—genderless sex workers, in the plural—at the official level, among his colleagues. He is beginning to question this because many a real-life *seks rabotnitza* (feminine sex worker) would rather be called *prostitutka*, the traditional term. Why, he asked, are his colleagues always compelling him to use politically correct, abstract words that aren't even authentic to the sex trade? Was this not a kind of bureaucratic hypocrisy?

Sex work is in use worldwide and in many languages. Americans who resist the terminology are not alone. And neither are the Russians.

5. *Feel Me* (Confluere Publications, 2002), a collection of poetry and prose by Leslie Bull, contains her thought-provoking commentary, "Being a Junkie Ho in Sex Worker World" (May 2001). This and other examples of Bull's work are discussed and accessible at http://www.confluere.com, or http://www.confluere.com/store/index.html.

CHAPTER FIFTEEN

Thinking Outside the Box
Men in the Sex Industry

JULIAN MARLOWE

☾

Prostitution and pornography are two highly divisive issues within the women's rights movement. The conventional stance is that both are harmful to women—prostitution is equated with sexual assault and commoditization, while pornography portrays women as submissive sexual objects and serves only to reinforce their subordinated status in this patriarchal society of ours. Relatively few people question these arguments since they do seem to hold some intuitive appeal to women—the majority of whom have no direct experience in the sex industry, it should be noted—and most men remain silent in order to avoid being labeled chauvinists or misogynists. Somewhere along the line, radical feminists have hijacked these issues and turned them into "women's issues" under the presumption that men aren't entitled to have a dissenting opinion because we aren't adversely affected. However, when men account for the vast majority of consumers as well as up to twenty percent of sex workers, it's somewhat short-sighted to deliberately exclude men from the debate altogether. More importantly, when the male perspective is fully factored into the debate, the underlying arguments against the entire sex industry are revealed to be less about the actual activities that take place and more about established gender roles that generalize how all men and all women think about sex.

ALL ABOUT ME

My first experience with commercial sex was purely accidental. I was a fresh-faced twenty-three-year-old walking home from a bar one night when a rather fetching man in his mid-thirties approached me at a stoplight and asked if I wanted to "have some fun". I initially declined, as it was late and I needed my beauty rest, but when he added "...there's some money in it for you", I figured it wouldn't kill me to stay out just a little bit longer. To make a long story short, I was paid fifty bucks for the inconvenience of letting a handsome man give me a hand job while we watched a porn flick in his living room.

After that initial encounter, I got to thinking that perhaps my preconceived notions about prostitution were biased by all the sensationalist claptrap that dominates any otherwise rational discussion about the sex trade. That one experience made me think that maybe there isn't that much difference between casual sex with a stranger you meet in a bar and casual sex with a stranger who happens to pay you—in both cases you're taking a calculated risk that the guy will turn out to be a psycho, and in both cases the anonymity is part of the appeal. Hoping for further encounters like that first one, I found myself taking detours around the boys' stroll on my way home from the clubs at night, thinking that maybe someone else would catch my eye. Suffice it to say, this strategy worked, and within a relatively short period this became a regular habit.

That fall I went back to graduate school, and escorting was an obvious source of income since it involved minimal time commitment, the pay was very good for the effort involved, and self-employment was ideal for accommodating an oft-unpredictable student schedule. And of course I thought it was kind of a cool way to make a living. As I had no desire to waste my time out on the street, I took out an ad in the local entertainment rag (which required photo ID and prohibited ads that listed prices or used explicit language), and made enough money to cover a month's rent within a week. I'd like to say the lifestyle was exotic, but it was really quite mundane when all is said and done: I went to classes, studied at home, and about five to ten times a day I'd get a call from someone asking me to prattle off the usual statistics and measurements. Only a small percentage of these calls turned into actual dates, which could range from a ten-minute quickie to sparkling conversation over dinner at an upscale restaurant.

While I made enough money through escorting to support a generous student lifestyle, I was hardly raking in the dough. Male escorts rarely, if ever, make as much money as their female counterparts due to basic economics: on the demand side, the pool of potential clients is significantly smaller for gay men than for straight women; on the supply side, there's no shortage of gay men willing to have sex with strangers for free, if one knows where to look. With the exception of other students, I knew of few male escorts who relied exclusively on prostitution for their entire income, using it instead as an income supplement. An argument often made is that women become trapped in prostitution because they can't see any viable alternatives—male prostitutes, on the other hand, are *forced* to find other alternatives since the money tends to be insufficient for the vast majority.

After completing my degree and starting a full-time job three years later, I withdrew my ads but still hooked up with the handful of clients who had kept my phone number. The call volume quickly diminished, but to this day I still get the occasional visit from one former client— a big, hunky straight-but-perpetually-questioning stud muffin who still refers to himself by a quaint pseudonym even though I figured out his real name years ago. At this stage it's purely recreational with no cash exchanged...although he did once give me a housewarming plant and a lovely Beaujolais.

That's the Reader's Digest version of my escorting career. The intent here is not to shock or titillate with graphic details about my sex life—I'll leave that to Jerry Springer—but rather to demonstrate that the prostitution biz is not nearly as one-dimensional as the Andrea Dworkins and Catharine MacKinnons of the world would have us believe. My reality is just as valid as the horror stories they present to support their abolitionist position. Unlike the Dworkins and MacKinnons, however, I'm not arrogant enough to presume that my experiences are representative of everybody else's, or that public policy should be determined on the basis of my perceptions alone.

ABOLITIONISM REVISITED

The conventional arguments against prostitution attempt to equate commercial sex with serial rape and slavery. Not only does this characterization assume that prostitutes are for various reasons incapable of consenting to commercial sex, but it also assumes that all prostitutes are women. Prostitutes are invariably portrayed as pathetic victims of sexual abuse and low self-esteem, often with drug addiction and poverty thrown in just to ensure that they are in no way accountable for their actions. Pimps and johns allegedly prey on these vulnerabilities, reinforcing the notion that prostitution is another example of (dominant) men exploiting (submissive) women for their own sinister purposes. It's not a coincidence that men in the business are excluded altogether, since the underlying arguments are considerably less compelling if the prostitute is assumed to be anything other than a weak, pitiable—and female—victim.

If one subscribes to the abolitionist ideology, prostitution is a manifestation of man's desire and ability to dominate a woman by procuring her subservience. It's taken for granted that no matter what fee she charges—even if she establishes it herself—she always ends up on the losing end of the transaction because she has been objectified and dehumanized solely for a man's sexual gratification. Underlying this hypothesis is the assumption that the act of paying another person for sex is dominant, and the act of receiving money for sex is submissive. Moreover, this activity is believed to be harmful to women in general because it reinforces the john's perception of women as commodities, which can be controlled merely by forking over a wad of bills.

When the exchange of sex for money takes place between two adult men, it is no longer obvious who is dominant and who is submissive. Is it the client who has the wherewithal to pay for sex, or is it the hustler whose youth and physical appearance allow him to charge a fee for his sexual services? On some level, the very act of paying another man for sex could be viewed as submissive, because the client is effectively conceding that his own attractiveness is insufficient to entice the hustler without a cash incentive. In the absence of any perceived power imbalance on the basis of sex, the roles become less clear—especially if the hustler happens to be younger and physically stronger than his client, as is often the case. From my own experience, I can recall no encounters in which I felt exploited or victimized, although there were a few clients who obviously weren't wealthy and I felt a little bit guilty for accepting their money because they probably needed it more than I did. As I'm not telepathic, I have no way of knowing whether my clients believed they were dominating me or not... but even if they did, why would I care as long as their cash made its way from their wallet to mine?

The prostitution-as-rape analogy is most easily understood in the context of female hookers because rape typically requires penetration. Abolitionists have argued that a woman is being raped whenever she engages in commercial sex since (a) her body is being invaded by the john in one manner or another, and (b) prostitution is never completely consensual by construction. In drawing male prostitutes into the argument, it is typically assumed for convenience that the actual acts performed are essentially the same as those performed by a female prostitute—hustlers are presumed to be the passive partners in both oral and anal sex, invariably without reciprocation. It would make the rape analogy much simpler if this were true, but gay sex simply isn't that regimented in practice, even when it's commercial. Gay sex typically involves a high degree of reciprocity, which makes the rape arguments appear kind of silly in this context: it's very difficult to argue that a hustler is being raped if he's the active partner. Male prostitutes with a female clientele present similar complications for the rape argument. The fact that these exceptions to the analogy exist is sufficient to demonstrate that at the very least, the argument cannot be applied to every encounter. Furthermore, if the prostitution can take place among men without anyone being raped, then presumably there should be some latitude for prostitution to take place among women without it automatically being viewed as rape.

The foregoing is not intended to argue that male and female prostitution are equivalent, because there are several notable distinctions between the two: men almost always work independently of pimps, are more likely to face violence from gay bashers than from clients, seldom have children to support, and in many cases merely use prostitution as a way to explore their sexuality. Moreover, it does not deny the existence of genuinely coercive situations in prostitution, both for women and for men. Rather, it demonstrates that if the same transaction takes place between two adult men, it is less likely to be viewed as coercive by default, and more likely to be regarded merely as sexual deviance and filed away under "private morality". The upshot of all this is that if prostitution can take place without being coercive—as it typically does for adult male prostitutes—how can one argue that the entire profession should be outlawed? Or to approach it from another angle, if men who have sex with male prostitutes in no way harm or degrade *women* through their actions, why would any feminist care?

KEEPING UP WITH THE JOHNS

While male hustlers tend to be overlooked in the prostitution debate, johns are virtually invisible despite the fact that they outnumber prostitutes by a vast margin. Not surprisingly, johns have largely chosen to remain inconspicuous, which makes it difficult to conceptualize who these people are, where they come from, or what their motivation is. Abolitionists fill in the blanks with a blanket characterization that casts all johns as misogynist sociopaths intent on expressing their contempt for women through commercial sex. The few famous johns who inadvertently stumble into the spotlight by getting arrested—such as Hugh Grant or Eddie Murphy—tend to salvage their public image either by pleading ignorance (as in the latter case) or by expressing profound regret (as in the former). Even Charlie Sheen, who reportedly spent over $50,000 on the services of Heidi Fleiss's escorts, is taking the repentant route and vowing never to go to a prostitute again. As I have never been a john, I cannot truly understand the thought process that drives a man to seek out a prostitute... but by the same token, neither can Andrea Dworkin or Catharine MacKinnon. I do, however, have enough direct experience with johns to know that everybody's story is unique and it is impossible to lump such a diverse demographic into one common group in order to speculate about their attitudes and motivation.

Treating johns as a single group becomes even more puzzling when male prostitutes are brought into the picture. After all, if johns hire prostitutes only to express contempt for women—as abolitionists insist—it doesn't make a whole lot of sense to hire a man. Many clients of male sex workers are married or lead otherwise heterosexual lives, and consequently have little or no opportunity to explore their same-sex inclinations. Those who identify as gay may be seeking out the company of a hustler simply because they have neither the time nor the inclination to find a partner in the more conventional ways, or they may be older men whose sexual tastes haven't aged in proportion to their years. Gay men and straight men are fundamentally different in their attitudes and experiences, yet abolitionists fail to make such distinctions when they characterize all johns as abusers and rapists. This does not deny the existence of misogynists who vent their anger on prostitutes—the hustler equivalent is the john whose internalized homophobia makes him hostile once his lust subsides and shame takes over—but such individuals are hardly representative of the entire john population and it is unfair to suggest that every john has malicious intent.

Although it makes the abolitionist arguments a lot more plausible if johns can be lumped into one homogeneous group, it simply doesn't reflect reality—johns include both straight men and gay men from the full range of socioeconomic backgrounds... and even a few women could be considered johns if you want to get technical. As with male prostitutes, one must also question why any feminist would care if a john only seeks out the services of men, because there's minimal risk that this will influence his attitude toward women if there's no woman involved in the transaction.

AND THEN THERE'S PORN

Pornography and prostitution are typically viewed by radical feminists as two sides of the same coin—prostitution provides direct sexual gratification, while porn provides the visuals by which the viewer can gratify himself. Both are deemed to be degrading to the women involved, because their bodies provide the entertainment value and everything beneath the surface is deemed superfluous. Further, both are deemed to be harmful to *all* women because they supposedly reinforce the notion that women were put on this earth solely for man's sexual amusement rather than as equal participants in society. Unlike prostitution, however, porn has much more representation on the other side of the debate, primarily from US First Amendment advocates concerned about censorship, and the government's ability to regulate private thoughts. Another distinction between the two issues is that the porn debate is more difficult to manipulate, with representations drawn from the most disadvantaged subset of the industry—most people have first-hand exposure to porn, whereas prostitution is largely out of sight. One cannot, for instance, insist that all women who engage in pornography do so only out of economic desperation, because anybody who's opened a Playboy centerfold can see that the women in question—with perfect teeth, Barbie proportions, and California tans—did not grow up in a Dickens novel.

The main objection to pornography is the objectification of women's bodies, so an obvious question to ask is whether the same objection still holds if it's a man's body that is being objectified through porn. Apparently it does, according to the same abolitionists who oppose prostitution. Their reasoning is that gay male porn is based on the same domination/submission theme as heterosexual porn, and even though no woman appears in front of the camera, it is harmful to women because it reinforces the inequality between the active (read masculine) partner and the passive (read feminine) partner. To wit:

'The sex act' means penile intromission followed by penile thrusting, or fucking. The woman is acted on; the man acts and through action expresses sexual power, the power of masculinity. Fucking requires that the male acts on one who has less power and this valuation is so deep, so completely implicit in the act that the one who is fucked is stigmatized as feminine during the act even when not anatomically female. In the male system, sex is the penis, the penis is sexual power, its use in fucking is manhood.
—Andrea Dworkin. 1989. *Pornography: Men Possessing Women*, p. 23. New York: E. P. Dutton.

Although this depiction of gay porn may seem plausible in the abstract, as a gay man I find it both bizarre and somewhat offensive. For starters, the very notion that gay men must choose between being "the man" or "the woman" during sex is patently heterosexist, and presumes that one cannot participate in receptive gay sex without forfeiting one's masculinity. It suggests that gay men strive to mimic heterosexuals when we have sex, and that a man cannot be both sexually "submissive" (for lack of a better term) and masculine at the same time, despite the fact that the roles in gay sex are specifically chosen rather than predetermined by anatomy. As with same-sex prostitution, it also seems a bit peculiar that feminists would care about objectification and domination that takes place between men, especially because the men who would be viewing homoerotic material probably don't regard women as sexual objects in the first place.

The biggest weakness in the anti-porn argument is that even if one accepts the questionable notion that gay porn reinforces masculine and feminine inequality, it fails to provide any insight into why porn involving a single man—beefcake photos or wanking videos, for example—is in any way degrading to women. Once again, abolitionists are relying on a subset of the industry to draw universal conclusions and are either disregarding men's involvement entirely or introducing oddball theories about gay sex in order to reconcile gay porn with their rigid position. Just as same-sex prostitution poses ideological problems for feminists, gay porn that doesn't involve women poses the same dilemma because it would be inconsistent for a feminist to argue that porn is permissible for gay men, while prohibited for all women.

CONCLUSION

Feminism is based on the principles of equality and independence, with responsibility being the inevitable corollary. Further, true independence for women means that their right to define their own moral standards should not be curtailed simply because someone else disapproves. The abortion rights issue is a clear example of how feminists fought for the right to choose, leaving it ultimately up to the woman herself to decide which choice is consistent with her personal beliefs and circumstances.

When it comes to prostitution, abolitionists seem to have forgotten these fundamental feminist principles, and without a trace of irony argue that some women are somehow incapable of making decisions about their own bodies and must be forcibly rescued from their predicament. Even those who state unequivocally that they voluntarily entered the profession and freely choose to remain are told condescendingly that they are victims but just don't know it yet. As for pornography, the most vocal opponents tend to be the same individuals who oppose prostitution, although the arguments against porn are based more on the indirect harm they supposedly inflict on all women rather than any direct harm imposed on the actual participants. In this instance the harm comes from the objectification of a woman's body, even if the creation of the images was completely consensual.

Both prostitution and pornography have come to be regarded as "women's issues", and contrary opinions voiced by men (as infrequent as they are) are dismissed as attempts by oppressors to maintain their dominance. Unfortunately, neither can truly be regarded as a women's issue since there are thousands of men earning a living in exactly the same manner as their female counterparts—perhaps not to the same extent, but in large enough numbers to represent a significant minority. So far, the abolitionist arguments that include male sex workers remain unconvincing, especially from my own perspective as someone who has actually worked in prostitution, and to a lesser extent, porn. The challenge is for abolitionists to come up with credible arguments that are gender-neutral and not based on stereotypes that cast men as sexual aggressors and women as defenseless victims. Once one discovers that the arguments make little sense when masculine and feminine pronouns are interchanged, it is only a short leap from there to postulate that perhaps there might be other exceptions to the underlying arguments even when the pronouns are switched back.

CHAPTER SIXTEEN

Prostitution and Sexual Autonomy

*Making Sense of the Prohibition of Prostitution**

SCOTT A. ANDERSON

INTRODUCTION

By now, it is well known that prostitutes in Western nations frequently live and operate in truly disastrous conditions. These conditions are typically worst for the many economically and/or racially marginalized women who earn their livelihoods through prostitution, but many other female as well as male prostitutes suffer gravely. Prostitution is also commonly thought to harm the public health and quality of life of many others not directly active in it. The extent of these problems varies across countries, in part due to differences in the regulations and social programs that govern and buffer prostitution in the developed West. Nonetheless, prostitution presents significant social problems in virtually every Western country and society, testifying to the seeming intractability of these difficulties.[1]

*Reprinted with permission from *Ethics: An International Journal of Social and Legal Philosophy*, The University of Chicago, Vol. 112 (July 2002), pp. 748–780. Copyright © 1995 by The University of Chicago. All rights reserved.

1. In this article, the term 'prostitution' refers to a kind of occasional, limited transaction in which a person purchases "live" physical sexual recreation from someone who provides it in order to receive tangible, nonsexual benefits as compensation, either directly from the purchaser or through an intermediate party (e.g., a pimp or procurer). Because prostitution necessarily involves at least two parties, and often a third, when this article discusses prostitution, it should be understood to include the combined activities of all of these parties and not just those of the prostitute.

The United States is one of the few Western nations in which all forms of prostitution are illegal almost everywhere.[2] Nonetheless, despite its prohibition, prostitution continues to occur widely; in fact, one might now reasonably question whether these laws have a purpose beyond simply controlling some aspects of the practice—mainly those that offend middle-class sensibilities—while underwriting a moralistic disdain for those who engage in it. Adding injury to insult, the prohibition of prostitution is widely believed to exacerbate its harms, especially in the United States. It contributes significantly to the hardships of prostitutes because it places them outside of legal protection, making them extremely vulnerable to predators who would exploit their relative powerlessness.

In the wake of these facts, liberals and radical feminists have been locked in debate about how best to respond to the problems associated with prostitution. On the liberal side, a number of authors have recently argued that we should adopt a reform program with respect to prostitution, one that would alter not just the practice and the laws that regulate it but also our attitudes toward it.[3] The authors in this group urge that we "normalize" prostitution, that is, treat it as just another recreation-oriented service industry. Opposing them, a number of authors often

2. In contrast to most of Western Europe, prostitution is currently illegal everywhere in the United States, except for rural counties in Nevada, where it is in some places legal, though strongly regulated. The illegality of prostitution in the United States typically includes prohibitions on the sale of sexual services, the purchase of sexual services, pimping or otherwise employing others to provide sexual services, operating a business where this is known to occur, and recruiting others into the business.

3. For representations of the liberal position, I will cite Martha Nussbaum, "'Whether From Reason or Prejudice': Taking Money for Bodily Services," in her *Sex and Social Justice* (New York: Oxford University Press, 1999), pp. 276–98; Sibyl Schwarzenbach, "Contractarians and Feminists Debate Prostitution," *New York University Review of Law and Social Change* 18 (1990–91): 103–30; and Lars Ericsson, "Charges against Prostitution: An Attempt at a Philosophical Assessment," *Ethics* 90 (1980): 335–66. Others whom I would line up on this side of the debate include D. A. J. Richards, Kenneth Shuster, and Laurie Shrage, though her position is considerably more ambivalent than that of the others. A considerable number of prostitutes and other sex workers also have argued strongly for normalization. See, e.g., Norma Jean Almodovar, "For Their Own Good: The Results of the Prostitution Laws as Enforced by Cops, Politicians and Judges," *Hastings Women's Law Journal* 10 (1999): 101–15; Carol Queen, "Sex Radical Politics, Sex-Positive Feminist Thought, and Whore Stigma," in *Whores and Other Feminists*, ed. Jill Nagle (New York: Routledge, 1997), pp. 125–35; and generally the discussions in Gail Pheterson, ed., *A Vindication of the Rights of Whores* (Seattle: Seal, 1989).

identified (by themselves and others) as "radical feminists" have attacked prostitution and the arguments in favor of its normalization.[4] In particular, they have spotlighted the severity of the problems faced by women in prostitution and have tried to show that prostitution is a retrograde institution which should not be condoned but eliminated through means including (though not necessarily limited to) its legal prohibition.[5]

The arguments on both sides of this dispute have force but leave serious doubts. This article is motivated in part by the concern that the radical feminists have failed to explain clearly why selling sexual recreation might itself be particularly problematic—that is, why open commerce in sex would make things worse for women than they are anyway in a patriarchal, capitalist society. In light of liberal proposals to reform prostitution, it is hard to see why, if such reforms were effective, we might

4. The position I'm identifying as "radical feminist" is so named because of the prominence among its defenders of authors such as Andrea Dworkin, Catharine MacKinnon, Kathleen Barry, Carole Pateman, Sheila Jeffreys, and Evelina Giobbe. While there are, of course, variation in their views, the position I develop out of their writings is, I think, more or less consistent with and recognizable in the work of all these authors. For representative and influential examples, see Andrea Dworkin, "Prostitution and Male Supremacy," in her *Life and Death* (New York: Free Press, 1997), pp. 138–216; Catharine MacKinnon, "Prostitution and Civil Rights," *Michigan Journal of Gender and Law* 1 (1993): 13–31; Kathleen Barry, *The Prostitution of Sexuality* (New York: New York University Press, 1995); Carole Pateman, *The Sexual Contract* (Stanford, Calif.: Stanford University Press, 1988); Sheila Jeffreys, *The Idea of Prostitution* (North Melbourne: Spinifex, 1997); Evelina Giobbe, "Prostitution: Buying the Right to Rape," in *Rape and Sexual Assault III: A Research Handbook*, ed. Ann Wolbert Burgess (New York: Garland, 1991), pp. 143–60. Some disciplinary philosophers also argue in this vein, including Debra Satz, "Markets in Women's Sexual Labor," *Ethics* 106 (1995): 63–85; and Christine Overall, "What's Wrong with Prostitution? Evaluating Sex Work," *Signs* 17 (1992): 705–24.

5. A note on the terms used in this debate: virtually all commentators on prostitution favor some reform of the laws prohibiting prostitution. Some advocate what I will call the "normalization" of prostitution, which involves at least making it legal and perhaps going so far as to treat it as just another sort of commercial enterprise (though one to which age restrictions apply). Among those favoring normalization, there are debates about the best course toward normalization (e.g., legalization vs. decriminalization), but this article will not be concerned with those issues. "Normalization" is opposed in this article to "prohibition," which will describe both the status quo as well as the reform position advocated by radical feminists, who would retain and even strengthen penalties on customers and middlemen, though not, perhaps, on prostitutes themselves.

still reasonably object to the institution. But liberal arguments for normalizing prostitution fail, I think, to make a compelling case, in part because they fail to understand how deeply problematic sexual relations are in our society and how normalization of prostitution would tend to obscure and entrench these problems, not solve them. Thus, while they raise what appears to be a significant challenge to the feminists' arguments, this challenge can be rebutted by a careful reconstruction of the grounds of the feminists' dissent.

This article attempts to give such a reconstruction by showing how the prohibition of prostitution is of a piece with a wide range of social regulations that serve to protect sexual autonomy. Although sexual autonomy may seem far from the minds of many radical feminists, properly understood, sexual autonomy is crucial to the feminist goals of achieving women's equality with men, as well as promoting a more general form of autonomy for women. By showing how, for us, sexual autonomy depends on a range of social restrictions on our individual practices, I will set out what I take to be the strongest set of considerations in favor of prohibiting prostitution. My arguments admittedly do not show that, all things considered, the prohibition of prostitution is justified, since this stronger result would require consideration of a large number of factors, many of them empirical, which lie outside the scope of this article's purview.[6] But by showing the weaknesses of the reform strategy, this article undercuts one of the main motivations for normalizing prostitution.

This article outlines the radical feminist critique of prostitution and then describes how liberals have responded to this critique, in particular, the suggestion that prostitution, including our attitudes toward it, can and should be reformed. To make progress in resolving this dispute, I first

6. The difficulties here include the fact that what kinds of practices we legally and socially condone may affect what kinds go on beyond the bounds of legal and social legitimacy. It is not always clear, for instance, that prohibiting a practice is the most effective way to quell its occurrence overall. Some evidence about the relationship of overt social regulation to actual social practice can be gained by surveying across different societies having different legal and social norms, and comparing cases. In nn. 38 and 40, I discuss some such evidence from European countries that have regulatory regimes for prostitution rather different from that of the United States. Yet such cases can be less than conclusive due to the numerous and obvious differences that combine to make each country and culture unique. Also of concern is the cost of enforcing any policy of prohibition. For one study showing a surprisingly high cost for current prohibitions, see Julie Pearl, "The Highest Paying Customers: America's Cities and the Costs of Prostitution Control," *Hastings Law Journal* 38 (1987): 769–90.

step back from a narrow focus on prostitution and examine the broader role that certain social regulations of sexual behavior play in protecting individual sexual autonomy throughout our society. These regulations serve as a barrier between sexual activity and the activities of production and commerce. After showing how sexual autonomy is protected by these sorts of barriers, I return to the radical feminists' critique and argue that a prohibition on prostitution can be justified because of the role it plays in defending the sexual autonomy of the poorest, least-powerful members of our society. This is important for those people most vulnerable to becoming prostitutes, but it is also necessary in order to pursue justice between rich and poor, as well as equality between women and men.

Before proceeding, it is important to be clear about what is not up for discussion here. There are businesses that literally enslave people, or subject them to violence, abuse, threats against loved ones, deceit, gross psychological manipulation, and so forth, in order to lure or keep them in the sex trade. Moreover, some sexual commerce involves children. These sorts of business practices cannot be defended, and no one I wish to debate defends them. When these kinds of violence and gross exploitation are excluded, there remains a segment of the sex trade in which all participants appear to exercise at least some continuing, minimal level of choice to engage in this practice. It is the propriety of sexual commerce under these circumstances (or better) about which there appears to be room to disagree and which serves as my topic.[7]

AN ANALYSIS OF THE RADICAL FEMINIST CRITIQUE OF PROSTITUTION

The radical feminists' criticism of prostitution flows from their more general analysis of social relations. In the broader picture, they have sought to publicize the extent to which women are disadvantaged in contemporary Western societies, connecting these disadvantages to our sexual practices. These practices, they argue, define a hierarchy in society, thus legitimating and enforcing the subordination of women as a class. Of the sexual practices thought to have this effect, feminists frequently cite prostitution as both an indicator and cause of the subordinate state of women, even as the epitome of that subordination. Christine Overall, for instance, claims

---

7. Please note also that the relevance of the arguments presented here may well be limited to the societies located in the developed West. In other parts of the world, the facts that would be most relevant for thinking about prostitution may be very different in both kind and substance.

that given the interweaving of sex, money and power, "dominance and submission, oppression and victimization are necessarily built into the practice [of prostitution]."[8] Although this view is hardly self-evident, if Overall and others are correct in it, then we would have the beginning of a rationale for attempting to suppress prostitution on the grounds that it is an objectionable *institution*. As such, one could not accurately evaluate the choices of prostitutes or their clients by focusing narrowly on the harms or benefits that result from such choices directly. Rather, such choices may be problematic for the contribution they make to sustaining a bad institution—in this case, one that frequently harms women and reinforces their subordination to men.

In showing prostitution to be a bad institution, feminist arguments generally offer a combination of the following three kinds of claims: (1) that the good purchased from a prostitute is frequently, in part, her own degradation; (2) that the existence of prostitution depends on the existence of an inequality in social or economic power between prostitutes and their customers; and (3) that prostitution contributes to the perpetuation of the inequalities that underlie the practice.

The first claim, that prostitution involves the sale of an individual's degradation, is given a powerful voice by Andrea Dworkin, herself a survivor of prostitution. She paints a harrowing picture of prostitution as a kind of inhumane violence targeted at the female body:

I think that prostitutes experience a specific inferiority. Women in general are considered to be dirty. Most of us experience this as a metaphor ... but a prostitute lives the reality of being the dirty woman....
She is perceived as, treated as ... vaginal slime. She is dirty; a lot of men have been there. A lot of semen, a lot of vaginal lubricant.... Her anus is often torn from the anal intercourse, it bleeds. Her mouth is a receptacle for semen, that is how she is perceived and treated. All women are considered dirty because of menstrual blood but she bleeds other times, other places. She bleeds because she's been hurt, she bleeds and she's got bruises on her.
When men use women in prostitution, they are expressing a pure hatred for the female body. It is as pure as anything on this earth ever is or ever has been. It is a contempt so deep, so deep, that a whole human life is reduced to a few sexual orifices, and he can do anything he wants.[9]
I want you to feel the delicate tissues in her body that are being misused. I want you to feel what it feels like when it happens over and over and over and over and over and over and over again: because that's what prostitution is. The repetition will kill you, even if the man doesn't.[10]

8. Overall, p. 722.
9. Dworkin, pp. 144–45.
10. Ibid., p. 140.

Although many people, including many prostitutes, deny that prostitution is always this brutal or degrading, one of the successes of feminist scholarship has been to uncover the extent of the suffering and brutalization endured by many prostitutes. These harms are far worse than attend almost any ordinary job and are arguably of a piece with rape, domestic battery, and sexual harassment.[11] Dworkin graphically describes the damaged body, the viscera, and the repetitive nature of prostitution in order to prevent her reader from achieving a detachment from these lived experiences or a retreat to a more abstract approach to them. The point, she claims, is that the subordination and degradation reflected in these harms are part of what men purchase in prostitution; hence, these harms are not incidental to nor easily separable from the practice of prostitution.[12]

---

11. Ibid., p. 141. In this same vein, see Giobbe, "Prostitution"; and Beverly Balos and Mary Louise Fellows, "A Matter of Prostitution: Becoming Respectable," *New York University Law Review* 74 (1999): 1220–1303.

12. Feminists, radical or otherwise, have succeeded in amassing a great deal of evidence and testimony on the dire conditions in which many prostitutes live their lives—before, during, and (if they survive) after their time in prostitution. These conditions include the following nonexhaustive list. Before: sexual abuse (as children or adults), child abuse or neglect, domestic violence, drug and alcohol abuse, poverty, divorce, and racism. During: rape, assault, murder, stigma, pregnancy, sexually transmitted diseases, discriminatory legal practices, drug and alcohol abuse, pimp control/slavery, poverty, psychosocial harms (distancing, dissociation, inability to form intimate relationships), and post-traumatic stress disorder (PTSD). After: stigma, psychosocial harms (distancing, dissociation, inability to form intimate relationships), PTSD, and poor employment prospects. For some works that document and/or catalog the harms suffered by prostitutes before, during, and after prostitution, see the following sources: Vednita Carter and Evelina Giobbe, "Duet: Prostitution, Racism and Feminist Discourse," *Hastings Women's Law Journal* 10 (1999): 37–57; Melissa Farley, "Prostitution in Five Countries: Violence and Post-Traumatic Stress Disorder," *Feminism and Psychology* 8 (1998): 405–26; Ine Vanwesenbeeck, *Prostitutes' Well-Being and Risk* (Amsterdam: Vrije Universiteit Press, 1994); Susan Kay Hunter, "Prostitution Is Cruelty and Abuse to Women and Children," *Michigan Journal of Gender and Law* 1 (1993): 91–104; Margaret Baldwin, "Split at the Root: Prostitution and Feminist Discourses of Law Reform," *Yale Journal of Law and Feminism* 5 (1992): 47–120; Evelina Giobbe, "Confronting the Liberal Lies about Prostitution," in *The Sexual Liberals and the Attack on Feminism*, ed. Dorchen Leidholdt and Janice G. Raymond (New York: Pergamon, 1990), 67–81; and Barry. Many of the harms described here seem to correspond to prostitution practiced at a lower socioeconomic stratum within the domain of prostitution. For an account by a prostitute who has escaped many of these attending difficulties while earning a good living in prostitution,

A second contention holds that in prostitution, men of relative privilege and power exploit the poverty, powerlessness, and history of sexual abuse that characterize the lives of many women. Radical feminists argue that the very existence of a supply of willing prostitutes should be seen as a mark of entrenched injustice. Since no rational person would willingly be consumed as a sexual object, prostitution is necessarily a form of exploitation: its existence depends on the role social inequality plays in ensuring that the socially more powerful have access to sexual objects of their choice.[13] While the conditions that lead people into prostitution are not unique to women, these conditions appear to occur in a pattern that is particularly gendered, to the disadvantage of women. Women are typically poorer than men and thus more vulnerable to economic exploitation and bad bargains in employment. In prostitution, pimps or procurers capitalize on their economic and social vulnerability, while law enforcement agencies treat them as outlaws—literally, people for whom the law's protections do not apply. Many prostitutes have also been abused as children, and these victims of abuse often become involved in prostitution at early ages, find it difficult to quit, and frequently lack the ability to defend their interests against other opportunistic abusers.[14] Thus, women who become prostitutes are often subject to men's worst treatment because those men know that prostitutes often lack the wherewithal to oppose it.

The third plank of the institutional criticism of prostitution holds that prostitution plays a key role in sustaining the social inequality of women. It does so by defining women in general as sexual objects, available to any man who desires them. One of the most obvious facts about prostitution in our society, yet perhaps the hardest to take into account, is the degree to which prostitution and prostitutes attract our interest and serve as a stimulus for talk, jokes, stories, gazes—in short, as a source of our

see the essay by Barbara [pseud.], "It's a Pleasure Doing Business with You," *Social Text* 37 (1993): 11–22.

13. See, e.g., Susanne Kappeler, "Liberals, Libertarianism, and the Liberal Arts Establishment," in Leidholdt and Raymond, eds., p. 180. To see the injustice in this, it helps to see the space of possibilities as Dworkin does when she writes, "Any man who has enough money to spend degrading a woman's life in prostitution has too much money. He doesn't need what he's got in his pocket. But there is a woman who does" (Dworkin, p. 150).

14. For one recitation of the exploitative background of prostitution, see the chapter on prostitution in Rosemarie Tong's *Women, Sex, and the Law* (Totowa, N.J.: Rowman & Allanheld, 1984), esp. pp. 51–53, 59–61. For another, see Priscilla Alexander, "Prostitution: A Difficult Issue for Feminists," in *Sex Work*, ed. Frédérique Delacoste and Priscilla Alexander (Pittsburgh: Cleis, 1987), pp. 184–214.

common titillation. But the stereotypes that are conjured by our common consciousness provide images not just of prostitutes but of women more generally.[15] Political theorist Carole Pateman connects this demonstrative effect of prostitution to the history of women's oppression: "When women's bodies are on sale as commodities in the capitalist market, the terms of the original [sexual] contract cannot be forgotten; the law of male sex-right is publicly affirmed, and men gain public acknowledgment as women's sexual masters—that is what's wrong with prostitution."[16] Prostitution thus supports a pernicious stereotype of what women are for and reinforces our society's tendency to view women first and foremost in sexual terms.

Although this description of the radical feminists' position is brief and lacks much of the detail and evidence in its favor, I think it describes accurately the kind of argument that they take to weigh against prostitution. These claims, if true, would together seem to give us good reason to treat prostitution as a suspect institution. Such a judgment should prompt us to examine critically the broader social structures that support the institution and the webs of choice and consequence it creates.

THE LIBERAL RESPONSE: REFORM THROUGH NORMALIZATION

Liberals can easily agree with radical feminists about many of the issues involved in prostitution, including the extent to which prostitutes currently suffer, the significance of women's social and economic inferiority, and the need to improve conditions for women generally. While they also agree that the United States should revamp the laws regulating prostitution, liberals disagree most directly with radical feminists over the question of how prostitution should be regulated under the less-than-ideal circumstances that typically confront women. Radical feminists generally favor maintaining and strengthening the prohibition of prostitution; although almost all favor exempting the activities of prostitutes from legal penalties, they advocate prohibiting the activities of the middlemen and customers. By contrast, while allowing for regulations with the health and safety of prostitutes and the public in mind, liberals do not in general aim to eliminate commercial sexual recreation as a way of making a living or as a pastime for those who can afford it. They hold that even successful

---

15. See Satz, pp. 77–81. For a similar though less well developed argument, see Overall, pp. 717–21.

16. Pateman, p. 208.

abolition may be only a very incomplete solution to the problems inherent in prostitution. In response to feminist arguments for prohibition, they can grant that prostitution as now practiced is a degrading institution, but they offer several rejoinders that seem to undercut calls for its prohibition. I will briefly mention two in passing and give a more extended discussion of a third.

The first rejoinder is that, even at the lowest rungs of voluntary prostitution, women still gain some benefits from it, and it may well be the best overall employment option they have. Eliminating prostitution might make things worse for the poorest women by denying them the benefits, small or large, that they gain from it. This objection may be sound, and if so, it may be decisive. If redress for women's economic conditions is not politically or otherwise feasible, we are pressed to consider what would provide the second-best, still-feasible option. The answer would depend on empirical and political facts about what would happen to those who are or might become employed in prostitution that lie beyond the scope of this article. I therefore take no stand on this objection.[17]

The second rejoinder notes that there is a great diversity of activity and participation within the bounds of prostitution. Even if we look just at those who become prostitutes (ignoring their customers and pimps/managers), we will find a great deal of heterogeneity among them (their genders, economic conditions, education, races, sexual histories, etc.) as well as significant heterogeneity in their business and sexual activities.[18] Therefore, it is not at all clear that prostitution amounts to a single institution; it may divide up into several institutions, which may or may not have any problematic characteristics in common. The questions raised by this challenge are difficult and interesting, but I will not attempt to answer them directly; however, some of the arguments below speak indirectly to the claim that (nearly) all forms of prostitution share an important common element.[19]

There is a third rejoinder that is potentially more damaging yet more amenable to a philosophical response. While the liberal respondents to radical feminism can and often do agree that prostitution is the site of many serious harms that merit social redress, what they dispute is that these harms derive specifically from the decisions of individuals to engage

17. Almodovar, former prostitute and former head of COYOTE (Call Off Your Old Tired Ethics), makes this objection forcefully (see Almodovar).

18. Some of the range of this diversity is brought out in Julia O'Connell Davidson, *Prostitution, Power and Freedom* (Ann Arbor: University of Michigan Press, 1998).

19. See esp. n. 49.

in *sexual commerce*, either as buyers or providers. Unless it can be made clear why *selling* sexual recreation to men contributes more to maintaining women's oppression than other forms of heterosexual relations, it would appear unjustified to bar individuals from engaging in voluntary sexual commerce. On the one hand, such a prohibition does not clearly improve the background circumstances in which women live, but it may well worsen the situation of those for whom prostitution is the best of a bad lot of choices. On the other hand, if society were to alleviate the harms that arise from women's economic and social inferiority, while also halting the problems created by prostitution's prohibition, we might well suppose that prostitution in such improved circumstances would be free from any remarkable harms. Thus, liberals can agree with radical feminists that prostitution as it exists now is a harmful, degraded institution, but they pointedly resist the conclusion that prostitution (or sexual commerce in general) is necessarily a bad institution.

This response seems to be at the heart of a number of liberal critiques of the radical feminist position. Those liberals whose work shows most concern with the lives of prostitutes argue that the best realistic hope for prostitutes is to seek to reform the circumstances in which prostitutes work. Although different writers have advocated different specific reforms, there is a general picture discernible in the work of several of these authors. They call for both re-envisioning what it is that prostitutes do as well as revising the typical attitudes of society at large toward prostitution, and prostitutes in particular. So, for instance, Sybil Schwarzenbach argues for legalization on the grounds that it is a necessary step to help destroy prostitution as we know it and to aid its metamorphosis into something she envisions as commercial "erotic therapy." As a practitioner of such therapy, "the prostitute could be respected for her wealth of sexual and emotional knowledge."[20] Lars Ericsson argues that prostitutes might "fulfill a socially valuable function by, inter alia, decreasing the amount of sexual misery in society."[21] In light of considerations such as these, Martha Nussbaum argues in a recent essay that the stigma accorded to prostitution is an unjust prejudice of the same sort that once denigrated the activities of women actors, dancers, and singers.[22]

The possibility that prostitution can be reformed calls into question the basis of the institutional critique. If so-called casual sex by heterosexuals is not always, everywhere bad for women, then it is natural to ask why an instance of casual sex should be suspect whenever the benefit attained

20. Schwarzenbach, p. 125.
21. Ericsson, p. 366.
22. See Nussbaum.

by one party (say, the woman) is remunerative rather than sexual. What difference does, say, a lack of mutual sexual attraction make to the ethical qualities of sexual relationships, if indeed one of the parties seeks and obtains other compensation for their sexual activity? If the liberals are right, then the harms that make us wary of prostitution seem to be severable from the essential nature of prostitution—the exchange of sexual for nonsexual goods. The exact means to achieve this severing may be somewhat obscure, but if it could be accomplished, even just in principle, then this would suggest that the harms we associate with prostitution are only contingently connected to it and need not determine how we evaluate prostitution itself.

While some authors have discussed this liberal/radical feminist debate usefully and at length, nothing seems to have ended it or to have shown the way forward to a resolution.[23] The radical feminists themselves have given little attention to options short of prohibiting prostitution outright and rarely consider what a reformed prostitution might look like or what sorts of supports would have to be in place to make such a thing conceivable.[24] In order to advance this debate, I shall now set out the basis for an answer to this third rejoinder by looking at ways our society aims

23. Some of the best recent work on this topic has been done by legal theorists, including Martha Chamallas, "Consent, Equality, and the Legal Control of Sexual Conduct," *Southern California Law Review* 61 (1988): 777–861; Margaret Jane Radin, *Contested Commodities* (Cambridge, Mass.: Harvard University Press, 1997), esp. pp. 123–36; and Baldwin; and by O'Connell Davidson, a sociologist. These authors have helpfully analyzed the difficulties leading to a stalemate in the debates. The author who I think comes closest to depicting accurately the stakes and difficulties in this debate is Sylvia A. Law, "Commercial Sex: Beyond Decriminalization," *Southern California Law Review* 73 (2000): 523–610. In this article, I will cover some of the same ground as these authors do, but I hope to give a fuller, more persuasive, and more philosophical defense of the radical feminist position than these authors have managed. My article also shares a number of the views and approaches found in the challenging and provocative essay by Balos and Fellows. The approach taken here departs from theirs in several respects, most notably in holding that sexual autonomy, while undoubtedly a liberal value, can and should be regarded as a proper goal of feminist social policy rather than as a problem for such policies. I also believe that the argument put forward here relies on premises more likely to find broader agreement, if only because the results I defend are considerably more modest in their ambitions. Nonetheless, their essay is worthy of serious attention and deserves a more complete response than I can provide here.

24. Responding to reform proposals, Jeffreys is typical of radical feminists when she writes, "If in fact the status of women were to change, then the sex of prostitution would likely become unthinkable rather than suddenly healthy. . . . If

to keep sex and commerce separate, giving rise to protections for a special form of autonomy in sex. In the final section, I will argue that the radical feminist criticism of prostitution makes most sense when understood against the background of this more general protection of sexual autonomy. So understood, I argue that radical feminists can and should deny that normalizing prostitution will suffice to render it an innocuous institution.

THE RELATIONSHIP OF THE GOODS OF SEX TO RESTRICTIONS ON OUR PRACTICES

At first face, it may seem paradoxical to suggest that restrictions or conventions constraining our activities could promote autonomy in them, since placing external controls on an activity would seem to reduce the individual's control of his or her activity. If we wanted to provide for sexual autonomy, it would seem that we should, as a society, forgo attaching any special significance to the sexual use of the body and instead leave it up to each individual to determine the proper meaning and uses of sex for him or herself. I want to suggest that this is a misunderstanding of the function of at least some of the social controls that regulate our sexual activities. Even though many of us now believe that sex is potentially valuable (and permissible) under a relatively wide range of circumstances—and, in particular, outside of the bounds of heterosexual marriage—the potential of sex to yield certain kinds of goods depends on the fact that, for us, sex has a place in a social framework, full of myriad restrictions and qualifications.

To illustrate the point, it will help to contrast some of our views about proper sexual conduct with the norms and regulations governing ordinary commerce and exchange. It is true of many ordinary human interactions that they will occur unproblematically on one side or the other of a transaction in the economic sense—for example, X gives Y a massage, X teaches Y logic, or X heals Y's illness, in return for which Y gives X money (or some similar service). Though commercial transactions are governed by a variety of legal and social norms, one of the principal governing norms is that of contract: one can be bound to honor one's commitments or forced to compensate the other party when one fails to do so. These commitments can even be tacit, implied, or conventional; for example, a seller may be understood to warrant that her product will have such and so

[the johns] had positive attitudes [toward women], they might not be able to conceive of using women in prostitution at all" (Jeffreys, pp. 229–30).

use or effect, or a consumer may be obligated to pay for a good he uses, without making such commitments explicit in either case. The possibility of making such commitments, and being held to them, is of course indispensable for the smooth, reliable conduct of virtually all commercial activity.

Now consider how the norms that govern commerce differ from those that apply in the following scenario. We have all heard tell of (and perhaps some of us have gone out on) a date where one person, usually a man, spends lavishly for an evening of food, drink, and entertainment, and his companion, usually a woman, is thereby expected to accede to his sexual overtures later in the evening. It is significant that these expectations may be shared by the people on the date and understood by them in advance, yet tacitly—possible, perhaps, because they both inhabit a social circle in which such dates are not unusual. Such dates continue to occur, we may suppose, because each party gets something he or she wants from them. This creates the appearance that what we have here is a transaction, like any other, where accepting the man's lavish expenditures means that the woman also accepts a subsequent obligation to let the man have sex with her.

Even if we recognize this pattern of behavior, in which expectations are often created and fulfilled, we do not think that spending lavishly on one's date creates anything like a moral or legal obligation for the date to have sex she does not want. While we may think it's a bad thing to knowingly accept an interested party's lavish attentions while having no intention of fulfilling his further sexual expectations, we don't hold that the frustrated party is entitled to enforcement of the bargain against the wishes of his date. Nor do we hold that he's entitled even to compensation for his efforts or expenditures, except perhaps the wisdom of experience. If, after his date refuses his sexual overtures, he continues assertively to press his demands, he will have harassed his date and perhaps even assaulted her. The fact that sex is a critical variable here comes out if we notice that we might be more willing to hold someone responsible for following through on such a bargain if the expected payback is, say, help with logic or a massage rather than sex.[25]

<hr/>

25. But not just any sort of expectation other than sex will generate the kind of obligations I'm thinking of here. For instance, lobbyists might treat congressional representatives and salespeople might treat prospective clients to lavish attentions yet generate no special obligation on the recipients' parts. It is, of course, their hope to generate a psychological feeling of obligation in their recipients, but this is not, we assume, underwritten by an actual moral obligation for the recipients to reciprocate.

I offer the example of the expensive date in order to suggest that some of the restrictions that govern our sexual practices serve to prevent certain kinds of pressures or incentives from being used against a person to alter her sexual choices. I believe we might best be able to see the value of the prohibition if we consider, hypothetically, how our lives and practices would be different without *any* such constraints in place—that is, if we were to treat sex as if it were not especially different from other kinds of activities that occur in commerce. Martha Nussbaum makes just such a proposal, when she defends the bold claim that we should see the prostitute's sex work as just another use of the body for purposes of earning a living—not especially different from other paid activities, such as chicken plucking, singing, massaging, or writing philosophical texts, in ways that matter for purposes of social regulation.[26] She argues that any residual reluctance to normalizing prostitution is based in an unjustifiable prejudice, one that we should strive to overcome, just as we have overcome prejudices against allowing women to work on the stage.[27] Although it might be appropriate to regulate prostitution for purposes of consumer or worker safety, fair trade practices, and so forth, it is unreasonable, and perhaps unjustifiable, to regulate or prohibit commercial sexual recreation just because of its *sexual* nature.

Part of the interest of Nussbaum's proposal is that it gives an account of just what might be behind the persistent, historical stigmatization of prostitution. Because I think something like her account is both plausible as well as necessary to justify the liberal position, it is all the more useful to take Nussbaum's claim at face value, rather than in a more cautious, circumspect way favored by most proposals for normalizing prostitution. If we take seriously the claim that sex is not especially different from other ways one can use one's body to make a living, then many more changes than just normalizing prostitution would be warranted—hence the boldness of her claim.[28] I propose to investigate here what it would mean to treat sex as just another use of the body. That is, I am not concerned at this point with limited proposals to normalize just prostitution or with hopes that a carefully constructed regulatory regime could minimize or localize the effects of sexual commerce. Instead, I mean to investigate what kind of thing sexual autonomy is and how certain social regulations foster it.

---

26. These are some of the occupations by comparison to which Nussbaum judges prostitution to be not especially problematic. See Nussbaum, pp. 278–85.

27. Ibid., esp. pp. 277–80, 285–88.

28. In fairness to Nussbaum, I should note that I am suggesting that we accept this one claim while disregarding the broader aims of her article, which do not, I believe, require one to endorse any of the scenarios I discuss below.

Once we understand this, we will be better placed to inquire whether some form of legalized prostitution (whether fully normalized or severely regulated) is really a more justifiable proposal than the prohibition favored by radical feminists.

If we take Nussbaum's claim at face value, then I believe that many readers will be troubled by some of the implications of this laissez-faire approach to the commercial uses of sex. Treating sex as just another use of the body in commerce would undermine perhaps three different aspects of sexual autonomy, illustrated by examples of the following sorts.

Category A: Incentives to Have Sex

1. Employees now shielded from performing sexual tasks as part of their conditions of employment may find their job descriptions redefined to include sexual duties. Also, some employees may be required to provide sexual services to other employees for either hiring or promotion.

2. Agencies dispensing welfare or unemployment compensations should be able to expect those who are capable of doing sexual work to take such work if it's available rather than to seek public relief.

3. One may make enforceable contracts to perform or obtain sexual services. Courts will be required to treat such contracts as they treat other personal-services contracts and uphold penalties or restrictions on nonperforming parties.

Category B: Control over Sexual Practices

4. Large, aggressive corporations may legitimately develop sexual services for consenting adults using whatever business practices are acceptable for other sorts of consumer goods (at least those such as alcohol or gambling, which are age restricted). In so doing, they may closely monitor and supervise the workplace sexual practices of those workers with sexual duties.

5. Workers with sexual duties may be required to adhere to standards of nondiscrimination with respect to their clients or coworkers.

6. The government may be entitled to inspect the health and sexual practices of prostitutes as this affects their safety and the safety of their clients. Risky sexual or other safety-affecting practices may be subject to blanket prohibitions, both while on the job and off.

Category C: Pressures on Sexual Attitudes and Values

7. Those large, aggressive corporations may, as part of their free-speech rights, market their product aggressively with the aim of overcoming

prejudices against paying for sex or having sex outside of a relationship, as well as other marketing objectives.

8. To the extent that special training may help prepare one for such a career, public schools, vocational schools, and colleges may/should offer such training. High school career counselors may/should advise those who seem differentially suited for this kind of work to consider it as a career.

My point in offering these scenarios is not to suggest that any of them is likely to come to pass in the wake of moves to normalize prostitution. Rather, these scenarios are simply exhibits of what it would mean to take the bold claim seriously—to treat sex as just another way to use the body to make a living—and so worth considering for the insights they might provide.

If these scenarios make us uneasy, I think it is because they illustrate various ways in which treating sex as just another use of the body for commercial purposes would lead to the undercutting of sexual autonomy. Undoubtedly, regulating the performance of a given activity (as the ban on prostitution regulates sex) takes away a certain range of choices from a person. Nonetheless, such restrictions may provide a sort of freedom within the activity by preventing it from coming into play with all of the other forces in life that can come to bear upon it. It is a brute necessity for most adults in our society that they earn a living by satisfying the economic demands of others. Rarely does anyone find a job where one does only the things one wants to do or a job in which all of one's duties are explicitly agreed to in advance. But as lamentable as these facts may be, they seem somehow of a different character than if the equivalent facts were transposed into our sex lives. The principal problem with treating sex as just another use of the body is that it is inconsistent with a number of the restrictions that make autonomy possible in sexual conduct.

A prohibition on exchanging sex for certain other sorts of goods should, if sufficient alternatives exist, provide us with a defense against various kinds of claims and intrusions that can be made against our sexual selves. Considering the kinds of pressures found in category A, if sexual autonomy means anything, it means that sex does not become a necessary means for a person to avoid violence, brute force, or severe economic or other hardships. Although this does not constitute the whole of sexual autonomy, it is surely an essential aspect of it. Were we seriously to treat sex as just another use of the body in commerce, doing so would first and most directly undercut sexual autonomy by exposing almost all workers (and job seekers) to the possibility of being pressured by employers to have unwanted sex as a condition of employment. On this hypothesis, there would be no principled justification for the existence of social barriers between sex and commerce, and hence such barriers should be removed. It is true that the removal of barriers between sex and commerce would vastly increase the number of goods which could be obtained by means of sexual activity.[29] At the same time, however, it would make it legitimate for others to demand, solicit, encourage, expect, and supervise our sexual activity by offering and withholding the ordinary goods within their control. The same necessity that sometimes compels us to take on unwanted tasks at work might be used legitimately by others to compel some of us to have sex. This seems to me to run counter to the basic commonplace against forced sex, just as it runs against prohibitions on quid pro quo sexual harassment.

We can perhaps make the point more vivid by noting two other protections against forced sex that, on our hypothesis, should fall by the wayside. First, to the extent that welfare and unemployment compensation are intended for persons who cannot find suitable employment, if sex work is available and a person is suitable for it (however that is judged), government should encourage people to take such work and cut off benefits if such work is refused.[30] Second, insofar as persons are allowed to

29. For a mundane example, imagine how things might be different—who would gain, and who would lose—if instead of taking their prospective clients to strip clubs (as is standard practice in some industries), companies could utilize their salespeople to proffer sexual services themselves.

30. The suggestion is meant to be provocative, but it's short of absurd. The principal objection to it is that, while government assistance may be conditional on one's willingness to take available work, one need only seek "suitable work." One can reject a job without losing unemployment compensation benefits if one does so on bona fide religious grounds, because it pays less than one is used to earning, because it interferes with family obligations, because it poses a health risk, or because it's a new line of work. Despite such protections, in the last nine months of 1999, until the press reported it, New York City's welfare-to-work program called "Business Link" made arrangements with the Psychic Network to train welfare recipients in Tarot reading and other skills and then to hire them as telephone psychics at $10–$12 per hour. See Nina Bernstein, "New York Drops Psychic Training Program," *New York Times* (January 29, 2000); and Michael Daly, "Veil of Secrecy Lifted: Program Training Poor to Be Phone Psychics Is Exposed," *New York Daily News* (March 19, 2000). (I am indebted to Jacob Levi for alerting me to this factoid.) It is also understood that, if one's unemployment drags on, the range of jobs one must consider suitable is expected to grow. Furthermore, former prostitutes might be required to consider such work suitable if it were available. Finally, welfare reform as we know it has imposed a number of fairly draconian conditions on eligibility, including work requirements that seem to pay little attention to the benefit recipients' suitability for the jobs they are required to take. As Sylvia Law has noted, "The state enjoys a large freedom to

make enforceable labor contracts, they should be allowed to make contracts for sexual services, including tacit or implicit agreements, and the courts would have to uphold them. This was the point in the expensive date scenario, discussed at the start of this section. As the lesson of that scenario suggests, the barriers established between sex and commerce not only function to keep the workplace free of sexual pressures but also to keep private sexual relations free of the norms of business, where broken promises and defeated expectations can bring enforced remedies.

The hypothesis we're considering puts sexual autonomy at risk in a second way by allowing outside parties to exert control over how some individuals conduct their sexual activities. Many of us hold at least as an ideal that we should enjoy a right to privacy "in the bedroom," where consensual sexual activities are no one else's concern. And U.S. courts have acknowledged at least a rudimentary form of that right. Some prostitutes, too, have asserted demands for the right to exercise control over their bedrooms. The World Charter for Prostitutes' Rights from 1985 demands with respect to working conditions that, "it is essential that prostitutes can provide their services under the conditions that are absolutely determined by themselves and no one else."[31]

Workers, however, do not enjoy such rights to privacy in the workplace, and hence this demand by prostitutes runs counter to the supposition that sex work is just another way of working. This problem is highlighted by the scenarios in category B above. Even supposing that some people would not be averse to sex work, treating sex work as if it were no special kind of work entails giving control over how one performs it to managers, corporate business tactics, and government regulation. Here it helps to imagine a brothel, though not the Hollywood sort, run by Dolly Parton or the Mayflower Madame, but rather one owned by the likes of McDonald's, Nike, or Philip Morris. As in other industries, companies who hire sex laborers would be justified in micromanaging the activities

condition receipt of public assistance upon the sacrifice of otherwise constitutionally protected rights. Perhaps courts would see a policy that conditioned aid on a requirement that a woman engage in commercial sex as so egregious that the policy would be found to violate constitutional liberty. But this conclusion is far from clear" (Law, p. 606). Hence, the suggestion in the text may be farfetched at present but is not inconceivable, especially given current trends in eligibility requirements for public assistance and social insurance. For a more general discussion of eligibility requirements for unemployment compensation, see Mark A. Rothstein, Charles B. Craver, Elinor P. Schroeder, and Elaine W. Shoben, *Employment Law*, 2d ed. (St. Paul, Minn.: West, 1999), pp. 767–70, 786–88.

31. Pheterson, p. 40.

of their employees, which might include closely monitoring a prostitute's health; rigorously training the prostitute; imposing strict standards for conduct while at work; insisting on nondiscrimination on the basis of age, sex, race, religion, or disability; and monitoring client contact to assure quality and efficiency of service. Civil authorities (e.g., the Chicago departments of health, business affairs, and police) might be required to inspect the health and sexual practices of prostitutes as this affects their safety and the safety and satisfaction of their clients. The control of prostitutes' activities might also be extended to include off-the-job behavior. For instance, employers might prohibit risky sexual practices or disclosure of work activities. They might also restrict sexual activity generally in the form of an "exclusive-services" contract.

The scenarios described above suggest that sex under such a regime is unlikely to be autonomous in the sense that applies to consensual sex in the privacy of one's own bedroom. Such autonomy depends on having the degree of control over one's sexual activities that prostitutes have demanded as a right but which has no basis within the norms of employer-employee relationships. It is only because of the specifically sexual nature of such work, and our beliefs that sex ought to be autonomously governed, that the assertion of such a right makes any sense at all.

Considering the scenarios in categories A and B together, it's apparent that the degree to which an individual would suffer from the removal of barriers between sex and commerce would likely depend on the individual's power and resources within society. If one has sufficient power and resources at one's command, one can accept desirable or reject unwanted sexual bargains with little lost and perhaps something gained. But if a person lacks the power and resources to maintain her sexual autonomy concurrently with a decent standard of living, she will find it thrust upon her to decide which she will protect and which she will give up. For example, if it became acceptable for a manager to demand (or at least to reward) sexual services from his subordinates, those lacking the wherewithal to find other work or to refuse his advances while retaining their jobs would be likely to find their situation made much worse by this institutional change. Those who accept their new sexual duties may lose a lot of their self-respect, integrity, and depth of feeling. At the very least, they will have lost the possibility of attaining a certain kind of good that can be achieved through sex, one that depends on a connection between sex and intimacy or between sex and commitment. Those who refuse may lose their jobs and what economic security they provided. Hence, allowing people to use sexual activity as just another means of making money may not actually increase autonomy on the whole but could instead spread a person's powerlessness into her sexual life and undermine her sexual autonomy. She may find her sexual autonomy tied directly, in a way it need not be, to her economic and political autonomy.

Although the poor and powerless are likely to experience the greatest losses of sexual autonomy if the institutional restraints that protect it are removed, the sort of change envisioned above would affect society broadly: the effects would include changing the way people experience and exercise control over their sexuality. Even those workers with relatively more power and economic resources may find that sex becomes less valuable for them as they come to experience their sexual ends as potentially at odds with their career and economic ends. If sex is something an employer might legitimately expect of at least some employees, a person who refuses to accept sexual tasks in her job knows that someone else might, thus lowering her chances for career advancement and success. Because managers are now prohibited from using their superior position to make sexual demands on (or offers to) their employees, there is rarely a causal link that puts one's sexual ends at odds with one's career ends.[32] Hence one can usually pursue each as one chooses without compromising the other. Correspondingly, under a regime that maintains a distinction between work activities and sex, one's work-related skills constitute a category of merit distinct from one's sexual qualities. But if employers were allowed to reward or punish employees for their sexual activities, it would be less clear than it is now that, when an employee succeeds, she does so based on what we now think of as her merits.[33]

There is a third way in which sexual autonomy can be undermined, somewhat more obscure than the other two but also important to consider. As things stand in this society, we face numerous actors and social forces that have an impact on our attitudes toward sex, including our sexual desires and the form in which they are expressed. These may influence us through advertising, entertainment, education, religion, peer pressure, and occasionally through more personal and pleasant contacts. The fact that things external to the self play a role in determining an individual's sexual desires is hardly a matter of concern in itself. But sexual autonomy involves an aspect of internal regulation of these desires as well, in accordance with the individual's understanding of the proper place of sex in a good life. This internal regulation of sexual desire is a notoriously fraught and unstable activity, and some people seem to abandon it altogether. Nonetheless, for most of us, there are times and places where we want to attend to and emphasize the sexual aspects of our selves and other

---

32. Of course, this is not true for everyone, as the continuing occurrence of sexual harassment cases makes clear. Still, it is the intention of sexual harassment laws and policy to end the threat of such trade-offs.

33. I owe the point of this argument to Candace Vogler.

times and places where we may not want to be reminded of our sexual selves, desires, possibilities, and so forth. This division is undoubtedly imposed differently by different people; paradoxically, however, the possibility of making such a division depends to some extent on the existence of cooperating external conditions. One way in which such cooperating conditions are secured is through limits on the ways and places in which external forces are allowed to manipulate our sexual desires.

You may well ask, "What limits?" since we seem to be bombarded by sexual innuendo everywhere, emanating especially from businesses that advertise to us and entertain us. Things are undeniably murky here. Nonetheless, advertisers and entertainers now uphold some limits on their uses of sex, and in these limits, such as they are, we might detect not just a reflection of prudery but perhaps an acknowledgment that it is not always desirable to have our desires tweaked. Furthermore, to the extent that businesses now use sex to sell to us, their goal is at least typically to sell us something other than sex—the appeal to libido is a means, not an end in itself. Such marketers may use and arouse our sexual desires in order to manipulate our other desires (say, the desire to buy cologne), but it's not clear that they have any special incentive to manipulate or alter the sexual desires themselves (though they may affect them as a secondary consequence).34

34. The marketing of pornography, of course, seems to provide a counterexample to this view, since the demand for pornography is significantly influenced by the quantity and kinds of sexual desires people have. There is, however, an ongoing debate over what limits are appropriate for the manufacture and sale of pornography. We can see both sides in this debate as making arguments about the ways in which our sexual desires should be subject to influence from external sources. This is obviously true in the case of those who wish to ban or restrict pornography, who argue that it harms and deforms such desires. But we should note that many of pornography's defenders respond in the same terms when they argue that pornography plays a valuable role in making us aware of the wide variety of forms in which desire can occur. They argue that it liberates desires, making them more genuine and imaginative. Hence we can see, even among defenders of pornography, that one main line of defense depends on a view of what kinds of external influences are valuable and/or harmful to our sexual autonomy. Yet these defenders need not defend a blanket right of pornography producers to market it everywhere, to everyone, all the time; they may support a ban on all sexual depictions of children as well as restrictions to prevent children from accessing pornography. In this vein, it is worth noting that, at least prior to the advent of the Internet, you couldn't acquire pornography just anywhere, which suggests that it has been regulated by convention if not by law. It remains to be seen whether some form of these conventions will take hold in cyberspace.

If I am right that we do generally support certain restrictions (legal or conventional) on how and when external forces are permitted to influence our sexual desiring, then I think we can see this as consistent with the idea of sexual autonomy developed so far. Because sexual autonomy depends in part on the internal regulation of our sexual desires, it is promoted by mechanisms that put certain reasonable limits on the degree to which external forces can seek to influence our desires. However, as scenario 7 in category C above illustrates, businesses that make their living off of sex itself have a significant incentive to speak to those desires directly. The economic well-being of such businesses would depend on their ability to create and keep a share of the market for sexual services, to which end they would naturally seek to develop and manipulate our desires. Under the hypothesis we've been considering, sex industries would be justified, as part of their free speech rights, to market their product aggressively with the aim of overcoming attachments to monogamy or one or another form of sexual practice. They might also employ marketing strategies aimed at developing brand loyalty, establishing tie-ins to other consumer/entertainment goods, and creating niche markets of underserved sexual desires. If these scenarios do raise some concerns about whether we want our sexual desires to be pressured in these ways, then it suggests that these pressures run counter to what we think of as good or healthy influences on our sexual desires.

There is also a great deal of dispute over what influences should be allowed to reach children regarding their sexual desires, morals, and practices. As with a number of other goods (e.g., alcohol, tobacco, and drugs), some degree of paternalism is clearly justified. And schools clearly don't attempt to train students for every possible, legitimate career. However, schools often take a role in preparing students for relationships or married life, for sexual activity, as well as for postgraduation careers. On our hypothesis, it would seem reasonable that they should also attempt to make students aware of legal career opportunities in sex work and provide training as necessary, as suggested in scenario 8. If we would object to schools playing this kind of role in career development, and object because of the sexual aspects of such careers, then such objections suggest that we do not believe sex is just another way of working or that training people to view it as such is in their best interests.[35]

35. Because high school students are in the process of developing into autonomous persons but are generally understood not to have arrived there yet, it is unclear to me whether this objection shows the place of sexual autonomy as clearly as the previous ones do. It might be useful to distinguish here between the practical and ideological functions of education in promoting autonomy and their

Even if one believes that our sexual mores ought to be revised, or that the above scenarios are not as problematic as I suggest, my point in this discussion has been to show that not all of the restrictions we might impose on sexual activity are simply vestiges of some now-abandoned, Victorian view of sex. Rather, the institutional restrictions on what sex can be used for serve to establish a special kind of autonomy in matters of sex and give a sense to the mundane view that sex is a kind of good distinct from those that are typically involved in commercial transactions.[36] If sexual activity needs to be couched in a set of institutional protections different from those that apply to work activities in general (such as OSHA regulations, nondiscrimination standards, fair labor laws, etc.), then we appear to share a desire for autonomy in our sexual activity that justifies these protections.

SEXUAL AUTONOMY AS A RADICAL FEMINIST VALUE

The point of the above discussion is to show that the legal and social discouragement of prostitution is just one of a large variety of ways in which our sexual activities are intentionally regulated or constrained by our

relationship to career choice. If people are prevented from taking up careers in sex work due to a lack of appropriate education (vocational training, counseling, etc.), then of course making such education available could also increase their autonomy. But it seems unlikely that the absence of vocational training is really a hindrance to making sex work a career-it is in part the ease with which it can be taken up that accounts for our disdain of it. So there would not seem to be much practical use for educating students about sex work. There might, however, be an ideological point to such training, aimed at reversing a prejudice, as, for instance, we desire schools to show women that they can be doctors and men that they can be nurses. If the reasons people are squeamish about sex work are based in prejudice, then fighting such prejudice would seem an appropriate role for schools to take up in training students for future work. Hence, with these caveats, I offer the scenario of high school vocational training as another case that is at least potentially consistent with the general pattern noted in the other scenarios.

36. Please note that I am not claiming, nor do I think it's true, that current attitudes toward sex have an unproblematic history or that they need be considered beyond criticism. Instead, I claim that even if our sexual views are problematic for historical or other reasons, it would require significant revision in the ways we think about sex and its relationship to personality before removing the barriers between commerce and sexual activity will seem, on the whole, ethically unproblematic.

communities; it is also one of the principal methods by which a separation is established between sexual activity and commercial activity. Hence, it helps to make possible a special kind of autonomy for agents with respect to their sexual activity. So far, I have suggested that we do indeed value sexual autonomy, but I have not tried to give a defense or explanation of this value. For some, its value may be obvious, yet surely some would think it a false or pernicious value. And though the arguments above suggest that we desire some separation of sexual activity from commerce in general, these arguments do not specifically speak to whether the prohibition on prostitution is merited. I want now to return to the arguments of liberals and radical feminists for and against normalizing prostitution, respectively, and to show how the above reflections on sexual autonomy help strengthen the latter side's case against normalization.

Keeping in mind the many points of agreement between liberals and radical feminists, we can begin to make sense of the prohibition of prostitution, as well as proposals to normalize and reform it, by separating out two different though related kinds of problems that, in combination, motivate their opposing responses to prostitution. The first kind, which I'll call the narrower set, consists in the specific acts of customers and pimps who harm, abuse, degrade, and exploit the prostitutes they employ. It also includes those harms and disadvantages that arise from state efforts to suppress prostitution, for example, the inability of prostitutes to organize collectively. These sorts of problems are ones that legal remedies (including perhaps altering or repealing some laws) are most likely to affect directly. The broader set of problems consists of the more general social facts that contribute to making prostitution a problematic institution. These facts include a number of things related one way or another to its sexual nature, for example, its gender-marked characteristics, the social stigma that attaches to both prostitutes and johns, and the feeling many prostitutes have of being demeaned and dirty. These social facts also include the circumstances that make (some) women and (a few) men particularly vulnerable to the worst aspects of prostitution without much say in the matter. Such circumstances include women's inferior economic status and specifically the lack of a range of better employment options. They also include the existence of social conditions that seem to undermine the ability of some people—mostly women—to resist or avoid the sorts of harms and abuses that characterize many prostitutes' lives. Finally, they include the fact that the plights of prostitutes, and women more generally, are rarely seen as injustices demanding social remedies. It should be clear that the two sets of problems are related: the need to consider special legal treatment for prostitution derives, it seems, from the more general social difficulties faced by (would-be) prostitutes. I'll consider the narrower and broader sets of problems in turn.

If we compare prohibition to normalization with respect to the narrower set of harms, it is clear that the current legal regime makes it difficult for many prostitutes to avoid the harms meted out to them by clients, pimps, psychopaths, and even many police officers. It also puts many prostitutes at a bargaining disadvantage in negotiating prices.[37] The normalization of prostitution would surely go some ways toward protecting prostitutes from such misconduct and exploitation by ending the prostitute's outlaw status.[38] What is less often noted is that we could achieve

37. Note, however, that prostitutes may at present reap some benefits from an artificial scarcity created by the prohibition of prostitution. If the prohibition is ended, the demand for sexual services might increase, but the supply of prostitutes might increase even more, resulting in lowered prices and leaving those who currently engage in prostitution worse off in absolute terms.

38. The experience of some European countries is of interest here since several have moved further toward the legal normalization of prostitution than has the United States while at the same time providing, on the whole, greater equality for women than exists here. That said, the European experience might not be especially helpful in settling debates over normalization in general. For one thing, although some countries have undone some of the most onerous strictures on prostitution, none have really gone so far as to treat it just like any other form of work. Among the legal strictures, prostitutes are typically confined to certain geographic areas (red-light districts), typically only small-scale businesses are allowed to proffer sexual services, and various ancillary regulations are often used to check the activities of prostitutes. Beyond the law, social stigma still attaches to being or hiring a prostitute even where prostitution is legal. For an overview of the situation in a number of European countries (among others), see the contributions in Nanette J. Davis, ed., *Prostitution: An International Handbook on Trends, Problems, and Policies* (Westport, Conn.: Greenwood, 1993). The most promising comparison case may be provided by the Netherlands, which has perhaps the most tolerance for and recent experience with prostitution in Europe. As in other countries, there is a great diversity in the types of prostitution practiced in the Netherlands, and the quality of life for prostitutes shows similar variance. According to the 1994 study of prostitution in the Netherlands by Vanwesenbeeck, the best off (roughly a fourth of the total number of prostitutes) seem to enjoy a high standard of living, better than the average for women in the Netherlands; the middle 50 percent are somewhat less well-off than their nonprostitute peers; and those in the bottom 25 percent are very badly off. "Their suffering was even greater than the average of the control group of heavily traumatized non-prostitute women" (Vanwesenbeeck, p. 147). Major determinants of a prostitute's quality of life were childhood experiences (particularly abuse), economic situation, working conditions, and her interactions with clients—in particular, whether the prostitute felt helpless or powerless relative to her clients. Those who were at the bottom of the prostitution hierarchy were thought to have the "most troublesome and recalcitrant customers" (ibid., p. 152), partially explaining why they seem to fare so much worse than those at the top of the hierarchy. Adding to the complexity of

significant progress in this direction without accepting the normalization of prostitution. As radical feminists have urged, society could undertake legal reform to ameliorate these problems by, for instance, removing the legal sanctions that now threaten prostitutes and instead increasing sanctions and enforcement against prostitutes' customers and exploitative pimps and procurers. We might also, as has occasionally been proposed, increase the ability of prostitutes to sue for damages those who harm or abuse them.[39] Finally, we might revise laws covering rape and other sex crimes to ensure that they protect prostitutes the same as anyone else and insist that police and prosecutors treat prostitutes with respect and concern. In other words, we could improve the lives of prostitutes by redirecting the onus of our legal system away from those who are already disadvantaged and placing it on those whose misconduct makes prostitution dangerous, degrading, and exploitative.[40]

this picture is the fact that, according to estimates, most of the women working in prostitution in the Netherlands are foreigners, and as many as 50 percent of the prostitutes are not European Union nationals and do not have valid work permits. Many of them, probably most, come from poorer parts of the world, and at least some sizeable portion of them are very likely to be working in prostitution nonvoluntarily. See Judith Kilvington, Sophie Day, and Helen Ward, "Prostitution Policy in Europe: A Time of Change?" *Feminist Review* 67 (2001): 78–93; and Donna M. Hughes, Laura Joy Sporcic, Nadine Z. Mendelsohn, and Vanessa Chirgwin, *The Factbook on Global Sexual Exploitation*, published on-line by the Coalition against Trafficking in Women at *http://www.catwinternational.org/factbook.htm* (1999). These facts suggest that the difficulties of prostitution may be hard to remedy through normalization. Furthermore, if the government cracks down on those immigrant prostitutes who are working in the Netherlands illegally, that by itself might serve to undo the benefits of normalization to those women by returning them to outlaw status and driving their activities back underground. It is perhaps also of interest that, at roughly the same time that the Netherlands, Denmark, and Germany have moved toward legal normalization, Sweden has decided to take an approach much more like that recommended by the radical feminists: it has recently increased the penalties and enforcement against the customers and employers of prostitutes while leaving prostitutes themselves more or less free from sanctions. See again Kilvington et al.

39. On the merits of this approach, see Balos and Fellows.

40. I do not mean to suggest, however, that simply shifting the burdens of prohibition from prostitute to customer, even if feasible, is without drawbacks. Looking at some places that have done more to prosecute customers, the evidence shows that targeting customers also serves to drive prostitution out of the public eye and into more obscure, isolated, and often more dangerous locations. For descriptions of some European results of such a policy, see Kilvington et al. (for Sweden); and Rosie Campbell and Merl Storr, "Challenging the Kerb Crawler

Although this sort of legal reform has some academic appeal, it is admittedly unrealistic. That is, as unlikely as we are to normalize prostitution anytime soon, we are surely less likely still to enact laws that punish only the (male) customers and pimps who use or abuse prostitutes while protecting prostitutes themselves. One might suppose that it's the asymmetry of this proposal that explains why it is so unlikely, but one should keep in mind that the current legal regime is almost equally asymmetrical, except that it punishes and constrains prostitutes while it effectively protects from prosecution those who rape or abuse them and punishes only rarely and mildly those who employ them. At any rate, our society could make prostitution safer and less exploitative by normalizing it, but to some extent, this goal can be achieved by redirecting the burden of the laws toward customers and pimps and by holding them responsible for the damages they inflict.

Turning now to the broader set of problems, it would seem that neither strategy can do much to rectify the background conditions that make prostitution, however bad it may be, still the best feasible option for some people, especially women. Normalizing prostitution, however, would seem to give women, especially, one option they do not now possess, while continued prohibition leaves them no better off. Let us suppose that with normalized prostitution, almost all women would have at least one job open to them that paid a decent wage or better. If so, making this option widely available might seem a significant improvement for many women.

Whether or not this supposition is defensible, the conclusion fails, I think, to understand the nature of the broader problems of which prostitution is a part. If indeed the harms suffered by women in prostitution derive largely from the underlying inequality and hardship they face, then the proposal to normalize prostitution is a mismatched solution. The fact that one additional economic option—namely, prostitution—might be offered to women is trivial in comparison to the many other opportunities that are denied and hardships that are imposed. Looking at the social facts underlying prostitution, we should ask why anyone should have to work as a prostitute just to be able to earn what an ordinary man would make doing an ordinary job. Even if normalization would improve the economic situation of prostitutes, as we're assuming it would, it seems highly unlikely to alter the more general problem of women's social and economic inferiority. Having one more economic opportunity than is now present will hardly solve the more general deprivations and disparities that help generate prostitution's more striking harms.

Rehabilitation Programme," *Feminist Review* 67 (2001): 94–108 (for the United Kingdom).

We might still ask, however, whether normalization could help to render the activity less problematic or at least whether it could avoid exacerbating those problems. In particular, we might hope that normalization would render the sexual aspects less traumatizing or stigmatizing, in part by making prostitution more like other jobs, in part by changing common attitudes toward prostitution. But such hopes are misplaced. Even if normalizing prostitution results in improved economic opportunity for would-be prostitutes, the improvement comes at the expense of their sexual autonomy, something that one gets to retain in most other kinds of work. Normalization would also undermine the ability to see this loss of sexual autonomy as a matter of injustice rather than as a matter of the prostitute's career choice. To the extent that sexual autonomy is important to us, making a person's economic viability conditional on giving up that autonomy is not a promising strategy for fixing the underlying circumstances.

To make this case, consider the objection that I am making too much of sexual autonomy—something that is, at any rate, a contestable value. Now it is certainly possible to imagine our society undergoing changes through which sex might become a relatively mundane activity, perhaps as inconsequential (under what would have to be the ordinary circumstances) as going out for dinner or acting on a solicitation to buy a newspaper. Were sex to become that ordinary, there would be no sense in proposing a special sort of autonomy with respect to it. At the same time, it would likely cease to play such a large role in the oppression of women and sexual minorities, and conceivably such oppression would die away, since its main organizing principle would have lost its punch.

While this possibility is perhaps a consummation devoutly to be wished, it is not how things are now.[41] Both in history and in the present, a person's sexuality almost always figures prominently as an aspect of his or her self-conception, status in society, and economic and social prospects. Being thought beautiful or ugly, being experienced or inexperienced,

---

41. The hope that someday the pressure might be taken off of sex is one of the most appealing goals of some recent prominent work in queer theory. See, e.g., Michael Warner, *The Trouble with Normal* (New York: Free Press, 1999). The suggestion is that if we could learn to transform sex into a not-terribly-portentous recreational activity, we might live better, happier lives in greater harmony with one another. Of course, there are tremendous difficulties in figuring out how to make the transition to this world without leaving large numbers of people vulnerable to horrible mistakes and exploitation. But if we could indeed let some of the air out of sex, it seems to me that this would be a very good thing by feminist standards.

being raped or impregnated, being sexually apathetic or adventurous—all of these factors can have significant impacts on how one's life goes, how one is treated by others, and how one thinks of oneself.[42] One cannot perhaps have total control over any of these factors, but there are varying degrees of control a person can exercise over his or her sexual activities and characteristics, and nearly everyone wants more control rather than less. It is because sex plays such a pivotal role in the lives of most adults, starting in their formative years, that it creates its own special subject as well as a realm within which one can be more or less autonomous.[43]

42. One indication of the separateness of this domain is that it cannot be reduced to or deduced from other important sources of autonomy. Being secure in one's possession of economic necessities, having a good education, and having a well-functioning, healthy body are all important for autonomy, but none of these provide much of a guarantee that one possesses sexual autonomy (one might, for instance, be pinned by terror into an abusive relationship, the victim of rape, or subject to pervasive sexual harassment). Moreover, it is at least conceptually possible that a person could lead a sexually autonomous life even if her economic, educational, and bodily autonomy are left insecure. (As a matter of practical reality, however, these other forms of self-determination are frequently conducive to maintaining one's sexual autonomy.)

43. Here is as good a place as any to note a different sort of objection that can be raised against prostitution and to ask whether it too might help the radical feminists' case. The suggestion is that selling sex is objectionable because it commodifies something that is not appropriately treated as a commodity. The central text for this objection is Radin's *Contested Commodities*, but similar complaints are raised by others. While I don't wish to rebut these arguments here, I'm not especially moved by them. It is thus perhaps useful to explain why the arguments I'm interested in making are different from an objection to the commodification of sex. In making my case, I have avoided trying to justify the special status that sex has for us, which is, I believe, contingent on many other facts about our form of social life. The point of my objection is that prostitution in our society helps institutionalize unequal access to sex having such special status, as well as unequal sexual autonomy—particularly inequality between men and women, and rich and poor. These inequalities are harmful to the weaker groups and help to perpetuate and reinforce broader inequalities between these people. But as I have just noted, the meaning and significance of sex are subject to change. Were sex to acquire a very different status for us, the problems associated with prostitution could well dissipate. By contrast, the objection to the commodification of sex depends on a view about the special characteristics of sex that distinguish it from ordinary commodities and a worry that if sex is mixed in commerce, it could lose its special characteristics. Whether or not the other difficulties with this argument can be solved, its essentialism about good and bad kinds of sex seems to me unnecessarily contentious. Furthermore, such reliance on essentialist views ought to be methodologically unappealing to radical feminists, whether or not they agree

Looking at the lives of prostitutes in particular, especially the women at the poorer end of the economic spectrum, it is clear that they do not exercise sexual autonomy in their sex work. As a result, they are subject to harms that society ordinarily makes great efforts to protect its members from. Many go into prostitution either because of prior brutalization or sexual abuse or because of homelessness, substance addiction, or financial emergency.[44] While some find the work easy and unobjectionable, even sometimes pleasant, many women find the work degrading or disgusting, their customers vile, and their sense of self-worth to be very low. Many would likely agree with Dworkin's assessment of prostitution in the passage quoted above, which sees prostitution as a dirty job where the dirt is intrinsically linked to a specific sort of male desire to use a woman's body. The fact that they have, in some sense, chosen or allowed others to use their bodies in these ways does not, it seems, mitigate the damage they suffer as a result. These women have traded their sexual autonomy for whatever economic benefit they can get for it: they do not exercise it by using sex as a means of survival.[45]

with its results. So while Radin-style arguments might reach conclusions similar to mine, the premises seem to me more contestable and less hospitable to other feminist concerns. (I am indebted to Leslie Francis for pressing me on this point.)

44. For documentation, see citations provided in n. 12.

45. Some prostitutes' rights advocates have objected that the prohibition of prostitution diminishes prostitutes' sexual autonomy by preventing them from using their bodies as they see fit. Whether or not this is so, the reader should note that nothing I have said so far would provide a rationale for placing restrictions on adult consensual sexual conduct per se when one uses sex for the sake of goods such as pleasure, intimacy, distraction, procreation, or even revenge or notoriety. Now no doubt some people might be attracted to work in prostitution for the sake of the sexual goods they can obtain or provide to others. In such cases—and I think only in such cases—a plausible argument can be made that the prohibition of prostitution decreases to some extent some people's sexual autonomy. Nonetheless, among the many arguments against prohibiting prostitution, we should not be too concerned that it prevents would-be prostitutes from achieving the sexual frequency, variety, and skilled expertise they would otherwise have. Were a person, man or woman, to set out to have a prostitute's sex life without its financial rewards, such action would go well beyond promiscuity, becoming nearly unintelligible. Working as a prostitute is not in general used as a means to these ends in the same way as, say, working as a philosophy teacher is used as a means to further one's philosophical activities—sex just isn't suited for that sort of role in most people's lives. Hence, ruling out one particular way sex can be used is a much smaller intrusion on autonomy than are circumstances where people have little choice other than to engage in sexual activity to earn a decent living.

When one reads Dworkin's description of prostitution, or the accounts of other former prostitutes looking back in horror, one need not suppose that these claims describe the life of every prostitute—even if the authors say so—in order to find in them compelling reasons to intervene against prostitution. Dworkin's depiction of the effect of sex on the prostitute's body is gripping because we do not think the visceral aspects of sexual commerce are just ordinary aspects of doing a job you don't much like. The fact that the harms Dworkin describes are bodily is not incidental; part of the point is that prostitution affects the body directly and integrally, and it stays with the prostitute long after her clients are gone and she has quit the trade. Of course, if we thought that sex was nothing out of the ordinary, then Dworkin's description of prostitution would lose much of its force, becoming something more like the complaint of a laborer who is bored, dirty, sore, and even a bit bloodied at the end of a day. Insofar as we see a special urgency in Dworkin's complaint, we have a reason to hold that sex warrants its own form of autonomy.

Although prohibiting prostitution does not by itself suffice to guarantee or restore sexual autonomy to those who now lack it, the prohibition can play a role in rejecting arrangements that result in its loss. Prohibition not only denies individuals the choice to sell sex for money, it also signals that no one should be expected to make choices about sex just to escape economic hardship. Given the current prohibitions on prostitution, it is within the reach of our present moral understanding to object to such trade-offs on the grounds that a person should be entitled to both a decent standard of living and the freedom to choose his or her sexual activities and partners by their special merits, whatever those may be. We are presently able to see such trade-offs as a problem different in kind from those involved in ordinary economic decision making. The prohibition on prostitution is, as much as anything, a restriction on what kinds of pressures or circumstances society will permit to bear on its members' sexual choices. It thus helps support the assertion of a right to sexual autonomy—something that does not depend on a person's command of economic or political resources—and thereby helps us to see that a prostitute's loss of sexual autonomy is a matter of social injustice.[46]

46. Of course, recognizing this, our society *ought* to be moved to create other economic opportunities for women and others when it turns out that prostitution is the best option available to them. Perhaps it is true that a society unwilling to take this further step should not prohibit prostitution. My point is simply that if prostitution is normalized, it becomes very difficult to see any need to act to create additional economic opportunities—that is, any more than we see such a need when workers in other fields face a constrained choice of jobs.

By contrast, normalizing prostitution would tend to undercut claims that sexual autonomy is a right and instead would make a prostitute's loss of sexual autonomy appear to be a matter of her choice of career—in part, a matter of *just how much* she values her sexual autonomy. But so long as social institutions protect most of us by preventing the sexualization of most kinds of jobs, prostitution would not be just any career. Those who choose to sell their sexual services will work in a very distinctive type of job. It will be a fact about people so employed that they exercise a liberty which is not open to most of us and that they contravene a standard of behavior which most of us uphold. They will also be subject to pressures and restrictions on their activities that cannot be placed on the rest of us. To the extent that, for instance, barriers against workplace sexual harassment help secure sexual autonomy for workers, this kind of protection simply won't extend to those whose economic situation makes prostitution their only viable economic option. Even if the legal prohibition on prostitution is ended, choosing to engage in that occupation will set one apart from other workers on these grounds alone, if on no others. Hence, leaving some people out of the protections most of us enjoy will serve to differentiate them from the rest of us and do so in a way that can reinforce, even seemingly justify, the harms they suffer.

An additional source of evidence for this last claim can be found by looking more broadly at how sexual activity and characteristics frequently serve as markers for a number of different sorts of hierarchical relations, including but not limited to those involving gender. For instance, one of the ways that members of oppressed classes and races can be stereotyped is according to their (presumed) sexual proclivities or activities, on the basis of which law or social norms can be used to impose costs or withhold benefits in ways that reinforce or sustain their oppression. To cite just two examples: in order to project an image of propriety, middle-class women and men in early nineteenth-century England were required to adhere to sexual double standards regarding proper conduct for men and women in order to distinguish themselves from the lower economic classes, who supposedly lacked such morals.[47] Closer to home, the supposed laxity of sexual ethics among African-Americans has provided both a stereotype and a justification for withdrawing welfare and other social benefits from

47. For instance, according to historian Jeffrey Weeks, "Sexual choice was hemmed in by simultaneous emphases on property, the survival (and even accentuation) of a differentiated standard of morality, and the growth of the ideology of 'respectability', with all its class connotations" (*Sex, Politics and Society*, 2d ed. [New York: Longman, 1989], pp. 26–27).

impoverished African-American communities in the last twenty years.[48] Thus sexual practices and qualities manifest a tendency to serve as defining characteristics, or "codings," not just of genders but also of other kinds of hierarchically defined groups. It is hard to say whether this sort of hierarchical coding of sexual activity can be avoided. But so long as sex and sexuality are invested with a high degree of significance, we will need to be wary that the roles of client and seller in prostitution may support and reinforce various forms of social oppression. Even if gender domination were miraculously to end, the kinds of roles established in prostitution may serve to support other equally unjust forms of social hierarchy.[49]

48. For one discussion of this phenomenon, see Patricia Hill Collins, *Black Feminist Thought*, 2d ed. (New York: Routledge, 2000), chap. 4.

49. In this spirit, we might consider whether the claims made in this article are as relevant to the situation of male prostitutes as they are to female prostitutes. There is no short and satisfactory answer to this question, but a list of differences and similarities between male and female prostitution might provide some insights. On the one hand, it is clear that male prostitution does not reinforce or reproduce so insidious an image of male sexuality in general as female prostitution seems to generate. This can perhaps be explained by several factors. For one thing, the gay-male subcultures in which many of these prostitutes operate are perhaps more tolerant and affirming of prostitution in general, so they may escape, at least locally, much of the stigma that attaches to women prostitutes. Also, the social significance of male prostitution is very different from that of female prostitution. Note, for instance, that there is no common epithet for men comparable in meaning or significance to that of "whore" hurled at a woman. Moreover, the harms associated with female prostitution (before, during, and after) are apparently less prevalent among male prostitutes. Finally, male prostitution has a considerably lower profile in our society than does female prostitution. To the extent that it has much visibility outside of gay-male subcultures, it is mainly because of transvestite prostitutes who work in the guise of women. (It is conceivable, however, that gay-male prostitution does contribute to a picture of what gay-male sexuality is like.) See Garrett Prestage, "Male and Transsexual Prostitution," in *Sex Work and Sex Workers in Australia*, ed. Roberta Perkins, Rachell Sharp, Garrett Prestage, and Frances Lovejoy (Sydney: University of New South Wales Press, 1994), pp. 174–90. For a subjective argument along these lines, see Julian Marlowe, "It's Different for Boys," in Nagle, pp. 141–44. On the other hand, even if male prostitution does not help to reproduce pernicious gender hierarchies, it still frequently reflects other sorts of hierarchy. Of those who become male prostitutes, a disproportionate number bear the marks of poverty, abuse, and rejection. In the trade, many male prostitutes suffer harms similar to those suffered by women, especially if they are younger and/or less secure. And one striking manifestation of hierarchy in prostitution has been the development, within sex

In the absence of a prohibition on prostitution, working in prostitution may come to be seen as just a career choice, appropriate for people who prefer other goods to sexual autonomy. But if this can be seen as a career choice, why not also suppose prostitutes *choose* to be treated in the way that Dworkin describes or at least suppose they are adequately compensated for such harms? After all, they're not like us; they do things we wouldn't dream of doing. If this last distinction reflects a mistake or a prejudice, it's connected to a thought many of us would nonetheless be very reluctant to give up: that our sexual choices are deeply important to us, and thus the ability to make them carefully, and autonomously, is something we aim to protect. Although normalizing prostitution might work to the economic advantage of prostitutes, it's not clear that it would or should change our views of the significance of sex or the importance of maintaining autonomy with respect to sexual uses of one's body. It would, however, greatly obscure the extent to which becoming a sex worker means, for many people, trading off control over their sexual choices for some measure of economic security. Normalizing prostitution will, for this group at least, amount to surrendering sexual autonomy as a distinctive good to which they should be entitled as a matter of basic social justice.

The arguments offered here thus set out what I think is the most compelling version of the institutional critique of prostitution. While most of us are fortunate to fall within a variety of social strictures that protect our sexual autonomy from various external forces, prostitutes—even under a normalized prostitution—manifestly lack one of the key protections. They thus tend to be marked as a distinctive group, targeted for certain

tourism, of a female demand from the developed world for male prostitutes in poorer regions, such as the Caribbean. This last suggests that the gendered nature of prostitution is less fixed than are the relations of dominance/subordination between client and provider. For a discussion of this last point, see O'Connell Davidson, pp. 180–83; and Kamala Kempadoo, "Freelancers, Temporary Wives, and Beach Boys: Researching Sex Work in the Caribbean," *Feminist Review* 67 (2001): 39–62. So, although there is within male prostitution a degree of variation similar to that within female prostitution, the above facts suggest that the difference between male and female prostitution may not be as great as my focus on female prostitution might suggest. Such differences as there are, however, seem to derive from the superior social position men, including male homosexuals, enjoy relative to women and from the different role that sex plays in a part of gay-male society. Hence, it seems to me that adding the evidence from male prostitution to my account enriches and ramifies the main argument of this article but does not significantly challenge its principal points. I thank Marcia Baron for pressing me to clarify this subject.

forms of abuse and stigma, and harmed in ways that materially and symbolically contribute to reproducing the social disparities that make some people, especially women, vulnerable from the beginning. These arguments therefore answer the liberal challenge noted above by showing why commerce in sexual activity is especially problematic for social justice and why normalizing and reforming prostitution would fail to address one of the central grounds for the radical feminists' complaint. They also show, I think, why it's important for feminists and others concerned with justice to pay explicit attention to this special sort of autonomy when evaluating and reforming our society's institutions and practices.

CHAPTER SEVENTEEN

Markets in Women's Sexual Labor*

DEBRA SATZ

☾

There is a widely shared intuition that markets are inappropriate for some kinds of human endeavor: that some things simply should not be bought and sold. For example, virtually everyone believes that love and friendship should have no price. The sale of other human capacities is disputed, but many people believe that there is something about sexual and reproductive activities that makes their sale inappropriate. I have called the thesis supported by this intuition the asymmetry thesis.[1] Those who hold the asymmetry thesis believe that markets in reproduction and sex are asymmetric to other labor markets. They think that treating sexual and reproductive capacities as commodities, as goods to be developed and exchanged for a price, is worse than treating our other capacities as commodities. They think that there is something wrong with commercial surrogacy and prostitution that is not wrong with teaching and professional sports.

*I am grateful to the support of a Rockefeller Fellowship at Princeton University's Center for Human Values. Earlier versions of this article were presented at Swarthmore College, Princeton University, and Oxford University. I am grateful to the audiences at these institutions and in particular to Elizabeth Anderson, Michael Blake, C. A. J. Coady, Amy Gutmann, George Kateb, Andrew Koppelman, Arthur Kuflik, Peter de Marneffe, Thomas Pogge, Adam Swift, Stuart White, and Elisabeth Wood. I also thank two anonymous reviewers at *Ethics*, as well as the editors of the journal. Reprinted with permission from *Ethics: An International Journal of Social and Legal Philosophy*, The University of Chicago, Vol. 106, Number 1 (October 1995), pp. 63–85. Copyright © 1995 by The University of Chicago. All rights reserved.

1. Debra Satz, "Markets in Women's Reproductive Labor," *Philosophy and Public Affairs* 21 (1992): 107–31.

The intuition that there is a distinction between markets in different human capacities is a deep one, even among people who ultimately think that the distinction does not justify legally forbidding sales of reproductive capacity and sex. I accept this intuition, which I continue to probe in this article. In particular, I ask: What justifies taking an asymmetric attitude toward markets in our sexual capacities? What, if anything, is problematic about a woman selling her sexual as opposed to her secretarial labor? And, if the apparent asymmetry can be explained and justified, what implications follow for public policy?

In this article, I sketch and criticize two popular approaches to these questions. The first, which I call the economic approach, attributes the wrongness of prostitution to its consequences for efficiency or welfare. The important feature of this approach is its treatment of sex as a morally indifferent matter: sexual labor is not to be treated as a commodity if and only if such treatment fails to be efficient or welfare maximizing. The second, the "essentialist" approach, by contrast, stresses that sales of sexual labor are wrong because they are inherently alienating or damaging to human happiness. In contrast to these two ways of thinking about the immorality of prostitution, I will argue that the most plausible support for the asymmetry thesis stems from the role of commercialized sex and reproduction in sustaining a social world in which women form a subordinated group. Prostitution is wrong insofar as the sale of women's sexual labor reinforces broad patterns of sex discrimination. My argument thus stresses neither efficiency nor sexuality's intrinsic value but, rather, equality. In particular, I argue that contemporary prostitution contributes to, and also instantiates, the perception of women as socially inferior to men.

On the basis of my analysis of prostitution's wrongness, there is no simple conclusion as to what its legal status ought to be. Both criminalization and decriminalization may have the effect of exacerbating the inequalities in virtue of which I claim that prostitution is wrong. Nonetheless, my argument does have implications for the form of prostitution's regulation, if legal, and its prohibition and penalties, if illegal. Overall, my argument tends to support decriminalization.

The argument I will put forward here is qualified and tentative in its practical conclusions, but its theoretical point is not. I will argue that the most plausible account of prostitution's wrongness turns on its relationship to the pervasive social inequality between men and women. If, in fact, no causal relationship obtains between prostitution and gender inequality, then I do not think that prostitution is morally troubling.[2] This

2. What would remain troubling would be the miserable and unjust background circumstances in which much prostitution occurs. That is, if there were

is a controversial claim. In my evaluation of prostitution, consideration of the actual social conditions which many, if not most, women face plays a crucial role. It will follow from my analysis that male prostitution raises distinct issues and is not connected to injustice in the same way as female prostitution.

On my view, prostitution is not wrong irrespective of its cultural and economic context. Moreover, prostitution is a complex phenomenon. I begin, accordingly, with the question, Who is a prostitute?

WHO IS A PROSTITUTE?

While much has been written on the history of prostitution, and some empirical studies of prostitutes themselves have been undertaken, the few philosophers writing on this subject have tended to treat prostitution as if the term referred to something as obvious as "table."[3] But it does not. Not only is it hard to draw a sharp line between prostitution and practices which look like prostitution, but as historians of the subject have emphasized, prostitution today is also a very different phenomenon from earlier forms of commercial sex.[4] In particular, the idea of prostitution as a specialized occupation of an outcast and stigmatized group is of relatively recent origin.[5]

While all contemporary prostitutes are stigmatized as outsiders, prostitution itself has an internal hierarchy based on class, race, and gender. The majority of prostitutes—and all those who walk the streets—are poor. The majority of streetwalkers in the United States are poor black women. These women are a world apart from prostitution's upper tier. Consider three cases: a streetwalker in Boston, a call girl on Park Avenue,

gender equality between the sexes but a substantial group of very poor men and women were selling sex, this would indeed be troubling. We should be suspicious of any :labor contract entered into under circumstances of desperation.

3. Laurie Shrage, "Should Feminists Oppose Prostitution?" *Ethics* 99 (1989): 347–61, is an important exception. See also her new book, *Moral Dilemmas of Feminism: Prostitution, Adultery and Abortion* (New York: Routledge, 1994).

4. The fact that monetary exchange plays a role in maintaining many intimate relationships is a point underscored ey George Bernard Shaw in *Mrs. Warren's Profession* (New York: Garland, 1981).

5. Compare Judith Walkowitz, *Prostitution and Victorian Society* (Cambridge: Cambridge University Press, 1980); Ruth Rosen, *Prostitution in America: 1900–1918* (Baltimore: Johns Hopkins University Press, 1982); B. Hobson, *Uneasy Virtue. The Politics of Prostitution and the American Reform Tradition* (Chicago: University of Chicago Press, 1990).

and a male prostitute in San Francisco's tenderloin district. In what way do these three lives resemble one another? Consider the three cases:

1. A fourteen-year-old girl prostitutes herself to support her boyfriend's heroin addiction. Later, she works the streets to support her own habit. She begins, like most teenage streetwalkers, to rely on a pimp for protection. She is uneducated and is frequently subjected to violence in her relationships and with her customers. She also receives no social security, no sick leave or maternity leave, and—most important—no control as to whether or not she has sex with a man. The latter is decided by her pimp.

2. Now imagine the life of a Park Avenue call girl. Many call girls drift into prostitution after "run of the mill promiscuity," led neither by material want nor lack of alternatives.[6] Some are young college graduates, who upon graduation earn money by prostitution while searching for other jobs. Call girls can earn between $30,000 and $100,000 annually. These women have control over the entire amount they earn as well as an unusual degree of independence, far greater than in most other forms of work. They can also decide who they wish to have sex with and when they wish to do so.[7] There is little resemblance between their lives and that of the Boston streetwalker.

3. Finally, consider the increasing number of male prostitutes. Most male prostitutes (but not all) sell sex to other men.[8] Often the men who buy such sex are themselves married. Unfortunately, there is little information on male prostitutes; it has not been well studied as either a historical or a contemporary phenomenon.[9] What we do know suggests that like their female counterparts, male prostitutes cover the economic spectrum.

6. John Decker, *Prostitution: Regulation and Control* (Littleton, Colo.: Rothman, 1979), p. 191.

7. Compare Harold Greenwald, *The Elegant Prostitute: A Social and Psychoanalytic Study* (New York: Walker, 1970), p. 10.

8. For discussion of male prostitutes who sell sex to women, see H. Smith and B. Van der Horst, "For Women Only—How It Feels to Be a Male Hooker," *Village Voice* (March 7, 1977). Dictionary and common usage tends to identify prostitutes with women. Men who sell sex to women are generally referred to as "gigolos," not "prostitutes." The former term encompasses the sale of companionship as well as sex.

9. Male prostitutes merit only a dozen pages in John Decker's monumental study of prostitution. See also D. Drew and J. Drake, *Boys for Sale: A Sociological Study of Boy Prostitution* (Deer Park, N.Y.: Brown Book Co., 1969); D. Deisher, "Young Male Prostitutes," *Journal of American Medical Association* 212 (1970): 1661–66; Gita Sereny, *The Invisible Children: Child Prostitution in America, West Germany and Great Britain* (London: Deutsch, 1984). I am grateful to Vincent DiGirolamo for bringing these works to my attention.

Two important differences between male and female prostitutes are that men are more likely to work only part time and that they are not generally subject to the violence of male pimps; they tend to work on their own.

Are these three cases distinct? Many critics of prostitution have assumed that all prostitutes were women who entered the practice under circumstances which included abuse and economic desperation. But that is a false assumption: the critics have mistaken a part of the practice for the whole.[10] For example, although women who walk the streets are the most visible, they constitute only about 20 percent of the prostitute population in the United States.[11]

The varying circumstances of prostitution are important because they force us to consider carefully what we think may be wrong with prostitution. For example, in the first case, the factors which seem crucial to our response of condemnation are the miserable background conditions, the prostitute's vulnerability to violence at the hands of her pimp or client, her age, and her lack of control over whether she has sex with a client. These conditions could be redressed through regulation without forbidding commercial sexual exchanges between consenting adults.[12] The second class of prostitution stands in sharp contrast. These women engage in what seems to be a voluntary activity, chosen among a range of decent alternatives. Many of these women sell their sexual capacities without coercion or regret. The third case rebuts arguments that prostitution has no other purpose than to subordinate women.

In the next section, I explore three alternative explanations of prostitution's wrongness, which I refer to respectively as economic, essentialist, and egalitarian.

10. Compare Kathleen Barry, *Female Sexual Slavery* (New York: Avon, 1979). If we consider prostitution as an international phenomenon, then a majority of prostitutes are desperately poor and abused women. Nevertheless, there is a significant minority who are not. Furthermore, if prostitution were legalized, it is possible that the minimum condition of prostitutes in at least some countries would be raised.

11. Priscilla Alexander, "Prostitution: A Difficult Issue for Feminists," in *Sex Work: Writings by Women in the Sex Industry*, ed. P. Alexander and F. Delacoste (Pittsburgh: Cleis, 1987).

12. Moreover, to the extent that the desperate background conditions are the problem it is not apparent that outlawing prostitution is the solution. Banning prostitution may only remove a poor woman's best option: it in no way eradicates the circumstances which led her to such a choice. See M. Radin, "Market-Inalienability," *Harvard Law Review* 100 (1987): 1849–1937, on the problem of the "double bind."

WHAT IS WRONG WITH PROSTITUTION?

The Economic Approach

Economists generally frame their questions about the best way to distribute a good without reference to its intrinsic qualities. They tend to focus on the quantitative features of a good and not its qualities.[13] Economists tend to endorse interference with a market in some good only when the results of that market are inefficient or have adverse effects on welfare.

An economic approach to prostitution does not specify a priori that certain sales are wrong: no act of commodification is ruled out in advance.[14] Rather, this approach focuses on the costs and benefits that accompany such sales. An economic approach to contracts will justify inalienability rules—rules which forbid individuals from entering into certain transactions—in cases where there are costly externalities to those transactions and in general where such transactions are inefficient. The economic approach thus supports the asymmetry thesis when the net social costs of prostitution are greater than the net social costs incurred by the sale of other human capacities.

What are the costs of prostitution? In the first place, the parties to a commercial sex transaction share possible costs of disease and guilt.[15] Prostitution also has costs to third parties: a man who frequents a prostitute dissipates financial resources which might otherwise be directed to his family; in a society which values intimate marriage, infidelity costs a man's wife or companion in terms of mistrust and suffering (and therefore prostitution may sometimes lead to marital instability); and prostitutes often have diseases which can be spread to others. Perhaps the largest

13. Sometimes the qualitative aspects of a good have quantitative effects and so for that reason need to be taken into account. It is difficult, e.g., to establish a market in used cars given the uncertainties of ascertaining their qualitative condition. Compare George Akerlof, "The Market for Lemons: Qualitative Uncertainty and the Market Mechanism," *Quarterly Journal of Economics* 84 (1970): 488–500.

14. For an attempt to understand human sexuality as a whole through the economic approach, see Richard Posner, *Sex and Reason* (Cambridge, Mass.: Harvard University Press, 1992).

15. Although two-thirds of prostitutes surveyed say that they have no regrets about choice of work. Compare Decker, pp. 165–66. This figure is hard to interpret, given the high costs of thinking that one has made a bad choice of occupation and the lack of decent employment alternatives for many prostitutes.

third-party costs to prostitution are "moralisms":[16] many people find
the practice morally offensive and are pained by its existence. (Note that
'moralisms' refers to people's preferences about moral issues and not to
morality as such.)

The economic approach generates a contingent case for the asymmetry thesis, focusing on prostitution's "moral" costs in terms of public
opinion or the welfare costs to prostitutes or the population as a whole
(e.g., through the spread of diseases). Consideration of the limitations
on sexual freedom which can be justified from a welfare standpoint can
be illuminating and forces us to think about the actual effects of sexual
regulations.[17] Nevertheless, I want to register three objections to this
approach to justifying the asymmetry thesis.

First, and most obvious, both markets and contractual exchanges function within a regime of property rights and legal entitlements. The economic approach ignores the background system of distribution within
which prostitution occurs. Some background systems, however, are unjust. How do we know whether prostitution itself is part of a morally
acceptable system of property rights and entitlements?

Second, this type of approach seems disabled from making sense of
distinctions between goods in cases where these distinctions do not seem
to reflect mere differences in the net sum of costs and benefits. The sale of
certain goods seems to many people simply unthinkable—human life, for
example. While it may be possible to justify prohibitions on slavery by
appeal to costs and benefits (and even count moralisms in the sum), the
problem is that such justification makes contingent an outcome which
reasonable people do not hold contingently. It also makes little sense,
phenomenologically, to describe the moral repugnance people feel toward
slavery as "just a cost."[18]

Let me elaborate this point. There seems to be a fundamental difference
between the "goods" of my person and my external goods, a difference
whose nature is not completely explained by appeal to information fail-
ures and externalities. "Human capital" is not just another form of capital.
For example, my relationship with my body and my capacities is more
intimate than my relationship with most external things. The economic
approach fails to capture this distinction.

---

16. See Guido Calabresi and A. Douglas Melamed, "Property Rules, Liability
Rules and Inalienability: One View of the Cathedral," *Harvard Law Review* 85
(1972): 1089–1128.

17. Economic analysis fails to justify the laws we now have regarding prostitution. See below.

18. See Radin, pp. 1884 ff.

Richard Posner—one of the foremost practitioners of the economic approach to law—illustrates the limits of the economic approach when he views a rapist as a "sex thief."[19] He thus overlooks the fact that rape is a crime of violence and assault.[20] He also ignores the qualitative differences between my relationship with my body and my car. But that there are such differences is obvious. The circumstances in which I sell my capacities have a much more profound effect on who I am and who I become—through effects on my desires, capacities, and values—than the circumstances in which I sell my Honda Civic. Moreover, the idea of sovereignty over body and mind is closely related to the idea of personal integrity, which is a crucial element of any reasonable scheme of liberty. The liberty to exercise sovereignty over my car has a lesser place in any reasonable scheme of liberties than the liberty to be sovereign over my body and mind.[21]

Third, some goods seem to have a special status which requires that they be shielded from the market if their social meaning or role is to be preserved. The sale of citizenship rights or friendship does not simply produce costs and benefits: it transforms the nature of the goods sold. In this sense, the market is not a neutral mechanism of exchange: there are some goods whose sale transforms or destroys their initial meaning.

These objections resonate with objections to prostitution for which its wrongness is not adequately captured by summing up contingent welfare costs and benefits. These objections resonate with moralist and egalitarian concerns. Below I survey two other types of arguments which can be used to support the asymmetry thesis: (1) essentialist arguments that the sale of sexual labor is intrinsically wrong because it is alienating or contrary to human flourishing and happiness; and (2) my own egalitarian argument that the sale of sex is wrong because, given the background conditions within which it occurs, it tends to reinforce gender inequality. I thus claim that contemporary prostitution is wrong because it promotes injustice, and not because it makes people less happy.

19. Posner, *Sex and Reason*, p. 182. See also R. Posner, "An Economic Theory of the Criminal Law," *Columbia Law Review* 85 (1985): 1193–1231. "The prohibition against rape is to the sex and marriage 'market' as the prohibition against theft is to explicit markets in goods and services" (p. 1199).

20. His approach in fact suggests that rape be seen as a "benefit" to the rapist, a suggestion that I think we should be loathe to follow.

21. I do not mean to claim however that such sovereignty over the body is absolute.

The Essentialist Approach

Economists abstract from the qualities of the goods that they consider. By contrast essentialists hold that there is something intrinsic to the sphere of sex and intimacy that accounts for the distinction we mark between it and other types of labor. Prostitution is not wrong simply because it causes harm; prostitution constitutes a harm. Essentialists hold that there is some intrinsic property of sex which makes its commodification wrong. Specific arguments differ, however, in what they take this property to be. I will consider two popular versions of essentialism: the first stresses the close connection between sex and the self; the second stresses the close connection between sex and human flourishing.[22]

Some feminist critics of prostitution have argued that sexual and reproductive capacities are more crucially tied to the nature of our selves than our other capacities.[23] The sale of sex is taken to cut deeper into the self, to involve a more total alienation from the self. As Carole Pateman puts it, "When a prostitute contracts out use of her body she is thus selling *herself* in a very real sense. Women's selves are involved in prostitution in a different manner from the involvement of the self in other occupations."[24] The realization of women's selfhood requires, on this view, that some of the capacities embodied in their persons, including their sexuality, remain "market-inalienable."[25]

Consider an analogous strategy for accounting for the value of bodily integrity in terms of its relationship to our personhood. It seems right to say that a world in which the boundaries of our bodies were not (more or less) secure would be a world in which our sense of self would be fundamentally shaken. Damage to, and violation of, our bodies affects us in a "deeper" way, a more significant way, than damage to our external property. Robbing my body of a kidney is a violation different in kind than robbing my house of a stereo, however expensive. Distributing kidneys

22. This section draws from and enlarges upon Satz.

23. Prostitution is, however, an issue which continues to divide feminists as well as prostitutes and former prostitutes. On the one side, some feminists see prostitution as dehumanizing and alienating and linked to male domination. This is the view taken by the prostitute organization Women Hurt in Systems of Prostitution Engaged in Revolt (WHISPER). On the other side, some feminists see sex markets as affirming a woman's right to autonomy, sexual pleasure, and economic welfare. This is the view taken by the prostitute organization COYOTE.

24. Carole Pateman, *The Sexual Contract* (Stanford, Calif.: Stanford University Press, 1988), p. 207; emphasis added.

25. The phrase is Radin's.

from healthy people to sick people through a lottery is a far different act than using a lottery to distribute door prizes.[26] But this analogy can only be the first step in an argument in favor of treating either our organs or sexual capacities as market-inalienable. Most liberals think that individual sovereignty over mind and body is crucial for the exercise of fundamental liberties. Thus, in the absence of clear harms, most liberals would reject legal bans on voluntary sales of body parts or sexual capacities. Indeed, the usual justification of such bans is harm to self: such sales are presumed to be "desperate exchanges" that the individual herself would reasonably want to foreclose. American law blocks voluntary sales of individual organs and body parts but not sales of blood on the assumption that only the former sales are likely to be so harmful to the individual that given any reasonable alternative, she herself would refrain from such sales.

Whatever the plausibility of such a claim with respect to body parts, it is considerably weaker when applied to sex (or blood). There is no strong evidence that prostitution is, at least in the United States, a desperate exchange. In part this reflects the fact that the relationship people have with their sexual capacities is far more diverse than the relationship they have with their body parts. For some people, sexuality is a realm of ecstatic communion with another, for others it is little more than a sport or distraction. Some people will find consenting to be sexually used by another person enjoyable or adequately compensated by a wage. Even for the same person, sex can be the source of a range of experiences.

Of course, the point cannot simply be that, as an empirical matter, people have differing conceptions of sexuality. The critics of prostitution grant that. The point is whether, and within what range, this diversity is desirable.[27]

Let us assume, then, in the absence of compelling counterargument, that an individual can exercise sovereignty through the sale of her sexual capacities. Margaret Radin raises a distinct worry about the effects of widespread prostitution on human flourishing. Radin's argument stresses that widespread sex markets would promote inferior forms of personhood. She says that we can see this is the case if we "reflect on what we

26. J. Harris, "The Survival Lottery," *Philosophy* 50 (1975): 81–87.

27. As an example of the ways in which the diversity of sexual experience has been culturally productive, see Lynn Hunt, ed., *The Invention of Pornography* (New York: Zone, 1993). Many of the essays in this volume illustrate the ways in which pornography has historically contributed to broader social criticism.

know now about human life and choose the best from among the conceptions available to us."[28] If prostitution were to become common, Radin argues, it would have adverse effects on a form of personhood which itself is intrinsically valuable. For example, if the signs of affection and intimacy were frequently detached from their usual meaning, such signs might well become more ambiguous and easy to manipulate. The marks of an intimate relationship (physical intimacy, terms of endearment, etc.) would no longer signal the existence of intimacy. In that case, by obscuring the nature of sexual relationships, prostitution might undermine our ability to apply the criteria for coercion and informational failure.[29] Individuals might more easily enter into damaging relationships and lead less fulfilling lives as a result.

Radin is committed to a form of perfectionism which rules out the social practice of prostitution as incompatible with the highest forms of human development and flourishing. But why should perfectionists condemn prostitution while tolerating practices such as monotonous assembly line work where human beings are often mere appendages to machines? Monotonous wage labor, moreover, is far more widespread than prostitution.[30] Can a consistent perfectionist give reasons for differentiating sexual markets from other labor markets?

It is difficult to draw a line between our various capacities such that only sexual and reproductive capacities are essential to the flourishing self. In a money economy like our own, we each sell the use of many human capacities. Writers sell the use of their ability to write, advertisers sell the use of their ability to write jingles, and musicians sell the use of their ability to write and perform symphonies. Aren't these capacities also

---

28. Radin, p. 1884.

29. An objection along these lines is raised by Margaret Baldwin ("Split at the Root: Feminist Discourses of Law Reform," *Yale Journal of Law and Feminism* 5 [1992]: 47–120). Baldwin worries that prostitution undermines our ability to understand a woman's capacity to consent to sex. Baldwin asks, Will a prostitute's consent to sex be seen as consent to a twenty-dollar payment? Will courts determine sentences in rape trials involving prostitutes as the equivalent of parking fine violations (e.g., as another twenty dollar payment)? Aren't prostitutes liable to have their fundamental interests in bodily integrity discounted? I think Baldwin's worry is a real one, especially in the context of the current stigmatization of prostitutes. It could be resolved, in part, by withholding information about a woman's profession from rape trials.

30. Radin is herself fairly consistent in her hostility to many forms of wage labor. She has a complicated view about decommodification in nonideal circumstances which I cannot discuss here.

closely tied to our personhood and its higher capacities?[31] Yet the mere alienation of the use of these capacities, even when widespread, does not seem to threaten personal flourishing.

An alternative version of the essentialist thesis views the commodification of sex as an assault on personal dignity.[32] Prostitution degrades the prostitute. Elizabeth Anderson, for example, discusses the effect of commodification on the nature of sex as a shared good, based on the recognition of mutual attraction. In commercial sex, each party now values the other only instrumentally, not intrinsically. And, while both parties are thus prevented from enjoying a shared good, it is worse for the prostitute. The customer merely surrenders a certain amount of cash; the prostitute cedes her body: the prostitute is thus degraded to the status of a thing. Call this the degradation objection.

I share the intuition that the failure to treat others as persons is morally significant; it is wrong to treat people as mere things. But I am skeptical as to whether this intuition supports the conclusion that prostitution is wrong. Consider the contrast between slavery and prostitution. Slavery was, in Orlando Patterson's memorable phrase, a form of "social death": it denied to enslaved individuals the ability to press claims, to be—in their own right—sources of value and interest. But the mere sale of the use of someone's capacities does not necessarily involve a failure of this kind, on the part of either the buyer or the seller.[33] Many forms of labor, perhaps most, cede some control of a person's body to others. Such control can range from requirements to be in a certain place at a certain time (e.g., reporting to the office), to requirements that a person (e.g., a professional athlete) eat certain foods and get certain amounts of sleep, or maintain good humor in the face of the offensive behavior of others (e.g., airline stewardesses). Some control of our capacities by others does not seem to be ipso facto destructive of our dignity.[34] Whether the purchase of a form

---

31. Also notice that many forms of labor we make inalienable—e.g., bans on mercenaries—cannot be justified by that labor's relationship to our personhood.

32. Elizabeth Anderson, *Value in Ethics and Economics* (Cambridge, Mass.: Harvard University Press, 1993), p. 45.

33. Actually, the prostitute's humanity is a part of the sex transaction itself. Whereas Posner's economic approach places sex with another person on the same scale as sex with a sheep, for many people the latter is not a form of sex at all (*Sex and Reason*). Moreover, in its worst forms, the prostitute's humanity (and gender) may be crucial to the john's experience of himself as superior to her. See Catherine MacKinnon, *Toward a Feminist Theory of the State* (Cambridge, Mass.: Harvard University Press, 1989).

34. Although this statement might have to be qualified in the light of empirical research. Arlie Hochschild, e.g., has found that the sale of "emotional labor" by

of human labor power will have this negative consequence will depend on background social macrolevel and microlevel institutions. Minimum wages, worker participation and control, health and safety regulations, maternity and paternity leave, restrictions on specific performance, and the right to "exit" one's job are all features which attenuate the objectionable aspects of treating people's labor as a mere economic input. The advocates of prostitution's wrongness in virtue of its connection to self-hood, flourishing and degradation have not shown that a system of regulated prostitution would be unable to respond to their worries. In particular, they have not established that there is something wrong with prostitution irrespective of its cultural and historical context.

There is, however, another way of interpreting the degradation objection which draws a connection between the current practice of prostitution and the lesser social status of women.[35] This connection is not a matter of the logic of prostitution per se but of the fact that contemporary prostitution degrades women by treating them as the sexual servants of men. In current prostitution, prostitutes are overwhelmingly women and their clients are almost exclusively men. Prostitution, in conceiving of a class of women as needed to satisfy male sexual desire, represents women as sexual servants to men. The degradation objection, so understood, can be seen as a way of expressing an egalitarian concern since there is no reciprocal ideology which represents men as servicing women's sexual needs. It is to this egalitarian understanding of prostitution's wrongness that I turn in the next section.

The Egalitarian Approach

While the essentialists rightly call our attention to the different relation we have with our capacities and external things, they overstate the nature of the difference between our sexual capacities and our other capacities with respect to our personhood, flourishing, and dignity.[36] They are also insufficiently attentive to the background conditions in which commercial

airline stewardesses and insurance salesmen distorts their responses to pain and frustration (*The Managed Heart: The Commercialization of Human Feeling* [New York: Basic, 1983]).

35. I owe this point to Elizabeth Anderson, who stressed the need to distinguish between different versions of the degradation objection and suggested some lines of interpretation (conversation with author, Oxford University, July 1994).

36. More generally, they raise questions about the desirability of a world in which people use and exploit each other as they use and exploit other natural objects, insofar as this is compatible with Pareto improvements.

sex exchanges take place. A third account of prostitution's wrongness stresses its causal relationship to gender inequality. I have defended this line of argument with respect to markets in women's reproductive labor.[37] Can this argument be extended to cover prostitution as well?

The answer hinges in part on how we conceive of gender inequality. On my view, there are two important dimensions of gender inequality, often conflated. The first dimension concerns inequalities in the distribution of income, wealth, and opportunity. In most nations, including the United States, women form an economically and socially disadvantaged group. The statistics regarding these disadvantages, even in the United States, are grim.

1. *Income inequality.*—In 1992, given equal hours of work, women in the United States earned on average sixty-six cents for every dollar earned by a man.[38] Seventy-five percent of full-time working women (as opposed to 37 percent of full-time working men) earn less than twenty thousand dollars.[39]

2. *Job segregation.*—Women are less likely than men to fill socially rewarding, high-paying jobs. Despite the increasing entrance of women into previously gender-segregated occupations, 46 percent of all working women are employed in service and administrative support jobs such as secretaries, waitresses, and health aides. In the United States and Canada, the extent of job segregation in the lowest-paying occupations is increasing.[40]

3. *Poverty.*—In 1989, one out of five families was headed by women. One-third of such women-headed families live below the poverty line, which was $13,359 for a family of four in 1990.[41] In the United

37. See Satz, *op. cit.*.

38. U.S. Department of Labor, Women's Bureau (Washington, D.C.: Government Printing Office, 1992).

39. D. Taylor, "Women: An Analysis," in *Women: A World Report* (London: Methuen, 1985). Taylor reports that while on a world scale women "perform nearly twothirds of all working hours [they] receive only one tenth of the world income and own less than one percent of world resources."

40. J. David-McNeil, "The Changing Economic Status of the Female Labor Force in Canada," in *Towards Equity: Proceedings of a Colloquium on the Economic Status of Women in the Labor Market*, ed. Economic Council of Canada (Ottawa: Canadian Government Publication Centre, 1985).

41. S. Rix, ed., *The American Woman, 1990–91* (New York: Norton, 1990), cited in Woman's Action Coalition, ed., *WAC Stats: The Facts about Women* (New York: New Press, 1993), p. 41.

States, fathers currently owe mothers 24 billion dollars in unpaid child support.[42]

4. *Unequal division of labor in the family.*—Within the family, women spend disproportionate amounts of time on housework and rearing children. According to one recent study, wives employed full time outside the home do 70 percent of the housework; full-time housewives do 83 percent.[43] The unequal family division of labor is itself caused by and causes labor market inequality: given the lower wages of working women, it is more costly for men to participate in household labor.

Inequalities in income and opportunity form an important part of the backdrop against which prostitution must be viewed. While there are many possible routes into prostitution, the largest number of women who participate in it are poor, young, and uneducated. Labor market inequalities will be part of any plausible explanation of why many women "choose" to enter into prostitution.

The second dimension of gender inequality does not concern income and opportunity but status.[44] In many contemporary contexts, women are viewed and treated as inferior to men. This inferior treatment proceeds via several distinct mechanisms.

1. *Negative stereotyping.*—Stereotypes persist as to the types of jobs and responsibilities a woman can assume. Extensive studies have shown that people typically believe that men are more dominant, assertive, and instrumentally rational than women. Gender shapes beliefs about a person's capacities: women are thought to be less intelligent than their male equals.[45]

2. *Unequal power.*—Men are able asymmetrically to sanction women. The paradigm case of this is violence. Women are subjected to greater amounts of violence by men than is the reverse: every fifteen seconds a woman is battered in the United States. Battering causes more injury

42. Report of the Federal Office of Child Support Enforcement, 1990.

43. Rix, ed. Note also that the time women spend doing housework has not declined since the 1920s despite the invention of labor saving technologies (e.g., laundry machines and dishwashers).

44. My views about this aspect of gender inequality have been greatly clarified in discussions and correspondence with Elizabeth Anderson and Elisabeth Wood during 1994.

45. See Paul Rosenkrantz, Susan Vogel, Helen Bees, Inge Broverman, and David Broverman, "Sex-Role Stereotypes and Self-Concepts in College Students," *Journal of Consulting and Clinical Psychology* 32 (1968): 286–95.

(excluding deaths) to women than car accidents, rape, and muggings combined.[46] Four million women a year are physically assaulted by their male partners.[47]

3. *Marginalization.*—People who are marginalized are excluded from, or absent from, core productive social roles in society—roles which convey self-respect and meaningful contribution.[48] At the extremes, marginalized women lack the means for their basic survival: they are dependent on state welfare or male partners to secure the basic necessities of life. Less severely marginalized women lack access to central and important social roles. Their activities are confined to peripheral spheres of social organization. For example, the total number of women who have served in Congress since its inception through 1992 is 134. The total number of men is 11,096. In one-third of governments worldwide, there are no women in the decision-making bodies of the country.[49]

4. *Stigma.*—A woman's gender is associated, in some contexts, with stigma, a badge of dishonor. Consider rape. In crimes of rape, the complainant's past behavior and character are central in determining whether a crime has actually occurred. This is not true of other crimes: "mail fraud" (pun intended) is not dismissed because of the bad judgment or naivete of the victims. Society views rape differently, I suggest, because many people think that women really want to be forced into sex. Women's lower status thus influences the way that rape is seen.

Both forms of inequality—income inequality and status inequality—potentially bear on the question of prostitution's wrongness. Women's decisions to enter into prostitution must be viewed against the background of their unequal life chances and their unequal opportunities for income and rewarding work. The extent to which women face a highly constrained range of options will surely be relevant to whether, and to what degree, we view their choices as autonomous. Some women may actually loathe

46. L. Heise, "Gender Violence as a Health Issue" (Violence, Health and Development Project, Center for Women's Global Leadership, Rutgers University, New Brunswick, NJ., 1992).
47. L. Heise, "Violence against Women: The Missing Agenda," in *Women's Health: A Global Perspective* (New York: Westview, 1992), cited in Woman's Action Coalition, ed., p. 55. More than one-third of female homicide victims are killed by their husbands or boyfriends.
48. I am indebted here to the discussion of Iris Young in *Justice and the Politics of Difference* (Princeton, NJ.: Princeton University Press, 1990).
49. Ruth Leger Sivard, *Women . . . a World Survey* (Washington, D.C.: World Priorities, 1985).

or judge as inferior the lives of prostitution they "choose." Economic inequality may thus shape prostitution.

We can also ask, Does prostitution itself shape employment inequalities between men and women? In general, whenever there are significant inequalities between groups, those on the disadvantageous side will be disproportionately allocated to subordinate positions. What they do, the positions they occupy, will serve to reinforce negative and disempowering images of themselves. In this sense, prostitution can have an effect on labor-market inequality, associating women with certain stereotypes. For example, images reinforced by prostitution may make it less likely for women to be hired in certain jobs. Admittedly the effect of prostitution on labor-market inequality, if it exists at all, will be small. Other roles which women disproportionately occupy—secretaries, housecleaners, babysitters, waitresses, and saleswomen—will be far more significant in reinforcing (as well as constituting) a gender-segregated division of labor.

I do not think it is plausible to attribute to prostitution a direct causal role in income inequality between men and women. But I believe that it is plausible to maintain that prostitution makes an important and direct contribution to women's inferior social status. Prostitution shapes and is itself shaped by custom and culture, by cultural meanings about the importance of sex, about the nature of women's sexuality and male desire.[50]

If prostitution is wrong it is because of its effects on how men perceive women and on how women perceive themselves. In our society, prostitution represents women as the sexual servants of men. It supports and embodies the widely held belief that men have strong sex drives which must be satisfied—largely through gaining access to some woman's body. This belief underlies the mistaken idea that prostitution is the "oldest" profession, since it is seen as a necessary consequence of human (i.e., male) nature. It also underlies the traditional conception of marriage, in which a man owned not only his wife's property but her body as well. It should not fail to startle us that until recently, most states did not recognize the possibility of "real rape" in marriage.[51] (Marital rape remains legal in two states: North Carolina and Oklahoma.)

---

50. Shrage ("Should Feminists Oppose Prostitution?") argues that prostitution perpetuates the following beliefs which oppress women: (1) the universal possession of a potent sex drive; (2) the "natural" dominance of men; (3) the pollution of women by sexual contact; and (4) the reification of sexual practice.

51. Susan Estrich, *Real Rape* (Cambridge, Mass.: Harvard University Press, 1987).

Why is the idea that women must service men's sexual needs an image of inequality and not mere difference? My argument suggests that there are two primary, contextual reasons:

First, in our culture, there is no reciprocal social practice which represents men as serving women's sexual needs. Men are gigolos and paid escorts—but their sexuality is not seen as an independent capacity whose use women can buy. It is not part of the identity of a class of men that they will service women's sexual desires. Indeed, male prostitutes overwhelmingly service other men and not women. Men are not depicted as fully capable of commercially alienating their sexuality to women; but prostitution depicts women as sexual servants of men.

Second, the idea that prostitution embodies an idea of women as inferior is strongly suggested by the high incidence of rape and violence against prostitutes, as well as the fact that few men seek out or even contemplate prostitutes as potential marriage partners. While all women in our society are potential targets of rape and violence, the mortality rates for women engaged in streetwalking prostitution are roughly forty times higher than that of nonprostitute women.[52]

My suggestion is that prostitution depicts an image of gender inequality, by constituting one class of women as inferior. Prostitution is a "theater" of inequality—it displays for us a practice in which women are subordinated to men. This is especially the case where women are forcibly controlled by their (male) pimps. It follows from my conception of prostitution that it need not have such a negative effect when the prostitute is male. More research needs to be done on popular images and conceptions of gay male prostitutes, as well as on the extremely small number of male prostitutes who have women clients.

The negative image of women who participate in prostitution, the image of their inferior status, is objectionable in itself. It constitutes an important form of inequality—unequal status—based on attitudes of superiority and disrespect. Unfortunately, this form of inequality has largely been ignored by political philosophers and economists who have focused instead on inequalities in income and opportunity. Moreover, this form of inequality is not confined to prostitutes. I believe that the negative image of women prostitutes has third party effects: it shapes and influences the way women as a whole are seen. This hypothesis is, of course, an empirical

52. Baldwin, p. 75. Compare the Canadian Report on Prostitution and Pornography; also M. Silbert, "Sexual Assault on Prostitutes," research report to the *National Center for the Prevention and Control of Rape*, November 1980, for a study of street prostitutes in which 70 percent of those surveyed reported that they had been raped while walking the streets.

one. It has not been tested largely because of the lack of studies of men who go to prostitutes. Most extant studies of prostitution examine the behavior and motivations of the women who enter into the practice, a fact which itself raises the suspicion that prostitution is viewed as "a problem about the women who are prostitutes ... [rather than] a problem about the men who demand to buy them."[53] In these studies, male gender identity is taken as a given.

To investigate prostitution's negative image effects on female prostitutes and on women generally we need research on the following questions: (1) What are the attitudes of men who visit women prostitutes toward prostitutes? How do their attitudes compare with the attitudes of men who do not visit prostitutes toward women prostitutes? (2) What are the attitudes of men who visit women prostitutes toward women generally? What are the attitudes of men who do not visit women prostitutes toward women generally? (3) What are the attitudes of women toward women prostitutes? (4) What are the attitudes of the men and women involved in prostitution toward themselves? (5) Given the large proportion of African-American women who participate in prostitution, in what ways does prostitution contribute to male attitudes toward these women? (6) Does prostitution contribute to or diminish the likelihood of crimes of sexual violence? (7) What can we learn about these questions through cross-national studies? How do attitudes in the United States about women prostitutes compare with those in countries with more egalitarian wage policies or less status inequality between men and women?

The answers to these questions will reflect social facts about our culture. Whatever plausibility there is to the hypothesis that prostitution causally contributes to gender status inequality, it gains this plausibility from its surrounding cultural context.

I can imagine hypothetical circumstances in which prostitution would not have a negative image effect, where it could mark a reclaiming of women's sexuality. Margo St. James and other members of Call Off Your Old Tired Ethics (COYOTE) have argued that prostitutes can function as sex therapists, fulfilling a legitimate social need as well as providing a source of experiment and alternative conceptions of sexuality and gender.[54] I agree that in a different culture, with different assumptions about men's and women's gender identities, prostitution might not have

---

53. Carole Pateman, "Defending Prostitution: Charges against Ericsson," *Ethics* 93 (1983): 561–65, p. 563.

54. See also, S. Schwartzenbach, "Contractarians and Feminists Debate Prostitution," *New York University Review of Law and Social Change* 18 (1990–91): 103–30.

unequalizing effects. But I think that St. James and others have minimized the cultural stereotypes that surround contemporary prostitution and their power over the shape of the practice. Prostitution, as we know it, is not separable from the larger surrounding culture which marginalizes, stereotypes, and stigmatizes women. Rather than providing an alternative conception of sexuality, I think that we need to look carefully at what men and women actually learn in prostitution. I do not believe that ethnographic studies of prostitution would support COYOTE's claim that prostitution contributes to images of women's dignity and equal standing.

If, through its negative image of women as sexual servants of men, prostitution reinforces women's inferior status in society, then it is wrong. Even though men can be and are prostitutes, I think that it is unlikely that we will find such negative image effects on men as a group. Individual men may be degraded in individual acts of prostitution: men as a group are not.

Granting all of the above, one objection to the equality approach to prostitution's wrongness remains. Is prostitution's negative image effect greater than that produced by other professions in which women largely service men, for example, secretarial labor? What is special about prostitution?

The negative image effect undoubtedly operates outside the domain of prostitution. But there are two significant differences between prostitution and other gender-segregated professions.

First, most people believe that prostitution, unlike secretarial work, is especially objectionable. Holding such moral views of prostitution constant, if prostitution continues to be primarily a female occupation, then the existence of prostitution will disproportionately fuel negative images of women.[55] Second, and relatedly, the particular image of women in prostitution is more of an image of inferiority than that of a secretary. The image embodies a greater amount of objectification, of representing the prostitute as an object without a will of her own. Prostitutes are far more likely to be victims of violence than are secretaries: as I mentioned, the mortality rate of women in prostitution is forty times that of other women. Prostitutes are also far more likely to be raped: a prostitute's "no" does not, to the male she services, mean no.

My claim is that, unless such arguments about prostitution's causal role in sustaining a form of gender inequality can be supported, I am not persuaded that something is morally wrong with markets in sex. In particular, I do not find arguments about the necessary relationship between commercial sex and diminished flourishing and degradation convincing.

55. I owe this point to Arthur Kuflik.

If prostitution is wrong, it is not because of its effects on happiness or personhood (effects which are shared with other forms of wage-labor); rather, it is because the sale of women's sexual labor may have adverse consequences for achieving a significant form of equality between men and women. My argument for the asymmetry thesis, if correct, connects prostitution to injustice. I now turn to the question of whether, even if we assume that prostitution is wrong under current conditions, it should remain illegal.

SHOULD PROSTITUTION BE LEGALIZED?

It is important to distinguish between prostitution's wrongness and the legal response that we are entitled to make to that wrongness. Even if prostitution is wrong, we may not be justified in prohibiting it if that prohibition makes the facts in virtue of which it is wrong worse, or if its costs are too great for other important values, such as autonomy and privacy. For example, even if someone accepts that the contemporary division of labor in the family is wrong, they may still reasonably object to government surveillance of the family's division of household chores. To determine whether such surveillance is justified, we need know more about the fundamental interests at stake, the costs of surveillance and the availability of alternative mechanisms for promoting equality in families. While I think that there is no acceptable view which would advocate governmental surveillance of family chores, there remain a range of plausible views about the appropriate scope of state intervention and, indeed, the appropriate scope of equality considerations.[56]

It is also important to keep in mind that in the case of prostitution, as with pornography and hate speech, narrowing the discussion of solutions

56. For example, does the fact that racist joke telling reinforces negative stereotypes and perpetuates racial prejudice and inequality justify legal bans on such joke telling? What are the limits on what we can justifiably use the state to do in the name of equality? This is a difficult question. I only note here that arguments which justify state banning of prostitution can be consistent with the endorsement of stringent protections for speech. This is because speech and expression are arguably connected with basic fundamental human interests—with forming and articulating conceptions of value, with gathering information, with testifying on matters of conscience—in a way that prostitution (and some speech, e.g., commercial speech) is not. Even if we assume, as I think we should, that people have fundamental interests in having control over certain aspects of their bodies and lives, it does not follow that they have a fundamental interest in being free to sell themselves, their body parts, or any of their particular capacities.

to the single question of whether to ban or not to ban shows a poverty of imagination. There are many ways of challenging existing cultural values about the appropriate division of labor in the family and the nature of women's sexual and reproductive capacities—for example, education, consciousness-raising groups, changes in employee leave policies, comparable worth programs, etc. The law is not the only way to provide women with incentives to refrain from participating in prostitution. Nonetheless, we do need to decide what the best legal policy toward prostitution should be.

I begin with an assessment of the policy which we now have. The United States is one of the few developed Western countries which criminalizes prostitution.[57] Denmark, the Netherlands, West Germany, Sweden, Switzerland, and Austria all have legalized prostitution, although in some of these countries it is restricted by local ordinances.[58] Where prostitution is permitted, it is closely regulated.

Suppose that we accept that gender equality is a legitimate goal of social policy. The question is whether the current legal prohibition on prostitution in the United States promotes gender equality. The answer I think is that it clearly does not. The current legal policies in the United States arguably exacerbate the factors in virtue of which prostitution is wrong.

The current prohibition on prostitution renders the women who engage in the practice vulnerable. First, the participants in the practice seek assistance from pimps in lieu of the contractual and legal remedies which are denied them. Male pimps may protect women prostitutes from their customers and from the police, but the system of pimp-run prostitution has enormous negative effects on the women at the lowest rungs of prostitution. Second, prohibition of prostitution raises the dilemma of the "double bind": if we prevent prostitution without greater redistribution

57. Prostitution is legalized only in several jurisdictions in Nevada.
58. These countries have more pay equity between men and women than does the United States. This might be taken to undermine an argument about prostitution's role in contributing to income inequality. Moreover, women's status is lower in some societies which repress prostitution (such as those of the Islamic nations) than in those which do not (such as those of the Scandinavian nations). But given the variety of cultural, economic, and political factors and mechanisms which need to be taken into account, we need to be very careful in drawing hasty conclusions. Legalizing prostitution might have negative effects on gender equality in the United States, even if legal prostitution does not correlate with gender inequality in other countries. There are many differences between the United States and European societies which make it implausible to think that one factor can alone be explanatory with respect to gender inequality.

of income, wealth, and opportunities, we deprive poor women of one way—in some circumstances the only way—of improving their condition.[59] Analogously, we do not solve the problem of homelessness by criminalizing it. Furthermore, women are disproportionately punished for engaging in commercial sex acts. Many state laws make it a worse crime to sell sex than to buy it. Consequently, pimps and clients ("johns") are rarely prosecuted. In some jurisdictions, patronizing a prostitute is not illegal. The record of arrests and convictions is also highly asymmetric. Ninety percent of all convicted prostitutes are women. Studies have shown that male prostitutes are arrested with less frequency than female prostitutes and receive shorter sentences. One study of the judicial processing of 2,859 male and female prostitutes found that judges were more likely to find defendants guilty if they were female.[60]

Nor does the current legal prohibition on prostitution unambiguously benefit women as a class because the cultural meaning of current governmental prohibition of prostitution is unclear. While an unrestricted regime of prostitution—a pricing system in women's sexual attributes— could have negative external consequences on women's self-perceptions and perceptions by men, state prohibition can also reflect a view of women which contributes to their inequality. For example, some people support state regulation because they believe that women's sexuality is for purposes of reproduction, a claim tied to traditional ideas about women's proper role.

There is an additional reason why banning prostitution seems an inadequate response to the problem of gender inequality and which suggests a lack of parallel with the case of commercial surrogacy. Banning prostitution would not by itself—does not—eliminate it. While there is reason to think that making commercial surrogacy arrangements illegal or unenforceable would diminish their occurrence, no such evidence exists about prostitution. No city has eliminated prostitution merely through criminalization. Instead, criminalized prostitution thrives as a black market activity in which pimps substitute for law as the mechanism for enforcing contracts. It thereby makes the lives of prostitutes worse than they might

59. Radin, pp. 1915 ff.
60. J. Lindquist et al., "Judicial Processing of Males and Females Charged with Prostitution," *Journal of Criminal Justice* 17 (1989): 277–91. Several state laws banning prostitution have been challenged on equal protection grounds. These statistics support the idea that prostitution's negative image effect has disproportionate bearing on male and female prostitutes.

otherwise be and without clearly counteracting prostitution's largely negative image of women. If we decide to ban prostitution, these problems must be addressed. If we decide not to ban prostitution (either by legalizing it or decriminalizing it), then we must be careful to regulate the practice to address its negative effects. Certain restrictions on advertising and recruitment will be needed in order to address the negative image effects that an unrestricted regime of prostitution would perpetuate. But the current regime of prostitution has negative effects on the prostitutes themselves. It places their sexual capacities largely under the control of men. In order to promote women's autonomy, the law needs to ensure that certain restrictions—in effect, a Bill of Rights for Women—are in place.[61]

1. No woman should be forced, either by law or by private persons, to have sex against her will. (Recall that it is only quite recently that the courts have recognized the existence of marital rape.) A woman who sells sex must be able to refuse to give it; she must not be coerced by law or private persons to perform.

2. No woman should be denied access, either by law or by private persons, to contraception or to treatment for sexually transmitted diseases, particularly AIDS, or to abortion (at least in the first trimester).

3. The law should ensure that a woman has adequate information before she agrees to sexual intercourse. The risks of venereal and other sexually transmitted diseases, the risks of pregnancy, and the laws protecting a woman's right to refuse sex should all be generally available.

4. Minimum age of consent laws for sexual intercourse should be enforced. These laws should ensure that woman (and men) are protected from coercion and do not enter into sexual relationships until they are in a position to understand what they are consenting to.

5. The law should promote women's control over their own sexuality by prohibiting brokerage. If what is wrong with prostitution is its relation to gender inequality, then it is crucial that the law be brought to bear primarily on the men who profit from the use of women's sexual capacities.

Each of these principles is meant to establish and protect a woman's right to control her sexual and reproductive capacities and not to give

61. In this section, I have benefited from reading Cass Sunstein, "Gender Difference, Reproduction and the Law" (University of Chicago Law School, 1992, unpublished manuscript). Sunstein believes that someone committed to gender equality will, most likely, advocate a legal ban on prostitution.

control of these capacities to others. Each of these principles is meant to protect the conditions for women's consent to sex, whether commercial or not. Each of these principles also seeks to counter the degradation of women in prostitution by mitigating its nature as a form of female servitude. In addition, given that a woman's choices are shaped both by the range of available opportunities and by the distribution of entitlements in society, it is crucial to attend to the inferior economic position of women in American society and those social and economic factors which produce the unequal life chances of men and women.

CONCLUSION

If the arguments I have offered here are correct, then prostitution is wrong in virtue of its contributions to perpetuating a pervasive form of inequality. In different circumstances, with different assumptions about women and their role in society, I do not think that prostitution would be especially troubling—no more troubling than many other labor markets currently allowed. It follows, then, that in other circumstances, the asymmetry thesis would be denied or less strongly felt. While the idea that prostitution is intrinsically degrading is a powerful intuition (and like many such intuitions, it persists even after its proponents undergo what Richard Brandt has termed "cognitive therapy," in which errors of fact and inference are corrected), I believe that this intuition is itself bound up with well-entrenched views of male gender identity and women's sexual role in the context of that identity.[62] If we are troubled by prostitution, as I think we should be, then we should direct much of our energy to putting forward alternative models of egalitarian relations between men and women.

---

62. Richard B. Brandt, *A Theory of the Good and the Right* (Oxford: Clarendon, 1979).

Obscene Division

Feminist Liberal Assessments of Prostitution Versus Feminist Liberal Defenses of Pornography

JESSICA SPECTOR

INTRODUCTION: FEMINISM, LIBERALISM, AND THE SEX INDUSTRY[1]

A review of the academic literature on both prostitution and pornography reveals a striking difference: while pornography has become a popular topic in the academy, there is still comparatively little written about prostitution *per se*. In philosophical circles, prostitution and pornography are thought to raise different sets of questions: pornography is discussed in the context of free speech issues and postmodern thought about subjectivity, while prostitution is typically only discussed (if at all) in the context of paternalism and gender oppression.

Historically, this has much to do with the development of classical liberal interest in speech issues and traditionally feminist interest in concerns about women's labor, set against a back-drop of changes in technology and the legal concept of obscenity.[2] But bound up with the differing legal,

---

1. I am grateful to Scott Anderson, Anne Eaton, Mark Gutzmer, Martha Nussbaum, and Debra Satz for their comments on earlier versions of this article.

2. "Obscene. Objectionable or offensive to accepted standards of decency. Basic guidelines for trier of fact in determining whether a work which depicts or describes sexual conduct is obscene is whether the average person, applying contemporary community standards would find that the work, taken as a whole, appeals to the prurient interest, whether the work depicts or describes, in a patently

social, and academic histories of prostitution and pornography,[3] there is a philosophical problem concerning the *justification* for their continuing different treatment, particularly by feminist liberals interested in women's sexual liberation and empowerment. Facing the different theoretical treatment of the two activities, and confronting the realities of the lives of those involved in them, we should wonder whether it makes sense to continue to compartmentalize real-person pornography as a speech issue relating to questions of obscenity, separate from discussions of the acts involved in prostitution.

The goal of this article is to tackle head-on the problem of the disparity between many feminist liberal assessments of prostitution and a frequent feminist liberal defense of live-actor pornography, and to suggest a remedy for it. The aim is both theoretical and practical: to understand and address some weaknesses in a common strain of many feminist liberal defenses of (certain aspects of) the sex industry, and to make some suggestions about how feminist liberalism might better address the conditions of the lives of the least well-off women. The theoretical points are made in the service of the ultimately practical end. For in order to improve the lives of a category of women typically left out of feminist liberal analysis, that analysis needs a change in focus and in tools.

offensive way, sexual conduct specifically defined by the applicable state law, and whether the work, taken as a whole, lacks serious literary, artistic, political, or scientific value." *Black's Law Dictionary*, 1990, 6th ed. (St. Paul: West Group), p. 1076. In addition to being a definitive source for Anglo-American legal terminology and phrasing, *Black's* is sometimes itself cited as legal authority. [Originally published as *Dictionary of Law, Containing Definitions of Terms and Phrases of American and English Jurisprudence, Ancient and Modern*, 1891, by Henry Campbell Black (1st edition).]

See also the Model Penal Code article on obscenity, which covers commercial material only: "Material is obscene if, considered as a whole, its predominant appeal is to prurient interest, that is, a shameful or morbid interest, in nudity, sex or excretion, and if in addition it goes substantially beyond customary limits of candor in describing or representing such matters." American Law Institute, Model Penal Code §251.4(1).Commentaries published 1980.

3. Despite its close connection to legally legitimate parts of the sex industry, prostitution remains illegal everywhere in the United States, except certain counties in Nevada. A popular misconception is that prostitution is legal in Las Vegas. In fact, it is illegal in all Nevada counties over a certain population; and streetwalking is illegal everywhere in the State. Currently, brothels are the only legal form of prostitution in Nevada, and they are legal only in ten out of Nevada's seventeen counties. For an account of working conditions inside Nevada's legal brothels, see Alexa Albert, 2001, *Brothel: Mustang Ranch and Its Women* (New York: Random House).

My argument about how to effect this change has two parts. The first concerns the degree to which the disparity between many feminist liberal treatments of prostitution and defenses of pornography are based on differing conceptions of freedom and the self, and the role that sex and sexuality play in those conceptions. The second part of my argument concerns the contrast I identify between the respective focus on worker and on consumer in many feminist defenses of the legal legitimacy of prostitution and live-actor pornography. I make the case that even though feminist liberal defenses of pornography tend to offer more satisfying accounts of the self as socially "situated" than do feminist liberal treatments of prostitution, they do so while ignoring the very worker who is supposed to be of such primary concern to the feminist liberal in the case of prostitution.

There are three central debates in the academic literature on prostitution and pornography: (1) the issue of harm and the possibility of consent (2) the question of prohibition, and (3) the liberating value versus oppressive function of the practices. In what follows, I argue that these debates are *not* (as many would have it) simply about sexual mores, but are more fundamentally disagreements about the relation between individual autonomy and society, as well as varying conceptions of the good life, and involve different perspectives on whose interests are relevant for discussion. I begin, in the first half of the paper, by sketching the outlines of the feminist debates about harms caused by the sex industry (See "THE QUESTION OF HARM AND THE POSSIBILITY OF CONSENT"). Then I deal with the individualism at the heart of the feminist liberal defense of the legitimacy of prostitution (See "LIBERAL INDIVIDUALISM"), and discuss the more Aristotelian approach feminist liberalism tends to take in its defense of pornography (See "HUMAN FLOURISHING AND THE VALUE OF EXPRESSIVE LIBERTY"). In the second half of the paper, I suggest a change in approach to both topics, combining an interest in the person whose body is needed for the production of live-actor pornography with attention to the social nature of self and its implications for appeals to individual consent (See "SOMEBODY SOMEWHERE").

This analysis has the potential to change the landscape of current thought not only about the sex industry, but also about the self and bodily commodification more generally, making room for a view that is both more complex and more practical, that looks at the context and harm of certain sorts of voluntary acts *for the participants*. As long as we are unclear about what, or who, is relevant to a discussion of commercial sex, there is little hope that we can be clear and consistent about other areas of bodily commodification where the sale of certain kinds of bodily services or products is considered suspect, such as surrogacy, cloning, stem cell research, etc. And if we should change our focus in feminist liberal investigations of commercial sex from consumer to the person whose body or labor makes the commercial product possible, then that may have implications for the realms of bodily commodification that involve even more complex questions about whose interests are relevant to the discussion.[4] Therefore, we begin with sex.

THE QUESTION OF HARM AND THE POSSIBILITY OF CONSENT

Traditionally, the central issue in academic discussions of the sex industry has been the question of harm and the possibility of consent, and following upon this, arguments about the merits of prohibition versus decriminalization or legalization.[5] Defenders of the legitimacy of prostitution and pornography argue that either nobody is harmed by them, or that the participants consent to these harms as part of an economic

4. I have in mind here questions about surrogacy versus the sale of eggs and sperm. But there are many other issues involving reproductive commodification that also share the same conceptually dicey ground as the issues of prostitution and pornography.

5. Legalization is distinguished from decriminalization. Advocates for legalization support government regulation of prostitution, whether as a job like any other or as a special kind of work. For instance, see Martha Nussbaum, 1999, "'Whether From Reason or Prejudice': Taking Money for Bodily Services." In *Sex and Social Justice*, pp. 276–98 (NY: Oxford). Advocates for decriminalization support removing criminal penalties for prostitutes, although not always for their customers or pimps. For an argument for the latter, see Margaret Jane Radin, 1996, *Contested Commodities*, pp. 134–36 (Cambridge, MA: Harvard University Press). Sweden recently instituted such policies. Many advocates for sex worker rights also support decriminalization rather than legalization because they are skeptical of any government involvement in prostitutes' lives. For instance, see Norma Jean Almodovar, Winter 1999, "For Their Own Good: The Results of the Prostitution Laws As Enforced By Cops, Politicians, and Judges." *Hastings Women's Law Journal* 10:1, pp. 113–114; and Pat Califia, 2000, *Public Sex: The Culture of Radical Sex*, 2nd ed., pp. 261–68 (San Francisco: Cleis).). Almost anybody who professes feminist concerns argues for the legal *status quo*. However, some have argued that the solution to the problem of harm requires, as a first step, equal enforcement of the laws that are already on the books. See Julie Lefler, Winter 1999, "Shining the Spotlight on Johns: Moving toward Equal Treatment of Male Customers and Female Prostitutes." *Hastings Women's Law Journal* 10:1, esp. pp. 16–35; and Dorchen A. Leidholdt, "The Sexual Exploitation of Women and Girls: A Violation of Human Rights." In Drucilla Cornell, ed., 2000, *Feminism and Pornography* (Oxford: Oxford), esp. p. 422.

trade-off that rational adults should be free to make. Opponents of the two activities argue that they are indeed harmful, and that the kinds of harms involved are not the kind to which one rationally consents. The view here is that consent is meaningless or absent in cases where what is being commodified is a form of abuse.

In the case of prostitution, the harm question primarily concerns both women who have sex for money as well as women in general. Possible harm to male prostitutes is typically subsumed under the harm to women, or dismissed as either not significant enough for attention or nonexistent, given the different gender dynamics involved in male versus female prostitution.[6] The harms to women who engage in prostitution themselves are thought to be direct: the woman who has sex for money is physically hurt and socially denigrated. These harms are so great that it is thought that she cannot reasonably be said to consent to them. She may be forced into the exchange by a need for money, or coerced by noneconomic means. MacKinnon calls the idea that women meaningfully submit to such harms "the myth of consent,"[7] arguing that consent is missing in the case of prostitution because harms like death and physical violence do not have a legitimate price, let alone the paltry price charged by street prostitutes in urban America, or the even more paltry amount left to them after pimps take their cut.[8]

6. For instance, see Scott Anderson, July 2002, "Prostitution and Sexual Autonomy: Making Sense of the Prohibition of Prostitution," esp.p. 49, *Ethics* 112, pp. 748–780; Carole Pateman, 1988, *The Sexual Contract* (Stanford: Stanford University Press), ch. 7, esp. pp. 192–94; Dorchen Leidholdt, 1993, "Prostitution: A Violation of Women's Human Rights," *Cardoza Women's Law Journal* 1, pp. 138–39; Catharine MacKinnon, 1993, "Prostitution and Civil Rights," *Michigan Journal of Gender and Law* 1, pp. 13–31; and Debra Satz, October 1995, "Markets in Women's Sexual Labor," *Ethics* 106:1, p. 64. Although MacKinnon calls the prostitution of women and girls "the paradigm" case, and says: "prostitution is overwhelmingly done to women by men," she asks us to remember that men and boys are also prostituted. For sociological examination of the problem of harm to male prostitutes in particular, see two English studies: Donald J. West and Buz de Villiers, 1993, *Male Prostitution* (London: Harrington Park Press); and Barbara Gibson, 1995, *Male Order: Life Stories from Boys Who Sell Sex,* (London: Cassell), esp. pp. 154–72.

7. MacKinnon makes this point in a variety of ways in a variety of places, but it is centrally the focus of Catharine MacKinnon (April 25, 2000) "Trafficking and the Myth of Consent," given as a public lecture at Trinity College, Hartford, CT.

8. MacKinnon's point is that, in fact, the consideration (i.e. payment) involved in the typical prostitution "contract" is too paltry to even be considered legitimate consideration. This is part of a larger argument she makes about the contract issues

For critics of prostitution *per se* (rather than of the poverty that under-girds the practice), such harms are of a different sort than harms resulting from other labor. This view is often confused with (and criticized as) a form of essentialism about a woman's sexual identity. But it need not be. Pateman makes the harms case by asking us to consider why there is, in social fact, a demand for commodified sex with women.[9] The prostitute's gender is pivotal, according to Pateman, who argues that prostitution is a "problem about women," not just a matter of commodified sex, in that it involves the purchase of a right over a woman's body. This is important for Pateman, because it means that prostitution is not simply a type of or-dinary wage labor. According to her, prostitution is unlike other physical labor, because it involves the unrestricted right to use a woman's body, not for the production of some further end, but for its own sake. As an in-herently gendered exchange, the prostitution contract is an instantiation of an over-arching sexual contract that trades patriarchal sexual rights over women. So, because sex and power are linked in this way, we cannot treat prostitution as just another form of wage labor.[10]

This position, often called "radical feminist," maintains that prostitu-tion is not merely the fallout of poor economic conditions, but is the *ur*-form of women's oppression.[11] A system of gender oppression corrupts the "free market" and prevents equal exchange between men and women, particularly regarding anything related to sex.[12] According to this view,

---

in prostitution. Typically, in contract law, what matters is the *fact* of consideration, not its adequacy. Inadequate consideration may be taken as evidence of undue influence, which could void a contract, but it is not an element in a case to rescind. MacKinnon's larger argument addresses this.

9. Carole Pateman, April 1983, "Defending Prostitution: Charges Against Ericsson," *Ethics* 93, pp. 561–65, p. 563.

10. Carole Pateman, "What's wrong with Prostitution?" *op. cit.*

11. Representatives of the radical feminist position include Margaret Baldwin, 1992, "Split at the Root: Prostitution and Feminist Discourses of Law Reform," *Yale Journal of Law and Feminism* 5, pp. 47–120; Kathleen Barry, 1995, *The Pros-titution of Sexuality* (New York: New York University Press); Andrea Dworkin, 1997, "Prostitution and Male Supremacy," in *Life and Death* (New York: Free Press), pp. 138–216; Evelina Giobbe, "Prostitution: Buying the Right to Rape," in Ann Wolbert Burgess, ed., 1991, *Rape and Sexual Assault III* (New York: Garland), pp. 143–60; Catharine MacKinnon, "Prostitution and Civil Rights," *op. cit.*; Christine Overall, Summer 1992, "What's Wrong with Prostitution? Evaluating Sex Work," *Signs,* pp. 705–24; and Carole Pateman, *The Sexual Con-tract, op. cit.*

12. See Kathleen Barry, "The State: Patriarchal Laws & Prostitution," from *The Prostitution of Sexuality, op. cit.*, p. 246.

the problem with arguments aimed simply at the economic coercion in prostitution is that they draw attention away from the gendered nature of this sex-power exchange.

Beyond the direct harms to the prostitutes from this sex-power exchange, the feminist critic charges that the practice of prostitution harms women generally.[13] If men think they possess a right to purchase dominion over a woman's body, then this cannot but affect the entire social and economic climate for women.[14] Some have even argued that part of the problem with the focus on consent is that, by misleading us into thinking that prostitution is the kind of thing one meaningfully chooses, it turns prostitution in particular into a problem about "other women" rather than a problem with gender and power relations for all women. If a woman chooses a life of prostitution, then "the rest of us" can distance ourselves from the harms that befall her. Baldwin charges that abstract academic arguments about prostitution perpetuate this "us/them, good-woman/whore" dichotomy, turning the problem of harm into an intellectual one about the conditions for consent.[15]

This critique of the meaningfulness of consent (or its sheer absence) goes to the heart of the feminist liberal view that prostitution can enable the disadvantaged to gain control of their own labor power. The standard liberal line on activities that are thought to be disreputable, degrading, or harmful is that it is up to the participants to decide whether or not they want to engage in them. So, even though prostitution might be

13. Catharine MacKinnon, "Prostitution and Civil Rights," *op. cit.*, pp. 30–31. MacKinnon's view is that the harms of pornography bring the harms of prostitution to all women, since "pornography is an arm of prostitution." For an early economic argument for how prostitution harms women generally, see Elizabeth Blackwell, "Preface and Chapter II: The Trade in Women," *Essays in Medical Sociology* pp. 135–41 and 155–74. [Originally in *The Human Element in Sex*, London: J.A. Churchill, 1884] (Interestingly, Blackwell happens to have been the first woman M.D.)

14. In his argument against the normalization of prostitution, Anderson runs a thought experiment about the bad consequences of treating prostitution as a legitimate form of work. See Scott Anderson, "Prostitution and Sexual Autonomy: Making Sense of the Prohibition of Prostitution," *op. cit.*

15. Margaret Baldwin, "Split at the Root: Prostitution & Feminist Discourses of Law Reform," *op. cit.* See also Margaret Baldwin, Winter 1999, "'A Million Dollars and An Apology:' Prostitution and Public benefits Claims," *Hastings Women's Law Journal* 10:1, pp. 189–224, where Baldwin makes the same general point, but without the emphasis on the power of anecdote versus abstract argument.

harmful (as are many forms of wage labor), it should be left as a matter of individual choice.

Many feminist liberals even acknowledge the gendered nature of the practice of prostitution in their defenses of the possibility of consent,[16] holding that prostitution is something women disproportionately do because our society generally fetishizes women's sexuality. But this, according to the liberal line, does not mean that sexual wage labor must be illegitimate. Indeed, the view goes, if we attend to past puritanical judgments about the appropriate sphere of women's labor, we see that prostitution is much like other traditionally stigmatized occupations for women. What is really needed, according to this view, is a sustained comparison between prostitution and other forms of wage labor, to try to identify precisely what might be troubling about prostitution, or rather, about the way that it is practiced. Schwarzenbach likens the prostitute as physical laborer to a dancer, while Nussbaum compares prostitution to a number of jobs that skew female, including domestic servant and masseuse, and Shrage points out the similar way that child care workers and prostitutes tend to come from disadvantaged socio-economic classes.[17] The point of such analogies is to show that the wage labor involved in prostitution is not so different from other traditionally women's wage labor in being potentially physically damaging and historically seen as degrading. Accordingly, since we treat other such jobs as legitimate choices, we should similarly treat prostitution. For feminist liberalism, it is the worst form of paternalism to preclude the choices of women whose options are already limited.[18]

16. The representatives of the feminist liberal position that I focus on in the following discussion are Laurie Shrage, January 1989, "Should Feminists Oppose Prostitution," *Ethics* 99:2, pp. 347–61; Sibyl Schwarzenbach, 1991, "Contractarians and Feminists Debate Prostitution," *NYU Review of Law and Social Change*, pp. 103–13; and Martha Nussbaum, "'Whether From Reason or Prejudice': Taking Money for Bodily Services," in *Sex and Social Justice op. cit.* I focus on these authors because they offer three very different and compelling arguments in defense of the legitimacy of prostitution that all maintain the possibility of consent, while still being sensitive to harms caused by the practice.

17. Sibyl Schwarzenbach, "Contractarians and Feminists Debate Prostitution," *op. cit.*, pp 114; Martha Nussbaum, "'Whether From Reason or Prejudice': Taking Money for Bodily Services," *op. cit.*, pp. 276–98; and Laurie Shrage, "Should Feminists Oppose Prostitution," *op. cit.*, esp. pp. 358–59.

18. I am grateful to Martha Nussbaum for our expanded discussions of these points. As she has rightly pointed out to me, her ultimate assessment of prostitution is not a romantic one—in fact, she describes the prostitute as more often

LIBERAL INDIVIDUALISM

So the radical feminist critique of prostitution is both an argument about the harms caused by prostitution and an argument about the fact (or sometimes, about the possibility) of consent to such harms, while the feminist liberal defense of the legitimacy of prostitution is an argument that the harms are not of a different kind than the harms caused by other jobs and, as such, can be subject to meaningful consent. This is not a disagreement to be resolved here (if anywhere). But it is one that reveals a deeper disagreement not only about the status of women, but also about the social elements of personhood and the conditions necessary for freedom. The radical and the liberal may agree about the pervasive nature of women's sexual oppression, and even about the generally deplorable conditions of the lives of many prostitutes, but they disagree fundamentally about the influence such oppression must have on the possibility of the self's integrity and the power of choice.

This is partly because the two views tend to differ concerning what constitutes free choice. The radical feminist sees the prostitute who appears to "consent" to prostitution as so affected by systematic gender oppression that her choices are distorted—and even her sense of self shaped—by it. Whereas the liberal believes in the individual's ability to transcend her oppressive circumstances somewhat by making a rational decision to do the best she can, considering. And to choose to do the best one can, considering, is to be free. The choices one has might be limited, and the circumstances one finds oneself in might be terrible, but one still can act as a rational agent, deliberating over options and choosing a course of action. Recently, Martha Nussbaum has critiqued what she terms this Kantian view of the individual moral agent, explicitly advocating a more Aristotelian conception of the self. But this is in the context of a critique of the Kantian-Rawlsian view of the family, not in the context of her discussion of prostitution. This is important, for I am about to argue that liberal feminist treatments of prostitution and pornography (including Nussbaum's) tend to employ different models of the self: Lockean in one case, and more Aristotelian in the other.[19]

According to Locke, the capacity for self-determination rests upon a proper prudential concern for oneself and the ability to rationally choose

---

akin to the capitalist wage slave than the creative artist. One of her points is that what feminism needs to do is discuss the conditions of the wage slave *generally*.

19. See Martha Nussbaum, 2000, "The Future of Feminist Liberalism," *Proceedings and Addresses of the American Philosophical Association* 74, pp. 49–79.

actions that further one's own good.[20] This Enlightenment conception of freedom as self directed (autonomous), prudential rational action is implicit in the liberal defense of the prostitute's ability to choose to sell sex and meaningfully consent to what may be degrading or dangerous work conditions. Liberals need not defend the form most prostitution takes (in the United States or elsewhere) in order to think that consent can still be meaningful. What is important to the liberal is that the *individual* surveys options, and reasons practically about which course of action will further her own ends. The feminist liberal may admit that a person's social context and relations are important, but it is still ultimately the individual person, or self, and her rational choices that are key here, rather than the good for a group of people, or a conception of human flourishing. That is why the feminist liberal defender of the legitimacy of prostitution focuses so heavily on the harms caused by the stigma surrounding prostitution. The social stigma oppresses the individual, preventing the exercise, without suffering social repercussions, of will concerning the use of one's own body. The stigma thus prevents the individual from expressing and exploring her own choices.

This view of the person, or self, as a discrete individual whose choices and actions come from within and can be analyzed somewhat independently of social practice, has of course been criticized from the Enlightenment onward. Much feminist liberal discussion of prostitution is sensitive to this and concerned with the problem of how to ensure that the individual's choices really are free and that a life of prostitution is truly a viable one. But despite a sensitivity to the influence on the self of social practices and context—typically expressed as a recognition of the constraining power of social stigma—feminist defenses of prostitutes' free choice to engage in the sex trade still tend to be based on a foundation of liberal individualism.[21] This is not only something that many feminist

20. A person who has the capacity to rationally reflect, deliberate, and adopt a course of action is *self*-determined. Without the capacity for self-determination, the agent cannot bind herself to an authorized course of action, so cannot be obligated or capable of law. See John Locke, 1975, *An Essay Concerning Human Understanding*, edited by Peter H. Nidditch (Oxford University Press) esp. p. 2.21 "Of Power," pp. 233–87.

21. For instance, compare Martha Nussbaum's (2000) critique of adaptive preferences and list of human capabilities as central political goals in *Women and Human Development: The Capabilities Approach* (Cambridge: Cambridge University Press) with her discussion of prostitution in particular in "'Whether From Reason or Prejudice': Taking Money for Bodily Services," *op. cit.* As mentioned above, Nussbaum explicitly critiques the Kantian-Rawlsian conception of the isolated individual self. But that critique makes no mention of the case of

liberals admit, but also something they are proud of: championing the rights and interests of the individuals who work in prostitution in order to secure for these individuals the same choices and economic opportunities as other individuals.

A main point of disagreement between the radical feminist critics of prostitution and feminist liberal defenders of its legitimacy is over this issue of an *individual*'s ability and right to choose a type of life that may not generally be considered a good one. Feminist liberals worry that sexual conservatism lies at the core of the social stigma surrounding prostitution, and are concerned that the feminist critics of prostitution play into the sexual conservatives' hands by limiting the type of sexual expression open to women. They argue that individuals with sexual desires and preferences outside of the romanticized norm are marginalized and their identities reduced to their sexual activities. Shrage and Schwarzenbach both claim that this tendency to identify persons with their sexual activities (e.g. slut, prude, lesbian, etc.) contributes to the stigmatization of women who exchange sex for money.[22] *But their suggested solution is not to give up the idea of a "true self;" rather, their suggested solution is to recognize that one's sexual activities do not in fact constitute that "true self."* One has a body, with which one engages in sexual activity, but the self, or person, is not that body or those activities, whether those activities are thought to liberate or constrain.

Notice here that for many feminist liberals, the entire discussion of prostitution rests on questions about the agency of the individual prostitute. Whether the issue is economic coercion, sexual expression, or differing notions of the good life, feminist liberalism focuses on the woman who is exchanging sex for money, and on the conditions of her labor. Her agency is typically thought to be isolable and separately analyzable—even while social stigma is recognized as a powerful influence—and the discussion is phrased in the terms of her options and choices, constrained though they might be. Yet this is not the case when it comes to pornography. As we shall see, this disparate treatment of prostitution and pornography reveals a tension in the feminist liberal view between an individualistic perspective and a more socially constructed view of agency—a tension coincident with a shift in focus from worker to consumer, and from

prostitution and, I maintain, her explicit defense of prostitution seems to involve a more Lockean than Aristotelian conception of the self.

22. Both Schwarzenbach and Shrage discuss the "reification" of one's sexual identity. See Schwarzenbach, "Contractarians and Feminists Debate Prostitution," *op. cit.*, p. 117; and Shrage, "Should Feminists Oppose Prostitution," *op. cit.*, esp. p. 356.

concern with the conditions of labor to concern with the liberty interests associated with speech.

HUMAN FLOURISHING AND THE VALUE OF
EXPRESSIVE LIBERTY

While the radical feminist concern in the case of live-actor pornography remains both the woman who is exchanging sex for money (whether directly or indirectly), and the condition of women generally, the feminist liberal focus shifts away from the individual worker and the conditions of her labor, to the consumer and the consumer's relation to the product of pornography. In the case of pornography, the traditional or classical liberal (in some degree of contrast with the feminist liberal) tells us that we need not watch it, read it, or listen to it if we do not like it. As rational adults, we make our own choices about the private activities in which we wish to engage, and any attempt to curtail those choices impinges on our freedom. According to the classical liberal, much pornography may be disturbing, but we can, at the least, turn away from it and, at the most, make our views heard in the free public realm so that we can convince others that it is disturbing and that they should turn away from it too.

This view has often been criticized by feminists of all stripes for predicating too much on a distinction between a private realm of free choice and a public one of free debate. As many have argued, this distinction between a private realm and a public one is problematic because it itself reinforces the gender hierarchy that is at issue.[23] The "private" is typically construed as the realm of the personal and the intimate. But if the worry is that the personal and the intimate are implicated in and affected by pornography in harmful ways, then it does no good to close off discussion of those harms through appeals to privacy.

However, the problem with privacy appeals is even more fundamental than this point about the gendered nature of "the private." The concept itself is too loose to form the basis of any solid defense of the liberal position. The classical liberal view is concerned with protecting privacy without being clear about the *sense* of private. If "private" means anything that is not the law's business, then it is circular to argue that the law should steer clear of the private realm. If "private" means what happens at home or what is not exposed to view, then further argument is required to show

23. For a sustained argument of this sort, see especially Susan Moller Okin, 1989, *Justice, Gender, and the Family* (New York: Basic Books).

that the law *should* stay out of it. Because of the looseness of the concept of "privacy," simply appealing to privacy is inadequate as a defense of the liberal position.

Yet, as problematic as the privacy defense is, it at least is meant to be broad enough to defend the legitimacy of both prostitution and pornography. It is when the more sophisticated feminist liberal accounts attempt to defend the legitimacy of pornography, including live-actor pornography, by means other than the privacy appeal that their approach to the two activities splits apart, shifting from an Enlightenment model of personhood and agency—with its emphasis on individual autonomy and rationality— to a view of the self as more socially embedded and fluid.

Many feminist liberals recognize the problems with the privacy appeal and seek to defend pornography's legitimacy by other means, as a form of expression representative of ideas rather than defending it as a legitimate type of bodily commodification. Instead of arguing that the sexual sphere of rational adults should be off limits to the law, people like Sally Tisdale argue that pornography's value is in what it teaches us about ourselves.[24] The "us" here is of course the viewer. Tisdale, for instance, is careful to note that (live-actor) pornography may have harmful effects on male viewers' attitudes about women, but she thinks this is balanced by the educational benefits it has for women like her.[25] The view is that pornography is fantasy, and as such, it comes wholly from within.[26] So, rather than being harmful to women, pornography can be liberating, enabling women to control their own sexuality.

This sort of defense often employs a legal model of obscenity to interpret pornography, treating the live-actor pornography product as a representation of ideas in the same way as a work of fiction.[27] For the liberal

---

24. Sallie Tisdale, 1989, "Talk Dirty to Me," in Alan Soble, ed., *The Philosophy of Sex* (New York: Rowman and Littlefield), p. 278.

25. Sallie Tisdale, "Talk Dirty to Me," *op. cit.*, p. 276.

26. Sallie Tisdale, "Talk Dirty to Me," *op. cit.*, p. 273. For a similar argument about the importance of pornography's being *fantasy*, but a very different conclusion about the significance of such fantasy, see Beverley Brown, "A Feminist Interest in Pornography—Some Modest Proposals" in *m/f*, 5/6 London: 1981. pp. 5–18.

27. Most of this discussion is focused on US obscenity law. The US Supreme Court has ruled that First Amendment protections of free speech and expression do not cover obscenity. This sense of 'obscenity' always refers to sex, and is defined by the Miller test, based on the 1973 Supreme Court ruling in Miller versus California that held that, in determining whether speech or expression could be labeled obscene, courts must consider all of three criteria:

defender of pornography's legitimacy, the difference between textual or virtual pornography and pornography that uses real, live human bodies is not significant. Even pornography that shows real people having real sex is considered to be part of the realm of ideas and fantasy. Thus, live-actor pornography is assimilated to speech with the additional defense that our *sexual identities* are partially formed by exposure to breadth and variety in such speech. Whether or not real people are laboring to produce the product is beside the point: what matters is the consumer's relation to the product of that labor.

Such a view of the value of pornography as sexual expression is compelling. If women's sexuality is constrained in a male-dominated culture, then it seems liberating to reclaim that sexuality and acknowledge one's own sexual identity. On this view, pornography can help "us" do that by showing us the good, the bad, and the ugly in our culture's sexual tropes and stereotypes. After all, knowledge is power, and the more we know about what arouses us and what does not, the more we can own and control our own sexual identities.

Joshua Cohen offers a more intellectual version of this argument, responding to the call for legal restrictions on live-actor pornography, by trying to make some space for societal interests in protecting pornography.[28] Cohen argues that the harm pornography does can be combated in a way that preserves sexual expression. He suggests treating some pornography as a subcategory of obscenity,[29] thus leaving room for discussions of its worth in the context of decisions about what might be regulated.[30] This is important, according to Cohen, because expression itself is part of liberty. So live-actor pornography is completely assimilated to speech

(1) whether the average person, applying contemporary community standards, would find that the work, taken as a whole, appeals to the prurient interest;

(2) whether the work depicts/describes, in a patently offensive way, sexual conduct specifically defined by applicable state law; and

(3) whether the work, taken as a whole, lacks serious literary, artistic, political, or scientific value.

See *Miller versus California 413 US 15 (1973)*. But see also the British *Obscene Publications Act*s (specifically 1959 and 1964) and the Limitations clause of the *Canadian Charter of Rights and Freedoms* (Clause One).

28. Joshua Cohen, 1996, "Freedom, Equality, Pornography," in Austin Sarat and Thomas Kearns, eds., *Justice and Injustice in Law and Legal Theory* (Ann Arbor: University of Michigan Press), pp. 99–137.

29. See reference, above, to *Black's Law Dictionary* and Model Penal Code for definitions of obscenity, under US law.

30. See Joshua Cohen, "Freedom, Equality, Pornography," *op. cit.*, p. 134.

and defended as involving distinct liberty interests for its producers and society at large.

This is the classic argument Mill gives for free speech in general in *On Liberty*. There Mill argues that one of the reasons that free speech is so important is because we need to hear a variety of opinions in order to know what is true and to hold true beliefs for the right reasons. The great thing about human judgment, according to Mill, is that it can be corrected—but only if we have access to a range of views. So free expression, of good or bad views, is helpful.

But Mill (and Cohen, to some extent) go beyond this argument based on the value of free expression for us as individuals searching for truth. Mill, the classical liberal, and some contemporary feminist liberals following him, argue that a free marketplace of ideas enables one to develop one's capacities and become a more fully realized person by providing information to guide choices and explore one's sense of self. What is needed for this is not just negative freedom, but a variety of ideas and experiences to have and choose from. Indeed, for Mill, this is what makes us human; such "experiments in living" help us figure out the best way of life for each of us.[31] And in a community with others, we learn from their choices and they learn from ours. In this way, a free society is the best facilitator of human flourishing.[32]

For Tisdale, Cohen, and other defenders of the value of pornography, the classical liberal defense of free speech, combined with this more Aristotelian appreciation for the centrality of choice in the formation of character, takes the form of a defense of the way pornography portrays *varieties* of sexual experience—for good and ill. So pornography—even nasty, hateful pornography—helps one develop a sense of who one is and who one is not. The value of live-actor pornography then, lies in its role of offering representations for its consumers to emulate or reject. Because desire is partly socially structured, limiting access to a variety of commercial pornographic representations can stunt the development of a person's own patterns of desire and sexual identification. For this reason, severe restrictions on live-actor pornography are not just impractical, but wrong, especially since it is women (and other oppressed groups, such as homosexuals) who have historically had such choices and experiences closed off to them.

31. See John Stuart Mill, *On Liberty*, ch. 3.
32. Mill is at his most Aristotelian here. For a discussion of Mill's "experiments in living," and a comparison of the differences between Mill and Aristotle on the role of choice in human flourishing, see John Gray, 1991, "Mill's Conception of Happiness and the Theory of Individuality," in *J.S. Mill's* On liberty *in Focus*, ed., John Gray and G.W. Smith (New York: Routledge), pp. 190–211.

Now, of course, the critic of commercial live-actor pornography would argue that your sexual awakening and development is not worth someone else's abuse and subjugation, even if one were to buy the idea that pornography facilitates the former (which most critics do not[33]). Nonetheless, the thing to notice here is that this liberal defense of the value of pornography does not make the self out to be an isolable object, available for individual analysis, in the way that the liberal treatment of prostitution does. On the contrary, this liberal defense is predicated on the self's developing partly in response to social constraints and experiences. Here the Lockean conception of a person as an individual standing alone and deciding to sell her labor power[34] has given way to a more Aristotelian defense of the value of an abundance of choices for a community of fully functioning moral agents.

This shift is made without much consideration of how such choices are distributed. And this encapsulates part of the problem with the feminist liberal shift from a discussion of the harms/benefits for the worker, in the case of prostitution, to a discussion of the value of pornographic speech for the consumer, even in the case of live-actor pornography. The worker[35]—the person whose labor power, or body, is needed for the

33. The most obvious objection to the claim that pornography is valuable as an aid in sexual awakening is the counter-claim that it is merely a masturbatory device. I do not wish to enter into a debate over whether or not something *can* be both things at once, or even a debate about whether any pornography is *indeed* both things at once. But it is important to note that many critics of pornography would object to all the high-minded talk of "human flourishing" and speech in this context. (See, for example, Mackinnon's famous remarks that one can't argue with an orgasm and that "an erection is neither a thought nor a feeling, but a behavior." Catharine MacKinnon, 1993, *Only Words*, ch. 1, Cambridge: Harvard).

34. For further discussion of the Lockean conception of ownership in the context of the prostitution exchange, see Sibyl Schwarzenbach, "Contractarians and Feminists Debate Prostitution," op. cit., §3. Of course Locke himself may have had a more nuanced conception of self than the version described. In any event, Hume certainly did. Nevertheless, it is the indivudualism of the Lock*ean* conception that has had so much influence on the liberal tradition.

35. The terms 'work' (in this context) and 'sex worker' are themselves controversial. The term 'sex work' is typically credited to Carol Leigh (aka Scarlot Harlot), who initially introduced it as a way to emphasize the legitimacy of commerce in sex and to reclaim some dignity for those who exchange sex for money. Although the term 'sex work' has become increasingly popular in some circles as a way of referring to those who make money as prostitutes, pornography actors, strippers, etc., it is still rejected by many. Some see it as a way of whitewashing the abuse suffered by many who are used in the sex industry, and thus

viewer of live-actor pornography to have the varieties of experience with different forms of speech that the liberal argues are so important—has dropped out of the account of the feminist liberal treatment of pornography. There are a number of pornography workers who offer defenses of what they do for money.[36] But even consideration of these accounts is missing from the liberal theorists' treatment of pornography. It is as if the person who is important in the case of pornography is not the worker at all, but the person who benefits from her labor. The worker herself, isolable rational agent or not, fades from view as if no pornography were live-actor pornography at all, but *mere* representation.

SOMEBODY SOMEWHERE

Leaving aside pornography that does not involve real human bodies having real sex, since that raises a host of different issues for both the critic and the defender of pornography's legitimacy,[37] we are here faced with

prefer terms like "prostituted woman," or "survivor." (For a general overview of the anti-prostitution objection to the term "sex worker" see Dorchen Leidholdt, "Demand and the Debate," a speech on trafficking and the history of the Coalition Against Trafficking in Women (CATW), given on October 16, 2003. Available on the CATW web site http://www.catwinternational.org. See also Janice Raymond, "Ten Reasons for Not Legalizing Prostitution," in *Prostitution, Trafficking and Traumatic Stress*, ed. Melissa Farley, 2003 (Binghamton: Haworth Press). Some criticize the term "sex work" as erasing what sets prostitution apart, in a good way, from regular "work": the sense of the forbidden, the special nature of what a prostitute does, even the very *badness* of it. And some point out that the term has class connotations and affiliations that the term "prostitute" does not. I only use the term "sex work" here when referring to the position of those for whom it is the term of choice. Where I refer to those who criticize the sex industry as being inherently exploitative and *not* involving legitimate "work," I do not use the term. After all, if somebody considers herself to have been a slave, then it is a terrible thing to re-describe her as a worker—terrible both for slave and worker alike.

36. For instance, see Nina Hartley, "In the Flesh: A Porn Star's Journey" in *Whores and Other Feminists, op. cit.*, pp. 57–65 and generally, the work of Annie Sprinkle, Susie Bright, and Theresa Reed.

37. In the case of pornography that does not involve the representation of real humans having real sex, the critic tends to focus on the question of harm to women generally. In this case, the issue becomes one of causation, the question of whether such pornography leads to mistreatment, degradation, and abuse of real people. For an excellent discussion of the various conceptions of causation

the question of whether or not the disparate treatments of prostitution and live-actor pornography are justifiable. In the one case, there is a fairly direct exchange of sex for money (although the "worker" may not ever see any of the money for her putative labor, in which case she is more properly classified a slave), while in the other case, the consumer's purchase is mediated by the camera. Both prostitution and live-actor pornography may involve a third party (pimp or pornography producer) or neither may (consider the pornographic work of Susie Bright, Annie Sprinkle, Carol Leigh, and others who market their own work). The difference is the different role the consumer plays in the transaction. In one case, the consumer purchases sexual interaction with another person, and in the other case, the consumer purchases the record of other persons' sexual interaction—a representation, as some would have it.

So it may not seem so strange after all that the feminist liberal treatment of pornography involving real persons should look very different from the feminist liberal treatment of prostitution: the *consumer* is engaged in a different activity in each case. In the case of prostitution, what is bought is—depending upon one's point of view—a sexual service, access to a body, or a person's sexual self. In the case of live-actor pornography, what is bought is a product, a record, a representation. What is of central importance to the feminist liberal is not the fact of commodification necessary for the making of this product, but its element of expression and its connection to liberty interests in speech. Where the debate over prostitution had been about whether or not sex was a proper candidate for commodification, the expressive liberty defense of pornography's legitimacy proceeds as if commodification were *necessary* for the human flourishing that it champions.

This presumption that commodification of sex is necessary for sexual expression is itself problematic for several reasons. First, it is problematic because nothing about the Millian/Aristotelian conception of identity as partly socially structured and developed through exposure to varieties of experience and choice requires that the *market* supply these experiences and choices. Not without further argument anyway. It may be that a (relatively) free market is the best way to ensure such variety, but then the case would seem to be for actively *promoting* sexual commodification, not just allowing us all to blossom in our own ways through unrestricted access to *ideas* about differing sexual tastes and identities. And *that* argument

at work in such a view, see Anne W. Eaton, "Might Pornography Cause Harm?" unpublished manuscript. On the liberal side, see Martha Nussbaum's discussion of literary pornography in "Objectification" in *Sex and Social Justice, op. cit.,* pp. 213–40.

simply is not made by the feminist liberal defenders of pornography's legitimacy, who assimilate live-actor pornography to speech and *thereby* justify it.

None of what I have just argued is a direct argument against pornography. For one thing, one could bite the bullet and argue in response that what we need is more commodification of sex, not less—a position that would probably trouble most liberals (let alone most feminist liberals). At the other end of the spectrum, one could accept that the modern pornography industry has gotten beyond the obscenity models used to analyze it, and agree that the sexual commodification involved in live-actor pornography is potentially, or even actually, harmful and yet *still* think that the harms of regulation are worse for the sort of human flourishing reasons raised, as well as for more practical reasons of politics and legal enforcement.[38]

Such arguments are commonly made about nonsexual matters, such as the use of drugs, the practice of euthanasia, and (less frequently) abortion. There is nothing incoherent about the view that some things that are harmful should not be disallowed. Perhaps the products of the pornography industry are like the products of the gun industry: weapons that can be used to harm, but access to which is intimately connected to other values we hold dear. According to such a view, we might consider various means of minimizing the potential for harm caused by these products (through restrictions like age limits, licensing, and trigger locks), but should also try to preserve access where we can, in order to maximize liberty.[39]

This may sound like a solution to the problem of harmful pornography. It is certainly appealing to this author's liberal intuitions. But the elephant in the room here is the fact that actual sex with real people—sexual labor or subjugation, as the case may be—is being exchanged for money in the case of commercial live-actor pornography. And this is the second problem with the presumption that commodification of sex is necessary for sexual expression. The product in such pornography depends upon a real person's having sex in exchange for somebody's making money. The person who is having sex in such a commercial context is thought to be of central importance in feminist liberal thought about prostitution, but is seemingly

38. One example of the dangers of regulation that is often cited, accurately or not, is the confiscation of Andrea Dworkin's writings under the MacKinnon-Dworkin anti-pornography regulations adopted in Canada.

39. This view, minus the connection to issues of gun control, is essentially the one put forward in various versions by Cohen, Nussbaum, and other feminist liberals who are concerned both about the status of women and about the value of expressive liberty.

irrelevant to feminist liberal thought about pornography. Academic discussions of expressive liberty typically center on the liberty interests of *consumers*, or possibly producers, but seldom on the people whose bodies are necessary to the making of pornography. This is not the case for feminist critics of pornography of course. For instance, MacKinnon and Dworkin famously argue that pornography is an arm of prostitution.[40] But very few feminist liberals who write about pornography even mention prostitution, and *vice versa*. Nussbaum is a notable exception here, but even her work on the two subjects seemingly preserves the same split between conceptions of the self and subjects of focus that is found in the rest of the feminist liberal discussion. The academic discussion of prostitution centers on the autonomy of the individual worker whereas the academic discussion of pornography centers on the value of expressive liberty, its relation to obscenity, and the social development of sexual identity.

This dichotomy is *not* generally preserved in the writings of those with practical experience working in or around the sex industry—whether they write in critique *or* defense of it.[41] A range of testimonials and social studies reveals a more fluid industry than the academic and legal compartmentalizations of prostitution and pornography (as well as other forms of sexual commerce) would seem to indicate. People who strip or perform in pornographic movies are very often also prostitutes off-camera and *vice versa*. Or they consider themselves such.[42] According to one study of

40. See their work generally. Specifically, see Catharine MacKinnon and Andrea Dworkin, 1998, *In Harm's Way* (Cambridge: Harvard), and Catharine MacKinnon, 1993, *Only Words* (Cambridge: Harvard).

41. See, generally, the discussions in Laurie Bell, ed., 1987, *Good Girls/Bad Girls: Sex Trade Workers and Feminists Face to Face* (Toronto: Women's Press); Leidholdt and Raymond, eds., 1990, *The Sexual Liberals and the Attack on Feminism* (New York: Pergamon); and Jill Nagle, ed., 1997, *Whores and Other Feminists* (New York: Routledge), as well as the writings of Carol Leigh, Jill Leighton, Theresa Reed, and many others.

42. See, for example, Traci Lords's description in her recent autobiography of work in the pornography industry and her attempts to leave it for work in the mainstream movie industry: "We were scripted prostitutes, performing for the camera." See Traci Lord's (2003) *Underneath It All* (New York: HarperCollins), p. 192. Of course, many people do not work in more than one department of the sex industry, but even those who testify to remaining on one side of a line or the other tend to emphasize that, by doing so, they differ from their peers. Tracy Quan often describes her work in prostitution as partly motivated by the secrecy and sense of the forbidden around prostitution that is not the same in the case of pornography. See Tracy Quan's various writings, especially her novel (2001), *Diary of a Manhattan Call-Girl* (New York: Crown). See also Lili Burana,

prostitution, thirty-eight percent of the women surveyed reported being used in child pornography.[43] Some estimates of the percentage of strippers involved in prostitution range from twenty-five to forty percent.[44] According to reports available from various anti-prostitution organizations, stripping is often used as a pipeline into prostitution, and women move, or are moved, between prostitution and pornography without restriction. In fact, many pro-prostitution activists decry the way the commercial pornography industry has tried to distance itself from prostitution in the public imagination in order to preserve its growing legitimacy, while hypocritically employing prostitutes and promoting the prostitution of its workers.

All of this stands in striking contrast to the academic feminist liberal treatment of prostitution and pornography as raising different ethical questions. The standard feminist liberal defense of prostitution's legitimacy maintains that prostitution is often harmful and degrading, but that we should work to eliminate the conditions that make women feel they have to do it rather than penalize them for doing it. While, on the other hand, the standard feminist liberal defense of the legitimacy of pornography maintains that pornography is generally beneficial and we can try to address its harms without curtailing the general practice, and so preserve what is generally good about it.

The problem is that this defense does not attend to the way live-actor pornography is produced and to the costs for those whose bodies are

2001, *Strip City* (New York: Talk Miramax Books); and Elizabeth Eaves, 2001, *Bare: On Women, Dancing, Sex, and Power* (New York: Crown). Burana and Eaves are part of recent spate of former workers chronicling their experiences at the no-contact peep show establishment "The Lusty Lady." Their accounts are especially revealing here for the time they spend discussing the authors' choices *not* to engage in sexual contact for money. Linda Lee Tracey, 1997, *Growing Up Naked* (Toronto: Douglas & McIntyre), describes the affect the growth of pornography had on the world of stripping during the 1970s. She is avowedly a former stripper, not a pornography worker or prostitute, but discusses how this contrasted with the behavior of many of her stripper peers who exchanged direct sexual contact for money. Tracey was also the subject of the controversial National Film Board of Canada documentary about pornography, "Not A Love Story."

43. Silbert and Pines, 1984, "Pornography and the Sexual Abuse of Women," *Sex Roles* 10, discussed in Margaret A. Baldwin (Spring 1989) "Pornography and The Traffic in Women," *Yale Journal of Law and Feminism* 1:1, pp. 111–55.

44. "Prostitution in Hartford," research compiled by Michele Kelly under the supervision of this author as part of an ongoing research project partially funded by the Hartford Metropolitan Research Program at Trinity College.

necessary for making it. As a thought experiment that should help illustrate what is wrong here, consider the following: a liberal defense of the legitimacy of prostitution based solely on the benefits prostitution has for the consumer, without any discussion of the role of the service provider. According to such an account, the legitimate sale of sex would be a good thing because it would aid "the rest of us" in our sexual development and exploration of our identities. Even nasty, harmful prostitution exchanges where prostitutes are abused could help teach us what we like or don't like, and traditionally marginalized sexual groups (such as sadomasochists) could find an outlet for sexual desires that might otherwise find improper outlet in the real (noncommercial) world of personal relationships. By enforcing other laws that are more narrowly targeted, such as those against kidnapping and underage sex, we could still weed out the forms of prostitution that are *truly* unacceptable, without preventing a person from exercising autonomy in deciding what to buy—which in a capitalist system, is central to human flourishing and the good life.[45] Although some prostitution may be unpleasant for the worker, the costs, for the sexual expressiveness of society at large, of limiting the practice would be too great to regulate it. So we should instead tolerate the bad and celebrate its value in helping consumers learn about their sexual identities.

Such an account would seem anathema to the broadest feminist concerns with the status of women and the conditions of the lives of the underprivileged because it leaves out a crucial element: the putative workers who may be trafficked or otherwise have so few options as to be unfree. (Neither would such an account satisfy pro-prostitution activists concerned with improving working conditions for those who choose to exchange their sexual labor for money, because such activists typically have, well, a worker in view.) It also treats prostitution as generally a good thing, in contrast with the standard feminist liberal treatment of prostitution, which either concedes to the critic that most forms of prostitution are troubling *as practiced*—arguing that they are just made worse through stigmatization and criminalization—or which refuses to essentialize the

---

45. This thought experiment is offered somewhat tongue-in-check of course. But similar defenses can be found in the literature. Ericsson and Califia, for instance, both defend the legitimacy of prostitution largely through such accounts of the benefits it offers to the consumer. See Lars O. Ericsson, April 1980, "What's Wrong with Prostitution?" *Ethics* 90:3, pp. 335–66; and Pat Califia, "Whoring in Utopia," *op. cit.* Schwarzenbach also offers a brief argument in this vein. See Sibyl Schwarzenbach, "Contractarians and Feminists Debate Prostitution," *op. cit.*

activity in any way at all. Even those feminists sensitive to queer theory, who recognize the value of nonheteronormative expressions of sexuality, would likely shy away from an argument that completely ignores all costs to the worker in such commercial transactions.

The problem is how to maintain a concern with individual women and the conditions of their lives, while not making the classical mistake of ignoring the effect that social practice has on a person's self-conception and very ability to make autonomous choices. This is an old problem for feminism, but it is at its sharpest in the different ways that prostitution and pornography are treated in academic discussion. It is here that feminist liberalism must come to grips with the tensions in its treatment of women as individuals and as a group, and with its traditional interest in the welfare of the "rest of us" that overshadows interest in bettering the lives of women who are the most marginalized.

I am not arguing that feminist liberalism lacks the tools to analyze prostitution or live-actor pornography, but rather that (1) different tools are being used to analyze each, undercutting the credibility and usefulness of both analyses, and (2) in defending the legitimacy of pornography, feminist liberalism is using the *wrong* tools. Using obscenity law to interpret live-actor pornography is not adequate for addressing concerns about the welfare of persons who are involved in the making of live-actor pornography. And privileging the interests of consumers to the exclusion of all else flies in the face of the values of both feminism and liberalism. At the same time, feminist liberal analyses of prostitution tend toward the simplistic when assessing individual choice and consent, simultaneously emphasizing the damaging effects of stigmatization and treating the individual's choice to exchange sex for money as problematic only in so far as it results from economic coercion. That is, only in so far as it is a symptom of poverty.

Feminist liberalism needs to do two things to remedy the troubling disparity between its treatment of prostitution and its treatment of pornography. It needs to be more critical of the meaningfulness of consent and choice in prostitution, given the social context. It should also combine the concern for the worker that is central to the defense of prostitution, with sensitivity to the social and cultural embeddedness of self that is central to the defense of pornography. Then it can look at live-actor pornography as a form of prostitution that raises additional questions about third-party consumption.

So first, what is needed is attention to the labor in live-actor pornography, rather than a concern, to the exclusion of all else, for the consumer. Examining the context for pornography workers rather than just consumers will present some difficulties. For instance, consent may be more meaningful for some persons and in some instances. Nevertheless, the point is to assess and justify *consent*, not the consumer's purchase right. We already do not permit consent to mutual combat with the idea that such "consent" is not rational. Apparent exceptions are more apparent than real, because they are highly regulated in a way that pornography is not, as in the case of boxing.[46] Even such apparent exceptions may be disappearing in the United States. Courts do not ask whether two hockey players consent to mutual combat when they throw off their gloves and fight. So-called "no holds barred" competitive combat, such as the Ultimate Fighting Championship (UFC), has been outlawed in many states. The big venue for Mixed Martial Arts (MMA) is now Japan, not the United States. Indeed, it seems that commercial live-actor pornography stands alone as a legally legitimate industry where interest in consumer access obviates concerns about the worker/participant.[47]

Traditional feminist liberal interest in preserving individual women's autonomy must be combined with a sensitivity to the fact that more options for some can sometimes mean less freedom for others.[48] Pornography that uses real people having real sex requires a supply of prostitutes to produce the product. That is something that feminist liberal defenders of the empowering potential of pornography for "the rest of us" need to take into account. We can recognize that persons are not isolable objects whose scope of choice is analyzable apart from social context, without losing sight of those who are least well-off and have the most to lose from

46. The recent epidemic of HIV/AIDs within the mainstream commercial pornography industry has brought some attention to the lack of regulations governing it. But even this concern is expressed more as a concern over public health issues than a specific concern for workers within the pornography industry.

47. Readers might consider the recent television "reality" shows about boxing. As attractive or repulsive (or both) as they may be, it is interesting to note that these shows have (so far, anyway) focused on the perspective of the boxing hopefuls rather than on the perspectives of promoters or audience.

48. For an excellent, detailed analysis of how sexual autonomy might be hindered by the normalization of prostitution, see Scott Anderson "Prostitution and Sexual Autonomy: Making Sense of the Prohibition of Prostitution," *op. cit.* Although Anderson's focus is solely on prostitution (indeed, preserving the same distinction between prostitution and pornography that I identify in much of the feminist liberal literature), I think his analysis of the ways in which prohibitions can preserve one's sexual autonomy can, in fact, also be applied to pornography.

the further commodification of the sexual sphere that evidently goes along with an increase in avenues for sexual expression.

Second, what is needed is for feminist liberalism to bring the same sensitivity to the social and cultural embeddedness of self that is central to its pornography analysis, to the concern for the worker that is the subject of its prostitution analysis. Combined with a more socially embedded view of the self, the feminist liberal argument about the harms done by stigmatization would then be made stronger. If the self is partly socially structured, and our identities are built in the context of exposure to a variety of experiences and expressions of sexuality, etc., then true freedom of choice and self-determination are near impossible when an entire sphere of activity (commercial sex) is so publicly stigmatized. Our very ability to develop and flourish is stunted by the opprobrium heaped on anyone who expresses his or her sexual self commercially. And it is the least well off who often suffer the most from such stigmatizations because they start out at a disadvantage.

We have these discussions about the tensions between freedom and protection all the time in other arenas, when debating the ethics and practicality of regulating "hate speech" and certain forms of group harassment, and remedies like affirmative action. It is not easy. But in other arenas aside from the sexual one, there does not seem to be such a striking bifurcation of thought for liberals between concern for the worker and concern for the consumer. The very different ways pornography and prostitution are viewed in our culture reveal something deeper about the way our culture views persons: the boundaries of persons, the proper functioning of persons, and the appropriate activity of persons. Sex seems to be the place where all these come together for us.

One option open to the feminist liberal is to offer a defense of pornography's legitimacy that combines the expressive liberty argument with an argument that workers do meaningfully choose to participate in such an enterprise commercially. The question then becomes one of whether having the "option" to exchange sex for money is more like having the option to sell one's (even nonessential) bodily organs, or more like having the option to be a ballet dancer, professional basketball player, or paid subject for medical experiments. As a society, we have decided that the former is not acceptable because it puts what are deemed undue incentives/economic pressures on the least well off. But we have apparently decided that the incentives/economic pressure on poor kids to try to excel at sports rather than academics is acceptable. If we decide that selling sex is more like organ selling, then we have decided that sex is an essential part of human identity, or a unique sort of activity in some way. If we decide that selling sex is more like being a professional athlete, then we have decided that, for the purposes of *public* morality, sex should not be cordoned off as a special sphere of human activity with a wholly different set of public rules than other physical activity/labor.

I do not believe that these issues need be cast in terms of a theoretical versus practical interest, as many critics of the sex industry charge.[49] Indeed, what I offer is a theoretical critique with practical consequences. What I identify as a theoretical disparity between feminist liberal treatments of prostitution and pornography means that the feminist liberal is not answering the charges against the two brought by the radical critic, and so not addressing the critic's practical concerns.

This is important if we ever *do* hope to resolve any of the disputes between feminist critics and defenders of the legitimacy of the sex industry. For if the critic keeps asking about the welfare of the worker, and the defender keeps answering with an argument about the benefits of pornography for "the rest of us," we will get nowhere. I remain hopeful that we can indeed get somewhere, and actually help improve the lives of those persons who are the subjects of feminist concern, while preserving the value of free expression and, yes, even the classical Millian value of varieties of experience. This will not be easy, for it means getting our hands dirty with some very tough philosophical and more globally moral questions: about what pornography is and what it does, what the significance is of real live bodies to pornography's function, and finally, what we want to say about the degree to which sex and sexuality are essential to the kinds of creatures we are.

I think, although I cannot argue the case here, that selling sex is neither like selling one's organs nor like being a professional athlete. My own view is that it is more like the case of the subject paid for medical experiments: it *can* be acceptable, depending on context, but it can also be unacceptable and especially harmful, depending on context, despite the participants all apparently freely choosing to be involved. In the current landscape of feminist liberal discussions about the sex industry, there is no room for such a view. That's the point.

49. For instance, see Margaret A. Baldwin, "Split at the Root: Prostitution and Feminist Discourses of Law Reform," *op. cit.*; or Vednita Carter and Evelina Giobbe, Winter 1999, "Duet: Prostitution, Racism, and Feminist Discourse," *Hastings Women's Law Journal*, 10:1, pp. 37–57.

Index

Index